June 26–28, 2018
Seoul, Republic of Korea

Advancing Computing as a Science & Profession

TVX 2018

Proceedings of the 2018 ACM International Conference on Interactive Experiences for TV and Online Video

Sponsored by:

ACM SIGCHI

In Cooperation with:

ACM SIGMM & ACM SIGWEB

Supported by:

Hanyang University, ATech, Nokia, Samsung C-Lab, & UXPA International

Advancing Computing as a Science & Profession

The Association for Computing Machinery
2 Penn Plaza, Suite 701
New York, New York 10121-0701

ISBN: 978-1-4503-5115-7 (Digital)

ISBN: 978-1-4503-6165-1 (Print)

Additional copies may be ordered prepaid from:

ACM Order Department
PO Box 30777
New York, NY 10087-0777, USA

Phone: 1-800-342-6626 (USA and Canada)
+1-212-626-0500 (Global)
Fax: +1-212-944-1318
E-mail: acmhelp@acm.org
Hours of Operation: 8:30 am – 4:30 pm ET

ACM TVX 2018 Chairs' Welcome

It is our great pleasure to welcome you to Seoul, Korea, for the fifth edition of the *ACM International Conference on Interactive Experiences for Television and Online Video – ACM TVX 2018.* We are certain that this is a great place to meet diverse research and industry communities from around the world, including those that have not previously been heavily involved in the TVX conference series. As such, we are incredibly excited to be able to present a stimulating program for ACM TVX 2018 in an equally magnificent part of the world; incidentally representing a first for this conference series – a host city in Asia!

As the leading international conference for the presentation and discussion of research and developments into interactive experiences for online video and TV, the conference brings together international researchers and practitioners from a wide range of disciplines, ranging from human-computer interaction, multimedia engineering and design to media studies, psychology and sociology, to present and discuss the latest insights in the field. The ultimate mission of the conference is to share novel ideas, concepts, and solutions that fulfill the needs of new media environments and identify new directions for future research and development.

This year's conference continues its tradition of being the premier forum in this field, following the success of the four previous editions of TVX (held in Hilversum, Chicago, Brussels and Newcastle upon Tyne), and building on the legacy of the EuroiTV conference series organized all across Europe, between 2003 and 2013. We continue to present research on topics in scope such as immersive experiences, user experiences & interaction design, content production, systems & infrastructure, devise & interaction techniques, media studies, business models & marketing, and innovative concepts & media art. In addition, we introduced two hot topics to the call for papers associated with ACM TVX 2018: "*AI/Big Data*" and "*Social Computing*".

The call for papers attracted 36 long and short paper submissions from Asia, Europe, North & South America across both academia and industry. Being the first edition in Asia, it received new submissions from China, Japan, and Korea which were less visible in the conference series until now. All submissions went through a rigorous double-blind peer review process. Each paper was assigned a primary Associate Chair (AC) and a secondary AC. The primary AC recruited at least two reviewers for each of their assigned paper, whilst the secondary AC recruited at least one reviewer for their assigned paper. Once the reviewers submitted their evaluation of the suitability of the paper, the primary AC wrote a meta-review summarizing the main points of each review. Authors of the submissions were then notified of the completed review and given the chance to respond to the reviewers' comments during a rebuttal phase. During the TPC meeting on March 16, 2018 in Lisbon, Portugal, each paper was discussed in-depth with the ACs, and the final decision on the accepted papers was made, resulting in a high-quality program of 12 accepted full and short papers, accounting for an acceptance rate of 33%. Full papers, Short papers, the abstracts of the 2 Workshops co-located with TVX (in addition to an industry workshop close to the public), and the 17 Work In Progress papers are part of the main proceedings and will be included in the ACM Digital Library. In addition to these submissions, there were several other tracks that attracted a considerable number of contributions, resulting in 8 TVX in Industry presentations, 8 Demonstrations, 3 Doctoral Consortium papers, and 2 Grand Challenge presentations, all made available in the adjunct proceedings, along with the papers from the Workshops.

This year we continued to put serious effort into Inclusion and Accessibility, a pioneer initiative at TVX, in three domains: 1) an Open Application process to become AC in the program committee; 2) a Mentoring Program to provide feedback and guidance from established researchers, aimed at those submitting to TVX for the first time, those in circumstances which are particular adverse, or at particularly novel submissions which might require additional input; and 3) Support for Accessibility in attending the conference.

The ACM TVX 2018 conference also features three interesting keynotes. We strongly recommend attendees attend these insightful keynote talks: "*Towards Smarter Cinematographic Drones*" by Marc Christie of the University of Rennes 1 in cooperation with Technicolor; "*Making Creative Content for Future TV: A Collaborative Ecosystem for Content-making in Korea & Asia*" by Ho Sung Kim, a record-holding movie producer in Korea; and the Industry invited keynote "*From a Fun Gadget to a Light of Hope*" by Junghoon Cho of Samsung.

It will be no surprise to you that assembling the program for ACM TVX 2018 was made possible through the hard work volunteered by quite a few generous folks. We would like to take this opportunity to thank all the contributors and volunteers who have made this conference possible. We thank the authors for all the submissions, the ACs who managed the whole review process and the reviewers who provided invaluable feedback for each paper. This conference could not have happened without our chairs in all the categories, and our committees putting their time and effort in making this conference a success. It is thanks to this joint team effort that we have been able to present the resulting remarkable program. We thank them and their institutions for sparing time to help move this important field forward. We extend our gratitude to the TVX Steering Committee for their support and guidance; and to Sheridan Proceedings Service for helping in getting the content together and published at the ACM Digital Library.

Last but not least, we thank you for registering and attending the conference, as you are an important part of our community and your participation makes these events possible. We also thank the hosting university **Hanyang University**; our sponsor **ACM SIGCHI** in cooperation with **ACM SIGMM** and **ACM SIGWEB**; and our supporters **Department of Arts & Technology (Hanyang University)**, **Nokia**, **Samsung c-lab** and **UXPA international**, for providing the means and the logistics to make this conference an enjoyable experience.

We trust that ACM TVX 2018 brings you a unique opportunity to share new perspectives with others interested in various aspects of TV and online media design, including TV manufacturers and media companies in Asia. We hope that altogether this program provides inspiration for noteworthy and thought-provoking conversations that raise interesting questions for the future, and that your experience in the conference provides you with a valuable opportunity to share ideas with other colleagues from around the world. Enjoy the conference and your stay in sensational Seoul!

Hokyoung Ryu
ACM TVX 2018 General Chair
Hanyang University, Republic of Korea

Jieun Kim
ACM TVX 2018 General Chair
Hanyang University, Republic of Korea

Teresa Chambel
ACM TVX 2018 General Chair
LASIGE, Faculdade de Ciências, Universidade de Lisboa, Portugal

Tom Bartindale
ACM TVX 2018 Program Chair
Newcastle University, United Kingdom

Vinoba Vinayagamoorthy
ACM TVX 2018 Program Chair
BBC Research & Development, United Kingdom

Wei Tsang Ooi
ACM TVX 2018 Program Chair
National Univ. of Singapore, Singapore

Table of Contents

Session 5: Systems

Session Chair: Rene Kaiser *(Know-Center - Research Center for Data-Driven Business & Big Data Analytics)*

Work-in-Progress

Session Chair: Hartmut Koenitz *(HKU University)*

Workshop Summaries

ACM TVX 2018 Conference Organization

General Chairs: Hokyoung Ryu *(Hanyang University, Republic of Korea)*
Jieun Kim *(Hanyang University, Republic of Korea)*
Teresa Chambel *(LASIGE, Fac. de Ciências, Universidade de Lisboa, Portugal)*

Program Chairs: Tom Bartindale *(Newcastle University, UK)*
Vinoba Vinayagamoorthy *(BBC Research & Development, UK)*
Wei Tsang Ooi *(National University of Singapore, Singapore)*

Work-in-progress Chairs: Hartmut Koenitz *(HKU University, The Netherlands)*
Donghun Chung *(Kwangwoon University, Republic of Korea)*

Demo Chairs: Tim Neate *(City, University of London, UK)*
Kyoungwon Seo *(Hanyang University, Republic of Korea)*

Workshop Chairs: Katrien de Moor *(Norweigian University of Science and Technology, Norway)*
Stanley Chang *(National Chiao Tung University, Taiwan)*
Britta Meixner *(Tiledmedia B.V., The Netherlands)*

TVX Industry Chairs: Shuichi Aoki *(NHK, Japan)*
Igor Curcio *(Nokia, Finland)*

Doctoral Consortium Chairs: Marianna Obrist *(University of Sussex, UK)*
Carlos Velasco *(BI Norwegian Business School, Norway)*

Local Production Chairs: Hyojin Kang *(Hanyang University, Republic of Korea)*
Dong-uk Ko *(Hanyang University, Republic of Korea)*

Inclusion and Accessibility Chairs: Pedro Almeida *(University of Aveiro, Portugal)*
Eunju Jeong *(Hanyang University, Republic of Korea)*
Jieun Han *(Hanyang University, Republic of Korea)*

Publicity Chairs: Gyu Hyun Kwon *(Hanyang University, Republic of Korea)*
Santosh Basapur *(Institute of Design, IIT, USA)*
Sung-woo Kim *(Kookmin University, Republic of Korea)*

Treasurer & Registration Chair: Ahreum Lee *(Hanyang University, Republic of Korea)*

Web Chair: Kyoungwon Seo *(Hanyang University, Republic of Korea)*

Steering Committee: Tom Bartindale *(Newcastle University, UK)*
Santosh Basapur *(Institute of Design, IIT, USA)*
Frank Bentley *(Yahoo, USA)*
Pablo Cesar *(CWI, The Netherlands)*
Teresa Chambel *(LASIGE, Fac. de Ciências, Universidade de Lisboa, Portugal)*
David Geerts *(KU Leuven-imec, Belgium)*
Marianna Obrist *(University of Sussex, UK)*

Program Committee:

Associate Chairs: Ahmed Arif *(University of California, USA)*
Diogo Cabral *(University of Madeira, Portugal)*
Lucia D'Acunto *(TNO, The Netherlands)*
Sid Ahmed Fezza *(National Institute of Telecommunications and ICT, Algeria)*
Chun-Ying Huang *(National Chiao Tung University, Taiwan)*
Rene Kaiser *(Research Center for Data-Driven Business & Big Data Analytics, Austria)*
Rodrigo Laiola Guimaraes *(Federal University of Espírito Santo, Brazil)*
Patrick Le Callet *(Université de Nantes, France)*
Diego Martinez-Plasencia *(University of Sussex, UK)*
Alan Said *(University of Skövde, Sweden)*
Guy Schofield *(University of York, UK)*
Wendy van den Broek *(SMIT, Belgium)*
Radu-Daniel Vatavu *(University of Suceava, Romania)*
Yonggang Wen *(Nanyang Technological University, Singapore)*
Maarten Wijnants *(Hasselt University, Belgium)*

Reviewers: Jorge Abreu
Imtiaj Ahmed
Pedro Almeida
Olivier Aubert
Werner Bailer
Mehmet Aydin Baytas
Suzanne Beer
Andrea Bellucci
Cynthia Bennett
Matthew Brooks
Sergio Cabrero
André Calero Valdez
Richard Carter
Marie Laure Cazin
Pedro Centieiro
Pablo Cesar
Liwei Chan
Sandy Claes
Gregoire Cliquet
Paulien Coppens
Sven Coppers
Romualdo Costa
Antoine Coutrot
Igor Curcio
Kamila Rios da Hora Rodrigues
Mike Darnell
Jolien De Letter
Simon Delaere
William Delamare
Jonas Demeulenaere
Yi Dong
Abdallah El Ali
Denzil Ferreira
Bruce Ferwerda
Christian Fuhrhop
Guanyu Gao
Thomas Gayler
David Geerts

Reviewers *(continued)*:

Katerina Gorkovenko
Rudinei Goularte
Philippe Guillotel
Philip Heslop
Jonathan Hook
Han Hu
Zixia Huang
Jack Jansen
Iris Jennes
Yichao Jin
Themistoklis Karavellas
Jieun Kim
Reuben Kirkham
Jan Willem Kleinrouweler
Bart Knijnenburg
Hartmut Koenitz
Zhicong Lu
Saeed Mahmoudpour
Matei Mancas
Jennifer Marlow
Robin Marx
Jennifer McNally
Jamie McRoberts
Ann Morrison
Mu Mu
Wolfgang Mueller
Ian Oakley
Maria da Graça Pimentel
Yannick Prié
Carlos Antonio Navarrete Puentes
Jacob Rigby
Maria Riveiro
Teresa Romão
Gustavo Rovelo Ruiz
Celso Saibel Santos
Tom Schofield
Auriana Shokrhpour
Carlos Soares Neto
Tobias Palma Stade
Aneesh Tarun
Matthias Traub
Marian Ursu
Jan Van den Bergh
Gina Venolia
Toinon Vigier
Mirjam Vosmeer
Yongjie Wang
Gerard Wilkinson
Doug Williams
Di Wu
David Zendle
Huaizheng Zhang
Juyong Zhang
Yuhang Zhao
Yan-Jie Zhong
Christoph Ziegler
Arkaitz Zubiaga

ACM TVX 2018 Sponsor & Supporters

Sponsor:

In Cooperation with:

Supporters:

Towards Smarter Cinematographic Drones

Marc Christie
Univ Rennes, IRISA, INRIA
marc.christie@irisa.fr

ABSTRACT

With the advent of stable and powerful quadrotors, coupled with high quality camera lenses, quadrotor drones are becoming new cinematographic devices in the toolbox of both professional and amateur filmmakers. Many sequences in recent movies and TV shows are now shot by drones due to the simplicity of the process compared to installing cumbersome and expensive camera cranes, and because of the new creative shooting possibilities it opens.

However, mastering the control of such devices in order to create cinematographic sequences in possibly evolving environments requires a significant amount of time and practice. Indeed, synchronizing the quadrotor and camera motions while ensuring that the drone is in a safe position and satisfies desired visual properties remains challenging. Professional film crews actually rely on two operators who coordinate their actions: a pilot focuses on controlling the motion of the drone, and a cinematographer focuses on motion and focus of the camera.

ACM CCS Concepts

• **Computing methodologies → Computer graphics**; *Animation; Graphics systems and interfaces*

Author Keywords

Virtual cinematography, quadrotor drones

TVX '18, June 26–28, 2018, SEOUL, Republic of Korea

ACM ISBN 978-1-4503-5115-7/18/06.
https://doi.org/10.1145/3210825.3212802

The challenge we address consists in easing the control of quadrotor drones for cinematography by proposing high-level interfaces adapted to cinematographers requirements. This can be performed by formalizing elements of cinematographic knowledge to make the drones smarter. This however raises a number of questions. How intelligent can these drones be made? Is it possible to encode filmic rules and conventions, or to even learn elements of filmic style? Can we define high-level behaviors so drones may react in real-time to scene changes? Can we therefore coordinate motions of multiple drones to cover scenes from multiple viewpoints in fully automated ways? We'll answer these questions and more by presenting the underlying principles of our approach to smarter cinematographic drones. We will present our advances and from there open to a more general discussion on the future of media and interactive media with drones.

BIOGRAPHY

Marc Christie is an associate professor at University of Rennes 1. His research focuses on virtual cinematography which is the application of real cinematography techniques to virtual 3D environments. The research covers a wide range of challenges like extracting data from real-movies, learning elements of film style (types of transitions, continuity between shots, editing patterns), proposing models and techniques to re-apply the learnt elements to virtual environments, computing camera angles and trajectories as well as optimal edits. Recently he focussed his research on how these models and techniques can be adapted to drones, opening the topic of cinematographic drones.

Making Creative Content for Future TV: A Collaborative Ecosystem for Content-making in Korea & Asia

Ho Sung Kim
Producer and Content Creator
Seoul, Korea
hosung819@gmail.com

ABSTRACT

Content makers need to make a concerted effort to escape from the conventional obsolete business model, and looking for new opportunities in the new media consuming platforms like 'YouTube' and 'Netflix.' In this keynote talk, I will highlight an innovative & collaborative ecosystem that I am now setting up in the Korea & Asia markets.

Motivation: In the Korea & Asia markets, television was a dominant platform to distribute films or TV contents, so the traditional business model of the big-budget movies or content was to simply sell their contents to the traditional distributors (e.g., Korea Broadcasting System, IPTV, OTT, and etc.), just after the wide releases in the cinema. However, people are now watching various kinds of videos on mobile devices or computers, not on TV, and want more personalized or lifestyle-matched contents than ever. In order to lead this future market trend, a new ecosystem for both content creators and media consumers is urgently needed.

Problem statement: In an actual fact, the reason why Disney has tried to merge 21st Century Fox (Film and television content division) can be seen in this regard. The Disney wants to monopolize the content distribution market in the traditional model (e.g., IPTV, OTT in Korea) and it wants to be a game-changer against emerging platforms such as YouTube and Netflix. No content distribution through Netflix or YouTube is a key to see the new power-game. A significant problem by this trend-setting is that small & medium budget content makers (content creators) cannot be afoot in the monopolized distribution markets by Disney, Netflix, and YouTube. This means that fewer content providers will survive by the next decade.

Approach: I will introduce the new ecosystem which aims to be beneficial for all the stakeholders (producer, director, screenwriter, CG technician, etc.), not for the best (i.e., big content providers) becomes the beast. My talk is about how to make such an ecosystem for the future content industry in Korea, by which new digital transformation in the media consumption can be soundly delivered for all of us.

TVX '18, June 26–28, 2018, SEOUL, Republic of Korea

ACM ISBN 978-1-4503-5115-7/18/06.
https://doi.org/10.1145/3210825.3212803

ACM CCS Concepts

• Human-centered computing → Collaborative content creation;
• Information systems → Multimedia content creation

Author Keywords

Content-making; Future TV; Collaborative Ecosystem; Platform; Industry in Korea & Asia

BIOGRAPHY

Ho Sung constantly creates a new paradigm shift in the Korean film industry with his innovative and creative initiatives in his commercial movie productions. He produced the recently released Along with the Gods which records second highest audience share in the all time box office in Korea. It is the first fantasy franchise movie which shot two movies at the same time. Another film produced by Ho Sung is Masquerade, a period piece which broke the record for audience share in its genre. At the 69th Cannes Film Festival, The Wailing got an official invitation to be presented in Out of Competition category. Ho Sung totally produced 8 commercial movies over 11 years and received 4 recognitions from major Korean Film Awards.

Gestures for Controlling a Moveable TV

Kashmiri Stec
Bang & Olufsen
Struer, Denmark
ksh@bang-olufsen.dk

Lars Bo Larsen
Aalborg University
Aalborg, Denmark
lbl@es.aau.dk

ABSTRACT

We investigate the effects of physical context on the preference and production of touchless (3D) gestures, focusing on what users consider to be natural and intuitive. Using an elicitation task, we asked for users' preferred gestures to control a "moving TV" display from a distance of 3-4m. We conducted three user studies (N=16 each) using the same premise but varying the physical conditions encountered, such as number of hands available or distance and orientation to the display. This is important to ensure the robustness of the gesture set. We observed two dominant strategies which we interpret as dependent on the user's mental model: hand-as-display and hand-moving-display. Across the varying conditions, users were found to be consistent with their preferred gesture strategy while varying the production (number of hands, orientation, extension of arms) of their gestures in order to match both their mental models and the physical context of use. From a technology perspective, this natural variation challenges the notion of identifying "the optimal gesture set" and should be taken into account when designing future systems with gesture control.

Author Keywords

Gesture interfaces; gesture variation; gesture manipulation of physical objects; natural user interfaces; human centric; user experience; perception; interaction design; models

ACM Classification Keywords

• **Human-centered computing~Gestural input** • Human-centered computing~Empirical studies in HCI • Human-centered computing~Empirical studies in interaction design • **Hardware~Tactile and hand-based interfaces.**

INTRODUCTION

Freehand gesture interaction for TV controls or content has been the subject of user studies for many years [1], with commercial products capable of freehand gesture interaction only recently emerging, for example Samsung's Smart TV [2] or LG's Magic Remote [3]. To our knowledge, no studies have so far reported on the manipulation of the TV sets' physical position and orientation, which is what we address in this work. Although not currently available, displays of this type are an inevitable consequence of the wide-spread adoption of mixed or augmented reality in the home. Like voice assistants today (Google Home, Siri, Alexa), 'visual' assistants (e.g. Piccolo [4]) will permeate the home environment, offering possibilities for content and object control. For this reason, we take a human-factors approach to investigating the gestures which can support object movements here: by understanding the human factor underlying gestures for object control, we can better design technology to empower users to control those objects in their homes.

Our aim is both to uncover the user's preferred gesture strategy and to investigate the consistency of the gesture choice and production in various naturalistic situations. This variation is important as everyday, in-home use of any system with gesture control will have to account for variations in user behavior, for example with respect to the user's ability to use one or two hands, to sit with different orientations and distances relative to the TV set, etc. Further, through our study, we hope to find evidence of the user's mental model of the TV manipulation task through their gesture preferences. Humans form mental models of the systems they interact with in order to predict and reason about their behavior [5,6]. As Norman points out [6, p8] a user's mental model is not readily observable. Instead, we aim to infer the user's mental model by observing the gesture strategies they employ to manipulate the display.

Thus, our work contributes to the area of identifying intuitive gestures for controlling TV displays from a distance – and by extension other large objects, e.g. tilting a window, turning a chair, etc. We believe this task is distinct from using gestures to manipulate content – to adjust sound, channel or other settings as addressed in gesture interaction studies such as [1, 7, 8, 9] – and thus needs special attention. The reason for this is that manipulating content addresses only virtual tasks and thus has no counterpart in the physical world. This allows gesture to be chosen with a large degree of freedom on both the designers' or users' part. In contrast, manipulating physical objects by freehand gestures entails an iconic match between the motions of the hands and the actions the user expects the device to perform. Because of this, users may expect the gestures to match and evoke what they would encounter in direct physical manipulation.

TVX '18, June 26–28, 2018, SEOUL, Republic of Korea

ACM ISBN 978-1-4503-5115-7/18/06…$15.00
https://doi.org/10.1145/3210825.3210831

Furthermore, elicitation studies rarely report on variations in the production of the identified gestures when changing the position, orientation and distance to the target device – all of which we can expect the user to encounter when using the device at home.

In this paper, we report results from three related studies investigating user preferences for gestures to control the orientation of the display itself, focusing on how production of the gestures changes with respect to the user's physical context. In so doing, we provide a methodological framework for investigating the effects of physical context on gestures. Thus, with this work, we contribute to the growing body of knowledge on touchless, freehand gesture interactions by investigating the effects of the user's physical context on the production of their device-oriented gestures.

In the following, we describe relevant work from human-human gesture studies and user-centered methods for eliciting gestures for smart devices within the fields of HCI and UX. This is followed by a presentation of our research questions, methods and findings. We end with a discussion on the implications of these results for the design and implementation of products with gesture interfaces.

RELATED WORK

Gesture description and analysis

Gestures (also called in-air gestures, 3D or freehand gestures, and touchless gestures) have been the focus of extensive research in the humanities and social sciences, particularly in the past twenty years (see [7] for a review). Although these studies focus on human-human interaction, their findings – which largely concern the extent to which gesture production is influenced by different contexts of use – are relevant to human-computer interaction both as a foundation for 'natural' and 'intuitive' gesture sets and for identifying the means by which gestures naturally vary.

Three aspects are of particular relevance for the studies we report on here: description and analysis of gesture form and location; iconicity and the relationship between visual input and gestured output; and consistency of gesture production.

In gesture studies, analysis of gestures is typically performed using manual annotation based on classification of the gesture according to one of any number of classification schemes (see [7] Section 5 for a review). We follow the approach of [13] and code the following: number of hands, handshape, gesture space using a 9-pt grid, direction of movement and extension. Together, these aspects encode the overall appearance of the gesture, and enable a human analyst to assess the extent to which one gesture resembles another.

Gestures are sensitive both to the type of information that is encoded, and to the way that information is presented in the environment. [18] find that users prefer gestures with hand-controlling-object over gestures with hand-as-object. Gestures are also typically found to mirror the environment: both [20] and [21] find that people use visual input to inform the physical appearance of the gestures that are produced, such that there is a visual match between what is seen and what it done with the hands. Further, [23] finds that this match is actually used to build accurate mental models of a given interaction. For gestures that manipulate physical objects, this iconic relationship is crucial.

The physical aspects of gesture production deserve a special comment: people are able to extend their arms and gesture quite far from their bodies in a roughly spherical shape with the arm as radius [14]. In general, people gesture as close to the centre of their torso as possible [13]. However, both the physical locations of multiple people [15] and the location of people with respect to objects in a room [17] affects the production of gestures, with people exhibiting sometimes quite drastic changes in the appearance of the gestures they perform. These effects are strongest with changes to the physical environment.

One question we can ask about gesture production is the extent to which it is consistent. As [24] point out, in the context of gesture studies, consistency is neither easy to define nor necessarily expected. Nonetheless, it's an important aspect to investigate as it can tell us the extent to which users will produce the same gesture in the same way, either with repetitions (e.g. because of poor system recognition) or across physical contexts of use; e.g. as users change location in the room. Any changes in the production of gestures that we can anticipate should become specifications for the system that makes use of them.

Gesture Control

Gesture interaction for the smart home is an increasingly attractive topic in both academia [25,7,26,27] and industry [2,3,28], with many studies focusing on how best to elicit or design gesture sets which are sufficiency natural and intuitive for users to incorporate in their daily lives, and sufficiently distinct and robust to satisfy current technology requirements. In this context, most UX work is based in the lab, where they try to match gesture forms with TV functions that control access to different kinds of content (play/pause, next/previous, zoom in/out, etc.), as, e.g., the discussion and experiments reported in [10,11] shows.

Products on the market typically have around 7 gesture-function pairs [7,28], while UX research has investigated anywhere from individual functions to sets of 12 or more [25,7,26,27]. This body of work exemplifies the difficulty in creating a satisfying gesture set, even on the human factors side, because of the huge variability in what feels good to people – whether physically or cognitively (e.g. [29,7,30]). Further, previous studies have noted that asking users to spontaneously develop gesture sets is a challenging task, e.g. [29,31,27], perhaps because communication with gestures is largely unconscious [13] and therefore hard to 'tap' into. This is arguably more true for gestures that control content than those that control movements, in large part due to the higher probability for a match in iconicity for the latter compared to the former; see Perniss & Vigliocco (2014) [22] and Müller et al. (2013) [12] for an extended discussions on iconicity in human-human gestures.

We know from prior user studies that users have a strong preference for producing gestures in which the hand '*holds*' an imagined object over gestures in which the hand '*is*' the object [18,32]. We are interested in the extent to which these findings intersect.

In our study, we infer users' mental models [6] of the manipulation task through observations of gestures and analyses of their spoken comments. As long as it allows them to solve a task, humans tend to stick with a mental model, even if it is incorrect or incomplete, although they may modify it [6]. This knowledge will in turn enable us to assess the consistency of the gestures they employ over time.

METHODS

This section explains the methods applied in the study. We first present the research questions and outline the corresponding studies. This is followed by an in-depth description of each study, focusing on the settings and coding schemes for each.

To address our research questions, we adopted a user-centered approach [29,7]. We conducted three user studies (N=16 participants each, no repetitions of test subjects across studies) with a similar premise that varied only with respect to the physical contexts encountered.

Research Questions

User Study 1: Which gestures feel best for controlling the movements of a large display from a near distance? To what extent do the number of available hands (two, one, none) affect gesture preferences for unidimensional adjustments? To what extent are users comfortable with multidimensional adjustments? We investigate this question using a lab setting.

User Study 2: How do gesture preferences and production vary with respect to the user's physical location in the room? We investigate this question using a lab setting.

User Study 3: Which gestures feel best for controlling the movements of a large display when varying the user's physical location and orientation to the display? We investigate this question using a naturalistic setting.

Across the three studies, participants first received a demonstration of how 'the moving TV' can move. In all studies, we used a mockup in the form of a wooden board the size of a 65" TV. This was mounted on a stand which was able to move sagittally, rotate horizontally and tilt vertically.

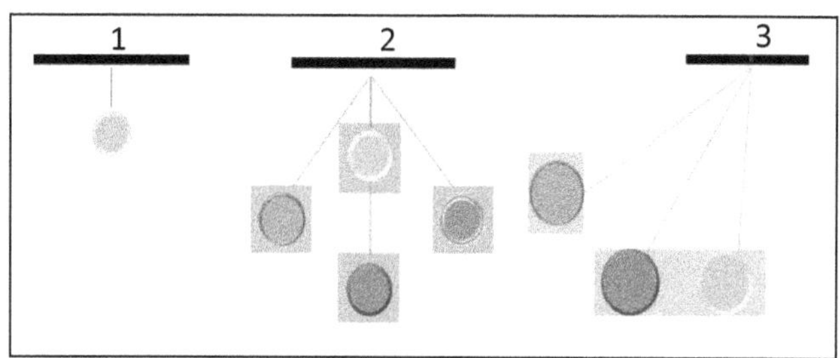

Figure 1. The relative positions for the display (rectangle) and users (circles) for studies 1, 2 and 3. The shaded areas in settings 2 and 3 denote a chair (green) and couch (pink and yellow); the lines denote the user's line of sight to the centre of the moving TV.

The setting is shown in Figure 1. Participants were told that we were interested in investigating possibilities for gesture control of the movements they had just seen. They were invited to use hand gestures that 'felt the best – the most natural' to them to control the display from a distance which varied between the studies. Participants could take as much time as they wanted to explore as many gestures as they wanted, and were asked to tell the experimenter which option(s) they preferred, and, whenever possible, why. For all gestures tried, regardless of overall preference, participants were asked to say what they liked and disliked. The tasks were designed to take 10-15 minutes; overall task length ranged from 6:15 to 21:31 minutes with an average length of 12:20 minutes.

Forty-eight participants (18 female) were recruited from within Bang & Olufsen, and had no prior knowledge about or experience with gesture interaction. Of these, 25 were 'mature' (above 30 years) and 23 were 'young' (30 years or younger). All had a high proficiency of English, provided informed verbal consent for both their participation in the task and recording of it for research purposes, and volunteered their time. Three participants self-identified as left-handed; the remainder self-identified as right-handed. All sessions were recorded with a professional video camera angled at approximately 45 degrees with respect to the participant. The data from one participant (a young female) had to be excluded because of a technical error with the recording.

Below, we describe the setting of the tasks and the coding schemes used; the codebook can be obtained by contacting the first author. All data (47 videos) were coded by the first author. Table 1 provides an overview of the coding schemes applied to the user studies. The majority of the codes describe the production of the user's gestures, which is necessary to understand how physical context affects a given gesture form. Handshape was coded following [13], and the direction of movement of the gesture following [13] and [33].

Code	Study 1	Study 2	Study 3
Handshape	X	X	X
Direction of Movement	X	X	X
Number of Hands	X	X	X
Gesture Space	X	X	X
Gesture Extension			X
Gesture Length			X
Physical Limitations	X		
(Competing) Social Associations	X		
No Hands Possible	X		
Likes	X	X	X
Dislikes	X	X	X
Action Sequence	X	X	X
Sequence of Adjustments	X	X	X
Action Sequence: Speech-Gesture Match	X	X	X
Consistency: Handshape	X	X	X
Consistency: Direction	X	X	X
Consistency: Hands	X	X	X
Consistency: Space	X	X	X

Table 1. The coding schemes used in studies 1, 2 and 3, respectively.

User Study 1

Setting. Participants in this task were invited to a large, empty meeting room where they stood 2.5m in front of the display (see setting 1 in Figure 1). They were asked to do the following: identify the gesture that 'felt the best – the most natural' to them for controlling unidirectional movements of the stand, i.e. sagittal (forward/backward), horizontal (left/right rotation) and vertical (up/down tilt) movements, using both hands, their dominant hand, their non-dominant hand, and no hands, respectively. They were then asked to sit in a chair to their left (approx. 3m from the display) and asked to make one multidimensional adjustment: move forward + rotate left + tilt down. For all gestures, participants were asked to say what they liked and disliked about their preferred strategy, as well as what they liked and disliked about strategies they had rejected.

Finally, after identifying each of their preferred gestures, participants were asked to place stickers on a mock-up of the display indicating where, if anywhere, they had imagined their hands controlling the display's movements. Task length varied from 11:27 to 17:30 minutes, with an average length of 14 minutes.

Coding Scheme The coding for study 1 is shown in the first column of Table 1. For the no hands condition, we coded whether users thought the adjustment was even possible without hands. Further, many users commented on physical constraints or associations they had with certain gesture forms, so we coded this as well. Finally, we coded whether there was a match between the strategy the user described and the one they performed. In gesture studies, a mismatch between speech and gesture usually points to active problem-solving as mental models are developed [34]; in these cases, the gestured strategy typically indicates the more mature mental model.

User Study 2

Setting. Participants in this task were invited to switch position between chairs (see setting 2 in Figure 1) in a large, empty meeting room while identifying gestures that 'felt the best – the most natural' to them for controlling multidimensional movements of the stand. In User Study 1, we identified 2 primary strategies for control: hands-as-display and hands-moving-display. In this study, participants were introduced to both strategies, and asked which, if either, they preferred, or if they would prefer to do something else entirely. As before, participants were invited to say what they liked and disliked about all strategies they tried.

Referring to Figure 1, setting 2: participants sat first in either the yellow chair (top, distance 3m from the display) or the pink chair (bottom, 6m from the display), where they adjusted sagittal and vertical dimensions (move forward + tilt down). Next, they sat in the green chair (4m and to the left of the display) then blue chair (4m and to the right of the display), where they adjusted the horizontal and vertical dimensions (rotate left or right + tilt down). Because gesture production is known to be affected by distance to the target (and by extension, device) [35,36], we used a balanced design whereby half of the participants sat first at a near distance (the yellow chair) and the other half sat first at a far distance (in the pink chair). Finally, after identifying each of their preferred gestures, participants were asked to indicate on a piece of paper with an image of the display where, if anywhere, they had imagined their hands controlling the display's movements. This was done at each chair, respectively, as soon as the preferred gesture was identified. Task length varied from 7:45 to 19:52 minutes, with an average length of 12 minutes.

Coding Scheme. To account for the different setting, we modified the coding scheme used in User Study 1 as indicated in the second column of Table 1.

User Study 3

Setting. Participants in this task moved between seats (see setting 3 in Figure 1) in a living room environment. They were asked to identify gestures that 'felt the best – the most natural' to them for controlling multidimensional movements of the stand, and were given similar instructions as in Study 2.

Because gesture production is known to be influenced by a need to 'match' visual input [21,20], this study varied the user's orientation to the display so that we could see the effect of 'mismatched' visual input. Participants first sat on the right side of the couch (3.5m from the display; yellow circle), then the left side of the couch (4m from the display; pink circle), then a side chair (3.5m from the display; green circle). In all positions, participants were asked to adjust the horizontal and vertical dimensions (rotate left + tilt down). In this way, both their orientation and distance to the display varied, with smallest adjustments needed from the yellow position and the largest adjustments needed from the green position.

Finally, after the primary adjustment described above had been made, participants were asked to hold an iPad mini in their non-dominant hand and describe what they would do to if they should have to move the display, i.e. whether they would put the iPad down to do a two-handed gesture or keep it in hand and attempt a one-handed gesture.

Task length varied from 6:15 to 21:31 minutes, with an average length of 11 minutes.

Coding Scheme. We modified the coding scheme used in User Study 2 as indicated in the rightmost column in Table 1. For gestures made while the iPad was held by the non-dominant hand, we coded the user's preferred handshape and whether the user preferred to put the iPad down or keep it in hand. If the latter, we further noted if they gestured with the iPad (e.g. as one can point with a pen or chopsticks in hand) or if they changed their strategy to one-handed.

RESULTS

This section presents the results of the three studies. The structure is as the previous section. Our main focus is on the analysis of the qualitative findings. Where appropriate, we also carried out statistical analysis to support the qualitative results.

User Study 1

Qualitative Findings Participants demonstrated two main strategies for controlling the display: hands-as-display and hands-moving-display, both produced with two hands. These are exemplified in Figure 2. Panel (A) shows hands-as-display: the palms of the hands are conceptualized as the display itself and movements of the palms are understood to be the motion of the display. Consequently, participants typically identified the center of the display as the mental landmark of their gestures. Panel (B) shows hands-moving-display, which is characterized by a grasping gesture. The motion of the hands is conceptualized as the user virtually controlling the motion of the display, as if they were doing so physically. Consequently, participants typically identified the edges of the display as the mental landmark of their gestures.

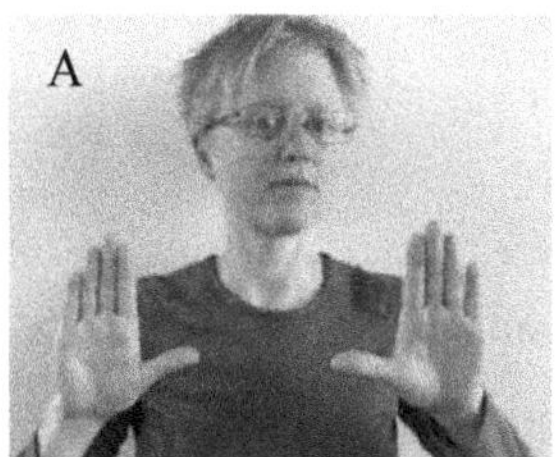

Figure 2. The two main strategies for controlling the display: hands-as-display (A) and hands-moving-display (B). The inset shows the top view.

The movements associated with these gestures are further exemplified in Figure 3 for hands-as-display and Figure 4 for hands-moving-display. For both strategies, the hands move forward and backwards simultaneously for sagittal movements and alternate forwards and backwards movements for horizontal rotational movements. As Figure 3 shows, for tilting with hands-as-display the hands move backwards from the wrist to tilt down (panel C1) and forward to tilt up (panel C2).

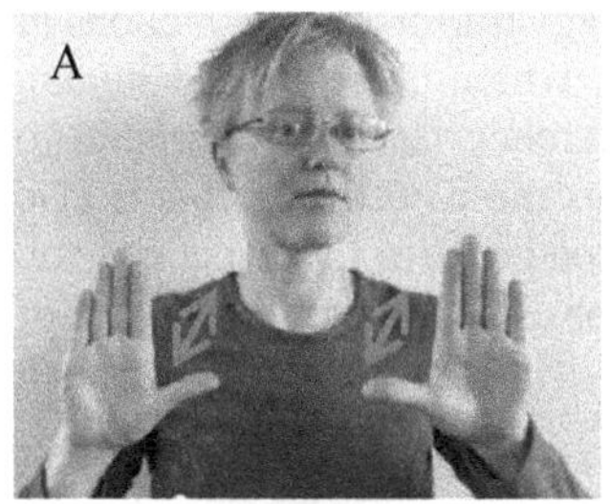

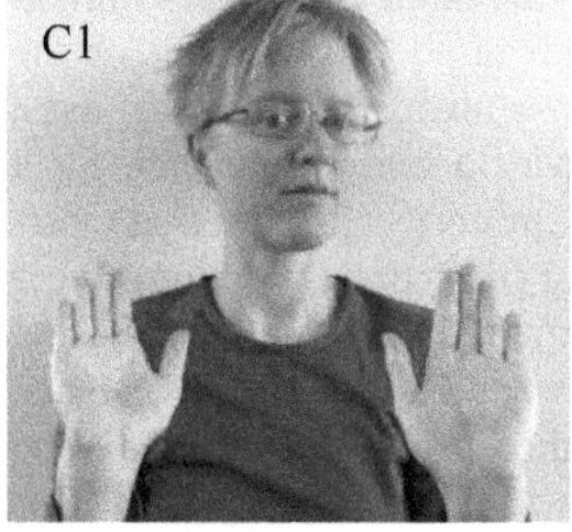

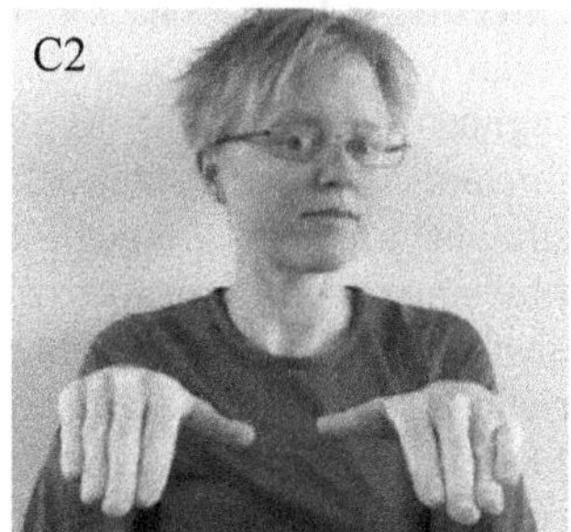

Figure 3. Primary movements for controlling the display with the hands-as-display strategy for sagittal (A), horizontal (B) and vertical (C1, C2) adjustments.

For hands-moving-display, there are two variations for tilting: one with arc traced from a horizontal position (panel C), and the other with hands moving forward and backward from a vertical position (panel D). In User Study 1, participants were equally divided between these strategies. In User Studies 2 and 3, the variation shown in panel D was favored.

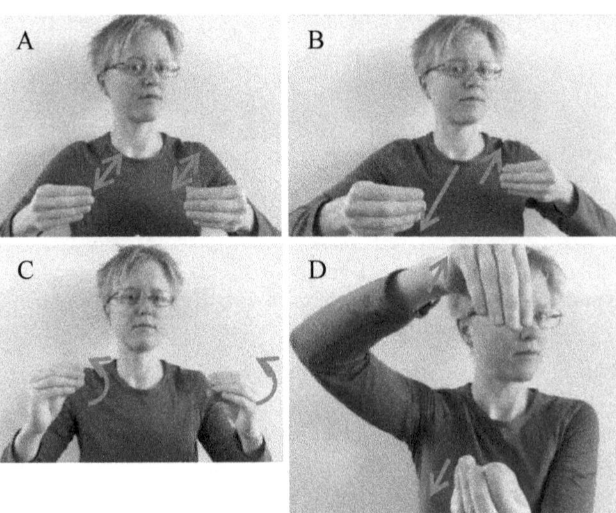

Figure 4. Primary movements for controlling the display with the hands-moving-display strategy for sagittal (A), horizontal (B) and two different vertical (C; D) adjustments.

This distinction in gesture strategy mirrors the distinctions in neuroscience and psychology, where neuro-typical human development evidences a preference for using the hand to control objects over the hand as the object [32]; this is also in line with findings from [18] on gestures for object control. Perhaps because of this, we observed that the majority of users preferred hands-moving-display because of the match to physical movements.

Direction of motion for both strategies was similar, regardless of number of hands used. Movements in the sagittal direction were always made with forwards/backwards motion, with a clear preference for a straight trajectory, though a minority preferred an arc. Movements in the horizontal direction (rotation) were always made with a straight trajectory in which the left and right hands alternated forwards and backwards movements. Movements in the vertical dimension (tilt) varied, and typically included forward/backward motion which was either straight or in an arc. For hands-as-display, this was realized as either the wrist rotation depicted in Figure 3 panels C1-2 or in an alternate form in which the entire forearm moves forward and backwards, protecting the wrist. For hands-moving-display, this was realized in the two forms depicted in Figure 4, panels C and D.

Handshape preferences exhibited more variability. All participants found control with two hands more satisfying; and all users thought that control with one hand should be possible, regardless of whether it changed the way the gesture is produced. For the condition without hands, some users jokingly suggested switching to head or feet control, but the majority said they would either give up or switch to voice.

When both hands were free, all participants performed gestures with two hands, saying that they needed to do so *for control* and *to understand* what was happening (we use *italicized text* throughout to indicate specific phrases our participants said). Seven participants proposed the same strategy to control the stand regardless of the number of hands used; the majority of these (five participants) preferred the hands-as-display strategy. These participants exhibited changes in the handshapes used. Those who preferred hands-as-display changed their handshape so that instead of having a vertical orientation, they had a horizontal orientation. Those who preferred hands-moving-display changed their gestures from grasping the left and right sides of the display to grasping only the top of the display. A majority (15) used the same strategy when controlling the stand with either their dominant or non-dominant hand, indicating that one-handed control is stable regardless of any potential handedness issues.

However, more participants (9) exhibited different preferences for control with one hand compared to two hands. This change in preference was typically realized as a switch from one strategy to another, and only when making a sagittal or vertical adjustment. For one-handed sagittal adjustments: Five participants switched to the hands-as-display strategy, commenting that it felt like asking someone to *come here*. For one-handed vertical adjustments: Three participants switched to hands-as-display because that strategy was *easier* and three switched to hands-moving-display because they felt like they *weren't strong enough* to support the 'mental weight' of the display on their wrists.

Overall, a majority of participants preferred hands-moving-display because of the match to the actions they would do if they were to actually move the display and not control its movements from a distance. Concerning hands-as-display, many noted physical limitations in wrist mobility which prevented them from performing their ideal gestures. At the same time, they also noticed interference from other gestures they would typically do. For example, many participants noted that hands-as-display *felt* like pushing someone or something away or like saying '*stop!*'. This social association conflicted strongly with the actions they were trying to perform, i.e. bring the display towards them, and pushed them to prefer a different strategy. For a deeper treatment of social context see, e.g., [19].

Perhaps because of this, we observed a lack of middle ground: participants had one clear preference for gesture strategy, and could neither understand nor empathise with an alternative. Those who preferred hands-as-display found it the more *elegant* solution and the alternative, more *brutal*. Those who preferred hands-moving-display found it *comfortable* because it matched the action they would normally do, and found the alternative *completely unrelatable*.

User Study 2

Qualitative Findings Participants demonstrated the same primary strategies for controlling the display as seen in User Study 1: hands-as-display and hands-moving-display, both with two hands. Participants drawings indicate similar mental landmarks as the previous study: users imagine their hands in the center of the TV for hands-as-display, and their hands on the edge of the TV for hands-moving-display. This is also supported by the gesture spaces used when producing the gestures: hands-as-display is typically accompanied by gestures in the center of the torso, while hands-moving-display is typically accompanied by gestures to either side of the torso. The majority of participants preferred hands-moving-display because of the match to physical movements.

In general, participants prefer two-handed gestures. They give a *better sense of control* and a *better understanding* of the real-time orientation of the display. However, some participants noted that one-handed gestures have the potential for being easier in social situations as they take less space. However, these participants also noted that it would *take time* to learn to use and trust the one-handed variations.

In the front (yellow) chair, participants tended to use a wider gesture space, while in the back (pink) chair, users tended to use a narrower gesture space. Many participants commented on this difference, saying that the distance was the source of the change – when they were close, their hands should be further apart so they could *grasp* the edge of the display; when they were far, their hands should be closer together so they could still grasp the edges. Thus, from a participant perspective, the model is the same (*grasp* the edge) but from a system perspective, the gestures look quite different: in the close chair, the size of the gesture is quite large, reaching into the extreme periphery of the user's gesture space – while in the far chair, the size of the gesture is quite small, often in the center of the user's gesture space.

As before, users exhibited a clear preference for one strategy, and could neither understand nor empathize with the alternative. Those who preferred hands-as-display found it *futuristic* and *techy cool*, while the alternative *was not natural because you're grasping air*. Those who preferred hands-moving-display found it *more powerful* because it matched the action they would normally and instinctively do, and found the alternative *completely unrelatable*.

Concerning gesture variations which stem from changes in the participants' physical location in the room: Gesture strategy (hands-as-display vs. hands-moving-display) was fairly consistent, with a majority preferring the same strategy across locations, and a minority changing strategies. The number of hands used was also largely consistent across locations. However, participants noted that for making horizontal adjustments, they would prefer to use *only* their dominant hand when it controlled the side of the display that should move (rotation from the green chair for righties and the blue chair for lefties) and that they would need *both hands* when controlling movements from the non-dominant side (rotation from the blue chair for righties and the green chair for lefties). Gesture space showed the most variation: the same gesture space was used in both the left (green) and right (blue) chairs, where the gestures were typically performed in the periphery of gesture space. For the front (yellow) and back (pink) chairs, however, different gesture spaces were used: periphery or extreme periphery for the front location and the center or periphery for the back location. While this might at first seem an inconsistency, from the user perspective, this is actually evidence of a consistent mental model: if their gestures grasp the edge of the display, their hands should of course be further apart when the display takes more space in the visual field.

User Study 3

Qualitative Findings Participants demonstrated the same main strategies for controlling the display as seen in User Studies 1 and 2: hands-as-display and hands-moving-display, both with two hands. Hands-as-display was typically accompanied by gestures in the center of the torso, while hands-moving-display was typically accompanied by gestures to either side of the torso. A majority preferred hands-moving-display because of the match to physical movements.

Participants tended to prefer the same gesture strategy across locations, and in every case but one performed the gestures in all three locations with the same number of hands (two). Most gestures were performed in the same gesture space across locations, typically the periphery. What differed was the extension of the gestures. In this task, participants were faced with an increasingly longer rotation challenge. As they moved from the 'easy' (yellow) to 'hard' (green) seat, the extension of the gestures increased. The length of the gestures also increased – but only for the right hand, which was the hand leading the rotation adjustment. For some participants, not only the length but the amount of body involved in the gesture increased, e.g. some leaned forward to start the movement and leaned back to finish it, others crossed the torso during the gesture and one even changed their gesture's handshape to accommodate the large distance the device (and therefore gesture) should travel. When asked, all participants who exhibited a change said that they had to do so in order to make a physical match to what they could see, i.e. that there should be an isomorphic match between their visual input and the gesture they produce (cf. [21,20]). This is strong evidence of a consistent mental model with different realizations that the system should be made aware of.

Finally, in this study, participants were asked for gesture preferences with both hands free or if one hand was occupied by a tablet. When both hands were free, participants preferred two-handed gestures as they give a better sense of control. When one hand was occupied by a device, participants had differing opinions. Some preferred to put the device down so that they could continue to enjoy two-handed control. However, more frequently, participants preferred to keep the device in their non-dominant hand and perform a one-handed gesture because it would be *annoying* or *inconvenient* to have to put the iPad down and then pick it back up. These participants performed the one-handed version of their otherwise preferred gesture strategy.

Quantitative findings

Although the focus has been on the qualitative findings, we carried out quantitative analyses where appropriate. Table 2 below shows a summary of the initially preferred gesture across all three studies:

Study	hands-as-display	hands-moving-display	Total
1	8	8	16
2	6	9	15
3	3	11	14
Total	17	28	45

Table 2. Summary of initially preferred gesture choice. One participant was omitted from Study 3 due to missing data.

The number of participants in Study 1 is (N=16), which is too low to analyze male-female, young-mature differences. However, in Study 2 and 3, participants were given exactly the same instructions, and thus we combine the studies when investigating their preferred initial gesture and whether they stick to their preference throughout the positions. Firstly, a X^2 test showed (X^2, N=31, p=0.025) that users stick to their initial selected strategy regardless of their relative position and rotation. Secondly, we found that males show a significant preference (X^2, N=17, p=0.05) for the hands-moving-display, whereas females showed no significant preferences. Similarly, young users exhibited no significant preferences, while mature users showed (X^2, N=16, p=0.0001) a clear preference for hands-moving-display.

DISCUSSION

Our findings show that users have a preferred strategy for gesture control which is both context invariant and context sensitive. User strategies are invariant in the sense that once a user has identified a preferred strategy – and thus formed a mental model of the gesture manipulation, that strategy 'works' for them regardless of environmental changes. In particular, all users performed gestures which drew on the iconic relationship between what the user saw and what they felt would be appropriate to do with their hands based on what they saw. In this sense, there was a 'match' to the mental model even though there was a 'mismatch' in the way the gestures were produced. Because of this, user strategies can be considered sensitive to context in the sense that features of the gestures they produce do change – sometimes quite substantially – depending on changes to their immediate environment. To summarize:

- Physical location influences the production of gestures, but not the choice; this is important from a technology perspective
- Preferred gestures are consistent across changes in physical locations; this is important from a UX perspective
- We observed two main strategies reflecting 2 distinct mental models: (1) hand-as-display vs. (2) hand-moving-display; this is line with the findings in [18] about gestures that encode transitive actions such as the ones investigated here. This is important for future work with mixed or augmented reality, where standards for this kind of object manipulation are being developed.

CONCLUSIONS

We carried out a series of three naturalistic gesture elicitation studies where parameters such as distance and orientation (angle) to the device and number of 'free' hands varied. Across all studies, we found a consistent choice of preferred gestures, as well as consistent changes to the production of those gestures which varied with respect to the user's location in the room. Thus, to successfully implement a gesture-controlled display, engineers must take this into account and support not only the gesture strategies identified, but also the changes to them which the user's environment evokes. As interest and demand for gesture interaction grows, possibilities to control objects with gestures (not only content) will grow as well. We believe it's important for UX to consider not only the relevant use cases, but also interactions which are contextualized and tailored to the user's home – allowing them as much or more freedom than they enjoy there today.

FUTURE WORK & LIMITATIONS

Our research focused on aspects of gesture production which could be easily coded by a human researcher watching video recordings. This was done both so that our results could be directly comparable to findings from gesture studies, and because of our focus on gesture recognition using visible data. Other aspects of gesture production – such as the speed of the gesture, the actual distances travelled by the hands and arms, and more subtle changes in handshape – could be made apparent with wearable devices, such as motion capture or accelerometers attached to the wrists. For pairing gesture speed to speed of the TV's movement, which is the next step needed with our current setup, this might even be appropriate as a starting point. We did not include them here as our long-term research goal focuses on freehand gesture control *without* wearables.

In user study 3, we noticed that users were orienting their gestures and body position to that of the device – some commented that adopting the frame-of-reference of the device (allocentric) was necessary to *understand* how the movement should happen, and one commented that they preferred to keep their own (egocentric) frame-of-reference because it was *easier*. Future work could investigate which frame-of-reference users find more natural, and in which contexts of use, or compare user feelings and success rates using allocentric vs. egocentric frames-of-reference when completing the same task.

We agree with [18] and [7] that 'a good gesture vocabulary is ... context-specific' to the extent that there is a 'match' between the proposed gesture and the response given by the device. However, as our work demonstrates, gestures which 'match' a specific context of use exhibit production variation which change as the user's physical context changes. We expect that this will be the case regardless of the gesture vocabulary tested. More work is needed to explore the full extent of this variation so that devices with gesture control can be made as robust as possible for detecting the full range of gestures which users 'naturally' and 'intuitively' produce. This is particularly true if devices should enter user's homes and move away from lab or game settings.

ACKNOWLEDGEMENTS

We thank our participants for their time and enthusiasm, and Søren Bech, Lyle Clarke, Tina Øvad and Ben Verbraak for comments on an earlier draft.

REFERENCES

1. William T. Freeman, Craig D. Weissman. 1995. Television Control by Hand Gestures. In: Proc. of IEEE Int. Workshop on Automatic Face and Gesture Recognition, Zurich.
2. Samsung Smart TV: TV Gesture book – Waving a Hand. http://www.samsung.com/ph/smarttv/common/guide_book_3p_si/waving.html
3. LG USA 2016. How to Use LG Smart TV Magic Remote (2016 - 2017). Youtube video by LG USA Home Appliances and Electronics, 2016. Link visited Jan 29 2018. https://www.youtube.com/watch?v=uoxYO9DslkA
4. Piccolo Labs. 2018. Retrieved from https://www.piccololabs.com.
5. Kenneth J. W. Craik. 1943. The nature of explanation. Cambridge: Cambridge University Press.
6. Don A. Norman. 1983. Some observations on mental models. Mental models, 7(112), pp.7-14.
7. Radu-Daniel Vatavu. 2012. User-defined gestures for free-hand TV control. In Proceedings of the 10th European conference on interactive TV and video (EuroITV'12), 45-48.
8. Jan Bobeth, Susanne Schmehl, Ernst Kruijff, Stephanie Deutsch, Manfred Tscheligi. 2012. Evaluating performance and acceptance of older adults using freehand gestures for TV menu control. In Proc. of EuroiTV '12, 35-44.
9. Oskar Juhlin, Elin Önnevall. 2013. On the relation of ordinary gestures to TV screens: general lessons for the design of collaborative interactive techniques. In Proc. of CHI '13. ACM, New York, NY, USA, 919-930
10. Jesper Kjeldskov, Mikael Skov. 2014 Was it Worth the Hassle? Ten Years of Mobile HCI Research Discussions on Lab and Field Evaluations. In Proc. of MobileHCI, 2014, Toronto, ON, Canada.
11. Celeste Groenwald et al. Understanding 3D mid-air hand gestures with interactive surfaces and displays: A systematic literature review. Proceedings of British HCI 2016, Bournemouth, UK.
12. Cornelia Müller, Alan Cienki, Elen Fricke, Silva Ladewig, David McNeill, Sedinha Teßendorf (Eds.) 2013. Body-Language-Communication. de Gruyter Mouton, Berlin.
13. David McNeill. 1992. Hand and mind: What gestures reveal about thought. University of Chicago Press, Chicago.
14. Matthias Priesters. 2013. Functional patterns in gesture space. Institut für Sprach- und Kommunikationswissenschaft der RWTH Aachen.
15. Asli Özyürek. 2002. Do speakers design their cospeech gestures for their addressees? The effects of addressee location on representational gestures. Journal of Memory & Language, 46: 688-704.
16. Wanhong Ling, Lear Du, Carisa Harris-Adamson, Alan Barr, David Rempel. 2017. Design of hand gestures for manipulating objects in virtual reality. In *Proceedings of the SIGCHI Conference on Computer-Human-Interaction* (CHI'17), 584-592.
17. Eve Sweetser, Marisa Sizemore. 2008. Personal and interpersonal gesture spaces: Functional contrasts in language and gesture. *Language in the context of use: Discourse and cognitive approaches to language*, 25-51.
18. Sukeshini A. Grandhi, Gina Joue, Irene Mittelberg. 2011. Understanding naturalness and intuitiveness in gesture production: insights for touchless gestural interfaces. In Proceedings of the *SIGCHI Conference on Human Factors in Computing Systems*, 821-824.
19. Julie Rico, Stephen A. Brewster. 2010). Usable gestures for mobile interfaces: evaluating social acceptability. In: Proceedings of the SIGCHI Conference on Human Factors in Computing Systems, Atlanta, Georgia, USA, 10-15 Apr 2010.
20. Raedy Ping, Susan Goldin-Meadow. 2010. Gesturing saves cognitive resources when talking about nonpresent objects. Cognitive Science, 34: 602–619.
21. Pamela Perniss, Asli Özyürek. 2015. Visible cohesion: A comparison of reference tracking in sign, speech, and co-speech gesture. Topics in Cognitive Science, 7: 36-60.

22. Pamela Perniss, Gabriella Vigliocco. 2014. The bridge of iconicity: from a world of experience to the experience of language. Phil. Trans. R. Soc. B 369: 20130300. http://dx.doi.org/10.1098/rstb.2013.0300

23. Thomas C. Gunter, J.E. Douglas Weinbrenner, Henning Holle. 2015. Inconsistent use of gesture space during abstract pointing impairs language comprehension. Frontiers in Psychology, 6, 80: 1-10.

24. Fey Parrill, Kashmiri Stec. 2017. Gestures of the abstract: Do speakers use space consistently and contrastively when gesturing about abstract concepts? Pragmatics & Cognition, 24, 1: 33-61.

25. Ionuţ-Alexandru Zaiţi, Ştefan-Gheorghe Pentiuc, Radu-Daniel Vatavu. 2015. On free-hand TV control: experimental results on user-elicited gestures with Leap Motion." Personal and Ubiquitous Computing, 19, 5-6: 821-838.

26. Arthur Theil Cabreira, Faustina Hwang. 2015. An analysis of mid-air gestures used across three platforms. Proceedings of the 2015 British HCI Conference, 257-258.

27. Sang-Su Lee, Jeonghun Chae, Hyunjeong Kim, Youn-kyung Lim, Kun-pyo Lee. Towards More Natural Digital Content Manipulation via User Freehand Gestural Interaction in a Living Room. In *Proceedings of the 2013 ACM joint conference on pervasive and ubiquitous computing (UbiComp'13)*, 617-626.

28. Micha Galor, Jonathan Pokrass, Bat-Yam, Amir Hoffnung. Apple Corp. 2013. Three Dimensional User Interface Session Control. United States Patent No.: US 8,933,876 B2

29. Michael Nielsen, Moritz Storring, Thomas B. Moeslund, Erik Granum. 2004. A procedure for developing intuitive and ergonomic gesture interfaces for HCI. In A. Camurri and G. Volpe (eds.). *Gesture-Based Communication in Human-Computer Interaction*: 5th International Gesture Workshop, GW 2003, LNCS 2915, Springer, Berlin, 409-420.

30. Debaleena Chattopadhyay, Davide Bolchini. 2015. Motor-intuitive interactions based on image schemas: Aligning touchless interaction primitives with human sensorimotor abilities. Interacting with Computers 27, 3: 327-343.

31. Haiwei Dong, Ali Danesh, Nadia Figueroa, Abdulmotaleb el Saddik. 2015. An elicitation study on gesture preferences and memorability toward a practical hand-gesture vocabulary for smart televisions. IEEE Access 3: 543-555.

32. Chris J. Boyatzis, Malcolm W. Watson. 1993. Preschool children's symbolic representation of objects through gestures. Child Development 64: 729-735.

33. Jana Bressem. 2012. Repetitions in gesture – structures, function, and cognitive aspects. PhD Dissertation, Universität Viadrina Frankfurt (Oder).

34. R. Breckinridge Church, Susan Goldin-Meadow. 1986. The mismatch between gesture and speech as an index of transitional knowledge. Cognition 23, 2: 43-71.

35. Chloe Gonseth, Anne Vilain, Coriandre Vilain. 2012. An experimental study of speech/gesture interactions and distance encoding. Speech communication 55, 4: 553-571.

36. Ielka van der Sluis, Emiel Krahmer. 2004. The influence of target size and distance on the production of speech and gesture in multimodal referring expressions. In Proceedings of the 5th International Conference on Spoken Language Processing (ICSLP'04), Jeju, Korea.

Frictional Realities:
Enabling Immersion in Mixed-Reality Performances

Asreen Rostami
Stockholm University
Stockholm, Sweden
asreen@dsv.su.se

Chiara Rossitto
Stockholm University
Stockholm, Sweden
chiara@dsv.su.se

Annika Waern
Uppsala University
Uppsala, Sweden
annika.waern@im.uu.se

ABSTRACT

This paper presents a case study of a Mixed-Reality Performance employing 360-degree video for a virtual reality experience. We repurpose the notions of friction to illustrate the different threads at which priming is enacted during the performance to create an immersive audience experience. We look at aspects of friction between the different layers of the Mixed-Reality Performance, namely: *temporal friction*, *friction between the physical and virtual presence* of the audience, and *friction between realities*. We argue that Mixed-Reality Performances that employ immersive technology, do not need to rely on its presumed immersive nature to make the performance an engaging or coherent experience. Immersion, in such performances, emerges from the audience' transition towards a more active role, and the creation of various fictional realities through frictions.

Author Keywords

Mixed reality performance; immersive video; immersion; priming; virtual reality; VR; interactive performance.

ACM Classification Keywords

• Human-centered computing~Mixed / augmented reality • Human-centered computing~Virtual reality • Human-centered computing~HCI theory, concepts and models • Human-centered computing~Collaborative interaction • Human-centered computing~Empirical studies in HCI • Applied computing~Performing arts • Applied computing~Media arts

INTRODUCTION

Over the past fifteen years, *Desert Rain* [30] has been the most emblematic example of a Mixed-Reality Performance (MRP) employing Virtual Reality (VR). As the technological barrier for using VR in performance art has drastically lowered, we are witnessing a renewed interest in the use of this technology. MRPs such as *Decompensation* [17], *Me and the Machine* [40], *Whist* [56], and trans-medial projects like *Orpheus* [52] provide examples of how artists adopt and appropriate 360-degree video.

TVX '18, June 26–28, 2018, SEOUL, Republic of Korea

ACM ISBN 978-1-4503-5115-7/18/06...$15.00
https://doi.org/10.1145/3210825.3210827

While VR and 360-videos are usually regarded as immersive technologies, in this paper, we argue that immersion is not an inherent quality of this medium that results from its technical properties. In so doing, we illustrate how artists enact performing strategies around the use of these media to create rich and meaningful audience experiences. We talk about these strategies as *frictions,* and we analyse how they are used within MRPs to create a dialogical relationship between the audience and performance, and create a meaningful, sensorial and embodied [38]. Within digital storytelling [2] frictions have been defined as inherent struggles in the plot that keep the audience engaged with the story. Here, we repurpose this notion to the domain of MRPs to discuss the audience participation to the narration of the performance, the fluctuation between the audience "real" (and physical) world and the "virtual" one of the 360-video, and between the physical and virtual presence of the audience in the performance. All these aspects of the audience experience –and not merely interacting with the technology- enable immersion with the 360-degree video and engagement with the performance as a whole. We regard the notion of friction as a "strong concept" [26] to talk about immersion and engagement within the application domain of Mixed-Reality Performances that use 360-degree video.

Of particular interest here are two related concepts of seamfulness and trajectories. Both concepts have broadly been explored and used in studies of mobile games and MRPs. Seamfulness explains how seams and gaps within the technology infrastructure can be used as features in the design of technology tools [5,11,15]. The concept of trajectories [8] describes instead the audience journeys through the performance, including narratives, spaces, times, roles and interfaces. Compared to seamful design that exposes glitches and transitions between one media to another, frictions are designed and enacted by the artists delicately to manipulate audiences' perception of time and space through the "live" experience. On the other hand, and compared to trajectories, friction shifts the focus from the audience journeys to blurring the boundaries between audience and performers, and how this can result in a sensorial and embodied experience of the 360-degree video and the performance itself.

VR has been defined "as virtual space to be visited and navigated through" [41], and which users can interact with through various interaction modalities (i.e., lifting objects and experiencing their texture). Yet the common understanding of VR also includes more static videos (i.e., 360-degree videos) and using Head-Mounted Displays (HDMs) that block our view from the surrounding environment.

This paper introduces *Strange Days,* as an example of a Mixed-Reality Performance that uses 360-degree video and HMDs to virtually recreate the experience of past events, allowing audience members to visually experience them from the performers' point of view. *Strange Days* is the re-enactment of memories that the performers and the audience members share with each other during a live experience, designed and performed by Bombina Bombast [57]. In the tradition of TVX in investigating real-world experiences, studying *Strange Days* provided us with a valuable opportunity to explore the existing artistic practices [33] around VR use that contribute to an immersive and meaningful experience, and to illustrate the analytical and design issues such a focus raises.

We contribute by introducing frictions as a frame to understand immersion with 360- degree video in relation to the broader experience of participating in the performance. Immersion emerges from the audience's transition towards a more active role in the narration, emotional engagement with the story, and the tension between the sense of presence in the 360-video and in the physical space that includes other audience members and performers. The relevance of the contribution in this paper lays at the intersection of MRP and VR, and in the growing discourse on 360-degree storytelling [55]. We also contribute to the design of interactions with VR technologies that try to merge the virtual world with physical one (i.e., commercial systems such as Microsoft HoloLens and Facebook Social VR).

After reviewing related literature, we offer a detailed description of the performance we have studied, its setup, and the research method employed. We analyse the collected data applying the lens of frictions to highlight temporal friction, friction between the physical and virtual presence of the audience, and friction between realities. By reflecting on these findings, we discuss different methods by which immersion can be enabled.

RELATED WORK

Our case study is grounded in two main research areas: the HCI body of work on Mixed-Reality Performances, and research exploring the use of VR and immersive technologies in performing arts.

Virtual Reality in the Performing Arts

Over the past, few years there has been significant technological developments in virtual reality devices, in terms of their commercial potential, cost, and availability. Systems that used to have niche hardware requirement can now be supported with commercially available devices ranging from the HTC Vive VR headset to Google Cardboard that transforms smartphones into 'Mobile VR' headsets. The increasing number of projects creating content for different fields (for example games [45], education [22] and healthcare [44]), are evidence of growing interest in this field. HCI researchers have particularly focused on studies illustrating technical aspects of using virtual reality. These include challenges in augmented reality environments (such as depth perception [14]), tools (such as HMDs [1,16]) or novel techniques for optical configuration [25] in order to ease the visual discomfort [31], or exploring human behaviour addressing the impact of AR and VR experiences for chronic pain patients [24].

In *History of Virtual Reality Performance* [18], Dixon provided a comprehensive survey of virtual reality for performing arts up to 2006. Over a decade later, and with a considerable technological improvement of VR equipment (360-degree video recorders, haptic sensors, head-mounted display with high resolution and low motion blur, etc.), we have witnessed a new wave of curators, filmmakers, and artists using this technology to create artistic experiences. Yet, despite the popularity, there is little of academic work about VR in performances. Unlike the old VR performances that heavily relied on computer generated 3D environments [18], most recent productions use real world images and videos to create more photo-realistic [42] virtual reality environments. The key technology advancement that made this possible was the adoption of panoramic video cameras which allow for 360-degree video recordings. This comes at the cost of limiting the opportunities for interaction, as the videos are pre-recorded and offer little or no opportunities for the audience member to touch or manipulate content in the environment. Some performances rely on 360-degree video as the main component of the performance for the audience. A characteristic example is *Decompensation* [17], a Mixed-Reality Performance in which the artist recreates different psychological stages that a "refugee perhaps pass through when moving and settling into a new social or cultural context over the span of many years". Dehghani used 360-degree video to create an experience, in which participants can experience displacement by physically changing the location and (moving from one scene to another).

This renewed interest in VR for the performing arts calls for the development of research studies that help us understanding and analyse audience' engagement with VR.

Immersion

The term immersion is widely used in a number of fields such as theatre, art installation, performance art or VR experiences. In theatre and performance art, immersion has been associated with audience participation and their intimate engagement with the piece or actors [35] as seen, for example, in promenade performances such as Sleep No More [58]. In these immersive performances audience becomes part of the performance and has the freedom (to some extent)[3] to interact with the performers, explore the space, and get engaged with performance activities [53]. In another reflection, several art installations (see for example *The Way Earthly Things Are Going* [49]) use the term to describe the sense of presence and how the art installation relies on one or multiple sensory inputs (i.e., hearing) to separate the spectator from "real world" and put her or him in an intimate moment in order to create an aesthetic experience. This exclusion from the "real world" (potentially) results in getting "immersed" in the artwork [35]. This definition, however, has been altered in those artistic practices that use digital technologies to immerse the audience [19]. In most of these digital immersive experiences, immersive technology (i.e., virtual reality) becomes the key feature to aid the immersion, often by recreating (or simulating) a lived experience for the audience. In this respect, Gordon Calleja [14] takes digital game studies as the main filed of exploration to highlight how the use of the term "immersion" varies from player's suspension of disbelief to player's perception of the designed world as well as players' engagement with the story, game world and characters. By this, he suggests the term immersion should be understood under the context it is used. In this regard and keeping digital games (that use interactive and 3-D designed environments) as the main context, Calleja looks at different level of player involvement with the game and how these involvements can enable an immersive game experience. While discussing these player involvements, he also looks at the immersion in three levels i) participation, ii) imagination, interpretation and interaction, and finally through player's iii) own narration of perceived experience.

Borrowing from Calleja's work on digital game studies, in this study we use the term immersion in the context of Mixed-Reality Performances as an interchange between the audience members' act of "absorbing" the art piece and artistic vision of MRP, and their transition towards a more active participation in the context of the performance [14].

Friction

Framing it within digital storytelling, Brayn Alexander defines friction as the inherent struggle in a plot in a story [2]. In this definition friction is not used with a negative connotation, rather it is the source of tension which grabs the attention of the audience, providing the energy that fuels their engagement beyond the curiosity sparked by interesting characters, style or world building. One example of this definition is different layers of mysteries and puzzles in a criminal story that the protagonist needs to uncover and solve in order to find the criminal (see for example, *The Killing* [59], a crime drama television series with twisted plots). While the complexity of the plot in this type of stories can keep the audience hooked to the stories, it should also have enough meaning for the audience to make sense and follow the story.

While Alexander sees frictions as a way to connect to the story, Stenros et al. [27] regard them as a source of disengagement. They associate the term with "issues" or "major cause of problems" in the narratives of a participatory drama. For Stenros et al. and their particular example of an alternate reality game, these problems can vary from character mismatches between online and live players, between fictional characters and production crew, or between aesthetics of online content and live events. They introduce these problems as frictions in narratives that disengages the player from the participatory drama and different beats of its story.

Having introduced these two different takes on the definition of friction, we adopt the term from Alexander's work to build upon the growing interest in VR and to discuss audience's engagement and immersion in the context of Mixed-Reality Performances that use 360-degree video.

Mixed-Reality Performance within HCI

Benford and Giannachi [7] introduced the term Mixed-Reality Performance to describe complex and hybrid artistic experiences which incorporate combinations of live and interactive performance where audience and performers interact with technology and digital media in real and virtual world. *Desert Rain* [6,30] is an emblematic Mixed-Reality Performance in which participants (players) experience virtual warfare in order to re-evaluate the boundaries between physical, fictional, real and virtual worlds. The "virtual world" in *Desert Rain*, is in fact, a combination of physical space and objects (designed for the purpose of the performance) and the projected video onto six rain curtains and screens. This setting was, however, different from those virtual environments that one can experience with recent VR technologies using HMDs. As a result of this performance and similar productions, the trajectories framework was developed [7,10]. In this analytical framework, performance experiences are viewed as journeys where the canonical narratives are intertwined with interpreted narratives, going through both spaces, times, roles and interfaces [8]. Several performance experiences have been designed using the trajectory framework, and researchers have illustrated how trajectories can be used in practice to analyse and control interactive performances and experiences [7]. This framework has been shown useful for both design and understanding of MRPs, such as enabling a dramaturgy for interactive experiences, identifying requirements for new technologies and for understanding better concepts within the overall performance experience [7,8,10].

Research on interactive performances have also investigated different modalities of audience participation such as audience's individual and social interaction with the artwork [16], audience's biodata as a source of input to interact with the performance [43] and audience's wittingness in relation

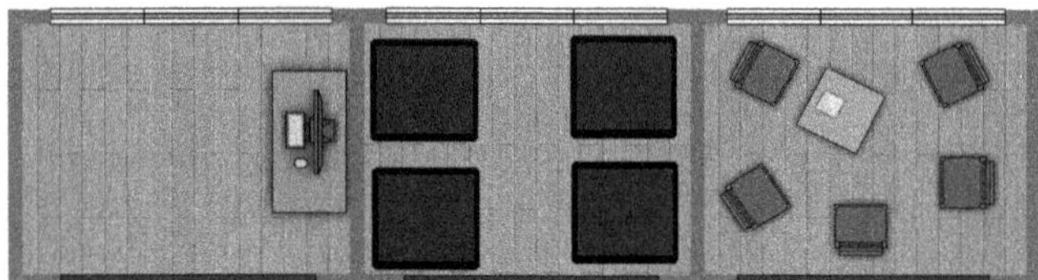

Figure 1. An illustration of the 3 rooms of the performance. Right: Room one, Middle: Room two, and Left: Room three.

to the performance [47]. The Humanacquarium [50,51], for instance, has focused on the mutual relationship between the performers and the audience and how participating can enable emotional encounters between different people and different roles.

In what follows, through analysis of a Mixed-Reality Performance we go beyond trajectories and seamful design to discuss how the notion of friction creates a dialogical relationship between the audience and performance in order to make the experience meaningful, sensorial and embodied. This relationship, we argue, enables immersion not only with the 360-degree video but the performance as a whole.

THE PERFORMANCE: STRANGE DAYS

Strange Days is a Mixed-Reality Performance that combines live performance with 360-degree video. It was designed and performed by Bombina Bombast, a leading performing arts company in Sweden that explores the use of innovative technologies (e.g., VR) in their work. Strange Days is inspired by a science fiction movie of the same name, directed by Kathryn Bigelow, in which the characters can re-experience the physical sensations of others. Bombina Bombast sought to realize this dystopian idea with currently available technology. The performance centres around the re-enactment of several memories and stories about important life events that the artists and the audience members share with each other. During the performance sharing is performed at three levels: through recounting the memories and the stories associated with them, through listening to songs associated with those memories, and through re-experiencing a memory using a 360-degree video.

Setup of "Strange Days"

This Mixed-Reality Performance is organized in three parts, each one taking place in a separate physical room (Figure 1). During the performance, audience members move through each room in sequence where they are met by a performer. When this study was carried out, audience members experienced the performance in groups of four; the rooms were fairly small (app. 10 m2) and located next to each other.

Room one

Strange Days starts with a facilitator leading participants into the first room (Figure 1, right). There, they meet the first performer, Steffan, who introduces himself and invites them to take a seat. On each chair there is a headphone set, all connected to a single iPad which is placed on the table and in front of the actor-performer (Figure 2 a). Stefan then sets out the narration by briefly introducing the performance and what they will experience in each room. Following this, he starts by sharing his own story and memory about his childhood, when he moved to Sweden from Serbia, during its civil war. He continues by describing how this ethnic childhood music suddenly became popular in the new country, and how the shared interest in this music genre helped him to connect to a new socio-cultural context. After this, he asks everyone to think about a song they value, then share the name of that song and the memories associated with it with the group. As audience members recall and retell their stories, he uses his tablet to find the song. Right after, he asks the audience to put the headphones on and listen to each song together, one by one. This part of the performance usually takes between 35-40 minutes, depending on the length of the songs and the conversation between the audience members and the performer.

Room two

In the second room (Figure 1, middle), audience members get invited by another performer, Emma, to sit or stand in the space that is covered by black rugs. These rugs are designed to resemble the floor in the 360-degree video that the audience members are going to explore. The performer then starts by sharing her story about a song that helped her face the grief and anguish of her parents' divorce. Then she describes an emotional and memorable day, when her partner surprised her by inviting a band to play that song just for her in their apartment. She gives a detailed account of that experience as she stood in the middle of the room, in the middle of the band which was playing for her, while her partner was holding her hand. Then she explicitly tells the audience that this is the memory that she wants to share with them.

After this line, she helps the audience put on the head-mounted displays and the headphones to watch and listen to the 360-degree video (Figure 2 b). In this video they experience the musical performance described from her point of view. A minute or two into the experience, the performer walks around the audience and holds each audience members' hand, one at a time, for 15-20 seconds. This is a way to share the special moment she experienced when her partner held her hand in the memory she recounts. The video is five minutes and 35 seconds long. The performance in the second room usually takes 10 up to13 minutes.

Room three

In the last room (Figure 1, left), Svante, the third performer, meets the audience and asks to choose who would receive a memory stick containing all the songs the group shared in the first room. After this, the performance ends and the audience members are led back to the waiting area.

RESEARCH METHODS

Over the last two years, *Strange Days* has been performed over 40 times in five different countries. However, this is, the first time that Bombina Bombast agreed to perform it for

Figure 2. (a) Performer (right) and audience members listening to each other's song (b) audience members viewing the musical performance in 360-degree video

research purposes. The artists' requirements were simply three small rooms located next to each other. The spatial setup was thus similar to the previous runs as the performances were designed and conceived to be portable. The layout of each room was organised to host four participants at a time, as well as one performer. Each group was scheduled to arrive at different times, thus minimizing the chance that they would meet and talk about the performance before experiencing it.

More than 300 people with different professional or amateur interest in performing arts, technology, design, or VR were invited, and heterogeneous group of 15 participants volunteered. They were 8 female and 7 male participants, ranging in age from 23 to 54 with a variety of professions including artists, researchers, students, developers, business directors and a retired teacher. We have given the participants pseudonyms to preserve their anonymity in relation to the quotes, however at the request of the artists we have used their real names throughout.

The purpose of our study was to explore the audience members' subjective experience of participating in the performance. This motivates our choice of data collection methods grounded in the social sciences (observations and interviews), drawing attention to the performance as an artefact (techniques and properties it embodies, see for instance [4]), or to the audience reception of the artistic vision.

Data collection

The empirical material was collected during four runs of the performance that took place on the same day. A total of four hours of observations was conducted while the participants experienced the performance. The observations focused on aspects of audience members' interactions with each other, and with the performing artists. We also looked at the participants' orientation towards the physical layout of the rooms in which the performance was experienced, and towards the other people present. For video recordings, one GoPro camera was placed in each room, which allowed us to capture an overview of the whole room, the people in it and the interactions between them. During the first run, one of the authors participated in the performance while observing the setting (participant observation). This was instrumental to gain a first-hand experience of the performance. To avoid being too intrusive, her interactions with the other audience members were limited to what was required by the artists.

When each performance was over, all the participants were interviewed individually through semi-structured interviews, in order to get immediate feedback from their experiences. Each interview lasted between 15-20 minutes and all recorded and transcribed. As the interviews were carried out immediately after the performance, they constituted the first occasion for the participants to discuss and share their experiences about the performance. We regard them as moments for the interviewees to utter their first impressions, and to start developing an opinion about the whole experience through talking to somebody else. We asked participants to describe their experience with the 360-degree video, and their experience in the different rooms, including their connection to the story or their contribution to the performance through sharing their personal memories and stories.

The authors of this paper were not involved in design of the performance nor its deployment. Our only contribution was to invite audience members and schedule their arrivals, and provide space and equipment for Bombina Bombast to reform and set the performance. In this respect, artists were not involved in designing the interview questions, collecting and analysing the data or suggesting anyone to participate in this study. While this collaboration provided us an opportunity to study existing MRP, for the artists it was a chance to advertise their work and performing in yet another venue. Artists did not receive any monetary compensation for this collaboration.

Data Analysis

The data were analysed recursively following principles of thematic analysis [13]. The authors started by collaboratively coding the transcribed interviews, focusing on participants' reflections on the experience of the 360-degree video as well as of their engagement with the performance as a whole. Being together vs. being alone in the experience, feeling uncomfortable, presence in physical and virtual rooms, re-experiencing and re-living, active vs. passive participation, physical awareness and encountering others and interacting with others (i.e., eye contact) were some of the initial themes identified during this first round of analysis.

During a second iteration, we turned to the notion of friction as a source of audience engagement [2] and we mapped it to the elements of the performance that we had identified as contributing (or not) to the i) audience involvement in the performance and ii) how they made sense of the 360-degree video in the context of the performance as a whole. This resulted in the three frictions that we present in this paper.

The video material was also used to analyse the moments of interactions that the participants had mentioned during the interview. This included, for instance, motivations for sharing a memory and how this was concretely instantiated in the narration, or verbal and non-verbal interactions between audience members. The video recordings offered an opportunity to examine how interactions between the artist-performers, the audience and the technology played out, and what challenges and opportunities these interactions provided for the experience [25,34].

RESULTS

Repurposing the notion of friction to be applicable for MRPs is relevant as it provides a key terminology to talk about immersion as emerging from audience's engagement with the whole performance and not merely with the VR. Our results span three aspects of friction that enable audience engagement with the performance. These frictions are explained below with representative quotes from our participants, describing their experience of time and memories, their virtual and real presence, and the different realities they experienced. We need to indicate that the quotes presented below stand for the majority of participants who discussed the relevant topic except two quotes that illustrate different experiences by two participants.

Therefore, the three frictions introduced here, are representative and inclusive of the whole corpus of data. Differences can however be found in the audience experience of these frictions as we describe them in relation to each friction.

Temporal Friction

The first instance of friction we discuss is the temporal friction. This is an invitation to the audience members to move towards a more active role in the performance and to directly participate with their own stories. In the case of the temporal friction, this transition occurs alongside a temporal dimension, as the present narration in the performance intertwines with the audience members' past experiences.

Meeting one of the performers in the first room (Figure 2 a) marks the audience's initial experience of the performance. As everyone sits around the same table, the artist-performer begins the narration by sharing a story about his youth and the importance of music during this period of life. The quote below, extracted from the dialogues in the first room, provides a concrete example of how the artist-performer relates to music to unpack the emotional dimension of past events.

"...It was quite hard at that time to be Serbian in this country, and I listened a lot to Balkan music...it became central for my life, early teenage life, which was kind of the only thing that I had, which was mine, and I was so proud of this, even though it was so sad and so much war was going on..." (Steffan)

Figure 3. Inviting the audience members to take part and share their memories

With these words, the artist-performer ends the personal account of past experience. Right after, he addresses the audience members and explicitly asks them to take the same retrospective journey through recounting their own memories and associating a song to them. The following quote is extracted from the video recordings of the part of performance described here:

"...now I'd like you to think of one song that has mattered sometime in your life, you can start by thinking of a band, and then maybe a song and what [it] makes you remember of a specific moment when you listen to that song. Or something happened...". (Figure 3)

We regard this invitation to directly participate and contribute to the performance as a friction that makes the audience members move towards a more active role in the performance. The quote below is transcribed from one of the video recordings in the first room, and it provides an example of how an audience member shared her song with the other people present. This act places her story in tandem with the performer's story.

"...the reason I chose this song, because ...still today when I hear it, it brings me back to those memories, kind of nostalgia. And it was the first time I actually had a song with someone, to say 'this is our song'." (Fera)

In this specific instance, the transition towards a more active participation modality occurs alongside a temporal dimension. Here the audience's present experience of the performance, their retrospection of meaningful past events, and the narrativization of those events (i.e., recounting them for other people) *come together* in the performance. In this process not only the performers', but also the audience members' pasts become central elements of the narratives and performance.

Different from temporal trajectories that looks into story lines designed by the artists and clock time in a real world [8], *temporal frictions blur the boundaries between audience and performers, thus allowing for a gradient of connection and engagement between the audience, the artist performer, and the performance as a whole.* The possibility to contribute with their own stories delicately set the audience members in the centre of the story, while turning the performance into a more intimate and *meaningful* experience.

The transition towards a more active participation was experienced as unexpected by all, but not necessarily uncomfortable [9]. It also contributed to a degree of self-consciousness in choosing and sharing certain stories with other people:

"It was unexpected, and you become a bit self-conscious when you need to choose something and share, and when you're not prepared". (Anna)

Resonating with what said by 12 participants, this quote also illustrates that the experience of a more active form of spectatorship intertwined with the audience members' awareness of their visibility in the performance.

"I was just thinking while the others were talking. Also trying to listen to them. It's also like you had to conduct how to tell the story. It was like the spotlight is on you. Go, tell your story" (Andrew).

Friction between Realties

The second type of friction we introduce is the one between the fictional realities emerging from the audience' experience of the performance and their experience of the "actual" world (i.e., the one they are located in). The adjective fictional simply indicates that it is part of the narrative [20]. This friction relates to the tension stemming from the audience projection into the fictional reality of the performance, both when memories and songs are shared, and when Emma's memory is replayed in the 360-degree video.

In the first room, collectively listening to the songs gave audience members the opportunity to empathize with the others, and to imagine them through the memories retold. As seen above, this was an unproblematic aspect of the audience engagement. As put by one of the interviewees, the memories retold were believable in the context of the performance, even if the events had not actually taken place. Listening together to the chosen songs was an opportunity to imagine the others, and see oneself in the situations recounted:

"When I listened to the songs I imagined them. Like, one guy was telling a story about when he was doing a road trip in America and I imagined him driving a car and I imagined another guy dancing. And I saw myself in my own songs." (Jason)

In the second room, however, the projection was not straightforward. Here, the 360-degree video provided a concrete visual layer to the performer's memory, as audience members could experience the physical layout of the room, and be surrounded by the band playing for Emma. By wearing the HMD, they could put themselves in Emma's original position in the room and (re-)experience the event from "her point of view":

"Now I would like to share this memory with you, and welcome you into it"

Narratology studies have extensively discussed the "suspension of disbelief" [20] as the agreement whereby readers (spectators in our case) pretend that the imaginary story being told has actually taken place and, thus, accept to believe in it. What is relevant for our analysis of a Mixed-Reality Performance is the role that digital media can play in suspending disbelief, or not.

Most of the interviewees (9 out 15) described their experience with the 360-degree video and with being present in someone's memory as strong and intimate. These people were also aware that their engagement with the story was not only connected to 360-degree video, but also to the story retold by Emma before they put on the HMD. The quote below represents this aspect of the audience' experience as they make sense of the relationships between Emma, the room and the song played, thus adding meaning to the content of the 360-degree video:

"It felt really private that you in a way could re-experience that memory. Strange to be present in someone else's memory because you can hear a memory in a story or someone telling you a memory, but this became another step. To be present, and get immersed in that because you have heard the story that she told me before. It became like I was there". (Tom)

Two of the interviewees reported a different experience with 360-degree video particularly regarding their projection with the fictional reality the medium was supposed to contribute to. One issue was the emotional disconnection between their personal past experience and the performer's (Emma) life.

"We were the [performer]character. In their past there was a song that would evoke an emotion of a life altering event, parents' divorce I think, without having any notion of that emotion there's a huge disconnect." (Verner)

Another disconnection stemmed from the technology, with respect to the technical properties and to people's concerns about what the technology could be used for (i.e., creating false memories). In the first quote below, Hanna explains that she did not experience any immersion in the 360-degree video because she is taller than the character in the video, that is the height of the camera when the video was recorded. This created a tension between the perception of her own body and presence in the actual world, and the first-person perspective mediated by the video in the virtual space. Hanna describes this experience as problematic from a technical perspective:

"I didn't like the immersion, I mean for the VR immersion is very important, I think immersion and the presence are not so good because I think the person is kind of smaller than the normal size, so the perspective is kind of weird."(Hanna)

The second quote below illustrates instead the disconnection between the audience' personal experience of the actual world and the fictional reality as determined by a meta-reflection on the role of technology:

"I felt like someone was trying to transplant memories into me ... it would be really creepy and just super weird. Actually being able to relive somebody's memory, ... that would be a really powerful and psychedelic experience. I can imagine that'd be very dangerous." (Verner)

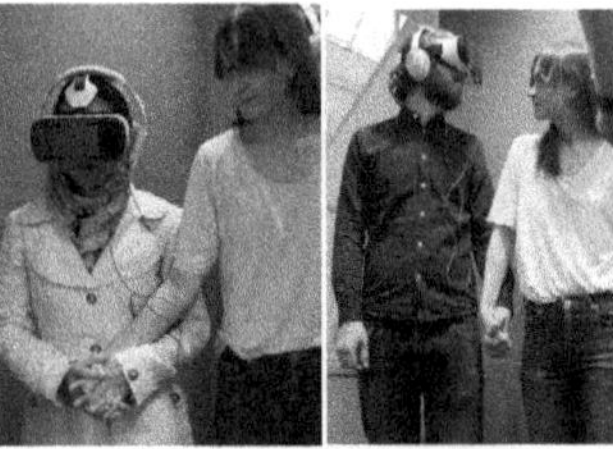

Figure 4. (a, b) One of the audience members is trying different angles of viewing 360-degree video (c, d) Embodied interaction between the performer and audience

In the following section we discuss how this disconnection was lessened by bringing back the sense of presence, through performer's interaction with the audience.

Friction between the Physical and Virtual Presence

The third friction we introduce is the one between the audience's physical and virtual presence in the performance. Discussing the audience members' sensorial experiences during the performance, and the awareness of their bodies, underlies this friction.

The audience experience of the performance was strongly influenced by their sense of presence in the physical room and in the virtual space reproduced by the 360-degree video. In the first room, audience members interacted with each other by recounting personal stories and memories. This created an intimate, sometimes emotional or awkward situation among a group of people who did not necessarily know each other. The quote below represents this aspect experienced by all audience members:

"I think it was a bit awkward because it was so close and I didn't know people" (Mary).

The physical proximity of others amplified the audience members' awareness of their presence in the room, their body movements, and how they physically oriented themselves towards the other people's present. This physical awareness and presence were even more intense when everybody listened to the song that was being shared, as audience members became aware to be at the center of the other people's attention:

"...Just the fact that they were there and the fact that I shared my story with them, it changed it quite obviously and their presence made me feel self-conscious. I was aware of my body for example. I was aware of whether I'm tapping my feet or where I'm looking. Just because of the other people that were there. Totally different experience to sitting by yourself at home and listening to music" (Verner)

In the second room, however, this sense of self-awareness and presence weakened as audience members put on the HMDs to revisit Emma's memory. The 360-degree video enabled the audience to experience a virtual place (the one represented in the video) which they could inhabit individually. Wearing the HMDs and headphones allowed audience members to isolate themselves from the sight and sound of the surrounding physical environment, and thus to be less concerned about the presence of other people and how they experience or influence the same performance. 11 participants described this aspect of the experience during the interviews. During the performance we could observe, for instance, that members of the audience took small steps, moved around the room, bent to explore the boundaries of the 360-degree video, or simply sat on the floor to experience the video (Figure 4 a,b).

The moment in the performance when Emma holds the hand of each audience member connects the audience's virtual presence in the immersive video to the physical world they inhabit. This moment is emblematic of the friction between the physical and virtual presence of the audience and performer. Emma tried to replicate the scene and the sensorial experience of her partner holding her hand, by establishing direct physical contact with the audience. When Emma reminds the audience of their physical presence, by touching their bodies and holding their hands, she adds this sensorial perception to what they see in the 360-degree video.

"...when she held my hand, I felt like I don't want to leave her hand...It was a very good feeling. I felt that I'm more connected to this experience. Somehow, I felt it might be the thing she [Emma] experienced for real... [he] grabbed her hand and this is actually what she experienced." (Nina)

Emma's *"ghost hand",* as one of the participants put it, resulted in an intimate moment for the audience, while she was virtually present but physically invisible to her presents. This contributed to blurring the boundaries between the physical and the virtual space and presence. These particular moments can be seen in Figure 4 (c,d), when audience members react to performer holding their hands by physically turning their head to her side, and trying to find her in the 360-degree video.

DISCUSSION

Immersive videos and VR technology provide a range of creative opportunities for MRPs (e.g., enabling the audience to re-experience a memory from the performer's point of view). Throughout this paper, we have argued that the audience immersion with the 360-degree videos, and engagement with the performance as a whole is not a given property of the video as a medium. This is relevant for the TVX community, as a growing number of academic (i.e., [12,36]) and industry work (i.e., [60]) explores the role of VR for entrainment as well as artistic purposes.

In the analysis of Strange Days, we have illustrated how the audience immersion and engagement with the 360-video stemmed from the experience of the performance as a whole, including the interactions with the performers and other audience members, and the audience participation in the performance. The concept of frictions has drawn attention to:

- the audience' emotional engagement with the story, and the possibility enabled at a discursive level to share their own memories;

- the tension between the audience' perception of reality, and the fictional reality of the performance;
- the tension between the audience sense of presence in the 360-video and the sensorial experience of one the performers holding their hands.

While 360-degree videos are conceived to provide immersive experiences [46], we argue that the qualities of this immersiveness are not given, but emergent and tightly connected to frictions and to the audience's transition towards a more active participation in the performance.

Frictions in Priming and Participation

Previous work [30] has described "behind the scenes activities" to engage participants with the performance, and to prepare them to be part of the experience. As we have seen in our analysis, temporal frictions can be regarded as invitations for the audience to transition towards a more active role in the performance. This reciprocal transaction of stories and memories primes the audience members while adding meaning to the 360-degree video and contributing to the audience engagement with the performance as a whole. Thus, drawing attention to frictions illustrates how priming can be a central element of the story and of the Mixed-Reality Performance, rather than confined to a set of behind the scene activities.

The experience of the temporal friction contributed to the audience's transition between *re-telling* and *re-living* a memory. These two modes of experiences were held together by the fact that re-telling primed the re-living, an aspect of the performance that the audience members became aware of. Similarly, the frictions between the physical and virtual presence blurred the boundaries between *inhabiting* the physical and the virtual spaces of the live performance and *being present* in the narration. The audience members associated the experience of this friction to a more central role in the performance as they became characters in the story rather than just witnessing it. Finally, the friction between the fictional reality and the audience's experience of the actual world redefines participation as characterised by *believing* and *projecting*. Both believing and projecting tightly relate to the concept of suspension of disbelief [20]. Believing in our case can be explained in terms of traditional narratology studies of narratives such as books, movies or theatre plays: the audience accepts to believe in a story containing fictive elements. Projecting, however, more tightly relates to the audience's empathy with the performance, and was intertwined with the digital media used. As seen in the analysis, for some audience members this projection was in fact hindered by technical qualities of the technology, and by concerns on the role such type of media might have in the future.

Designing Immersion Through Frictions

Strange Days, as the artists themselves explained, was designed and performed using the Brechtian method of acting [39] to create a dialogue and interaction between the performer and the audience within the performance. This form of directly addressing the audience is what James Mcteague [39] considers *"breaking the fourth wall"*. In the second room however, when the performer asked her audience members to put on HMDs to take her place in the 360-degree video simulating her memory, the audience's role shifts from active and engaged towards a more passive and less interactive one. In fact, the audience became the 'observer' of the performance rather than making any interactions with the performer. This lack of interaction–and limited opportunity for action–with technology or a live performance can disturb the audience's suspension of disbelief (belief or projection). Experiences that rely on the technology to make the audience feel immersed are most susceptible to this disruption [41]. However, by establishing an embodied interaction between the performer and audience the experience became once again interactive, tangible and kinesthetic through friction. This bodily interaction, actuated by a human agent with tactile input, not only broke the forth wall, but also recreated the audience engagement with the space around.

Many strategies for creating immersive experiences, including breaking the fourth wall, have been used in the design of MRPs (i.e., *Situation Rooms* [61]). However, many performances that incorporate 360-degree video or VR do not exploit the full potential of such strategies because of the presumed "immersiveness" of the technology itself. The "successful" immersive experience in such performances are not far from experiencing, for example, the Circle-Vision theatre installed by Walt Disney Company in their theme parks, in late 60s. The main difference between this early 360-degree projection room (and the VR caves that followed it) and the types of experience discussed in this paper is the use of a headset. A Head-Mounted Display enables a more intimate experience, but it also isolates audience members from one another. Creating an immersive experience in MRPs however, does not need to rely on the technology or immersive media intrinsically. Immersion can emerge from props and technologies, how they are designed and used by the artists in the MRP, the audience's spatial and emotional engagement with the scene, with the narratives, and with the characters as performed by artists and performers. Immersion is, therefore, an emerging quality of the performance enabled by the interactions between the performer and the audience.

Reflecting on the role of frictions can lead to design strategies that aim to break the fourth wall, thus contributing to the audience transition towards an active role in the performance, and, ultimately, an immersive experience. New technological improvement in VR equipment (i.e., VR motion platforms or haptic controllers) are driven by similar goals–to create subtle connections between realities and their associated characters. This can be seen in those VR devices that add a layer of AR to the experience (i.e., Microsoft HoloLens) or in a more novel way by breaking the fourth wall with "merging the realities" as we can see in, for example, Intel's Project Alloy [60] or Facebook's Social VR

[62]. Adopting the notion of frictions provide us with an analytical lens to investigate such upcoming VR experiences, and opportunities to design interactive and embodied experiences for and with them.

Frictions in the Wild

While performance art has made inroads into HCI research, notably with works presented in [7,48,50], there are also opportunities for HCI to learn more from "real" world productions and how practitioners use different methods and technologies in their art piece.

While frictions are designed and enacted by the artists, they are experienced by the audience through participation in the performance. It is the "live" experience of frictions that creates them. The practitioners use frictions to manipulate audiences' perception of time and space, through the "live" experience and in order to create different worlds and realities in an immersive experience. These frictional realities can twist, tangle and sometimes unravel but they always connect again and come together, as they present an immersive experience. In these regards, we argue that an engaging successful immersive Mixed-Reality Performance does not merely stem from the experience of the immersive technology or media. It emerges instead from the intertwinement of the **technology** together with other dimensions, namely: the **audience's participation and contribution** to the performance and different types of **frictions** enacted by the artists to contribute to the audience's experience of the performance as a cohesive narration and frictional reality.

CONCLUSION

In this paper, we have presented the analysis of a Mixed-Reality Performance, *Strange Days*. In our analysis, we retrospectively applied the lens of frictions to better understand how artists created a more emotionally and physically immersive experience for the audience, and to better understand the audience members' experience. We use this MRP as an example of increasing interest in using 360-degree videos in artistic productions. Such performances, we have argued, do not need to rely on immersive technology to be considered as a fully immersive experience, but instead can draw on the frictions between different layers of design to prime the audience members, and engage the audience with the performance, enabling immersion with the 360-degree video and the performance itself.

ACKNOWLEDGMENT

We are grateful to Emma Bexell, Stefan Stanisic and Svante Back from Bombina Bombast for their collaboration. We would also like to thank Charles Windlin as well as our participants.

REFERENCES

1. Deepak Akkil and Poika Isokoski. 2016. Gaze Augmentation in Egocentric Video Improves Awareness of Intention. In *Proceedings of the 2016 CHI Conference on Human Factors in Computing Systems* (CHI '16), 1573–1584. https://doi.org/10.1145/2858036.2858127
2. Bryan Alexander. 2011. *The New Digital Storytelling: Creating Narratives with New Media*. Praeger, Santa Barbara, Calif.
3. Adam Alston. 2013. Audience Participation and Neoliberal Value: Risk, agency and responsibility in immersive theatre. *Performance Research* 18, 2: 128–138. https://doi.org/10.1080/13528165.2013.807177
4. Jeffrey Bardzell and Shaowen Bardzell. 2015. *Humanistic HCI*. Retrieved January 18, 2016 from http://dx.doi.org/10.2200/S00664ED1V01Y201508HCI031
5. Louise Barkhuus, Matthew Chalmers, Paul Tennent, Malcolm Hall, Marek Bell, Scott Sherwood, and Barry Brown. 2005. Picking Pockets on the Lawn: The Development of Tactics and Strategies in a Mobile Game. In *Proceedings of the 7th International Conference on Ubiquitous Computing* (UbiComp'05), 358–374. https://doi.org/10.1007/11551201_21
6. Steve Benford, Mike Fraser, Gail Reynard, Boriana Koleva, and Adam Drozd. 2002. Staging and Evaluating Public Performances As an Approach to CVE Research. In *Proceedings of the 4th International Conference on Collaborative Virtual Environments* (CVE '02), 80–87. https://doi.org/10.1145/571878.571891
7. Steve Benford and Gabriella Giannachi. 2011. *Performing Mixed Reality*. The MIT Press, Cambridge, Mass.
8. Steve Benford, Gabriella Giannachi, Boriana Koleva, and Tom Rodden. 2009. From Interaction to Trajectories: Designing Coherent Journeys Through User Experiences. In *Proceedings of the SIGCHI Conference on Human Factors in Computing Systems* (CHI '09), 709–718. https://doi.org/10.1145/1518701.1518812
9. Steve Benford, Chris Greenhalgh, Gabriella Giannachi, Brendan Walker, Joe Marshall, and Tom Rodden. 2012. Uncomfortable interactions. In *Proceedings of the SIGCHI Conference on Human Factors in Computing Systems*, 2005–2014. Retrieved January 18, 2016 from http://dl.acm.org/citation.cfm?id=2208347
10. Steve Benford, Irma Lindt, Andy Crabtree, Martin Flintham, Chris Greenhalgh, Boriana Koleva, Matt Adams, Nick Tandavanitj, Ju Row Farr, and Gabriella Giannachi. 2011. Creating the spectacle: Designing interactional trajectories through spectator interfaces. *ACM Transactions on Computer-Human Interaction* 18, 3: 1–28. https://doi.org/10.1145/1993060.1993061
11. Gregor Broll and Steve Benford. 2005. Seamful Design for Location-based Mobile Games. In *Proceedings of the 4th International Conference on Entertainment Computing* (ICEC'05), 155–166. https://doi.org/10.1007/11558651_16
12. Andy Brown, Jayson Turner, Jake Patterson, Anastasia Schmitz, Mike Armstrong, and Maxine Glancy. 2017.

Subtitles in 360-degree Video. In *Adjunct Publication of the 2017 ACM International Conference on Interactive Experiences for TV and Online Video* (TVX '17 Adjunct), 3–8. https://doi.org/10.1145/3084289.3089915
13. Alan Bryman and Bob Burgess (eds.). 1994. *Analyzing Qualitative Data*. Routledge, London ; New York.
14. Gordon Calleja. 2011. *In-Game: From Immersion to Incorporation*. The MIT Press, Cambridge, Mass.
15. Matthew Chalmers and Areti Galani. 2004. Seamful Interweaving: Heterogeneity in the Theory and Design of Interactive Systems. In *Proceedings of the 5th Conference on Designing Interactive Systems: Processes, Practices, Methods, and Techniques* (DIS '04), 243–252. https://doi.org/10.1145/1013115.1013149
16. Peter Dalsgaard, Christian Dindler, and Kim Halskov. 2011. Understanding the Dynamics of Engaging Interaction in Public Spaces. In *Human-Computer Interaction – INTERACT 2011*, 212–229. Retrieved January 15, 2017 from http://link.springer.com/chapter/10.1007/978-3-642-23771-3_17
17. Nima Dehghani. Decompensation. Retrieved August 28, 2016 from http://www.nimadehghani.com/
18. Steve Dixon. 2006. A history of virtual reality in performance. *International Journal of Performance Arts and Digital Media* 2, 1: 23–54. https://doi.org/10.1386/padm.2.1.23/1
19. Steven P. Dow. 2008. *Understanding user engagement in immersive and interactive stories*. ProQuest.
20. Umberto Eco. 1995. *Six Walks in the Fictional Woods*. Harvard University Press, Cambridge, Mass.
21. Daniel J. Finnegan, Eamonn O'Neill, and Michael J. Proulx. 2016. Compensating for Distance Compression in Audiovisual Virtual Environments Using Incongruence. In *Proceedings of the 2016 CHI Conference on Human Factors in Computing Systems* (CHI '16), 200–212. https://doi.org/10.1145/2858036.2858065
22. M. Elboim Gabyzon, B. Engel-Yeger, S. Tresser, and S. Springer. 2016. Using a virtual reality game to assess goal-directed hand movements in children: A pilot feasibility study. *Technology and Health Care* 24, 1: 11–19. https://doi.org/10.3233/THC-151041
23. Çağlar Genç, Shoaib Soomro, Yalçın Duyan, Selim Ölçer, Fuat Balcı, Hakan Ürey, and Oğuzhan Özcan. 2016. Head Mounted Projection Display & Visual Attention: Visual Attentional Processing of Head Referenced Static and Dynamic Displays While in Motion and Standing. In *Proceedings of the 2016 CHI Conference on Human Factors in Computing Systems* (CHI '16), 1538–1547. https://doi.org/10.1145/2858036.2858449
24. Diane Gromala, Xin Tong, Amber Choo, Mehdi Karamnejad, and Chris D. Shaw. 2015. The Virtual Meditative Walk: Virtual Reality Therapy for Chronic Pain Management. In *Proceedings of the 33rd Annual ACM Conference on Human Factors in Computing Systems* (CHI '15), 521–524. https://doi.org/10.1145/2702123.2702344
25. Christian Heath and Paul Luff. 2000. Technology in Action. *Cambridge Core*.
26. Kristina Höök and Jonas Löwgren. 2012. Strong Concepts: Intermediate-level Knowledge in Interaction Design Research. *ACM Trans. Comput.-Hum. Interact.* 19, 3: 23:1–23:18. https://doi.org/10.1145/2362364.2362371
27. Stenros Jaakko, Holopainen Jussi, Waern Annika, Montola Markus, and Ollila Elina. 2011. Narrative Friction in Alternate Reality Games: Design Insights from Conspiracy For Good. Retrieved from http://www.digra.org/wp-content/uploads/digital-library/11301.54362.pdf
28. Izabelle Janzen, Vasanth K. Rajendran, and Kellogg S. Booth. 2016. Modeling the Impact of Depth on Pointing Performance. In *Proceedings of the 2016 CHI Conference on Human Factors in Computing Systems* (CHI '16), 188–199. https://doi.org/10.1145/2858036.2858244
29. Han-Jong Kim, Ju-Whan Kim, and Tek-Jin Nam. 2016. miniStudio: Designers' Tool for Prototyping Ubicomp Space with Interactive Miniature. In *Proceedings of the 2016 CHI Conference on Human Factors in Computing Systems* (CHI '16), 213–224. https://doi.org/10.1145/2858036.2858180
30. Boriana Koleva, Ian Taylor, Steve Benford, Mike Fraser, Chris Greenhalgh, Holger Schnädelbach, Dirk vom Lehn, Christian Heath, Ju Row-Farr, and Matt Adams. 2001. Orchestrating a mixed reality performance. In *Proceedings of the SIGCHI Conference on Human Factors in Computing Systems*, 38–45.
31. Robert Konrad, Emily A. Cooper, and Gordon Wetzstein. 2016. Novel Optical Configurations for Virtual Reality: Evaluating User Preference and Performance with Focus-tunable and Monovision Near-eye Displays. In *Proceedings of the 2016 CHI Conference on Human Factors in Computing Systems* (CHI '16), 1211–1220. https://doi.org/10.1145/2858036.2858140
32. Arun Kulshreshth and Joseph J. LaViola Jr. 2016. Dynamic Stereoscopic 3D Parameter Adjustment for Enhanced Depth Discrimination. In *Proceedings of the 2016 CHI Conference on Human Factors in Computing Systems* (CHI '16), 177–187. https://doi.org/10.1145/2858036.2858078
33. Kari Kuutti and Liam J. Bannon. 2014. The Turn to Practice in HCI: Towards a Research Agenda. In *Proceedings of the 32Nd Annual ACM Conference on Human Factors in Computing Systems* (CHI '14), 3543–3552. https://doi.org/10.1145/2556288.2557111
34. Dirk vom Lehn, Christian Heath, and Jon Hindmarsh. 2001. Exhibiting interaction: conduct and collaboration

in museums and galleries. *Symbolic Interaction* 24, 2: 189–216.

35. Josephine Machon (ed.). 2013. *Immersive Theatres: Intimacy and Immediacy in Contemporary Performance*. Palgrave, Houndmills, Basingstoke, Hampshire.
36. Andrew MacQuarrie and Anthony Steed. 2017. Cinematic virtual reality: Evaluating the effect of display type on the viewing experience for panoramic video. In *2017 IEEE Virtual Reality (VR)*, 45–54. https://doi.org/10.1109/VR.2017.7892230
37. Yasutoshi Makino, Yoshikazu Furuyama, Seki Inoue, and Hiroyuki Shinoda. 2016. HaptoClone (Haptic-Optical Clone) for Mutual Tele-Environment by Real-time 3D Image Transfer with Midair Force Feedback. In *Proceedings of the 2016 CHI Conference on Human Factors in Computing Systems* (CHI '16), 1980–1990. https://doi.org/10.1145/2858036.2858481
38. John McCarthy and Peter Wright. 2004. Technology As Experience. *interactions* 11, 5: 42–43. https://doi.org/10.1145/1015530.1015549
39. James Mcteague. 1994. *Playwrights and Acting: Acting Methodologies for Brecht, Ionesco, Pinter, and Shepard*. Praeger, Westport, Conn.
40. Me and the Machine. 2010. When We Meet Again (introduced as friends). Retrieved August 28, 2016 from http://www.meandthemachine.co.uk/works/whenwemeetagain/
41. Janet H. Murray. 2016. Not a Film and Not an Empathy Machine. *Immerse*. Retrieved July 17, 2017 from https://immerse.news/not-a-film-and-not-an-empathy-machine-48b63b0eda93
42. William T. Neale, James Marr, and David Hessel. 2016. Nighttime Videographic Projection Mapping to Generate Photo-Realistic Simulation Environments. https://doi.org/10.4271/2016-01-1415
43. Asreen Rostami, Donald McMillan, Elena Márquez Segura, Chiara Rossitto, and Louise Barkhuus. 2017. Bio-Sensed and Embodied Participation in Interactive Performance. In *Proceedings of the TEI '17: Tenth International Conference on Tangible, Embedded, and Embodied Interaction* (TEI '17). https://doi.org/10.1145/3024969.3024998
44. Gustavo Saposnik. 2016. Virtual Reality in Stroke Rehabilitation. In *Ischemic Stroke Therapeutics*, Bruce Ovbiagele (ed.). Springer International Publishing, 225–233. Retrieved September 21, 2016 from http://link.springer.com/chapter/10.1007/978-3-319-17750-2_22
45. Maeve Serino, Kyla Cordrey, Laura McLaughlin, and Ruth L. Milanaik. 2016. Pokémon Go and augmented virtual reality games: a cautionary commentary for parents and pediatricians. *Current Opinion in Pediatrics* 28, 5: 673–677. https://doi.org/10.1097/MOP.0000000000000409
46. Alia Sheikh, Andy Brown, Zillah Watson, and Michael Evans. Directing attention in 360-degree video. *IET Conference Proceedings*: 29 (9 .)–29 (9 .)(1).
47. Jennifer G. Sheridan, Nick Bryan-Kinns, and Alice Bayliss. 2007. Encouraging Witting Participation and Performance in Digital Live Art. In *Proceedings of the 21st British HCI Group Annual Conference on People and Computers: HCI...But Not As We Know It - Volume 1* (BCS-HCI '07), 13–23. Retrieved January 15, 2017 from http://dl.acm.org/citation.cfm?id=1531294.1531297
48. Jocelyn Spence. 2016. Introducing Performative Experience Design. In *Performative Experience Design*. Springer International Publishing, 1–23. Retrieved August 15, 2016 from http://link.springer.com/chapter/10.1007/978-3-319-28395-1_1
49. Tate. Nigerian artist Emeka Ogboh makes a connection between the volatility of financial markets and the movement of people seeking better lives. *Tate Modern*. Retrieved February 8, 2018 from http://www.tate.org.uk/visit/tate-modern/display/voices/emeka-ogboh
50. Robyn Taylor, Guy Schofield, John Shearer, Jayne Wallace, Peter Wright, Pierre Boulanger, and Patrick Olivier. 2011. Designing from Within: Humanaquarium. In *Proceedings of the SIGCHI Conference on Human Factors in Computing Systems* (CHI '11), 1855–1864. https://doi.org/10.1145/1978942.1979211
51. Robyn Taylor, Guy Schofield, John Shearer, Jayne Wallace, Peter Wright, Pierre Boulanger, and Patrick Olivier. 2011. Humanaquarium: Exploring Audience, Participation, and Interaction. In *CHI '11 Extended Abstracts on Human Factors in Computing Systems* (CHI EA '11), 1117–1122. https://doi.org/10.1145/1979742.1979723
52. Mirjam Vosmeer and Ben Schouten. 2017. Project Orpheus A Research Study into 360° Cinematic VR. In *Proceedings of the 2017 ACM International Conference on Interactive Experiences for TV and Online Video* (TVX '17), 85–90. https://doi.org/10.1145/3077548.3077559
53. Gareth White. 2012. On Immersive Theatre. *Theatre Research International* 37, 03: 221–235. https://doi.org/10.1017/S0307883312000880
54. Robert Xiao and Hrvoje Benko. 2016. Augmenting the Field-of-View of Head-Mounted Displays with Sparse Peripheral Displays. In *Proceedings of the 2016 CHI Conference on Human Factors in Computing Systems* (CHI '16), 1221–1232. https://doi.org/10.1145/2858036.2858212
55. 2016. Exploring VR and immersive video. *About the BBC*. Retrieved April 15, 2018 from http://www.bbc.co.uk/blogs/aboutthebbc/entries/a792a4ad-f1d4-4f95-a26a-18c03ff29b27

56. WHIST. *AΦE*. Retrieved August 2, 2017 from http://www.aoiesteban.com/whist/
57. Bombina Bombast. Retrieved April 16, 2018 from http://bombinabombast.blogspot.com/
58. Sleep No More. *McKittrick Hotel*. Retrieved July 25, 2017 from https://mckittrickhotel.com/sleep-no-more/
59. The Killing(Danish TV series). *Wikipedia*. Retrieved from https://en.wikipedia.org/w/index.php?title=The_Killing_(Danish_TV_series)
60. Intel Unveils Project Alloy. *Intel Newsroom*. Retrieved January 16, 2017 from https://newsroom.intel.com/chip-shots/intel-unveils-project-alloy/
61. Rimini Protokoll - Situation Rooms. Retrieved January 16, 2017 from http://www.rimini-protokoll.de/website/en/project_6009.html
62. Facebook Social VR Demo. Retrieved January 16, 2017 from https://www.facebook.com/zuck/videos/10103154531425531/

Narrative Bytes: Data-Driven Content Production in Esports

Florian Block, Victoria Hodge, Stephen Hobson, Nick Sephton,
Sam Devlin, Marian F. Ursu, Anders Drachen, Peter I. Cowling
{firstname.lastname}@york.ac.uk,
Digital Creativity Labs, University of York, UK

ABSTRACT

Esports – video games played competitively that are broadcast to large audiences – are a rapidly growing new form of mainstream entertainment. Esports borrow from traditional TV, but are a qualitatively different genre, due to the high flexibility of content capture and availability of detailed gameplay data. Indeed, in esports, there is access to both real-time and historical data about any action taken in the virtual world. This aspect motivates the research presented here, the question asked being: can the information buried deep in such data, unavailable to the human eye, be unlocked and used to improve the live broadcast compilations of the events? In this paper, we present a large-scale case study of a production tool called *Echo*, which we developed in close collaboration with leading industry stakeholders. *Echo* uses live and historic match data to detect extraordinary player performances in the popular esport Dota 2, and dynamically translates interesting data points into audience-facing graphics. *Echo* was deployed at one of the largest yearly Dota 2 tournaments, which was watched by 25 million people. An analysis of 40 hours of video, over 46,000 live chat messages, and feedback of 98 audience members showed that *Echo* measurably affected the range and quality of storytelling, increased audience engagement, and invoked rich emotional response among viewers.

Author Keywords

Esports, Data-Driven Storytelling, Content Production.

CCS Concepts

Information systems → Information systems applications → Multimedia information systems → Multimedia content creation

INTRODUCTION

Esports is the term used for describing video games that are played competitively and watched by, normally large, audiences [34]. Over the past decade, esports have evolved from a niche segment of the games culture into a mainstream global phenomenon. In 2017, over 388 million people worldwide played or watched esports, and the number of esports fans is projected to grow a further 50% by 2020 [11].

ACM ISBN 978-1-4503-5115-7/18/06.
https://doi.org/10.1145/3210825.3210833

Esports take a variety of shapes, from digital versions of traditional sport, such as *FIFA* [4] to first-person shooters (e.g. *Counter Strike: Global Offensive* [16]) and magic-themed fantasy games, such as *Dota 2* [22] and *League of Legends* [15]. Many esports titles have associated amateur and professional online leagues and tournament, some of which feature prize pools exceeding those of many traditional sports [43, 52]. Coverage of esports borrows many elements from traditional sports broadcasting. Pre-game coverage features expert panels and follows the athletes as they enter the arena. During matches, virtual in-game footage is accompanied by audio commentary. After the match, coverage typically consists of interviews with the players and post-match analysis.

Esports also introduce a set of interesting changes to content production and delivery that sets them apart from traditional sports. In esports, live broadcast and on-demand content is almost exclusively delivered online, via video-platforms such as Twitch [18] and YouTube. Many esports titles also deliver live and on-demand matches as *raw data streams* that capture every aspect of the virtual world, such as the movement of the players. On the PC of a viewer, this data can be reassembled to create an interactive view of the match in which spectators can change camera angles, rewind, and interact with virtual objects. Match data also contains many statistics, timings and other additional layers of information that are not usually visible to the naked eye. Using specialised tools, such data can be extracted and translated into audience-facing content, such as graphs and statistics, enhancing the viewing experience.

In traditional sports, *tracking data* [44, 24, 46] has been used for a while to augment the viewers' experiences [75, 37], for instance, to better illustrate the performance of an athlete or make complex strategies visible to the viewer. In esports, the use of data and statistics have particular potential to benefit coverage and to help mainstream audiences enjoy and extract meaning from watching professional esports [34, 75, 37]. Compared to many traditional sports, gameplay in esports can be much more complex, making it hard for non-expert viewers to follow the action [34]. At the same time, as esports audiences grow rapidly, content creators increasingly need to make those complexities palatable and entertaining to casual audiences [13]. How can esports data be used by content producers to better engage their audience and make watching esports more meaningful to broader audiences?

In this paper, we present the first large-scale case study of *data-driven content production* in esports – i.e., the use of data analytics and data mining to inform the production of esports live coverage. We developed a production tool, called *Echo*, which uses large volumes of historic match data to detect highlights in live matches of the game Dota 2 [22], and provides mechanisms for automatically translating these highlights into audience-facing graphics. We deployed *Echo* at one of the largest international esports tournaments – ESL One Hamburg 2017, watched by 25 million people online – which allowed us to gather a wealth of experimental data consisting of: observational ethnographic data on how *Echo* impacted commentary and content production, materialised as 40 hours of video footage, 9 million chat messages and feedback from 98 directly surveyed audiences members, which we used to infer how *Echo* influenced the audiences' experience. We conclude that even simple graphical overlays of data-driven insights, such as the ones implemented by *Echo*, can have measurable effects on the commentary and quality of coverage. Many of *Echo's* graphics provoked elaborate discussions among commentators, and elicited strong emotional engagement among viewers. This is, indeed, the expected outcome, but, here, we provide strong experimental evidence coming from a significant case study – one of the largest esports tournaments in the world in whose production we deployed our *narrative byte tool*, *Echo*.

RELATED WORK

While the scientific relevance of esports has been highlighted over a decade ago [69], academic research in the area has been relatively sparse, with pockets of work ranging from economics [76, 63], to social practices [62, 26], regulation [36], and gender inequality [33, 41, 57]. Only a small number of studies directly address aspects of content production [25, 29, 65]. Studies in game-design have focused on optimising the visual presentation and user interface of esports games for observers [25, 29]. Work in machine learning has presented new mechanism for automatically extracting highlights from esports videos [65]. Outside of content production, most relevant to our work are studies of viewer needs and consumer practice in esports, technical work that leverages esports data for game analytics, as well as literature from traditional sports that inform our work. Each is presented in the following sections.

Consumer Needs and Practices in Esports

A series of prior work focuses on understanding viewer needs and consumer practices [34, 42, 72, 66], finding a variety of motivations for why people watch esports, including escapism, novelty and acquiring knowledge about the games being played. The latter motivation is particularly relevant for this paper, and translates into clear practical implications that make the case for data-driven content production esports. Hamari et al. [34] point out that content producers need to develop "better ways for the spectators to acquire knowledge from the eSport", explicitly pointing out the need to "more effective ways of displaying the game states", and highlighting the potential of overlay statistics. A comparison of consumption motives of esports and traditional sports found that one of the predominant motives for engaging with esports are competition and skill building [42], lending further importance to fostering skill acquisition as part of the viewing experience. In this paper, we expand on prior work by contributing the first survey of how data-driven content affects viewers' experience.

Esports Analytics

Esports data is often publicly available, and in terms of its detail and volume rivals even the most data-rich traditional sports, such as Formula One. The data-rich ecosystem surrounding esports has attracted attention by a series of work in the area of Game Analytics – the practice of extracting insights from data generated through digital games [32]. Esports are particularly conducive to the study of new techniques in Machine Learning and Artificial Intelligence, which require large volumes of training data to perform well. Examples of such application include identifying team encounters in esports data [59], predicting match outcome [38, 39, 35, 40, 47, 61, 64, 71], identifying factors that determine success in professional play [31, 55, 56, 74], as well as recommender systems that help players make better tactical decisions [23, 27]. Our work draws on similar analytical techniques. However, our focus is on studying the use of data and analytics as a *narrative tool*, which involves the translation of live data into formats that mainstream audiences can understand. Aside from academic work, we draw on an emerging landscape of esports data portals that seeks to make large volumes of esports data accessible. For instance, for the popular esport Dota 2, various data portals exist, such as Dotabuff [3], OpenDota [12] or DatDota [2], that essentially aggregate match data from tens of thousands of games and identify the most successful strategies over time. In line with the remit of our work, these platforms are targeted at mainstream audiences, and cater for the information appetite observed among the esports audience, as highlighted in the previous section. In this paper, we conceive a new category of applications that leverages data as a *real-time narrative tool for engaging live mainstream audiences*, with profound implication on the underlying design principles and implementation.

Data-Driven Content in Traditional Sports

Esports borrows many elements from traditional sports broadcast, making work relating to data-driven content relevant to the current investigation. From a commercial viewpoint, infographics and augmented views are part of most sports coverage today, such as Hawk-Eye Vision in tennis, visualisations of player's distance from the goal in football, or superimposing visual markers of current records in Olympic swimming competitions. Recent trends focus on the capture and visual representation of live sports tracking data, including 3D reconstructions, event and highlight detection, as well as ball and player tracking [28, 75]. Such techniques enable broadcasters to give their viewers new insights into the performance, strategy and style of athletes [75] as well as "explain things that weren't explicable previously" [37]. In this paper, we explore the foundations for data-driven content production in esports, with the aims of both opening up a new area of academic inquiry and contributing to the professionalisation of data-driven content production in the esports industry.

CASE STUDY

We conceived *data-driven content production* as the process of translating raw match data into audience-facing content. In the absence of existing commercial products, standards and prior academic work in this space, it was crucial that our research involved close collaboration with industry. Working with industry was key to acquiring an understanding of current practices, gathering requirements, and to co-design new technology [58]. Industry collaboration is also vital for creating opportunities for deploying and evaluating new tools in an ecologically valid setting, such as an esports tournament, involving expert crews that typically plan and execute such events.

Between June 2016 and March 2017 we ran a series of workshops and meetings, in which we recruited key stakeholders in the esports industry for participation in our co-design process. We recruited 17 senior experts across leading organisations within esports:

- *ESL* – Electronic Sports League [5] – is the globally leading esports company, producing events in two dozen countries and hosting some of the largest international esports tournaments, reaching tens of millions of viewers every year. Participating representatives from the company included several high level executives, senior product managers, and technical leads across TV, technology and pro gaming divisions.
- *Fnatic* [7] is one of the most successful esports organisations, having leading professional teams in a variety of esports, with players from all over the world. Participating representatives included senior executives as well as a former coach and data analyst.
- Prominent online celebrities that are regularly involved in some of the largest international esports events, including a leading commentator, two celebrity analysts, and two casters (individuals who broadcast their own games online), with a combined total of over 2 million online followers.

The research team working with the domain stakeholders consisted of experts in interactive storytelling, user-centred design, interactive data visualisation, game analytics, and machine learning.

Requirements Gathering

To inform the design of a concrete prototype, we wanted to obtain insight into any existing practices of using data during the production of live esports events. Our initial set of workshops provided the following insights:

Data = USP (Unique Selling Point). A consensus across representatives from big esports companies and freelance talents was that esports data has significant potential to augment and advance current broadcasting practice. Large content producers see data-driven content as a potential means of generating USP that will more deeply engage the tech-savvy fan base, and potentially make esports more attractive to watch for new viewers. Individual content producers echoed this sentiment, highlighting that innovations in augmenting in-game footage could help them individualise their content.

Data is already used, but clunky to work with. Various members of our expert team, in particularly our stage analysts and commentators, routinely use historic data for storytelling, mostly taken from existing data portals, self-made tools and pre-assembled databases. However, it was lamented that drawing on data involves significant manual labour. Many existing tools only provide very basic ways of probing and visualising data, while more sophisticated tools are hard to operate. Moreover, most tools do not provide flexible options for presenting the data in audience-friendly way, making them unsuitable for real-time storytelling.

Crews are small, data expertise is rare. Esports productions have very small profit margins. Compared to regular sports broadcasts, crews are extremely streamlined and data expertise is rare. It is desirable that new data-driven production tools can be operated by existing production staff.

Simplicity is key. Esports broadcast are already overloaded with information (see for instance Figure 1). Any additional messaging has to be simple enough to be consumed and understood by the audience in seconds.

Feedback by our domain experts provided a clear set of design requirements. Tools for data-driven content production in esports need to: 1) provide a high level of automation in data acquisition and processing, 2) integrate mechanisms that help operators identify interesting patterns within complex data, and 3) support a 'one-click' mechanism for translating data into extremely simple graphics that audiences can instantly understand.

Context – Defence of the Ancients 2

Having elicited basic design requirements we needed to choose a specific esports game to contextualise our case study. In consultation with our experts, we chose the game *Dota 2* [22]. Not only is Dota 2 one of the most popular esports [49], it also provided the most comprehensive public access to both live and historic match data. Dota 2 also features rich and complex gameplay, with high potential for data-driven content production to enhance the viewer's experience. Lastly and somewhat more pragmatically, our pool of experts included a high-profile caster, analysts and commentator specialising on Dota 2, giving us access to game-specific domain-knowledge during the design process.

Dota 2 is a fantasy-themed game in which two teams of five players compete (think 5-a-side football with various weapons and endowed with magic). Each player picks from a pool of 115 distinct *hero* avatars (or characters), each

Figure 1. In-game view of Dota 2 as seen by the players and the audience (© Valve Corporation).

having unique skills and play styles. At the start of the game, heroes find themselves in their own base (one base per team) located at opposite corners of a square-shaped virtual arena, consisting of forests, three roads and a river. The overall aim of the game is for teams to defend their own base while destroying the enemy base. To fulfil this objective, players need to first strengthen their heroes, by collecting two basic types of in-game currencies: gold and experience. Gold can be used to purchase virtual items that make heroes more powerful. Experience (XP) allows heroes to level up, increasing their overall strength. Gold and XP are obtained by killing enemy heroes, or computer-controlled monsters called *creeps* that are scattered across the arena. In their effort to compete for resources and conquer each other's base, teams often clash. When taking too much damage, heroes can "die", rewarding the enemy team both gold and XP, as well as sending the dead hero back to its base. Killing enemy heroes allows teams to temporarily outnumber the enemy team, creating further tactical advantage and opportunities to break down the enemy's defence. Matches have no predetermined length, but typically last anywhere from 20 minutes to over 1 hour.

It's All About the Player

Our experts stressed that many key stories of Dota 2 broadcasts gravitate around "the player" (analogous to traditional sports [75]). However, tracking each player's performance, even for expert viewers and commentators, is often challenging. Unlike the strongly simplified account given above about Dota 2's game mechanic, gameplay in Dota 2 is extremely complex, with players performing various parallel objectives while mostly being dispersed across the map. During a live match, commentators often resort to a set of basic statistics built into the game that captures each player's performance according to a set of *Key Performance Indicators* (KPIs). One of the most important KPIs, for instance, is a player's *Net Worth* - the total gold value the hero has acquired. Seeing an ordered list of Net Worth gives some basic understanding on which player is doing well at the current time. However, an issue is that Net Worth is only indicative of good performance for some heroes. Other heroes have different objectives, such as helping their team-mates or scouting portions of the terrain that is controlled by the enemy. However, these objectives are not captured by out-of-the box KPIs.

Another issue with the game's built-in statistics is that they only reflect data from the current game. Relative comparison between different heroes, however, is often not meaningful due to vast differences in playstyle. Some heroes for instance, are strong early into the game, while others start off weak and get stronger later in the game. In order to fully judge how well each player is performing with their chosen hero, one has to rely on previous experience of observing the same hero being played. Not every viewer, however, has this knowledge for all 115 heroes. Some broadcasts have used historic comparison to better illustrate live performance to audiences. For instance, Ben Steenhuisen, Dota 2 analyst and developer of DatDota [2], cross-references historic databases with real-time data during a game, and creates small text snippets illustrating players' performances that are shown to the audience in form of a small popups. This process involves a set of exclusive expert tools, significant technical skill, expertise in data science, and manual labour and to be operated effectively. Another limitation of the process is that the way information is presented to the audience cannot be customised. Reflecting our design requirements, we wanted to expand existing practices by creating a production tool that is easy to operate, assists with identifying extraordinary data points based on historic data, provides an entirely automated data pipeline, and allows free customisation of audience-facing visuals.

Echo – Capturing the Extraordinary

To improve the audience's ability to track hero performance, we developed a new tool called *Echo* (see Figure 2). *Echo* is a production tool that can monitor data from a live match and, for each minute into the game, compare performances of each player to thousands of historic performances. *Echo* displays one column per player, five per team. Within each column, *Echo* shows a list of 12 KPIs that capture various aspects of the player's performance, significantly expanding Dota 2's out-of-the-box statistics. The KPIs were chosen as a result of technical availability (what we could access in the live data stream) and our expert's advice for covering a range of different playstyles and roles. *Echo* calculates the percentiles of the live performances – or how many percent of historic performances are exceeded in the live game. For each KPI and player, *Echo* provides three values: 1) The first percentile expresses how the player's performance at the current minute relates to thousands of previous performances of the same hero. For instance, the magnified portion of Figure 2 shows that 42 minutes into the live match, the player named "inYourdreaM" has reached a Net Worth that is higher than 98% of values previously recorded of all players that chose the same hero. 2) The second percentage shows how the player's live performance compares to the player's personal match history. This column is suitable to detect if a player has a particularly good or bad game compared to their historic performance. 3) The third column shows how the current performance is situated within *all* matches within the reference data, including performances by any player and any hero. This column is particularly suited to track "all

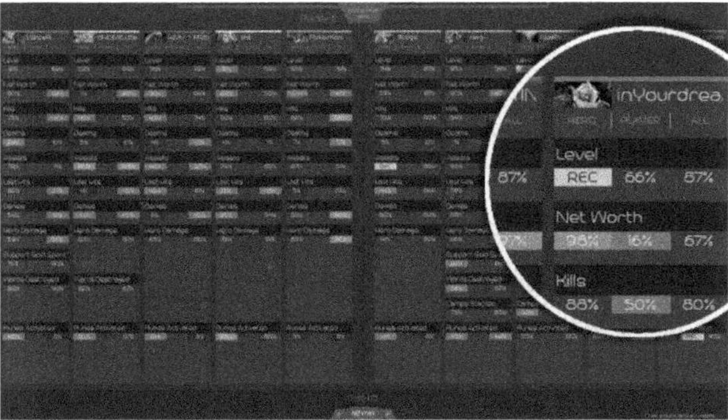

Figure 2. Basic view of *Echo*, showing each Player's live performances as percentiles of historic data.

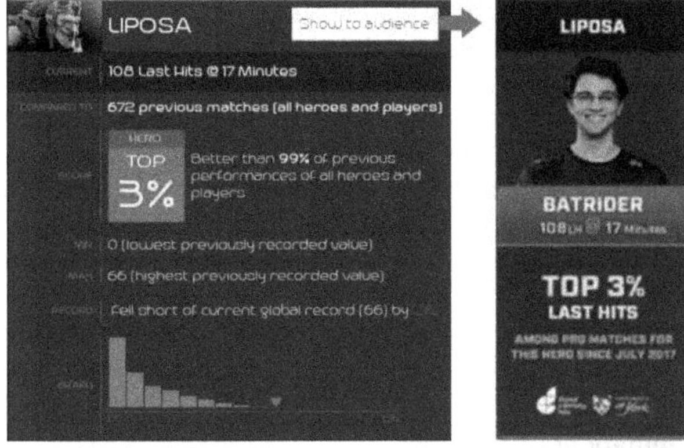

Figure 3. Detailed view of a particular KPI. If "Show to audience" button is pressed, *Echo* triggers the graphics system to show a graphical overlay to the audience (© ESL).

time" records or extraordinary performances across heroes. Values that exceed any value in the scope are marked with "REC" = record. Negative records (worst values ever observed in each respective scope) are marked as "LOW". Values that exceed certain thresholds are colour coded (yellow = record, purple = top 1%, blue = top 5%, red = negative record). The colour coding assists the operator with identifying interesting constellations. For instance, in the row Networth highlighted by the magnified portion of Figure 2 one can deduce that for the hero, the player lies within the top 2% of historic performances, but does relatively poorly (bottom 16%) compared to their personal match history. This indicates that this player usually picks heroes that are capable of obtaining gold faster. The third column tells us that in the global reference frame, taking into account all heroes and players, the player performs only above average.

Clicking any percentile opens a more detailed information dialog, giving the operator additional information for the specific performance, including a histogram, current minimum and maximum records and a preview of the type of core messaging that would be shown to the audience (see Figure 3, left). Pressing the button in the top right corner of the preview will automatically generate an audience-facing graphic, which can then be superimposed over the in-game footage (see Figure 3, right).

The main goal of the design of the graphics was to reduce complexity and to provide a single, clear message to the audience. As stories revolve around players, a natural part of the visual design would be a portrait, and the player's *gamer tag* (the in-game nickname). The more difficult task was to wrap the core message into a clear presentation. As it is well established, special care needs to be taken when conveying statistics to the public, as statistics literacy may widely differ and even basic statistical concepts, such as percentiles, may not be well understood [51]. Consequently, we presented the percentile with a qualitative cue "Top X%" or "Bottom X%", including an adjusted percentage that creates a correct representation of the percentile. For instance, In Figure 3, *Echo* would have identified the player's performance as being in the 97th percentile, translating into the phrase "Top 3%". While we did not expect most viewers to read information beyond the core messaging, we did want to provide a second level of information that commentators and quick readers could access, essentially describing the scope of the performance. The percentiles depend on the current minute in the game as well if one compares current performance to all games of a certain hero, the player's match history, or all games in the database. To visually break up this information, we added two sets of information to the graphics. Above the core message, we displayed the current value of the KPI (e.g. "X gold") and the time the graphics referred to ("@ minute X"). Below the graphics, we added small print that described the scope (hero, player, or all games) as well as the range of games that are considered in our database. As part of our evaluation, we will assess how those different components were perceived.

Implementation

Echo was implemented in C# and WPF, utilising a local SQLite database [17] for storing the historic match data. The historic match data was compiled to include all professional games for the current season, including a total of 13,550 performance metrics (across 1,355 matches, each containing 10 player performances). Raw match data was obtained using the official Dota 2 match history API [20] in conjunction with APIs from Datdota's match API [2] to obtain a url for the raw replay file (storing the full recording of the match). We then downloaded all 1,355 raw replay files and processed them using a customised version of Clarity [16], an open-source match parser for Dota 2. The parser allows to traverse match data in a chronological way, and extract time series of all KPIs per player.

EVALUATION

Echo was deployed at ESL One Hamburg 2017, one of the largest Dota 2 tournaments of the year, which featured a $1m prize pool and attracted over 25 million online viewers as well as 20,000 fans onsite [6]. With a schedule stretching across four days, the event provided an ideal environment to collect rich observational data about how *Echo* impacted the viewers' experience, and to gather explicit audience feedback on *Echo* as well as the general importance of data-driven content in Dota 2.

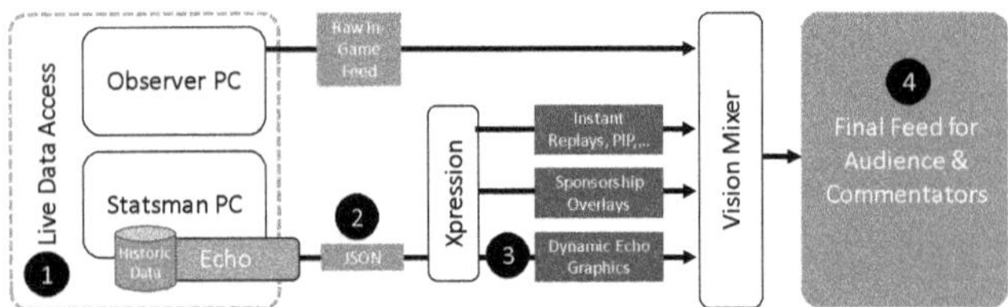

Figure 4. Schematic of Echo's integration: (1) Echo accesses real-time data through the Statsman's PC, (2) sends selected data points to Xpression via JSON http request; (3) Xpression generates a graphic and overlays the final feed (4).

Integration with Production Workflow

Esports coverage is structured very much like traditional sports coverage. A pre-game panel introduces the match, giving background on teams and players, followed by the players entering the arena and taking their gaming station on stage. This sequence is produced in line with traditional broadcast. The actual in-game coverage, is produced by a separate team, most notably the audience-facing talents – usually two commentators. Behind the scenes, the primary roles for the production of in-game coverage during an esports tournament are the *statsman*, the *spotter* and the *graphics operator*. The statsman is responsible for technically setting up matches and monitoring statistics during the match. The spotter is the virtual camera operator. The statsman and spotter work on independent PCs, which both run Dota 2's observer mode, allowing them to watch the players in real-time, control camera angles and navigate across the virtual environment, and access to the built-in statistics tools. The spotter's in-game view is the main footage going into the vision mixer. Analogous to traditional sports broadcast, the graphics operator is responsible for enriching the raw in-game footage with visual overlays, such as sponsorship information, instant replays, or picture-in-picture segments. The mentioned observer mode in Dota 2 also provides a real-time data API, which is the entry point for *Echo*, which was installed on the statsman's PC. *Echo*'s dashboard was displayed on a secondary monitor. *Echo* was integrated with the graphics software used by the production [12] (see Figure 5), enabling the statsman to bypass the graphics operator and directly push graphics to the audience.

The preparation of the graphics-integration, including visual and animation design was carried out by ESL, to reflect their visual design language used throughout the tournament. The statsman had full editorial control over timing and selection of what performances from *Echo*'s data dashboard he wanted to show to the audience. As a general practice, graphics were shown during quiet moments of the match, to not distract viewers from important events. As *Echo*'s graphics always related to an individual player, the statsman frequently coordinated with the spotter, so that the in-game view focused on the player who the graphics related to.

Data Collection

The four-day tournament provided various opportunities for collecting observational data and gathering audience feedback. The unedited live footage, as seen by the audience, was made freely available on Youtube after each day, capturing every occurrence of *Echo's* graphics and how it affected commentators' narrative – our first data source. The majority of viewers watched the event coverage live, via Twitch [18], which provided them with a real-time chat in which they could communicate with each other during the broadcast. We recorded all these time-stamped messages for analysis. Between matches, we recruited onsite viewers for in-person interviews. On the fourth event day, we also conducted an online survey, and recruited participants via social media. In total, we collected 40 hours of broadcast footage, 46,000+ chat posts from twitch, 69 online audience survey responses and 29 in depth interviews with visitors of the event. We also collected user activity logs of *Echo*, recording which graphics the operator showed to viewers, when they were shown and for how long. This allowed us to accurately time-align the display of *Echo*-generated graphics with both the audience chat log and the actual tournament footage.

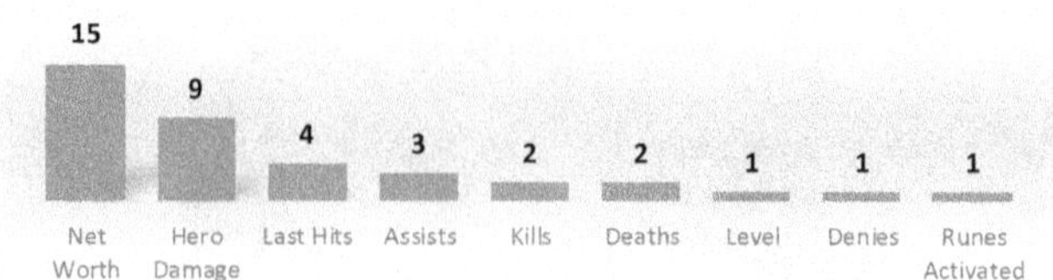

Figure 5. Frequency of graphics by KPI

Summary of Use

Across 27 matches played at ESL One Hamburg, *Echo* generated 38 audience-facing graphics (average 1.4 / match). In the majority of matches (21), *Echo* produced 1 or two graphics. In two matches, *Echo* did not produce any graphics, due to a lack of extraordinary stats. In three matches, three graphics were shown, while in one game, four graphics aired. The average air time per graphic was 10 seconds, totalling in 7.5 minutes of airtime received during over the course of the whole tournament. Of all graphics shown, 27 graphics (71%) illustrated *positive* performances, such a player performing in the top 5% or breaking a top record. 11 graphics (29%) highlighted *negative* performances, such as poor records.

Figure 5 shows the frequency of graphics by specific Key Performance Indicators (KPIs). This distribution yields various insights. The most frequently used KPI – Net Worth – is widely acknowledged to be the most important statistic used by experts to gauge hero performance, so it is unsurprising that it became a popular choice for the data operator. The second most frequently used KPI – damage done to enemy heroes – is not usually exposed through the game client. This provides good indication that *Echo* was effective in expanding the built-in statistics, and that this information was deemed relevant to the audience by an experienced statsman. There was also a good breadth of KPIs used at the tail end of the distribution – while the two most frequently used KPIs make up for exactly 50% of the alerts, the other 50% are distributed across 7 different KPIs. This shows that *Echo*'s vocabulary of KPIs generate narratives that brought a more varied aspects of performance to the fore.

Impact of *Echo* on Commentary

Based on review of video footage showing the occurrence of all 38 graphics generated by *Echo*, we evaluated the qualitative effect the graphics had on the commentators' narrative. Overall, out of the 38 total graphics, 14 of the graphics elicited commentators to make direct verbal reference to the contents of the graphic. In six cases the graphics were aired in direct response to the commentators' narrative. In four instances, both effects interleaved, creating a dialog between commentators and statsman. Following an ethnographic approach of data analysis [70, 67], the following paragraphs aim to highlight the *quality* of different effects observed. We do not claim representativeness or general validity of our findings. Rather, we wanted to identify and characterise an initial set of categories of impact that can inform future theory and experimental study in the area of data-driven content production.

Shaping Narrative, Eliciting Surprise. In various instances, the graphics highlighted an aspect of a player the commentators had not been aware of, or apparently had not considered. When a graphic about a *Net Worth Record* was displayed (placing the player at the top 1%), the commentators noted:

> *Commentator 1: "Look at that....look at that"*
> *Commentator 2: "Yeah, he's really fat [high networth]"*

The first statement captures a degree of surprise, indicating that the commentators had not been aware of this extraordinary performance. The graphics triggered an elaborate subsequent discussion about the player's strategy and performance. In another instance, *Echo* generated a graphic highlighting that a player was performing in the *Top 2% of Assists*. Assists are the number of enemies killed in presence of this player. This graphic indicated that the player's involvement in team-fights was very high. This triggered the following consideration by the commentator:

> *Commentator 1: "Here we can see his early levels may have been a little slow, in terms of experience, but just his involvement, his movements... always where the action is"*

Again, the statement provides evidence of a degree of surprise, moving focus from a KPI in which the player was underperforming, to a KPI that brought out a different aspect of the player's contribution that had thus far gone unnoticed. Overall, we observed 8 instances in which the reaction of commentators indicated a certain element of surprise. In some instances, *Echo*'s graphics shaped the commentators narrative minutes after they appeared.

Doing Poorly: highlight bad performances. Eleven graphics pointed out poor performances, sometimes eliciting strong reactions by the commentators. One graphic pointed out the very poor level of a player named "Solo" (levels indicate progress of a player) eliciting an emotional response by the commentator:

> *"I mean, Solo [=player's name], bless him... "*
> *[continued]... he's had a lot of deaths... ", and it's the levels, as you pointed out earlier, really holding him back. Level 13, 43 minutes in."*

The initial comment was followed by an elaborate discussion between commentators about the reasons for this poor performance, bringing out various insights to the audience. Stats also brought out comic moments. 16 minutes into a match, a certain player had only killed a single creep (this is roughly equivalent to a tennis player not having scored a single point in a whole set). The graphics, marked a "poor record", invoked amusement among the commentators:

> *Commentator 1: "Look at this stat man." [Both chuckling]*
> *Commentator 2: "Poor record, one last hit – bless him."*

Data-Dialogs. In four cases, we observed clear dialogs between commentators and statsman. In one instance, the commentators are talking about how well the hero named "Rubick" is doing:

> *Commentator 1: "Look at the money on Rubick!"*
> *Commentator 2: "This is gotta be one of the richest Rubicks I've seen in a long time."*

While commentator 2 finishes the sentence, an *Echo* graphic pops up showing that Rubick is breaking the Net Worth record (= how "rich" a hero is), prompting an immediate reaction by the other commentator:

> *Commentator 1: "Top record for net worth – 21 thousand on him at the 61 minute mark [...]"*

In another match, the graphics slots in perfectly with the commentators narrative about a hero named "Chen" performing very well in terms of his Net Worth:

> *Commentator 1: "This Chen is getting very rich... " [Graphic popping up showing that the hero "Chen" is within the top 5% of Net Worth] "...statistically rich."*

Overall, the graphics generated by *Echo* stimulated vivid discussions between the commentators, producing informative and entertaining background facts to the audience. Data-dialogues were observed, in which statsman and commentators engaged interactively to shape a coherent narrative. There was clear evidence that *Echo* brought aspects to the fore that surprised commentators and diversified the usual narrative toolbox of statistics.

Impact of *Echo* on Twitch Chat

To analyse the impact of *Echo*'s graphics on the audiences' engagement on Twitch chat, we applied a combination of quantitative and qualitative measures on the twitch chat data. *Frequency of Posting* has been proposed as a quantitative proxy measure for engagement [53]. For each graphics shown on the stream, we calculated frequency of posting 30 seconds before and after the graphics appeared. A repeated measure factorial design (ANOVA) with two factors *Timing* (before / after) and *Graphics Type* (positive performance / negative) showed a significant effect for *Timing* ($F_{1,33}$=11.616, p=.002). On average, frequency of posting rose from a baseline of 3.7 contributions just before the appearance of the graphic, to 4.9 after the graphic aired. There was also a significant interaction between *Graphics Type* and *Timing* ($F_{1,33}$=17.448, p=.027), showing that the increase in chat activity was significantly more pronounced for negative performances (87.1% increase in frequency of posting) compared to positive ones (12.5% increase).

To get a qualitative understanding of how *Echo*'s graphics affected chat engagement, we conducted an analysis of all 30 second chat excerpts, comprised of 5091 chat posts. The following paragraphs describe our findings:

Repetition, Repetition. A substantial portions of chat entries replicate either the value of the KPI (e.g. "95 net worth"), or the percentage (e.g. top 5%). Among the 5091 analysed chat posts, a total of 1,242 (~20%) contained one or more repetition of the graphics content (487 repetitions for content of "top performances", 755 repetitions for content of "bottom performances"). This means that a substantial percentage of overall chat contribution focused on re-sharing the messaging of the graphics on chat.

Rich emotions. To characterise the makeup of the other 80% of chat messages, as well as to characterize the conversational context in which the graphics contents were shared, we conducted a word frequency analysis. Of the top 20 most frequently used words (accumulatively making up almost half of all word occurrences), 10 words were abbreviations, such as "LOL" (=laughing out loud), or "Clap". The other ten words were iconic in nature. Chat users commonly express their emotions explicitly in form of memes or emoticons, which we interpreted using a variety of online sources [1,9,19]. For instance, when typed in twitch chat, the word *PogChamp* is represented with the icon (head of a person with a wide open mouth), which is commonly used to express shock and disbelief [1]. The observed memes reflected a range of emotions, including surprise, tension, frustration, upset and amusement.

Effectiveness of Visual Design

The presented findings so far suggest that the design of *Echo*'s graphics was effective in bringing out the central message to the audience (e.g. "Top 5%"). Across commentary and Twitch chat, there was also evidence that other details had been picked up. For instance, after a player broke a top record, the following dialog ensued:

> *Commentator 1: "Hey look, here we go. Top Networth"*
> *Commentator 2: "Top record."*
> *Commentator 1: "At 8 minutes."*
> *Commentator 2: "8 minutes."*
> *Commentator 1: "I mean [mumbles] it's crazy. We are pre 9 minutes and we are seeing heroes reaching [...]"*

In this and three other instances, commentators picked up on the timing aspect contained in smaller letters above the main message, and utilized this information from the graphics to emphasise the core message. However, commentators never picked up on the "small print" below the main message, and there was also no indication that commentators picked up the difference between scopes. In one instance, this led to the commentators portraying a performance as global record, even though the graphics depicted only a personal record (referencing only a single player's match history). A handful of Twitch users did, however, pick up on the small text, expressing concern with the phrase *"since July 2017"*, with some users expressing confusion or disagreement: "SINCE JULY 7 MAN NOT ALL TIME WTF[=outrage]", "top 5% damage since july?". While there were only three total instances among 5091 chat posts, this evidence suggests that a small number of users do scrutinise even "the small print", and raise questions of the validity of the stats. We only include matches since July, since then a major patch (update that changes the game) had significantly impacted various KPIs, making it questionable to compare data collected before and after the patch. An alternative wording "since patch 7.07" may have addressed those concerns.

As for visual language, evidence showed that we were successful in contextualising players performance in respect to historic data, and current time of the match. However, we were not successful in bringing out differences between the different scopes, or reference frames, that *Echo* provides. In future iterations, this information should be more clearly visible, possibly even integrated with the core message (e.g. "PLAYER TOP 5%" vs. "HERO TOP 5").

Online Survey

To elicit explicit feedback on how the graphics were received we used an online questionnaire. The two aims of the online questionnaire were a) to identify generally what role data-driven content plays in viewer's experience of Dota 2 broadcasts, and b) to capture specifically how they rated the graphics generated by Echo. Participants were recruited through advertisement via Twitter, which was re-tweeted by the official ESL account and the tournaments hashtag #ESLOne. The following sections discuss the main findings. 106 people responded to the survey, with 69 people fulfilling the criteria of being over 18. 63 participants fully completed the survey. Figure 6 shows all questions and the results.

The majority of respondents (70%) felt that statistics were 'very important' or 'extremely important' to their experience of Dota 2 (Q1). When asked about how important statistics are when *watching* a Dota 2 broadcast, 81% of subjects responded with 'very important' or 'extremely important' (Q2). In addition, another 16% of subjects chose 'moderately important'. Notably, none of the subjects responded with 'not at all important'. After the two general questions, subjects were shown a sample graphic generated by Echo, followed by four questions specifically referring to the sample graphic. The majority of respondents (76%) leaned towards finding *Echo*'s graphics easy to understand, where as 15% leaned towards the opposite (Q3). 10% did not feel strongly either way. 56% did not find *Echo*'s graphics distracting, opposed by 27% of participants who did (16% neutral, Q4). The majority of subjects (84%) found that the graphics contained useful information. When asked about whether subjects wanted to see more of this information in the future, 84% subjects responded with 'strongly' agree (55%) and 'somewhat agree' (29%).

The results capture an interesting design trade-off between distracting audiences and delivering useful value-add information. Data from the online survey provided evidence that overall, *Echo* was successful in its core aim of bringing useful and meaningful information to the majority of respondents, even to some of those who perceived Echo as distracting. The responses also captured high demand and appetite among viewers for data-driven content in Dota 2.

Semi-Structured Interviews

To complement the quantitative findings from the online survey, we conducted 29 semi-structured interviews with fans in the arena to shed light on *the possible qualitative aspects* of data and statistics for the purpose of storytelling. In line with our analysis of commentary, our focus was not on representativeness or general validity. Instead, we wanted to extend prior statistical findings in consumer demand by providing a more facetted picture of potential motives for the like or dislike of data-driven content. Individuals or groups were randomly approached to participate in the study. Audio of all interviews were recorded. The questions were:

Q1. What role do statistics play in your experience of Dota 2?

Q2. What role do statistics play as part of broadcasts such as ESL ONE?

- showing subjects a sample graphic generated by Echo -

Q3. Did you notice those graphics during the event?

Q4. What did you think of them?

Broadly, answers to Q1 and Q2 echoed results from the online survey. 25 interviewees of the 29 made references to statistics having an important role in their experience of Dota 2 as players and viewers. As theorised by prior studies of consumer demand in esports [34], our data confirms that statistics in Dota 2 help both novice and experienced viewers *better understand the current state of the game*, and keep track of the many intricacies of professional play: *"[statistics are] important because you can't keep track of everything"*. Along the same lines, a novice viewer remarked: *"For me it's totally interesting to get a better overview of the game"*.

One group of participants expressed that statistics let them better predict likely outcomes: *"[live statistics] help us to guess on what will happen in the future"*. This points to the potential of statistics to foster the audience's *anticipation,* which, in turn, sets the stage for viewers to be surprised, e.g. when an anticipated outcome does not occur.

Using *Echo* as an exemplar, Q3 and Q4 brought out additional nuances of how data-driven content can enrich a live event. Concretising advantages of "keeping track", interviewees expressed that *Echo* helped them get *"a better look at the players and how they are doing"*. Another

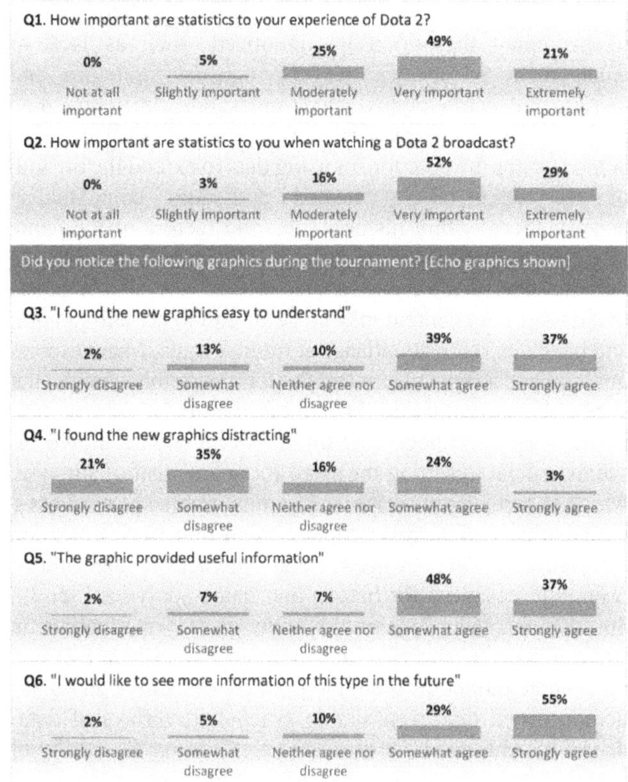

Figure 6. Results from the online Survey, see text for details.

participant felt *Echo*'s graphics helped enhance his appreciation for professional play: "*"I think it's quite impressive to see what level they are reaching in the playing skills"*. Entertainment was also brought out as a quality of *Echo*'s graphics: *"It's fun! Yeah, I like it"*. Particularly the negative performances provoked some explicit mention: *"Particularly when watching the ESL One, you can really see when people really fail at the game [...] it's funny"*.

DISCUSSION & CONCLUSION

Echo provides substantial evidence for the importance of data-driven content production in esports. Our audience survey shows that data and statistics are central to the viewing experience, and audiences have a clear appetite for more data-driven content, such as is presented by Echo. Through co-designing *Echo* with leading industry partners, and conducting a large-scale observation of how it was used in one of the world's largest esports tournaments – we generated a range of detailed insights that extend existing research on consumer motives in esports and traditional sports [34, 37, 42, 72, 66, 75]. We provide observational evidence confirming that data-driven content can indeed be an effective tool to make the gameplay more transparent to viewers [34], to cater for the audience's desire for skill building [42], as well as to enable audiences to more effectively follow the performance of the athletes [75].

Our data paints a more facetted picture of consumer demand for data-driven content in esports. Data-driven content not only allows content producers to *"explain things that weren't explicable previously"* [37], but also brings to light aspects of gameplay that often go unnoticed, such as lack of engagement of specific players, unusual strategies and tactics, and behaviour which is measurably different than what has gone before (particularly record-breaking). This demonstrates the potential of using data to extend the breadth of storytelling. Echo helped audiences contextualise performances within historic data, and factors of the game (e.g. how much time has passed). Beyond illustrating the current state of the game, audience feedback also suggests that data-driven content may be helpful to foster anticipation and hence increase attendance at future events. Many esports neither have a fixed match length, nor a clear mechanism that shows the current "score" – making it hard for audiences to know what to expect. The ability to anticipate, however, seems crucial to setting the stage for an element of surprise, which in turn, characterises many memorable sports event – anticipation and surprise being crucial ingredients of good storytelling. This suggests that prediction algorithms, originally designed for betting and game analytics [38, 39, 40, 47, 61, 64, 71], could have useful application in storytelling, e.g. showing audiences a simple display of win percentage that helps them judge likely outcomes. *Echo* has demonstrated that even simple graphical overlays of data-driven insights can have measurable effects on the quality of commentary and coverage. Many of *Echo*'s graphics provoked elaborate discussions among commentators, and invoked strong emotional engagement among viewers.

It is important to note that the presented findings are generated in the concrete context of Dota 2 and do not necessarily generalise to other esports games. However, Dota 2 has almost identical game mechanics to League of Legends [15], another representatives of the MOBA genre (Massive Online Battle Arena). Dota 2 and League of Legends make up two of the three most popular esports [49], having an estimated combined following of 113 million people [73]. Arguably, this makes our findings relevant for a substantial portion of the ecosystem in esports content production. Further studies will have to be conducted to study the relevance of data-driven storytelling in other popular genres, such as first person shooters. Another area of future study is how we can translate insights from esports, which is data-rich today, to the broadcast of traditional sports and other live events that may in the foreseeable future have access to data-streams of similar quantity and quality.

While *Echo* currently generates static content, in our future work we will explore how data can engage audiences in a more interactive fashion. For instance, companion apps could offer a personalised experience of data-driven content that adapts to the needs and interests of individual viewers. In contrast to traditional sports, gameplay data in esports not only exists for professional matches, but for *all* matches. This would enable forms of engagement that were not possible in traditional broadcast, for instance, by comparing professional performance with each individual viewer's personal performance to give individualised insights and coaching tips.

The high volumes of esports data also provides a unique environment to study the role of Machine Learning and Artificial Intelligence as creative tools for storytelling. In our future work, we will explore the use of more sophisticated AI to help content creators identify unique moments in gameplay, and to provide an AI assistant making it possible to generate personalised, interactive data-stories. We also aim to create data-driven tools that help small production crews and individual streamers create rich coverage.

Our case study has also demonstrated that esports provides a unique ecosystem for capturing audience feedback and behavior. Each esports event inherently generates a rich set of digital observational data, much of which can be automatically collected and analysed. While still more men watch and play esports than women, the esports audience is racially diverse [13], and much more inclusive in regards to disabilities than traditional sports [68]. This makes esports a fertile environment for experimentation, for creative production, social enquiry, and cultural analysis. Our findings highlight the appetite of esports fans to engage with data as a creative tool – involving not only large production companies, but millions of individual content producers that could share data-driven stories peer-to-peer. In many ways, one could conceive data-driven storytelling as a tool for millions of esports fans to connect with each other creatively. From an educational perspective, this opens up a set of attractive possibilities for study. Esports constitutes a unique environment to study how mainstream audiences wish to engage with and extract meaning from data. An unexplored educational benefit of content-driven storytelling in esports may thus be its ability to foster data literacy and "mental fitness" by motivating vast young audiences to learn through telling stories with esports data about which they care deeply.

ACKNOWLEDGEMENTS

We want to thank ESL for their support and providing access to ESL One Hamburg. Special thanks go to Marcel Menge, Tobias Grieser, Christian Eikermann and James Lampkin for their time and help during the design, deployment and evaluation of Echo. We also want to thank Ben "Noxville" Steenhuisen and Jonathan "JJ Pimpmuckl" Liebig for their careful and creative operation of Echo during ESL One Hamburg, as well as to Ted "Pyrion Flax" Forsythe, Kevin "Purge" Godec and Tobi "TobiWan" Dawson for sharing their advice and expertise during the design of Echo. We also thank Fnatic's Patrik "cArn" Sättermon, as well as Luis "Deilor" Sevilla and Fabien Ungerer for their thoughtful input. Last but not least, our gratitude goes to the members of the ESL One Hamburg audience who have taken part in the study. This work was conducted at Digital Creativity Labs (www.digitalcreativity.ac.uk), supported by EPSRC / AHRC / InnovateUK under grant no EP/M023265/1.

REFERENCES

1. A beginner's guide to the most-used Twitch emotes: https://www.dailydot.com/unclick/twitch-emotes/
2. Datdota. https://www.datdota.com/
3. Dotabuff. https://www.dotabuff.com/
4. EA. FIFA Video Games. https://www.ea.com/games/fifa
5. ESL, https://www.eslgaming.com/
6. ESL, Press Release ESL One Hamburg, 2017. https://www.eslgaming.com/press/esl-one-hamburg-powered-intel-debuts-20000-fans-onsite-and-25-million-online-viewers
7. Fnatic. https://www.fnatic.com/
8. Java Script Object Notation, ECMA-404 The JSON Data Interchange Standard. https://www.json.org/
9. Know your meme http://knowyourmeme.com/memes/monkas
10. Newzoo. Esports revenues will reach $696 million this year and grow to $1.5 billion by 2020 as brand investment doubles (2017). https://newzoo.com/insights/articles/esports-revenues-will-reach-696-million-in-2017/
11. Newzoo. Global Esports Market Report (2017). https://newzoo.com/insights/trend-reports/global-esports-market-report-2017-light/
12. OpenDota. https://www.opendota.com/
13. PWC. The burgeoning evolution of eSports (2016). https://www.pwc.se/sv/pdf-reports/the-burgeoning-evolution-of-esports.pdf
14. Ross, Real-Time Motion Graphics, Xpression. https://www.rossvideo.com/graphics-system/xpression/
15. Riot Games, League of Legends. http://leagueoflegends.com/
16. Skadistats. Clarity Parser for Dota 2. https://github.com/skadistats/clarity
17. SQLite Consortium, SQLite. https://www.sqlite.org/
18. Twitch. https://www.twitch.tv/
19. Twitch-A-Speak http://mashable.com/2014/08/08/twitch-emoticons/#pQdQuLh3HGqc
20. Valve, Dota 2 Match History WebAPI. https://dev.dota2.com/showthread.php?t=47115 (accessed 30/01/2018)
21. Valve, Counter-Strike Global Offensive. http://blog.counter-strike.net/
22. Valve. Dota 2.http://www.dota2.com/play/
23. Agarwala, A. and Pearce, M., 2014. Learning DotA 2 team compositions. Technical report, Stanford University.
24. Alamar, B. and Mehrotra, V. (2012, February). Beyond Moneyball: The Future of sports analytics. Analytics Magazine. Retrieved from: http://www.analytics-magazine.org/special-articles/525-beyondmoneyball-the-future-of-sports-analytics
25. Carlsson, C. and Pelling, A., Designing Spectator Interfaces for Competitive Video Games. Master's thesis, Report No. 2015:129, Chalmer University of Technology, Gothenburg, Sweden 2015.
26. Carter, M. and Gibbs, M.R., 2013, May. eSports in EVE Online: Skullduggery, fair play and acceptability in an unbounded competition. In FDG (pp. 47-54).
27. Conley, K., Perry, D., 2013. How does he saw me? A recommendation engine for picking heroes in DotA 2. Technical report, Stanford University.
28. Dietrich, C., Koop, D., Vo, H.T. and Silva, C.T., 2014, October. Baseball4d: A tool for baseball game reconstruction & visualization. In Visual Analytics Science and Technology (VAST), 2014 IEEE Conference on (pp. 23-32). IEEE.
29. Ditmarsch, van, J.L., 2013. Video games as a spectator sport (Master's thesis). Report no 3268969, Utrecht University, 2013.
30. Dove, G. & Jones, S. (2012). Narrative Visualization: Sharing Insights into Complex Data. Paper presented at the Interfaces and Human Computer Interaction (IHCI 2012), 21 - 23 Jul 2012, Lisbon, Portugal.
31. Eggert, C., Herrlich, M., Smeddinck, J. and Malaka, R., 2015. Classification of player roles in the team-based multi-player game DotA 2. In: International Conference on Entertainment Computing. Springer, pp. 112-125.
32. El-Nasr, M.S., Drachen, A. and Canossa, A., 2016. Game analytics. Springer London Limited.
33. Fox, J., & Tang, W. Y. (2016). Women's experiences with general and sexual harassment in online video games: Rumination, organizational responsiveness, withdrawal, and coping strategies. new media & society, 1461444816635778.
34. Hamari, J. and Sjöblom, M., 2017. What is eSports and why do people watch it?. Internet research, 27(2), pp.211-232.
35. Hodge, V., Devlin, S., Sephton, N., Block, F., Drachen, A., & Cowling, P. (2017). Win Prediction in Esports: Mixed-Rank Match Prediction in Multi-player Online Battle Arena Games. *arXiv preprint arXiv:1711.06498.*
36. Hollist, K.E., 2015. Time to be grown-ups about video gaming: the rising eSports industry and the need for regulation. Ariz. L. Rev., 57, p.823.
37. Horky, T., & Pelka, P. (2017). Data Visualisation in Sports Journalism: Opportunities and challenges of

data-driven journalism in German football. Digital Journalism, 5(5), 587-606.

38. Johansson, F., Wikström, J., 2015. Result prediction by mining replays in DotA 2. Master's thesis, Blekinge Institute of Technology, Karlskrona, Sweden.

39. Kalyanaraman, K., 2015. To win or not to win? A prediction model to determine the outcome of a DotA 2 match. Technical report, University of California San Diego.

40. Kinkade, N., Jolla, L. and Lim, K., 2015. Dota 2 win prediction. Technical report, University of California San Diego.

41. Kim, S. (2017) Gender inequality in eSports participation : examining League of Legends . Unpublished Masters Thesis, Univeristy of Texas at Austin. http://hdl.handle.net/2152/62914

42. Lee, D. and Schoenstedt, L.J., 2011. Comparison of eSports and traditional sports consumption motives. ICHPER-SD Journal of Research, 6(2), pp.39-44.

43. Lewis, L. and Bradshaw, T. 2017. Esports: Is the gaming business ready to come of age? Financial Times, Noveber 5th, 2017. URL: https://www.ft.com/content/ef8539b6-be2a-11e7-9836-b25f8adaa111

44. Lewis, M. (2004). Moneyball: The Art of Winning an Unfair Game. W. W. Norton and Company.

45. Lim, Y.K., Stolterman, E. and Tenenberg, J., 2008. The anatomy of prototypes: Prototypes as filters, prototypes as manifestations of design ideas. ACM Transactions on Computer-Human Interaction (TOCHI), 15(2), p.7.

46. Lindsey, G. R. (1959). Statistical Data Useful for the Operation of a Baseball Team. Operations Research, 7(2), 197-207.

47. Makarov, I., Savostyanov, D., Litvyakov, B. and Ignatov, D. I., 2018. Predicting Winning Team and Probabilistic Ratings in DotA 2 and Counter-Strike: Global Offensive Video Games. Springer International Publishing, Cham, pp. 183-196.

48. Medlock, M. et al. The Rapid Iterative Test and Evaluation Method: Better Products in Less Time. Cost Justifying Usability, An Update for the Internet Age. Boston, Morgan Kaufmann, 2005.

49. Meola, A. Here are the most popular eSport games of 2017 and the companies behind them. Business Insider, Dec 2017. http://uk.businessinsider.com/top-esports-games-developers-2017-11

50. Millington, B. and Millington, R. (2015).'The Datafication of Everything': Toward a Sociology of Sport and Big Data, Sociology of Sport Journal 2015 32:2, 140-160

51. Murray, S. and Gal, I., 2002, July. Preparing for diversity in statistics literacy: Institutional and educational implications. In Proceedings of the Sixth International Conference on Teaching of Statistics. Ciudad del Cabo: IASE.

52. Nordmark, S. The top 10 highest prize pools in esports, The OP, 24th December 2017. URL: https://dotesports.com/the-op/news/biggest-prize-pools-esports-14605#list-1

53. Pan, R., Bartram, L. and Neustaedter, C. TwitchViz: A Visualization Tool for Twitch Chatrooms. In Proceedings of the 2016 CHI Conference Extended Abstracts on Human Factors in Computing Systems (CHI EA '16). ACM, New York, NY, USA, 1959-1965.

54. Pingali, G., Opalach, A., Jean, Y. and Carlbom, I., 2001, October. Visualization of sports using motion trajectories: providing insights into performance, style, and strategy. In Proceedings of the conference on Visualization'01 (pp. 75-82). IEEE Computer Society.

55. Pobiedina, N., Neidhardt, J., Calatrava Moreno, M. d. C. and Werthner, H., 2013. Ranking factors of team success. In: Proceedings of the 22nd International Conference on World Wide Web. ACM, pp. 1185-1194.

56. Rioult, F., Métetivier, J.-P., Helleu, B., Scelles, N. and Durand, C., 2014. Mining tracks of competitive video games. AASRI Procedia 8, 82-87.

57. Salter, A., & Blodgett, B. (2012). Hypermasculinity & dickwolves: The contentious role of women in the new gaming public. Journal of broadcasting & electronic media, 56(3), 401-416.

58. Sanders, E.B.N. and Stappers, P.J., 2008. Co-creation and the new landscapes of design. Co-design, 4(1), pp.5-18.

59. Schubert, M., Drachen, A. and Mahlmann, T., 2016. Esports Analytics Through Encounter Detection Other Sports.

60. Segel, E. and Heer, J., 2010. Narrative visualization: Telling stories with data. IEEE transactions on visualization and computer graphics, 16(6), pp.1139-1148.

61. Semenov, A., Romov, P., Korolev, S., Yashkov, D., and Neklyudov, K. (2016). Performance of Machine Learning Algorithms in Predicting Game Outcome from Drafts in DotA 2. In International Conference on Analysis of Images, Social Networks and Texts (pp. 26-37). Springer, Cham.

62. Seo, Y. and Jung, S.U., 2016. Beyond solitary play in computer games: The social practices of eSports. Journal of Consumer Culture, 16(3), pp.635-655.

63. Seo, Y., 2016. Professionalized consumption and identity transformations in the field of eSports. Journal of Business Research, 69(1), pp.264-272.

64. Song, K., Zhang, T. and Ma, C., 2015. Predicting the winning side of DotA 2. Technical report, Stanford University.

65. Song, Y., 2016. Real-time video highlights for yahoo esports. arXiv preprint arXiv:1611.08780.

66. Sjöblom, M. and Hamari, J., 2017. Why do people watch others play video games? An empirical study on the motivations of Twitch users. Computers in Human Behavior, 75, pp.985-996.

67. Spradley, J.P., 2016. Participant observation. Waveland Press.

68. Usmani, B. This is Your Brain on Esports, Motherboard, Vice, 2014. https://motherboard.vice.com/en_us/article/mgbe9x/this-is-your-brain-on-esports

69. Wagner, M.G., 2006, June. On the Scientific Relevance of eSports. In International Conference on Internet Computing (pp. 437-442).

70. Walsh, D., 1998. Doing ethnography. Researching society and culture, pp.217-232.

71. Wang, W., 2016. Predicting multiplayer online battle arena (MOBA) game outcome based on hero draft data. Master's thesis, Dublin, National College of Ireland.

72. Weiss, T. and Schiele, S., 2013. Virtual worlds in competitive contexts: Analyzing eSports consumer needs. Electronic Markets, 23(4), pp.307-316.

73. Wolmarans, Kyle. Dota 2 vs. League of Legends: Updating the numbers. Criticalhit, 2016. https://www.criticalhit.net/gaming/dota-2-vs-league-legends-updating-numbers/

74. Yang, P., Harrison, B. E. and Roberts, D. L., 2014. Identifying patterns in combat that are predictive of success in MOBA games. In: Proceedings Foundations of Digital Games.

75. Yu, X. and Farin, D., 2005, July. Current and emerging topics in sports video processing. In Multimedia and Expo, 2005. ICME 2005. IEEE International Conference on (pp. 526-529). IEEE.

76. Zarrabi, S. A., & Jerkrot, H. N (2016). Value creation and appropriation in the esports industry. Department of Technology Management and Economics Division of Innovation Engineering and Management, CHALMERS UNIVERSITY OF TECHNOLOGY, Gothenburg, Sweden. Report No. E 2016:090

Facts, Interactivity and Videotape: Exploring the Design Space of Data in Interactive Video Storytelling

Jonathan Hook
Digital Creativity Labs, Department of Theatre, Film & TV
University of York, UK
jonathan.hook@york.ac.uk

ABSTRACT
We live in a society that is increasingly data rich, with an unprecedented amount of information being captured, stored and analysed about our lives and the people we share them with. We explore the relationship between this new data and emergent forms of interactive video storytelling. In particular we ask: i) how can interactive video storytelling techniques be employed to provide accessible, informative and pleasurable ways for people to engage with data; and ii) how can data be used by the creators of interactive video stories to meet expressive goals and support new forms of experience? We present an analysis of 43 interactive videos that use data in a noteworthy fashion. This analysis reveals a design space comprising key techniques for telling engaging interactive video stories with and about data. To conclude, we discuss challenges relating to the production and consumption of such content and make recommendations for future research.

Author Keywords
Data; interactive documentary; interactive video; narrative visualization; object-based media; perspective media.

CCS Concepts
• Human-centered computing → Visualization theory, concepts and paradigms.

INTRODUCTION
The rise of personal informatics (e.g. health, fitness and sleep tracking), consumer Internet of Things (IoT) (e.g. smart thermostats and connected cars), social media and the open data initiative means people now have access to an unprecedented amount of data about their lives, environments and the people they share them with. This proliferation of data is set to continue, with wearable technology adoption forecasted to reach 28% by this year, two thirds of consumers planning to purchase an in-home IoT device by 2019 [1], global social media adoption reaching 37% [43] and the G8 countries signing a charter to make government data open by default [34].

TVX '18, June 26–28, 2018, SEOUL, Republic of Korea

ACM ISBN 978-1-4503-5115-7/18/06.
https://doi.org/10.1145/3210825.3210826

In parallel with these developments, we have seen the emergence of new forms of interactive video. Key examples include: interactive documentaries (iDocs) [15], ShapeShifting TV [42] and, most recently, experiments in object-based [4] and perceptive media [11]. These new interactive forms enable the creation of video experiences where content is varied based on viewers' interactions, context and other data about them, and, in turn, reveal new possibilities for non-linearity, responsiveness and personalization not possible in traditional video storytelling.

In our research we ask whether these emergent forms of interactive video can be used as a platform to tell stories about, and with, the data that is proliferating our modern society. We hypothesize that the development of such data-driven interactive video experiences can offer two key, interconnected, benefits: i) presenting data in interactive video stories can provide an alternative means to reveal, contextualise and explain data, to those who are uninspired or unable to engage via existing presentation forms; and ii) equipping filmmakers to exploit modern data sources as a new *material* in interactive videos can reveal new ways to meet expressive goals and support new viewer experiences.

Despite this potential, we know very little about the form that such data-driven interactive videos should take; what tools, processes and underpinning technologies are required to craft them; and what issues will affect viewer reception, perception and experience. In this paper, we aim to develop a foundational understanding of these issues by exploring how data has been employed in existing interactive video content. We present an analysis of 43 items of interactive video content that use data in a prominent or otherwise noteworthy fashion when telling a story. Based on this analysis, we present a design space that comprises key techniques that can be employed to tell interactive video stories with and about data, and challenges that will affect their production and reception.

In mapping such techniques and challenges, our findings can guide the creation of future data-driven video content; inform future research into tools and underpinning technologies for its production and delivery; and support the development of ethical production guidelines that ensure data use is appropriate and sensitive to issues of viewer perception, experience and privacy.

MOTIVATION AND RELATED WORK

The Challenge of Engaging the Public with Data

Empowering the public to understand and act upon the unprecedented amount of data that exists about us in modern society can provide wide-ranging personal and societal benefits. For example, by transforming the way people engage with their diet, fitness, mental and physical health, transport and energy use [25, 33] and fostering civic awareness and participation [20]. However, motivating and facilitating mass, inclusive public engagement with data remains an unsolved challenge. Making data available (e.g. for download from open data portals or devices) isn't enough. Exploring raw data requires significant motivation, time and skill with tools not held by most people [16]. Rather, more inclusive methods are needed to motivate and enable a broader demographic to access, understand and take action in response to data about them [19].

The prevalent approach for making data accessible to the public is to provide interfaces that make the direct exploration of sources more manageable, usually by placing them in a structured graphical form. A substantial body of research in the field of data visualization has demonstrated that exploring data in these ways can be intuitive, visually compelling and, as a result, highly engaging for many users [e.g. 6]. For example, mobile applications displaying interactive graphs have proved a popular way for users to understand data from wearable health monitors [40] and other interactive visual representations have been shown to have great potential in enabling members of the public to explore open data released by governments [12].

Despite the success interactive data visualizations have had in engaging many users, research suggests that they may not be the right way to motivate and enable *all* people to find insight in data that exists about them. Concerns have been raised about whether the activity of seeking out and directly exploring data in graphical form, even with easy to use interfaces, will have sufficient mainstream appeal to stimulate mass engagement [24, 32]. Moreover, previous research has shown that many people, in particular those from low-education backgrounds [10], may struggle to determine appropriate actions to take in response to data presented in primarily graphical form, as this can require an understanding of how low-level facts and trends, often represented across multiple different visualisations [23], relate to contextual factors and expert knowledge [8, 31].

Story-based Approaches for Data Engagement

Previous work has explored how activities and media forms popular with the public can be used to broaden the appeal and accessibility of data. For example, art [17] and artistic installations [36], craft activities and products [3], gamification [38] and the fabrication of bespoke souvenirs [30] have been proposed as alternatives to reveal and explain insights within data. One approach with great potential for bringing data to people in a form that they can, and will want to, consume is storytelling [18, 21]. This stands to reason, few forms of communication are as accessible, informative and engaging as a well-told story. Skilled storytellers employ established narrative techniques (e.g. genres, structures, devices, characters) in the context of their audience's knowledge and experience to provide easily understood and remembered paths through complex, expansive and conflicting sources of information [5, 46]. Moreover, good stories don't just inform they entertain. Forms like documentary can make engagement with information exciting, intriguing and challenging through the creative application of narrative techniques.

Data journalism has already demonstrated how skilled storytelling techniques from established media forms can be applied to support data engagement, and a public appetite to consume data in story form [14]. Data journalism articles allow people to gain individualised insight from complex data sources, by blending the presentation of interactive visualisations with storytelling techniques from text-based print and online journalism [39]. Moreover, the awards and critical acclaim received by such articles (including a Pulitzer Prize [28]) shows how data-driven storytelling can open up new opportunities for creative expression and lead to content that is highly compelling in its own right.

Interactive Video for Data Engagement and Expression

We hypothesize that video-based storytelling forms have especially strong potential for facilitating broader public engagement with data. Few storytelling forms are consumed so regularly by such a large segment of the population. For example, 91% of adults in the UK watch television each week, viewing an average 3 hours and 36 minutes per day, and the appeal of video content continues to grow in the online age with consumption of paid video-on-demand services rising to 26% in 2015 [35]. Additionally, video offers a diverse range of genres (e.g. documentary, drama, comedy) with different storytelling techniques that can be applied to appeal to different groups.

Presenting data through stories is, of course, central to existing video genres, such as news and documentary [2]. However, traditional broadcast distribution, where the same content is transmitted to all viewers, has meant video stories must feature aggregate data relevant to large, homogenous audiences. Consequently, the insight that a person can receive about their data from current video storytelling approaches is significantly limited in terms of personal relevance and depth, compared to what is available to those motivated and able to use analytics tools and interactive visualisations. Recent developments in interactive video, such as web-based interactive documentaries [e.g. 15] and object-based media [e.g. 4] allow for the creation of video stories that are dynamically reconfigured in response to information about each viewer and their context. As a consequence, there are now opportunities to create interactive videos that present each viewer with an individually tailored perspective on their data.

We argue that such interactive data-driven videos can offer new ways to present data to the public that a large and diverse section of the population will be able to, and equally crucially, want to use. Moreover, we expect that equipping filmmakers to exploit modern data sources as a *material* in interactive video productions can reveal new ways to meet expressive goals and support the creation of new forms of media experience.

METHOD

While the coming together of data from modern sources with emergent forms of interactive video presents opportunities for increased public data engagement and new forms of expression, the form, production and reception of such data-driven interactive videos are not yet understood. In particular, the production of video content depends on established aesthetic techniques for telling effective and engaging stories. It isn't yet clear what form the equivalent techniques that incorporate data into video stories should take and how they should be tailored in response to different data sources, genres, production goals and audiences. In this paper, we seek to address this knowledge gap by developing a foundational understanding of the ways that data from modern sources has been incorporated into existing interactive video content.

To develop this understanding, we conducted an analysis of existing examples of data-driven video content. Our analysis followed a two-stage process. In the first stage, we identified a set of interactive videos that use data in a prominent or otherwise noteworthy fashion. In order to identify this set we reviewed 300 interactive videos from the following sources: 262 from MIT's Docubase, 27 from i-docs.org, 6 from open web searches (e.g. with terms such as "data visualization video") and 5 items that the author was previously aware of. Each item was watched by a researcher and included or excluded based on the following criteria: 1) the content must be primarily video-based; 2) data must feature prominently in what is presented to the viewer; and 3) the presentation of data must extend beyond what is possible in a non-interactive video (e.g. content showing only static graphical visualizations similar to those seen on television news were excluded). This final criterion was chosen to focus our study on the relationship between data and *interactive* video content (see [2] for a review of data-driven storytelling in non-interactive videos).

Our first stage analysis resulted in a set of 43 interactive videos. In the second stage, the examples in this set were subjected to a more detailed review. Each item was viewed again by a researcher in order to determine information in the following categories: the genre of video story; the type of data used; the approach employed for presenting the data in the story; any role that data played in supporting the story; any role that the story played in supporting the viewer in understanding data; any notable challenges for data-driven stories raised; and examples of best-practice for addressing such challenges. It was not possible to access a working version of 4 examples. However, we were able to include these in the sample by reviewing secondary sources (e.g. videos showing their experience that were available). Where multiple items were part of a series, these were reviewed as individual items. This decision was made because we found that different episodes in a series could often employ and pose divergent approaches and challenges. Where an item is an episode in a series, the naming convention "Series Title (Episode #: Title)" is used.

To conclude our review, we analyzed the information recorded for each category to identify, and classify the examples in terms of, a set of recurrent design features. These features were determined by grouping examples based on observed similarities, and by cross-referencing these emergent groups with storytelling literature [e.g. 13, 45, 46]. This process was iterative, with examples reconsidered in light of emergent features during multiple passes through the data.

CASE STUDIES

Our analysis revealed a design space of data-driven video stories that is presented in Table 1. This space maps the examples reviewed in terms of: i) design strategies that were employed to tell engaging interactive video stories about, and with, data; ii) presentation structures that were used to combine data and video together into cohesive narrative experiences; and iii) a set of further recurrent features observed (e.g. genre, form of data presentation, type of data). In presenting our design space, we draw inspiration from the method employed by Segel and Heer in their related review of data journalism content [39]. We first describe a set of detailed case studies, which each illustrate a selection of design space features. When describing each case study, we highlight the design space features described **in bold**. We then present further analysis of the design space that reveals additional features and challenges that span the sample in a subsequent section.

Unspeak

In this web-based interactive **documentary** the viewer is introduced to Stephen Poole's concept of "Unspeak" – the careful choice of language "to say something without saying it, without getting into an argument and so having to justify itself" [37]. The video portion of the experience is a traditional linear film, in which a narrator explains the concept of Unspeak drawing on a set of examples from politics and popular culture. While watching this video, the viewer has the option to pause playback and view a set of interactive data visualizations. These visualizations allow the viewer to explore data about the prevalence of different Unspeak terms on **social media** in the three years preceding the film's release. This data is presented in a variety of **graphical** forms. The data included is **static** (i.e. not dynamically sourced at the time of viewing) and **the same for all viewers**, having been recorded at production time.

"Unspeak" illustrates perhaps the most rudimentary presentation structure observed in the design space: **loosely**

coupled data. In this structure (used in 5 examples) video content and data are presented across two distinct, companion experiences. While interacting with either experience the viewer is given the option to switch to the other, usually by clicking on a link or icon. The example also illustrates one of the most prevalent design strategies employed in the sample (30 examples), the use of video to provide **contextualization** for data. In "Unspeak", if the viewer were to interact with the data visualizations in isolation they may find them comparatively uninteresting. However, by accompanying these visualizations with a video that offers a rich explanation of the rhetorical power of words, the viewer is motivated to investigate how the otherwise innocuous terms shown in the graphs have been employed to frame major political events. This, in turn, gives the data a new meaning and heightened credence.

Frontline: Targeting the Electorate

"Frontline: Targeting the Electorate" is a web-based interactive **documentary** that explores how the electorate is targeted during political campaigns. The film provides each viewer with a personalized perspective on how they may have been targeted with information during the 2012 US presidential campaign. At the start of the experience, the viewer is informed that their **location** has been automatically detected from their browser. They are then asked to complete a short interactive quiz about their demographics, political views and lifestyle. This **dynamic** and **individual data** is used to assemble a bespoke video comprising interviews with experts explaining the particular strategies used to target the viewer during the campaign.

This case exemplifies the **adaptive narrative** presentation structure, which was observed in 3 examples. With this structure, decisions about the selection and order of video content shown to the viewer are made based on a data source. In "Frontline: Targeting the Electorate", this presentation structure is used to implement one of the most commonly observed design strategies (22 examples): the use of **personal data as a device** that supports and amplifies the filmmaker's intent. In the film, the intent is to make viewers aware of the concerning tactics that can be employed by politicians during elections. Adapting the narrative shown to each viewer in response to their individual data supports this in two ways. Firstly, the filmmaker creates a strong personal connection between the issue of targeting and the viewer by presenting videos that refer to the actual tactics that would be employed to target them. Secondly, by adapting the content of the film using the same data used to target voters during elections, the filmmaker is able to reinforce the authenticity of their argument by demonstrating that such targeting is viable.

Coal: A Love Story

This web-based interactive **documentary** presents the viewer with a collection of video and other media that highlights America's dependence on coal. One section of the film, "Coal & You", allows the viewer to explore how their own lifestyle and behavior influences the issues discussed in the film, by calculating their own annual coal consumption. The viewer is presented with a linear video that shows people doing everyday activities, such as web browsing and cooking. These are overlaid with **static** text stating the amount of coal each activity depends on. At the end of the video, the viewer is told that the average American family burns 6,500 lbs. of coal per year, and asked how they compare. An interactive quiz then enquires about the viewer's location and everyday habits (e.g. number of hours spent on a mobile device). The answers are used to provide an **individual perspective** on **static** energy consumption data (classified as **factual** in our design space), which is presented as a personal coal use estimate shown via a combination of **graphics** and **text**.

"Coal: A Love Story" demonstrates a presentation strategy that was observed in 18 examples in the design space: **interleaved data**. With this strategy, the viewer is shown a series of videos in a linear structure. At points between these videos the viewer is asked to interact with data in a format that is not video-based (e.g. a graphical interactive data visualization). This differs from the loosely coupled structure, because the viewer is not given a choice of when to interact with data, but is actively directed to explore it at defined points in the narrative. In the film, this presentation structure is used to support a design strategy found in 8 examples: the use of **video to create intrigue** about the content of a data source. In this case, video is not primarily used to present or explain data. Rather, the preceding video is used to heighten the viewer's interest in and, therefore, motivate their engagement with data that is subsequently presented in a different form. In this way, the strategy can be seen to leverage a crucial feature of video storytelling to engage the viewer with data: plot structure. By arranging the presentation of information into two phases of exposition (in the preceding video) and denouement (in the ensuing interactive quiz), the viewer's interest in exploring the data source is heightened. The film is also a further example of using video to provide **contextualization** and **personal data as a device**.

Do Not Track

"Do Not Track" is a 7 episode web-based interactive **documentary** series that aims to inform the viewer about the proliferation of web tracking and its implications. The third episode, "Like Mining", explores some of the problematic ways that companies might profile people based on the information they post on social networks. The episode is structured around a television **advertisement** for "Illuminus", a fictional company that uses social network profiling to make decisions about insurance policies and loans. Using an **interleaved data** presentation structure, the viewer is shown segments of the advert's linear video narrative. These are followed by interactive web pages that use **text**, **graphics** and a personalized **image** to demonstrate to the viewer that many features of the fictional product shown in the advert could actually be implemented by

Figure 1: Viewers' responses to different video segments are used to evidence a point made by the filmmaker in "The Risk Taker's Survival Guide" (© Rubber Republic [C12])

analyzing their **individual social network** data. This data is accessed **dynamically** from the Facebook API, if the viewer provides authorization.

This case illustrates a design strategy that was observed only in this example, which we refer to as **fiction made real** through data. In this strategy, video is used to illustrate a fictional scenario, which is then demonstrated to be a realistic proposition using a data source. The result in this case is that the authenticity of the fictional scenario illustrated in the video advert, and the conceivable risks it shows, is established more strongly than may be possible if it was shown on its own in a non-interactive video. While examples employing this approach could be subsumed into **personal data as a device**, we feel they should be marked as a distinct strategy in the design space. This is because they demonstrate how a key feature of video storytelling – the capability to richly depict fictional situations – can be exploited to increase a viewer's level of interest in data and its implications and, conversely, how individualized data can enhance the impact of fictional scenarios when included as a device in documentaries.

The Risk Taker's Survival Guide

This web-based interactive **documentary** explores the topic of risk. In one section of the film, a combination of **adaptive narrative** and **interleaved data** presentation structures is used to illustrate how poor many people are at assessing risk in everyday life. Half of the film's viewers are shown a video of a backpack in a busy crowd in New York's Grand Central Station, while the other half are shown a bag on an empty rural station platform. Both groups are asked to decide whether they would report this bag to station staff using an interactive quiz. Data about the percentage of viewers that chose to report each bag is then shown on the screen (Figure 1). At the time of viewing, this was much higher for the bag on the isolated platform than the busy one. In a following video segment, a narrator explains that it would be logical for more people to report the bag in the busy station, as if this contained an explosive device it could cause harm to a larger number of people.

This section of "The Risk Taker's Survival Guide" illustrates a design strategy that was observed in 8 examples in the design space: using **peer data as a device**. In such examples, the possibility of gathering data about, and from, viewers through their interactions with an interactive video is exploited to assemble an evidence base that supports the filmmaker's intent. In "The Risk Taker's Survival Guide" this **viewer engagement data** helps the filmmaker illustrate how poor people can be at assessing risk in two important ways. Firstly, by asking the viewer to participate in the creation of the data that evidences a point, the filmmaker is able to create a stronger personal connection between, and perspective on, the results than might be possible with the inclusion of pre-set statistics in a traditional video. Secondly, the use of actual data gathered from the viewers of the film to evidence arguments, rather than general statistics, has the potential to give that evidence a greater sense of authenticity.

Netwars

In this 5 episode web-based interactive **documentary**, the viewer is confronted with current and future risks posed by cyber warfare. All episodes in the series are narrated by an unnamed, unidentified and potentially untrustworthy character that introduces and explains a range of cyber security threats. For example, in the first episode, "Out of CTRL", the narrator introduces the risks posed by vulnerability scanning in a video segment. The viewer is then presented with an interactive page that uses **text** and **graphics** to show how vulnerable their computer configuration (e.g. their operating system) makes them to attack. This data is **dynamic** and **individual** to the viewer, having been detected automatically from their web browser.

In addition to further demonstrating the **interleaved data** presentation structure, **personal data as a device** and **video to create intrigue** strategies, this case also illustrates a further strategy evident in 16 of the examples reviewed: the **use of character** to support data engagement. The narrator in Netwars is not a neutral figure that simply introduces and explains the data presented. Rather, he is a mysterious, erratic and potentially untrustworthy figure, whose dramatic performance evokes a sense of unease and apprehension about the issues discussed. When combined with the presentation of individual data that illustrates how such issues personally affect the viewer, this application of character serves as a powerful device to grab the viewer's attention and emphasize the importance of the film's topic.

Here at Home

The topic of this web-based interactive **documentary** is an experiment designed to reduce homelessness in five Canadian cities. Viewers are presented with an interactive graphical visualization of data from the study, which is **the same for all viewers**. Scattered amongst this visualization float small pictures of people involved in the study. Clicking on a picture plays a short video interview about that person's experiences of the project.

"Here at Home" illustrates two recurrent, and closely linked, features evident in the design space that have not been seen in the case studies discussed so far. Firstly, the example illustrates a further presentation structure: **augmented visualization**. In the 6 examples employing this structure, the viewer experience most closely resembles exploring an interactive visualization. However, the viewer is presented with the option to view linear video content while exploring the data by, e.g., clicking on thumbnails. The result, in this case study, is that the videos connect otherwise abstract and sterile statistics to the lives and experiences of real people. This makes the case a further example of the **use of character** to support data engagement and video to provide **contextualization**.

The example also illustrates a design strategy that was exhibited in 6 examples in the design space: the use of **data as a narrative structure**. In "Here at Home", data doesn't just provide additional evidence and information about the individual stories shown in the videos. It also offers a meaningful route through them. Previous accounts of database documentaries have noted how the design of interfaces for exploring collections of video clips can provide an opportunity for filmmakers to *"preserve narrative and argument in the documentary text"* [29]. Examples employing this strategy demonstrate how interactive data visualizations can be used as the basis of such interfaces, providing a meaningful path through which a viewer can navigate and come to understand an otherwise loosely connected collection of films.

Holy Mountain

This web-based interactive **documentary** tells residents' stories of Montreal's Mount Royal. Using an elegantly illustrated web-based interface, the viewer can navigate between five locations on Mount Royal. At each, a selection of videos and photo essays, which each tell a Montrealer's story of the place, can be viewed. While the viewer explores each location, short messages about Mount Royal from the **social network** site Twitter are displayed in the corner of the screen. These messages are sourced **dynamically** using the Twitter API, by searching for the keywords "Mont Royal". Clicking on these messages takes the viewer to Twitter where they can interact further (e.g. by reading replies or by sending a response to the author). This case illustrates a design strategy that was observed 5 times in the design space: the use of **data for liveness**. Here, the filmmaker not only creates a static record of past memories of Mount Royal recorded in video form, but also employs live data to create an experience that is more closely connected with current Montrealers' lives.

Take This Lollipop

This web-based interactive film sits in the genre of **horror**. The short film begins with a scene in which an angry and deranged **character** is stalking a victim on Facebook. The video incorporates **social network** data (e.g. **images** and **text** messages) gathered **dynamically** from the viewer's **individual** Facebook page into shots of the protagonist's computer screen. Additionally, the character is shown to look up directions on Google Maps, which are based on

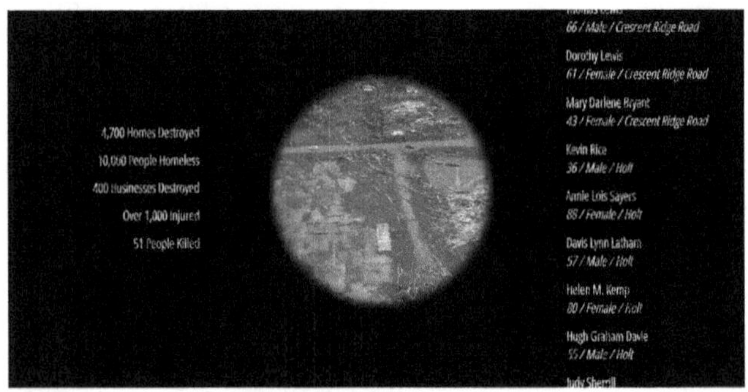

Figure 2: Viewers must scroll to the end of the data before the narrative progresses (© Andrew Beck Grace [C13]).

individual data about the viewer's **location**. As a consequence, it is made clear to the viewer that the potential victim of the character is, in fact, them. In the final scene, the character is seen to drive to their victim's location and get out of his car – where the film ends.

"Take This Lollipop" employs a number of the strategies discussed in previous case studies to support the filmmaker's intent to scare the viewer, including: **personal data as a device** and the **use of strong character**. In addition, it illustrates a further presentation structure not discussed so far: **dynamic video**. In this structure, the primary viewer experience resembles a traditional video (i.e. a story is told through the linear presentation of video frames). However, the data shown in this sequence varies depending on the viewer, through the inclusion of, e.g., dynamic graphics, text or images. The film also illustrates a further design strategy employed in 5 examples: the **use of atmosphere** to re-contextualize data. By employing established horror tropes including dramatic sounds, close-up framing, erratic cutting, hard lighting and prominent shadows, the filmmaker creates an atmosphere of unease and dread. When the viewer's own social network data is juxtaposed with this atmosphere it takes on a new meaning; frightening the viewer and, in turn, stimulating them to reflect on the data they share online.

After the Storm

"After the Storm" is a web-based interactive **documentary** that combines videos with interactive elements to tell one person's story of a devastating tornado. At two points in the story, viewers must scroll through lists of hurricane deaths and locations that are shown as **text** (Figure 2). While video plays and the spoken narration continues as the viewer scrolls, the story will not progress until the viewer reaches the end of the list. In addition to providing another example of the **dynamic video** presentation structure, this case illustrates a strategy only seen in this example: the use of data **interaction as a device**. Scrolling through the lists takes time and effort, which, in turn, stresses the scale of the damage resulting from tornados and their frequency across the US. This supports the filmmaker in making the argument that such events "could happen to you". In this way, interacting with data is not just a means to view information, but a device supporting the telling of the story.

DESIGN SPACE ANALYSIS

Types of Data and Level of Personalization

We classify the types of data featured into 8 categories. The data employed in the majority of examples (62.8%) is classified as **factual**. The topics of these datasets were diverse and included: energy, health, social program outcomes, risks and piracy attacks. Other popular types used included **social media** (used in 27.9% of examples), the viewer's **location** (30.2%) and data about **viewers' engagement** with the experience (20.9%). Less common types of data included information about the **viewing device** (7%); **other personal** data such as the viewer's emails and music listening habits (4.7%); **news** articles (2.3%); and data from **IoT** devices (2.3%).

We also classified the data featured in terms of its level of personalization to the viewer. We found the majority of examples (60.5%) featured data that was the **same for all viewers**. However, a reasonably large percentage (34.9%) did employ data that was **individual** to the viewer. Where individual data was used, we observed that data types were limited to the categories of: **social media, location, viewing device**, **other personal** data and **IoT**. An interesting hybrid between individual and shared data was observed in 23.3% of examples, which we classify as **individual perspective**. Here, the main dataset featured in the experience is the same for all viewers. However, individual viewer data is used to present a personal perspective on it. For example, the "Risk Taker's Survival Guide" uses data about a viewer's age and behavior to provide a life expectancy estimate based on shared data.

58.1% of examples featured data that was sourced **dynamically** during the experience, from sources such as data APIs or from information available found via the viewer's browser. In the majority of cases where data was dynamically included in an experience, we observed that little or no analysis was performed on it as part of its presentation in the story. Rather, in 68% of examples employing dynamic data this was presented in its raw form (e.g. by showing a viewer's location on a map rather than drawing a meaningful inference from that location). Despite analysis of dynamic data being rare in the sample, its potential value as a storytelling strategy was illustrated in "Do Not Track (EP3: Like Mining)" where data sourced dynamically from the viewer's Facebook page was analysed to determine aspects of the viewer's personality.

Challenges and Emergent Best Practice

A number of the design strategies relied on the **availability of data** individual to the viewer to create a bespoke experience. If this data doesn't exist, is partially complete, or the viewer doesn't allow access, there is potential that the film may not be viewable as intended. For example, the personal impact of the fictional Illuminus reports in "Do Not Track (Episode 3: Like Mining)" is reduced if the viewer does not have, or is not willing to provide access to, Facebook data. In examples employing peer data as a device, the potential for a **cold start problem** [c.f. 22] was noted, where arguments based on peer data cannot be made until that data has been amassed.

While some examples simply displayed an **error message** or made **content unavailable** when data was unavailable, others offered solutions to allow the viewer to engage. In "Frontline: Targeting the Electorate" if the viewer's location isn't available or within the US, they are given the option to **manually input** their own, or an imaginary, location. This solution is likely to only be practical in cases where video stories are based on simple forms of data that can be entered easily by the viewer. A potentially more scalable solution was observed in Do Not Track. Here, social network **data from an alias**, the film's narrator, is used to illustrate the fictional Illuminus advert. This means the film can be experienced by all viewers, but is still problematic as the impact of basing the film's fiction made real strategy on individual viewer data is lost.

The **relevance of data** to different viewers was also identified as a potential challenge. Multiple examples implemented the personal data as a device strategy by highlighting an individual connection between the viewer's personal data and a shared data set. Such cases rely on each viewer's individual data having sufficient relevance to the shared data for a meaningful connection to be made. This may not always be the case. For example, in "God's Lake Narrows" the viewer's location is correlated with First Nations reserves in Canada, to suggest that the problems experienced by such communities are 'closer to home' than the viewer might think. This message is undermined if the film is viewed outside of Canada, and the data shows the viewer is actually a long distance from the nearest reserve. In such cases, the use of **data from an alias**, which is more relevant, may provide a way to give all viewers a meaningful experience.

In examples where dynamically accessed data was used to create a sense of liveness, a further challenge was posed by the **lack of control** that the filmmaker has over that data. For example, in "Mount Royal", there is a risk the social network data included may be inappropriate or offensive. This could, for example, prove a barrier to the assignment of classifications to data-driven films. Where dynamic data is used as the basis of argumentation, as in examples employing the peer data as a device strategy, there is a further risk that the data will not support or otherwise conform to the filmmaker's intended message.

Offering viewers **informed consent** about how their data will be used in the telling of a story was also a crucial challenge revealed in the design space. In "In Limbo" the viewer provides authentication to the Gmail API at the start. Text from their emails is subsequently shown on screen with no prior warning. This unexpected display of private data could be problematic, especially if the film is viewed in a social situation. Providing viewers with a clear explanation of how their data will be used, so that they can

Category	Feature	After the Storm [C13]	Are You Happy? [C22]	Bar Code [C28]	Boron Mon Amor [C3]	Coal: A Love Story [C23]	Crisis Guide Pakistan [C5]	Do Not Track (EP 1: Morning Rituals) [C11]	DNT (EP 2: Breaking Ad)	DNT (EP 3: Like Mining)	DNT (EP 4: The Spy in My Pocket)	DNT (EP 5: Big Data Inside the Algorithm)	DNT (EP 6: The Daily Me)	DNT (EP 7: To Change the Future Click Here)	Facebook Friendship Videos [C20]	Frontline: Targeting the Electorate [C24]	Goa Hippy Tribe [C7]	God's Lake Narrows [C4]	Happy World [C2]	Hazardous Hospitals [C1]	Here at Home [C16]	Hollow [C25]	Holy Mountain [C8]	In Limbo [C30]	Land of Opportunity [C6]	Last Hijack Interactive [C32]	Media of Things [44]	Netwars (EP1: Out of CTRL) [C29]	NW (EP2: Remote Attack)	NW (EP3: Back Up Your Life)	NW (EP5: The Industry of Fear)	Oil to Die For [C17]	Planet Money Makes a T-Shirt [C15]	Seven Deadly Digital Sins [C26]	The Industry [C9]	The Network Effect [C14]	The Risk Taker's Survival Guide [C12]	The Shirt on Your Back [C21]	The Test Tube [C27]	The Wilderness Downtown [C18]	This Land [C31]	Take This Lollipop [C33]	Unspeak [C19]	Visual Perceptive Media [C10]
Structure	Dynamic video	+	+					+	+			+	+	+	+			+						+				+	+							+	+	+	+	+		+		
Structure	Interleaved data					+				+	+	+		+			+			+		+	+					+	+	+	+	+	+	+			+			+				
Structure	Augmented data			+			+														+								+						+						+			
Structure	Loosely coupled data				+														+						+	+																	+	
Structure	Adaptive narrative															+											+																	+
Design Strategy	Contextualization	+			+	+	+	+	+	+	+	+	+	+		+			+	+	+	+		+	+	+		+	+	+	+	+	+		+		+	+			+		+	
Design Strategy	Personal data as device					+		+	+	+	+	+	+	+	+	+	+	+		+				+				+	+	+							+		+	+		+		+
Design Strategy	Video creates intrigue					+		+								+				+								+	+	+					+		+							
Design Strategy	Fiction made real									+																																		
Design Strategy	Peer data as device			+										+	+	+						+												+			+		+					
Design Strategy	Use of character	+						+			+										+	+				+		+	+	+	+	+		+	+		+	+				+		
Design Strategy	Data as narrative structure			+			+														+								+						+						+			
Design Strategy	Data for liveness		+					+					+										+																+					
Design Strategy	Use of atmosphere																												+		+					+				+		+		
Design Strategy	Interaction as device	+																																										
Genre	Advertisement									-																																		
Genre	Comedy																																	-										
Genre	Cookery																										+																	
Genre	Documentary	+	+	+	+	+	+	+	+	+	+	+	+	+		+	+	+	+	+	+	+	+	+	+	+		+	+	+	+	+	+	+	+		+	+	+		+		+	
Genre	Drama																																											+
Genre	Horror																																									+		
Genre	Music																																							+				
Genre	Science Fiction																												-		-													
Genre	Unclassified														+																					+								
Form	Graphical			+	+	+	+	+	+	+	+	+				+			+	+	+	+			+	+			+			+	+	+	+	+	+		+		+		+	
Form	Image							+		+		+	+		+		+							+																+		+		
Form	Text	+	+	+		+		+	+	+	+	+	+	+	+			+	+	+	+	+	+	+	+			+	+	+	+	+	+		+	+	+	+	+			+		
Form	Speech							+																																				
Data Type	Social media		+							+			+	+	+		+			+			+	+															+			+	+	
Data Type	News												+																															
Data Type	Viewing device																							+				+		+														
Data Type	Location					+		+			+	+				+		+						+				+	+	+					+					+		+		
Data Type	Viewer engagement			+								+	+	+		+						+												+			+		+					
Data Type	Other personal																							+																				+
Data Type	Factual	+		+	+	+	+	+	+		+					+		+	+	+	+	+			+	+		+	+	+	+	+	+		+	+	+	+			+			
Data Type	Internet of Things																										+																	
Perso.	Individual							+		+	+	+			+	+	+							+			+	+	+	+										+		+		+
Perso.	Same for all viewers	+	+	+	+		+		+		+		+	+					+	+	+	+	+		+	+					+	+	+	+	+	+	+	+			+		+	
Perso.	Individual perspective					+		+						+		+		+										+	+	+							+		+					
Sou.	Static	+		+	+	+	+		+		+					+		+	+	+	+				+	+		+	+	+	+	+	+			+	+	+			+		+	
Sou.	Dynamic		+			+		+		+	+	+	+	+	+	+	+	+				+	+	+			+	+	+	+				+			+		+	+		+		+
Challenge	Availability of data									+	+					+	+							+																+				
Challenge	Relevance of data			+				+								+		+		+		+																						
Challenge	Cold start			+									+	+		+						+												+			+		+					
Challenge	Lack of control		+										+										+														+		+					
Challenge	Informed consent																							+																		+		
Solution	Error message										+																																	
Solution	Content unavailable																							+																+		+		
Solution	Manual input															+																												
Solution	Data from an alias									+							+																											
Ana.	Primary	+	+	+			+	+	+	+	+	+	+	+	+	+	+	+	+	+	+	+	+	+	+	+		+	+	+	+	+	+	+	+	+	+	+	+	+	+	+	+	
Ana.	Secondary				+	+																					+																	+

Table 1: Design space showing recurrent features (rows) and which examples they were observed in (columns). Blue cells (+) indicate the presence of features and green cells (-) indicate features in a secondary role. Some labels are abridged: "Level of Personalisation" (Perso.), "Sourcing of Data" (Sou.) and "Analysis based on Primary or Secondary Source" (Ana.).

make an informed choice about progressing, may be a way to avoid such problematic situations. However, this simple approach to consent may be incompatible with examples like "Take This Lollipop", "Netwars" and "Do Not Track", where feeling surprised about the unexpected, but creative, ways data is used is a compelling feature of the experience.

DISCUSSION

Interactive Video Can Tell Engaging Stories with Data

At the beginning of this paper we hypothesized that presenting data in interactive video stories could provide an alternative means to reveal, contextualise and explain data, to those who are uninspired or unable to engage via existing presentation forms. While empirical studies with viewers will be needed to fully explore this hypothesis, our findings provide initial evidence of the potential of this approach. Our analysis has demonstrated a range of structures and strategies (summarized in Table 2) through which video storytelling techniques can be employed to motivate and enable audiences to engage with data sources. The examples reviewed, in particular those using the contextualization strategy, show us how situating the presentation of data within the narrative of a video story can aid in communicating the meaning, importance and implications of that data to viewers. Moreover, further strategies revealed in our analysis demonstrate how the application of video-storytelling devices such as strong characters, plot structures of intrigue and resolution, genre tropes and cinematic atmosphere can make data sources and the insights they contain interesting, exciting and even unnerving for viewers. We argue that by transforming data presentation into something that is not just informative, but entertaining, these particular *dramatic* strategies could make video storytelling an especially effective way to inspire a large section of the population to engage.

Interactivity and Personalization Add Significant Value

The application of video storytelling techniques to make information attractive, engaging or otherwise enjoyable for viewers has, of course, been demonstrated throughout the history of documentary film. However, what is novel in the examples reviewed is how they exploit opportunities posed by *interactivity* to engage viewers with data in new ways. The most prominent opportunity of interactive video demonstrated by the examples was the possibility of delivering personalized experiences to different viewers based on the content of a data source. In examples such as "Netwars", "Do Not Track" and "Frontline: Targeting the Electorate", this allowed the filmmaker to draw on established video techniques to tell a compelling story about data, but without the restriction imposed by non-interactive video that this data should be the same for all viewers. The possibility of personalizing video stories in response to viewer data was observed to underpin a number of the design strategies, including personalization as a device and fiction made real. Additionally, it was seen to enhance the effect of other strategies including the application of atmosphere and character. For example, the effect of the erratic and unreliable narrator in Netwars is heightened by the use of viewers' personal data in the story.

Presentation Structures	Dynamic video	Different data presented to each viewer in an otherwise linear video.
	Interleaved data	Data presented in interactive intervals between video segments.
	Augmented data	Data visualization augmented with video.
	Loosely coupled data	Video and data presented across companion experiences.
	Adaptive narrative	Selection and order of video content changed based on data.
Design Strategies	Contextualization	Video contextualizes a data source.
	Personal data as device	Personalization supports and amplifies the filmmaker's intent.
	Video creates intrigue	Video creates intrigue about data.
	Fiction made real	Fictional video scenario shown to be authentic using data.
	Peer data as device	Data captured from other viewers support's filmmakers intent.
	Use of character	Characters support viewer's engagement with data.
	Data as narrative structure	Data offers a path to navigate videos.
	Data for liveness	Dynamic data provides contemporaneity for video.
	Use of atmosphere	Cinematic atmosphere re-frames the viewer's experience of data.
	Interaction as device	Interaction with data as a device that supports the filmmaker's intent.

Table 2: Summary of Presentation Structures and Design Strategies identified in the design space.

Genre Tropes Were Central to the Design Strategies

All but two examples conformed to the norms and traditions of an established genre and three examples were seen to employ characteristics from a secondary genre when engaging the viewer with data (e.g. advertising in "Do Not Track (EP 3: Like Mining)"). This application of tropes and conventions from existing genres of video storytelling was observed to be a key way in which compelling viewer experiences could be built about and around data sources. Examples of the role played by genre ranged from the broader placement of personal data within the context of established narrative structures from documentary film to the combination of docudrama traditions [27] with a viewer's individual data in the fiction made real strategy.

The prevalent application of genre tropes demonstrates that the potential value of video storytelling doesn't just lie in the inherent features of the video form (e.g. moving image, structured presentation of information over time). Rather, our findings highlight the important role that the rich history of techniques for exploiting these features to tell compelling stories, and filmmakers' skilled application of them, can play in engaging people with data. We feel this is an important observation to make in the context of previous research on data storytelling, which has tended to focus on the value of visual storytelling and narrative structure [e.g. 2, 39] and not what can be gained by building on a broader range of genre conventions and their skilled application.

One genre, documentary, was particularly prevalent in the design space, representing 86% of all examples reviewed. This is not surprising, as building on the traditions of a non-fiction genre would seem to be a natural choice when seeking to present data to a viewer. However, the limited examples that do deviate from documentary demonstrate the rich potential that other genres can play in engaging people with data. For example, "Take This Lollipop" shows how tropes from horror can be used to make the viewer reflect on the privacy and security risks posed when posting personal data to social media. Examples in the design space also almost exclusively conform to genres of *entertainment*. However, our findings suggest that data-driven video stories might have value outside of this context, such as in the communication of design ideas and possibilities. For example, the fiction made real strategy demonstrates the potential for data-driven video stories to form the basis of design fictions [41], where the authenticity and implications of imagined futures illustrated in video form [e.g. 26] could be reinforced through the inclusion of a viewer's own data.

The Potential of Adaptive Narrative is Underexplored

One of the most promising presentation structures revealed in the design space was that of adaptive narrative. The examples employing this structure demonstrated the rich and exciting possibility of creating data-driven video stories in which the fundamental narrative structure is changed by selecting and rearranging video content based on a data source. By changing the narrative structure of a video story in response to a data source the filmmaker may be empowered to profoundly tailor how it is contextualized and analyzed, and the conclusions and recommendations that are drawn. In doing so, the expressive and rhetorical power of the design strategies identified in this paper might be significantly enhanced. For instance, in "Coal: A Love Story" rather than presenting each viewer's personal coal use estimate as text and graphs, they might be shown a bespoke adaptive video that makes individualised behavior change suggestions based on aspects of their energy use.

While highly promising, the adaptive narrative presentation structure was the least prevalent in our analysis (7% of examples). The design space was instead dominated by examples where the extent of personalization offered to the viewer in response to their data was limited to including dynamic text, graphics and images within an otherwise static and linear narrative structure. In our future work, we are interested in exploring why this rich category of data-driven video stories is as yet so underexplored and how barriers to its production might be addressed by building on the wealth of prior research in non-linear content authoring, production and distribution offered by the TVX community.

The Variety of Data Sources Employed is Limited

While the design space illustrates a rich and diverse range of strategies for incorporating data into interactive video stories, the variety of data included in examples was quite limited. We were particularly surprised to find that only one example featured data from the IoT devices that account for an increasing amount of data produced in our society. Where data individual to the viewer was incorporated into a video story the variety of sources was even more limited. Such examples only used data about viewers' social media, location, browser and viewing device. We posit that the reason for this limited data variety stems from the fact that some data sources are easier to include in an interactive video from a technical and viewer perspective. A viewer's social network data or location can be easily included using established APIs, with only a simple authentication step. In contrast, including data from a home IoT device would be technically complex and may require the viewer to conduct a complex process to configure the transfer of data from device to content. For this reason, we believe that the development of tools and infrastructure [e.g. 7] that make it easier for a broader variety of data to be included in video stories will be an important avenue for future research. This will, in turn, enable a richer variety of data-driven video content and, most crucially, allow for the design strategies identified in this paper to be used to help people understand a broader range of data. Developing tools that enable the creation of films that draw inferences from dynamic data sources, rather than just displaying data in raw form, may also open up a wealth of new production opportunities (e.g., for the personalization as a device strategy).

There is a Need to Establish Ethical Production Practice

The examples highlighted a number of ethical challenges posed by data-driven video stories. These include the lack of control over the appropriateness of content that includes dynamic data (e.g. as with the live social network data included in examples such as "Mount Royal") and the need to make viewers aware of how personal data will be used before they consent (e.g. as with the unexpected on-screen display of personal email data in "InLimbo"). Furthermore, the centrality of personalization to the design strategies suggests that data-driven videos, if not designed responsibly, may enforce the harmful information filter bubble effects seen in other forms of personalized online media [9]. We hypothesize that research exploring how to negotiate these and other complex issues of ethics, privacy and data ownership will be crucial for creating positive audience perceptions and responses to interactive video content that is based on personal data. We argue that research establishing ethical production practices for data-driven video stories will also be particularly vital, if we are to ensure that content is not damaging to audiences or society. This will be especially important if data-driven video stories extend into areas (e.g., advertising) where there is potential for the nefarious application of personalization based on viewer data.

ACKNOWLEDGEMENTS

This research was funded by the EPSRC "Perspective Media: Personalised Video Storytelling for Data Engagement" project (EP/R010919/1).

REFERENCES

1. Accenture. 2014. The Internet of Things: The Future of Consumer Adoption.

2. Fereshteh Amini, Nathalie Henry Riche, Bongshin Lee, Christophe Hurter, and Pourang Irani. 2015. Understanding Data Videos: Looking at Narrative Visualization through the Cinematography Lens. In *Proceedings of the 33rd Annual ACM Conference on Human Factors in Computing Systems* (CHI '15). ACM, 1459-1468. https://doi.org/10.1145/2702123.2702431

3. Swamy Ananthanarayan, Nathan Lapinski, Katie Siek, and Michael Eisenberg. 2014. Towards the crafting of personal health technologies. In *Proceedings of the 2014 conference on Designing interactive systems* (DIS '14). ACM, 587-596. https://doi.org/10.1145/2598510.2598581

4. Mike Armstrong, Matthew Brooks, Anthony Churnside, Michael Evans Frank Melchior, and Matthew Shotton. 2014. Object-based broadcasting - curation, responsiveness and user experience. In *Proceedings of the 2014 International Broadcasting Convention (IBC '14)*. IET, 12.2-12.2. http://dx.doi.org/10.1049/ib.2014.0038

5. Paul Ashton. 2011. *The Calling Card Script: A Writer's Toolbox for Screen, Stage and Radio*. A & C Black Publishers Ltd.

6. Florian Block, Michael Horn, Brenda Caldwell Phillips, Judy Diamond, Margaret Evans, and Chia Shen. 2012. The DeepTree Exhibit: Visualizing the tree of life to facilitate informal learning. *IEEE Transactions on Visualization and Computer Graphics,* 18, 12, 2789-2798. https://doi.org/10.1109/TVCG.2012.272

7. Amir Chaudhry, Jon Crowcroft, Heidi Howard, Anil Madhavapeddy, Richard Mortier, Hamed Haddadi, and Derek McAuley. 2015. Personal data: thinking inside the box. In *Proceedings of The Fifth Decennial Aarhus Conference on Critical Alternatives* (AA '15). Aarhus University Press, 29-32. http://dx.doi.org/10.7146/aahcc.v1i1.21312

8. Eun Kyoung Choe, Nicole Lee, Bongshin Lee, Wanda Pratt, and Julie Kientz. 2014. Understanding quantified-selfers' practices in collecting and exploring personal data. In *Proceedings of the 32nd annual ACM conference on Human factors in computing systems* (CHI '14). ACM, 1143-1152. http://doi.acm.org/10.1145/2556288.2557372

9. Seth Flaxman, Sharad Goel and Justin M. Rao. 2016. Filter Bubbles, Echo Chambers, and Online News Consumption. *Public Opinion Quarterly*, 80, S1, 298-320. https://doi.org/10.1093/poq/nfw006

10. Mirta Galesic, and Rocio Garcia-Retamero. 2011. Graph literacy: A Cross-Cultural Comparison. *Medical Decision Making*, 31, 3, 444-457. https://doi.org/10.1177/0272989X10373805

11. Adrian Gradinar, Daniel Burnett, Paul Coulton, Ian Forrester, Matt Watkins, Tom Scutt, and Emma Murphy. 2015. Perceptive Media – Adaptive Storytelling for Digital Broadcast. In *Proceedings of the INTERACT 2015 Conference on Human-Computer Interaction* (INTERACT '15). Springer, 586-589. https://doi.org/10.1007/978-3-319-22723-8_67

12. Alvaro Graves and James Hendler. 2013. Visualization tools for open government data. 2013. In *Proceedings of the 14th Annual International Conference on Digital Government Research* (dg.o '13). ACM, 136-145. https://doi.org/10.1145/2479724.2479746

13. Harry M. Geduld, and Ronald Gottesman. 1973. An illustrated glossary of film terms. Holt, Rinehart and Winston.

14. Jonathan Gray, Lucy Chambers, Liliana Bounegru. 2012. *The Data Journalism Handbook: How Journalists Can Use Data to Improve the News*. O'Reilly Media.

15. David Green, Simon Bowen, Jonathan Hook, and Peter Wright. 2017 . Enabling Polyvocality in Interactive Documentaries through "Structural Participation". In *Proceedings of the 2017 CHI Conference on Human Factors in Computing Systems* (CHI '17). ACM, 6317-6329. https://doi.org/10.1145/3025453.3025606

16. Michael Gurstein. 2011. Open data: Empowering the empowered or effective data use for everyone? *First Monday,* 16, 2. http://dx.doi.org/10.5210/fm.v16i2.3316

17. Tiffany Holmes. 2007. Eco-visualization: combining art and technology to reduce energy consumption. In *Proceedings of the 6th ACM SIGCHI conference on Creativity & cognition* (C&C '07). ACM, 153-162. https://doi.org/10.1145/1254960.1254982

18. Jessica Hullman, and Nick Diakopoulos. 2011. Visualization Rhetoric: Framing Effects in Narrative Visualization. *IEEE transactions on Visualization and Computer Graphics*, 17, 12, 2231-2240. https://doi.org/10.1109/TVCG.2011.255

19. Marijn Janssen, Yannis Charalabidis, and Anneke Zuiderwijk. 2012. Benefits, adoption barriers and myths of open data and open government. *Information Systems Management*, 29, 4. http://dx.doi.org/10.1080/10580530.2012.716740

20. Maxat Kassen. 2013. A promising phenomenon of open data: A case study of the Chicago open data project. *Government Information Quarterly,* 30, 4, 508-513. https://doi.org/10.1016/j.giq.2013.05.012

21. Robert Kosara and Jock Mackinlay. 2013. Storytelling: The Next Step for Visualization. *IEEE*

Computer, 46, 5, 44-50. https://doi.org/10.1109/MC.2013.36

22. Xuan Nhat Lam, Thuc Vu, Trong Duc Le, and Anh Duc Duong. 2008. Addressing cold-start problem in recommendation systems. In *Proceedings of the 2nd international conference on Ubiquitous information management and communication* (ICUIMC '08). ACM, 208-211. http://dx.doi.org/10.1145/1352793.1352837
23. Ian Li. 2011. *Personal informatics and context: Using context to reveal factors that affect behavior*. PhD Thesis, Carnegie Mellon University.
24. Ian Li, Anind Dey, and Jodi Forlizzi. 2010. A stage-based model of personal informatics systems. In *Proceedings of the SIGCHI Conference on Human Factors in Computing Systems* (CHI '10). ACM, 557-566. https://doi.org/10.1145/1753326.1753409
25. Ian Li, Yevgeniy Medynskiy, Jon Froehlich, and Jakob Larsen. 2012. Personal informatics in practice: improving quality of life through data. In *CHI '12 Extended Abstracts on Human Factors in Computing Systems* (CHI EA '12). ACM, 2799-2802. http://dx.doi.org/10.1145/2212776.2212724
26. Joseph Lindley and Robert Potts. 2014. A Machine Learning: An Example of HCI Prototyping with Design Fiction. In *Proceedings of the 8th Nordic Conference on Human-Computer Interaction* (NordiCHI '14). ACM. 1081-1084. https://doi.org/10.1145/2639189.2670281
27. Steven N. Lipkin. 2002. *Real emotional logic: Film and television docudrama as persuasive practice*. Southern Illinois University Press.
28. Ewen Macaskill, and Gabriel Dance. 2013. NSA Files Decoded: What the Revelations Mean for You. *The Guardian*. Retrieved October 25, 2017 from https://www.theguardian.com/world/interactive/2013/nov/01/snowden-nsa-files-surveillance-revelations-decoded
29. Kate Nash. 2012. Goa Hippy Tribe: Theorising Documentary Content on a Social Network Site. *Media International Australia*, 142, 1, 30-40. https://doi.org/10.1177/1329878X1214200105
30. Bettina Nissen, John Bowers, Peter Wright, Jonathan Hook, and Christopher Newell. 2014. Volvelles, domes and wristbands: embedding digital fabrication within a visitor's trajectory of engagement. In *Proceedings of the 2014 conference on Designing interactive systems* (DIS '14). ACM, 825-834. https://doi.org/10.1145/2598510.2598524
31. Jeungmin Oh, and Uichin Lee. 2015. Exploring UX issues in Quantified Self Technologies. In *Proceedings of the Eighth International Conference on Mobile Computing and Ubiquitous Networking* (ICMU '15). IEEE, 53-59. https://doi.org/10.1109/ICMU.2015.7061028
32. John Rooksby, Mattias Rost, Alistair Morrison, and Matthew Chalmers. 2014. Personal tracking as lived informatics. In *Proceedings of the 32nd annual ACM conference on Human factors in computing systems* (CHI '14). ACM, 1163-1172. http://doi.acm.org/10.1145/2556288.2557039
33. UK Government, Cabinet Office. 2012. Open Data: Unleashing the Potential
34. UK Government, Cabinet Office. 2013. Policy paper: G8 Open Data Charter and Technical Annex.
35. Ofcom. 2016. The Communication Market Report, Aug 2016. Retrieved October 30, 2017 from https://www.ofcom.org.uk/research-and-data/multi-sector-research/cmr/cmr16
36. Open Data Institute. 2016. Data as Culture. Retrieved October 25, 2017 from https://theodi.org/culture
37. Stephen Poole. 2007. *Unspeak: Words Are Weapons*. Abacus.
38. Byron Reeves, James Cummings, James Scarborough, June Flora, and Dante Anderson. Leveraging the Engagement of Games to Change Energy Behavior. 2012. In *Proceedings of the International Conference on Collaboration Technologies and Systems* (CTS '12). IEEE, 354-358. https://doi.org/10.1109/CTS.2012.6261074
39. Edward Segel, and Jeffrey Heer. 2010. Narrative Visualization: Telling Stories with Data. *IEEE Trans. Vis. Comput. Graph.*, 16, 6, 1139-1148. https://doi.org/10.1109/TVCG.2010.179
40. Ben Shneiderman, Catherine Plaisant, and Bradford Hesse. 2013. Improving Healthcare with Interactive Visualization. *IEEE Computer*, 46, 5, 58-66. https://doi.org/10.1109/MC.2013.38
41. Bruce Sterling. 2009. Design fiction. *Interactions* 16, 3, 20-24. https://doi.org/10.1145/1516016.1516021
42. Marian Ursu, Maureen Thomas, Ian Kegel, Doug Williams, Mika Tuomola, Inger Lindstedt, Terence Wright, Andra Leurdijk, Vilmos Zsombori, Julia Sussner, Ulf Myrestam, and Nina Hall. 2008. Interactive TV narratives: Opportunities, progress, and challenges. *ACM Trans. Multimedia Comput. Commun.* Appl., 4, 4, 39 pages. https://doi.org/10.1145/1412196.1412198
43. We Are Social & Hootsuite. 2017. Digital in 2017 Global Overview Report.
44. Gerard Wilkinson, Tom Bartindale, Tom Nappey, Michael Evans, Pete Wright, and Patrick Olivier. 2018. Media of Things: Supporting The Production of Metadata Rich Media Through IoT Sensing. In *Proceedings of the SIGCHI Conference on Human*

Factors in Computing Systems (CHI '18), ACM. https://doi.org/10.1145/3173574.3173780

45. World Heritage Encyclopedia. 2018. List of Narrative Techniques. Retrieved March 30, 2018 from http://self.gutenberg.org/articles/eng/Literary_technique
46. John Yorke. 2014. *Into The Woods: How Stories Work and Why We Tell Them*. Penguin.

REFERENCES TO CONTENT EXAMPLES IN REVIEW

C1. Marshall Allen, Olga Pierce and Tom Jennings. 2013. Hazardous Hospitals. Retrieved 15th January, 2018 from http://www.happy-world.com/en

C2. Gaël Bordier and Tristan M. France. 2011. Happy World. Retrieved 15th January, 2018 from http://www.happy-world.com/en

C3. John Burgan. 2013. Boron Mon Amor. Retrieved 15th January, 2018 from http://old.react-hub.org.uk/future-doc-sandbox/projects/2013/boron-mon-amour

C4. Kevin L. Burton. 2011. God's Lake Narrows. Retrieved 15th January, 2018 from http://godslake.nfb.ca

C5. Council on Foreign Relations. 2010. Crisis Guide: Pakistan. Retrieved 15th January, 2018 from https://www.cfr.org/interactives/CG_Pakistan

C6. Luisa Dantas. 2013. Land of Opportunity. Retrieved 15th January, 2018 from http://landofopportunityinteractive.com

C7. Darius Devas. 2011. Goa Hippy Tribe. Retrieved 15th January, 2018 from http://www.sbs.com.au/goahippytribe

C8. Gilbert Ducxzlos and Hélène De Billy. 2010. Holy Mountain. Retrieved 15th January, 2018 from http://holymountain.nfb.ca

C9. Mirka Duijn. 2017. The Industry. Retrieved 15th January, 2018 from https://deindustrie.vpro.nl

C10. Ian Forrester. 2015. Visual Perceptive Media. Retrieved 15th January, 2018 from http://www.bbc.co.uk/rd/projects/visual-perceptive-media

C11. Brett Gaylor. 2015. Do Not Track. Retrieved 15th January, 2018 from http://donottrack-doc.com

C12. Matt Golding. 2015. The Risk Taker's Survival Guide. Retrieved 15th January, 2018 from http://risktakersguide.com

C13. Andrew B. Grace. 2015. After the Storm. Retrieved 15th January, 2018 from http://www.pbs.org/independentlens/interactive/after-the-storm

C14. Greg Hochmuth and Jonathan Harris. 2015. The Network Effect. Retrieved 15th January, 2018 from http://networkeffect.io

C15. Caitlin Kenney, et al. 2013. Planet Money Makes a T-Shirt. Retrieved 15th January, 2018 from http://apps.npr.org/tshirt

C16. Mental Health Commission of Canada. 2012. Here at Home. Retrieved 15th January, 2018 from http://athome.nfb.ca

C17. Todd Melby. 2015. Oil to Die For. Retrieved 15th January, 2018 from http://blackgoldboom.com/oil-to-die-for

C18. Chris Milk. 2010. The Wilderness Downtown. Retrieved 15th January, 2018 from http://thewildernessdowntown.com

C19. Tommy Pallotta. 2013. Unspeak. Retrieved 15th January, 2018 from http://unspeak.submarinechannel.com

C20. Chris Plante. 2016. A summary of every Facebook friendship anniversary video. Retrieved 15th January, 2018 from https://www.theverge.com/2016/8/30/12709938/facebook-friendship-anniversary-video

C21. Lindsay Poulton. 2014. The Shirt on Your Back. Retrieved 15th January, 2018 from https://www.theguardian.com/world/ng-interactive/2014/apr/bangladesh-shirt-on-your-back

C22. Mandy Rose. 2010. Are You Happy? Retrieved 15th January, 2018 from http://theareyouhappyproject.org

C23. Laura Ruel. 2011. Coal: A Love Story. Retrieved 15th January, 2018 from http://www.poweringanation.org/coal

C24. Sabrina Saccoccio. 2012 Frontline: Targeting the Electorate. Retrieved 15th January, 2018 from http://www.pbs.org/wgbh/pages/frontline/campaign-targeting

C25. Elaine M. Sheldon. 2013. Hollow. Retrieved 15th January, 2018 from http://www.hollowdocumentary.com

C26. Alicia Smith, et al. 2014. Seven Digital Deadly Sins. Retrieved 15th January, 2018 from http://sins.nfb.ca

C27. David Suzuki. 2010. The Test Tube With David Suzuki. Retrieved 15th January, 2018 from http://testtube.nfb.ca

C28. Hughes Sweeney and Joël Ronez. 2011. Bar Code. Retrieved 15th January, 2018 from http://barcode.tv

C29. Lena Thiele. 2014. Netwars. Retrieved 15th January, 2018 from http://www.netwars-project.com

C30. Antoine Viviani. 2015. In Limbo. Retrieved 15th January, 2018 from http://inlimbo.tv/en

C31. Dianne Whelan. 2010. This Land. Retrieved 15th January, 2018 from http://thisland.nfb.ca

C32. Femke Wolting and Tommy Pallotta. 2014. Last Hijack Interactive. Retrieved 15th January, 2018 from http://lasthijack.com

C33. Jason Zada. 2011. Take This Lollipop. Retrieved 15th January, 2018 from http://www.takethislollipop.com

How Users Perceive Delays in Synchronous Companion Screen Experiences – An Exploratory Study.

Vinoba Vinayagamoorthy
BBC R&D
London, United Kingdom
vinoba.vinayagamoorthy@bbc.co.uk

ABSTRACT

A lot of work has been focused around enabling accurately synchronised companion screen experiences. The challenge has been to ensure that the delays between the presentation of programme content to the TV and the delivery of the relevant companion screen content to a mobile device are kept to a minimum. This is mainly driven by the need to ensure that the integrity of the editorial design of companion screen experiences can be maintained at the users' end. This paper presents a 32-participant study which sought to explore the impact of delays between the presentation of programmes on a TV and the presentation of companion content on a Tablet. Three types of experiences: 1) video-to-slideshow using Factual content, 2) video-to-alt-video using Sports content, and 3) video-to-AD (audio description) using Drama content; were tested across eight levels of delays. Participant responses suggest different factors influence their evaluation of the different types of experiences tested.

Author Keywords

Companion screen; connected experiences; interaction techniques; second screen; television; synchronisation; delays.

Categories and Subject Descriptors

• Human-centered computing~User studies • Human-centered computing~Laboratory experiments • Human-centered computing~Empirical studies in HCI

INTRODUCTION

It is a truth universally acknowledged, in the media sector, that a user in possession of a TV presenting a programme, must probably be in want of a mobile device to use for various activities. A couple of well cited reports, one by Accenture for UK viewers [19] and another by Google for US viewers [26], have cited 87% and 77% respectively, as estimates for the percentage of viewers that watch TV while simultaneously using their mobile device. Broadcasters have been conscious of the opportunity this presents with respect to delivering content in even more ways to audiences [12]. Broadcast delivers content to large audiences allowing everyone to see the same thing, however, enabling audiences to easily access programme-related online content through their mobile devices has the potential to deliver richer personalised experiences to individuals.

There are different technologies that can be used achieve synchronisation between two devices each with its merits and drawbacks [5, 16, 25, 28, 30]. On the one hand, the user can indicate what they are watching and rough estimates can be made to ascertain the right type of content to display on a companion screen. This might be sufficient for relatively slow paced companion screen content such as an EPG. On the other hand, the DVB project [12, 13] published an open communication standard between Internet-connected TVs and companion screens, which enabled responsive, reliable and frame-accurate synchronisation between devices over a home network. It has been theorised that users 'watching' *richer* companion screen experiences might be *less tolerant* to asynchrony [14, 28]. Limited research has been conducted to understand how the perception of delays between devices impact the users' response to supposedly synchronised companion screen experiences. Knowing where the limits of user tolerance, to delay between the TV and a companion mobile device, is for different types of experiences will allow broadcasters and content makers to judge how to create the optimal experience given the technologies available to the user in their home or another environment.

During the course of the study, reported in this paper, three types of experiences were selected to test as first probes. They were chosen based on prior knowledge on what type of companion screen experiences are commonly considered as potential offerings for different programme genres [8]. Different levels of delays were injected into the three types of companion screen experiences to see how user responses changed using questionnaires and interviews.

RELATED WORK

Companion screen experiences come in many shapes, sizes and form [5, 14]. There is a wide research space, spanning over ten years, into what types of experience makes an immersive, entertaining, useful or viable one [25, 27].

TVX '18, June 26–28, 2018, SEOUL, Republic of Korea

ACM ISBN 978-1-4503-5115-7/18/06…$15.00
https://doi.org/10.1145/3210825.3210836

These include work into understanding user behaviour and interactions with companion screen [7, 9], research into figuring out how the visual attention of a user might flow when using companion screens [18, 23], design explorations into the relationship between different design elements of companion content and user responses to the experience [11, 24], studies into genre-specific motivations to using companion screens [1, 7, 15], thought provoking design of companion apps to enhance TV programmes [20, 21] and user research into how delays between devices used in companion screen experience affect users [29, 30].

As part of 2-Immerse [1], an EU project focused on understanding the delivery of multi-screen experiences to audiences, Ziegler et al. [30] studied user tolerances to perceived delays between a TV presenting a Shakespearean play and a Tablet presenting the associated script (in the form of a synchronised textbook) with different interaction capabilities. Their results indicated that although users did not notice the delays, for the textbook kind of experience tested, they felt significantly more distracted by the tablet content for increasingly higher delays. Similarly, Wei Liang et al. [29] studied the impact of relative time delays (3s and 10s), made to look like a buffering issue, in companion screen experiences on user responses. Although there were no significant results uncovered in most of the user responses collected, post study interviews revealed that users felt frustrated over the 10s delays.

Due to the complexities in designing companion screen experiences, such as the multifaceted relationship between individuals and their content, the uncertainty of user intent or motivation while using companion devices, the variety of environments in which users might be based and so on, it's difficult to focus scope into one research study.

RESEARCH OBJECTIVES

The objective of this study was to test how tolerant users are to different levels of simulated time delays using a representative set of passive, non-interactive experiences presented on two supposedly synchronised screens – a TV and a Tablet. The delay was simulated by injecting a prescribed time offset into the presentation of the companion content on the Tablet relative to the corresponding programme content presented on the TV. The Tablet would either be in sync with the TV or lag behind it. The two main research questions are; a) How *perceptible* are users to simulated delays in synchronised companion screen experiences? b) How much delay is *tolerable* while viewing different types of synchronised companion screen experiences?

METHOD

Independent Variables

There were two independent variables in this study; a) the type of companion screen experience and b) level of delay between the programme on a TV and the companion content on a Tablet.

Type of Companion Screen Experiences

During the course of this study, there has been a focus on trying to tease out what type of experience best suits the programme content or genre. A companion screen experience will always require the user to manage splitting their attention between two streams of content. Therefore, the design of companion screen experiences has to consider the rhythm of the programme content, the pace of information on the TV, the social issues related to the programme and an understanding of how the service is used in a home environment [27].

Taking into account lessons learnt in previous studies, informal conversations with programme makers and audience research explorations, six genres were initially chosen as being suited to companion screen experiences: '*Factual (Documentaries)*', '*News*', '*Sports*', '*Drama*', '*Gameshows*' and '*Childrens*' [8]. Gameshows were an obvious candidate for companion screen experiences. The pace of information is, generally, manageable and constant through the program. However, a play-along experience normally involves the user interacting with it which is out of scope for this study. Similarly, companion experiences designed for children programmes have the potential to allow novel, imaginative and interactive experiences but unproven formats. Plus, working with kids in a user testing environments introduces its own set of special challenges.

At first glance, News seems to afford a lot of scope for design and innovation w.r.t transformation into a companion screen experience. However, News is tied to specific dates and locations which means it will always be late at delivery in a study. It was better to look at simple companion experiences which a broadcaster might offer as a regular but useful service with minimal additional effort involved in the production pipeline.

In the end, the three genres chosen for the study were *Factual*, *Sports* and *Drama*. Even with a constrained focus on genre, companion screen experiences come in different forms. In order to limit the number of conditions tested in an exploratory study and present a variety of experience types, the design has been whittled down to three (3) experiences:

- *Video-to-Slideshow*: A Factual programme on a TV with a complimentary slideshow on a Tablet,
- *Video-to-Alt-Video*: A Sports programme on a TV with a video stream filmed from an alternative camera angle on a Tablet,
- *Video-to-AD*: A Drama programme on a TV with an audio description stream on a Tablet.

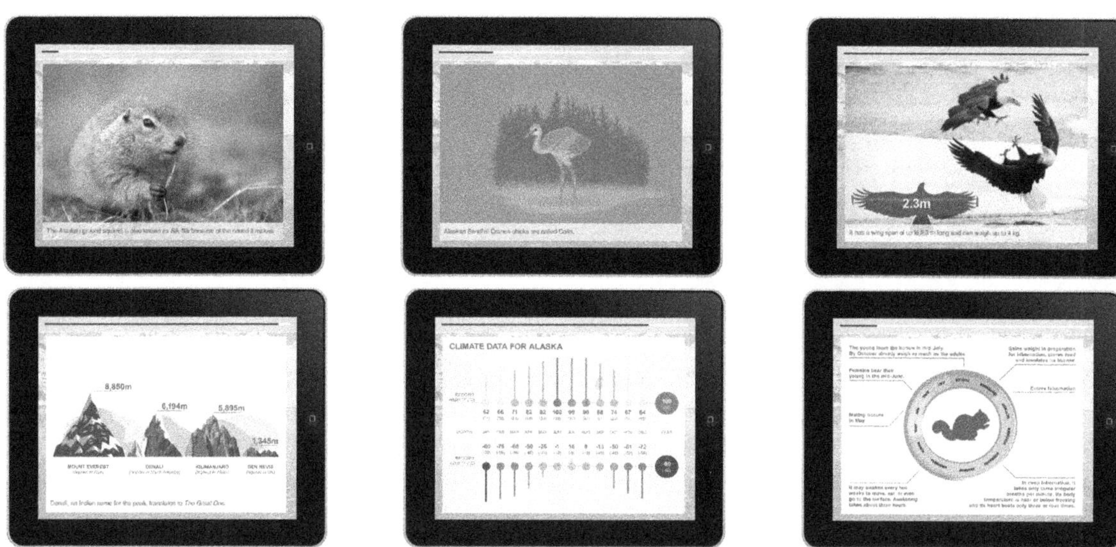

Figure 1. Sample slides, of varying visual complexity, from the companion slideshow content for *Alaska: Earth's Frozen Kingdom*

Levels of Delay

Vinayagamoorthy et al. [28] theorised on the variation of synchronisation accuracy requirements across different companion screen experiences. Initially, a wide range of delays were chosen to cover the three very different types of experiences chosen for this study. The 0ms delay was chosen to represent the *control* condition in the study. Near frame time delays of 10ms, 20ms and 50ms were chosen to cover the video-to-alt-video condition. Near word time delays of 100ms and 200ms were chosen to cover the video-to-AD condition. Near event/context (and much larger) time delays of 500ms, 1000ms, 2000ms, 3000ms, and 4000ms were chosen to cover the video-to-slideshow condition. Other than the control condition, this came up to ten levels of delay that were of interest.

BBC R&D colleagues were asked to take part in pilots in which all these levels of delay were tested with the three types of companion screen experiences. The pilots concentrated on two main questions. Firstly, the extent to which colleagues noticed a delay between the programme on the TV and the content on the Tablet. Second, the extent to which colleagues were able to follow the content on both screens. None of the pilot participants noticed 10ms, 20ms, and 50ms delays in the video-to-slideshow and video-to-AD conditions. Similarly, a 10ms delay was not noticed in video-to-alt-video condition. On the other hand, 3000ms and 4000ms were noted as glaring obvious out-of-sync values for the video-to-alt-video conditions. In order to balance the time and effort needed to test a large number of combinations against the need for statistically robust results, these levels of delay were excluded in the final design of the study.

Eight level of delays were chosen for each type of companion screen experience (Table 1). In addition to the control condition (0ms), 100ms, 200ms, 500ms, 1000ms, 2000ms, 3000ms and 4000ms were chosen for the video-to-slideshow and video-to-AD conditions. The levels of delay chosen for the video-to-alt-video conditions were 0ms, 20ms, 50ms, 100ms, 200ms, 500ms, 1000ms and 2000ms.

Levels of Delay Label	Video-to-Slideshow (Factual)	Video-to-Alt-Video (Sports)	Video-to-AD (Drama)
Level 0	0ms	0ms	0ms
Level 1	100ms	20ms	100ms
Level 2	200ms	50ms	200ms
Level 3	500ms	100ms	500ms
Level 4	1000ms	200ms	1000ms
Level 5	2000ms	500ms	2000ms
Level 6	3000ms	1000ms	3000ms
Level 7	4000ms	2000ms	4000ms

Table 1. 8 Level of Delays vs. 3 Types of Experiences. Level labels used in all charts due to the differing delay value for the different experiences in the design of the study.

Design of Content

Broadcasters often have access to vast archives of content, some of which remain relevant to modern rehash of programme ideas or help add context to continuing storylines. Furthermore, in making programmes, it is normal to shoot more material than necessarily used for the main broadcast. These stores of content remain mainly inaccessible to the general public and majority of the research material is thrown away. The prospect of somehow preserving, digitising and utilising this content in some form is hugely tempting. The overarching aim behind creating companion content for this study was to ensure near production quality authenticity and try to reuse as much of the existing content produced, broadcasted or published by a broadcaster, in this case the BBC.

Figure 2. Screenshots, of varying camera shots (close up zoomed in & wide zoomed out panning), from the muted companion video content for *Six Nations Rugby*

The programme chosen to represent *Factual* was the "Winter" episode of '*Alaska: Earth's Frozen Kingdom*' [3] due to its slow pace and predictable easy-to-digest rhythm. This was put together with a slideshow that gave complimentary information about the subject being covered in the programme scene. Previous work has indicated that there is some appetite for this type of companion screen experience for this genre [27]. Although a lot of background information and surplus images existed, there was a need to re-craft the raw content to attain a production-quality and a digestible set of slides.

A programme producer, an illustrator and a UX designer were recruited to collate and craft a suitable companion slideshow experience for the broadcasted programme. Eight ~2.5 minute clips from the programme material were 'cut' into self-contained test material. In keeping with, Neate et al. [23], depending on the complexity of the programme content shown on the TV, the producer created a storyboard which guided the illustrator and the UX designer in crafting the companion slideshow. The resulting slides differed in visual complexity depending on the ebb and flow of the programme (Figure 1). The slides relevant to each 2.5 minutes of content were presented in increasing visual complexity. Eventually, 4 slides were created as companion content for each 2.5-minute clip. This amounted to about 1 slide per half a minute or so with slightly increasing time allocated for the more complex slides. An integrated progress bar on the top of each slide indicated how much time was left before a new slide was presented.

Coverage of the '*England versus France six nations 2015*' rugby match [22] was chosen to represent *Sports* due to number of tries (11 tries from both sides leading to a 55-35 win for the English team but more importantly enough options to create test material). The broadcasted coverage of the match, on the TV, was coupled with a video stream of an alternative camera coverage of the tries on the companion screen. Broadcasters often capture popular sports events with multiple cameras, the feeds of which are edited and stitched to provide a more rounded coverage of the event. However, only a select number of clips from the cameras are stored in a 'sports library' for potential reuse. These tend to be coverage of unusual or exciting snippets of the event. In Rugby, tries, huddles or a particularly good run may be covered and stored in ≤1 minute clips.

In order to create a suitable set of video to video experiences, the sport library provided 2-3 clips from alternative camera coverage of the 11 tries. These clips were analysed and a variety of different camera shots were chosen to pair along with the broadcasted programme content. Eight clips were chosen to act as companion content to 8 of the 11 tries in the broadcasted match. The clips varied in duration between 18 seconds and 56 seconds. Unfortunately, the fast paced action of Rugby did not warrant a longer recording on the alternative cameras during the original coverage.

The "Crows" episode of '*Wolf Hall*' [4] was used to represent *Drama* due to the candlelit scenes and longer than usual non-verbal (wordless) interactions between characters. This was coupled with an audio description stream on the companion screen.

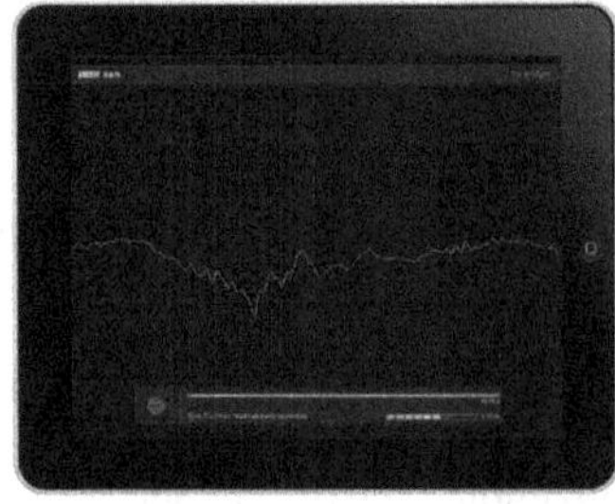

Figure 3. Sample screenshot of the visualisation accompanying the companion audio description content for *Wolf Hall.*

This was the most straightforward experience to craft. The existing audio description of the programme was simply stripped off the broadcasted material and delivered on the companion screen. Once again, eight self-contained segments of the programme were selected as test material. Each clip averaged out at 1.5 minutes of content. There were about 3-4 distinct audio descriptions of scenes to act as companion experiences in the chosen content. A simple visualisation was added to the companion app in order to provide some form of feedback to the participant.

There were eight clips of content chosen for each of the three genres of programmes (*Factual*, *Sport*, *Drama*) selected for this study amounting to 24 clips in total. Each of the 24 clips was associated with companion content.

Figure 4. Set-up: a) living room space with "TV" (laptop hidden behind 40 inch HD TV); b) Tablet (iPad Air); c) sitting area for administering questionnaires and observation room behind mirrored wall.

Design of Study

Considering there were 3 types of experiences presented against 8 levels of synchronisation delays, a full repeated measure study would have required each participant to watch 24 varying experiences. In order to minimise participant fatigue, a modified Latin square with repeated measure experiment design was chosen, similar to Ziegler et al [30]. Each participant was administered a pre-assigned randomised set of 12 clips out of a set of 24 possible clips, of varying delays, of which 4 were *Factual*, 4 were *Sports* and 4 were *Drama*. The design allows for each clip ('type of experience' x 'level of delay') to be viewed 16 times.

Apparatus

Figure 4 depicts the setup used for the study in a user lab. Participants were presented the companion experiences on a 40 inch HD TV and an iPad Air. Similar to Ziegler et al. [30], a JavaScript based TV emulator, running on a laptop connected to the TV, was used to simulate the media presentation and DVB-CSS [12, 13] synchronisation functionalities of an HbbTV 2 device [17]. In this paper, the TV refers to this "laptop + TV" setup.

A companion application also implemented DVB-CSS, similar to those described by Vinayagamoorthy et al. [28]. The system was used as designed to present the control conditions with 0ms injected delay. For the test conditions, appropriate timing offsets were injected to the timestamps sent from the TV (laptop + TV), over a home network, to the companion apps on the Tablet. This resulted in the right level of delayed experience prescribed in that test condition.

A remote control web app was used to trigger the right type of experience with the right level of delay for the test condition the participant was scheduled to experience. All control of the video playback on the Tablet (and TV) were disabled.

Questionnaire

Two questionnaires were designed for this study: a post *condition* questionnaire and a post *study* questionnaire. The post condition questionnaire was administered to the participant after they experienced *each* condition while the post study questionnaire was administered after the participant had watched *all* of their pre-assigned conditions.

The post condition questionnaire asked participants to rate their experiences on a 7-point Likert-type scale that ranged from strongly disagreeing (1) to strongly agreeing (7) to statements. The statements queried two things; a) if participants noticed any delays between the TV and the Tablet, b) if they felt the experience was difficult to take in.

- Q1: *I felt I was missing part of the programme on the TV because of the Tablet.*
- Q2: *I felt I was missing content on the Tablet because of the TV.*
- Q3: *I felt the content of the Tablet was relevant to the programme being shown on the TV.*
- Q4: *I felt the Tablet did not add anything to the experience.*
- Q5: *I felt the TV and the Tablet were well timed to each other.*
- Q6: *I felt like I was waiting for the TV to "catch up" to the Tablet.*
- Q7: *I felt like I was waiting for the Tablet to "catch up" to the TV.*
- Q8: *I felt frustrated with the whole experience (TV + Tablet).*
- Q9: *I felt the whole experience was easy and natural.*
- Q10: *I felt I had to keep shifting between screens a lot in order to not miss out on seeing the content on either the TV or the Tablet.*

The post study questionnaire focused on what participants thought of companion screen experiences, within the context of the three types of experiences presented in this study, as did the semi-structured interview administered to each participant at the end of the study. The objectives were to discern reasons behind participants' responses to the post condition questionnaire during analysis.

Participants

An agency was used to recruit 32 participants with a 50/50 gender split between the ages of 19 to 53 (M=36, SD=10), all fluent in the English language, mostly computer literate and an even distribution of gaming experience. They were all regular watchers of TV (> 10 hours per week) and held no biases against the genre of programmes being tested (*Factual, Sports & Drama*) or the BBC.

Participants self-evaluated as being very familiar with using touchscreen devices like smartphones and tablets All of the participants owned a TV and a smartphone while 27 of the participants also owned a tablet. A lot of the participants (29) admitted to being easily distracted by content (≥5 on the 7-point scale), such as social media, on their mobile devices while watching TV and miss something on the TV while engaging on mobile devices. Most of the participants (28) also admitted to having the TV on in the background while doing other things (≥5 on the 7-point scale). The distribution of participants who felt they got easily absorbed in TV was even across the board. Participants were paid £60 for 1.5 hrs of their time.

Procedure

One experimenter supported the participant through the study while another remained in the observation room. Participants were video (& audio) recorded while undertaking the study. Participants were briefed on what to expect and given a consent form to sign. Participants were also administered a form designed to capture demographics and information about their usage of TVs and mobile devices. Afterwards, the participants were taken through a 'training' session in which they were shown examples of the three types of synchronised experiences used in the study. This was to manage the effect novelty might have on participants' responses. It was also a way to deal with any questions participants might have about the experience. None of the content used in the training session was reused in the test conditions.

After training, the experimenter asked the participant to sit and wait for the first of twelve experiences to begin shortly. The experimenter then went to the observation room to trigger the first test condition using the remote control web app. Once the experience ended, the experimenter came back into the living space to help administer a post-condition questionnaire. The participant was then asked to watch the second of twelve experiences followed by the post-condition questionnaire and so on until the participant watched all twelve of their pre-assigned experiences.

After the participant finished answering the twelfth post-condition questionnaire, they were asked to complete a post-study questionnaire which focused on their thoughts on the three different types of experiences. The participants were then interviewed in a semi-structured manner, guided by specific themes, by one experimenter.

- T1: *General feedback on the three types of companion experiences*
- T2: *How easy did they feel the companion experiences were to watch.*
- T3: *Did the participant notice any changes in how synchronised the companion experiences they saw were.*
- T4: *Did they have preferences within the content on the Tablet: different shot types for the video stream (Sports) and different visual complexity of the slides (Factual).*

Participants were always asked to give their feedback in a free form style after which the experimenter followed the prescribed themes. After the interview, the participant was debriefed and recordings were ended.

RESULTS

After processing the data, there was a complete balanced set of 16 responses for each level of delay for the video-to-alt-video (Sports) experience. However, there were only 15 responses for the video-to-AD (Drama) experience with the 500ms delay condition and 17 responses for the video-to-AD experience with the 200ms delay condition. In the video-to-slideshow (Factual) experience with the 200ms delay, there were only 15 responses while there were 17 responses in the control condition (0ms) of the video-to-slideshow experience.

Overall the same strategy was used to analyse the *post condition* questionnaires. The data was grouped into three sets, one for each type of experience and each set was separated into the 8 levels of delay associated with the experience. A non-parametric Friedman test was conducted to ascertain if there were statistically significant difference in the means of participant responses associated with the level of delays tested. Levene's test was used to confirm homogeneity of variance. A series of post-hoc binomial sign tests were performed to examine pairwise differences between each condition. Descriptive statistics was conducted on participant responses to the *post study* questionnaires. The data was considered as a whole for these. Interviews with the participants were transcribed using a specialist agency, coded through thematic analysis and grouped into key themes. The major themes were drawn out and summarised.

Post Condition Responses

As mentioned, the 8 level of delays used in the study differs depending on the type of experience (Table 1).

Missing Content: Q1 & Q2

Although some participants felt they were missing part of the programme on the TV due to the Tablet, especially in the video-to-alt-video conditions (Figure 5), no significant effect was uncovered in participant responses to Q1.

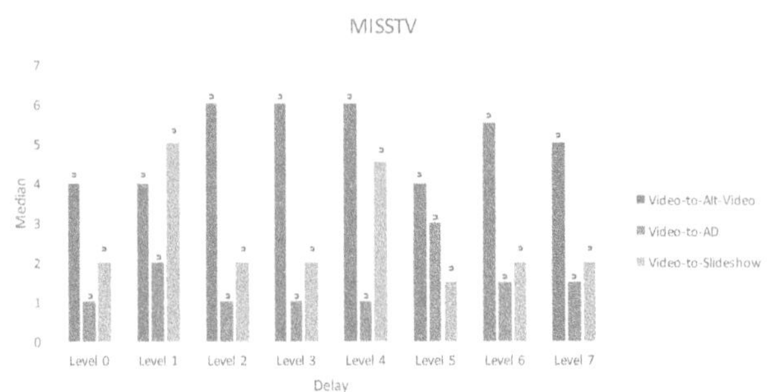

Figure 5. Median of responses – "*I felt I was missing part of the programme on the TV because of the Tablet*" (Q1).

There was a statistically significant difference between groups in participant responses to Q2 (Figure 6) in the video-to-alt-video conditions: $\chi^2(7) = 20.68$, $p < 0.005$. Post hoc analysis revealed that participant responses to Q2 for the video-to-alt-video conditions with 20ms delay (M=2.06,

SD=1.48) was significantly smaller than the conditions with 50ms (M=4.50, SD=1.97), 100ms (M=4.56, SD=2.22), 200ms (M=5.25, SD=1.98), 1000ms (M=4.00, SD=2.06) and 2000ms (M=3.88, SD=2.16) delays. Responses for the 0ms (M=3.31, SD=2.18) control and 50ms delay conditions were significantly smaller than conditions with 200ms delay.

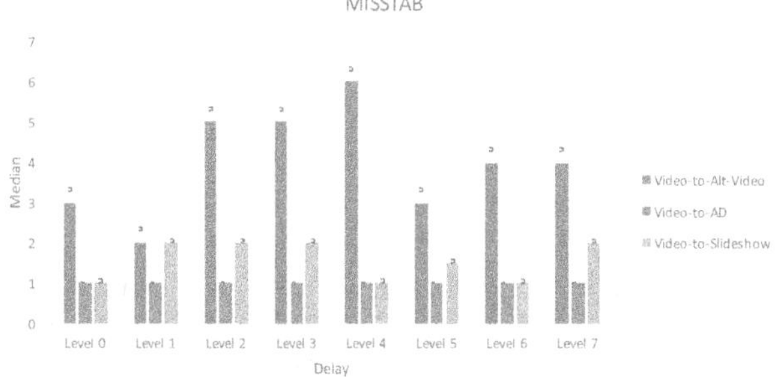

Figure 6. Median of responses – "*I felt I was missing content on the Tablet because of the TV*" (Q2).

Relevance: Q3 & Q4

There were no significant differences uncovered within conditions in the analysis of participant responses to Q3 which dealt with how relevant the content on the tablet was to the programme shown on the TV. However, participant responses to Q3 was quite favourably high across all conditions (Figure 7). No differences across conditions were uncovered in participant responses to Q4 which stated that the Tablet didn't add anything to the experience.

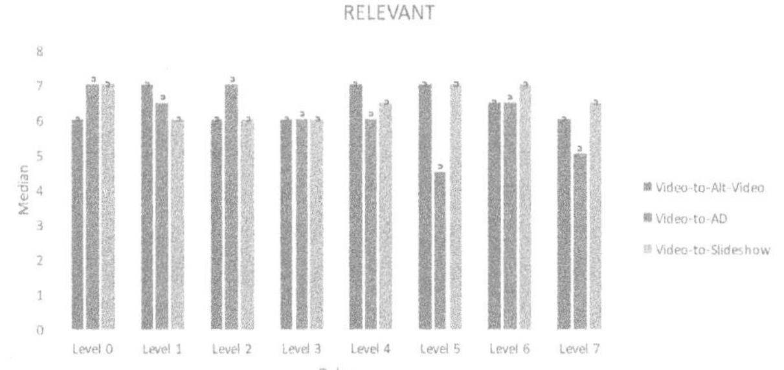

Figure 7. Median of responses – "*I felt the content of the Tablet was relevant to the programme being shown on the TV*" (Q3).

Level of Synchronisation: Q5, Q6, & Q7

There were no significant differences in participant responses to the Q5 which asked them to rate how well timed the TV and Tablet were to each other (Figure 8). Similarly, participant responses to the question of one device lagging behind the other were not significantly different across conditions (Q6, Figure 9 & Q7, Figure 10).

Very few participants strongly agreed that they felt like the TV was lagging behind the Tablet (Q6) and not many participants felt strongly that the Tablet lagged behind the TV (Q7) as depicted in Figure 10.

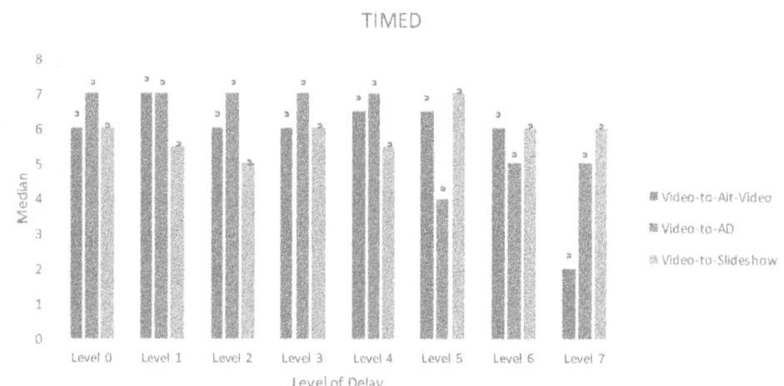

Figure 8. Median of responses – "*I felt the TV and the Tablet were well timed to each other*" (Q5).

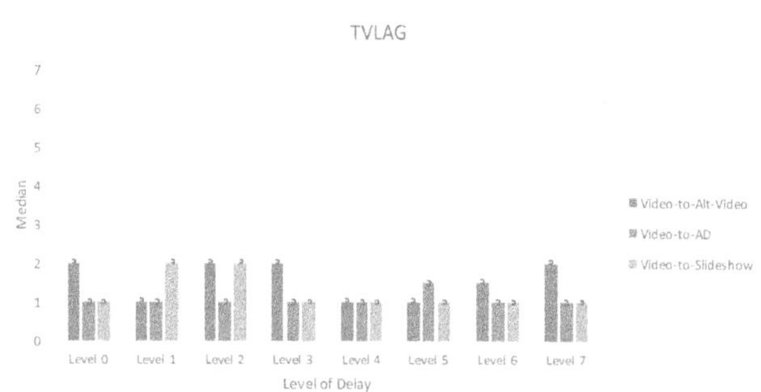

Figure 9. Median of responses – "*I felt like I was waiting for the TV to 'catch-up' to the Tablet*" (Q6).

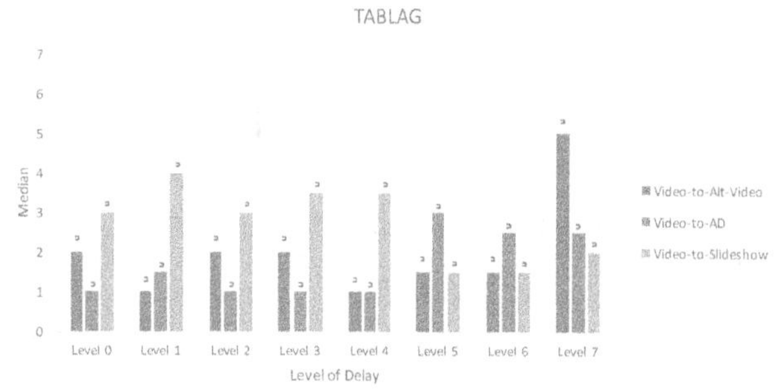

Figure 10. Median of responses – "*I felt like I was waiting for the Tablet to 'catch-up' to the TV*" (Q7).

User Experience: Q8, Q9, & Q10

There was a statistically significant difference between groups uncovered in participant responses to their feelings of frustration with the experience (Q8) in the video-to-alt-video conditions: $\chi^2(7) = 15.85, p < 0.05$. Participant responses for the video-to-alt-video conditions with 500ms delay (M=2.00, SD=1.26) was significantly smaller than the conditions with 1000ms (M=3.38, SD=2.06) and 2000ms delay (M=4.13, SD=1.96).

There was a statistically significant difference between groups uncovered in participant responses to how easy and natural the experience felt (Q9) in the video-to-alt-video conditions: $\chi^2(7) = 15.25, p < 0.05$. Post hoc analysis indicate that participant responses for the video-to-alt-video conditions with 200ms (M=3.50, SD=2.07) delay was significantly smaller than the conditions with 500ms (M=5.25, SD=1.81) delay.

There were no significant differences uncovered w.r.t level of delays within types of experiences in the analysis of participant responses to Q10. However, participants' self-reported rating of how much they had to shift attention from the TV and the Tablet, regardless of the level of delays, is quite different between the types of experiences (Figure 11). The video-to-alt-video conditions demand more shifts of attention between the devices, followed by the video-to-slideshow and video-to-AD conditions.

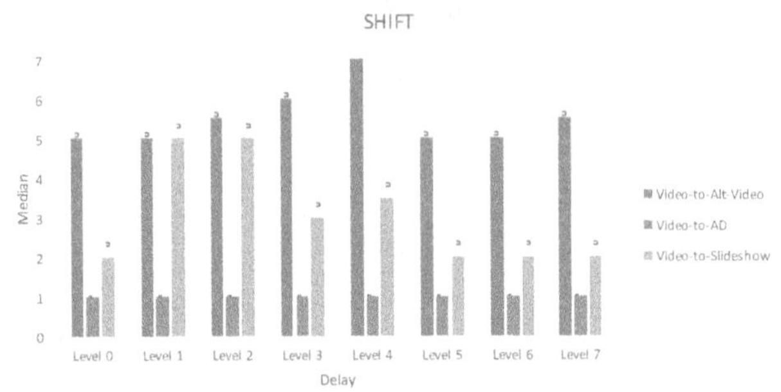

Figure 11. Median of responses – "*I felt I had to keep shifting between screens a lot in order to not miss out on seeing the content on either the TV or the Tablet*" (Q10).

Post Study Insights

All participants indicated that having a Tablet changed the way they watched TV, 25 of whom said it was in a good way and 21 of those did not expect that. The Tablet changed the way 2 participants watched TV in a bad way, as they expected, while 5 participants said it was changed in a bad way unexpectedly. Most of the participants (27) indicated that they like the way the Factual companion experience was presented while only 16 participants indicated the same towards the Sports or the Drama companion experience. Only 2 participants strongly indicated not wanting to be able to have a companion screen experience in their homes while 18 participants strongly agreed that they would want to be able to have companion screen experience in their homes.

Interview Findings

Characterising Companion Experiences: T1 & T2

Only a few participants (9) mentioned that the companion screen experiences emulated behaviour they would have carried out at home. Out of all three experience, the video-to-AD experience (audio description accompaniment to Drama) was found the most useful (21) due to its implication for visually impaired users: "*I didn't even have to watch the program I knew what was going on you know, and everything was very direct, so I think in terms of people you know that suffer from really bad eye sight like or are blind I think yeah it works very well so I'd say that's probably the best one. - P12*". Although some participants found it added an extra dimension to the programme (11) and thought it was done well (6): "*I looked at an expression on the guy's face, then the thing said, he looks tired. I thought, oh I didn't think he looked tired, I thought he looked angry, but then that did add to it and it makes you think about something else. - P10*". As expected, a few participants found it irritating or not pleasurable (6). A good number of participant did not like it (16) and found it distracting (15). Participants felt that, if they were not visually impaired, it was not needed (10), not relevant (5), confusing (4) and intrusive (2): "*I mean, I didn't need to be told they were riding over the drawbridge sort of thing, because I could see that. – P17*".

The video-to-slideshow (information accompaniment for Factual) was evaluated as useful to themselves (22), engaging (15) and relevant (13) due to the additional information given: "*The Alaska one I thought that was ingenious I thought it was great to have information that you really wouldn't think you needed. – P11*". Participants mentioned or agreed that it was a good application for children (27) for its educational value, especially since their children liked interacting with touchscreen devices, and as a way to foster conversations while watching TV: "*That would be useful to all, all ages of children. Sorry, no all ages of, uh, human beings, and for children all the way to, you know, grown-ups. – P8*". A few participants found the experience frustrating (6) since they missed out on some scenic content on the TV because of paying attention to the Tablet: "*I was watching that bit and I kept looking back to see when it was gonna change so that was quite hard – P20*".

In comparison to the other two experiences, the video-to-alt-video was rated as useful by only a few participants (7) since it allowed them to see a different viewpoint: "*So it almost felt like I was sort of in a bit of a privileged position as a fan, as a viewer. Almost like I was kind of... I could have been on the bench, could have been a manager. - P5*". However, this type of experience was the most distracting (16), frustrating (8), and/or confusing (9) due to the participants having to shift attention more frequently between the TV and the Tablet.

Differences in Delays: T3

None of the participants mentioned noticing a delay between the TV and the Tablet in the video-to-slideshow experiences. In fact, some participants evaluated the timing for the video-to-slideshow experiences as being spot on w.r.t timings (10) and well-paced (15): "*I knew I could concentrate on the documentary, that there was information there and then I had awhile before the next screen came up. So I, I liked that idea of the slide shows being slower. – P17*". Participants did not notice any differences in timings across the four video-to-slideshow clips they watched.

A good number of participants specifically noted *one* out of four clips as being out of sync in both the video-to-alt-video (14) and video-to-AD (17) conditions. Some participants mentioned some of the four clips being out of sync in video-to-alt-video (10) and video-to-AD (5) conditions.

Other participants didn't find any differences in timings between the four clips they watched in the video-to-alt-video (8) and the video-to-AD (10) conditions.

The main contributing factor to participants noticing an out of sync video-to-AD condition was an overlap (15) of running of the audio description stream on the Tablet over the audio stream on the TV. In addition to the evaluation of the experience being out of sync, this overlap led to frustration, distraction, reduction of enjoyment and dislike of the experience: "*Some of them were a little bit out of sync where I think one of the characters said something and then the guy blurted out his sentence. – P19*". In the case of the video-to-alt-video conditions, a few participants thought the delayed clips afforded a replay functionality (4) which allowed them to re-watch the 'highlights' on the Tablet: "*I thought it, it wasn't timed well but it was better, because I was able to watch it, and then watch it again almost instantly. – P16*".

Preferences: T4

Other than acknowledging its usefulness and problems caused during overlap of audio streams, participants didn't feel anything needed to be done differently with regards to the video-to-AD experiences.

In the video-to-alt-video conditions, there were different types of shots (close in zoomed or wide panning) streamed to the Tablet (Figure 2). Additionally, there were different angles shown in the alternate camera video stream. Participants felt that having a context dependent shots (12) would lead to a better experience: "*I preferred the like when they're tackling on the ground I liked to...if I'm watching it on the screen you can't really see what's going on, but I like the zoomed in, how you can really see what was happening in the tackle. Um I was more drawn to watching the tablet then I was the big screen for those ones – P21*". Participants didn't see the point (11) to having two views from the same angle. They felt it was too similar to each other (9) and found it more compelling (5) if they had different options. Participants wanted more options of alternative views (9) in which they could choose and control (7) their experience with better editing to ensure both views are easier to follow in terms of shots (7). Some participants thought a Sports companion experience could have statistics about the event (7): "*I mean, sometimes you might want to have some extra knowledge around, like the ability to, to key into maybe different players and what's gone on during the season or just other like little parts that might add to the commentary – P1*". A few participants (6) suggested a re-watch application for Sports in which they would be able to see a highlighted part of the event on demand.

Participants responded positively to video-to-alt-video companion experiences in which the programme content on the TV was shown in a wide angle zoomed out fashion while the video stream on the Tablet was a close up zoomed in alternative, preferably from two different angles (10). A few participants (3) liked having it the other way around, with the close up shot on the TV while the Tablet showed a zoomed out shot. A couple of participants (2) reported that they found it difficult to make spatial sense of the game when the TV and the Tablet showed two different angles.

Compared to video-to-alt-video (15) and video-to-AD (12), video-to-slideshow conditions were the most positively talked about experience (25). Participant still mention being distracted (18) and that it demanded attention (17) from the TV programme but this is tied to the visual complexity of the content on the Tablet (Figure 1). Although, overall participants thought the content was well-paced (15) and in sync (10), some participants felt the simpler slides (one image + one line of text) was too slow/static (5), not engaging (11) and rather basic (10). The slides of higher visual complexity (last two slides on temperature and hibernation cycle in Figure 1) were seen as too detailed (15) with too much information which contributed to feelings of giving too much attention to the Tablet at the expense of the TV (10 of 17), distracting (7 of 18) and too little time (8) to digest the content on the Tablet. Participants who didn't mention the slides being too detailed didn't find the video-to-slideshow demanding (15). Some participants suggested designing video-to-slideshow companion experiences which affords more control to the user (12) which would allow them to control the speed of content delivery to the Tablet: "*I thought it would be quite good if you could make that more interactive. Um, maybe that dragging or maybe that clicking in that it gives you like, I don't know, like how long the actual distance is. - P26*". A few participants thought it needed better crafting (7) related to how long slides were kept on screen and affording control so the user can choose to read them later or choose what level of detail they preferred in their experience.

DISCUSSION

At the beginning of the study, the expectation was that participants would be less tolerant to perceived delays, relative to the TV, in more fast paced companion content (video-to-alt-video) in comparison to the slower paced companion content (video-to-slideshow).

Unfortunately, participant responses to the questions querying if they noticed delays between the Tablet and the TV didn't yield any numerical insight across conditions. However, participants felt that the 20ms level of delay was the one in which they didn't miss content on the Tablet because of the TV (Q2), in comparison to 50ms, 100ms, 200ms, 1000ms and 2000ms. It's possible that the higher level of delays allowed participants to use the companion screen experiences as a re-watch/recap application as suggested by participants in the interview. Furthermore, the 20ms level of delay scored the least w.r.t participants noticing a lag in the Tablet compared to the TV. However, the post hoc tests didn't uncover a pattern across the full range of level of delays consider in this study and the significant results don't get mirrored in the control conditions (0ms) which is puzzling.

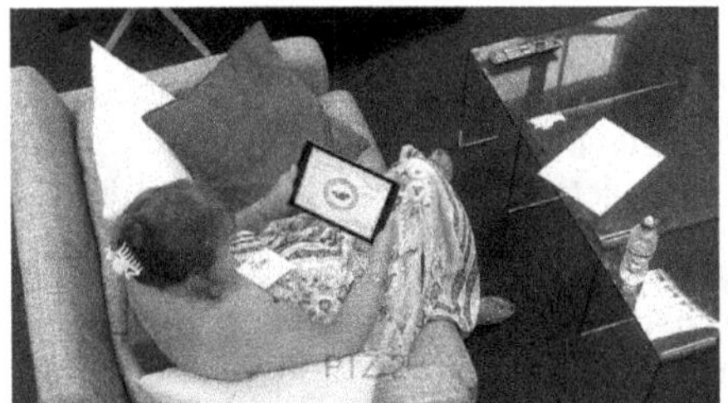

Figure 12. a) Watching a video-to-slideshow clip b) Watching a video-to-AD clip c) Watching a video-to-alt-video clip.

So it appears that for this type of video-to-alt-video experience, participants might prefer to have very little levels of perceived delay between the TV and the Tablet but more research is needed to fine-tune the specifics. Also some participants prefer to have a recap application instead of attempting to watch two different videos at the same time. Additionally, there was some quite interesting shot preferences given for alternative video streams in companion content for Rugby matches – zoomed in close ups on the Tablet while a zoomed out panning shot on the TV, preferably from a different angle.

In the video-to-AD conditions, there were no significant differences uncovered across conditions. However, during interviews, participants pointed out that an overlap between the audio description stream on the Tablet and the audio stream on the TV was the most important factor to evaluating a video-to-AD condition as being out of sync. Audio descriptions are crafted to fit carefully within the silence in between conversations in the programme so it is understandable that the tolerance levels of participants are sorely tested when the delay cause an overlap between two audio streams.

Participant didn't detect any delays in the video-to-slideshow conditions. However, given the rhythm of the companion screen experience designed – 1 slide per half a minute with a 4 second delay at worst, it is possibly unsurprising that the level of delays tested, for this type of experience, didn't affect the participant responses collected especially since the test material were all focused on the same subject in the 2.5 minutes tested. The most important feedback participants gave us was with regard to the visual complexity that they could comfortably handle and their desire to have more control in video-to-slideshow companion screen experiences.

CONCLUSION

This study explored the impact of different levels of perceived delay in three specific companion screen experiences. As always extrapolating conclusions for the mass audiences based on laboratory studies with small sample sizes has its own well known issues. Therefore, results can't be generalised across all experiences, of course, but it appears that participants do notice delays in some companion screen experiences and their tolerance to these delays is dependent on the type of experience. Current synchronisation technologies, such as DVBCSS, certainly have the potential to enable the types of experiences tested.

The video-to-alt-video conditions were quite short and fast paced. Some participants mention finding it difficult to get spatial understanding of the match using the video streams from two different angles. This type of experience was also the most distracting and demanded the most shifts in attention. So for longer experiences which allow participants to acclimatise and for experiences which have more similar (or the same) video on both the TV and the Tablet, the level of tolerance towards perceived delays can be expected to go less than 20ms. Additionally, participants seem to use the alternative video experience in different ways, so what is traditionally seen as a delay might be accepted as a function by participants.

The video-to-AD condition, albeit useful and the easiest to create, was more difficult to test since it was being evaluated by participants who were not visual impaired. If the conditions were tested on participants who were visually impaired or if the audio stream on the companion device was from the main programme or part of some spatial audio effect, the sensitivity to delay could be much lower since any overlap would be much more noticeable.

The video-to-slideshow conditions took the most effort to make in order to retrospectively match the high production values emulated in the original programme. Participants gave some interesting feedback, some of which collided with the direction the experience designers took in making a synchronous companion screen experience.

A brief skim of the video recordings of the participants revealed differences in how they held the Tablet during different types of experiences. (Figure 12). How do these behaviours change for longer experiences? Much of these insights and issues will have to be explored in future work. As one participant put it, there is still some way to go: "*I found that the tablet made the experience better for some but worse for others. – P14*".

ACKNOWLEDGMENTS

The research leading to these results received funding from the European Union's H2020-ICT-2015 programme under grant agreement number 687655 (2-IMMERSE). Matt Hammond, Rajiv Ramdhany, Christoph Ziegler, Michael Evans, Inez Torre, Stephen Anderson and Shaun Holsgrove all generously gave invaluable support, skills and advice.

REFERENCES

1. 2-Immerse Home Page. 2-Immerse. Retrieved February 9, 2018 from https://2immerse.eu/.
2. Edward Anstead, Steve Benford, Robert J. Houghton. 2014. Many-Screen Viewing: Evaluating an Olympics Companion Application. In *Proceedings of the 2014 ACM international conference on Interactive experiences for TV and online video (TVX 2014)*, 103-110. http://dl.acm.org/citation.cfm?id=2602299.2602304.
3. BBC Two - Alaska: Earth's Frozen Kingdom. BBC /programmes page. Retrieved January 24, 2018 from http://www.bbc.co.uk/programmes/b0520nyz.
4. BBC Two – Wolf Hall. BBC /programmes page. Retrieved January 24, 2018 from http://www.bbc.co.uk/programmes/p02gfy02.
5. BBC R&D - Companion Screens: Creating a viewing experience across more than one screen. BBC R&D Blog Post. Retrieved February 9, 2018 from http://www.bbc.co.uk/rd/projects/companion-screens.
6. R. A. Bailey. 2008. *Design of Comparative Experiments*. Cambridge University Press, Chapter Row-column designs, 105–116.
7. Frank R. Bentley. 2017. Understanding Secondary Content Practices for Television Viewing. In *Proceedings of the 2017 ACM International Conference on Interactive Experiences for TV and Online Video (TVX 2017)*, 123-128. https://doi.org/10.1145/3077548.3077554.
8. Alison Button. 2012. Second Screens: How people are actually using them to enhance their TV viewing. Retrieved September 29, 2015 from http://audiencesportal.co.uk/article_list/digital_media_articles/second_screens.aspx.
9. Pablo Cesar, Dick CA Bulterman, A. J. Jansen. 2008. Usages of the secondary screen in an interactive television environment: control, enrich, share, and transfer television content. In *European Conference on Interactive Television*. Springer Berlin Heidelberg. 168-177. http://dx.doi.org/10.1007/978-3-540-69478-6_22.
10. M. Oskar van Deventer, Hans Stokkinh, Matt Hammond, Jean Le Feuvre, Pablo Cesar. 2016. Standards for Multi-Stream and Multi-Device Media Synchronization. In *IEEE Communications Magazine – Communications Standards Supplement*. 54, 3 (2016), 16-21.
11. John Dowell and Edward Anstead. 2017. Interaction with a TV Companion App as Synopsis and Supplement. In *Proceedings of the 2017 CHI Conference on Human Factors in Computing Systems (CHI 2017)*. 2264-2268. https://doi.org/10.1145/3025453.3025459.
12. Digital Video Broadcasting (DVB); *Companion Screens and Streams; Part 1: Concepts, roles and overall architecture*. 2015. DVB BlueBook A167-1, ETSI TS 103 286-1. Retrieved September 29, 2015 from https://www.dvb.org/standards.
13. Digital Video Broadcasting (DVB); *Companion Screens and Streams; Part 2: Content Identification and Media Synchronization*. 2015. DVB BlueBook A167-2, ETSI TS 103 286-2. Retrieved September 29, 2015 from https://www.dvb.org/standards.
14. David Geerts, Rinze Leenheer, Dirk De Grooff, Susanne Heijstraten, Joost Negenman. 2014. In Front of and Behind the Second Screen: Viewer and Producer Perspectives on a Companion App. In *Proceedings of the 2014 ACM international conference on Interactive experiences for TV and online video (TVX 2014)*, 95-102. http://dl.acm.org/citation.cfm?id=2602299.2602304.
15. Katerina Gorkovenko and Nick Taylor. 2016. Politics at Home: Second Screen Behaviours and Motivations During TV Debates. In *Proceedings of the 9th Nordic Conference on Human-Computer Interaction* (NordiCHI 2016), https://doi.org/10.1145/2971485.2971514.
16. Matt Hammond. 2015. Standardising companion screen synchronisation - tools and testing. Retrieved October 9, 2015 from http://bbc.in/1z2JNg5.
17. HbbTV Specification FAQ. HbbTV. Retrieved October 9, 2015 from https://www.hbbtv.org/wp-content/uploads/2015/07/HbbTV-Specification-2.0-FAQ.pdf.
18. Michael E. Holmes, Sheree Josephson, and Ryan E. Carney. 2012. Visual attention to television programs with a second-screen application. In *Proceedings of the Symposium on Eye Tracking Research and Applications (ETRA '12)*, Stephen N. Spencer (Ed.), 397-400. https://doi.org/10.1145/2168556.2168646.
19. Gavin Mann, Francesco Venturini, Robin Murdoch, Bikash Mishra, Gemma Moorby, Bouchra Carlier. 2015. *Digital Video and the Connected Consumer*. Accenture. Retrieved September 29, 2015 from http://bit.ly/TechRepAccenture_2015.
20. Janet Murray, Sergio Goldenberg, Kartik Agarwal, Tarun Chakravorty, Jonathan Cutrell, Abraham Doris-Down, and Harish Kothandaraman. 2012. Story-map: iPad companion for long form TV narratives. In *Proceedings of the 10th European Conference on Interactive TV and Video (EuroITV 2012)*, 223-226. https://doi.org/10.1145/2325616.2325659.
21. Abhishek Nandakumar, Janet Murray. 2014. Companion Apps for Long Arc TV Series: Supporting New Viewers in Complex Storyworlds with Tightly Synchronised Context-Sensitive Annotations. In *Proceedings of the 2014 ACM international conference*

on Interactive experiences for TV and online video (TVX '14), 3-10. http://dl.acm.org/citation.cfm?id=2602317.

22. Six Nations 2015: England 55-35 France - BBC Sport. Retrieved January 24, 2018 from http://www.bbc.co.uk/sport/rugby-union/31974720.
23. Timothy Neate, Matt Jones, and Michael Evans. 2015. Mediating Attention for Second Screen Companion Content. In *Proceedings of the 33rd Annual ACM Conference on Human Factors in Computing Systems (CHI 2015)*, 3103-3106. https://doi.org/10.1145/2702123.2702278.
24. Timothy Neate, Michael Evans, and Matt Jones. 2016. Designing Visual Complexity for Dual-screen Media. In *Proceedings of the 2016 CHI Conference on Human Factors in Computing Systems (CHI 2016)*, 475-486. https://doi.org/10.1145/2858036.2858112 The DVB Project – about page. DVB. Retrieved September 24, 2015 from https://www.dvb.org/about.
25. Timothy Neate, Matt Jones, and Michael Evans. 2017. Cross-device media: a review of second screening and multi-device television. *Personal Ubiquitous Computing*. 21, 2 (April 2017), 391-405. https://doi.org/10.1007/s00779-017-1016-2.
26. The New Multi-screen World: Understanding Cross-platform Consumer Behaviour. Google. Retrieved September 24, 2015 from https://think.withgoogle.com/databoard/media/pdfs/the-new-multi-screen-world-study_research-studies.pdf.
27. Vinoba Vinayagamoorthy, Penelope Allen, Matt Hammond, Michael Evans. 2012. Researching the User Experience for Connected TV – A Case Study. In *CHI'12 Extended Abstracts on Human Factors in Computing Systems (CHI 2012)*, 589-604. http://dl.acm.org/citation.cfm?doid=2212776.2212832.
28. Vinoba Vinayagamoorthy, Rajiv Ramdhany, and Matt Hammond. 2016. Enabling Frame-Accurate Synchronised Companion Screen Experiences. In *Proceedings of the ACM International Conference on Interactive Experiences for TV and Online Video (TVX 2016)*, 83-92. https://doi.org/10.1145/2932206.2932214
29. Chua Wei Liang Kenny, Jacob M. Rigby, Duncan P. Brumby, and Vinoba Vinayagamoorthy. 2017. Investigating the Effect of Relative Time Delay on Companion Screen Experiences. In *Adjunct Publication of the 2017 ACM International Conference on Interactive Experiences for TV and Online Video (TVX 2017 Adjunct)*, 21-26. https://doi.org/10.1145/3084289.3089918.
30. Christoph Ziegler, Christian Keimel, Rajiv Ramdhany, and Vinoba Vinayagamoorthy. 2017. On Time or Not on Time: A User Study on Delays in a Synchronised Companion-Screen Experience. In *Proceedings of the 2017 ACM International Conference on Interactive Experiences for TV and Online Video (TVX 2017)*, 105-114. https://doi.org/10.1145/3077548.3077557.

"I Can Watch What I Want": A Diary Study of On-Demand and Cross-Device Viewing

Jacob M. Rigby[1], **Duncan P. Brumby**[1], **Sandy J.J. Gould**[2], **Anna L. Cox**[1]
[1]UCL Interaction Centre, University College London, London, WC1E 6EA, UK
[2]School of Computer Science, University of Birmingham, Birmingham, B15 2TT, UK
[1]{j.rigby.14, d.brumby, anna.cox}@ucl.ac.uk, [2]s.gould@cs.bham.ac.uk

ABSTRACT
In recent years, on-demand video services, such as Netflix and Amazon Video, have become extremely popular. To understand how people use these services, we recruited 20 people from nine households to keep a viewing diary for 14 days. To better understand these household viewing diaries, in-depth interviews were conducted. We found that people took advantage of the freedom and choice that on-demand services offer, watching on different devices and in different locations, both in the home and outside. People often watched alone so they could watch what they wanted, rather than coming together to watch something of mutual interest. Despite this flexibility, the evening prime time continued to be the most popular time for people to watch on-demand content. Sometimes they watched for extended periods, and during interviews concerns were expressed about how on-demand services make it far too easy to watch too much and that this is often undesirable.

CCS Concepts
•Human-centered computing → Empirical studies in HCI; *Human computer interaction (HCI);*

Author Keywords
On-demand video; film; television; video; streaming; diary study; mobile viewing; IPTV; VoD; SVoD; binge watching

INTRODUCTION
Consuming video through on-demand video services has become a popular activity in recent years. According to the Nielsen company, 43% of people globally watch some kind of on-demand video at least once a day [3]. Subscriptions to paid services (e.g., Netflix and Amazon Video) are rising year on year, and total on-demand viewing as a percentage of all viewing (including viewer-recorded content) is also increasing annually in the UK [12].

With the rise in popularity of on-demand services, what impact is this having on how people consume video content? Large-scale surveys, such as those from Ofcom [12] and Nielsen [3], are useful for giving a general impression of the popularity of on-demand services. However, such surveys can lack the necessary level of granularity to unpick what is driving these viewing practices. For example, Ofcom [12] suggest that the TV is still the most popular way to view, but that 21% of the online population choose to watch on a phone, 23% on a tablet and 33% on a computer at least once a month. These surveys provide useful data but do not ask about important contextual and situational factors that might be affecting why people choose to watch on one device over another. Does this decision of which device to use depend on where the person is watching? Who they are watching with? What time of day they are watching? What they are watching? We focus here on what motivates such decisions that people take when viewing.

In this paper, we describe the results of a diary study conducted to provide a detailed snapshot of everyday viewing behaviours using on-demand services. The work presented here extends an initial analysis of these viewing diaries [16] by describing the prevalence of different practices surrounding on-demand viewing. In particular, we focus our analysis on unpicking differences in viewing behaviour on handheld mobile devices and non-mobile devices. In this paper we also present the results of in-depth interviews that were conducted to better understand these household viewing diaries. These interviews focused on understanding what motivated different viewing behaviours: why people choose to view on particular devices, watch in different locations, and watch alone or together. We also develop an understanding of people's positive and negative perceptions of on-demand services.

RELATED WORK
Prior to the advent of on-demand video services, viewers had limited choice about what they watched, and when and where they watched it. Previous research from this era gives us an insight into "traditional" linear TV viewing practices. For instance, evening viewing after the working day was especially popular, particularly in the living room [18]; people watched TV regularly, often for multiple hours per day [8]; and personal viewing schedules were based around broadcast schedules, which in turn influenced other household activities [6].

Considering the current popularity of on-demand video services and mobile viewing, surprisingly little HCI literature has addressed it. An early study by O'Hara et al. [13] sought to better understand how watching video on mobile devices fits into people's lives. In agreement with similar findings by Ofcom [11], O'Hara et al. [13] found that portability and fitting

TVX '18 June 26–28, 2018, SEOUL, Republic of Korea

ACM ISBN 978-1-4503-5115-7/18/06.
DOI: https://doi.org/10.1145/3210825.3210832

in with other peoples' schedules were important factors. They also found other reasons for watching, such as simply passing time, and being able to be present with others while still consuming video privately. Conversely, O'Hara et al. [13] also found that mobile video was used to disengage with others and signifying the wish to be left alone. This study mainly focused on the motivations rather than establishing prevalence, perhaps due to being conducted back in 2007, before powerful mobile devices and on-demand video services were commonplace.

McNally and Harrington [9] conducted a more recent study on how teens and millennials consume mobile video, again focusing on motivations rather than prevalence. They found that motivations depended on mood and emotional state. McNally and Harrington also investigated how content was chosen, finding that it was based on the level of stimulation provided, as well as video length and amount of engagement required.

Bury and Li [2] conducted a survey study in 2013 into different ways of consuming TV. They found that mobile viewing was unpopular, with 70% of respondents never having used mobile devices for viewing. Those that participated in mobile viewing mainly did so when travelling and commuting. However, this seems to have changed in recent years, with mobile viewing growing in popularity [12]. This study also clearly shows a general shift away from live TV viewing to online viewing.

Barkhuus and Brown [1] conducted in-depth interviews to understand how TV watching was changing as a result of new technologies. In particular, they focused on personal video recorders (PVR) and internet downloads, as this study was conducted in 2009, before on-demand video services were common. They found that most participants who used a PVR system had moved away from watching live TV almost entirely, preferring to queue up recordings from their downloaded library. This freedom from the TV schedule was particularly valued by those with non-standard work schedules.

Irani et al. [7] conducted a diary study of people's viewing habits. This study examined the temporality of viewing in 14 households, which included the use of time shift and early on-demand services. They found that viewing was typically based around the rhythms of individuals' lives, households, and peers. The ability to choose when to watch could help align televisual schedules, allowing members of a household to watch together. There was also much discussion in households about what to watch and about the content of a show. Irani et al. also found that TV content was used as a background to other tasks, and to fill gaps of unscheduled time.

A study by Vanattenhoven and Geerts [20] also looked at how different ways of consuming media occurred around the house via qualitative interviews, including on-demand content. They noted that viewing depended on the context of other things happening in the household. They found that on-demand viewing typically involved "heavier" content requiring more focus (e.g., films and TV series), and took place in the evening. In contrast, broadcast TV typically involved "lighter" content (e.g., news), which was watched while doing other tasks.

Nogueira et al. [10] analysed a large dataset from a Portuguese IPTV operator. While the insights from this work are largely concerned with the technicalities of delivering video to consumers, it does offer some high-level insights into viewer behaviour. Nogueira et al. found that users interacted with this service throughout the day, though viewing was most popular in the evening. They also found that users exhibited a large amount of "zapping" behaviour in order to select content, similar to "channel surfing", taking on average 2.5 minutes to settle on something. However, their data does not offer insights into mobile viewing, and only covers use of a single video service.

In summary, previous research has provided useful perspectives into how people use on-demand video services. A common theme is that people value and and take advantage of freedom from the broadcast schedule, allowing them to choose viewing times that suit them. Furthermore, much of the literature reveals a strong social element to watching TV. Be it watching together, selecting content together, or discussing shows with friends and colleagues, social factors appear to affect viewing practices. Prior research also gives us a limited perspective on viewing on mobile devices, specifically regarding motivations for doing so, which are many and varied.

While the phenomena of on-demand viewing and mobile viewing are strongly coupled, they have not been investigated together from an HCI perspective using recent, real-world data, which would allow us to develop deeper behavioural insights. Furthermore, we do not know exactly how people are using these services throughout the day over longer periods of time, across different devices and services, and what motivates particular viewing behaviours. In the following sections, we present the results of a diary study with interviews that was conducted over a 14-day period with 20 people from nine households. We asked people to record the details of each time someone viewed on-demand content in the household. These diaries focused on when and where viewing took place, as well as which services and devices were being used. Pre- and post-study interviews were also conducted to further probe and understand these present-day viewing practices.

METHOD

Participants

Ten UK households who watched at least five hours of on-demand content a week were recruited through word of mouth and advertisements (see Table 1 for breakdown). One (household C) withdrew, leaving 20 remaining participants from nine households. Mean age was 29.8 ($SD = 13.8$). Households were paid £100 (~$137) for 14 days of continuous participation.

Materials

Households chose either a paper or digital diary. Seven chose digital and two chose paper. For the digital diary, data was entered into an online form using any device with a web browser. Results were stored in a spreadsheet. For the paper diaries, custom diary booklets were created for each household. After data collection, they were digitised in the same format as the digital ones for ease of analysis. Diaries were designed to make data entry as easy as possible, e.g. with checkboxes for names, locations, and services.

Participants completed information about each viewing session, defined as a period of viewing with at least 30 minutes of

Household	Responses	Location	Notes	Participant	Age	Gender	Nationality
A	27	Birmingham	Cohabiting couple	A1 A2	57 68	F M	British British
B	36	Birmingham	Parents and their children	B1 B2 B3 B4 B5	33 38 8 4 2	M F M F M	British British British British British
C	-	-	Withdrew	-	-	-	-
D	22	London	Cohabiting couple	D1 D2	32 29	M F	Spanish Spanish
E	18	London	Cohabiting couple	E1 E2	31 29	M F	Danish Danish
F	24	London	Cohabiting (others not participating)	F1	27	F	Mexican
G	14	London	Cohabiting couple	G1 G2	32 32	M F	Italian Italian
H	15	Oxford	Cohabiting friends	H1 H2	27 30	F F	British British
I	7	London	Cohabiting couple	I1 I2	27 35	F M	German British
J	15	London	Cohabiting couple	J1 J2	31 33	M M	German British

Table 1: Participant household profiles

non-viewing activity either side to allow for short to medium breaks. Participants were required to fill in basic information about their viewing: who was present, start and finish times, what was watched, how long for, devices and services used, location, and breaks they took. They were also asked to justify and explain their responses, where appropriate.

For this study, on-demand content is defined as that which is accessed at the viewer's convenience. This includes catch-up services (e.g. BBC iPlayer), subscription services (e.g. Netflix, Amazon), short-form content (e.g. Youtube, Facebook), and content downloaded or recorded onto computers or personal video recorders (e.g. TiVo). We also focus on two groups of devices: non-mobile devices (TV, desktop computer, laptop computer) and handheld mobile devices (phone and tablet).

Procedure

After recruiting participants, a preliminary interview was conducted to ascertain their general on-demand viewing habits and motivations. They were then briefed on how to enter data in their diaries. Participants were requested to create at least one diary entry per day, but this could simply be to say that no viewing took place. For each household, one participant was nominated to be responsible for the diary and complete it on behalf of others if necessary, though other household members were encouraged to fill in the diary as well. During the study, participants were sent SMS reminders every evening to encourage participation. After the study was over another interview was conducted to ask them about their experiences with using the diary, as well as to explain particular behaviours.

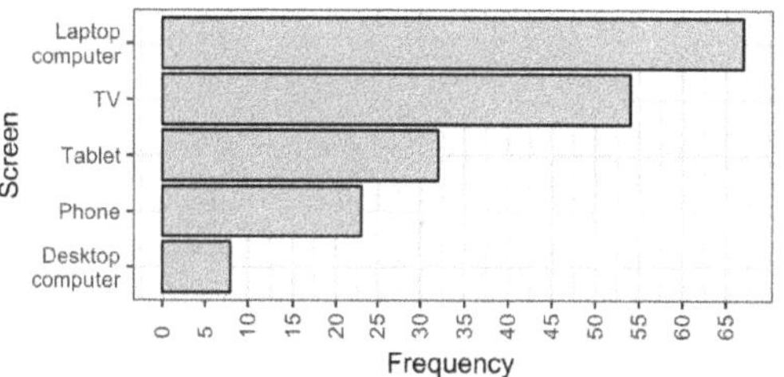

Figure 1: Distribution of viewing screens

RESULTS

Participants created 202 diary entries in total. Of these, 24 said that no on-demand service usage occurred that day, leaving 178 remaining entries describing on-demand viewing. Mean entries per household was 20.6 (SD = 9.1). These diaries captured 188:36:00 (HH:MM:SS) of viewing time, with a mean of 20:57:20 per household (SD = 08:10:11). We provide both a quantitative and qualitative analysis of diary entries. For all statistical analysis we opted to aggregate data by household rather than at the level of the individual participant. Interviews were also conducted with participants at the end of the study to learn more about their diary entries and on-demand viewing habits. These interviews were transcribed and were analysed thematically using an inductive coding approach.

In this section, we present data from both the diary entries and direct quotations from the thematic analysis of our interview data. We cluster this around eight different headings. First, *viewing screens*, is where we consider which devices people chose for viewing and why. Second, *viewing location*, where we consider the places both inside and outside of the home where people chose to view. Third, *viewing time of day and duration*, where we consider how viewing fits into people's daily activities and how long they view for. Fourth, *services used*, where we consider exactly which on-demand services people used to access content. Fifth, *watching alone and watching together*, where we consider participants' co-viewing habits. Sixth and seventh, *positive perceptions of on-demand viewing* and *negative perceptions of on-demand viewing*, where we explore what people like and dislike about these platforms. Finally, *binge watching*, where we focus on how on-demand services can facilitate viewing a lot of content in one session, and how people think about and define binge watching.

Viewing Screens

We first focus on the kind of screen that participants used to view content. Diary entries fell into five distinct viewing device categories, pre-specified in the participants' diaries. These are shown in Figure 1. We further collapsed these device categories into two distinct groups: non-mobile devices (TV, desktop computer, laptop computer) and handheld mobile devices (phone and tablet). Of the 178 entries, 55 (29.9%) contained viewing on a handheld mobile device (i.e., phone or tablet). Households reported more viewing sessions on non-mobile devices (M = 14.0, SD = 8.3) than on handheld mobile devices ($M = 5.8$, $SD = 6.7$). However, this difference was not significant, $t(8) = 1.98$, $p = 0.08$.

To further understand how people chose a viewing device, we next look to diary their entries and what was said during the end of study interviews. It became clear that different viewing devices were chosen for different reasons. For example, participant A1 described how she and A2 (her partner) would choose their tablets when they wanted to watch content individually, while still being together in the same room.

A1: [We watch] the stuff on the tablet singly — we both watch different things on that — but on the TV we tend to put something on that we both want to watch.

This was later clarified:

A1: I can watch what I want to watch. We both put our earphones on and we can then watch our own watching[...]. The TV, that's our bit of relaxation together. But our little bit of YouTube is what we do on our own.

Portability was another factor. Participant B1, an eight-year-old child, said he liked to be able to watch anywhere, instantly:

Interviewer: Why do like to watch it on a tablet?

B3: Because I can take it anywhere. TV, [...] you have to leave it there. And [other devices] take loads of time to set up if you take it somewhere.

Participant J1 said that the device could dictate the content that was viewed, with phone viewing only being for short clips:

J1: Most of the time the phone is usually for only shorter snippets it's like YouTube, or Twitter things... like really short up, to five minutes or so. [...] if I'm taking the time to watching something for longer, I can also take the time to just sit on the couch and relax.

Participant F1 said the phone was her preferred device in many cases, also due to the immediacy of it:

Interviewer: You seem to watch on your phone quite a lot. Is that your preferred device?

F1: Yeah, I mean that's when I'm at home. I think when I'm [at work] I use my laptop.

Interviewer: So what do you like about the phone for watching stuff on?

F1: That it's just more immediate.

However, mobile viewing was consistently seen as being unfavourable and was often avoided if possible. This was typically due to small screen sizes, as stated by household I:

Interviewer: So do you ever watch on tablets or phones?

I2: No.

Interviewer: Never? Absolutely never?

I2: Never.

Interviewer: Okay and why is that?

I1: Screen is too small.

Participant B1 spoke in disbelief that someone could watch for long periods on a small screen:

B1: I was talking to [my friend] about this earlier and he said every night he'll sit and watch a film on his phone. He'll sit there, like, next to [his wife] and she'll sit there watching something he's not interested in and he'll sit there and watch a film or watch videos on YouTube, something to do with work, whatever. And his phone is the same size as mine. I couldn't imagine watching a whole film, just because it's too small.

When asked further about mobile viewing, he clarified:

B1: I don't really get much pleasure holding the tablet to watch something. [...] It doesn't interest me, I'd rather sit and watch it on the telly or not bother. [...] One, you've got to hold it and two, the size of the screen.

However, he did see a benefit to mobile viewing in keeping children occupied:

B1: What I would say about the tablet and the phones, though, is having the kids, when you're out and, say you're going for a meal or something like that, having the phone or tablet with video or like you say, YouTube, is really quite handy because it does keep them occupied.

While the laptop was the most popular viewing screen, participants consistently said that they would prefer to watch on a television. One of the main reasons for this was the bigger screen, but participants also liked the associated comfortable seating. Household A said how watching on the TV was just part of their routine:

Interviewer: Why do you watch, for instance, Better Call Saul on the TV?

A2: Bigger screen.

A1: Bigger screen, yeah. [...] And it's our sort of evening routine, we come in [the living room], we sit down and we watch TV and that's... yeah, it's our routine really.

Participant D1 said watching on a TV is the ideal situation, even though he did not own one himself:

Interviewer: In an ideal world what would you choose to watch on?

D1: A really cool and expensive and nice TV.

Interviewer: And why is that?

D1: Because the quality is quite nice, and if everything is integrated with the streaming service and all that then... lying down on the sofa is the best option.

Viewing Locations

We next consider the location where participants viewed content. As shown in Figure 2, viewing occurred in 10 distinct locations, with the living room and bedroom being the most popular locations. We can again further collapse these locations into two distinct groups: watching in the home (living room, bedroom, kitchen, etc.) and watching outside of the home (workplace, public transport, public place). Households reported more viewing sessions inside the home ($M = 17.7$, $SD = 8.9$) than outside of the home ($M = 2.1$, $SD = 2.2$), and this difference was significant, $t(8)=4.82$, $p = .001$. Moreover, four

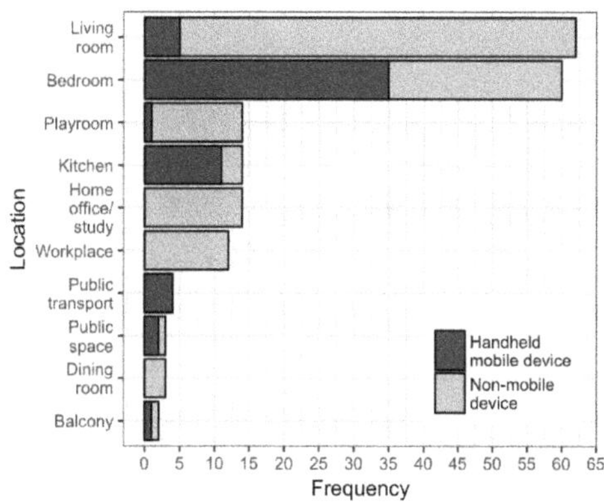

Figure 2: Distribution of viewing locations

of the nine households never once reported watching content outside of the home. Most viewing sessions were reported to have taken place in a single location; there were just five diary entries (2.8%) in which participants reported moving between two locations, and all of these were entirely inside the home.

Diary entries and interview data suggest that viewing location was often not a concious choice, but a result of situational and contextual factors. Participant F1, living in a shared house in London (where it is common to convert communal living spaces into extra bedrooms), spoke about how she could not watch in the living room:

Interviewer: Why do you prefer to watching the bedroom than in the living room for instance?

F1: Because I don't have a living room.

While small screens on mobile devices were often seen negatively, some participants spoke favourably about being able to view on public transport due to their portability, such as H1:

H1: You can use it on a plane.

Interviewer: Why is that?

H1: Because you can just put it on the little table.

Interviewer: Because it's smaller?

H1: It's smaller.

Viewing Time of Day and Duration

We next consider the times at which participants watched during the day, and how long their viewing sessions lasted. A histogram of viewing start times can be seen in Figure 3. It can be seen in the figure that late evening tended to be the most popular time to start viewing, though lower levels of viewing also took place throughout the day, apart from in the very early hours of the morning. In terms of total viewing time, 105:08:00 (55.7%) of viewing took place in the evening period between 18:00 and 00:00. It can also be seen in the figure that viewing on handheld mobile devices was particularly popular in the morning, and during late night and the early hours of the morning. There appears to be a noticeable transition from the pre-bed social ritual of watching on a TV to personal viewing on mobile devices at bedtime.

When considering how long participants viewed for, we found that mean viewing session duration was 01:03:00 (SD = 00:55:56). A histogram of session durations can be seen in Figure 4. Of all the sessions, 122 were one hour or less (69%), and 158 sessions (89%) were two hours or less. Figure 5 shows a detailed view of these sessions, where the most common durations is 30 minutes (often the length of one episode). Only 22 (12%) viewing sessions were over two hours. The longest session was six hours, and the shortest two minutes. On average, households reported longer viewing sessions on non-mobile devices (M = 01:15:37, SD = 00:34:42) than on handheld mobile devices (M = 00:38:24, SD = 00:18:58). However, this difference was not significant, $t(6) = 2.14$, $p = 0.076$.

Amount of Content Viewed

To better understand what was being watched during a session, we also consider the amount of content that was watched. For this analysis we consider each episode or separate video to a different item that is watched. Participants reported watching 481 items across 178 sessions; watching 2.7 items per session (SD = 2.7, range: 1–20). The largest number of items viewed in a single session was 20 YouTube videos over 90 minutes. We found that households tended to watch more items on non-mobile devices ($M = 38.1$, $SD = 33.1$) than on handheld mobile devices ($M = 15.3$, $SD = 23.4$). However, this difference was again not significant, $t(8) = 1.59$, $p = 0.15$.

On-demand Services Used

Participants were also asked to record which on-demand services they used for viewing. They reported using 13 distinct services. These are shown in Figure 6 along with the number of sessions they featured in. We divided these services into two categories: short-form, which consisted of YouTube, Facebook, Lynda iOS app (a training course app), Vimeo, WhatsApp, and The Guardian website (news); and long-form, which consisted of Netflix, Raiplay (Italian on-demand service), BBC iPlayer, unofficial streaming services, home recordings, and Amazon Video. There was no difference in the number of sessions reported by households for using either only long-form services ($M = 10.6$ $SD = 7.3$) or only short-form services ($M = 8.6$, $SD = 6.5$), $t(8) = 0.56$, $p = 0.59$. Households reported longer viewing sessions when sessions featured only long-form services (M = 01:21:49, SD = 01:04:40) than with sessions containing only short-form services (M = 00:38:13, SD = 00:30:40), and this difference was significant, $t(8) = 3.75$ $p = 0.006$.

Watching Alone and Watching Together

We also explored whether people watched alone or with others (i.e., co-viewing). Watching alone was more common than co-viewing. In total, 135 sessions (75.8%) were watched alone, and 43 (24.2%) by multiple people. In this context, co-viewing refers to more than one person actively watching.

Motivations for watching alone were explored during the interviews. A common theme was differing interests. For example, household E (a cohabiting couple with 88.9% of their sessions viewed alone), had very different tastes:

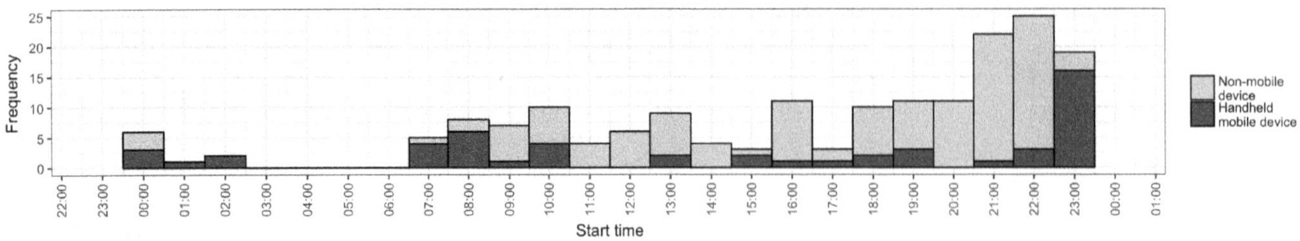

Figure 3: Histogram of viewing start times

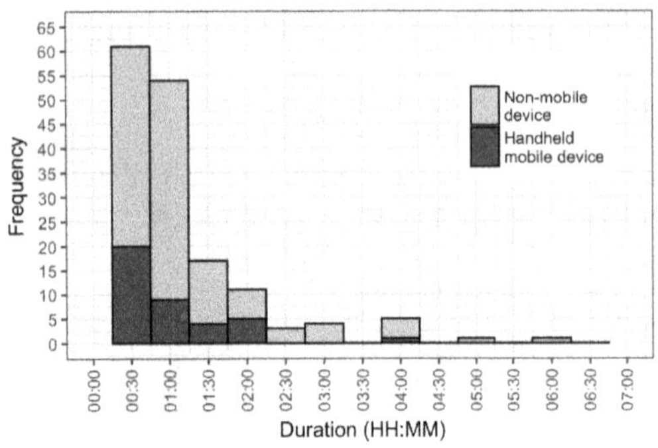

Figure 4: Histogram of viewing session durations

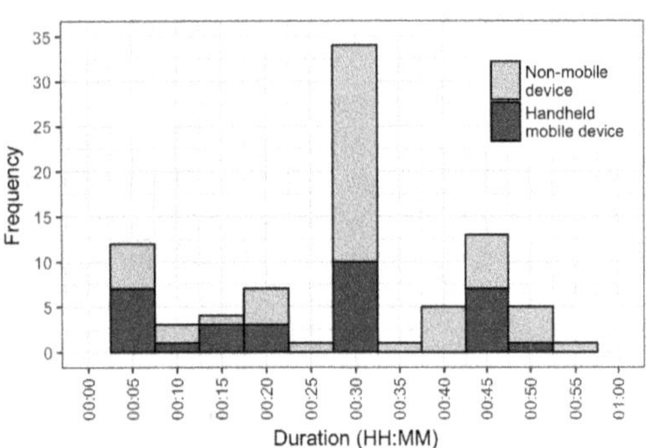

Figure 5: Histogram of viewing session durations for sessions with a duration of one hour or less

> *Interviewer: So what affects whether you watch together? Is it that you like different things, is it that you're just around at different times?*
>
> *E1: Yeah I think I like watching it more than [E2] does, and different things. I really enjoy watching House of Cards whereas he's more, I guess, logical with what he chooses to watch.*

Household D (53.3% of sessions viewed alone) also cited similar differences in personal tastes:

> *Interviewer: And you said you don't ever watch things together?*
>
> *D1: Not really. [My girlfriend] falls asleep all the time.*
>
> *Interviewer: [...] apart from that is there another reason? Do you like different things?*

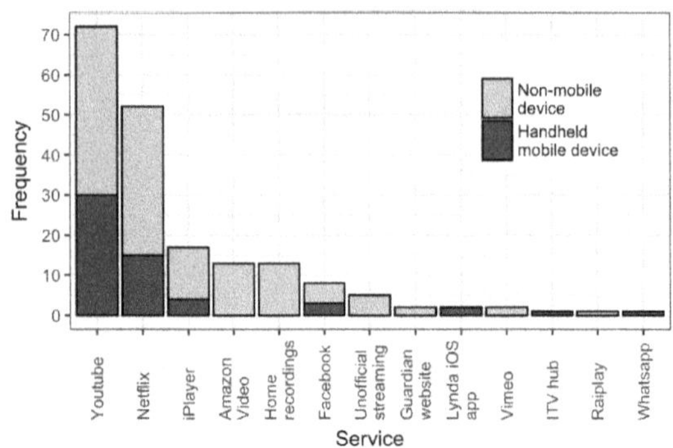

Figure 6: Popularity of different services

> *D1: We do really like very different things, and I think the rare occasion we watch something together is... Well actually, we do watch quite often The Big Bang Theory during dinner. But it's fifteen minutes and we watch the same episodes all the time. So it's more as kind of a background thing... We tried watching other TV series that we might enjoy watching together but those haven't existed to this point.*
>
> *Interviewer: Okay, so you said she goes to sleep all the time. Is it because she sleeps early and you go to bed late? Is that a factor?*
>
> *D1: No no, it's more that she only wants to watch what she likes, and if I don't adjust to it she really finds it really boring and just falls asleep.*

Household A had a more even split of watching alone (58.33%) versus together (41.67%), but still expressed different tastes which influenced whether or not they viewed together:

> *Interviewer: So, why don't you want to watch what [A2] wants to watch?*
>
> *A1: Because it's food programmes...*
>
> *A2: Health...*
>
> *A1: (Laughing) I can answer it myself. Yeah, it's generally food programmes, health programmes...*
>
> *Interviewer: Okay. And [A2], why don't you want to watch what [A1] wants to watch?*
>
> *A2: I can't watch another camper van conversion [on YouTube]!*
>
> *Interviewer: (Laughing) Okay.*

A2: And [A1]'s tutorials, he watches an awful lot of tutorials, which wouldn't interest me.

However, often watching alone was driven by situational factors rather than conscious choice — sometimes people just happened to be alone when they watched. Participant F1 (90.91% of sessions watched alone), an international student, discussed how she often watches alone when in the UK, but with family when back in her home country:

Interviewer: Do you normally watch alone then, when watching on-demand stuff?

F1: Yeah well, when I'm here, yes. ... If I go for holidays back home then I might do it with my, I don't know, with my sister, or my mom.

Participant G1 discussed how watching at work for a break meant they often watched alone:

G1: ...we like some similar shows and therefore we watch them together, but also because, I mean even for instance, [...] during lunch break if I'm alone, I watch something and therefore I am alone!

Participant H1 also referenced her living situation, having recently moved into a different household with new housemates:

H1: But maybe that's just because of my living circumstances. Before I used to just watch TV with other people.

Interviewer: So which would you prefer? Or does it depend?

H1: It depends, but I prefer to watch stuff with other people I think.

Positive Perceptions of On-Demand Video Services

Participants generally had favourable opinions about on-demand services. One of the most obvious themes from the data was the benefits provided by these services in terms of freedom, convenience, and choice for viewers. The results presented above show this clearly — participants watched in a variety of locations, at different times and on different devices. They also spoke about this in interviews, such as the following quote from participant A1:

A1: You can choose when you watch it then can't you? You know you don't have to say "ooh it's on at 8 o'clock tonight, we've got to be there for 8 o'clock". If we watch it on-demand you can think "I'll watch it at 10 o'clock if I want".

A number of households spoke about the catalogue of content available, which can make it easy to find something to watch:

E1: I think I watched the first thirty minutes of it but didn't really... And that's the thing about on-demand — if you don't really like it, you can just find something else.

F1: It's been so long since I watched the TV that I don't even remember how it is that you have to wait every week for a new episode or whatever, for the series, right? So now I just watch them whenever I want, whenever I have the time.

J1: I can always find something [more easily] on on-demand, because on broadcast TV I am limited to [...] forty different channels? And most of it is just reruns, and on-demand I have the selection of fifteen-thousand videos or something.

Participants also remarked on the quality of content available via on-demand services in comparison with broadcast TV, which was generally seen as similar if not better:

D1: I think I went into Netflix because of the catalogue they had, and a couple of their own productions like House of Cards, Orange Is the New Black, and the fact [that] they had a lot of stuff [...]. I tried it out and I enjoyed it.

However, participant J1 did note how broadcast TV was still useful for time-sensitive content:

J1: I think that quality is quite similar, I think. Broadcast TV also has some more things to offer like as news coverage which you don't get on demand.

Negative Perceptions of On-Demand Viewing

While opinions were generally positive, participants noted some negative aspects. Typically these were in relation to watching large volumes of content, or at least the potential to. Some participants spoke about being addicted to particular shows. Household A spoke about AMC's *Better Call Saul*:

A1: Yeah, well we like to watch two or three at a time, don't we?

A2: Yeah.

Interviewer: Why is that?

A1: We can't stop watching them because they're addictive.

A2: The trouble is, when you watch one that's on for almost an hour... you just, you feel as though you've been short-changed, you need to watch some more.

A1: Yeah, you're drawn in aren't you? You just want to watch more.

Participant F1 also spoke about a compulsion to watch:

F1: It becomes a bit addictive now. At least on the TV if you missed an episode you will be like "Oh okay, I'll just watch it next week" and then you will do other stuff. But now, I have this theory about habits. Because I can watch whenever I want, and it's the sort of thing where I need to be watching now to go to sleep.

Other participants also spoke about becoming hooked on a show, and how certain services made it very easy to watch another episode:

E2: Normally when you watch something you have to say "Should we see one more?". Then we would actually take an active choice to press next button, but Netflix there's like five seconds countdown. So often we [think] "Should we see one more?", "Hmm, I don't really know" and then, the intro screen is on and Netflix started.

E1: It made the choice for us.

E2: Yeah, I think if it didn't start automatically and we actually had to push the button, then I think we would talk. I probably would talk about if we should see one more, because now it was the fourth in a row.

Participants also spoke about trying to control their viewing to ensure they didn't spend more time watching than intended:

E1: You also want to see a lot of these like, Suits, or whatever... We don't want to get dragged into it because I can't get out of it (laughing). [...] I know myself too well that I'll end up spending half a day there.

Participant H1 said something similar:

H1: I didn't want to start a series one time because I knew I would just waste so much of my time watching it.

This type of boundary setting was also mentioned by other participants. Participant F1 thought that excessive viewing might be having a detrimental effect on other areas of her life, and so spoke about creating hardware boundaries to combat it:

F1: No I don't have Netflix on my phone, and I don't want to put Netflix on my phone.

Interviewer: Why is that?

F1: Because at least with the tablet you know I leave it at home, and I know that I won't use it unless I am at home at night.

Interviewer: So that's one way of setting a boundary?

F1: Yes, I mean I always feel to set these boundaries and they work, but the problem is for the last few months I've become an addict to YouTube. I don't think I was like that last year. I was a bit more able to control myself.

Interviewer: How about watching outside of the office and outside of home? So, maybe in a public place or while you were travelling for instance. Can you talk about if you did any of that?

F1: No, because so first of all I don't have enough data to watch videos, and I also deliberately don't pay more [...] so that I can restrict myself from watching videos, because otherwise I would just be watching everything.

Participants also said how watching too much content often meant they wasted time or ended up going to bed too late:

A2: I think sometimes we normally stay up a bit late with on-demand.

H1: Um, well, because then I'll watch maybe three episodes in an evening...well, on a bad evening or like I'll watch two and the next evening I'll watch two. If there are lots of episodes in the series then that's a big waste of time.

Binge Watching

Discussions of consuming too much content often brought the subject specifically to binge watching, which was discussed with all of the participants. Most of the participants were familiar with this behaviour and said they participated in it themselves. It seemed that this phenomenon could be thought of as a particular type of excessive viewing. However, when pushed to define binge watching, few participants had a clear idea of what binge watching was. Some would define it as being based on the number of episodes of a show that was watched, e.g. participant G1 defined it as three or more episodes, but only when watching TV shows:

G1: I have always thought about it in terms of TV shows [...]. So, watching many more than just one single episode, in one sitting.

Interviewer: So how many episodes is it before you are binge-watching?

G1: I would say from three.

Interviewer: So if I watch three five minute YouTube videos, is that binge-watching?

G1: Not exactly. My understanding was [...] that you are watching episodes of 45 minutes each.

Participant J1 also agreed with this:

J1: I think binge watching should be sort of a TV series episode length. An hour, or 45 minutes, or 42 minutes... and you watch more than two of those in a row.

Others said it was based on the amount of overall time spent, such as participant D1:

Interviewer: How many episodes do you think is binge watching?

R: Ooh, erm, anything that goes above four or five hours.

Interviewer: Okay, so it's more about the time than the number of episodes for you?

R: Yeah, because it's not the same to watch a whole TV mini-series that has 10 episodes [that are] an hour and 15 minutes each, [as it is to watch] ten episodes of The Big Bang Theory or Friends.

Participant I2 also agreed with this, specifically noting how the number of episodes was inconsequential. He also seems to think that it is possible binge watch shorter content:

I2: Well, the [time and number of episodes] are synonymous, right? So if the programme was 10 minutes per episode, then I would go through [many] more episodes probably to achieve the same amount of time.

Household B also thought it was based on the amount of time spent, but disagreed about the actual definition.

Interviewer: So how would you define it? Is it the number of episodes or is it the amount of time that you watch?

B2: The amount of time. [...]

Interviewer: So, how many episodes would have to watch and how long would you have to watch for, for it to be binge watching?

B3: I don't know. I guess if you sit there, waste your whole night. [...]

B3: Yeah, I've never thought about it before, so I don't know. Um, four or five hours I guess. [...]

B2: I'd go for three.

Such disagreement as to what constitutes a televisual binge was also present in other households, such as in household A:

A1: Didn't we watch three [episodes] in the last couple of weeks? We watched three [episodes].

A2: Oh three... yeah, but I wouldn't say that constituted binge watching, but maybe it does.

R1: I think three is, yeah. Three is, I would say, yeah.

R2: I don't know... but yeah we did watch three.

Interviewer: So would you say that that's binge watching?

R2: I wouldn't say that's binge watching.

Interviewer: Why not?

R2: I don't think there are enough episodes there.

Interviewer: Okay.

R1: I would say... I think more than two is binge watching.

Unlike some, H1 did not think that episodes necessarily had to be watched back-to-back or even on the same day:

H1: I think it's watching multiple episodes compulsively. [...] it could be one episode but you watch an episode per evening or it could be within a shorter space of time...

Participant J1 also suggested that watching one episode per evening could be binge watching, but was not entirely sure:

J1: Maybe it is... maybe seven episodes in seven days is binge watching [...] it's difficult to say. I think... like in a short period of time, watching something that was made for once a week maybe.

Participant I1 thought binge watching was more related to viewing intentions:

I2: It depends, yes, because if I'm supposed to work and I tell myself, "Okay, one. One video" and then I end up watching six, then it's kind of binge watching too, because I was supposed to take just a 10 minute break.

I: So does it depend on what you are supposed to be doing, for you?

R2: Yeah, I guess what the intention was. If I really just want a fifteen-minute break and I end up, you know, watching something for thirty minutes, then I kind of escalated there, so in a way that would be binge watching. If it's a lazy Saturday afternoon and it's raining and I end up watching three or four episodes, then yeah I think four or five is turning into binge watching, but otherwise if I have the time and nothing else to do...

DISCUSSION

The findings of this study show that although on-demand video platforms have the potential to change viewing behaviour, viewers still often conform to traditional viewing habits. For instance, in terms of viewing time, most viewing occurred during the evening "prime time" slot. Furthermore, the most common session duration was 30 minutes, typically the length of one episode of content. The TV was also still a popular viewing screen. However, changes as a result of new technology can also be seen. YouTube was the most common viewing platform, showing how shortform content has become popular. We also found that a third of viewing happened on a mobile device, and instances of very long viewing sessions.

When considering viewing screens, we can see that the laptop was slightly more popular as a viewing device than the television, which may not be possible without the cross-device availability of on-demand services. This could be due to the ease of access to different services via the internet, as well as the balance of screen size and portability that laptops provide. However, for the purposes of viewing they function similarly to a TV — a fairly large screen that can be placed in a comfortable location, with the ability to watch with others. Though most viewing occurred on larger screens, a third of viewing sessions were on handheld mobile devices. This was generally seen as unfavourable, and mostly seemed to be down to necessity — in interviews, participants expressed their dislike for viewing on mobile devices, citing the small screen as a reason. This agrees with previous work showing how viewing on small screens can lead to a reduced viewing experience [15]. However, participants said that they would watch on a mobile device if no other device were available (e.g. when travelling). Most said they preferred to watch on a TV, due to large screen size and comfortable seating typically found nearby. Individual differences were evident however, with some participants entirely discounting watching content on phones, and others sometimes preferring it.

We found that viewing device often depended on people's locations. The majority of viewing (89.9%) took place inside the home, and the living room was the most popular location. It is perhaps then not surprising that people tended to watch on larger display TVs and laptops rather than smaller mobile screens when in the living room. Mobile devices tended to be used in the home in locations where there may not be access to a TV, such as the kitchen or bedroom. Our participants did report watching on mobile devices when outside of the home, particularly when travelling and commuting to work. In recent years the lower cost of mobile data has made easier to watch on-demand services on the move. These instances of mobile viewing tended to be during longer journeys, possibly because it allows for an entire episode of content to be watched.

Participants spoke very favourably about on demand services, especially about how they have allowed them more freedom and choice than broadcast TV. However, a study by Vanattenhoven and Geerts [20] found that some consumers found the amount of choice available to be an annoyance, especially with regard to the number of different services available. Interestingly, we did not find this sentiment in any of our data.

This freedom also allowed participants to select content that matched their personal tastes. Our interview data revealed that these differing tastes among household members could lead to people choosing to view alone, which was reflected in the diary data showing that 75.8% of sessions were watched alone. This shows a stark turnaround of events when compared with an observational study by Saxbe et al. [17], who found that watching TV with at least one other person happened for 61% of the time, and that the TV provided a platform for togetherness in the household. While participant D1 said he and his partner generally watched different content in different rooms due to differing tastes, participant A1 described how she and her partner used tablets and earphones to watch different content, but still be in the same room together. This agrees with Ofcom's findings [12] who found that people often turn to on-demand services for some "alone time".

Although we observed that only a quarter of sessions were co-viewed, we know from previous research that viewers value the way new broadcasting technologies can enhance the social aspect of viewing [1, 7]. While watching alone was more common than co-viewing, it may be that the sessions watched alone were driven by other latent social factors, such as being able to discuss the show with friends. Finally, it could be that co-viewing and other social factors work differently in different household configurations, e.g. we observed that the households with the highest percentage of co-viewing were household A, an older couple (42.1% of sessions co-viewed) and Household B, a family (41.7% of sessions co-viewed), while the household with the lowest percentage was household H, two young professional cohabiting friends (6.7% of sessions co-viewed). We cannot speculate beyond this with our data, but it would be an interesting focus of future research.

However, participants were often wary of the way instant access to large amounts of content could mean watching for long periods. This led to some participants creating boundaries to prevent this behaviour, either by simply not starting to watch a new show, or by restricting viewing in some other way, e.g. not installing Netflix on their phone. While it may in the interests of service providers to make it as easy as possible to view large volumes of content for revenue and engagement purposes, this was often troubling to our participants, some of whom commented that Netflix "made the choice for [them]" when deciding whether to watch another episode. As such, the introduction of small "design frictions" to combat automatic behaviours could lead to a better user experience [4], either by design or manually by the users themselves.

Discussing consuming large amounts of content typically led to talking about binge watching, which most of the participants said they participated in. However, when pushed to define what binge watching was, there were widely different responses and definitions often seemed to change depending on the context. This is reflected in other studies, where binge watching is defined differently by different authors. For example, some participants said it was watching two or more episodes in a row (as in [14, 12]), and said three or more episodes in a row (as in [5, 21]). Others said it was not so much the number of episodes watched but the total time spent watching, while others said it was a combination of these two features. Others said that it depended on their intentions when they started to watch. In summary, different people seemed to have different ideas of what binge watching is, and this disagreement reflects the diversity of definitions that appear in the literature on this topic. Such varying definitions suggest that it could defined on a scale, and vary with context and type of content, as suggested by Trouleau et al. [19].

While we took effort to recruit participants of various ages and living in different parts of the UK, most of our participants were London-based millennials without children. This bias in the sample may have affected our results. For instance, some participants lived in shared housing without a communal living room or TV. In place of this, viewing occurred on laptops and tablets in bedrooms. Considering millennials' typically high level of interaction with technology, we might have expected more activity that differs from traditional notions of TV viewing. This may have seen an increase if our sample featured more teenagers and children. Viewing mainly in the evening is perhaps to be expected, as our sample was mostly adults in full-time employment. However, there was a steady amount of daytime viewing, resulting from one household with children being at home and people viewing during work breaks.

Our sample consisted of 20 individuals from nine households. This could be argued to be a small sample size, however it is similar to that of comparable studies (e.g. [13, 1, 20, 9]). It also reflects the challenges of conducting this type of research, where prolonged studies with involved tasks for participants can deter participation, even when well compensated.This may have influenced the results of the statistical tests we employed — while the differences between means were often quite large, the high variance and low sample size did return some non-significant results. Notwithstanding, as the present study is qualitative in nature, we argue that the sample size is sufficient to illuminate many of the behaviours surrounding on-demand and mobile viewing, especially given the study duration.

A limitation of the diary study method is that some participants may not have recorded everything they watched. During interviews some participants did remark that they sometimes did not record very short viewing sessions (e.g., a short Facebook video) because of the effort involved. However, this was fairly uncommon, with most participants saying they recorded the vast majority of content they watched.

CONCLUSION

This paper extends our understanding of how on-demand viewing occurs in daily life. The results of a diary study show that this technology leads to new behaviours such as mobile viewing, viewing for long periods, and consuming shortform content. However, our sample still often conformed to traditional viewing habits. Viewing was mostly in the evening on a large screen, though this sometimes happened in new ways, such as by using a laptop. While mobile viewing did account for a third of all viewing sessions, in general this was seen as less favourable than watching on a large screen. Typically, mobile viewing seemed to occur for contextual reasons, such as being a practical device to use while travelling, or wanting to watch content privately when in the presence of others. We also found that viewing alone was far more common than viewing with other people. Participants had largely positive opinions about on-demand video services, but generally seemed to be wary about the ability watch for long periods and the impact it could have on other areas of their lives.

ACKNOWLEDGEMENTS

This research was supported by EPSRC grant EP/G037159/1.

REFERENCES

1. Louise Barkhuus and Barry Brown. 2009. Unpacking the Television: User Practices around a Changing Technology. *ACM Transactions on Computer-Human Interaction (TOCHI)* 16, 3, Article 15 (Sept. 2009), 22 pages. DOI:http://dx.doi.org/10.1145/1592440.1592444

2. Rhiannon Bury and Johnson Li. 2015. Is It Live or Is It Timeshifted, Streamed or Downloaded? Watching Television in the Era of Multiple Screens. *New Media & Society* 17, 4 (2015), 592–610. DOI: http://dx.doi.org/10.1177/1461444813508368

3. The Nielsen Company. 2016. On-demand Demographics: VOD Viewing Across Generations. (2016). http://www.nielsen.com/uk/en/insights/news/2016/on-demand-demographics-vod-viewing-across-generations.html

4. Anna L. Cox, Sandy J.J. Gould, Marta E. Cecchinato, Ioanna Iacovides, and Ian Renfree. 2016. Design Frictions for Mindful Interactions: The Case for Microboundaries. In *Proceedings of the 2016 CHI Conference Extended Abstracts on Human Factors in Computing Systems (CHI EA '16)*. ACM, New York, NY, USA, 1389–1397. DOI: http://dx.doi.org/10.1145/2851581.2892410

5. Dimph de Feijter, Vassilis-Javed Khan, and Marnix van Gisbergen. 2016. Confessions of a 'Guilty' Couch Potato Understanding and Using Context to Optimize Binge-watching Behavior. In *Proceedings of the ACM International Conference on Interactive Experiences for TV and Online Video (TVX '16)*. ACM, New York, NY, USA, 59–67. DOI: http://dx.doi.org/10.1145/2932206.2932216

6. David Gauntlett and Annette Hill. 2002. *TV Living: Television, Culture and Everyday Life*. Routledge.

7. Lilly Irani, Robin Jeffries, and Andrea Knight. 2010. Rhythms and plasticity: television temporality at home. *Personal and Ubiquitous Computing* 14, 7 (01 Oct 2010), 621–632. DOI: http://dx.doi.org/10.1007/s00779-009-0280-1

8. Robert J. Logan, Sheila Augaitis, Robert H. Miller, and Keith Wehmeyer. 1995. Living Room Culture - an Anthropological Study of Television Usage Behaviors. In *Proceedings of the Human Factors and Ergonomics Society Annual Meeting*, Vol. 39. SAGE Publications Sage CA: Los Angeles, CA, 326–330. DOI: http://dx.doi.org/10.1177/154193129503900507

9. Jennifer McNally and Beth Harrington. 2017. How Millennials and Teens Consume Mobile Video. In *Proceedings of the 2017 ACM International Conference on Interactive Experiences for TV and Online Video (TVX '17)*. ACM, New York, NY, USA, 31–39. DOI: http://dx.doi.org/10.1145/3077548.3077555

10. João Nogueira, Lucas Guardalben, Bernardo Cardoso, and Susana Sargento. 2017. Catch-up TV Analytics: Statistical Characterization and Consumption Patterns Identification on a Production Service. *Multimedia Systems* 23, 5 (01 Oct 2017), 563–581. DOI: http://dx.doi.org/10.1007/s00530-016-0516-7

11. Ofcom. 2016. Linear Vs. Non-linear Viewing: A Qualitative Investigation Exploring Viewers' Behaviour and Attitudes Towards Using Different TV Platforms and Services Providers. (2016). http://www.ofcom.org.uk/research-and-data/tv-radio-and-on-demand/tv-research/linear-vs-non-linear-viewing

12. Ofcom. 2017. The Communications Market Report 2017. (2017). http://www.ofcom.org.uk/__data/assets/pdf_file/0017/105074/cmr-2017-uk.pdf

13. Kenton O'Hara, April Slayden Mitchell, and Alex Vorbau. 2007. Consuming Video on Mobile Devices. In *Proceedings of the SIGCHI Conference on Human Factors in Computing Systems (CHI '07)*. ACM, New York, NY, USA, 857–866. DOI: http://dx.doi.org/10.1145/1240624.1240754

14. Matthew Pittman and Kim Sheehan. 2015. Sprinting a Media Marathon: Uses and Gratifications of Binge-watching Television through Netflix. *First Monday* 20, 10 (2015). DOI: http://dx.doi.org/10.5210/fm.v20i10.6138

15. Jacob M. Rigby, Duncan P. Brumby, Anna L. Cox, and Sandy J.J. Gould. 2016. Watching Movies on Netflix: Investigating the Effect of Screen Size on Viewer Immersion. In *Proceedings of the 18th International Conference on Human-Computer Interaction with Mobile Devices and Services Adjunct (MobileHCI '16)*. ACM, New York, NY, USA, 714–721. DOI: http://dx.doi.org/10.1145/2957265.2961843

16. Jacob M. Rigby, Duncan P. Brumby, Anna L. Cox, and Sandy J.J. Gould. 2018. Old Habits Die Hard: A Diary Study of On-demand Video Viewing. In *Proceedings of the 2018 CHI Conference Extended Abstracts on Human Factors in Computing Systems (CHI EA '18)*. ACM, New York, NY, USA. DOI: http://dx.doi.org/10.1145/3170427.3188665

17. Darby Saxbe, Anthony Graesch, and Marie Alvik. 2011. Television As a Social or Solo Activity: Understanding Families' Everyday Television Viewing Patterns. *Communication Research Reports* 28, 2 (2011), 180–189.

18. Alex Taylor and Richard Harper. 2003. Switching off to Switch On. In *Inside the Smart Home*, Richard Harper (Ed.). Springer London, London, Chapter 7, 115–126. DOI:http://dx.doi.org/10.1007/1-85233-854-7_7

19. William Trouleau, Azin Ashkan, Weicong Ding, and Brian Eriksson. 2016. Just One More: Modeling Binge Watching Behavior. In *Proceedings of the 22nd ACM SIGKDD International Conference on Knowledge Discovery and Data Mining (KDD '16)*. ACM, New York, NY, USA, 1215–1224. DOI: http://dx.doi.org/10.1145/2939672.2939792

20. Jeroen Vanattenhoven and David Geerts. 2015. Broadcast, Video-on-demand, and Other Ways to Watch Television Content: A Household Perspective. In *Proceedings of the ACM International Conference on Interactive Experiences for TV and Online Video (TVX '15)*. ACM, New York, NY, USA, 73–82. DOI: http://dx.doi.org/10.1145/2745197.2745208

21. Emily Walton-Pattison, Stephan U. Dombrowski, and Justin Presseau. 2016. 'Just One More Episode': Frequency and Theoretical Correlates of Television Binge Watching. *Journal of Health Psychology* 23, 1 (2016), 17–24. DOI: http://dx.doi.org/10.1177/1359105316643379

Utilitarian and Hedonic Motivations for Live Streaming Shopping

Jie Cai, Donghee Yvette Wohn, Ankit Mittal, Dhanush Sureshbabu
New Jersey Institute of Technology
Newark, NJ, USA
jc926@njit.edu, wohn@njit.edu, ds676@njit.edu, am2272@njit.edu

ABSTRACT

Watching live streams as part of the online shopping experience is a relatively new phenomenon. In this paper, we examine live streaming shopping, conceptualizing it as a type of online shopping that incorporates real-time social interaction. Live streaming shopping can happen in two ways: live streaming embedded in e-commerce, or e-commerce integrated into live streaming. Based on prior research related to live streaming and consumer motivation theories, we examined the relationships between hedonic and utilitarian motivations and shopping intention. We found that hedonic motivation is positively related to celebrity-based intention and utilitarian motivation is positively related to product-based intention. A content analysis of open-ended questions identified eight reasons for why consumers prefer live streaming shopping over regular online shopping.

Author Keywords

Live streams; live streaming shopping; e-commerce; Technology Acceptance Model (TAM); hedonic and utilitarian motivations; behavioral intentions.

ACM Classification Keywords

Human-centered computing; Human computer interaction (HCI); Empirical studies in HCI.

INTRODUCTION

Live streaming is an increasingly popular form of media, with growing research around this topic, ranging from technical research about live streaming systems [21,31,32] to behavioral studies about streamers' motives and viewers' motives across different platforms, including YouTube Live [9,21], Twitch [10,12,21,33], and Periscope [8,30].

Nowadays, if we open Twitch (which is primarily gaming content but is quickly expanding into other areas as well) and view a recommended streamer who is streaming a video game, we can see all kinds of technology product links on their channels to shopping sites such as Amazon and Newegg. Sometimes streamers are paid to promote these products in stream; other times the shopping sites such as Amazon give the streamers commissions for sales generated by links on their channels. On the live video platform "Live.me," which was established in 2016, users could buy the items promoted by their favorite streamers while viewing the stream.

In the U.S., the incorporation of shopping into live streams is relatively new and has not always been successful. In March 2016, Amazon launched "Style Code Live" to broadcast fashion and beauty tips via mobile, but the live television show was cancelled in May 2017. In Dec. 2016, Livby launched the first mobile live streaming shopping app in the U.S. [23] but has yet to become mainstream. As of February 2018, no other large U.S. online shopping site has live streaming channels on their websites.

In contrast, almost all main e-commerce platforms in China such as Taobao.com, JD.com, and VIP.com have live streaming channels for their online vendors or brands. For example, users on Taobao.com (similar to eBay) can create an online store and demo products through a live stream with product links on the right side that can be clicked to purchase. In the middle of the screen there is a chatroom for viewers to communicate. Brands often promote events by inviting social media influencers or internet celebrities to broadcast products and increase sales. Sometimes, store owners themselves live stream for their small businesses. In 2016, Meili Inc., a leading fashion e-commerce platform in China, held its first overseas live streaming show in New York [22].

There is very little research, however, on live streaming shopping, perhaps due to it being a relatively new phenomenon. We thus conducted this study to understand why people watch live streams when they shop and why they would prefer shopping on e-commerce websites that have live streams as opposed to those that do not. Understanding the motivations of users would enable us to identify current pros and cons related to existing live streaming shopping sites, opportunities for live streaming platforms to incorporate elements of e-commerce, as well

TVX '18, June 26-28, 2018, SEOUL, Republic of Korea

ACM ISBN 978-1-4503-5115-7/18/06...$15.00
https://doi.org/10.1145/3210825.3210837

as e-commerce sites to incorporate elements of live streaming.

In this paper, we first introduce live streaming from a social media perspective. Then, we summarize current live streaming research related to motives and integrate them with shopping motivation theories to form our hypotheses. Finally, we present survey results of closed and open-ended questions.

LIVE STREAMING SHOPPING DEFINITION

Live streaming is a new type of social media, some research called it mixed media [10], which was different from traditional social media such as Facebook and Twitter. Scheibe et al. [25] mentioned that social networking site was a narrower term of social media and could be categorized into asynchronous [13] and synchronous. Live streaming is a primarily synchronous social media form. It contains some unique features such as simultaneity [25] and authenticity [30].

Shopping through live streams is a new way of shopping and contains not only lots of social commerce attributes but also unique media attributes. Social commerce refers to a way of commerce mediated by social media [26]. Kim and Park [14] defined social commerce as a subset of e-commerce that used social network sites for social interactions to facilitate online shopping. In this study, we refer to *live streaming shopping* as having attributes of social commerce that integrates real-time social interaction into e-commerce. It can be achieved in two ways: live streaming is embedded into e-commerce, such as Amazon live style code, Taobao.com, and JD.com or e-commerce is integrated into live streaming, such as Live.me and Livby.

MOTIVATIONS TO WATCH LIVE STREAMS

In this section we examined the most current research about streamers' motivations. Friedländer [8] measured streamers' motivations on social live streaming services (*N*=7,667) across different platforms and countries and found out that the top six motives were boredom, socializing, to reach a specific group, need to communicate, fun, and self- expression. Hamilton et al. [10] studied streaming on Twitch and concluded that there were two reasons for people to engage in live streaming: unique content, and interaction and participation. For the streamers, desire to build community and encouragement of participation with viewers were their motivations. For the viewers, three motives were identified through interviews: intention to learn about a particular game, friendliness of the streamers, and social interaction.

Other related research did not distinguish the motives between streamers and viewers and just used the general motives of users. For instance, research about YouNow (a social live streaming service) showed that the main motives to use this platform were ease of use, satisfaction of the need of self-presentation, boredom and acceptance by the community [25].

MOTIVATIONS OF LIVE STREAMING SHOPPING

Because live streaming shopping is a new form of mixed media and shopping, it is important to consider both existing consumer literature on why people shop and user experience literature on why people watch live streams. As it has both technology related attributes and general online shopping features, our research drew from previous motivation theories related to acceptance of information technology as well as theories about online shopping.

For consumers' shopping motivations, most research explored utilitarian and hedonic motivations [2,3,7,19,20]. Utilitarian means functional, instrumental, and practical and hedonic means multisensory and emotive [11]. Babin et al. [1] documented that utilitarian outcome was a result from "conscious pursuit of an intended consequence" while utilitarian value could explain "shopping trips described by consumers as 'an errand' or 'work' where they were happy simply to 'get through it all'." Utilitarian benefits could be ease of use and satisfactory outcomes while hedonic benefits could be enjoyment of the shopping experience[2]. Utilitarian motivations included convenience and cost reductions (i.e., money, time, and effort) [15].

Hedonic values are subjective and can be generated from playfulness and fun [11]. Falode et al. viewed hedonic shopping as "a positive experience where consumers may enjoy an emotionally satisfying experience related to the shopping activity regardless of whether or not a purchase was made"[7], and it pertained to hedonic fulfillment such as fun, amusement, and sensory stimulation [1]. Hirschman and Holbrook depicted shoppers as "problem solvers" or "fun, fantasy, arousal, and enjoyment" seekers [11]. Other research described shopping motives as either work [29] or fun [28].

For technology-related motivations, the Technology Acceptance Model (TAM) in information systems is widely adapted and used for research related to understanding why people adapt and use technology. Davis in 1989 developed two scales (perceived usefulness and perceived ease of use) for system usage and defined perceived ease of use as "the degree to which a person believes that using a particular system would be free of effort" and perceived usefulness as the extent that people believe using a particular system would enhance their job performance [4].

Individuals' behavioral motivations are differentiated into extrinsic (behaviors prompted by external contingencies) and intrinsic (perceived pleasure and satisfaction) motivation [6]. From this perspective, both ease of use and usefulness are perceived as extrinsic motivations [16,27]. Therefore, the TAM was extended by many research with enjoyment as an intrinsic motivation [5,16,17]. Thus "hedonic" and "utilitarian" not only applied to consumer motivations but also used to systems and user experiences [19].

TAM has been applied in the e-commerce context. Childers et al. applied TAM in online retail shopping and postulated that the usefulness referred to the outcome of the shopping experience and ease of use referred to the process resulting to outcome [3]. They also proposed that usefulness could reflect utilitarian motivation and enjoyment embodied hedonic aspect. Shang et al. [27] also applied TAM in online shopping and found the intrinsic motivations were the major reason to shop online.

Using the framework of utilitarian and hedonic motivations, we incorporated the original TAM to understand the utilitarian aspects. But since this model only covers utilitarian motivations, we had to add hedonic motivations. There could be many different types of hedonic motivations, but we decided to focus on the aspect of the live streamer, as that was a novel component to live streaming shopping in comparison to regular shopping. We chose interpersonal attractiveness as a measure of how much the viewer thinks the streamer is interesting as a person, and physical attractiveness as a measure of how much the viewer likes the streamer's outwardly appearance.

Integrating the reasons and motives summarized from previous literature to use live streams with the TAM and motivation theories, we finally refined four motivations for live streaming shopping: two utilitarian motivations (ease of use and usefulness) and two hedonic motivations (physical attractiveness and interpersonal attractiveness). Correspondingly, we developed two types of intentions for these motivations: one is utilitarian intention (intention to watch because of the product), and another is hedonic intention (intention to watch because of the streamer).

> **RQ1:** How do utilitarian (product-related) motivations and hedonic motivations (streamer-related) explain intention to watch a live stream for shopping?

Because live streaming shopping is a new phenomenon in online shopping domain, we wanted to understand not only why people engage in it but also why they would prefer it over other modes of shopping. Because we did not find a good theoretical framework for this, this was a preliminary attempt to get some idea of users' preferences. Thus, we posed an open-ended question:

> **RQ2:** Why do people prefer live streaming shopping as opposed to regular online shopping sites?

METHODS

Participants

An online survey was designed and approved by IRB, then distributed on Amazon Mechanical Turk. Only English-speaking participants that were 18 years or above and with an approval rate higher than 90% were qualified to complete the task. Since our questions were about shopping experiences that involved live streaming, in order to avoid missing data, two qualifier questions were set: "Have you ever used a shopping website that had a live stream?" and "Have you ever watched a live stream about a product before purchasing it?" Only participants who answered "yes" for both were qualified. Thus, all our respondents had some live streaming shopping-related experience. Because we encouraged our participants to explain more in open-ended questions, we gave them $2.

We collected a total of 220 responses. We cleaned the dataset by looking at the open-ended question answers and removing cases where people wrote gibberish. We also eliminated cases where there were substantial missing values. The final dataset contained 199 valid answers. Most of respondents were from United States (78.4%), followed by India (14.6%); the rest were from 11 different countries. The average age was 31.7 (SD=7.89), but most of them were between 25 and 34 years old (64.8%). In our survey, there were more male (61.8%) than female (37.2%) participants. Most of them had a bachelor's degree or higher (58.2%) and were full-time employees (73.4%).

Survey Measures

All the items for motivations were borrowed from prior research. Interpersonal attractiveness (M=4.13 SD=.64, α=.73) was from [24] and had three items: "The streamer was likeable," "The streamer was approachable," "The streamer was very warm." Physical attractiveness (M=3.62 SD=.88, α=.88) was from [18] and had three items: "The streamer was quite handsome/pretty," "The streamer was attractive physically," "The streamer was very good looking."

Usefulness (M=4.19 SD=.55, α=.81) and ease of use (M=3.92 SD=.60, α=.77) were adapted from [1,3,27] to fit the context of live streaming shopping. Usefulness contained seven items such as: "It was useful in getting information about the product," "The live stream shows the effectiveness of the product," and "It would improve my shopping ability." Ease of use contained seven items such as: "It would allow me to save time when shopping," "It would be convenient for me," and "I could find products easier through live streaming." We prefaced all the items with "I watched a live stream before purchasing a product because ..." and measured them with a 5-point Likert scale from "Strongly disagree" to "Strongly agree".

For our dependent variable, we had two types of intention: intention to watch a live stream if an individual is searching for a product online and just happens to find a live streaming event (M=4.25, SD=.70) and intention to watch a live stream if a shopping website invited their favorite internet celebrity to stream an event for an hour (M=4.10, SD=.81). These were single item measures on a 5-point Likert scale from "Very unlikely" to "Very likely".

Besides the major independent variables and dependent variables, we also asked questions about the streaming content and their decision-making factors with the question: "How important are the following factors in your decision to buy the product?": "how much I like the streamer" (M=3.56, SD=1.11), "how much I need the product" (M=4.12, SD=.83), and "how much I like the product" (M=4.19, SD=.82). These three items were on with a 5-

point Likert scale from "Not at all important" to "very important."

We also had two open-ended questions. In the beginning of the survey, we asked, "What are some examples of products you bought after seeing it on a live stream?" Toward the end of the survey, we asked, "Why did you shop on a live streaming site rather than other online shopping sites that don't have live streaming?"

RESULTS

Descriptive Data

We asked questions about how often they shop online and watch live streams to understand general shopping frequency (see Table 1). When asked about which live streaming shopping sites they have used (check all that apply), participants had used Amazon style live code the most (62.4%), followed by Live.me (23.6%), VIP.com (7.5%), Taobao.com (7%), JD.com (4%), Livby (4%), and other (34.7%).

When asked which platforms they watched live streams on before purchasing a product (multiple choices allowed), participants reported Facebook Live (62.8%), followed by YouTube Live (46.2%), Twitch (25.6%), Instagram (21.1%), Periscope (8.5%), and other (10.1%). The products they bought after watching a live stream were: Electronics, Computer, and Office (30.2%), Clothing, Shoes, and Jewelry (24.1%), Home, Garden, and Tools (14.1%), Music, Movies, and Games (11.1%), and Beauty and Health (10.1%).

Relationship Between Motivation and Intention

For the relationship between motivations and intentions, we put the four motivations and the decision-making factors as independent variables, and two scenario-related intentions as dependent variables. Results are shown in Table 2.

For the utilitarian intention, which was whether they would watch a live stream if an individual was searching for a product online and just happened to find a live streaming event, 24% of the variance were explained by the model, $F(7,191) = 10.15$ and $p < .001$. Usefulness was the only significant motivation and liking product was the only significant decision-making factor, indicating that if the users were goal-oriented and looking for a specific item, the more useful they thought the product info was and the more they liked the product, the more likely they would go watch the live stream in this situation.

For the hedonic intention, which was whether they would watch a live stream if a shopping website invited their favorite internet celebrity to stream an event for an hour, the model accounted for 23% of total variance, $F(7,191) = 9.40$ and $p < .001$. Physical attractiveness of the streamer and liking the streamer were significant, meaning that if users were driven by hedonic motivations, the more attractive the streamer was and the more they liked the streamer, the more likely they would watch a live stream promotion event.

Frequency	Q1	Q2	Q3	Q4
Never	.5	4	8.5	.5
Once	5	24.6	22.6	6.5
Two to three times over six months	25.6	28.6	24.1	20.6
Four to five times over six months	15.1	11.6	10.1	13.6
About once a month	11.6	12.6	12.1	8.5
Two or three times a month	14.1	10.6	10.1	12.1
About once a week	16.1	5.5	6	14.6
Two or three times a week	8.5	2.5	6.5	15.1
Four or more times a week	3.5	0	0	8.5
Total	100	100	100	100

Percentage %

Note: "In the past six months, how frequently did you (Q1) shop online through a website or shopping app, (Q2) shop online AFTER watching a live stream on a shopping website, (Q3) shop online after watching a live stream that was not part of the shopping website, and (Q4) watch live streams (in general)".

Table 1: Live streaming and online shopping frequency

	Product Scenario	Celebrity Scenario
Streamer related		
Interpersonal attractiveness	.13	.03
Physical attractiveness	.04	.14*
Liking streamer	.06	.29***
Product related		
Usefulness	.27**	.11
Ease of use	.01	.07
Needing product	.03	-.03
Liking product	.17*	.14
Adjusted R^2	.24***	.23***

*$p<.05$, **$p<.01$, ***$p<.001$. Values are standardized beta coefficients

Table 2: Linear regression models explaining intention to use live streaming shopping in the future in two scenarios.

Comparison to Traditional Online Shopping

RQ2 inquired into why individuals would shop on a live streaming shopping site rather than other online shopping sites that don't have live streaming. Two of the authors sat down together and sorted participants' short answers into groups without any prior categories in mind. The categories were then reviewed by all authors and best examples were selected to present in the results. We identified eight reasons: product demos, product information, excitement about novelty of live streaming, interaction, convenience, hype about the product, wanting other opinions, and deals. Some participants reported more than one reason.

Product demonstrations (37%): By far the most popular reason was the ability to see demonstrations of how products worked. Participants could see how the product looked, how it was assembled, or how to properly use the product. P24 (male, 35) said, "I could get a good visual examination of the product and how it is used." In particular, people wanted to see demos of software. "You can't really tell how useful it'll be to you without seeing it in action," said P90 (male, 33).

Product information (27%): The second frequent response participants gave was that they wanted more information about the product they were interested in. They said that the short product descriptions or photos on many shopping sites might not give all the information a person needs when making a purchase or not be timely. For example, P22 (female, 52) said, "Live streaming is up to date and gives me much more information about the product."

Excitement about novelty (26%): Participants also thought the idea of shopping via a live stream was an exciting new idea or found it entertaining. P12 (male, 23) said live streaming shopping was "a fun new way to shop" while P98 said live streaming shopping was "more entertaining" than regular online shopping. The participants wanted a new, engaging way to shop for products. P38 (male, 28) said, "Most of the times when I want to buy something, I rather search for the live streams because it is more fun than just surfing through shopping websites."

Interaction (23%): Interacting with other people was the third reason why participants shopped on a live streaming site. Having the ability to directly communicate with the streamer and other viewers in real time helped facilitate their decision to purchase a product. As P197 (female, 50) put it, "If I want to see someone interact with the product and be able to ask questions, it makes it more immediate than going to a website and sending an email, for example." P147 (female, 23) also made comparisons to other services: "If I don't understand something about the product (especially with tech products) you can ask all the questions you want until you get a satisfying answer (which you rarely have with customer service)." Interacting directly with the product maker was also a reason. P94 (male, 26) said that they would watch live stream shopping "if it was an exclusive product, like one that someone had invented/ manufactured themselves and therefore were the experts."

Participants also appreciated the opportunity for more personal questions. P22 (female, 52) said that they seek live streams when buying food products, so they can question relevant to their dietary restrictions. Finally, participants noted that they can get benefits and supports from other viewers as well. P194 (female, 42) said that having many people in a chat interested in the same product led to unique questions that they may not have thought of.

Convenience (15%): Participants liked being able to view and buy a product they were interested in without having to leave their home. As P54 (female, 49) put it, a live stream "showed me all about the product and how it works from the comfort of my home." P1 (male, 50) said that live streams helped him save time: "For a more expensive product such the iPhone it saves me time when I can't get to the store, but the item is expensive and important, so I need to make a good decision but save time in the process." P151 (female, 25) said purchasing products through a live stream was easier for them because they have kids, so it is hard to get out of the house.

Hype (7%): Only a few participants purchased something on a live stream because of a lot of other people were interested in it, which made them curious. In the case of P116 (male, 28), watching a live stream made them want the product more. For example, someone could be interested in a new video game but is unsure of purchasing it. Watching someone play the game and talking to the chat on a live streaming service like Twitch could push them to purchase the game.

Wanting other opinions (4%): Some participants wanted a review or opinion for the products they were interested in. This was different from objective product information in that participants were specifically seeking opinions. In particular, they sought out reviews from streamers they trusted. P105 (male, 26) said, "It also allows me to get an opinion of the product from a person that I have trusted with other similar products." Participants also wanted reviews from people that do not work for the company selling the product they were looking to buy because they believed that the streamers would be unbiased and knowledgeable. They also wanted to see live streams for opinions when online written reviews were mixed.

Deal or discounts (3%): A few participants said they watched a live stream to get a deal on an item they were interested in. For example, P66 (male, 34) described that popular streamers had partnerships with companies where the company gave streamers a unique discount code to share with their viewers. When a viewer of the stream used the code to purchase an item, a portion of the sale went to the streamer. In this business strategy, the company got more exposure, the streamer got additional money, and viewers saved money and supported the streamer.

DISCUSSION

Our research showed that different intentions were associated with different motivations. Specifically, utilitarian motivations were only associated with utilitarian intention (product scenario), and only hedonic motivations significantly predicted hedonic intention (celebrity scenario) in live streaming shopping domain. This paper might provide some hints for current e-commerce businesses that planned to jump into live streaming shopping in the near future. For example, in the regression model, only physical attractiveness and liking streamer could significantly predict celebrity-related intention, suggesting that e-commerce could catch this type of customer and launch a campaign to promote new products/brands by inviting micro celebrities from other live streaming platforms because this type of customer cared only about their admired celebrities. It could be an economical approach to market and expose products instead of using commercial ads and inviting superstars. The potential disadvantages of this approach might be that it attracted a lot of viewers to watch but the actual purchase might happen at very low rate because intention did not equal to actual behavior. Future research can try to identify and measure the difference between the strength of intention before and after watching live streams, or the strength of intention after watching and the actual purchase. Results also showed that if consumers really needed the product, they would not use live streaming shopping because needing product was non-significant for both intentions. Instead, if they think the info is useful and they also like product, they want to watch it and potentially buy it, indicating that e-commerce business can also target these undecided, info-seeking, wobbly customers and convince them to make a purchase.

We found that most viewers watched live streams on Facebook Live (62.8%) and YouTube Live (46.2%) and shopped on other websites. There was a gap between live streaming platforms and online shopping platforms, suggesting huge business opportunities. E-commerce businesses could partner with and add interfaces to live streaming platforms. This method could import the viewers to be potential customers. Alternatively, if the live streaming platforms wanted to expand their business into e-commerce, they could just open a shopping channel on their platforms. For example, Facebook Live can just add a shopping channel on its streaming site.

We can also think of this in another way. For e-commerce businesses, instead of having partnerships with live streaming platforms, they could directly create their own live streaming channels such as Taobao, JD, and VIP, the top three Chinese e-commerce companies. We also noticed that there was a huge variety among categories and electronics and computers (30.2%) and clothing, shoes, and jewelry (24.1%) were the most popular ones. Hence, if an e-commerce wanted to integrate live stream to expand its business, categorization might need to be considered. For example, if an e-commerce business currently focuses on tech products and wants to expand to beauty category, it might need to partner with live stream platforms that have plenty of beauty content and streamers instead of opening a channel on its current tech website.

In Table 1, if we looked at the frequency of equal and more than once a week, 28% of our participants shopped online through a website or shopping app and 38% watched live streams in general. However, only 8% shopped online *after* watching a live stream on a shopping website and 12.5% shopped online after watching a live stream that was not part of the shopping website. The data also indicated a huge potential market for live streaming shopping.

From the results of content analysis of why people prefer live streaming shopping over regular online shopping, we found many product-related motives such as information seeking and product demonstration, indicating that current e-commerce might incorporate more information-oriented features, especially for some complex and new products such as software products that were mentioned by our participants. Interaction with streamers to get consultation and reliable product reviews is unique for live streaming shopping, suggesting that the potential opportunities for traditional e-commerce businesses.

We had a convenience sample of Mechanical Turkers who all had some experience with live streaming shopping, so this sample is not representative of all online shoppers and is most likely biased toward those who are more tech-savvy. Most of the participants were from the U.S. so our results can only be limited to the boundaries of our sample. However, since live streaming shopping is a mainstream phenomenon in China future research may want to look specifically at the Chinese market. Finally, this study used a survey methodology, which answers "what" but not "why." This was a first attempt at trying to understand live streaming shopping and should be paired with other methodologies in the future.

CONCLUSION

In this study, we used utilitarian and hedonic motivations as a theoretical framework and incorporated the technology acceptance model (TAM) to investigate how these two types of motivations are related to intention to engage in live streaming shopping in the future. Consistently, utilitarian motivations (usefulness) predicted utilitarian intentions while hedonic motivations (physical attractiveness) positively and significantly predicted hedonic intention. We also identified eight motives through qualitative analysis about why people would prefer live streaming shopping over regular online shopping: product demos, product information, excitement about novelty of live streaming, interaction, convenience, hype about the product, wanting other opinions, and deals.

These results are a preliminary investigation into the new phenomenon of shopping with live streams. Our results may give insight into design of both e-commerce and live streaming systems.

REFERENCES

1. Barry J Babin, William R Darden, and Mitch Griffin. 1994. Work and/or Fun: Measuring Hedonic and Utilitarian Shopping Value. *Journal of*

Consumer Research 20, 4: 644. https://doi.org/10.1086/209376

2. Eileen Bridges and Renée Florsheim. 2008. Hedonic and utilitarian shopping goals: The online experience. *Journal of Business Research* 61, 4: 309–314. https://doi.org/10.1016/j.jbusres.2007.06.017
3. Terry L. Childers, Christopher L. Carr, Joann Peck, and Stephen Carson. 2001. Hedonic and utilitarian motivations for online retail shopping behavior. *Journal of Retailing* 77, 4: 511–535. https://doi.org/10.1016/S0022-4359(01)00056-2
4. Fred D. Davis. 1989. Perceived Usefulness, Perceived Ease of Use, and User Acceptance of Information Technology. *MIS Quarterly* 13, 3: 319. https://doi.org/10.2307/249008
5. Fred D. Davis, Richard P. Bagozzi, and Paul R. Warshaw. 1992. Extrinsic and Intrinsic Motivation to Use Computers in the Workplace. *Journal of Applied Social Psychology* 22, 14: 1111–1132. https://doi.org/10.1111/j.1559-1816.1992.tb00945.x
6. Edward L. Deci. 1975. *Intrinsic Motivation.* Springer US, Boston, MA. https://doi.org/10.1007/978-1-4613-4446-9
7. Bukola Olamidun Falode, Adetoun Adedotun Amubode, Mojisola Olanike Adegunwa, and Sunday Roberts Ogunduyile. 2016. Online and Offline Shopping Motivation of Apparel Consumers in Ibadan Metropolis, Nigeria. *International Journal of Marketing Studies* 8, 1. https://doi.org/10.5539/ijms.v8n1p150
8. Mathilde B Friedländer. 2017. JISTaP Streamer Motives and User-Generated Content on Social Live-Streaming Services. *J Inf Sci Theory Pract JISTaP* 55, 11: 65–84. https://doi.org/10.1633/JISTaP.2017.5.1.5
9. Oliver L Haimson and John C Tang. 2017. What Makes Live Events Engaging on Facebook Live, Periscope, and Snapchat. In *Proceedings of the 2017 CHI Conference on Human Factors in Computing Systems - CHI '17*, 48–60. https://doi.org/10.1145/3025453.3025642
10. William A Hamilton, Oliver Garretson, and Andruid Kerne. 2014. Streaming on twitch: fostering participatory communities of play within live mixed media. *Proceedings of the SIGCHI Conference on Human Factors in Computing Systems*: 1315–1324. https://doi.org/10.1145/2556288.2557048
11. Elizabeth C. Hirschman and Morris B. Holbrook. 1982. Hedonic Consumption: Emerging Concepts, Methods and Propositions. *Journal of Marketing* 46, 3: 92. https://doi.org/10.2307/1251707
12. Mehdi Kaytoue, Arlei Silva, and Loïc Cerf. 2012. Watch me playing, i am a professional: a first study on video game live streaming. *Proceedings of the 21st international conference companion on World Wide Web*: 1181–1188. https://doi.org/10.1145/2187980.2188259
13. Christopher S G Khoo. 2014. Issues in Information Behaviour on Social Media. *Proceedings of the ISIC Workshop on Information Behaviour on Social Media* 24, 2: 75–96.
14. Sanghyun Kim and Hyunsun Park. 2013. Effects of various characteristics of social commerce (s-commerce) on consumers' trust and trust performance. *International Journal of Information Management* 33, 2: 318–332. https://doi.org/10.1016/j.ijinfomgt.2012.11.006
15. Y. K. Kim and J. K. Kang. 1997. Consumer perception of shopping costs and its relationship with retail trends. *Journal of Shopping Center Research* 4, 2: 27–62. Retrieved January 28, 2018 from http://173.254.37.135/JSCR/IndArticles/Kim_N297.pdf
16. Matthew K.O. Lee, Christy M.K. Cheung, and Zhaohui Chen. 2005. Acceptance of Internet-based learning medium: The role of extrinsic and intrinsic motivation. *Information and Management* 42, 8: 1095–1104. https://doi.org/10.1016/j.im.2003.10.007
17. Hsi-Peng Lu and Philip Yu-Jen Su. 2009. Factors affecting purchase intention on mobile shopping web sites. *Internet Research* 19, 4: 442–458. https://doi.org/10.1108/10662240910981399
18. James C. McCroskey and Thomas A. McCain. 1974. The measurement of interpersonal attraction. *Speech Monographs* 41, 3: 261–266. https://doi.org/10.1080/03637757409375845
19. Heather Lynn O'Brien. 2010. The influence of hedonic and utilitarian motivations on user engagement: The case of online shopping experiences. *Interacting with Computers* 22, 5: 344–352. https://doi.org/10.1016/j.intcom.2010.04.001
20. Jeffrey W. Overby and Eun Ju Lee. 2006. The effects of utilitarian and hedonic online shopping value on consumer preference and intentions. *Journal of Business Research* 59, 10–11: 1160–1166. https://doi.org/10.1016/j.jbusres.2006.03.008
21. Karine Pires and Gwendal Simon. 2015. YouTube Live and Twitch: A Tour of User-Generated Live Streaming Systems. In *Proceedings of the 6th ACM Multimedia Systems Conference on - MMSys '15*, 225–230. https://doi.org/10.1145/2713168.2713195
22. PR Newswire. 2016. Meili Inc. Publicized its First Overseas Live-streaming Show in Times Square,

New York. *PR Newswire*. Retrieved October 26, 2017 from http://eds.b.ebscohost.com.libdb.njit.edu:8888/ehost/detail/detail?vid=6&sid=c83b1947-0faa-40fc-9d58-0ac21e28e5ac%40pdc-v-sessmgr01&bdata=JnNpdGU9ZWhvc3QtbGl2ZQ%3D%3D#AN=201607140527PR.NEWS.USPR.CN45767&db=bwh

23. PR Newswire. 2016. Livby Launches The First Mobile Live Streaming Shopping App. *PR Newswire*. Retrieved October 26, 2017 from http://eds.b.ebscohost.com.libdb.njit.edu:8888/ehost/detail/detail?vid=18&sid=c83b1947-0faa-40fc-9d58-0ac21e28e5ac%40pdc-v-sessmgr01&bdata=JnNpdGU9ZWhvc3QtbGl2ZQ%3D%3D#AN=201612130900PR.NEWS.USPR.LA67806&db=bwh

24. Stephen Reysen. 2005. Construction of a New Scale: The Reysen Likability Scale. *Social Behavior and Personality: an international journal* 33, 2: 201–208. https://doi.org/10.2224/sbp.2005.33.2.201

25. Katrin Scheibe, Kaja J Fietkiewicz, and Wolfgang G Stock. 2016. Information Behavior on Social Live Streaming Services. *Journal of Information Science Theory and Practice* 4, 2: 6–20. https://doi.org/10.1633/JISTaP.2016.4.2.1

26. Mahdi Shadkam and James O'Hara. 2013. Social commerce dimensions: The potential leverage for marketers. *Journal of Internet Banking and Commerce* 18, 1. https://doi.org/10.1007/978-3-531-92534-9_12

27. Rong An Shang, Yu Chen Chen, and Lysander Shen. 2005. Extrinsic versus intrinsic motivations for consumers to shop on-line. *Information and Management* 42, 3: 401–413. https://doi.org/10.1016/j.im.2004.01.009

28. John F. Sherry, Jr. 1990. A Sociocultural Analysis of a Midwestern American Flea Market. *Journal of Consumer Research* 17, June: 13–30. https://doi.org/10.1086/208533

29. John F. Sherry, Mary Ann McGrath, and Sidney J. Levy. 1993. The dark side of the gift. *Journal of Business Research* 28, 3: 225–244. https://doi.org/10.1016/0148-2963(93)90049-U

30. John C Tang, Gina Venolia, and Kori M Inkpen. 2016. Meerkat and Periscope: I Stream, You Stream, Apps Stream for Live Streams. In *Proceedings of the 2016 CHI Conference on Human Factors in Computing Systems - CHI '16*, 4770–4780. https://doi.org/10.1145/2858036.2858374

31. Eveline Veloso, Virgílio Almeida, Wagner Meira, Azer Bestavros, and Shudong Jin. 2006. A hierarchical characterization of a live streaming media workload. *IEEE/ACM Transactions on Networking* 14, 1: 133–146. https://doi.org/10.1109/TNET.2005.863709

32. Alex Borges Vieira, Ana Paula Couto da Silva, Francisco Henrique, Glauber Goncalves, and Pedro de Carvalho Gomes. 2013. SopCast P2P Live Streaming: Live Session Traces and Analysis. In *Proceedings of the 4th ACM Multimedia Systems Conference on - MMSys '13*, 125–130. https://doi.org/10.1145/2483977.2483993

33. Donghee Yvette Wohn, Guo Freeman, and Caitlin McLaughlin. 2018. Explaining Viewers' Emotional, Instrumental, and Financial Support Provision for Live Streamers. In *Proceedings of the 2018 CHI*. https://doi.org/10.1145/3173574.3174048

A Data-driven Approach to Explore Television Viewing in the Household Environment

Minjoon Kim[1], Jinyoung Kim[2], Sugyo Han[2], Joongseek Lee[2]
Department of Computer Science and Engineering[1]
Department of Transdisciplinary Studies, GSCST[2]
User Experience Lab, Seoul National University, Seoul, South Korea
{minjoon.kim, daisy0, subook2, joonlee8}@snu.ac.kr

ABSTRACT
The rise of small, IoT-related devices and sensors have enabled us to sense and collect data than ever before. In this study, we walk through our attempt of a data-driven approach in collecting behavioral data on television viewing, an activity thought as passive and habitual. We conducted a 14 day experiment with 13 households in the wild using a data logger installed at each house. Television-related data in IR log data and IPTV packets, and contextual data in Bluetooth signal data and brightness data are collected through the data logger. The data is supplemented by the qualitative situational information that participants provided via in-situ chatbot surveys. Our non-intrusive data logger has enabled behavioral data collection in a natural, comprehensive manner. Detailed television viewing behaviors recorded through IR data logs, volume of viewing sessions, and in-situ chatbot responses show how television viewing is heavily context-dependent than previously thought.

CCS Concepts
•**Human-centered computing → Empirical studies in HCI;** *Field studies;*

Author Keywords
Television viewing behavior; social context; experience sample method (ESM); in-situ data collection

INTRODUCTION
The television is now a vastly different device compared to the ones that have come years before. The appliance that defined household pastime cultures like family evening gatherings and TV dinner has vastly improved technologically throughout the years. The size and resolution of the television is now larger than ever, and the addition of computer-like "smart" capabilities has made the television the entertainment hub of the household. Services like YouTube, Netflix, and other Video-on-Demand (VOD) platforms are being integrated into the television, allowing users to access various content when they wish [2].

With these developments, the TV experience can no longer be described with adjectives such as single-screen, passive, and family-oriented. Users are constantly distracted from the television, and also simultaneously engaged on other devices such as laptops, mobile phones and tablets. Such behavioral patterns bring in the need to discover new ways to measure and understand, in detail, what modern families' TV related behaviors are.

Traditional television studies have focused solely on the channels and programs that the users are watching through self-reporting diaries, but this method makes it difficult to anticipate results and also suffers from reliability. Instead, the use of small-sized computers, sensors, and gadgets that have brought upon the Internet-of-Things can be utilized. These devices have made it much easier to sense and collect various sources of data [19], and can prove to be an effective way of detecting events of interest. Devices like the Raspberry Pi can be used to automate data collection, providing a non-intrusive way of collecting data [18]. This way, the burden and fatigue put on users can be minimized while at the same time ensuring natural, in-the-wild collection of data.

In this paper, we present a non-intrusive, in-the-wild data collection method using various sensors which allows us to observe user behaviors and patterns through sensor data. In addition, the use of event-triggered user surveys improve upon previous methods that rely on self reporting. Much like existing works on viewer behavior during television viewing, we investigate how the interactions between family members and the context of the household affect users' behaviors when watching television, and extend it through a data-driven approach.

We start by reviewing previous studies related to television behavior, and methods on how to record user behaviors and activities. Using an implemented data logger, we then collect various behavioral data related to TV watching that includes television remote controller IR (infra-red) logs, IPTV (Internet Protocol Television) packets and program information, bluetooth tracker signal data, and brightness data near the television from a photo-resistor. We also collect in-situ surveys in the form of chatbots in order to investigate the needs and wants

TVX 2018, June 26–28, 2018, Seoul, Republic of Korea.

http://dx.doi.org/10.1145/3210825.3210829

during a TV viewing session. Both quantitative and qualitative data sets are collected and used to present our findings on the television viewing behaviors of 13 households.

RELATED WORK

Television Viewing Studies

Early studies have focused on how the individual watched the television. Ethnographic studies [20] were mainly carried out to study individuals and their viewing habits. These studies have characterized television viewing as either a primary or secondary activity [4, 15]. More recent studies have continued the trend of individual television viewing behaviors [29], pointing out how television viewers' TV-related activities were mainly passive behaviors such as eating or drinking [12].

The rise of the smartphone and other hand-held devices drew interest in how users would use second-screen devices while watching television [15], while simultaneously enabling easier methods to record group viewings and how focused the viewers are watching TV [22]. Vanattenhoven and Geerts [27] have studied how the different composition of family members watching TV determines the programs watched. The authors have also discovered how the time of day, in relation to the actual week and on personal schedules affect their television viewing behaviors through a diary study.

A similar study based on data has been conducted by Chaney et al [7]. The authors presented a large-scale study of television viewing habits between individual and group viewing sessions. While using Nielsen's US household data collected from their electronic People Meter system, this dataset also included supplemental data from paper diaries. While not the same domain, Taylor, et al. attempted to see what kind of implications and insights could be sought from an abundance of behavioral data [25].

Other studies have used cameras and recording devices to analyze user behaviors around the television. Shokrpour and Darnell [23] used cameras in order to record and analyze users' simultaneous tasks performed in front of the television. The authors defined eye gaze elsewhere from the TV as a multitask event, and also set certain time periods for actual recording in light of privacy issues. Rigby et al [17] also used cameras in order to investigate how users interact with their mobile devices while watching television. While both papers argue that video analysis provides deep insight, they also note that this method is also time and labor intensive. The intrusiveness of the cameras and the reliability of the cameras to film properly has also been raised as an issue.

Experience Sampling Methods

The ESM was originally developed in the field of psychology, and widely adapted in diverse fields in both academia and industry [10, 14, 28]. In the HCI field, many researchers have utilized the ESM to build a comprehensive understanding of how and why people interact with technologies under natural conditions [5, 6, 9].

There are three components that define the characteristics of ESM according to previous studies [1, 3, 8]: 1) in-situ data collection of 2) self-reported behaviors and experiences 3) for a long period of time. In-situ data collection can be useful for exploration of contexts associated with human-computer interactions, which can complement data- driven research methods. Researchers have used the ESM for daily gathering of first-person experiences and human needs such as daily mobile use [11, 13] and mobile information needs [24]. Such human-computer interactions tend to occur habitually and they do not make a lasting impression to the users. In these cases, in-situ data collection helps researchers capture mundane yet significant interaction moments and contexts that retrospective recollection might not provide.

The two remaining components of ESM, self-reporting and longitudinal investigation, often create challenges in its implementation and the collection of valid in-situ dataset. Among various concerns raised by researchers, the significant commitment and dedication required to the participants has been regarded as a major challenge that prevents researchers from obtaining useful information [5].

While the event-triggered ESM is not new [16], ubiquitous sensors and enabling platforms have made the implementation of this protocol possible ever before. For instance, Froelich et al. [13] developed an open-source platform (MyExperience) for conducting the event-triggered ESM. This platform uses sensing technologies embedded in the mobile phone and sends out preset questionnaires that depend on the mobile usage contexts.

STUDY DESIGN

Through this study, we want to establish a thorough understanding on how the television is used in households nowadays. Observing behavioral patterns through data provides the most grounded approach, yet in television viewing further contextual information is needed. Previous works have pointed out how television preferences and viewing differ between groups and individuals [7, 27, 4]. In addition to the viewer composition, television can be turned on in the background while individuals are doing some other main activity [21]. We have determined that such situational information can have an effect on the observed data. Thus in designing the experiment, we take a data-driven approach by collecting various types of data related to television viewing, while at the same time obtaining contextual information that aids in understanding the circumstances of the data utilizing a chatbot. We present further details below.

Sensor Data

We have collected four distinct logs of data: 1) television remote controller IR logs, 2) IPTV packets (later matched with pro- gram information), 3) Bluetooth tracker signal data, and 4) brightness data near the television from a photo-resistor. Collecting such data has also given us the opportunity to look at television watching behaviors through detailed data points. Through IPTV packets and in-turn television program data, we wanted to see what each household and its family members were watching at certain times of the day, and days of the week.

By collecting television remote controller logs, we wanted to see exactly how family members were watching television.

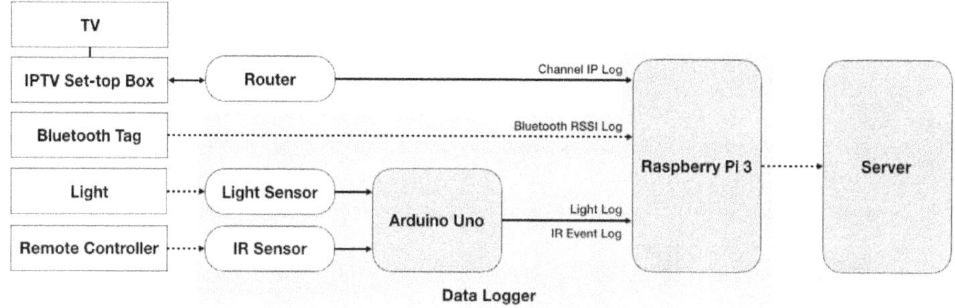

Figure 1. Data logger design

We are interested in the volume levels when a certain program is being watched. We also wanted to know how users settle on a channel after turning the television on. For example, do users mindlessly zap through the channels until they find something interesting? Or do they only turn on the television when they are trying to catch a certain program?

The bluetooth tracker signal data and brightness data near the television were collected in order to collect further context on how people were watching television inside the household. Through the bluetooth tracker signals, we wanted to gauge how active family members were while watching TV. Were they moving around, doing household chores? Or were they simply sitting near the sofa and dedicating their attention to the TV? Brightness data was collected in order to see if users preferred dark or bright lights when watching different television contents such as movies or news.

We have designed an automated data logger as shown in Figure 1 to collect the data logs mentioned above. The implementation of a data logger offers various advantages over previous studies that have relied on human observations and active diary recordings. First, this automated setup has allowed the collection of data with minimal home intrusion. It has been observed that researchers present in experiment setups can affect the behavior of participants, causing uncomfortableness and, more importantly, feigned interactions that may have a big impact on the study [5]. The use of an always-on data logger would be able to mitigate this effect.

Second, the data logger is designed to not burden the participant with active data collection during the duration of the study. Previous methods have required participants to actively record their television viewing behaviors in detail [26, 27]. This method relies much of the data collection on recording the details in the right moment and format, which may require a learning curve and may suffer from inaccurate records. The data from self-recording studies are sometimes ignored for the first few and last days of the experiment due to incompleteness of the data, usually caused by the learning curve of the experiment [5]. In contrast, the use of an automated data logger allows the data collection to be processed in the back without explicit knowledge of the user.

Collected data

The data logger implemented, as shown in Figure 1, utilizes a Raspberry Pi 3[1] module with two sets of Arduino Uno[2] sensors connected to the device. One Arduino board obtains the IR signals of the remote controllers via an infra-red receiver, and produces a time-stamped log with the button's name when a certain button is pressed. The second Arduino board is connected to a photo-resistor, which will record high numbers under bright light, and low numbers under dim light.

Bluetooth data is collected via the transmit signal of a Bluetooth-enabled life-style logging armband called Misfit. Each experiment participant is given a Misfit for the duration of the experiment. Each Misfit armband has its own MAC address that we use to roughly track a person's movement inside their house. The closer the participant is to the data logger, the higher the recorded transmission power will be. For the IPTV packet data, which includes information about which channels are being watched at what time, we link our Raspberry Pi 3 module to the same AP (Access Point) router that the TV set-top box is connected to. The Raspberry Pi 3 is able to track multicast IP packets used for data transfer in IPTV systems[3]. In this study, we were only able to track packets from live television.

The Raspberry Pi 3 module acts as the central computer and data storage unit of the data logger. All four types of log data are timestamped and stored onto the Raspberry Pi 3. At the end of each day, the data logger uploads all obtained data over to a server, which then can be accessed only by the researchers.

Chatbot Surveys

A survey chatbot was implemented with the data logger to collect contextual information related to TV watching. Collecting various data without affecting the experiment participants' behavior is important when collecting data in the wild. A direct observation method would mean some sort of researcher presence would be inevitable, which may affect participant behaviors. Meanwhile, self-reporting methods have issues in data reliability. In order to circumvent these issues, we have incorporated the use of participants' smartphones and a mobile

[1] https://www.raspberrypi.org/products/raspberry-pi-3-model-b/
[2] https://store.arduino.cc/usa/arduino-uno-rev3
[3] https://www.tcpdump.org/

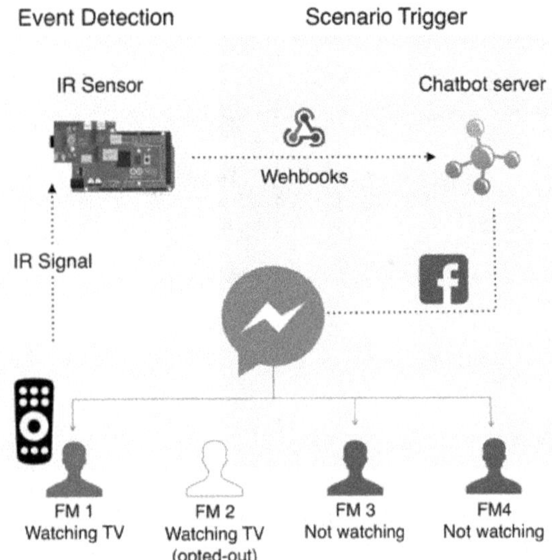

Figure 2. Event detection and chatbot scenario triggering

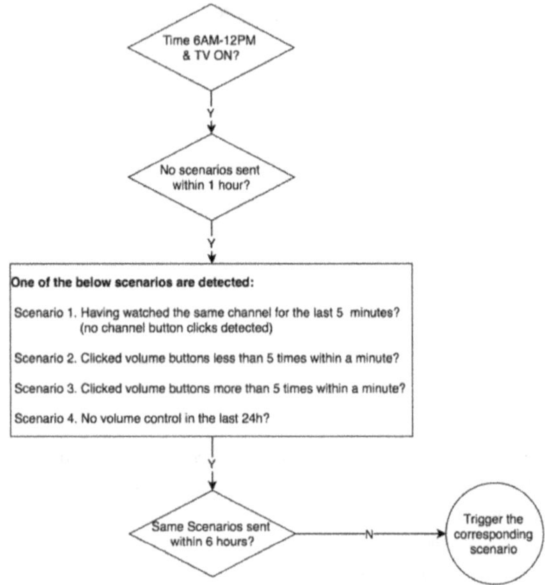

Figure 3. Event-triggered chatbot logic

chatbot, as a previous study has mentioned the prevalent use of smartphones while watching television [15].

As the data logger would collect live data within a household, we have used this stream of data as our method of observation. A python script was implemented and installed on the data logger, and would continuously monitor the remote controller IR record logs coming in. Based on certain events-of-interest, explained later in this section, would act as triggers for the script to determine which kind of chatbot survey scenario would be sent to the family members of the household. This way, we can send survey responses immediately when an event-of-interest is registered (Figure 2).

Design logic

Family members in each household were asked to like the same Facebook page so we could identify their Facebook IDs and register them as the recipients of the messages. The registered family members in each household received the same Facebook messages whenever triggers were activated. Each survey started with a landing question asking "Are you watching TV right now?", which users could reply "Yes" or "No". The survey would not continue if the participant answers "No". This measure was taken to ensure that 1) we could get contextual information of everybody in the household, regardless of what they were doing, and 2) recipients could opt not to partake in the survey if they were not inside the household.

We have set up four event-triggered survey scenarios and two user-triggered survey scenarios to be sent to the event participants. The four event-triggered scenarios include 1) a 'Landing' scenario where the user views a channel or program for more than five minutes, 2) a 'Small Volume Change' scenario in which the user changes the volume levels less than five times in a minute, 3) a 'Large Volume Change' scenario where the user changes the volume levels more than five times in a minute, and lastly 4) a 'No Volume Change' scenario, which was sent to participants at the end of the day if they have watched television without adjusting the volume. Each chatbot scenario is composed of no more than 15 questions per survey, and would ask participants of their audio preferences, who they were watching TV with, concurrent activities done while watching TV, remote controllership, and their general satisfaction of the TV watching experience in both multiple choice and open-ended questions. All four of the events were observable with the IR log data.

There is a possibility that the four events-of-interest may happen frequently, bombarding participants with chatbot survey notifications. This was an important issue to consider, as participant fatigue could factor in the survey responses. In order to mitigate such annoyance and burden of the participants, we added time limits on the chatbot surveys. The same types of triggers were spaced out six hours apart, and no event-triggered survey was issued within an hour of each other (see Figure 3).

In order to find the right balance between collecting more data and participant fatigue, we have included two user-triggered surveys which are sent only when participants would press a certain button on the remote indicating 'satisfied' and 'unsatisfied'. These surveys would ask why the participant felt satisfied or unsatisfied with the current television viewing session. In contrast with the event-triggered surveys, we did not put a number limit on user-triggered surveys so that this could serve as an option to obtain contextual information about the television viewing session when the event-triggered chatbots are on rest.

Experiment Setup

Recruiting

We conducted the study to understand the TV watching contexts and interactions that people engage in during TV watch-

Figure 4. Research team installing the data logger at a participant household. The red box indicates the location of the data logger.

ing. Because the main study was designed for a two-week-long data collection period, we needed to devise a couple requirements to ensure "good" data collection.

First, households eligible for the study had to be subscribed to an IPTV provider and use an IR-based remote controller. Without an IPTV provider, it was impossible to obtain logs which channels the family was watching. The same goes with an IR-based controller. The controller had to be IR-based in order for successful data collection. Second, households had to watch more than 4.5 hours of television per day on average in order to be eligible for the study. The average viewing times for Korean households was 191 minutes in 2015, a statistic reported by the Korea Communications Commission[4], which would make 4.5 hours a safe cut for a fair amount of data to be collected for a two-week participation period.

After recruiting, 16 initial households were selected from and near Seoul, South Korea for the study. A total of 30 individuals from 13 households[5] participated in the study. We have selected families of diverse household types in order to observe the varying social contexts within a household. The 13 households consist of one single member household, five one-generational households, and seven two-generational households. The largest family had five members, consisting of two parents and their three teenage children. The age of participants ranged from 16 to 59 years old.

Each household would participate in the experiment for 14 days. In cases of family vacations and other unforeseen circumstances (e.g., power outages) that resulted in missing data, the participants were asked to continue the experiment until 14 days worth of data were collected. During the two weeks of experimentation, participants were asked to answer Facebook Messenger chatbot surveys when prompted. Participants were given a copy of the signed IRB document, and were compensated $250 for their participation when the two weeks was over.

[4]http://news.joins.com/article/19894246

[5]Three households withdrew from the study during the experiment.

Preparing for experiment participation

At the start of the experiment, two members from the research team would visit the household to conduct the pre-experiment interviews and install the data logger. The two researchers would survey the house for the idea location of the data logger. The data logger must be 1) connected to the IPTV set-top box for packet recording, 2) at a location where the light sensor would not be affected by the television, and at the same time, 3) at a location where the IR sensor would be able to register remote controller button presses without registering noise from other sources like fluorescent lights (Figure 4).

The researchers would then educate the participants on how to answer chatbot surveys through their smartphones. A majority of participants did not want to use their own Facebook ID for the experiment, so we provided test accounts to be used. While it did not take much time for the participants to understand how to reply to the chatbot survey through their phones, some older participants needed getting used to Facebook Messenger, which is a relatively less popular messenger platform in Korea.

Lastly, participants had to wear the Misfit bluetooth fitness tracker for the experiment. This particular device was chosen due to its long battery life, thus participants did not have to recharge the device during the experiment duration[6]. As mentioned before, the bluetooth signals were measured to see where the participants were sitting to watch television and to roughly track their movement in the house. Some participants did not want to wear the fitness tracker, and while most of them reluctantly accepted to wear it, there were 7 participants who opted out of the study because of it. When all preparations were taken care of, the pre-experiment interview was conducted. Researchers also recorded the TV volume and IPTV volume (IPTV systems have its own volume system on top of the actual television volume) as a part of the interview to make tracking volume levels possible. The researchers would come back after the experiment was done to collect the data logger and conduct the final interview.

RESULTS

TV Viewing – by the numbers

Over the course of 14 days from 13 participant households, the average time spent watching television was 538 minutes per day. Within these numbers, the experiment participants turned the TV on 2.1 times on average per day during the experiment. Each time they turned on the television, it remained on with an average of 258 minutes. Participants recorded an average of 7.9 channels viewed each day, while staying on a single channel for 45.6 minutes on average. This number is equivalent to watching 1.3 TV programs on a single channel. We defined watching a single program or channel for more than five minutes as a 'landing' session. A total of 2,027 'landing' sessions were recorded from 13 participant households. The three most-watched genres were Entertainment (640 sessions), News (401 sessions), and Society and Culture (309 sessions). The three most-watched genres in terms of viewing minutes were Entertainment (22,580 minutes), News (13,071 minutes), and Drama (9,975 minutes).

[6]https://misfit.com/products/misfit-shine?color=grey

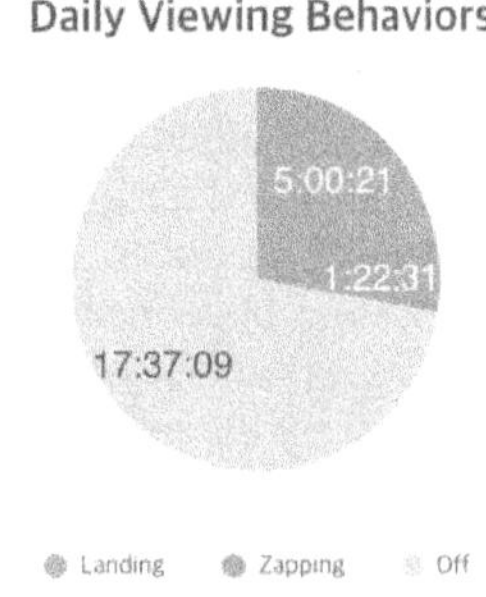

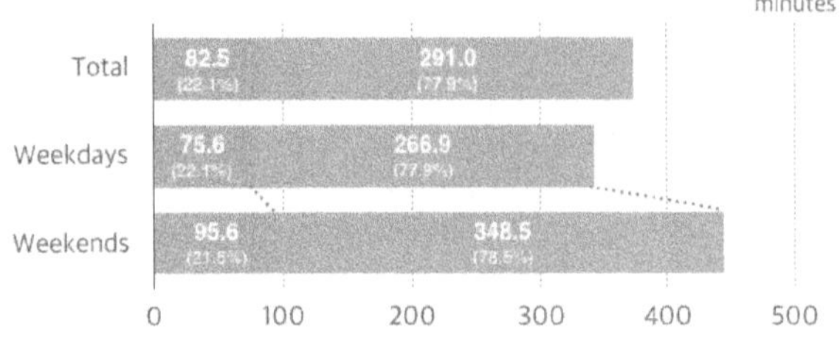

Figure 5. Zapping vs. Landing sessions

TV Viewing – Zapping vs. Landing

As mentioned before, we defined watching a single program or channel for more than five minutes as a 'landing' session. As the opposite, we consider any viewing session less than five minutes as a 'zapping' session. The five-minute mark is adopted by Korea's national broadcasting station, KBS[7] in television related surveys. By comparing these two types of viewing sessions, we wanted to see if television viewing goal-driven (e.g. turning on the TV to watch the Super Bowl), or spontaneous (e.g. habitually turning on the television after coming back from work).

By analyzing the packet data and remote controller IR logs, we can see the ratios between landing and zapping sessions (Figure 5). It is interesting to see how users rapidly zap through channels for almost a quarter of the time. This behavior seems to be consistent, as observed by the negligible difference between the weekend and weekdays.

Remote Controller Events

The 13 participant households have recorded a total of 45,296 remote controller IR logs during the duration of the experiment. 49.5% of the IR logs have turned out to be channel related. Channel related buttons include the channel up and down buttons and the num-pad numbers (0 – 9) on the remote controller. Separating the values, the channel up and down buttons registered 18,524 logs, roughly about 4.5 times the amount of the num-pad buttons (4,006 hits). The next frequent button category was 'Other' with 36.7% of the IR logs, but we suspect this abnormal high number is due to the existence of Electronic Program Guides (EPGs). Controlling EPGs must be done through the arrow keys on the remote controller, and

[7]https://survey.kbs.co.kr/survey/index/end

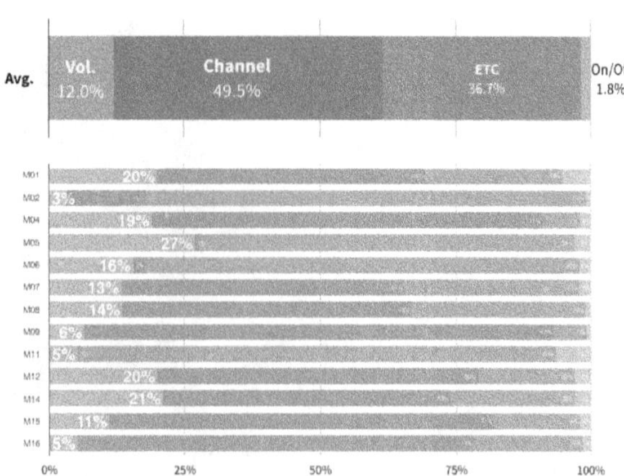

Figure 6. Ratios of remote controller button types. Each household displays distinct button pressing behaviors

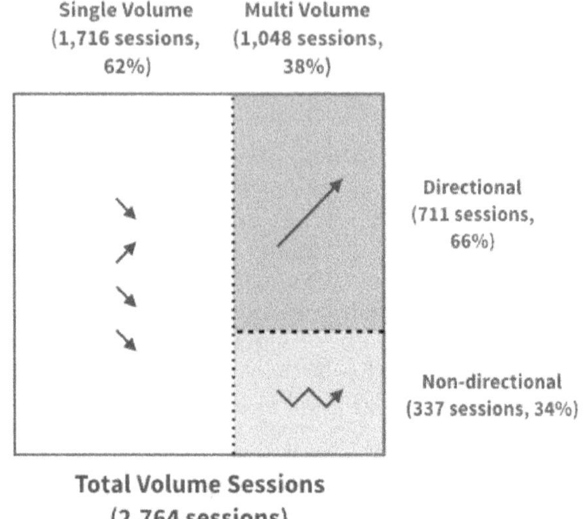

Figure 7. Details on how volume buttons are pressed. Viewers have more single volume sessions compared to multi volume sessions.

because we were not able to determine which arrow-and-enter-key combination was used for channel switching, this may have skewed the numbers towards the Other category.

Across 13 households, volume logs have been recorded a total of 5,475 times for 12.0% of the total remote controller logs, an unexpectedly high number of hits. While the percentages vary vastly by each household, with the lowest volume button percentage being as low as 5% and the highest recording 27%. (Figure 6), it is the way how people change the volume that caught our attention. To our knowledge, we have not found how volume data, or volume change has been generally recorded in previous television behavior studies.

By grouping the 5,475 volume logs into one-minute sessions have resulted in 2,764 separate volume sessions. By taking a look at these sessions, we have observed that 62.1% of the sessions (1,716 sessions) were single volume presses, while 37.9% (1,048 sessions) were consisted of multiple volume

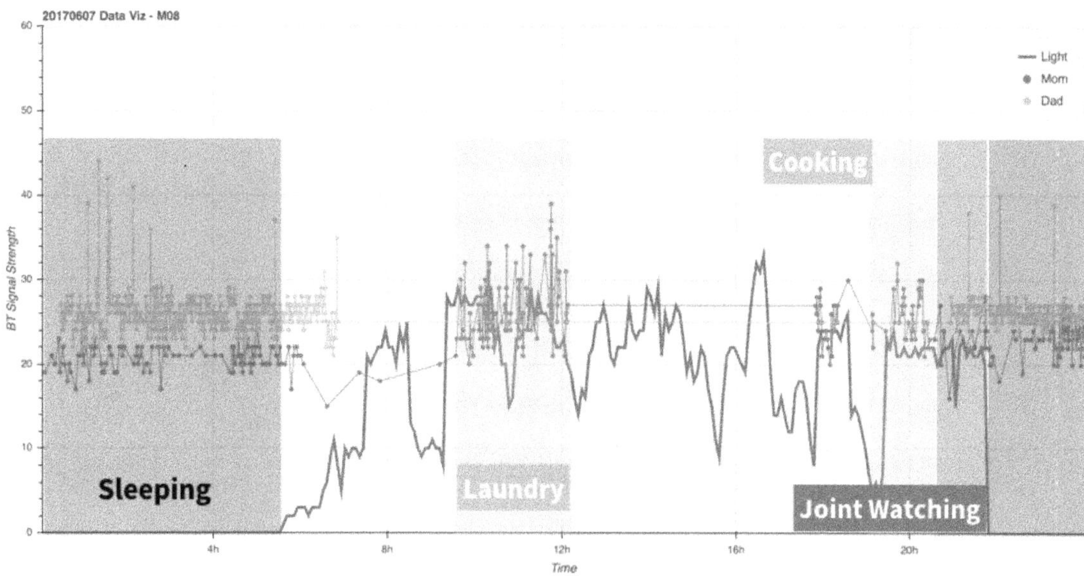

Figure 8. Bluetooth signal and brightness visualization of Jun. 6th, 2017 for Household M08. Brightness data show how the family woke up around 7:30 am and went to sleep near 10:00 pm. Bluetooth data shows how active the participants were. Labels are added from chatbot responses.

presses. Within these multiple presses, 67.8% (711 sessions) have been shown to be directional (Figure 7). Also, the distribution of volume buttons in the IR logs have shown that after an initial volume change, viewers tend to re-adjust the volume within a three minute window 46.0% (1,271 sessions) of the time.

Bluetooth and Brightness Data

As mentioned in the previous section, data on Bluetooth signal strength and brightness of the living room were collected as a means to see further contextual information regarding television viewing. Both data sets have given us a big picture on user behaviors (Figure 8). The brightness data can indicate the general lifestyle patterns of each household. By looking at time periods of high values (when lights were turned on) over the course of two weeks, we were able to recognize when a certain household would go to sleep, or wake up.

Bluetooth power signals helped in mapping whether a participant was inside the house, or how active the participant was while watching television. The bluetooth signal values also indicated certain zones where television viewing would mainly take place. This band could be interpreted as the area in front of the television such as the sofa where television viewing is most likey to happen. While this study was first piloted by Seo, et al. [22], to our knowledge this is the first attempt in deploying this system in a comprehensive, in-the-wild experiment. The bluetooth data coupled with chatbot survey responses have allowed for detailed analysis, which will be explained in the following section.

FINDINGS

Group vs. Individual Viewing Patterns

Genres in group viewing

In line with previous studies on group versus individual viewing patterns, we have identified individual and group viewing sessions from our data set to see how different combinations of users affect the kinds of television programs watched. For individual viewing sessions, we characterize each user as either an adult or child, and male or female. Group viewing sessions are categorized by age (all adults/only children/family viewing). From the total amount of sessions, we have identified 356 sessions where user compositions are clearly known.

Results show, in line with previous works, that individual and group viewing behaviors are different. Fathers of the households generally watched more Entertainment (36.4%), Society and Culture (19.7%), and Sports (15.2%) genres the most, while mothers have watched more Entertainment (30.5%) and News (25.7%). Interestingly, mothers recorded more than twice the number of viewing sessions than the fathers of the household. This may be a cultural and generational issue, as in Korea men tend to be at their work while the women take care of the household. This can also show why News viewing of women is higher than the men. Similarly, as the children must be at school for a majority of the day, individual viewing events were almost non-existent. For children, there were only seven sessions identified for it to be further divided into gender, and not much can be read from the data.

In group viewing settings, we have identified 72 sessions through chatbot responses and bluetooth data where the mother and father would watch television together as a couple, and 43 sessions where the entire family would watch together. All numbers appear to be similar minus the News genre, which increased dramatically in family viewing settings. This may be attributed to the fact that family viewing sessions usually happened later in the evening. Or simply, the news can be a relatively easier content to consume for all age groups, with families defaulting to this genre when there is nothing else to watch on the television. While there may be some cultural elements that affect the general viewing tendencies, overall

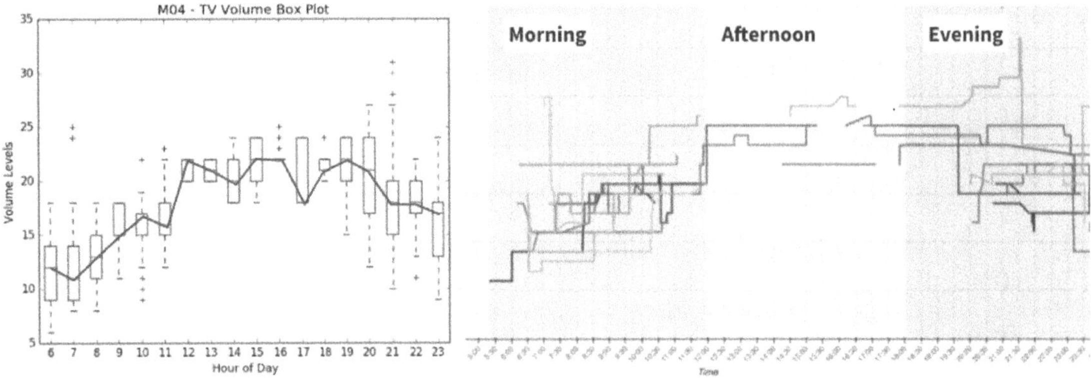

Figure 9. Volume level graph (right) of all landing sessions of household M04. Notice the differing volume levels depending on the time of day. A box-and-whiskers plot on the left shows the most frequent volume levels of each hour. A curve running through the median values show a curve.

our findings match with previous studies[7, 27] in that family member composition affects contents watched.

Volume change in group viewing

As a pair with genres, we have further investigated on how user composition affects volume change. From the same group of sessions, we have identified 46 adjacent session pairs (within 2 hours of each other, 87 total sessions) in which viewer composition has changed. When group composition has changed, 31 pairs out of 46 recorded volume changes. The average volume change was 4.12 for TV volumes, and 5.00 for IPTV volumes[8]. The changes of group composition can be classified as group-to-individual, individual-to-group, and group-to-group, with the last being two group viewing sessions comprised of different groups of individuals.

In order to confirm that volume changes were affected by viewer composition and not the program genre, a social factor within the household, we have analyzed each household's volume change versus the television genre watched. We calculated the conditional probability (as below) of volume change when the viewing genre has changed, attempting to find if genre had an impact on volume changes.

$P = (A|B)$, where A is the volume change and B is 'when the genre has changed'.

Results my be seen in Table 1. While the results for each household is different, the overall consensus leads to the change of genre having no strong relation with volume change.

Household	*Volume Change Probability*
M01	0.602564103
M02	0.697674419
M04	0.348484848
M05	0.705882353
M06	0.534883721
M07	0.487179487
M08	0.401869159
M09	0.636363636
M11	0.666666667
M12	0.25974026
M14	0.515384615
M15	0.622047244
M16	0.822580645

Table 1. Volume chage probability for each household when the genre of the viewing session has changed

Dedicated vs. Background Viewing

Chatbots indicated that virtually half (48.9%, 150 out of 307 responses) of television viewing is done in the background. Background viewing describes the act of having the television on while doing some other main task. These tasks could be categorized into 'stationary' tasks (56.7%, 85 out of 150 responses) that included eating, smartphone usage, and folding laundry, and 'mobile' tasks (34.7%, 52 out of 150 responses) such as cooking, cleaning, getting ready for work. Similarly, from a total of 304 chatbot responses that indicated group viewing, experiment participants recorded 45% group viewing sessions (137 out of 304 responses) compared to 46% individual viewing.

The bluetooth data could be used to confirm the chatbot responses. Visualizing the bluetooth signal data and measuring how much fluctuation occurs during a timeframe can give us information whether the participant is moving while watching television or is staying relatively stationary. As shown in Figure 8, we can see the signal difference between sitting down and watching versus moving around and having the television on in the background.

Social Context Affecting TV Volume

External surroundings affecting television viewing

An interesting revelation from the chatbot surveys was that participants seemed to be mindful of their television volume levels, and noise in the house in general for the fear of disturbing neighbors. Participants have stated that they pay attention to their volume levels because they "live in an apartment, and

[8]IPTV sets have their own volume. We tracked both volume sets, focusing on whichever one a household would use as the main volume

sometimes [we] can hear noises from other households. [I] wouldn't want cause trouble" (M14). Participant M05 mentioned how he was "aware of the sound levels" despite living alone. "I think I may lower it too much, but I know that my neighbor is sensitive and I want to be safe".

We wanted to see how the data actually supported the findings from chatbot survey responses. We have visualized the volume levels of a household in Figure 9. Each color band represents a TV viewing session, defined by TV on and off events. In a household, it could be seen that the volume level of the television rises and falls depending on the time of the day. Television viewing is usually concentrated in the morning and evening, compared to the afternoon. This can be attributed to the fact that people are out and working during the day, which leaves the house empty or with only one person, usually the wife, at home. This relative freedom also allows the volume to reach higher levels in the afternoon.

Both the volume log data and chatbot responses indicate how societal norms and daily patterns have an impact on how people watch the television, which can be visible in volume levels. By mapping the most used volume level during television viewing hours, we can see how the volumes of a household rises and falls. Household M04 (Figure 9, left) observed the most "typical" curve. Other households have also registered different volume patterns while following the general rule. While in some it was difficult to discern a pattern, these households have watched the television for a lesser amount of time compared to household M04.

Domestic situations affecting television viewing

Out of all chatbot survey responses, 279 were related to specific volume changes during a TV viewing session. A majority of the responses (35.8%, 100 out of 279) recorded that these volume changes were due to social situations within and around the house. Looking into the social dynamics that have directly affected volume change, the biggest reasons were 'Family Interactions' (29 responses), followed by 'Noises from Inside the House' (23 responses), and lastly 'Noises from Outside the House' (13 responses), as seen on Figure 9. Volume change from social interactions was double the amount of answers compared to volume change from 'internal' TV factors (17.9%, 50 out of 279), which can be categorized as sounds relevant to the current TV program. This includes the quality of the sound mix, the clarity of the voices, and the background music that sets the mood of a scene.

From the 29 responses that said the volume change was due to family and social interactions, one participant noted that "The house is really busy right now so I had to turn up the volume just to hear the television" (M07), and another mentioned that "The baby is asleep right now so I need to turn the volume down. I don't like it when I have to listen to the TV with basically no sound but it is better than the baby waking up" (M12).

Noises from inside the house was the next highest number of responses. Here, participants pointed towards the sounds of cooking, family members taking a shower, doing the laundry and using the vacuum cleaner as the main reasons why. One

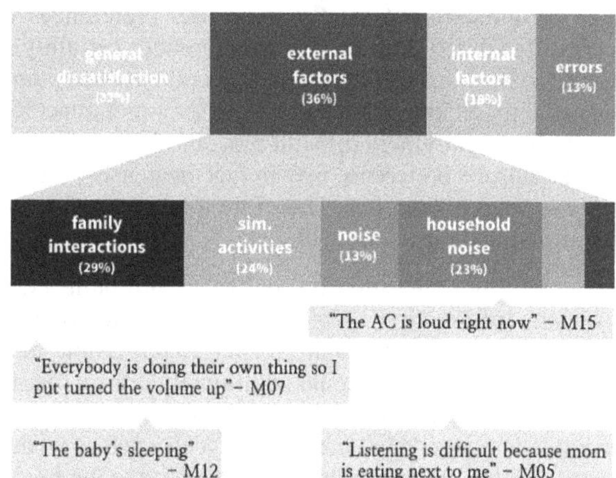

Figure 10. The social situations inside the house are cited as reasons for volume change.

participant noted that: "I really want the television to turn itself up when there's water noise coming from inside the house." (M05). Another pointed out how "the television is too loud but my wife wants to hear the television while cooking" (M03).

When other household activities were taking place simultaneously in the house, it was clear that the other activities had a higher priority than television viewing. Participant M08 mentioned how "my son is studying right now, so I can't have the television volume as high as I want it to." Being mindful of other family members' activities such as sleeping or cooking was a key factor especially in the volume levels.

Other notable responses informed of specific volume preferences between the family members. One participant has noted that "I like to turn up the volume, but my mom likes it quieter. When I turn on the TV and the volume is set lower then I know that mom has been watching the television before me" (M08). Another has mentioned that "When turning off the TV late at night, I always lower the volume. I don't like being surprised with loud noises when I turn on the television early in the morning and I also don't want to wake anybody up" (M04). These types of responses show that participants have their own set of volumes that they like to listen to, and further validate the findings of the previous section.

DISCUSSION

We have shown the possibility on how a data-driven approach coupled with in-situ qualitative data can provide much deeper insights surrounding device usage behaviors. By looking into both the quantitative and qualitative data, we have discovered how domestic social elements such as family interactions and activities inside the house further complicate device usage.

Studies on device usage tend to focus on how to line up user preferences with a particular setting or utility. On a personal device like a phone, this may be the right direction to go by. On the contrary, shared devices like the television contain multiple user preferences; and while it may be easier to differentiate who is using the device, our study has shown that usage patterns are not merely about user preferences when it comes to shared devices. User preferences certainly exist, but due to the various environmental contexts users operate the device in, picking out a particular user's preference would seem to be an extremely difficult task. Furthermore, what we know as a user's preference may in fact mean user preferences *within a certain situation*. Therefore it is essential to define such situations, especially with data.

At the baseline, our study has collected and built a dataset of various information. While we have tried to collect various data from sources that are related to television viewing, through our analysis we could additionally draw a rough outline on the general daily activities of each household. We were able to gauge "big" household events such as what time a family wakes up, when does the father leave the house for work, and what time does everybody goes to sleep. While we were not aiming to look for this kind of information through the data, we were able to see more than expected.

This can be approached into two different ways. By collecting more data, we can precisely know the surrounding situations when the television is on and being watched. For example, scenarios like the television automatically adjusting the volume depending on how many people are in the house, exactly who is watching, and what is that person doing while watching, may be possible. This can also be expanded to other household devices. If a device can collect various data regarding the user and its surroundings, knowing when to activate a certain setting, knowing when to automatically adjust itself can enhance the product to fit the user even more.

On the other hand, one can look at the privacy issues when collecting data from a shared device. Data from personal devices can be used to show a single user's behavior patterns, but in the case of a shared device like the television, much more information can be extracted, as our study, albeit briefly, has shown. We believe the general location of the television, and how the shared nature of the television and its social significance in a household may contribute to showing unwanted data patterns of a house. Similarly, data collected from other shared household devices may show a bigger picture than it appears.

LIMITATIONS

There are some limitations to our study. First of all, the timeframe of the study is somewhat short. An argument can be made that the two-week duration of the study may not be representative of the "general" television viewing behaviors of a household. Unplanned schedules and the turn of events (in news, for example) in societal issues may have contributed to viewing patterns that are not representative of a particular participant. While we have tried to mitigate this by screening participants with a television viewing average of 4.5 hours per day, this may have caused other complications in the data as well.

Another limitation of the study is the general attrition of participants. While our study was aimed to be non-intrusive by nature, the collecting of the data itself was somewhat of a hurdle with the participants. Especially when dealing with the bluetooth fitness tracker, this issue became more apparent. While other data logs such as IPTV packets and remote controller IR logs were easily collected with continuity, the bluetooth signal data was the most unreliable out of the four data logs. Participants let us know how it was cumbersome to put on the fitness tracker, and towards the end of the experiments, some participants did not wear the armband. Also, as mentioned briefly before, the data collected from the armbands had a lot of noise, and it took meticulous cleaning to see where inside the house were the users watching television.

Finally, the chatbot utilized for in-situ event triggered surveys also gave us food for thought in this study. While a decline in response percentage was not observed, many users pointed out that they knew what kind of questions the chatbot would ask within the first week of the study. The participants mentioned how they got somewhat "bored" of the questions, despite our efforts on diversifying chatbot questions and responses. The design implications and agent-ness of the chatbot should be further investigated when it is used as an ESM tool.

CONCLUSION

We believe this study has shown an effective method to track user behavior. We have implemented and deployed a data logger capable of collecting various behavioral and contextual data in a non-intrusive way, allowing for data to be logged in a natural setting. By adding a few sensors, we were able to see, with data, how households watch and interact with the television.

Our findings show that television viewing behaviors in the household have a tendency to be either focused and dedicated, or in the background or distracted. Qualitative and quantitative data both have shown how users interact with the TV in a domestic environment. Television viewing itself appears to be a very social and context dependent activity as well. With data, we were able to observe previously hidden details in television viewing behaviors, especially about details of the remote controller data and volume changing behaviors. We have also shown how contextual and environmental surroundings have a bigger-than-expected effect on television viewing behaviors.

ACKNOWLEDGMENTS

This research was conducted in joint with Samsung Electronics. The authors would like to thank all experiment participants for diligently taking part in the experiment. Also, we would like to extend our thanks to our lab interns.

REFERENCES

1. Lynda Andrews, Rebekah Russell Bennett, and Judy Drennan. 2011. Capturing affective experiences using the SMS Experience Sampling (SMS-ES) method. *International Journal of Market Research* 53, 4 (2011), 479. DOI:http://dx.doi.org/10.2501/IJMR-53-4-479-506

2. Bastiaan Baccarne, Tom Evens, and Dimitri Schuurman. 2013. The Television Struggle: an Assessment of Over-the-Top Television Evolutions in a Cable Dominant Market. *Communications & strategies* 92, 4 (2013), 43–61. http://bit.ly/1QFLX9g

3. Lisa Feldman Barrett and Daniel J Barrett. 2001. 10-Experience Sampling in Psychology. *Social Science* 19, 2 (2001), 175–185. DOI: http://dx.doi.org/10.1177/089443930101900204

4. Regina Bernhaupt, Marianna Obrist, Astrid Weiss, Elke Beck, and Manfred Tscheligi. 2008. Trends in the Living Room and Beyond : Results from Ethnographic Studies Using Creative and Playful Probing. *ACM Computers in Entertainment* 6, 1 (2008), 1–23. DOI: http://dx.doi.org/10.1145/1350843.1350848

5. Scott Carter and Jennifer Mankoff. 2005. When Participants Do the Capturing : The Role of Media in Diary Studies. *Human-Computer Interaction* 05 (2005), 899. DOI:http://dx.doi.org/10.1145/1054972.1055098

6. Scott Carter, Jennifer Mankoff, and Jeffrey Heer. 2007. Momento: Support for Situated Ubicomp Experimentation. *Proceedings of the SIGCHI conference on Human factors in computing systems - CHI '07* (2007), 125–134. DOI: http://dx.doi.org/10.1145/1240624.1240644

7. Allison J B Chaney, Mike Gartrell, Jake M Hofman, John Guiver, Noam Koenigstein, Pushmeet Kohli, and Ulrich Paquet. 2014. A Large-scale Exploration of Group Viewing Patterns. *Proceedings of the 2014 ACM International Conference on Interactive Experiences for TV and Online Video* (2014), 31–38. DOI: http://dx.doi.org/10.1145/2602299.2602309

8. Cynthia Christensen. Tamlin Conner; Barrett, Lisa Feldman; Bliss-Moreau, Eliza; Lebo, Kirsten; Kaschub. 2003. A Practical Guide to Experience-Sampling Procedures. *Journal of Happiness Studies* 4, 1 (2003), 53–78. DOI:http://dx.doi.org/10.1023/A:1023609306024

9. Sunny Consolvo, Ian E Smith, Tara Matthews, Anthony LaMarca, Jason Tabert, and Pauline Powledge. 2005. Location Disclosure to Social Relations: Why, When, & What People Want to Share. *CHI 2005 Conference on Human Factors in Computing Systems* (2005), 81–90. DOI:http://dx.doi.org/10.1145/1054972.1054985

10. Bob Evans. 2016. Paco-Applying Computational Methods to Scale Qualitative Methods. *Ethnographic Praxis in Industry Conference Proceedings* 2016, 1 (2016), 348–368. DOI: http://dx.doi.org/10.1111/1559-8918.2016.01095

11. Denzil Ferreira, Jorge Goncalves, Vassilis Kostakos, Louise Barkhuus, and Anind K. Dey. 2014. Contextual experience sampling of mobile application micro-usage. *Proceedings of the 16th international conference on Human-computer interaction with mobile devices & services - MobileHCI '14* (2014), 91–100. DOI: http://dx.doi.org/10.1145/2628363.2628367

12. Ulla G Foehr. 2006. Media multitasking among American youth: Prevalence, predictors, and pairings. *The Henry J. Kaiser Family Foundation* December (2006), 1–39. DOI: http://dx.doi.org/10.1111/j.1460-2466.2012.01641.x

13. Jon Froehlich, Mike Y Chen, Sunny Consolvo, Beverly Harrison, and James a. Landay. 2007. MyExperience: a system for in situ tracing and capturing of user feedback on mobile phones. *Proceedings of the 5th international conference on Mobile systems, applications and services* San Juan, (2007), 57–70. DOI: http://dx.doi.org/10.1145/1247660.1247670

14. Wilhelm Hofmann and Paresh V. Patel. 2015. SurveySignal: A Convenient Solution for Experience Sampling Research Using Participants' Own Smartphones. *Social Science Computer Review* 33, 2 (2015), 235–253. DOI: http://dx.doi.org/10.1177/0894439314525117

15. Yoori Hwang, Hyoungjee Kim, and Se Hoon Jeong. 2014. Why do media users multitask?: Motives for general, medium-specific, and content-specific types of multitasking. *Computers in Human Behavior* 36 (2014), 542–548. DOI: http://dx.doi.org/10.1016/j.chb.2014.04.040

16. Stephen S Intille, Emmanuel Munguia Tapia, John Rondoni, Jennifer Beaudin, Chuck Kukla, Sitij Agarwal, Ling Bao, and Kent Larson. 2003. Tools for Studying Behavior and Technology in Natural Settings. In *UbiComp 2003: Ubiquitous Computing*, Anind K Dey, Albrecht Schmidt, and Joseph F McCarthy (Eds.). Springer Berlin Heidelberg, Berlin, Heidelberg, 157–174.

17. Jacob M. Rigby Duncan P. Brumby Sandy J.J. Gould Anna L. Cox. 2017. Media Multitasking at Home: A Video Observation Study of Concurrent TV and Mobile Device Usage. *Proceedings of the 2017 ACM International Conference on Interactive Experiences for TV and Online Video (TVX '17)* (2017), 3–10. DOI: http://dx.doi.org/10.1145/3077548.3077560

18. Gierad Laput, Yang Zhang, and Chris Harrison. 2017. Synthetic Sensors. *Proceedings of the 2017 CHI Conference on Human Factors in Computing Systems - CHI '17* (2017), 3986–3999. DOI: http://dx.doi.org/10.1145/3025453.3025773

19. Mirjana Maksimović, Vladimir Vujović, Nikola Davidović, Vladimir Milošević, and Branko Perišić. 2014. Raspberry Pi as Internet of Things hardware : Performances and Constraints. *Design Issues* 3, JUNE (2014), 8.

20. Jon O'Brien, Tom Rodden, Mark Rouncefield, and John Hughes. 1999. At Home with the Technology : An Ethnographic Study of a Set-Top-Box Trial. *ACM Transactions on Computer-Human Interaction* 6, 3 (1999), 282–308. DOI: http://dx.doi.org/10.1145/329693.329698

21. Kelly L. Schmitt, Kimberly Duyck Woolf, and Daniel R. Anderson. 2003. Viewing the viewers: Viewing behaviors by children and adults during television programs and commercials. *Journal of Communication* 53, 2 (2003), 265–281. DOI:http://dx.doi.org/10.1093/joc/53.2.265

22. Jehwan Seo, Hyunchul Lim, Changhoon Oh, Hyun-Kyu Yun, Bongwon Suh, and Joongseek Lee. 2016. A System Designed to Collect Users' TV-Watching Data Using a Smart TV, Smartphones, and Smart Watches. *Proceedings of the ACM International Conference on Interactive Experiences for TV and Online Video - TVX '16* (2016), 147–153. DOI: http://dx.doi.org/10.1145/2932206.2933562

23. Auriana Shokrpour and Michael J. Darnell. 2017. How People Multitask While Watching TV. *Proceedings of the 2017 ACM International Conference on Interactive Experiences for TV and Online Video - TVX '17* (2017), 11–19. DOI:http://dx.doi.org/10.1145/3077548.3077558

24. Timothy Sohn, Kevin a. Li, William G. Griswold, and James D. Hollan. 2008. A diary study of mobile information needs. *Proceeding of the twentysixth annual CHI conference on Human factors in computing systems CHI 08* (2008), 1–10. DOI: http://dx.doi.org/10.1145/1357054.1357125

25. a. S. Taylor, S. Lindley, T. Regan, and D. Sweeney. 2014. Data and life on the street. *Big Data & Society* 1, 2 (2014), 1–7. DOI: http://dx.doi.org/10.1177/2053951714539278

26. Jeroen Vanattenhoven and David Geerts. 2015a. Broadcast, Video-on-Demand, and Other Ways to Watch Television Content: A Household Perspective. *Proceedings of the ACM International Conference on Interactive Experiences for TV and Online Video* (2015), 73–82. DOI:http://dx.doi.org/10.1145/2745197.2745208

27. Jeroen Vanattenhoven and David Geerts. 2015b. Contextual aspects of typical viewing situations: a new perspective for recommending television and video content. *Personal and Ubiquitous Computing* 19, 5-6 (2015), 761–779. DOI: http://dx.doi.org/10.1007/s00779-015-0861-0

28. Alladi Venkatesh. 1996. Computers and Other Interactive Technologies for the Home. *Commun. ACM* 39, 12 (1996), 47–54. DOI: http://dx.doi.org/10.1145/240483.240491

29. Anke Wonneberger, Klaus Schoenbach, and Lex van Meurs. 2009. Dynamics of Individual Television Viewing Behavior: Models, Empirical Evidence, and a Research Program. *Communication Studies* 60, 3 (2009), 235–252. DOI:http://dx.doi.org/10.1080/10510970902955992

Explicating the Challenges of Providing Novel Media Experiences Driven by User Personal Data

Neelima Sailaja, Andy Crabtree, Derek McAuley
University of Nottingham
Nottingham, UK.
first.last@nottingham.ac.uk

Phil Stenton
BBC R&D
Salford, UK.
phil.stenton@bbc.co.uk

ABSTRACT
The turn towards personal data to drive novel media experiences has resulted in a shift in the priorities and challenges associated with media creation and dissemination. This paper takes up the challenge of explicating this novel and dynamic scenario through an interview study of employees delivering diverse personal data driven media services within a large U.K. based media organisation. The results identify a need for better interactions in the user-data-service ecosystem where trust and value are prioritised and balanced. Being legally compliant and going beyond just the mandatory to further ensure social accountability and ethical responsibility as an organisation are unpacked as methods to achieve this balance in data centric interactions. The work also presents how technology is seen and used as a solution for overcoming challenges and realising priorities to provide value while preserving trust within the personal data ecosystem.

Author Keywords
Media; personal data; data; interviews.

ACM Classification Keywords
Human-centered computing~Field studies

INTRODUCTION
With media becoming increasingly online and ubiquitous, it has shifted from traditional scenarios of audiences consuming from service provider dictated schedules to the freedom of consuming customised and context-sensitive content available at the user's demand. This transformation has led to a turn towards personal data to help media service providers[39] meet audience expectations.

Research has identified a number of challenges introduced by the use of personal data which include loss of user trust[20], privacy compromises[44] and asymmetry of power over data[25]. While there is a growing call within academia to explore the socio-technical underpinnings of data[7], the consequences of these challenges within the domain of new media, are yet to be explored.

Recent research heralds a number of diverse opportunities pioneered by the use of diverse types of user data[5,13,34]. While such research contributes primarily to the design and evaluation of the user experience of new media experiences, the challenges and shifting priorities presented by the use of data to power these innovations are not often accounted for. To ensure sustainable growth of data driven media technologies, there is a need for understanding the drivers and challenges shaping their growth. Here, there is an explicit call to unpack and understand these priorities to help explore solutions that maximise the potential of personal data while minimising the challenges introduced by it.

This paper takes up this challenge by studying the present-day practices within a large U.K. based media organisation which has very recently shifted to technological frameworks powered by personal data. As part of this initiative, we interviewed employees working in varying capacities, serving and managing a diverse range of data driven media services.

The results of this study, while deeply rooted in varying perspectives and contexts, reveal the unified need for improved interactions in the user-data-service ecosystem where user trust and value are to be consistently balanced to ensure sustainable innovation in data driven new media experiences. While maintaining this balance manifests in diverse manners for different stakeholders, three priorities were identified as potential pathways to ensure the same. The results unpack being legally compliant and going beyond just the mandatory to further ensure social accountability and ethical responsibility as an organisation as the means to achieve and preserve this balance. Here, technology is often seen and utilised as a solution for overcoming challenges and realising priorities successfully to ensure sustainability within the personal data ecosystem.

Thus, the contributions of this paper include :

- Explicating the need for better interactions in the user-data-service ecosystem in data driven media

TVX '18, June 26–28, 2018, SEOUL, Republic of Korea

ACM ISBN 978-1-4503-5115-7/18/06.
https://doi.org/10.1145/3210825.3210830

experiences, where trust and value (to both the user and the service provider) are balanced.

- Unpacking how various legal, social and ethical considerations play out as key contributors that could help achieve and maintain this balance.
- Presenting how technology is used as a mechanism to embody solutions that preserve this balance.

BACKGROUND

Personal data and new media

The utilisation of personal data to drive new media experiences translates itself into a shift from traditional forms of broadcasting to a mass audience towards the practise of narrowcasting where individual users with unique user profiles are provided with tailored and interactive user-specific experiences.[6,10,19,22].

Interactivity in media has traditionally been a much-deliberated concept. Steur's definition of interactivity in a media experience was one where 'users can participate in modifying the form and content of the mediated environment in real time' [48]. Markus's version of the same stated that an 'interactive medium is a vehicle that enables and constrains multidirectional communication flows among the members of a social unit'[29]. Rada added the capabilities of computer-mediated information sharing systems including multi-media and hypertexts[35]. Today, personal data has emerged as an enabler that helps realise all of these definitions of interactivity to provide users with multifaceted interactive experiences that removes 'old constraints' and offers users 'new liberties of action'[11], through interactivity that respects every individual user's requirements.

Examples of such experiences are dissimilar in nature with respect to the data collected, sources of collection, use of data and the very essence of the experience itself. There are movies that adapt themselves continuously to user reaction learned through real time physiological data[34]. Formats where news programmes are personalised on user televisions to provide more relatable and relevant content, are being explored[5]. Personalisation of broadcast[12], a necessary methodology and tool that supports varied forms of tailored experiences are also currently gaining much momentum in media research. Other forms of experience enhancement supported by personal data include tailoring of recommendations[2], personalised electronic programme guides[24], recommendations made based on user emotions[13] etc.

Current Challenges

While the use of personal data leads to considerable appreciation in technological growth in media, the shift also entails caveats that dictate careful management of the many challenges this shift introduces into the system.

While personal data affords "new horizons for personalised, interactive and immersive entertainment as well as marketing...[...].... At the same time, some such proposals may be at variance with human values many of us hold dear, including privacy, trust, and control."[18]

A World Economic Forum report on personal data[20] details the current crisis in trust associated with the service providers' use of personal data. "The widespread loss of trust is unmistakable: security breaches, identity theft and fraud; concern from individuals and organizations about the accuracy and use of personal data; confusion from companies about what they can and cannot do; and increasing attention and sanctions from regulators."[20]

In 2006, Netflix was forced to cancel the sequel to their $1 million personal data driven recommendation algorithm improvement contest[47] following a warning from privacy advocates that notified the new dataset to be easily de-anonymised. This was also coupled with a suit filed by a privately homosexual mother who was "alleging that Netflix violated fair-trade laws and a federal privacy law protecting video rental records, when it launched its popular contest in September 2006"[46], further affecting user trust in media organisations adversely. The current political allegations of 'fake news'[51] also renders itself into this scenario where users are questioning media organisations and their trustworthiness, leading them to depend on alternate sources of news media like Facebook, Twitter and YouTube that delivers more user generated content, potentially undermining the situation further, as these channels are not subject to media regulation.

Along with the challenges of loss of privacy, trust and legal implications is the lack of control given to the user. Lanier[25] had mentioned an asymmetry of control in the digital economy where the users, who are both the producers and consumers of the data commodity, exercise very little control over it. While research has highlighted the importance of allowing data legibility, negotiability and agency through control[32] to the users, there still remains an explicit call for the technological embodiment of these principles. Users are continued to be presented with incomprehensible privacy statements[31,37], followed by acceptance statements where the users are constrained to binary choices[45] dictated by service providers often leading to low levels of understanding and very little space to exercise control[43].

Therefore, in order to ensure continued innovation in media research supported by user personal data, there requires a better understanding of the current landscape of the personal data ecosystem, it's priorities, opportunities and challenges. This work intends to explore these domains by identifying the current challenges and potential methods and pathways that help overcome these challenges to ensure sustained innovation in data driven media experiences.

THE STUDY

The study method consisted of interviews and was performed in collaboration with a large publicly funded media organisation within the U.K.. After years of resistance, the organisation is currently in the process of shifting to mandatory user sign-ins and collection of personal data. They serve a diverse variety of media experiences catering to audiences of varying demographics. This includes News, Sports, Children's entertainment, Knowledge and Learning, Radio, Video on Demand, 360 experiences, Virtual Reality experiences, Live Broadcast etc.

Participant Recruitment

The recruitment began with the help of a gatekeeper who enabled access to certain key teams. The majority of the participants were contacted individually through recruitment emails that outlined the aims of the research and their involvement in it. The rest were recruited by snowballing references through participants who identified potential candidates who worked within the same team, but in a role starkly different from theirs.

Interview Method

Since the participants hailed from teams that served vastly different kinds of experiences and hence had different priorities, in order to successfully achieve the goal of the study, the interviews had to accommodate the diversity in the views of the participants. Simultaneously, the interviews also had to accommodate dialogue around the issues that the study aimed to learn about.

These priorities resulted in an interview design which was unstructured, consisting of a set of topics that helped guide the conversations if they ever stalled[38]. The three areas of interest that were used as seeds to drive the conversations were:

- the current collection and use of personal data,
- the benefits and risks of using personal data, and
- the future of personal data in new media.

The conversations flowed where the respondents directed them making the method "informant"[27] in nature. In instances where topics that were aimed to be discussed were ignored, the researchers ensured that they seeded them into the conversations through questions, follow up questions, comments or queries. Given the highly complex nature of the topics discussed wherein the attitudes towards personal data are wide and varying with the reasoning for the same being highly contextual, we believe the exploratory approach helped accommodate the complexity and multifaceted nature of the data in its full richness.

With the view of using the results of the study in design endeavours that would enable future data driven media experiences, the conversations were often encouraged to be deeply rooted in current technologies that the participants were contributing to. This helped demonstrate the current practises and also worked as probes[17] to visualise future scenarios that the participants envisaged would help overcome the current challenges they face.

Data Gathering

A total of 20 interviews were conducted with stakeholders who work in diverse teams, which included Sports, News, Children's content, Education, Video-on-Demand platforms, Radio, Research and Development, Audience Platform, Marketing and Audiences and Data Management. These participants serve varying roles within these teams which includes engineers, technical architects, digital planners, analysts, UX practitioners, designers, producers etc. These participants also work in diverse capacities and hierarchical levels within the organisation which includes, directors and executives (4), department leads and heads (5), senior professionals (7) and relatively newer recruits (4). The group included 6 females and 14 males with ages ranging from 20s to 50s. This mix of teams and experience ensured representation of the varying priorities raised at different levels of work organisation while serving a wide range of media experiences. The common connection that served in the selection of participation was the individual's involvement with data driven technologies and personal data.

The interviews were either in person, by telephone or Skype, and lasted thirty to forty five minutes. All interviews were audio recorded and the recordings transcribed for data analysis purposes. The data collection and transcription was done simultaneously where the collection was discontinued once the data reached saturation, as the responses and discussions became repetitive.

Data Analysis

Reflecting Sacks' analytic commitment[40,41] we believe "that the warrant for any given assertion should be visible in the data"[36]. Hence, the analysis of transcribed data was done in a qualitative data driven manner. Owing to the open ended and unstructured nature of the conversations and the varying contexts addressed by the participants, the topics of discussion and the data formed a spectrum of perspectives. Therefore, we adopted endogenous topic analysis[36] through close reading of the transcripts to identify discrete topics that had manifested in the participants talk that demonstrate how they reason about personal data and its challenges.

In the first round of analysis, all topics discussed by the participants were marked out. In the second round, common topics of discussion were grouped while those that did not overlap were treated with equal weight independently. The focus here was to attend to the talk's topics, which is different from traditional forms of open coding where the text is analysed and any interesting phenomena in the data is coded and marked up[27]. By adopting endogenous topic analysis, it is not the questions that are relevant any more but the responses and how they are opened up. This helps eliminate one of the weaknesses of traditional grounded theory, the researchers' pre-conceived notions of what is "interesting"[27] and what is not. Instead, the onus is on the data itself as it churns out the topics it has embodied within it. Theoretically, this is in line with the documentary method of interpretation used in sociology, which in Mannheim's words is a "search for an identical homologous pattern of meaning underlying a variety of totally different realizations of that meaning."[28] Here, an actual appearance is considered "as the "document of", "as pointing to", as "standing on behalf of", a presupposed underlying pattern [14]."

This ethnomethodologically inspired method[4] also helped accommodate the heterogeneity in the topics discussed, due to the diversity in participants' roles associated with personal data. It ensured that the very unique practical reasonings presented in the data were not discarded because of lack of overlap or absence of patterns (cf. traditional thematic analysis[8]). In contrast, here the contextual distinctions help form, support and add to the richness of the emerging topics. This is a deviation from the "development of concepts"[27] stage in grounded theory analysis where a metric of evaluation of the outcome is "the number of instances in the data that support the specific concept"[27]. Instead, the analysis here is sensitive to the situational variations embodied within the data, which might otherwise be considered outliers or distractions, due to lack of overlap.

Trying to reduce and transform this data moves away from the goal of efficiently mapping this emerging scenario of personal data use in media, which demands the need for exploration that is rooted in the practicalities of the real world.

RESULTS

In the following section we present the results of the data analysis catalogued under five major topics that emerged from the interviews.

Business Priorities

The results show that the use of personal data helps achieve and regulate a range of organisational business priorities.

Fulfilling the business mission

Ensuring delivery of valuable service to every single user is one of the organisation's premier missions. Personal data is expected to become a key tool in this process.

"It has to do especially with the [***]'s mission of delivering value to everyone. So, by having an idea of the location and age and gender, we can make sure that we are delivering something for everyone.[P12]"

Use of personal data is expected to shift the relationship between the service provider and the user from the antiquated one to many broadcast model to one to one relationships that cater to each users' particular needs and interests.

"Optimally the world is changing where rather than one to many, its one to one relationships that organisations create with their audiences and customers. And so, we have to move into that world.[P14]"

Personal data provides opportunities to understand consumption trends across various demographic segments, based on age, location, etc. This helps as an evaluative tool in learning how different content is consumed across the spectrum of audiences, identifying gaps in consumption and making amends to future content creation to ensure consumption across all cohorts.

"And so we also use this case for tracking consumption, so that we can say how well we are doing on a geographic basis, and also, to an extent, if we cross reference against other available data sources, so demographic, using the geo-demographic dataset. So there's some element of use within the product, the digital products themselves, but also a great deal of value from a reporting point of view.[P2]"

With the introduction of social media, measuring reach of services is not contained within service provider platforms. Media is liked, shared and discussed by users through multiple social media platforms. Understanding who a user is, is expected to help reach out to social media profiles, providing possibilities for exploring the reach of the organisation's services on these profiles and platforms.

Provide symmetrical exchange of value

Providing users with a good exchange of value is vital to the success of any business. Provision for user accounts and profiles are expected to give users opportunities to express themselves better online and to be more active participants in the data economy. This enhanced contribution from the users could then be reflected to them in the experiences that they receive in return. These reflections could go beyond traditional media services to educational initiatives that help with personal growth, self-reflection programmes that help the user make sense of his/ her personal data with regards to contexts frequented by the user, interactive experiences that show a comparison of user data against the rest of the audiences etc.

"So, we are going around public service remit for data so where Amazon and commercial organisations it is very much about how they can market it back to you, so our question was what was a public service organisation, that's not making money do? So, we are looking at what's the most meaningful feedback? If you give us your data, how can we give you something back? That is enhancing for you, as opposed to just for us.[P8]"

Help with product development

Product development in media is based on input from many different sources within the organisation with the user having very little participation in the process. With the use of personal data, users can play a more central role in this process with the service providers being able to understand user needs down to the granularity of the specific devices used.

"So, I guess it informs the development of the product. So, it basically helps to inform staff, so for example, this is the kind of stuff that can help tell us, you know, TV platforms for example, are becoming more and more, are becoming a bigger and bigger part of [Video on Demand] usage. That's then really important for us to say, ok, should we then be putting in more refills on TV, should we be trialling more stuff on TV, that kind of thing.[P4]"

Staying relevant

With the high level of entropy in the number of products and services that are available to users, it is an existential need for every business to stay relevant in the users' everyday lives in order to ensure their sustained success and growth. Personal data, is currently considered to be a tool that would help understand the users' changing wants and needs and hence help the business and its products stay relevant to the user in the current day.

"I also think that there's a risk though in a sense to avoiding collecting personal data .....[....]...... I think what I'm saying is that consumers demand personalised experiences and that requires personal data. And if you cannot supply them what they expect, then they will consider you to be irrelevant.[P3]"

Importance of Trust

Trust was stressed as one of the key values of the organisation and as an international brand, it represents a public service entity that has always worked in ways that upheld user trust as a priority. This trust, that has been built over the years, is part of the organisation's legacy and is very important to the organisation. As a business, they recognise the possible erosion of user trust the mismanagement of user personal data could lead to and hence are very careful that their experiences reflect this value at all levels and dimensions.

"There's another risk which is.... and this is back to our relationship with our audience. So, we, the [***] is a very well trusted brand and you know to maintain that trust we need to ensure that we are not doing anything weird with the data that people provide to us.[P2]"

Legalities of using personal data

The General Data Protection Regulation was referred to as a guide for designing future media experiences. It was acknowledged that future regulation supports provision of higher levels of data legibility to the user which is aimed to empower the data subjects with an understanding of data practises around services offered by the organisation. This puts more pressure on service providers to deliver valuable services where the need, use, consent and control of personal data is easily justifiable not just to the user but legally as well.

"I think what the GDPR is bringing is a bigger literacy about us, of users giving away our data to get better benefit, but we need to be conscious about to whom we give that data and what is the actual value we get from that. Because if we are much more literate, people will have to treat our data with care, with much more care. And if we end up in a situation where this information would be lost, that would be a bad thing for the organisation and we might just lose completely, the trust.[P5]"

Personalisation

Enhancement of experiences and user journeys through personalisation was identified as one of the key uses of personal data in new media. The creative contribution of personalisation in crafting current and future experiences was often acknowledged, the legal implications of the same was also recognized.

Personalising the media experience

Personalisation is used to enhance new media experiences in various ways including both personalisation of recommendations and notifications, as well as the content served, e.g., video, audio, news, sports etc.

"It's not about recommendations like, because we know about you, you might like to buy this book. It's more like we know that you live in wherever it is you say that you live in off Facebook and we know that the main football team there is and that kind of thing. So the football team in the story, it's the team that's closest to you....we think you like that.[P3]"

Personalisation is also extended to scenarios where the user collaboratively engages with the experience to drive it in a unique and personalised fashion. An example of this is a "cook along" kitchen experience where data from smart utensils and/ or user input are used to continuously tailor the content to match user expertise and pace.

Personalisation for enhancing user journeys

Personalisation is expected to help in the process of exposing the audiences to the breadth of the content available to them.

"So, you know we have many many hours of TV and radio every single day. Both international and regional radio stations and TV networks. And we create about one and a half thousand new webpages every single day. Most of all that content...... it would be impossible for any individual to be across it all...[..]... Its just packages of information or content, that may well be of interest to an individual but they are not going to know that its even available... I mean in the digital era just because something goes up in a regional radio station, it might be about a subject that somebody who doesn't live in that region is interested in.[P14]"

Personalisation also helps go beyond just the serving of content of interest. It could also be applied to curate and enable entire user journeys to suit the users' wants and needs.

Personalisation introduces the possibility of new "genres of experiences" which otherwise would not have been possible. Each user, through their own, unique set of personal data would be able to create and experience exclusive and novel genres of experience.

"What it does is that every day it gives you sort of an on this day in the past view of your social media accounts in the past and what you posted....[....]....I think what I guess what I'm trying to get at there is that's a whole experience that's based only on my personal data and it's based on my personal data not yours. Or rather yours is based on your personal data and mine is based on mine. And it's a kind of genre of experience that I think is very powerful.[P3]"

Personalisation and the Law

In the U.K. it is expected that not all individuals are exposed to the same degree and type of personalisation. Service providers are sensitive to this gradation in personalisation services and are considering design alternatives that accommodate such legal constraints.

"In the UK there is a, we have this idea of not every single user will get the personalisation on the same level as others. In line with the future regulation GDPR, we would not be able to serve personalised

recommendations, personalised experiences, without the consent of a parent or a guardian, for anyone under 13. So, currently, for under 13 years old have their personalisation disabled by default which means that when they register and they are signed in, they are not receiving any personalised experiences as we are not able to use any of their data for personalisation.[P5]"

Crafting future content

Personalisation is considered as a *"research tool for the creative process[P5]"*. It could help rethink the crafting of future content creation to help enhance experiences.

"Its more giving the content commissioners the capability, tools and information to enhance the decision making process. To be more in line with what people actually need. And then, as a result of that, we are much more likely to target better content. And show a wider content which might be in line with peoples' kind of expectation.[P5]"

Forming Cohorts

Forming user cohorts based on demographic data or user behaviour was often discussed as a method of leveraging personal data that afforded a range of possibilities, like abiding by legislation, delivering relevant content and evaluating the reach and response to disseminated content.

To abide by legislation

The formation and use of user cohorts based on age was adopted to ensure alignment with legislative constraints regarding the different types of personal data that was collected from signed up users. Cohorts also help manage users' age transitions, which is accompanied by changes in the jurisdiction with respect to their personal data use.

"For children under 13 we do not collect full post code, we collect town, the town where they live. And, we also, for practical purposes today, if you are under 18 we collect your year of birth, sorry your date of birth so that we can work out when you transition from being under 13 to over 13 and when you transition from being under 18 to over 18, so that we can track those transitions.[P2]"

Cohorts also ensure that every user has, by default, available to him/ her the legally allowed grade and form of services for their age.

To deliver relevant content

Cohorts help target content that is relevant to users. Targeting is enabled across diverse types of content, including television shows, online programmes, radio shows and even marketing emails that are served to audiences. Forming cohorts helps with the personalisation of these varied types of content to make more targeted decisions about the material to be served to a user based on his/ her membership in various cohorts.

"So, personalisation comes in many types and forms. So, it's creating um, improved websites, it improves programming, it's giving recommendations to people what they might want to watch, depending on which cohort they sit in and even sending newsletters out to people. So, if I, for example, if I'm middle aged and if I really like nature programming and I like Radio 4, but I don't like Sports, why would you be sending me emails about sports or why would you be sending me emails about Radio 1 extra when you know that I'm a Radio 4 listener.[P10]"

To measure response and reach

Cohorts also perform the function of evaluation of disseminated content. It is used *"to measure our conversion rate and measure how we succeeded with the making of better experiences.[P5]"* It also helps to highlight gaps in content consumption, especially helping uncover flaws that might be preventing delivery of service to specific sets of audiences that belong to particular demographic groups.

"In terms of developing new services, understanding which bits of those new services are reaching audiences that we are not currently reaching. Or we are just building things that are super serving our existing audiences. Helping us understand if there are gender imbalances, if we are serving people in different parts of the world in different ways. You know, we are doing particularly well with women in the South of England but we are doing very poorly with women in India.[P16]"

Risks

Concerns like reputation damage, loss of user trust and data security concerns were flagged as potential risks of using personal data. Current risk mitigation measures like anonymisation, encryption and prioritisation of transparency were also discussed in parallel.

Reputation Damage

The potential of personal data, if not used in a judicious manner leading to possible maligning of reputation was highlighted as a risk.

"The main risk is that you could really screw up as an organization....[....]..... And your reputation would be ruined as an organisation you know.[P3]"

The stakeholders recognise their role as a data controller and the importance of being legally and ethically responsible for their use of personal data, so that the legacy and reputation of the organisation is preserved.

"Ok legal risks, in the sense of, if we are thinking in terms of the audience then, in the data protection law, we are the data controller, I think that's the terminology. And I think we have certain legal obligations to look after, in our role as the data controller, that we do appropriate things with people's data. And then there's also just..... I think from our own point of view, what we want to do our own ethical things as far as the [***]'s reputation is at risk.[P17]"

Trust

While the importance of using personal data is undeniable, there is also the risk of being intrusive as a service provider during the collection and use of this data. They consider being *"creepy[P2]"* as a risk that would undermine the trust the audiences have on the organisation and its services.

"So, we, the [***] is a very well trusted brand and you know to maintain that trust we need to ensure that we are not doing anything weird with the data that people provide to us...[...]... And we also have the informal mission of don't be creepy.[P2]"

Constraining and biasing user attitudes

An interesting comparison of a user's browsing space in the internet to that of a neighbourhood, helped highlight the risk of such personal data being used to bias and change user behaviour to match and benefit organisational expectations.

"If you think about back in the days, you lived in a neighbourhood, this neighbourhood has a specific group of people associated with it and so socio-economic kind of status. This information has been then aggregated and sold to advertising when you are walking in a specific neighbourhood you have a different advertising. The same thing happens right now online, however, we can be much more specific. You know much more latest precision targeting specific people.[P5]"

The fear of pushing irrelevant content to groups of users based on inaccurate decisions made due to their membership in a particular cohort was also considered a risk that constrained and biased user experiences.

Serving appropriate content

The ethical need to serve users with appropriate content is further emphasised with the involvement of users below the age of eighteen. With the use of shared devices and tailored user profiles, the risks of children being exposed to content inappropriate for them is increased and calls for attention.

"I suppose the other thing is, this is probably less.... for the [***], which is a trusted brand, meaning that people have lots of faith in what we do and all sorts of consideration behind the scenes to make sure our services are appropriate for the intended audiences, you know....more so in the case of Children's content, where we go to great lengths to make sure that our online users who are children, doesn't necessarily have access to certain aspects of what we do. And then we think about parental approval etc. When you have signed in users or signed in devices that are potentially shared, there are risks there.[P14]"

Creative challenge

Another risk outlined was the creative challenge of utilizing data to its fullest potential.

"And then there's also the risk that people aren't trained well enough to understand how to use that data for the benefit of all audiences, because it's kind of a new thinking and it's new and so there's a lot of change needed in people's minds and the ability to understand how to utilise and exploit this data for good, rather than it just adding to the noise of information that's there.[P18]"

Data Security

The importance of securing the personal data collected was highlighted continuously in discussions about risks. The potential to become a target for hackers was perceived as a high-stake risk.

"If its exposed for other purposes that wasn't designed to be collected, or if it is exposed for purposes outside of the [***] that is bad on our part both reputationally and legally that's wrong on our part. So, we have got to put lots of security around it.[P6]"

Risk Management

Along with the discussion of the various risks posed by personal data, risk mitigation strategies undertaken were also mentioned.

Anonymisation of usernames, data minimization[49,50] and encryption were all technological measures that were discussed as part of current risk management strategies.

The emphasis on transparency was also highlighted as part of the current risk mitigation process. "*So, we have worked with the information commissions office to come up with a strategy that helps our users to understand how we use our data. So, our mitigation for that trust question is that we try to get really transparent in how we use the data.[P2]"*

User empowerment

Dialogue around personal data renders it as a tool that enables improved interactions through user empowerment by helping understand the user, including the user in the creative processes and exploring the potential of consent models that are user-focused.

Understanding the User

One of the most notable benefits of using personal data for a service provider was its capacity to help understand users better.

"Being able to understand who somebody is at a more granular level than what you can do without being signed into something and without capturing personal data is a huge benefit. So, being able to kind of go, this worked for this kind of audience and we can prove it through kind of statistical data. That's really massive.[P13]"

Behavioural data which helps understand actual user activity and consumption on a platform would uncover user interests and habits related to media consumption. This adds considerable value to user online identities, resulting in interactions influenced by the users themselves.

Also, understanding user intentions and delivering experiences that are aligned with every user visit is expected to be a radical novelty that would help transform the current service delivery norms.

"It will, what will we use it for, again it's about providing useful experiences to people. So, if you are just wasting time, so you just want to be entertained, then we might provide you with smaller, more upbeat, more light hearted news. But if you want to be informed about a topic, then we would offer you more deeper, more related content and deeper related content to the same content that you are interested in.[P15]"

Deliver to the user

Personal data contributes to various techniques that make content delivery more efficient and appropriate to the users. Understanding the users with the help of personal data, by combining content from differing temporal, geographic and contextual sources helps collate the most appropriate experiences for every user.

"So, if we take full post code, in our digital products, we resolve that to things like what TV region are you in, so that on [Video on Demand platform] we can show you the appropriate version of your TV. We also use it to determine your local radio station, we also use it to determine the weather forecast for your location. And, when we have any local news or local news alerts we can update you based on your location.[P2]"

With the increase in popularity of internet television like Netflix etc, the popularity of broadcast television has seen a drop[3]. One of the biggest challenges this shift has introduced is the need to stay relevant to younger audiences. The learnings gained from the use of personal data is expected to help maintain relevance over all demographic bands by ensuring delivery of relevant content to everyone.

Include the user in crafting future media content

Using personal data could help involve user priorities when making decisions regarding crafting future media experiences. By using personal data to shape media experiences, the scope of decision making essentially broadens from that of just editors and content commissioners to the users themselves.

"I'm actually quite interested in moving beyond that involving users with the algorithms, instead of us trying to guess what people are interested in. I'm more interested in them telling us. And that's what so much personal data and indicating preference and storing people's preferences and being able to go back and edit those and update them as they change.[P15]"

User centred consent models

User consent is one of many legal bases for any technology to collect, store or use personal data[15]. Consent has been translated into design by allowing the users with the choice of opting in or out of personalisation. Also, to ensure user consent happens through user empowerment the need for the user to be knowledgeable about data practises was agreed upon. The provision of alternative models of layout for the organisation's privacy policy was considered a response to this scenario.

"We publish information at three different levels. In the UX, in the user experience, as you are entering your fields of why kind of question. Then you can drop down to a short summary. That makes through to a more detailed description, still written in English rather than legalese that describes what is the.... how do we use the data, why are we collecting it and that sort of thing. And then that works through to our privacy policy which is a kind of legal document.[P2]"

DISCUSSION

Organisational Concern: Striking the balance

Research has shown the use of data to increase productivity and performance[9,26], help with management decisions[30] and contrastingly, sometimes even disempowerment[7], depending upon the nature of the service provider. The results of this study reflect that while personal data used in new media technologies is a significant contributor to creativity and innovation, there is the desire for improved interactions in the user-data-service ecosystem to ensure a healthy balance between the value produced by the use of personal data and the potential loss of user trust it could result in.

Value

The value created by personal data to both the media service provider and the user is multifarious in nature. Ranging from providing novel creative affordances to helping support business interests, it is highly dependant upon the context, the audiences catered to and the services offered.

Personalisation of varying types (providing new genres of experiences, user specific experiences, holistic experiences, curated user journeys) is one way of providing value through enhancement of the creative aspects available. Staying 'relevant' by keeping up with competition through the use of personal data is considered another way of producing value, here, by catering to the business interests of the organisation. The ability to form and manage cohorts to support communities and extend the reach and relevance of content was also identified as a means to value derivation. Also, the availability of user personal data further unfolds the challenge of promoting the identification of alternative methods of value producing measures presented by personal data that extend beyond just the content and the business to more user-focused experiences like customised self-reflection and feedback initiatives.

Trust

While personal data increases the potential channels for value creation, it also simultaneously introduces the risk of loss of user trust, emphasising the need to foster trusted relationships with the users during this process.

Access to personal data has led to the demand for more data and an increase in the resolution of potential data. When data becomes increasingly granular and detailed, the dangers could start outweighing the benefits as users become increasingly sensitive to mismatches and errors. The ability to cohort users further introduces the risk of bad stereotyping leading to lowered user satisfaction and trust in the organisation. Also, the need to stay relevant by keeping up with competition demands constant focus on user priorities to ensure interactions that compromise on user trust are not adopted in the process. Thus, the availability of user personal data, while affording a number of possibilities, also increases the need for ensuring preservation of user trust while putting these novel methods to practise.

Need for balance

The World Economic Forum has already detailed a crisis in trust associated with personal data use in technologies[20]. Previous research also specifically demonstrates decreased levels of user trust while using media technologies driven by personal data[42].

The results of this study further uncovers various diverse practical manifestations of the opportunities and threats introduced by the use of personal data that contribute to the loss of user trust. While it affords service providers with multifarious channels for value creation, including better support for business priorities, providing increased service affordances through personalisation, understanding the users better through cohort formation etc., it also presents, in parallel, various risks that undermine user trust in the organisation. This demands the need for user empowerment through interactions that balance both trust and value in the user-data-service ecosystem.

Response Mechanisms

This study reveals the considerations contributing to this scenario to be legal, social and ethical in nature. While the legal priorities often arise from the impending GDPR that acts as a response to the trust crisis, the findings reveal that service providers acknowledge the need to think beyond mandatory legal obligations to cater to social and ethical concerns raised by the use of personal data, in order to preserve user trust in data driven services.

Legal

Legal requirements are a prominent sculpting force while designing and delivering personal data driven technologies as they enforce accountability into the scheme in a mandatory manner. The near future introduction of the GDPR aims to bring user trust back into the digital economy through the enforcement of legislation. Hence, aligning with legal requirements plays an important role while using personal data in media experiences.

"With the younger audiences, we are allowed to keep the data in order to be able to say that so many people do this, that or the other, but we are not allowed to keep that data attributed to one person, that says because you watched this, you can then watch that, because that becomes marketing, we are not supposed to be using that data for in that sense. So, there are all sorts of legal frameworks that we are trying to sort of... to work within.[P18]"

In the U.K., legislation dictates stark distinction between the grade of personal data collection and personalisation served to users under the age of eighteen and over eighteen. The introduction of shared entities like media devices, data sources, social spaces and settings further highlight the many nuances of the interactions within this legal need that calls for immediate attention.

Reflected in the findings were the measures required for the realisation of the GDPR. Providing transparency about data practises was identified as a method for translating legislation into design. Currently, transparency is enabled through introduction of new websites that present information to users in simple and engaging ways, a shift in the format of the terms and conditions statement, general use of simple language when discussing data practises etc. Thus, realisation of transparency is a goal that is expected to be achieved through legible interaction strategies.

Social

The turn towards personal data in new media experiences highlights several challenges that places the call for better social accountability. Social accountability, while not regulated like in the legal scenario, is considered a requirement to help build user trust in personal data environments. It refers to being accountable as a societal entity, respecting and mitigating the social implications of using personal data that could lead to loss of user trust.

"And I am not sure how comfortable they would be in answering what is your ethnic background or your religious beliefs and things like that. I would like for us to deliver value for everyone but I'm not so sure that I would like to ask for that information. So, it's a rather tricky situation...[...]....to put it bluntly, it would be a bit creepy to ask for that kind of information.[P12]"

Fear of reputation damage, due to the organisation not being able to be fully accountable for its use of personal data was a challenge that triggered many actions, precautions and decisions. This fear is often associated with the fear of loss of user trust from the use of personal data and thus becomes a social challenge that constrains the complete realisation of the creative potential offered by data driven media.

Personal data can act as a tool that enables understanding the audiences or the society in many ways that help accurate delivery of appropriate content to users. It helps explore user wants and needs on an individual level and allows for uncovering cohort behaviours. However, knowing the balance of when to utilise information about user membership in a particular service-created cohort versus when to respect user individuality is a social challenge which requires further attention.

Ethical

Ethical considerations are responses to both legal and social accountability challenges. While not dictated, or regulated by any specific entity in the media space, ethical data practises have been recognised by service providers as a key necessity in building user trust in personal data ecosystems.

"I think that you can do it the right way and the wrong way. For me, I think that if you are asking something, if you are asking people for more information about who they are, or what they think about stuff, then you need to give something back, or you need to justify why you are asking for it.[P13]"

The possibility of using information about the audiences to constrain their consumption and bias and prime them to align with the service providers' wants and needs surfaced as an ethical challenge that could contribute considerably to the current crisis in trust[20]. Thus, the challenge of using the collected data in ethical ways and the effective communication of these interactions to build user trust demands further consideration.

While age appropriateness of broadcast is often legally regulated, with the expansion of media moving beyond just broadcast coupled with the previously discussed involvement of shared media consumption settings, the ethical need to regulate the appropriateness of the content served in these social scenarios is also highlighted.

Personal data is currently considered by some as an asset class[44] on the same lines as oil and gold, but in contrast to these fungible assets, personal data is highly contextual and raises the creative challenge of ethically utilising it to its fullest potential. The challenge then is to innovate as a service provider and provide services that are on par with the competition while not compromising on user trust through unethical behaviour.

Technological reasonings

The response to some of these legal, social and ethical challenges are currently enabled through the use of technology. Thus, technology becomes a medium that embodies solutions that lead to more trustworthy data interactions.

Examples of such technological reasonings include data security where techniques such as anonymisation, data minimisation, encryption etc are adopted to avoid realising loss of user trust and reputation damage. Thus, investing in interactions that provide and communicate higher user data security are expected to lead to increased user trust.

Use of cohorts is a technological translation of the need to manage legal requirements, evaluate content consumption, deliver relevant content and identify and cater to underserved audiences. The challenge of recognising the difference between contexts that require cohort use and those where cohorts are dysfunctional requires further attention. Here, further research could make valuable contributions by developing interaction strategies that overcome erroneous stereotyping by exploring the socio technical effects of cohorts and identifying scenarios where they disempower versus empower users.

Transparency was highlighted as one of the legal requirements of the GDPR that is hoped to result in increased user trust. Terms and conditions statements are a classic example of transparency provision where despite active research in both industry[52] and academia[21,43], the adoption of alternative forms of privacy statements that empower the user, still remain a challenge. Thus, designing data interactions that lead to increased awareness and understanding of the underlying data practises are prioritised as a means for building user trust.

Using user personal data to understand audiences to help craft future content was discussed previously. The user is now a participant in the creative, editorial and commissioning processes, making future media experience design and dissemination procedures more user centric. Such initiatives that help address the concern of biases by involving actual user behavioural and consumption data in the crafting process are expected to increase the relevance of services and build user trust.

Providing meaningful feedback in the form of self-reflection summaries, quantified-self initiatives or visualisations that demonstrate the user's role in the digital economy have been identified as alternatives for trust creation. Helping the users feel more empowered through experiences that encourage user trust is expected to open potential avenues for improved value exchange.

CONCLUSION AND FUTURE WORK

The turn towards personal data in driving novel media experiences is resulting in changing priorities and challenges when delivering these experiences to audiences. This interview study explores these current challenges and priorities of media service providers working on a diverse range of data driven media experiences within a large U.K. based media organisation.

The results of this study unpack a call from the service provider's perspective for improved mechanisms and interactions within the user-data-service ecosystem where trust and value are consistently upheld and balanced as priorities. This balance has been identified to be preserved through being legally compliant and going beyond just the mandatory to also ensure social accountability and ethical responsibility as an organisation. With media and broadcast ranging diversely in terms of content, services and audiences catered to, the manifestation of these priorities are diverse and highly context dependant. But here, technology is often seen as a solution for realising many of these diverse priorities successfully to ensure sustainability within the personal data ecosystem.

While this research uncovers the priorities and potential pathways that would ensure continued innovation in new media experiences driven by personal data, there is still the call to explore further practical alternatives that add value to the interactions between stakeholders within the ecosystem in a trusted manner. Previous research like Human Data Interaction[32] provides theoretical frameworks that support such interactions, through the recommendation of application of principles like data legibility, negotiability and agency. But, there is still the call for practical solutions and design recommendations that could be used in everyday contexts. To fully understand the technological and social viability of such alternatives we intend to further extend this research through the use of technological probes that involve personal data driven media experiences supported by alternative technological solutions like personal data management systems[1,23,33].

We are currently exploring an IoT data driven adaptive media experience contexualised in the living room of the home, which applies the legal, social and ethical priorities highlighted in this study. Here, the Databox, a personal networked device that allows users to regain agency of their online presence[16] through active control and management of their personal data, would be used to enable legal, ethical and socially accountable interactions to ensure trustworthy data transactions that users could actively engage with. We aim for such novel alternatives to probe audiences and solicit insights and practical possibilities for the future that provide value to both the user and the service provider in the personal data ecosystem, while preserving user trust.

ACKNOWLEDGEMENTS

This work was supported by the BBC R&D and EPSRC [grants EP/L015463/1, EP/M001636/1]. Data supporting this publication is not openly available as our ethics approval does not allow for the release of transcripts to third parties.

REFERENCES

1. Yousef Amar, Hamed Haddadi, and Richard Mortier. 2016. Privacy-Aware Infrastructure for Managing Personal Data Personal Data Arbitering within the Databox Framework. Proceedings of the 2016 conference on ACM SIGCOMM 2016 Conference: 571–572.
2. Xavier Amatriain. 2013. Big & personal: data and models behind netflix recommendations. Proceedings of the 2nd International Workshop on Big Data, Streams and Heterogeneous Source Mining Algorithms, Systems, Programming Models and Applications - BigMine '13, 1–6. http://doi.org/10.1145/2501221.2501222
3. Jonathan Bacon. 2016. Young viewers choosing VOD over pay TV. Marketing Week. Retrieved September 18, 2017 from https://www.marketingweek.com/2016/02/11/young-viewers-choosing-vod-over-pay-tv/
4. Douglas Benson and John A Hughes. 1983. The perspective of ethnomethodology. Longman Publishing Group.
5. Frank Bentley, Karolina Buchner, and Joseph "Jofish" Kaye. 2014. MyChannel: Exploring City-based Multimedia News Presentations on the Living Room TV. Proceedings of the ACM International Conference on Interactive Experiences for TV and Online Video., ACM, 71–78. http://doi.org/10.1145/2602299.2602302
6. Fernando Bermejo. 2009. Audience manufacture in historical perspective : from broadcasting to Google. New Media & Society 1–2, 11: 133–154. http://doi.org/10.1177/1461444808099579
7. danah boyd and Kate Crawford. 2012. Critical Questions for Big Data. Information, Communication & Society 15, 5: 662–679. http://doi.org/10.1080/1369118X.2012.678878
8. Virginia Braun and Victoria Clarke. 2006. Using thematic analysis in psychology. Qualitative research in psychology 3, 2: 77–101.
9. Eric Brynjolfsson, Lorin M Hitt, and Heekyung Hellen Kim. 2011. Strength in numbers: How does data-driven decisionmaking affect firm performance?
10. Matt Carlson. 2006. Tapping into TiVo : New Media & Society 8, 1: 97–115. http://doi.org/10.1177/1461444806059877
11. Colin Cherry. 1977. The telephone system: creator of mobility and social change. The social impact of the telephone: 112–126.
12. Tony Churnside. 2013. Object-Based Broadcasting. Retrieved September 10, 2016 from http://www.bbc.co.uk/rd/blog/2013-05-object-based-approach-to-broadcasting
13. Paula Falco, Christina Noonan, and Ge Cao. 2016. REFLEX: Face Micro-Expression Recognition System for TV Content Curation. Proceedings of the ACM International Conference on Interactive Experiences for TV and Online Video, ACM, 163–169. http://doi.org/10.1145/2932206.2933564
14. Harold Garfinkel. 1996. Studies in Ethnomethodology. Polity Press, London, United Kingdom.
15. Article 7 GDPR. 2016. Regulation (EU) 2016/679 of the European Parliament and of the Council of 27 April 2016 on the protection of natural persons with regard to the processing of personal data and on the free movement of such data, and repealing Directive 95/46/EC (General Da. Official Journal of the European Union L119, 1–88.
16. John Haddadi, Hamed, Howard, Heidi, Crowcroft. 2015. Personal Data: Thinking Inside the Box. 8.
17. Hilary Hutchinson, Wendy E. Mackay, Bo Westerlund, et al. 2003. Technology probes: inspiring design for and with families. Proceedings of the SIGCHI Conference on Human Factors in Computing Systems - CHI '03, 17–24.
18. Wijnand IJsselsteijn and Wijnand. 2017. Here's Looking At You, Kid. Proceedings of the 2017 ACM International Conference on Interactive Experiences for TV and Online Video - TVX '17, ACM, 1–1. http://doi.org/10.1145/3077548.3077562
19. Iris Jennes. 2017. The Social Construction of Targeted Television Advertising : The Importance of " Social Arrangements " in the Development of Targeted Television Advertising in Flanders. Proceedings of the 2017 ACM International Conference on Interactive Experiences for TV and Online Video, ACM, 41–50.
20. Carl Kalapesi. 2012. Rethinking Personal Data : Strengthening Trust.
21. Patrick Gage Kelley, Joanna Bresee, Lorrie Faith Cranor, and Robert W Reeder. 2009. A "nutrition label" for privacy. Proceedings of the 5th Symposium on Usable Privacy and Security SOUPS 09, 4. http://doi.org/10.1145/1572532.1572538
22. Pyungho Kim. 1999. A machine-like new medium – theoretical examination of interactive TV. Media, Culture & Society 25, 2: 217–233.
23. Tom Kirkham, Sandra Winfield, Serge Ravet, and Sampo Kellomaki. 2013. The personal data store approach to personal data security. IEEE Security and Privacy 11, 5: 12–19. http://doi.org/10.1109/MSP.2012.137
24. Christopher Krauss, Lars George, and Stefan Arbanowski. 2013. TV predictor: personalized program recommendations to be displayed on SmartTVs. Proceedings of the 2nd international workshop on big data, streams and heterogeneous source mining:

Algorithms, systems, programming models and applications. ACM, 2013., 63–70.

25. Jaron Lanier. 2014. Who owns the future? Simon and Schuster.
26. Steve LaValle, Eric Lesser, Rebecca Shockley, Michael S Hopkins, and Nina Kruschwitz. 2011. Big data, analytics and the path from insights to value. MIT sloan management review 52, 2: 21.
27. Jonathan Lazar, Jinjuan Heidi Feng, and Harry Hochheiser. 2017. Research methods in human-computer interaction. Morgan Kaufmann.
28. Karl Manheim. 1952. On the interpretation of Weltanschauung. From Karl Manheim.
29. M. Lynne Markus. 1987. Toward a "critical mass" theory of interactive media: Universal access, interdependence and diffusion. Communication Research 14, 5: 491–511. http://doi.org/10.1177/009365087014005003
30. Nan L Maxwell, Dana Rotz, and Christina Garcia. 2016. Data and Decision Making: Same Organization, Different Perceptions; Different Organizations, Different Perceptions. American Journal of Evaluation 37, 4: 463–485.
31. Aleecia M. McDonald and Lorrie Faith Cranor. 2008. The Cost of Reading Privacy Policies. I/S - A Journal of Law and Policy for the Information Society 4, 3: 1–22.
32. Richard Mortier, Hamed Haddadi, Tristan Henderson, Derek Mcauley, and Jon Crowcroft. 2014. Human-Data Interaction : The Human Face of the Data-Driven Society.
33. Min Mun, Shuai Hao, Nilesh Mishra, et al. 2010. Personal data vaults: a locus of control for personal data streams. Proceedings of the 6th International COnference on - Co-NEXT '10: 17.
34. Matthew Pike, Richard Ramchurn, Steve Benford, and Max L. Wilson. 2016. # scanners: exploring the control of adaptive films using brain-computer interaction. Proceedings of the 2016 CHI Conference on Human Factors in Computing Systems, ACM, 5385–5396.
35. Roy Rada. 1995. Hypertext. In Interactive Media. Springer New York, New York, NY, 21–47. http://doi.org/10.1007/978-1-4612-4226-0_3
36. Dave Randall, Liz Marr, and Mark Rouncefield. 2001. Ethnography, ethnomethodology and interaction analysis. Ethnographic Studies 6, 1: 31–44.
37. Joel R Reidenberg, Travis Breaux, Lorrie Faith Carnor, et al. 2014. Disagreeable Privacy Policies: Mismatches Between Meaning and Users' Understanding. Berkeley Technology Law Journal 30, 1: 39–88. http://doi.org/10.15779/Z384K33
38. Colin Robson. 1993. Real world research: A resource for social scientists and practitioners-researchers. West Sussex: John Wiley & Sons.
39. John Rose, Olaf Rehse, and Björn Röber. 2012. The Value of our Digital Identity.
40. Harvey Sacks. 1984. Notes on methodology. Structures of social action: Studies in conversation: 21–7.
41. Harvey Sacks. 1992. Lectures on conversation. 2 vols. Edited by Gail Jefferson with introductions by Emanuel A. Schegloff.
42. Neelima Sailaja, Andy Crabtree, and Phil Stenton. 2017. Challenges of using personal data to drive personalised electronic programme guides. Proceedings of the 2017 CHI Conference on Human Factors in Computing Systems, ACM, 5226–5231. http://doi.org/http://dx.doi.org/10.1145/3025453.3025986
43. Florian Schaub, Rebecca Balebako, Adam L Durity, and Lorrie Faith Cranor. 2015. A Design Space for Effective Privacy Notices. Eleventh Symposium On Usable Privacy and Security (SOUPS 2015), 1–17.
44. Klaus Schwab, Alan Marcus, J. O. Oyola, William Hoffman, and M. Luzi. 2011. Personal Data : The Emergence of a New Asset Class.
45. Paul M Schwartz and Daniel Solove. 2009. Notice & Choice.
46. Ryan Singel. 2009. Netflix Spilled Your Brokeback Mountain Secret, Lawsuit Claims. Wired. Retrieved September 18, 2017 from https://www.wired.com/2009/12/netflix-privacy-lawsuit/
47. Ryan Singel. 2010. NETFLIX Cancels Recommendation Contest after Privacy Lawsuit. Retrieved March 29, 2018 from https://www.wired.com/2010/03/netflix-cancels-contest/
48. Jonathan Steuer. 1992. Defining Virtual Reality: Dimensions Determining Telepresence. Journal of Communication 42, 4: 73–93. http://doi.org/10.1111/j.1460-2466.1992.tb00812.x
49. European Data Protection Supervisor. 1995. Data Minimization Article 6.1(b) and (c) of Directive 95/46/EC. Retrieved from https://edps.europa.eu/node/3080
50. European Data Protection Supervisor. 2017. Data Minimization Article 4.1(b) and (c) of Regulation EC (No) 45/2001. Retrieved from https://edps.europa.eu/taxonomy/term/133

51. Amy B Wang. 2017. Trump renews attack on “Fake News CNN” after retraction. Retrieved March 29, 2018 from https://www.washingtonpost.com/news/the-fix/wp/2017/06/27/trump-renews-attack-on-fake-news-cnn-after-retraction/?utm_term=.6a2087289e12

52. Zynga. 2011. PrivacyVille. Retrieved September 18, 2017 from https://www.zynga.com/privacy/privacyville

A New Production Platform for Authoring Object-based Multiscreen TV Viewing Experiences

Jie Li
CWI
Amsterdam, Netherlands
jie.li@cwi.nl

Thomas Röggla
CWI
Amsterdam, Netherlands
t.roggla@cwi.nl

Maxine Glancy
BBC R&D
Manchester, United Kingdom
maxine.glancy@bbc.co.uk

Jack Jansen
CWI
Amsterdam, Netherlands
jack.jansen@cwi.nl

Pablo Cesar
CWI & TU Delft
Amsterdam, Netherlands
p.s.cesar@cwi.nl

ABSTRACT

Multiscreen TV viewing refers to a spectrum of media productions that can be watched on TV screens and companion screens (e.g., smartphones and tablets). TV production companies are now promoting an interactive and engaging way of viewing TV by offering tailored applications for TV programs. However, viewers are demotivated to install dozens of applications and switch between them. This is one of the obstacles that hinder companion screen applications from reaching mass audiences. To solve this, TV production companies need a standard process for producing multiscreen content, allowing viewers to follow all kinds of programs in one single application. This paper proposes a new object-based production platform for authoring programs for multiscreen. The platform consists of two parts: the preproduction tool and the live editing tool. To evaluate whether the proposed workflow is appropriate, validation interviews were conducted with professionals in the TV broadcasting industry. The professionals were positive about the proposed new workflow, indicating that the platform allows for preparations at the preproduction stage and reduces the workload during the live broadcasting. They see as well its potential to adapt to the current production workflow.

Author Keywords

Multiscreen TV viewing; Object-based broadcasting; Production tools; Graphical interface design.

TVX '18, June 26–28, 2018, SEOUL, Republic of Korea

ACM ISBN 978-1-4503-5115-7/18/06…$15.00
https://doi.org/10.1145/3210825.3210834

ACM Classification Keywords

• **Human-centered computing~User studies** • **Human-centered computing~Field studies**

INTRODUCTION

Traditional studies on TV viewing considered viewers' relaxation and passivity as important factors that contribute to their enjoyment [7]. Lately, with the prevalence of smart companion devices (i.e., smartphones and tablets), it is common to see that people's attention is easily distracted from the TV screen to companion screens [19, 21]. TV viewing is no longer a lean-back experience. The media industry foresees the potential of multiscreen. They are promoting an interactive and engaging way of viewing TV by offering auxiliary content and interactive functions on companion screens [1, 4, 8, 18, 20, 25]. These applications were all tailored for specific TV programs, becoming impractical for viewers to install and switch between dozens of inconsistent ones. Much efforts have been invested in companion applications, but hardly any of them reached mass audiences [5].

Conventional ways of TV production are well established. The processes for preproduction, live and recorded broadcasting to TV screens is standardized [23]. However, there is no standard process for producing companion screen content. Instead of developing applications in an ad-hoc manner, Geerts et al. [10] suggested providing a single application with which viewers could follow all the companion screen shows of a broadcaster. In a previous study [16], a preproduction tool was designed for authoring TV programs for multiscreen. The tool was evaluated by professionals in the TV broadcasting industry. They indicated that preproduction for live broadcasting is radically different from that for recorded broadcasting. Live broadcasting is time critical and always has a certain unpredictability. Even for broadcasting to TV screens only, it is a challenge for the director and the production team to react to live events or search databases for new materials [12, 15]. The professionals suggested that only a preproduction tool is not sufficient to guarantee successful broadcasting of multiscreen content. An integrated platform that includes both preproduction and live broadcasting was proposed [16].

The focus of this paper is on an object-based production approach [2] for authoring multiscreen content. The goal is to design a live editing tool, together with a preproduction tool, to form an integrated platform that supports the authoring and broadcasting of multiscreen content. To do so, the first step is to understand the current workflows of live broadcasting. A field study was conducted at a live OB (Outside Broadcasting) truck covering the MotoGP 2017 race at Silverstone. Due to the rapid pace of MotoGP races and various types of live events (e.g., crashes, overtakes), this field study offered us a good opportunity to observe the intense workflow and rapid decisions needed for live broadcasting. Afterwards, a live triggering tool and a proposed workflow for authoring and broadcasting multiscreen content were designed. Finally, validation interviews with professionals in the broadcasting industry were conducted with three research questions:

1) Is the proposed workflow for multiscreen production appropriate? Does it fit into the current production workflow?

2) Are the tools (preproduction & live editing) adequately designed? What are the suggestions from the professionals for improvement?

3) Who is the right person in the production team to use such new tools?

The paper is organized as follows. First, related work introduces several object-based production concepts and multiscreen viewing experiences. It also summarizes a typical production workflow, highlighting the differences and challenges of live and recorded broadcasting. Next, the background section recalls the results of one previous study and the design of a preproduction tool. Then, we describe the field study at MotoGP 2017 (Silverstone) and visualize the current workflow of live broadcasting for a MotoGP racing event. Based on the insights from the field study, a live editing tool is designed. In the end, the validation interviews of the production platform and the results are presented. We conclude that the workflow proposed by the platform was appreciated by the professionals. They indicated that the user interfaces of the platform are straightforwardly designed, so they can be easily mastered by the production team. The platform allows preparations at the preproduction stage and reduces the workload during live broadcasting. They foresaw the potential of the platform in producing multiscreen contents and provided feedback to improve the interface design. They suggested that the current production team needs to hire additional staff to operate the platform. The platform can run in parallel with the existing production workflows. However, it might require time and effort to get the production team to accept and trust a new system.

RELATED WORK

This section describes some recent research about object-based broadcasting and production workflows.

Object-based Broadcasting

The concept of object-based media is not new. The field of computer games is advanced in applying this approach, allowing game players to follow customized playing modes and to fully interact with the game world. What is an object-based production process? Here, "object" refers to different media units that are used to make a TV program. The object-based approach involves breaking down a program into separate content objects, typically including graphics, audio, video, background music, dialogues, subtitles, sound/visual effects, etc., and describing how they can be rearranged. With this approach, a program can be adapted to fulfill the needs of different individual viewers [15, 26].

Some recent studies have explored object-based production in different use cases. Cox et al. [6] developed a personalized interactive cooking application called CAKE. CAKE supports an interactive dialogue between a viewer and a cooking show. CAKE can integrate multiple recipes selected by the viewer and automatically generate a step-by-step cooking plan. In this way, the show is adjustable according to the viewer's pace. *Squeezebox* developed by BBC Research & Development [3] is an object-based tool that enables rapid re-editing the duration of the content. *Squeezebox* can automatically analyze and segment the footage into individual shots. The production team can mark up the priority of each shot, determining whether the footage will be cut or preserved as the duration is reduced. Most recently, Puentes et al. [22] developed a flexible visual authoring tool. By dragging and dropping static or dynamic "components" (e.g., texts, images, videos, audio, fonts, etc.) into "containers" (e.g., defined regions on the screens). Developers and designers become time-and-cost-efficient in creating interactive TV applications.

As a summary, Figure 1 compares the traditional linear TV program broadcasting and the object-based broadcasting. The two broadcasting approaches both start with preparing all content objects. The linear broadcasting transmits the same program to every viewer, resulting in a passive and lean-back viewing experience. It remains difficult for content providers to make different versions of the program to fit different screen formats, audiences and environments. In contrast, object-based broadcasting transmits content objects independently to viewers along with the metadata describing how they should be assembled. The devices controlled by the viewers optimally assemble the content objects [2, 17, 26].

The object-based production platform proposed in this paper consists of a collection of interactive media units configured to work together to deliver the look and feel of a single tool. This collection is called Distributed Media Application (DMApp) [15]. Reusable media units (DMApp Components) are assembled during the preproduction to create coherent multiscreen experiences and be aired during the live broadcasting. The set of DMApp components are actually a set of content objects as shown in Figure 1, which can also be configured to have some interactive and novel functions, such as "like" widget (for expressing "like" preference), real-time video chat or text chat, which can stimulate viewers' engagement. The DMApp components are one of the essential elements of the production tool design.

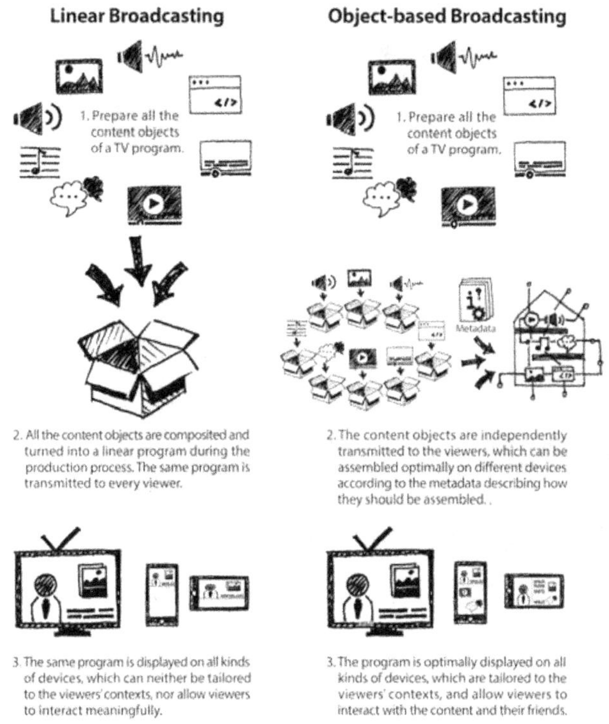

Figure 1. Compare the traditional linear broadcasting with the object-based broadcasting.

Typical Television Production Workflow

A production workflow typically consists of three phases, namely preproduction, production and postproduction [23]. Pre-production contains all kinds of preparations for the production. The main activity at this phase is to break down the script into individual scenes. All the media content (audio, video, graphics, visual and sound effects, etc.) are prepared accordingly. The primary task of the production phase is to film live shows or raw footages for postproduction. The goal of postproduction is to make precise edits and to select the best shots for broadcasting. However, for live broadcasting, the time for postproduction is limited. Instead of extensive postproduction, what the director does is called "live editing", which involves quickly mixing live camera feeds, selecting and editing some shots to prevent undesirable materials being aired. For recorded broadcasting, there can be iterations between postproduction and filming. The director may request to shoot extra video footages or reshoot some unsatisfying scenes. Due to the time limit and unpredictability of the live broadcasting, live editing is the most overwhelming task for a TV production team, even for broadcasting only to TV screens. Figure 2 shows a summary of the main tasks of the three phases. We believe that current working practices will need to evolve to accommodate the requirements of multiscreen production.

BACKGROUND

In a previous study, semi-structured interviews with professionals in the TV production industry were conducted to collect requirements concerning the tool design for multiscreen TV production [17]. According to the requirements, four wireframe concepts of a preproduction tool were designed. Professionals from the broadcasting industry were invited to evaluate these concepts. One of the concepts was selected and redesigned based on the consensus of the professionals [16].

The professionals specifically pointed out that the preproduction tool should differentiate the authoring for live and recorded broadcasting, due to the time limitation and unpredictability of live broadcasting. During live broadcasting, the whole team works like a symphony orchestra. Mistakes do happen, but every effort is made to minimize their occurrence. One of the professionals recommended a simplified live triggering tool to reduce the burden. The professionals also advised that the production team should be able to quickly build up events during live broadcasting, using data packages such as the drivers' profiles, live statistics, and camera feeds. Once live events happen (e.g., riders crash and overtake in a motorcycle race), the live broadcasting team needs to quickly trigger replays of the events. Customized templates should be adopted in this situation rather than to create things from scratch.

Figure 2. A typical television production workflow. Main tasks of each phase are described.

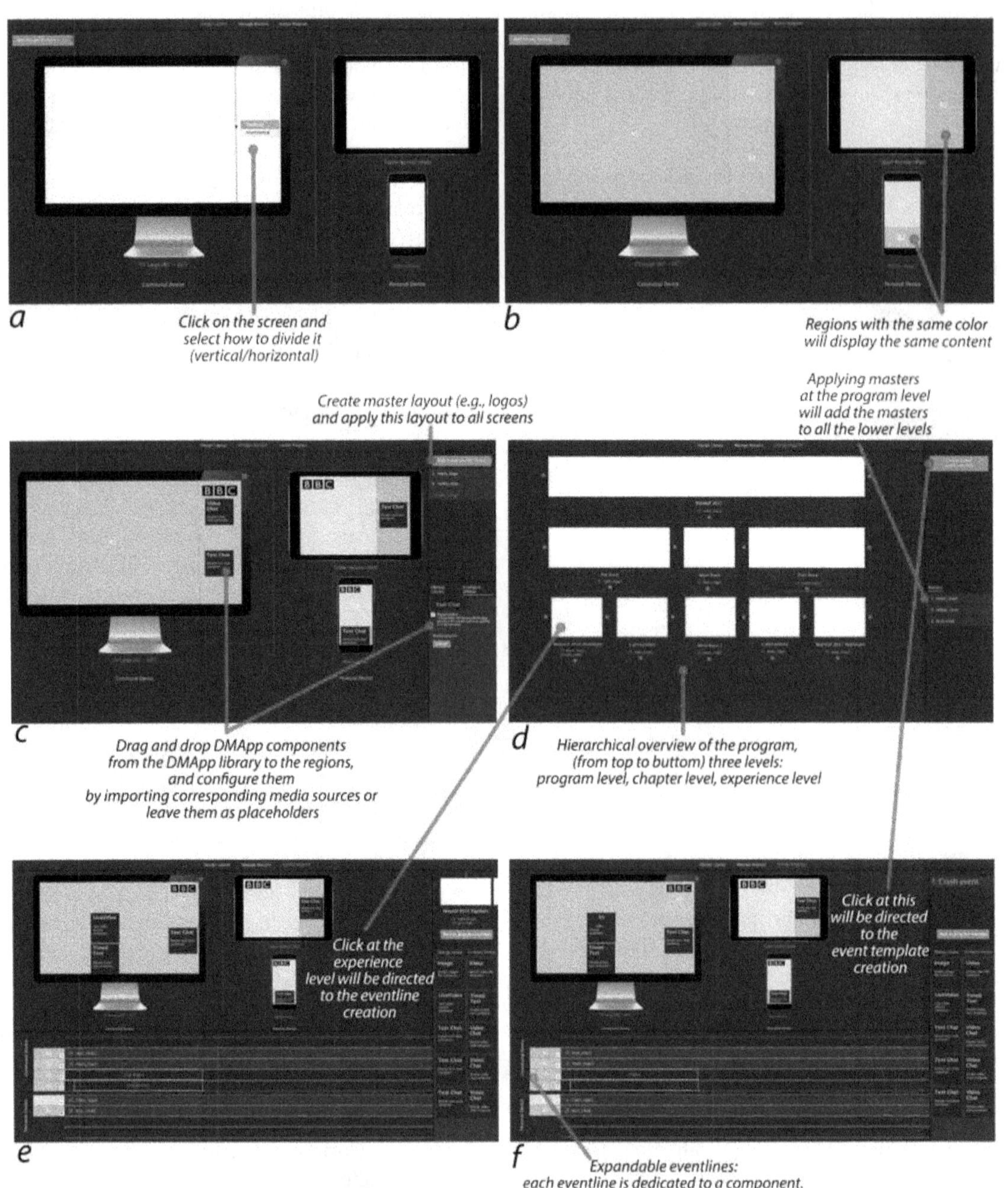

Figure 3. The advanced mode of layout design: (a) Click on the screen to divide it vertically or horizontally; (b) Label the regions with names and colors. Regions with the same color will display the same content. The eventline and event templates creation: (c) Create master layout, (d) Hierarchical overview of the program, (e) Create and edit content at the experience level, and (f) Create and edit content for live events.

Figure 3 shows featured screenshots of the re-designed preproduction tool, based on the feedback from the professionals [16]. Creating templates for live events is also included in the preproduction tool. Figure 3a and 3b illustrate the layout design mechanism in the advanced mode. The easy mode of layout design is to incorporate existing brand templates. The advanced mode allows program authors to flexibly divide regions on screens and label the regions with different colors. Regions with the same color will display the same content. For instance, the yellow and blue regions on the screens of the tablet and the phone. Figure 3c-3f depicts the eventline and event templates creation. Figure 3c shows the way to create a master layout, for example, a master layout of the "main logo". Figure 3d exhibits a three-level hierarchical overview of the program. From top to bottom, these levels are the program level, the chapter level and the experience level. Once created, the master layout can be applied at the program level. Then, the same master will be automatically added at the chapter level and the experience level. The master layout reduces repetitive work. Figure 3e and 3f are very similar, both including previews on multiple screens, eventlines and a library of DMApp components. Clicking on one of the documents at the experience level will direct to the "interface" shown in Figure 3e, where experience can be created, previewed and edited. The interface shown in Figure 3f has the same function, but for creating, previewing and editing live events, such as a crash at a motorcycle race or a goal in a football match.

As suggested by professionals, apart from the preproduction tool, a live editing tool should be designed to reduce the workload of live broadcasting, especially when broadcasting for multiscreen. All kinds of anticipated events and DMApp components can be prepared in the preproduction tool. With the live editing tool, the director can trigger the prepared events and components to multiscreen at adequate moments and remove them when the program requires. To design such a live tool, a field study was conducted at MotoGP 2017, to observe the live broadcasting workflow at an outside broadcasting (OB) truck. The next section will present the methods and results of the MotoGP study.

A FIELD STUDY AT MOTOGP

The goal of the study is to understand the workflow and challenges of live broadcasting. We chose to conduct the study at a representative event: the MotoGP 2017 racing event. MotoGP is the premier class of motorcycle racing events and is overwhelming for broadcasters due to the rapid pace of the races and unpredictable live events (overtake, crash, etc.). Due to the complexity, the MotoGP live broadcasting workflow adequately represents live sports broadcasting.

The commercial and television rights of the MotoGP have been exclusively held by Dorna, an international sports management and media company. Dorna provides the "World Feed" (i.e., IPF=International Program Feed) of the MotoGP racing to all other broadcasters worldwide. North One Television is the production company responsible for producing the presentation of Dorna's IPF for all the BT Sport's MotoGP broadcasts including the British MotoGP at Silverstone. North One Television hosted the field study, which was conducted in their OB truck gallery, their OB truck has standard setups for on-site broadcasting.

Methods

Four researchers participated in the three-day field study, from August 25 to 27, 2017, following a field data gathering technique called contextual inquiry [14]. When everyday work becomes habitual and unconscious, people are usually unable to articulate it. Contextual inquiry reveals these unconscious and tacit aspects of work. It guides researchers and designers to stay with people at their working place and talking with them about their work while observing them [14]. Due to the intense live OB broadcasting, the researchers were not allowed to talk to the staff during their work.

The first two days were the MotoGP warm-ups, and the third day was the official race. The four researchers were divided into two groups, which took turns to do the observations, swapping every two hours. A production manager who was not working in the OB truck was sitting together with the researchers during the first 30 minutes of the observation, assisting the researchers in understanding the set-ups, roles and workflows in the OB truck. Researchers were allowed to ask the production manager questions in a low voice. The OB live broadcasting of the warm-up races and the official race were observed, and the conversations between the staff were noted. The official race was video recorded.

Data analysis

The notes of the researchers and the video recordings were analyzed right after the field study. The notes of the four researchers were combined, with many overlapped content such as the OB truck set-ups, the transcripts of the conversations between the staff, and the workflow descriptions. The researchers discussed and rationalized the overlapped content, reaching a shared understanding of challenges in live broadcasting. The video recordings and conversations between staff were further analyzed to reveal the workflow.

Results

The results first illustrate the set-ups and roles of people who participated in the live broadcasting. Then, it visualizes the workflow and explains what is crucial for quickly reacting to live events.

The OB truck set-ups and roles of staff

In the OB truck, staff were arranged into two rows as shown in Figure 4. Apart from the OB truck, three InVision teams were working near the racing track, which consist of a presenter, a producer, and a cameraman. The director or the producer at the OB truck gallery can communicate with the InVision teams and send them instructions about what to do (e.g., instruct the presenter to talk about a particular topic and the cameraman to shoot certain scenes).

The role and tasks of the OB truck staff are described as follows:

1) Assistant producer. Keep up with the schedule, counting down with a stopwatch.

2) Producer. Decide together with the director, and inform the whole team about, a sequence of content that will be presented next, typically during a break. Work together with the production coordinator about what replay clips should be made.

3) Director. Decide the look and feel of the program. Instruct the whole team. Communicate with the presenters and the cameramen.

4) Graphic operator. Make graphics (results, name labels, etc.) in real-time. Usually use a template and type in texts (Preview on the GRAF PW on the Screen 2, see Figure 5).

5) Graphic editorial. Check the graphics before sending them on air. Make and edit more complex graphics and commercial clips (preview on the TOG of the Screen 2, see Figure 5).

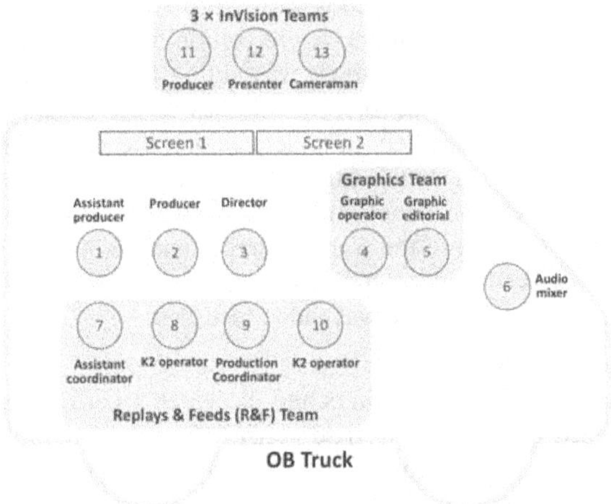

Figure 4. Roles of staff on an OB truck and the InVision teams on the tracks.

6) Audio mixer. When the program is on air, making sure it has the correct audio signal.

7) Assistant coordinator. Have a good knowledge of MotoGP, help production coordinator to decide on the making and selection of the replay clips.

9) Production coordinator. Direct the K2 operators to make replay clips (e.g., deciding when the clip starts and how long it should be).

8) & 10) K2 operators. K2 is a replay making and archiving system. Two operators are constantly working with it during the live broadcasting.

In the OB truck, two 55-inch screens were placed in front of the director. The main preview screen is the Screen 2. A quarter of the screen was the actual live feed of the program on a TV screen. Another quarter of the Screen 2 was taken by the preview of the program. The rest of the Screen 2 was filled up by four preview channels (named by different colors as GREEN, PINK, BLUE, RED), the upcoming feeds and replays were placed in these four channels. The Screen 2 also had a mini-preview for graphics (GRAF PW), and the camera feeds from the three InVision teams. The Screen 1 had the same four channels (GREEN, PINK, BLUE, RED) for upcoming feeds and replays. One quarter of the Screen 1 was the "World Feed" from Dorna. The Screen 1 also exhibited the local time, helicopter feeds and commercial previews. Details of the two screens divisions are illustrated in Figure 5.

The workflow in the North One OB truck

The broadcasting work of North One Television is written down as a "running order document". The document consists of the pre-race warming ups, the in-race commentary, the replays and graphics in addition to Dorna's, and the post-race commentary, which is specified with a minute by minute schedule. The staff use the minutes as reference points throughout the live broadcasting process. The document also defines where graphics, visual sources, and sound come from and when they are "on-air". It contains the duration of each

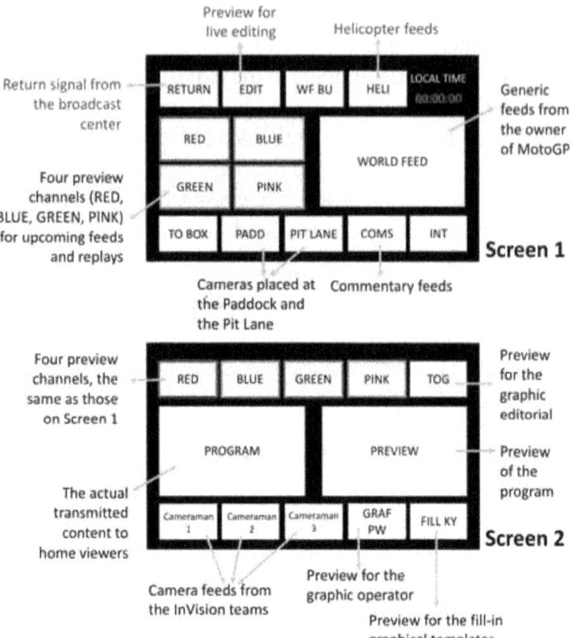

Figure 5. Two screens in front of the director.

item and the approximate time it starts. Table 1 presents a brief example of such a document. A program is segmented into many parts with 3-minute commercial breaks in-between. During the breaks, the producer announced the sequence of content that would be aired in the coming period. The workflow within each part was the same. The main tasks involved in the workflow are visualized in Figure 6 and explained as follows:

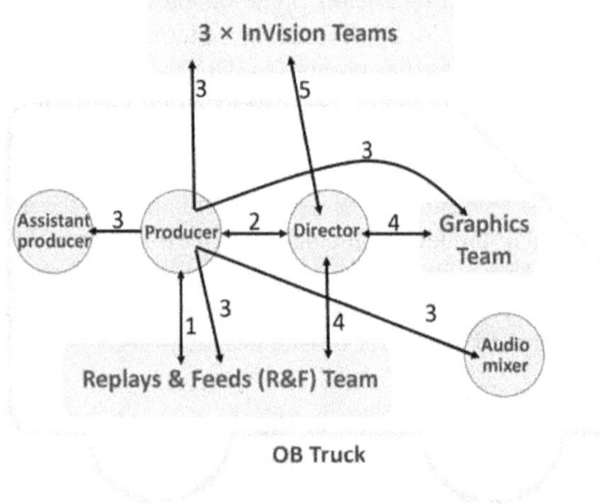

Figure 6. The workflow of the live broadcasting.

1) The producer communicates with the R&F team, collecting interesting materials to include in the broadcast. The R&F team "sells" the interesting feeds and replays to the producer.

2) The director works closely with the producer, checking all feeds, and deciding together with the producer the sequence of events for the coming 10-15 minutes.

ITEM	GRAPHICS	SOURCE	SOUND	DESCRIPTION	DURATION	TIME OF DAY
				WARM UP SHOW 5'00		08 45 00
1	Opening animation	VT	Bubble	Opening	00:00:08	08 45 08
2	Presenter name	CAMS	PRES MICS	LIVE: Presenter welcome	00:00:20	08 45 28
3		VT	SOVT	VT: Welcome	00:00:36	08 46 04
4		CAMS/VT	PRES MICS/SOVT	LIVE: Presenter interview VT: Player introductions	00:03:30	08 49 34
...	...	...	...	...	...	...
n				**OFF AIR-08:50:45**		08 50 45

(VT: Videotape; CAMS: Cameras; PRES MICS: Presenter microphones; SOVT: Sound of videotape.)

Table 1. An example of a "running order document" for live broadcasting.

3) The producer announces the decisions to the rest of the team.

4) When events happened, the director asks for particular feeds from the R&F team and requests the graphics team to create specific graphics based on the templates.

5) The InVision teams may be requested by the director to shoot particular scenes or talk about particular topics.

Challenges of live broadcasting

During the live broadcasting, especially for such an intense sports event, the team members were utterly focusing on their own tasks. The workload of the producer, the director and the replay operators was extremely heavy. We believe that it would be difficult for the team to use current equipment to produce extra content for multiscreens. Thus, the next section proposes a multiscreen production platform, for both authoring and broadcasting live content to TV screens as well as companion screens.

A MULTISCREEN PRODUCTION PLATFORM

As introduced in the "background" section, a preproduction tool was designed and evaluated in previous studies. This section will present the design of the live editing tool. The two tools, namely the preproduction tool and the live editing tool, are two parts of the proposed multiscreen production platform.

The Live Editing Tool

The goal of the live editing tool is to enable the production team to do live broadcasting for multiscreens, to reduce their workload and to quickly react to events. Compared with the preproduction tool, the interface of the live editing tool is rather simple and straightforward. There are two tabs. The left tab (Figure 7a) contains all the components and events prepared in the preproduction tool (e.g., logos, name tags, live event replays etc.). The right tab (Figure 7b) contains the components and events being triggered at the moment. Under the right tab, the triggered components can be removed during live broadcasting. For instance, when the leaderboard takes too much space and hides something of interest, the director can decide to remove the leaderboard for the time being. Figure 7 exhibits some examples of the prepared and triggered components in the live editing tool, and a preview on a TV screen.

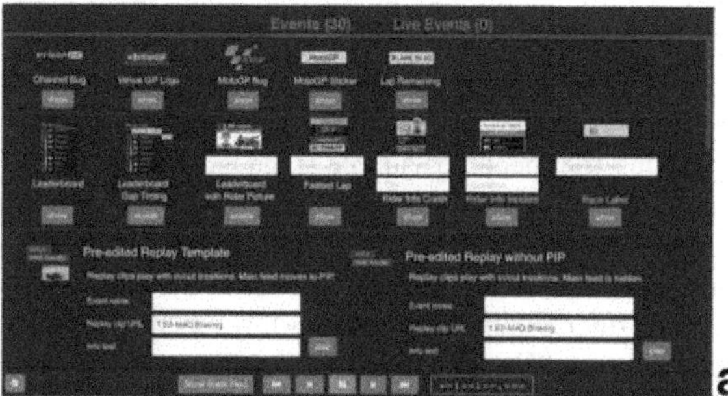

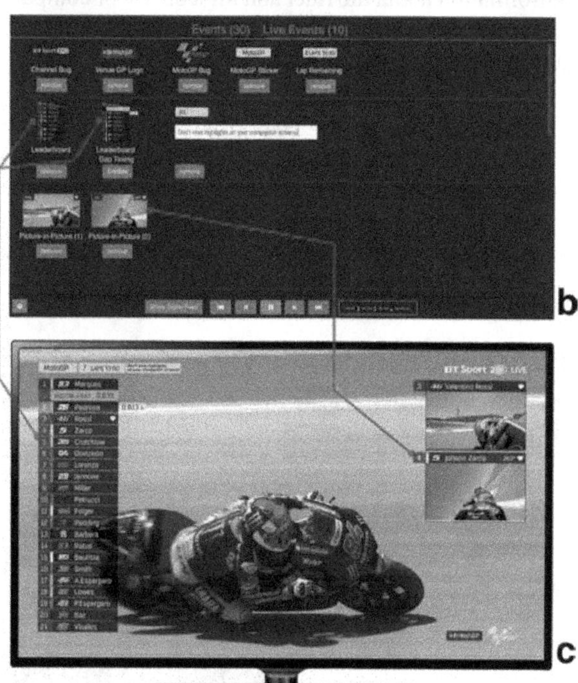

Figure 7. Some examples of (a) the prepared components and (b) triggered components in the live editing tool and (c) a preview on a TV screen.

A proposed workflow

The production platform proposes some changes to the typical TV production workflow (see Figure 2). The changes focus on the preproduction and the live editing parts, enabling the production team to create and broadcast for multiscreen, both for live and recorded content. The preproduction tool digitalizes the "running order document"

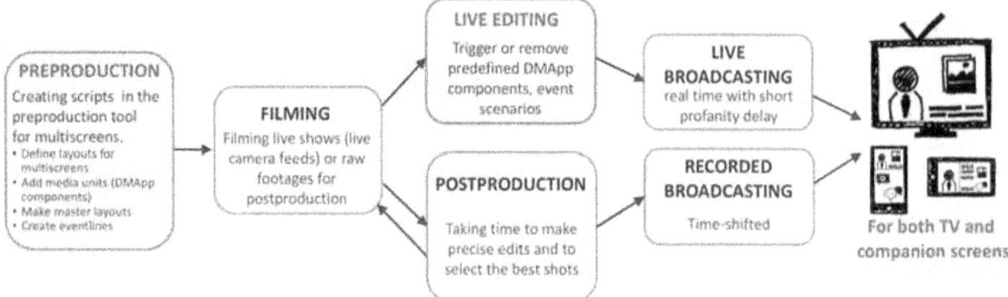

Figure 8. The changes (in orange color) made by the production platform to the typical television broadcasting workflow.

or script and allows the production team to prepare for anticipated live events (e.g., a crash in MotoGP or a goal in football). It also enables the team to preview the created experience on multiscreen without having a video feed. The live editing tool becomes simple since most of the work has been done at the preproduction phase. The team only needs to trigger the prepared components and live events at the right time. The editing task is simple. For instance, the team chooses a rider's name from a drop-down menu, and click on "show", the profile component will automatically generate the information about the rider and air it on TV or companion screens. The changes in the workflow are highlighted in Figure 8. The new set of tools for preproduction and live editing of a program are sketched in Figure 9.

To validate whether the workflow proposed by the production platform is appropriate, the next section presents validation interviews with professionals who are experienced in producing live interactive TV program, developing companion screen applications, doing research about new production workflows and so on.

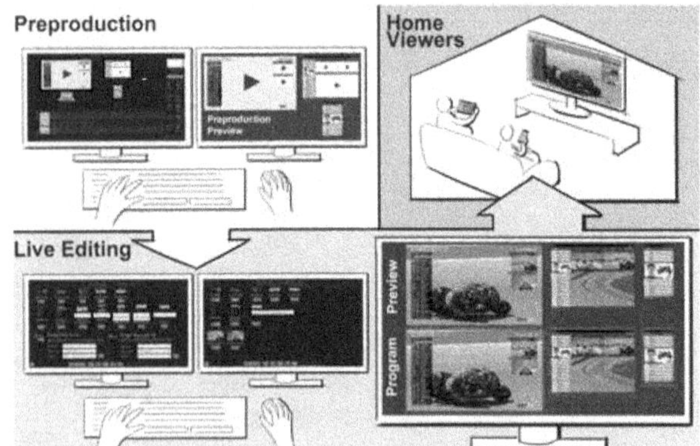

Figure 9. Preproduction and live editing of a program.

VALIDATION INTERVIEWS

The goal of the validation interviews is three folds. The first is to validate whether the proposed workflow for multiscreen production is appropriate (e.g., whether it fits into the current production workflow). The second is to collect suggestions from professionals for improving the tools. The third is to find out who is the right person in the production team to use such new tools.

Methods

Six semi-structured interviews [24] were conducted at the BBC usability lab, on Jan 18 and 19, 2018. This section introduces the selection of the interviewees, the procedure of the validation interviews, the data collection and the analysis.

Interviewees

Ten broadcasting professionals (P1-P10) with related backgrounds were invited to validate the workflow and the platform. They are either experienced in producing interactive TV, developing companion screen applications or doing research on multiscreen immersive TV experience and new production workflows (see Table 2). Most interviews were one-to-one conversations except two, which was conducted with two (P2 & P3) and four professionals (P6, P7, P8 & P9), due to their limited time availability.

P1	Interactive TV researcher at BT, researching on next generation multiscreen and immersive TV application, and experienced in UX design and evaluations.
P2	UX designer at BBC, developing companion screen applications and websites.
P3	Creative director at BBC, creating online content for TV programs.
P4	Senior UX designer at BBC, doing researching about workflows and roles in a production team.
P5	Computer scientist at BBC, researching on HCI and UX.
P6	TV series producer at BBC, producing live interactive TV programs and working in production studios
P7	Broadcast journalist and assistant producer at BBC, creating online and interactive content for TV programs.
P8	Assistant producer at BBC, creating online and interactive content for TV programs, working in production studios
P9	New workflow researcher at BBC, working with production studios, developing innovative tools for the production of subtitles and shot planning for multi-camera TV direction
P10	Creative director for production systems at BBC, developing and testing production tools

Table 2. Ten professionals and their daily work.

Procedure

The prototype of the production platform was installed at the usability lab. Two interviewers facilitated the interviews. The interviews lasted about one hour, mainly consisting of three steps as follows:

1) One interviewer introduced some related topics, including, among others, multiscreen viewing and object-based broadcasting. At the end of the introduction, the new workflow and the goals of the interviews were explained.

2) With the interview goals in mind, the prototype of the production platform was played by one facilitator and presented to the professionals. The preproduction tool was shown first, then the live editing tool. Open discussions were encouraged around whether the new workflow is appropriate or not.

3) The professionals were requested to give improvement suggestions of the interface and indicate the suitable person(s) that can use the tool in the future.

Data collection and analysis

The interviews were video and audio recorded. The audio records were transcribed into text. The video records were used to clarify ideas during the transcription process. Relevant quotations from the transcripts were selected and coded according to the goals and the discussions of three researchers in the project. Figure 10a shows an example of the coded texts. It consists of a quotation from a professional (e.g., P3) selected from the transcripts and an interpretation of the researcher (the handwritten texts). The coded texts were then sorted into four main categories, namely positive aspects of the platform, ways to fit into the current production workflow, suitable staff to use the platform, and improvement suggestions. The results section presents the four main categories (Figure 10b).

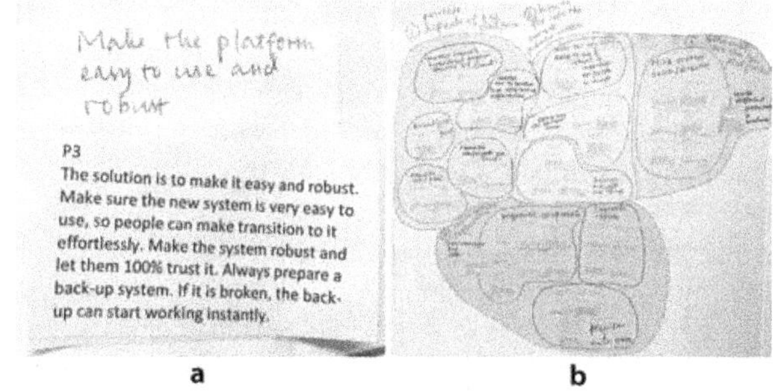

Figure 10. (a) One example of the coded texts; (b) The coded texts were sorted into four main categories.

Results

According to the research questions, the results were sorted into four main categories. The first category describes the positive aspects of the production platform complimented by the professionals. The second category gathers the comments about how to fit the platform into the current production workflow. The third one consists of suggestions for suitable staff to operate the platform. The last category presents the recommendations from the professionals for improvement. The four categories are presented in the following subsections.

Positive aspects of the platform

P1, P2 and P3 liked the master layout design and hierarchical overview of the program chapters, which reduce the repetitive work. They also indicated their preference for the re-usable DMApp components, since keeping a short list of re-configurable components can save the effort of searching. Another aspect they considered as appropriate is the "eventline" (P2, P3, P5 &P10). Components and events are arranged in sequence on the eventline because a program is based on a sequence of components and events. For some events, especially the live ones, it is impossible to know their length during preproduction. P4 pointed out that the dark interfaces can bring a sense of familiarity to most production team members since they are frequent users of video editing tools. Most of these tools have a dark interface (e.g., Adobe Premiere). P4 also mentioned that the live editing tool is very *"light"*, *"it may not need a level of expertise to be able to use it"*, which is a good sign for the production team to be motivated to try it. P6, P7 and P8 thought the platform worked very much in parallel as their *Live Lessons* (a live education program). They saw opportunities to offer live interactive lessons to students. P6 also indicated an opportunity to use the platform for pre-recorded programs, but make it feel like a live interactive experience. As P6 explained, "*It will be more cost-effective to do recorded broadcasting than live broadcasting, but we do not want to sacrifice viewers' live interactive experience.*"

How to fit into the current production workflow

The professionals had consistent opinions about how to fit the platform into the current production workflow. They believed that it might be difficult to replace the current workflow (P3, P4 & P9). As P3 explained, "*People tend to use the old-fashioned software. Once they get trained to use it, they do not want to change to new systems.*" "*It might be quite some barriers to let people who work on TV screens switch to multiscreen* (P9)."

To change this reluctance to adopt a new production platform, the professionals suggested two ways. The first is to "*make it easy and robust*" (P3). As P3 explained, "*Make sure the new system is straightforward, so people can make a transition to it effortlessly. Make the system robust and let them 100% trust it. Always prepare a backup system. If it is broken, the back-up can start working instantly.*" The second is to convince the production team that multiscreen TV view is valuable (P3, P6 & P9). "*It will be good to let the production team to play with the platform, to try out different scenarios of multiscreen TV viewing experiences* (P3)." "*Specify scenarios of audience experiences. Some of them might have no companion screens but a TV screen, some of them might have a tablet, a phone and a TV, others might have two phones, and so on. Give the director a list of new audience experiences. Let him feel that this is new, and they want to try* (P9)."

Suitable staff to use the platform

P2, P3, P4, P6, P7, P8, P9 and P10 all gave similar ideas about who will use the platform. "*Practically, it makes more sense that a separate team or a person to be trained to operate this platform. It lacks space in the current production team, to really work for companion screens* (P3)." P4 suggested that "*It seems to me that this should be another team working on this platform, a team with a focus on social, online and companion content, not on TV* (P4)." P6 and P9 recommended a new role called "an interactive director" or "an interactive direct team", to use this platform. P2 and P10 further specified that people within this interactive team should also clearly divide the tasks. "*For example, a person decides to show or to remove components, and another person decides where the components go, to companion screens or to TV screens* (P10)." P10 also suggested inviting different production teams (e.g., small or big, different genres) to use the platform. For example, a small and young production team that makes relatively simple program might adopt this new system more easily than the well-established and sophisticated production teams.

Improvement suggestions

Improvement suggestions were mainly about the interface design. A few professionals questioned about the layout mechanism in the preproduction tool (P2, P3 & P10). They were confused about the regions and overlays of components. Frequently asked questions include "Does the content take the entire space of the region it assigns to (P2)?"; "Is there a way to specify the exact positions of certain components, to prevent they overlap undesirably (P10)?"; "How to arrange components that are placed in the same region (P3)?" In the end, three modes of layout design were proposed based on the feedback from the professionals. The first mode is the easy mode, where a library of templates is prepared. The second mode is region mode, where TV screens and companion screens are divided into several regions. Every region can only hold one component at a time, and the component will take up all the space in that region. Components in different regions will not be overlapped. The third mode is the advanced mode, where the exact positioning of every component can be specified. The main video stream is overlaid by all the components. Figure 11 shows the region mode and the advanced mode.

Figure 11. Advanced mode of layout design for a TV screen, where the video stream is overlaid by components with accurately specified positions (above); region mode of layout design for a tablet screen, where a screen is separated into multiple regions (below).

Another consistent feedback is about organizing the components in the live editing tool (P1, P4, P5, P6, P7, P8 & P9). The professionals complained that the list of the prepared components is very long with a lot of scrolling to find a component. P10 suggested thinking about several drop-down lists instead of a scrolling list. Within each drop-down list, there can be selections of components that can be grouped together, such as the icons, logos and statistic graphics are under one list. Name tag templates and statistics templates are under another list.

The professionals also indicated that the two tabs in the live editing tool are counterintuitive (P6, P7 &P8). People need to constantly switch between two tabs in order to trigger or stop certain components. They suggested to use only one button for triggering and stopping a component, like a switcher for light: click once to trigger and click again to stop. Adding preview to the live editing tool was also requested by three professionals (P2, P4 & P10). "You do not need to show all the content in the preview on a big screen. A mini-preview that gives ideas about the position of the triggered component is sufficient.

DISCUSSION AND CONCLUSION

This paper proposes a production platform and a new workflow for authoring and broadcasting TV programs to multiscreen. The platform was validated by ten professionals in the TV broadcasting industry. They indicated that the user interfaces of the platform are straightforwardly designed and allows well preparations at the preproduction stage and reduce the workload during the live broadcasting. They foresaw the potential of the platform in producing multiscreen contents for both live and recorded broadcasting and provided feedback to improve the interface design, such as clarifying the layout design mechanisms in the preproduction tool, organizing components and adding previews in the live triggering tool. The study process has some limitations. For instance, during the field study at Silverstone, we did not have opportunities to have a conversation with the production team while they were working. Some valuable insights may be neglected. The prototype was not fully implemented, so it was impossible to ask the professionals to operate the platform during the interviews. The future evaluations will be conducted with a fully developed platform in real live broadcasting context.

Apart from the limitations, the validation interviews provided useful insights for the redesign and implementation of the platform. The professionals specifically pointed out several aspects that need be carefully considered, such as how to make the digitalized "running order documents" as flexible as the paper documents. In other words, when something happened during live broadcasting, the team needs to quickly delete some pre-authored content and quickly build new content to replace it. Another aspect is about whether multiple members of the team can work on the platform together. In this case, the task dividing among team members is important, to avoid conflict in editing. The third aspect is to think about the "responsive design" like a website. The authored content can automatically rescale to fit into different sizes of screens; or the same content has different modes (e.g., novice versus expert) that are customized to personal interest. The viewers have some flexibility in selecting modes or resolutions. The production team should have the editorial control (e.g., decide the recommended screen size for a program, and decide how many modes a program has). They indicated that the current production team needs to hire extra staff to use the platform. The platform can run in parallel with the existing production workflows. However, it might require time and effort to get the production team to accept and trust a new system.

Both end viewers and production companies are believed to benefit from the proposed new platform. For end viewers, the platform offers interactive contents and personalized and immersive watching experiences. For production companies, the platform helps reduce the workload of live broadcasting, making authoring and broadcasting possible for multiscreen. The next step of the project is to accomplish the development of the production platform and test it at a stadium, for real live football broadcasting. Meanwhile, it will be tested with end viewers to evaluate their experiences. The tests will happen in the summer of 2018.

ACKNOWLEDGEMENT

This work is supported by European Union's Horizon 2020 research and innovation program under grant agreement No 687655, project 2-IMMERSE.

REFERENCES

1. Edward Anstead, Steve Benford, and Robert J. Houghton. 2014. Many-screen viewing: evaluating an Olympics companion application. In *Proceedings of TVX '14*, 103-110.
2. Mike Armstrong, Matthew Brooks, Anthony Churnside, Michael Evans, Frank Melchior, Matthew Shotton. 2014. Object-based broadcasting- curation, responsiveness and user experience. In *Proceedings of IBC 2014 Conference*, Amsterdam, The Netherlands, p. 12.2.
3. BBC Research & Development. 2015. *Squeezebox: A production tool that can edit for you.* Retrieved December 5, 2017, from http://www.bbc.co.uk/rd/projects/squeezebox
4. Frank R. Bentley. 2017. Understanding Secondary Content Practices for Television Viewing. In *Proceedings of TVX '17*, 123-128.
5. Pablo Cesar. 2015. From secondary screens to socially-aware and immersive experiences (invited talk). In María José Abásolo, Francisco J. Perales and Antoni Bibiloni (Eds.), *Applications and Usability of Interactive TV*, p. VII-VIII.
6. Jasmine Cox, Rhianne Jones, Chris Northwood, Jonathan Tutcher, and Ben Robinson. 2017. Object-Based Production: A Personalised Interactive Cooking Application. In *Adjunct Publication of TVX '17*, 79-80.
7. Mihaly Csikszentmihalyi and Robert Kubey. 1981. Television and the rest of life: A systematic comparison of subjective experience. *Public Opinion Quarterly, 45*(3), 317-328.
8. John Dowell, Sylvain Malacria, Hana Kim and Edward Anstead. 2015. Companion apps for information-rich television programmes: representation and interaction. *Personal and Ubiquitous Computing, 19*(7), 1215-1228.
9. K. Anders Ericsson and Herbert A. Simon. 1980. Verbal reports as data. *Psychological Review, 87* (3), 215–251.
10. David Geerts, Rinze Leenheer, Dirk De Grooff, Joost Negenman, and Susanne Heijstraten. 2014. In front of and behind the second screen: viewer and producer perspectives on a companion app. In *Proceedings of TVX '14*, 95-102.
11. Christian Holz, Frank Bentley, Karen Church, and Mitesh Patel. 2015. "I'm just on my phone and they're watching TV": Quantifying mobile device use while watching television. In *Proceedings of TVX '15*, 93-102.
12. Jianmin Jiang, Joachim Kohler, Carmen Williams, Janez Zaletelj, Georg Guntner, Heike Horstmann, Jinchang Ren, Jobst Loffler, and Ying Weng. 2011. "Live: An integrated production and feedback system for intelligent and interactive TV broadcasting." *IEEE Transactions on Broadcasting, 57*(3), 646-661.
13. Hans Jonasson. 2012. *Determining Project Requirements*. ESI International Project Management Series. CRC Press.
14. Holtzblatt, K. and Beyer, H., 2014. Contextual design: evolved. *Synthesis Lectures on Human-Centered Informatics*, 7(4), pp.1-91.
15. Ian Kegel, James Walker, Mark Lomas, Jack Jansen and John Wyver.2017. 2-IMMERSE: A platform for orchestrated multiscreen entertainment. In *Adjunct Publication of TVX '17*, 71-72.
16. Jie Li, Zhiyuan Zheng, Britta Meixner, Thomas Röggla, Maxine Glancy and Pablo Cesar. 2018. Design an Object-based Preproduction Tool for Multiscreen TV Viewing. Accepted by *CHI 2018*, late-breaking work.
17. Britta Meixner, Maxine Glancy, Matt Rogers, Caroline Ward, Thomas Röggla and Pablo Cesar, P., 2017, June. Multi-Screen Director: a New Role in the TV Production Workflow?. In *Adjunct Publication of TVX '17*, 57-62.
18. Janet Murray, Sergio Goldenberg, Kartik Agarwal, Tarun Chakravorty, Jonathan Cutrell, Abraham Doris-

Down, and Harish Kothandaraman. 2012. Story-map: iPad companion for long form TV narratives. In *Proceedings of EuroITV '12*, 223-226.

19. Abhishek Nandakumar and Janet Murray. 2014. Companion apps for long arc TV series: supporting new viewers in complex storyworlds with tightly synchronized context-sensitive annotations. In *Proceedings of TVX '14*, 3-10.
20. Timothy Neate, Matt Jones, and Michael Evans. 2015. Mediating Attention for Second Screen Companion Content. In *Proceedings of CHI '15*, 3103-3106.
21. The Nielson Company. 2017. *The Nielson total audience report Q1 2017*. Copyright © 2017 The Nielsen Company. Retrieved December 5, 2017 from http://www.nielsen.com/us/en/insights/reports/2017/the-nielsen-total-audience-report-q1-2017.html
22. Carlos Antonio Navarrete Puentes and José Tiberio Hernández Peñaloza. 2017. HEd: A Flexible HbbTV WYSIWYG Visual Authoring Tool. In *Adjunct Publication of TVX '17*, 15-20.
23. Jim Ownens and Gerald Millerson. 2009. *Television production (The 15th edition)*. Focal Press.
24. Marina Remington and P. Tyer. 1979. The social functioning schedule: A brief semi-structured interview. *Social Psychiatry, 14*, 151-157.
25. Pedro Silva, Yasmin Amer, William Tsikerdanos, Jesse Shedd, Isabel Restrepo, and Janet Murray. 2015. A Game of Thrones Companion: Orienting Viewers to Complex Storyworlds via Synchronized Visualizations. In *Proceedings of TVX '15*, 167-172.
26. Doug Williams, John Wyver and Maxine Glancy. 2016. *Evaluating the potential benefits of object-based broadcasting.* Retrieved December 5, 2017 from https://nem-initiative.org/wp-content/uploads/2016/11/doug-willams-obb.pdf

Digital Authoring of Interactive Public Display Applications

Ryan Mills
Lancaster University
Lancaster, England
r.mills2@lancaster.ac.uk

Matthew Broadbent
Lancaster University
Lancaster, England
m.broadbent@lancaster.ac.uk

Nicholas Race
Lancaster University
Lancaster, England
n.race@lancaster.ac.uk

ABSTRACT
HbbTV (Hybrid broadcast broadband TV) is an emerging force in the entertainment industry, and proper standarisation of technologies would be hugely beneficial for the creation of content. HbbTV aims to realise this vision and has been widely successful thus far. This paper introduces MPAT (Multi Platform Application Toolkit), which is the result of multiple organisational entities effort and dedication to extend the capabilities and functionality of HbbTV, in order to ease the design and creation of interactive TV applications. The paper also showcases the versatility of MPAT, by describing a series of case studies which provide digital storytelling and visual authoring of interactive applications which transcend traditional TV use cases, and instead provide a gripping interactive experience via integration with public displays.

Author Keywords
Public Display Infrastructure; Interactive TV Applications; Authoring Tool

CCS Concepts
•Human-centered computing → User interface management systems;

INTRODUCTION
Interactive TV applications require a lengthy process of authoring, reviewing and publishing which remains expensive with significant upfront investment typically needed. Furthermore, expertise in this technical field also requires trained specialists capable of implementing bespoke complex architectures. In addition to the lengthy review process, applications naturally take extensive time before they are fit for deployment. MPAT [13] is described in [15] as "an open-source authoring and publishing tool, based on the WordPress content management system and provides an easy-to use solution to existing publishing systems that supports rapid expert review and professional online publishing". Both WordPress and MPAT are open source projects, and the latter extends the functionality of WordPress to enable the creation of powerful interactive TV applications. The use of WordPress as a base Content Management System (CMS) has various advantages over a bespoke system designed to achieve the same goal, namely that it is a hugely popular tool, with a dominant market share compared to other CMS options [6]. This aspect alone presents a strong argument in favour of the use of this system, as there is a substantial likelihood that users will already have familiarity in the creation of similar pages. Similarly, Wordpress is robustly tested, and has a vibrant community who continually build additional functionality. As a visual alternative to the creation of web pages, WordPress has been demonstrably shown to be easy to learn and is ideal for simple web pages. This simplicity is advantageous when designing TV applications as complexity and verbosity will often confuse the end-user. MPAT aims to enable the creation of, otherwise very technical and expensive, TV applications by users who lack the expertise to do so. This is done in an attempt to increase the number of applications for TV, and reduce the time taken.

During the design, testing and implementation of MPAT, it became clear that it would support a myriad of potential use cases outside of the TV traditional broadcast settings. This is in part due to the nature of the application created; simple and intuitive in use. The applications that MPAT creates are HbbTV compliant; a standard adopted by manufacturers to ensure cross-compatibility of TV applications. Current uses of this application include additional and interactive content, which complement a relevant broadcast TV programme. However, due to the power and ease of use that this visual editor provides, it is feasible for use outside of the TV application domain. There exists similarities between the way in which interactive TV and public display applications are consumed, including the size of the displays, the necessity to display information clearly and concisely, and the distance between the display and the viewer. The interaction techniques are also similar: operated by one person whilst having multiple viewers. Furthermore, both public displays and TV share components within their problem domain. The design of public display applications is inherently difficult due to the careful choices needed to ensure engagement, while TV applications must subtly, yet effectively, imply the notion that an application is available for execution whilst the broadcast is in the background. Moreover, the creation of said applications is demanding in itself as these displays often operate on a diverse range of hardware, and the application must be implemented using disparate guidelines depending upon the ownership. This issue has been recently remediated through the standardisation of HbbTV technology for TV environments, yet no such standard exists for public displays. As MPAT offers simultaneous availability for multiple platforms, whilst also streamlining the creation process, it becomes a viable candidate for creating public display applications.

TVX '18, June 26–28, 2018, SEOUL, Republic of Korea

ACM ISBN 978-1-4503-5115-7/18/06.

DOI: http://dx.doi.org/10.1145/3210825.3210835

PUBLIC DISPLAY INFRASTRUCTURE

The context for the development of MPAT for public displays was Lancaster University, which hosts a large-scale PDI (Public Display Infrastructure) [14]. This infrastructure consists of a number of connected displays that are capable of presenting personalised content to each individual user, which is achieved by an integration of iBeacon technology. This effort to personalise content on the various displays allows for more engaging content, and allows students the means to find specific information on demand. The current implementation requires use of an iOS application developed by researchers at Lancaster University: 'Tacita' [12].

The technology underpinning this has also been merged with the hugely popular 'iLancaster' application, which is available for both Android and Apple devices and is installed by the majority of Lancaster University students and staff. Tacita aids developers in the creation of custom applications which communicate with the PDI to display personalised content on individual screens across campus when a user has come into contact with them. If enabled, Tacita will periodically check to see if a user is in the vicinity of a public display that provides applications matching the users preferences. If so, the mobile application contacts the relevant web-based display application, specifying the desired display and personalisation parameters. The web application then contacts the display component in order to ensure that the relevant content was shown on the display.

Mobile devices which act as interaction gateways may alleviate problems relating to engagement and interaction inherent within public displays. These displays often do not give the feeling of ownership to their users in the same way that a personal device does, which in turn imposes difficulties for user engagement [5]. In comparison to other interaction procedures such as touch enabled interactions, mobile devices grant the user a certain level of privacy and familiarity.

In this paper, we aim to design and implement a number of public display applications using MPAT. Two distinct use cases are investigated, as we highlight both the build and deployment processes for each. Finally, we explore the interaction possibilities, as well as conducting a preliminary evaluation of the use of these applications.

At present, it is believed that no applications using HbbTV's library and specifications have been adopted for use by public displays. As a result, research into this area is very scarce and careful consideration of the implications that this transition creates must be taken into account when designing such applications. At MPAT's core lies a fundamental objective to allow its service to be be available on multiple platforms. This paper outlines the design and interaction procedure relating to this process.

RELATED WORK

There exists a large amount of tools which aim to reduce the time spent designing interfaces for applications. However specialised applications, such as ones applicable to interactive TV and PDIs, are less well known. While the HbbTV foundations are built using accepted standards, they require some expertise in order to properly extend their functionality. Nevertheless, tools of this nature have been developed, and are documented below.

Other products exist that compete with MPAT, which all aim to extend upon the HbbTV library and provide a comprehensive visual authoring environment. HEd [8] is a WYSIWYG (What You See Is What You Get) visual authoring tool which facilitates the creation of interactive TV applications in a similar manner to MPAT. Generic components can be placed at will within a visual interface, representing the application within a broadcast stream upon rendering on a display. This variant provides an interface for the customisation of displayable elements by the allowing an author to specify the CSS properties that they desire. These components can also be modified to include custom functionality that a specific application requires by the utilisation of JavaScript (JS) functions. While services such as these exist and provide much of the functionality present within MPAT, none of them been implemented within the sphere of public displays.

There has been substantial research into pervasive display design patterns, which aim to successfully draw attention and engage with viewers to ultimately begin the interaction procedure. Bendinelli [7] identifies many of these patterns through the evaluation of public display utilisation. These patterns outline certain recurring situations and provide insight into how to address them, while also providing a starting point for the application development process. While a useful starting point, these guidelines must be extended in order to provide a meaningful experience for users upon consideration of a specific application. A development environment which realises these guidelines was also created. This environment aims to highlight the most important aspects that compose the structure of such applications, by allowing an author to exploit a list of patterns and apply them to their application. As this environment does not allow for visual arrangement and addition of components, the development process can be seen as less intuitive in comparison to the editor provided by MPAT. While MPAT does not provide guidelines for development, many high level components are packaged with MPAT, and an author is free to experiment with many possible design scenarios. These components are also readily customisable within the MPAT editor, and also extensible by the modularity which WordPress provides.

The choice of a web based framework to produce interactive public display applications is not an uncommon approach, as this method is at a high level of abstraction and allows content to be shared from a number of sources. These applications conform to common web technology standards such as HTML and JS. An example of this is the UBI hotspots, which is a pervasive display infrastructure which bases its design on the web paradigm. This abstraction grants services which reside on the Internet and accessed using a URL to be consumed by the various public display deployments situated in Oulu, Finland [9]. Akin to the deployment lead by Lancaster University, users can initiate interaction using personal mobile devices.

Although the number of public displays is large and continues to grow, there exists a small percentage which can actually be interacted with. Cardoso states that this is due to the fact that there exists no clear abstraction for interaction modality, and this leads to specific work, outside of the core application functionality, having to be undertaken and replicated by each developer working on a separate project [10]. With this lack of abstraction impacting the quality of public display applications, a clear standard implementation for such systems would be beneficial. Cardoso also creates an environment which allows developers to ignore the lower level details of interaction implementation, and instead focus on core functionality. Although this product exists, it is very bespoke and doesn't offer a wide range of functionality. MPAT offers its services on multiple platforms and its base, HbbTV, has been rigorously tested by industry leading organisations as it is not a drastically new implementation. This mature technology provides an open API for interaction, and could be a clear contender for the standard abstraction service for public displays.

DESIGN

As part of an ongoing initiative to improve HbbTV adoption across the UK, Lancaster University have conducted two very different pilot projects. Each of these aims to draw attention to the emerging technology while providing end-users the opportunity to interact with MPAT enabled HbbTV applications.

Overview of Pilots

The pilots demonstrated and documented in this paper consist of one which caters to prospective students and one for the general collegiate. The former is focused on building an electronic prospectus for students visiting Lancaster University on one of our open days. The latter integrates with the existing PDI lead by Lancaster University, to create a storytelling narrative for staff and students. They will receive a piece of content, visible on the multiple displays located around campus as they are encountered. For the purposes of this paper the former pilot will be referenced as the digital prospectus pilot, and the latter will be referenced as the presence detection pilot.

The presence detection pilot follows the interior lives of three characters: The Scientist, The Artist and The Historian until the egress of a celestial event overlooking Bowland Tower within Lancaster University. The narrative is distributed and non-linear in nature, allowing users to explore the various possible story lines possible. The story will evolve depending upon the order of displays visited by, in essence this means that each individual user will explore a different narrative across campus. A visual representation of this is depicted in Figure 1. In the example, each display is attributed to one of the three story lines, meaning that when a user encounters a display, they will receive a video depending upon how far into the story they are and also which story line the display is connected to. The overall story has five separate instances which users can experience, with the ability to see parts from each of the three overarching character narratives, dependent upon which displays the user encounters around campus. While each character has it's own narrative, the content within each storyline seamlessly flow into one another to create a unique experience encompassing the different thematic representations a celestial event.

Figure 1. The three narratives of the storytelling application

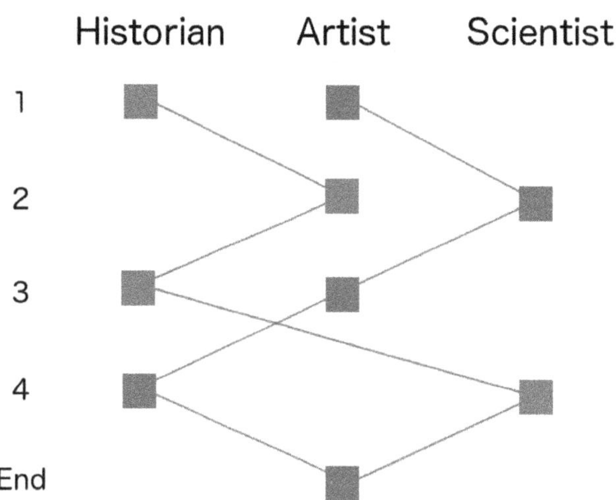

The digital prospectus pilot, while deployed in a public location, does not integrate with the display infrastructure Lancaster University has developed. The application is launched on a standard digital TV, with a traditional broadcast stream being produced by a connected computer, which provides a looping informational video. This pilot showcases MPAT in its traditional format, while also being in a public setting. Because of the fact that the application is not broadcast with terrestrial TV and is not to be consumed in a home environment, several choices in design must be made that accommodate this.

Firstly, as it is a public settings and there are multiple stimuli in close surroundings, it must be easy to identify that the display exists and is providing information, and furthermore that there is an additional application which exists and can be interacted with. The display must be situated in such a manner to catch the eye of prospective students as they enter and also maneuver around the various attractions on offer by the University. The method of input must also be made easily accessible and intuitive to use, and care must be taken to increase engagement which also neither obstructs or is obtrusive to other potential interacting users [5]. The latter pilot is centered around integrating the existing PDI offered by Lancaster University with MPAT. Research into correct substantiation of content for viewing within pervasive display infrastructures is vast and encompasses multiple view points. Linden et al [2] propose a web-based framework to cater the process of content instantiation and interaction. The paper describes how concurrent applications can be rapidly deployed and managed through means of a web framework, which acts as a broker, carefully considering which applications need to be shown by use of a web browser. Other work [1] has led to the development of bespoke applications which launch on individual devices to display specific content, which has been demonstrably shown to lack openness and scalability. This approach is largely due to the fact that most public displays are proprietary technology, in which the network acts as an "isolated island, each with its own concepts and technologies". This is both a problem for users and developers alike, with the latter requiring huge

Figure 2. An overview of our open pervasive display ecosystem..

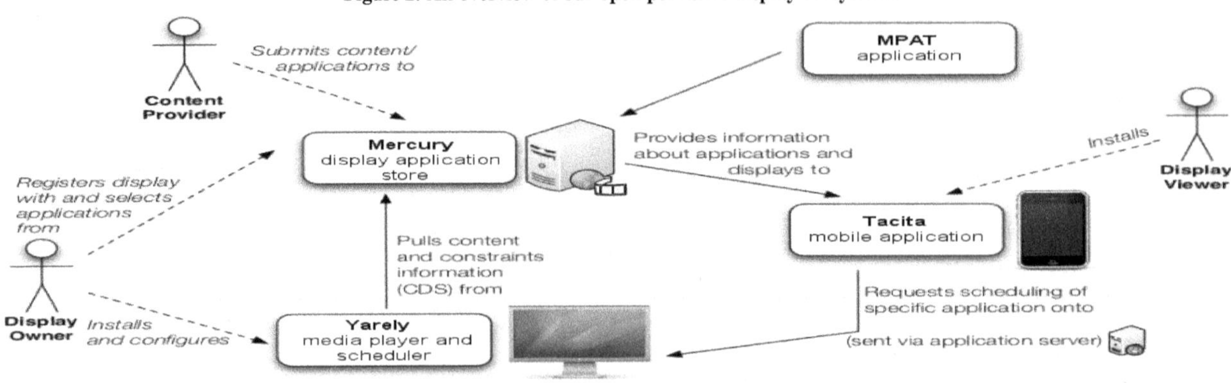

amounts of effort to build the foundations of the infrastructure and the interaction mechanism, within the limitations of the architecture. For the users, the bespoke nature of these infrastructures precipitates unfamiliarity with both identifying a public display and also the interaction model.

Due to the lack of abstraction within the sphere of public displays, the infrastructure adopted by Lancaster University is itself bespoke, however it offers abstraction in terms of application development by allowing 3rd parties access to a RESTful API which in turn aids the development process. Figure 2 depicts the ecosystem of the architecture and the interaction mechanism contained within. The MPAT application developed resides within mercury's application store, and can be instantiated upon demand via integration of web servers which serve requests. As shown, Yarely [4], a software player for open pervasive display networks, dictates the scheduling of application to be launched on specific displays. This technology allows accessibility for a range of different media types, including video and pdf. The application server is responsible for providing Yarely with a CDS (Content Descriptor Set). This is described in [4] as "a method to provide a description of a set of content items to be played by the node, the circumstances in which they should be played, and the location of any required media". This CDS is in XML format, which allows for a range of implementations, as from a transmission perspective it is protocol agnostic. The CDS must be rendered and manipulated for each individual scheduling request, and provides a layer of abstraction for application developers, whom only have to consider adhering to the API standard. This architecture also allows for web applications to be deployed on the various displays situated around campus, by specifying the type and URL within the CDS. This integral functionality allows MPAT applications to be natively launched on the displays, as MPAT itself is web-based and pages within the application have their own URL. Furthermore, encompassing MPAT applications within a web framework allows integration for all other PDIs which allow applications from a web source. As the pilot is fundamentally providing a non-linear story to users who traverse campus, the application server developed must distinguish between individuals and enumerate how many displays they have visited, in order to create a CDS which contains a hyperlink to the MPAT application where the correct video is stored. This CDS is then sent to the infrastructure, where the request is scheduled and eventually displayed. Upon receipt of a content request, the display launches a WebKit instance, which is directed to URL specified in the CDS.

Application Development

An MPAT application is a set of pages that are distributed with a piece of broadcast content, which should have a single style, entry point (the URL specified by the Application Information Table), origin, and which is created from a single application model. Each page is composed of multiple predefined components, which are bundled with the MPAT editor. Using this editor, components can be placed in locations on the page at the developers will, which will eventually create the desired application. There are two fundamental stages that a developer must traverse in order to make an MPAT application, the first being the creation of a page model.

The page model, shown in Figure 3, acts as a template for the various pages within the application, and is achieved in a visual fashion. Designers of the application can drag and drop boxes to the desired position within the page, which represent the various components that the MPAT editor offers. This avenue of application development is advantageous in multiple ways, however, one of the main advantages is the fact that no code will need to be written in order for a new application to be developed. This saves both time and money for prospective businesses wishing to create interactive TV applications, as expertise is not needed in this instance.

Figure 3. Page model editor.

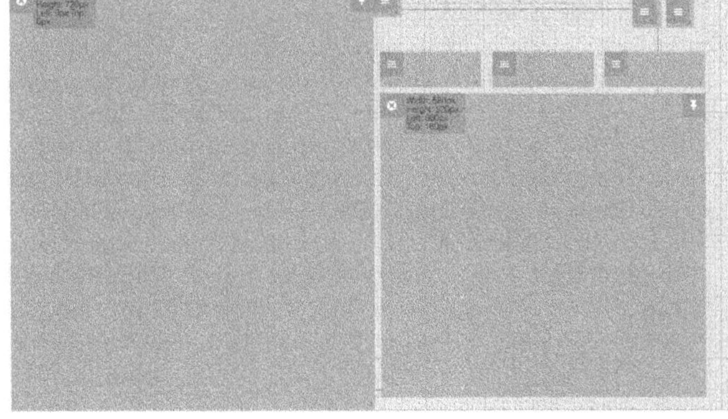

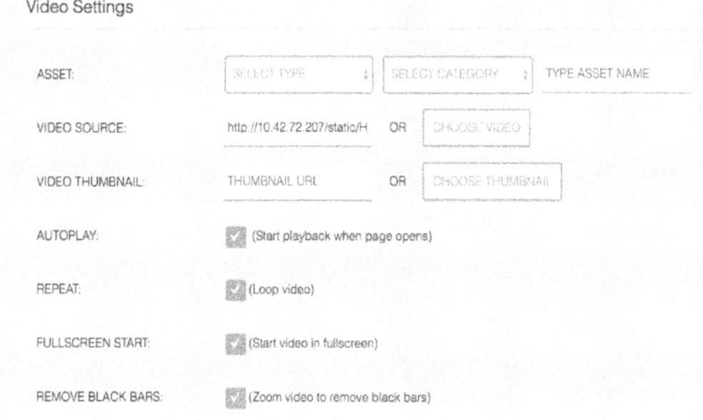

Figure 4. Component editor interface.

Once the overall layout page is satisfactory and suits the purpose of the application, the designer must then traverse the second stage of the authoring process, and navigate to the page editor within WordPress. The page editor requires a page model in order to build a template for the selected page. Once selected, components can be placed at will in the predefined positions set within the page model. Clicking on a components template within the editor will load the relevant component options menu, and will allow the user to specify which component is to be used and to customise the component at their will. For simple components such as text, the customisation options are limited and only provide basic support such as dictating the style and whether it can be navigable. However, more complex components such as video allow for a wider range of customisation ability, with the MPAT editor including optional functionality for autoplay, repetition, fullscreen start, and video thumbnails. Figure 4 illustrates the interface utilised by authors by customise the componenets.

This method of development not only vastly decreases the time and cost for the creation of interactive HbbTV applications, but also provides the functionality needed for applications within the sphere of public displays. As the digital prospectus pilot is a relatively complex application, with lots of different information needing to be displayed, the number of different components is vastly superior to the presence detection pilot. For the presence detection pilot, multiple pages within the same application were created to store the various videos, created by a digital artist, which make up the overarching storyline. These pages do not link to each other and have no method of navigation, and only contain a single video component.

Three different navigation models have been incorporated into the MPAT editor to create applications with different narrative approaches. The first is the website model, which migrates the link based navigation experience that the consumers are used with in mobile and computer web browsers; users will be able to navigate through the application and click on hyper links, using a remote control unit, to advance to the next stage. This method of navigation encompasses most non-specialised applications, and as it is in the same ilk as traditional web pages it is a popular choice among creators utilising the toolkit. Many varied types of applications have been created using this model, and allows creators much freedom in terms of design and navigational pathways.

Slideflow offers a more appealing story telling approach, where users can follow the narration scrolling in predefined directions. This approach assumes pages are located next to each other, and each page naturally leads to the next. This is achieved by implementation of HbbTV APIs, namely using the Key Events [3]. Hooks to the directional keys on the RCU (Remote Control Unit) are used by MPAT to ensure that they are only available to scroll through the application, and cannot be used by developers utilising the page editor.

Finally, the Timeline editor allow the developers to hook creative content, and therefore govern its appearance and behavior, to predefined events. This approach allows multiple pages to be displayed on the screen at any time, with the broadcast video present behind the application. This navigation scheme covers applications that are time oriented and is described in [16] as "either dependent upon media time in the case of applications such as VoD and catch-up, or on stream events in the case of live broadcasts where the precise synchronization of HbbTV elements is provided through stream events". One of the main driving factors for this style of navigation was for the vast popularity of 'red button' style applications. This style will periodically notify the existence of an application by means of an alert visible in front of the broadcast media. This is often used to indicate that additional context is available for consumption; whether that be the showcasing of contextual information relevant to current events within the broadcast content, such as social media integration, or some other form of entertainment medium that users can consume. Once the red button has been pressed, an MPAT application will be dynamically loaded onto the TV which will deliver the additional content.

Consideration of the type of application which needs to be created must be applied when deciding which navigation style is to be implemented. For some applications such as ones which make use of the "red button", this decision is fairly straightforward, however, for most this choice involves the weighing and evaluation of multiple aspects concerning the application architecture, requirements, and most importantly the setting in which the application will be deployed.

For the digital prospectus pilot, the Timeline navigation model was chosen. This was largely chosen due to it requiring ambient video, with notifications suggesting the presence of an application which provides more specific contextual information. This was the obvious choice, as this model was fundamentally developed for this style of application. For the presence detection pilot, a standard website model was chosen. Whilst any model would have fit this application, as the PDI simply creates a web request and displays a page from an unnavigable application, there is no need for implementation of the more heavyweight counterparts.

IMPLEMENTATION

As mentioned previously, the first use case focuses on building an electronic prospectus for students visiting Lancaster University on one of our open days. This study makes use of a looping video showing different aspects of the School and Computing and Communications, as well as red button functionality, which allows prospective students to find out more information about the content currently being displayed. The video being shown was situated in a room filled with staff members from individual departments within Lancaster University, with the intention that prospective students shall navigate to the department they are interested in, in order to communicate with staff to gain relevant knowledge. Naturally, with the number of students attending being many more than the amount of computing staff available at the even, students may have to wait a period of time until a staff member is available to talk to and gain the relevant information that they require. Due to this, the prospectus application was devised to give students, whom would be otherwise standing and waiting in line, an opportunity to find information about the University and the courses offered within, without direct contact with faculty members.

As this pilot did not utilise the existing public display infrastructure, the method of loading the application was more trivial, and required the use of BRAHMS [11], which is an industry standard transport stream multiplexer and provides the broadcast channel for the display to play. This also provides an easy way to load the MPAT application, which is done by entering a URL, which is then subsequently parsed into the DVB-T2 Application Information Table (AIT), which is a table holding relevant information needed to execute an application. This allows the HbbTV enabled display to load the application remotely, using a network connection.

The application created consists of two parts, firstly, the red button which takes an end user to the corresponding page within the electronic prospectus, and the electronic prospectus itself. An informative message is displayed at predefined time slots within the video which informs students that additional contextual information is available. A remote control unit was utilised by the students to initially gain access to the prospectus, when a notification of additional context appears upon the display, and then to navigate through the pages located within.

Figure 5. Notification of additional context.

The standard functionality of this case study consists of looping video which contains footage of several aspects within Lancaster University and the School of Computing and Communications itself, including aerial footage of InfoLab21, a building housing researchers and other faculty members involved in the computing department, and research projects spearheaded by the various students within the department. Notifications of additional context are pushed to the display once relevant content within the video is shown, and if a user decides to press the red button during that period, MPAT will load the relevant page within the prospectus application. This is achieved by utilisation of the aforementioned Timeline feature. The Timeline editor enables applications to be visible in front of the looping video at specific periods of time.

Figure 5 shows an example banner which is pushed via time events within the Timeline editor. This banner appears within certain time periods of the broadcast video, and is set to predefined times within the editor. This banner loads the relevant application once a user presses the red button on the remote control unit. Based on an overview of the courses offered within the School of Computing and Communications, the prospectus offers the visitors a chance to gain additional information about subject areas they are interested in. The various pages contained within the application can be navigated by selecting the link components, which serve as pathways between content areas.

Grouping of related information is achieved by the aforementioned hotspot component. The different courses offered by the School of Computing & Communications can be chosen within the disparate standalone pages. Selecting a hotspot component invokes a state change, which updates the page to show relevant information about the hotspot selected.

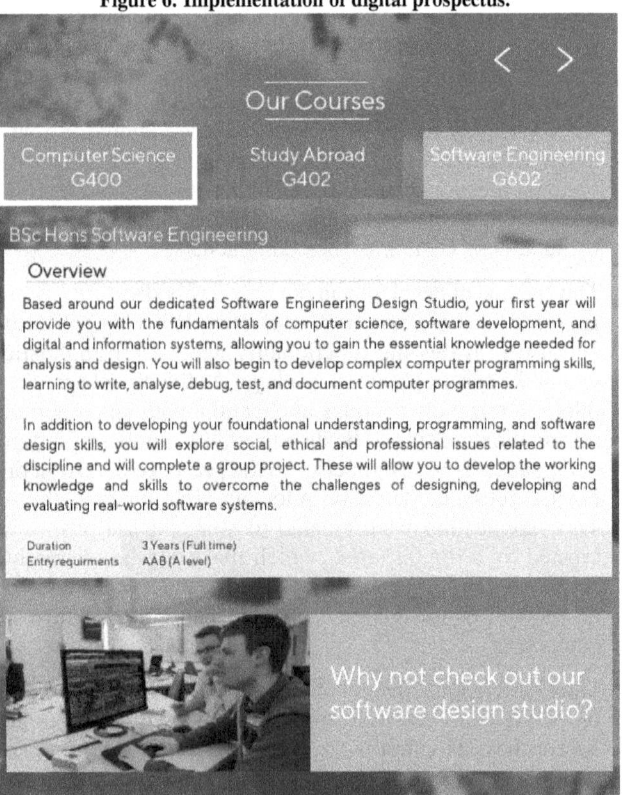

Figure 6. Implementation of digital prospectus.

Figure 6 shows a page within the digital prospectus application created, and shows the functionality of the hotspots which have been implemented in the form of navigable boxes which represent a course available on the currently viewed page.

Figure 7. Communication between entities.

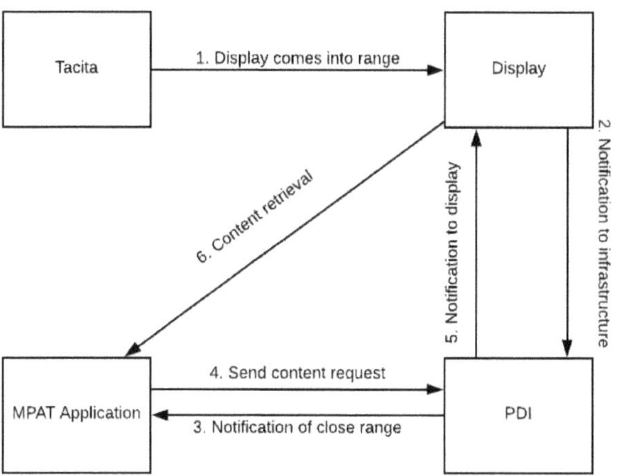

The presence detection pilot aims to demonstrate the possibilities of HbbTV outside of the traditional broadcast format, whilst also simultaneously promoting interactivity amongst collegiate and visitors around campus. This large scale pilot showcases content created by MPAT to a significant number of end-users.

The pilot relates to presence of users, and requires the use of Tacita's API to receive events from the iOS application, individual displays and the submission of content requests. In order to conform to the API standards Tacita upholds, a web server was created which accepts various requests from the PDIs RESTful interface. The architecture of the system, and the steps which need to be undertaken in order to display content on a display is outlined below in Figure 7.

The application server which was created, implemented a bespoke user management system which tracked the individuals route around campus, noting the displays which they passed along the way. Each time a request from a device with Tacita installed was received, a cookie was attached which uniquely identified the user. If this cookie had not been processed before, then a new user had initiated contact with the application server, and a new user object was created which also appended the display which triggered the request. This functionality enabled the application server to dictate which video that a user should receive.

Once a request for content is received, the application server first checks how many displays they have been to previously, and then which storyline group the display belongs to. Once this information has been retrieved, a response to the displays GET request is formulated. The response will be a 302 redirect to an external MPAT application which contains the correct video. Upon receipt of this response, the display will open a WebKit instance of the MPAT application, and the video will begin playback. This pilot showcases the capacity for MPAT to extend beyond the traditional TV broadcast medium, and provide an interactive storytelling narrative across heterogeneous devices.

INTERACTION

The digital prospectus pilot implemented the same method of interaction that is traditionally used in digital TV applications, by means of a remote control unit. While this could be seen as advantageous, as many users would be familiar with this style, there are also noticeable drawbacks. Many public displays are now touch screen or have some other method of input, and as a result, the general public may have difficulty correctly identifying that it is a TV displaying the broadcast, and that a remote is required. Several avenues were explored to remedy this, and have been discussed in the design section. While the interaction procedure may be verbose, the method of input can be seen as a simple task. The users of the application were able to correctly launch the initial application, and then intuitively navigate through the pages to gather the information that they require. The procedure required involves initially pressing the red button on the RCU, in order to launch the main functionality of the application. Once displayed, navigation through the pages is also achieved by using the RCU. Focus to different elements within the page is achieved by a white border around the piece of content, which indicates which element is currently selected. Standardised navigation between page elements has been implemented in such a way that keys can change the selected element by direction: clicking on the left arrow passes the focus to the nearest element to the left of the current focused zone. If there is none, nothing happens. Enter is used to trigger the action of the current focused zone, for example initiating playback of multimedia.

The interaction with the PDI is very different from the previous pilot and focuses on the combination of the Tacita application and RFID technology to detect the presence of subscribed users. Once installed, a list of sub-applications is visible from the user interface, in which the user can subscribe to. If a subscription to the application is enabled, once a user comes into close proximity to a display and it's corresponding iBeacon, the Mercury application store which houses the applications used by Tacita, receives a request for content, and the relevant video is displayed. This method of interaction is completely hands-free and requires little input from the user other than the initial installation of the application. Due to this minimal interaction procedure, users will not feel frustrated in attempting to learn new verbose and bespoke methods in order to make use of the functionality provided.

Figure 8. Still image of a part of the artist narrative.

Figure 9. Utilisation of the digital prospectus application.

EVALUATION

Digital Prospectus Pilot

The digital prospectus pilot has been deployed in two separate instances. The pilot was active during two university open days and enabled prospective students to witness the capabilities of the digital authoring tool in a public setting. The display was situated at the fore of the respective departmental stalls, in an attempt to capture the attention of potential users. Large banner notifications were chosen as means to notify the existence of an application, and a remote control unit was placed in plain sight close to the relevant department's informational desk, with a large note stating that it can be used to interact with the display.

Figure 9 showcases the environment in which the application was deployed, and the setup of the display. Prospective students who were otherwise incapable of speaking directly to a member of staff would actively be drawn to the informational display, and correspondingly make use of the application. Other prospective students who would require information that is provided by the application would also be allocated time with the application after engaging in conversation with a member of staff. Users were receptive to the application and spent varying periods of time traversing the various pages held within, in order to find the information they require. Access logs of the system where the MPAT instance is installed were parsed, and subsequent requests for the various web pages within the application were accumulated.

Page	Pilot 1	Pilot 2	Total
Landing Page	28	24	52
Undergraduate Courses	19	19	38
Masters Courses	17	12	29
Combined Degrees	11	7	18
Final Year Project	6	4	10
Our Facilities	11	6	17
Total	92	72	164

As shown, the most popular pages were the landing pages at the start of the application. This indicates that many users did not fully traverse the application, and instead selected only content that was relevant to them. The number of users who interacted with the system can be said to be approximately equivalent to the number of hits to the landing page. However, as mentioned previously other pages can be launched into directly, depending upon the context currently within the ambient video. As such, the number of total users is likely in excess of the reported 52.

The application development process was understandably a rapid experience, consisting of no more than 24 hours until completion of the application. A collaborative effort was made by the development team using the MPAT visual editor to concurrently create the web pages contained within using a single page model. The editor allows for cloning of pages and the components contained within, which grants separate entities the chance to easily reuse similar page styles for faster creation.

User Evaluation

A number of participants were involved in a user evaluation which aimed to gauge the overall satisfaction of the product. The usability of the application is evaluated in multiple aspects, which include questionnaires, specific tasks to undertake, and open-ended interview questions. While the questionnaire aims to gather both an understanding of the users background and the vital usability ratings, the interview questions additionally grants the accumulation of rich qualitative data. Ten people participated in the evaluation, all of whom are prospective students and between the ages of 18 to 25, which were chosen to represent the population of potential users of the application. The number of users involved in the evaluation contained more males (7) than females (3).

The evaluation was conducted over a 2 day period, with each day having a fraction of the participants interacting with the study. Participants were first given written instruction on how to operate the application, and then encouraged to become familiar with the process. They were then instructed to perform tasks such as finding a piece of information from the prospectus. All of the participants were successful in navigating through the application and correctly identifying the required information. Participants were then asked to fill out a questionnaire, which included a 7-point Likert type scale to examine specific usability metrics. A subset of the specific user satisfaction questions are listed below:

Q1 The application positively affects my view of the University.

Q2 The application allows me to find information I am interested in.

Q3 The application gives me a better understanding of the University.

Six participants (60%) reported a rating of $\geq$5 when asked if the application positively affects their view of the University, while only one (10%) reported a rating of $\leq$3. In relation to whether the application allows the participants to find information they are interested in, eight (80%) declared a score of $\geq$5, and no participants gave a rating of $\leq$3. Seven participants (70%) gave a rating of ≥5 when asked whether the application grants a better understanding of the University, while one (10%) gave a rating of ≤3. All of the participants also declared that they were familiar with public displays.

During the interview stage of the evaluation, a common comment was that having the ability to find additional information about the building they were located inside, was valuable in providing contextual information which was previously unknown to them. Furthermore, a large portion of participants described that gaining this information without the need to communicate with members of staff was beneficial. The participants who gave a rating of ≥5 for Q1, listed above, were asked to elaborate on the reason why they gave that response. A prevalent opinion by the participants was that they were excited to see useful products which benefit student wellbeing being spearheaded by the University. The qualitative evaluation also highlighted some areas where confusion may arise for participants. The landing page, which was used to gauge the amount of users interacting with the application, was seen by many users as being obtuse. The landing page consisted of a splash screen with the MPAT logo and a button which the user must press in order to continue to the main content of the application. This piece of functionality was expressed to be unimportant when compared to the rest of the application. Moreover, the lack of an on screen explanation was said to detriment the understanding of the users.

Upon reflection of the usability evaluation, changes were made to the application which aim to accommodate the points of concern raised by the users. Amendments to the interface were included in a revised prototype, which include textual on screen instructions which aid the user navigate to the main functionality. It is recommended for future deployments to remove the landing page, and instead specify the entry point of the application to be the first page of the informational content.

Presence Detection Pilot

The presence detection pilot, which utilised personalisation and mobile sensing, was active for a month, and yielded many results due to active participation by collegiate members. As the 'iLancaster' application is a prerequisite for undergraduate students and thus installed on multiple devices, they had the option to use the external applications and engage with the pilot. The pilot made use of all 45 connected public displays situated around the University campus, and allowed students to create their own narrative dependent upon the route taken. During the period in which the application was live, 256 unique video requests were served by the PDI. This equates to over 50 possible unique narratives which have been explored by various faculty members.

The data collected from this pilot also grants insight into usage patterns, as a log of each display interaction is recorded inside a database. Analysis of the results indicate the vast majority of videos served by the PDI were between lecture periods. Furthermore, only a minute portion of video requests were served after lectures had finished for the day. This naturally leads to the conclusion that the students who were active in the pilot wanted to engage with it in between periods of learning when otherwise unoccupied. This notion is reinforced by the location of the displays accessed. The data collected reveals that a large portion of accessed displays were located within close proximity to Bowland College, the main hub for lecture theatres within Lancaster University.

The web based development framework has been shown to be a suitable approach for public display applications, as this method allows for multi-platform implementation. Furthermore, this aspect opens up possible integration with other PDIs which accept content from third-party sources through publication of services. Content creation via instantiation of functionality provided by MPAT has been shown to be successfully utilised, and engaged in by multiple members of the public, from various backgrounds, which have garnered both useful statistics and user experience metrics. The results gained coupled with the correct utilisation of the implemented MPAT applications suggest encouraging results and promising further deployment of newly created applications.

FUTURE WORK

The success of the digital prospectus application suggests similar MPAT application could be created and operated in other informational institutions which allow patrons to find contextual information without requiring communication with external entities. Interest has been garnered within the computing department to house the application permanently in InfoLab21, the building which houses computer science researchers and staff, as a tool for visitors outside of open day events. A proposed solution is to install a display in the foyer, which is constantly executing the MPAT application, in an attempt to attract individuals for interaction purposes, whilst also gaining ambiance for frequenters of the building.

This informative style of application allows for multiple avenues to be explored upon examination of suitable environments. Suitable venues could include, but are not limited to, recreational facilities with an emphasis on learning such as aquariums or museums. It is proposed that these institutions create applications for individual exhibits, which will allow patrons the opportunity to find contextual information about the pieces they are currently viewing in an interactive manner. Due to the ease of use that MPAT provides, creation of said applications will not require large up front costs for technicians with expertise, whilst also providing a comprehensive learning experience for visitors.

The ability to create public display applications in an efficient manner by leveraging the functionality which MPAT provides paves the way for organisations to utilise the open source tool and implement their own infrastructure. Due to the lack of abstraction inherent within PDIs, standardisation of technology which allows rapid and multi-platform deployment would be truly beneficial. This abstraction layer provides fundamental changes in application development life cycle and intrinsically depreciates the effort required to create complex interactive public display applications, while also maximising possible compatibility across devices. This compatibility could lead to future implementation of MPAT applications tailored towards integration with other PDIs that support web based applications.

CONCLUSION

This paper presents the design, implementation and evaluation of MPAT applications catered towards instantiation upon public displays. Several challenges have been identified through research into the problem space, and through real world case studies these have been mitigated through correct utilisation of application design and interaction procedure. Creation of public display applications from the visual authoring environment that MPAT provides has been demonstrably shown to be comparable to other much more bespoke alternatives, while greatly diminishing the deployment cost.

ACKNOWLEDGMENTS

This work was supported by the Collaborative Project Multi-Platform Application Toolkit (www.mpat.eu) funded by the European Commission through the Horizon 2020 Programme (H2020-ICT-2015, call ICT19-2015) under grant agreement number 687921. The authors would also like to thank Mateusz Mikusz for his assistance with this work.

REFERENCES

1. Jorge C. S. Cardoso and Rui Jose. Interaction Tasks and Controls for Public Display Applications. In *Advances in Human-Computer Interaction*. 2014. DOI=10.1155/2014/371867
2. Tomas Linden, Tommi Heikkinen, Timo Ojala, Hannu Kukka, and Marko Jurmu. Web-based framework for spatiotemporal screen real estate management of interactive public displays. In *Proceedings of the 19th international conference on World wide web*. 2010. DOI=http://dx.doi.org/10.1145/1772690.1772901
3. HbbTV Specification 2.0 `https://www.hbbtv.org/wp-content/uploads/2015/07/HbbTV_specification_2_0.pdf`
4. Sarah Clinch, Nigel Davies, Adrian Friday and Graham Clinch. Yarely : a software player for open pervasive display networks. In *PerDis '13 Proceedings of the 2nd ACM International Symposium on Pervasive Displays*. 2013.
5. Thomas Kubitza, Sarah Clinch, Nigel Davies, and Marc Langheinrich. Using mobile devices to personalize pervasive displays. In *SIGMOBILE Mob. Comput. Commun.* 2013. DOI=http://dx.doi.org/10.1145/2436196.2436211
6. Market share trends for content management systems for websites `https://w3techs.com/technologies/history_overview/content_management`
7. Alessandro Bendinelli and Fabio Paterno. Authoring Public Display Web Applications: Guidelines, Design Patterns, and Tool Support. In *Proceedings of the 11th Biannual Conference on Italian SIGCHI Chapter*. 2015. DOI=http://dx.doi.org/10.1145/2808435.2808457
8. Carlos Antonio Navarrete Puentes and Jose Tiberio Hernandez Penaloza. HEd: A Flexible HbbTV WYSIWYG Visual Authoring Tool. In *Adjunct Publication of the 2017 ACM International Conference on Interactive Experiences for TV and Online Video*. 2017. DOI=https://doi.org/10.1145/3084289.3089917
9. Tomas Linden, Tommi Heikkinen, Vassilis Kostakos, Denzil Ferreira, and Timo Ojala. Towards multi-application public interactive displays. In *Proceedings of the 2012 International Symposium on Pervasive Displays*. 2012. DOI=http://dx.doi.org/10.1145/2307798.2307807
10. Jorge C. S. Cardoso and Rui Jose. Creating web-based interactive public display applications with the PuReWidgets toolkit. In *Proceedings of the 11th International Conference on Mobile and Ubiquitous Multimedia*. 2012. DOI=http://dx.doi.org/10.1145/2406367.2406434
11. BRAHMS `https://www.irt.de/en/products/media-services-and-applications/brahms/`
12. Tacita `https://itunes.apple.com/gb/app/tacita/id1131274089?mt=8`
13. MPAT. `http://www.mpat.eu/`.
14. Sarah Clinch, Nigel Davies, Adrian Friday, Miriam Greis, Marc Langheinrich, Mateusz Mikusz, Thomas Kubitza and Christopher Winstanley. Demo : an ecosystem for open display networks. In *PerDis '14 Proceedings of The International Symposium on Pervasive Displays*. 2014.
15. MPAT Initial Plan for the Dissemination and Exploitation of Results `https://ec.europa.eu/research/participants/documents/downloadPublic?documentIds=080166e5ae913e09&appId=PPGMS`
16. MPAT System Architecture and API Documentation `https://ec.europa.eu/research/participants/documents/downloadPublic?documentIds=080166e5abb3cc63&appId=PPGMS`

Companion Screen Architecture for Bridging TV Experiences and Life Activities

Hisayuki Ohmata, Masaya Ikeo, Hiromu Ogawa, Tohru Takiguchi, Hiroshi Fujisawa
NHK (Japan Broadcasting Corporation)
Tokyo, JAPAN
{oomata.h-ik, ikeo.m-je, ogawa.h-ju, takiguchi.t-io, fujisawa.h-ja}@nhk.or.jp

ABSTRACT

The diversification of personal lifestyles has complicated the roles of media and associated service consumption. In our current era, when people start to use new services by transitioning from one service or device to another, bothersome operations can decrease their motivation to use the new services effectively. For example, even though companion screen services are now available on integrated broadcast–broadband systems, broadcast accessibility from mobile service remains suboptimal because existing architectures remain television (TV)-centric and cannot use these services effectively. In response to this issue, we propose a user-centric companion screen architecture (CSA) that can tune to a specified TV channel and launch broadcast-related TV applications from mobile and Internet of Things (IoT)-enabled devices. We confirmed the general versatility of this CSA by prototyping multiple use cases involving various broadcasters and by evaluating broadcast accessibility from mobile devices via user tests. The obtained results showed that 86% of the examinees expressed improved user satisfaction and that 78% the examinees reported a potential increase in the number of broadcasts they would watch. Thus, we conclude that our proposed CSA improves broadcast accessibility from mobile and IoT services and can help bridge the gap between TV experiences and life activities.

Author Keywords

Companion Screen; Integrated Broadcast–broadband System; IoT; Content Targeting.

ACM Classification Keywords

H.5.m. Information interfaces and presentation (e.g., HCI): Miscellaneous.

TVX '18, June 26–28, 2018, SEOUL, Republic of Korea

ACM ISBN 978-1-4503-5115-7/18/06…$15.00
https://doi.org/10.1145/3210825.3210828

INTRODUCTION

The proliferation of Internet services, smartphones, and Internet of Things (IoT)-enabled devices has diversified human lifestyles, with multiple service providers now designing and deploying cross-device and mash-up services in order to provide appropriately tailored content for various users. Furthermore, time spent on media has changed significantly in the last decade. In particular, although time spent watching television (TV) has decreased, time spent on smartphones has increased [1].

However, broadcast television services still have significant influence on our daily lives, and TV viewing is often intimately connected with our daily activities. For example, it is commonplace to see persons standing in line at a shop or restaurant which is played on a popular TV drama, and TV programs are often popular topics in our daily conversations. Furthermore, TV advertisements (ads) broadcast in conjunction with popular programs are an effective method for inducing purchases. In terms of ad spending, even though digital ads overtook TV ad spending in 2016, TV-based ad expenditures in the US are expected to continue growing, albeit at a slower pace [2], and TV ads are still said to be more effective than Internet ads for creating and growing brands [3].

Focusing on the relationship between broadcast and mobile media, we find that there is a good level of basic affinity. For example, when people multitask while watching TV, 36% of those viewers use personal devices, usually smartphones [4], and it is common practice to learn about new TV programs from comments on social networking services (SNSs). Additionally, integrated broadcast–broadband (IBB) systems can provide companion screen (CS) services that enhance the provision of broadcast-related content from TV to smartphone in front of a TV. Considering such situations, numerous touch points toward broadcast services have been located on mobile services, and it can be seen that there are significant opportunities for assisting users who want to reach broadcast services.

However, there is currently no method that can help users to transit smoothly from mobile to broadcast services. For example, if a user who is sitting on a sofa in front of a TV finds an interesting on-air program via a mobile application, he/she must find the remote control, turn the TV on, and then tune into the program to watch. This cumbersome process has the potential to reduce a user's motivation to watch the newly discovered TV programs. In terms of consumer services, user experience (UX) design is of primary importance when attempting to provide a better experience and increase user satisfaction. Furthermore, it is commonly known that complicated operations at service touch points reduce the likelihood that the service will be used.

With these points in mind, we propose a system model for extending an IBB system to bridge broadcast, Internet, and real-life services using a CS, the core technology of which is a companion screen architecture (CSA) that can tune to a specified TV channel and launch broadcast-related applications from a CS. The proposed architecture allows various mobile applications to smoothly access broadcast services through a simple one-tap action. In addition, since the CSA also can be implemented in smart speakers, smart watches, and other devices, it enhances the bridge between broadcast and IoT services.

The general versatility of the system model and CSA was verified through prototyping. Specifically, we prototyped CS software that supports the proposed CSA and upgraded Hybridcast TV, and then implemented this software on Hybridcast-compliant companion applications for smartphones, smart watches, and smart speakers. We then demonstrated various use cases that involved connecting broadcast, Internet, or real-life services using the proposed CSA with various broadcasters.

Moreover, we evaluated broadcast accessibility from a mobile application with our CSA via an online questionnaire of 1000 people and field test involving 103 users. The results show that 86% of the examinees experienced increased user satisfaction, while 78% of the examinees reported it would probably increase the number of broadcasts that they viewed.

Based on the above, we conclude that our proposed CSA has an acceptable level of general versatility, and thus the potential to improve the UX of TV viewers. This, in turn, has the potential to stimulate an increase in the number of broadcasts watched. In addition, the CSA enhances the connection among broadcast, mobile, and IoT services and helps bridge the gap between TV experiences and real-life activities.

RELATED WORK

Companion Screen Technologies

CS technology is one of the more effective solutions to bridging TV and mobile device experiences. Standard IBB systems, such as Hybridcast [5] and Hybrid Broadcast Broadband TV (HbbTV) [6], have enabled broadcast and Internet services to be linked by Web applications launched on TVs which are indicated by a broadcast signal. Furthermore, multiscreen services using CSAs also can be provided by TVs and smartphones [7][8].

In the current architecture, a Web application running on a TV sends a command message and URL to a CS on a smartphone that launches a separate Web application in the CS. Both applications can then communicate with each other directly by text messages on the same segment of a local network. However, the current architecture is designed using a TV-centric model, which means that when a user is not in front of the TV, he or she cannot connect with the CS. Since no services can be provided to the CS at such times, it is not helpful for users.

In addition, if a user in front of a TV operating a multiscreen service wants to use a CS, he/she must turn on the TV and launch the TV application using the TV remote control because it is impossible to access the service from the CS alone. Moreover, only TV and smartphones are currently connected on existing IBB systems, and as we look forward to the growth of IoT services, we can see it would be advantageous to build an architecture that would connect TVs and IoT-enabled devices.

On the other hand, a number of mobile-centric CS technologies are also available. For example, DIscovery And Launch (DIAL) [9] is an open protocol for device discovery and application launch that is supported by Smart TVs that come with preinstalled YouTube or Netflix applications, as well as dongle devices such as Chromecast. Additionally, users can cast streaming videos or share their smartphone screens to TVs.

Hybridcast and HbbTV also use this protocol to discover TVs from the CS, and HbbTV 2.0 allows the launch of broadcast-independent applications from the CS. However, this type of application is currently designed for TV portal and program guide services, and it cannot handle broadcast channels and data. This inability to handle broadcast services or broadcast-related applications makes it impossible for users to use them to smoothly reach broadcast services from mobile applications.

Collaboration for Broadcast and IoT-enabled Devices

It is currently expected that the IoT market, which includes smart TVs, will continue growing year by year [10]. The World Wide Web Consortium (W3C) is the primary driver behind Web-based IoT, which it calls the Web of Things, and is striving to create an environment in which IBB systems and IoT-enabled devices can connect seamlessly. This is expected to provide immense opportunities for new services that work across TVs and various connected devices.

Some collaboration systems for broadcast services and physical devices have already been proposed. For example, the proposed method for creating immersion in TV programs in [11] provides a tactile-sense presentation system for smart TVs, while an interactive robot that enables chat with a viewer while watching TV programs is proposed in [12]. However, these systems are designed for particular devices, and thus lack versatility. Furthermore, since they are designed solely for use in front of a TV, it is impossible to provide cross-device services that include various types of TVs and IoT-enabled devices.

SYSTEM MODEL

Service Requirements

Since the motivation behind our system model is to provide viewers with enhanced experiences in front of their TVs and help bridge the gap between TV experiences and real-life activities, we began by redesigning the current IBB system, which has already been deployed with CSA. The following are our newly designed service requirements:

- Ensure broadcast and Internet or real-life services can be connected to each other.
- Ensure broadcasters and various enterprises are able to provide common or individual services.
- Provide a way for people to use various services anytime, anywhere, regardless of whether a network-connected TV is present.
- Ensure each service is usable across multiple devices: TVs, smartphones, and IoT-enabled devices.
- Ensure the interface used to access services is as simple as possible.
- Ensure the ease for enterprises to develop applications without difficulty.
- Implement an access policy for personal data and system functions.

Proposed Model

Our proposed system model, which fulfills all the requirements described above, is shown in Figure 1. Since people use a variety of connected devices in each situation, it is important to create touch points for broadcast content on diversified devices so that they can help users bridge their TV experiences with other life activities.

Accordingly, we began by deciding that CSs would be at the center of this system so that content could be provided to users in situations that take advantage of their device characteristics. For example, the mobility provided by smartphones or smart watches make them useful in various outdoor settings, while smart speakers are suitable for users inside the home.

Next, noting that more than seven million Hybridcast-compliant TVs have already been sold, we redesigned the Hybridcast IBB system for closer interaction with CS services that were launched ahead of HbbTV. This is important because existing Hybridcast CSAs (CSAv0 and CSAv1) were designed based on TV-centric models. More specifically, CSAv0 uses the device-connection protocol of each TV manufacturer and companion applications provided by those manufacturers, while CSAv1 defines a common protocol that can connect various manufacturers' TVs via a common companion application called "Hybridcast Connect" (HCApp).

Our proposal, hereafter referred to as CSAv2, is an extension of CSAv1 that supports both TV- and CS-centric connections. In addition, we designed CSAv2 for implementation ease on not only HCApp but also various other smartphone applications and devices, because it has the potential to add value to existing applications or devices that are not related to broadcast services. This means that, from the standpoint of broadcast services, it has the potential to attract new customers from other services.

In our proposed system model, CSs work as device connectors and data routers over TVs, mobile applications, and IoT-enabled devices. Broadcasters or enterprises provide TV-related content or services to the CSs that are implemented in CSAv2. This means those same broadcasters or service providers can also advertise various services and contents targeted specifically to CS users based on their broadcast program or TV viewing activities. For their part, CS users can access various contents and services across the devices by using the CSAv2 device connection function.

To help CSAv2 optimize content for each user, a personal history function manages user information on TV viewing and daily activities, which it then provides to broadcasters or service providers based on user agreements. Viewing history refers to data on when and what broadcasts or video-on-demand (VoD) programs were watched. Activity history includes location data and a history of purchases, travel, etc. Since various applications and devices that have implemented CSAv2 will be at work near users in numerous settings, it is expected that they will encounter numerous touch points for accessing broadcast contents, and thus numerous opportunities to utilize the available data.

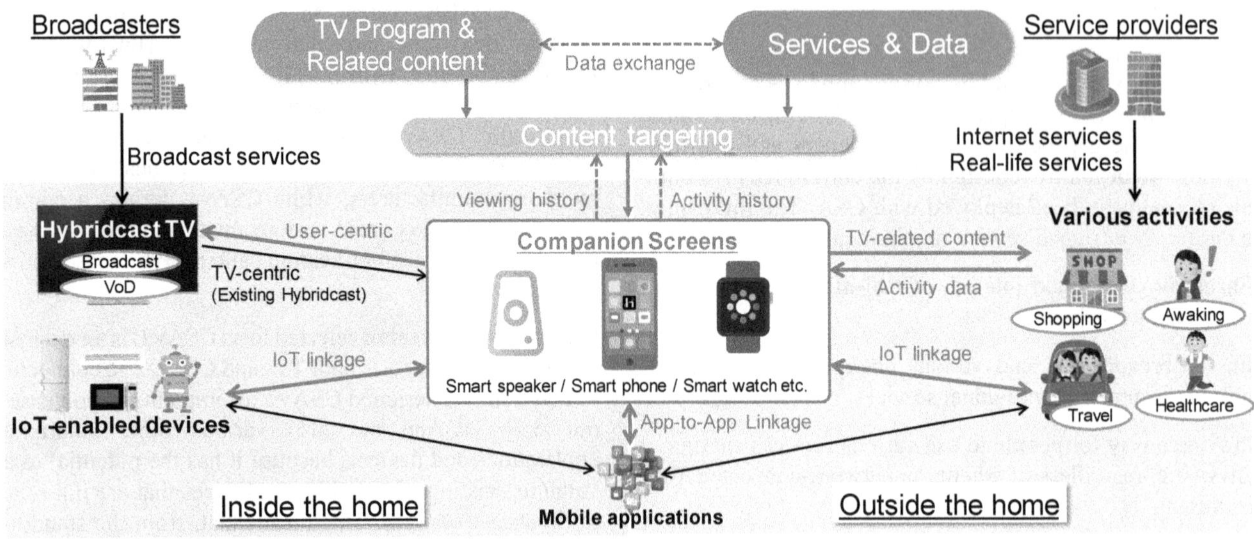

Figure 1. System model for bridging TV experiences and life activities

COMPANION SCREEN ARCHITECTURE

As explained above, we designated CSAv2, a function model of which is shown in Figure 2, as the core technology of our proposed system model. As can be seen in this figure, CSAv2 is composed primarily of three modules: a TV-link module, a service-link module on the CS, and a CS-link module on the TV. The TV-link module is essential for linking the CS with the TV. The TV-link and the CS-link modules are extensions of CSAv1, which uses the architecture of existing Hybridcast systems. In contrast, the service-link module is composed of multiple functions designed to enhance the linking of devices, services, and experiences, many of the implemented functions of which may be different depending on the designs or requirements of each service. Since the CSs are at the center of the proposed system, broadcast services, as well as other Internet or real-life services, can be connected via both modules.

TV-Link Module and Companion Screen-Link Module

The TV-link module runs alongside the CS-link module. CSAv1 provides the device-linkage protocol, including device discovery and the handshake, between the TV and companion applications. Application program interfaces (APIs) for applications launched from the TV to the companion application and app-to-app communications between the TV and CS are also defined. These are implemented in the TV-link and CS-link modules.

However, since CSAv2 is an extension of CSAv1, we designed the CS-centric protocol, combined it with channel tuning and application launch function on the TV, and upgraded the TV-link and CS-link modules. DIAL was adopted to launch the new application because most Hybridcast capable smart TVs already support it. In addition, since our goal is to provide a way to expand TV experiences, it was decided that broadcast service applications running on TVs should be broadcast-related rather than broadcast-independent.

Therefore, this protocol defines the execution order for applications that are to be launched after tuning into a channel. To make it possible for this protocol to be used by Web application on CS or by the native functions of mobile applications or smart devices, we also define TV-control APIs. In order to support these TV-control APIs, CSAv2 supports both Web-based and native implementation, as well as Web browser upgrades for the companion application.

Service-Link Module

The service-link module is composed of multiple functions designed to enhance linkages between devices, services, and experiences. Each function is provided by a common API for native applications or Web applications running on CS. The use of a simple interface ensures that broadcasters and various service providers can provide cross-device services when linking multiple services using these APIs. This is expected to reduce application development costs.

Device-linkage function

The device linkage function used for link CS and IoT-enabled devices applies our proposed architecture to control IoT-enabled devices via broadcasts [13]. More specifically, it discovers and authenticates devices near the CS and establishes a connection in order to transmit data. By managing connection logs, it enhances the convenience of users and ability of service providers to select available devices. Additionally, this function abstracts the differences in the device model, type, or communication protocol to the greatest extent possible in order to enhance the ease of CS application development. We currently support two communication protocols: HTTP and Bluetooth Low Energy (BLE), because most typical existing devices support one or both protocols.

App-to-app-linkage function

The app-to-app-linkage function enables app-to-app communications on smartphones by using the intent function provided by the operating system. This allows a CS application to launch other mobile applications using the appropriate parameters, and vice versa.

Event trigger function

The event trigger function is a simple matching engine between broadcast-related content and user context, such as location, time, or device connection status. Personal data, as explained below, are available as context. Users or service providers can use the data to set conditions that trigger events and actions.

Personal data management function

TV viewing history and life activity history for locations visited and items purchased are managed as personal data. In addition, the device connection and app-to-app communication status are also recorded as system logs.

Access Control Mechanism

Web applications running on CS or native applications can access each function easily by using APIs. However, since this mechanism increases security concerns about privacy and device control, a built-in function that authenticates applications when calling APIs according to user and service provider policies is provided. This mechanism protects personal data and system functions from incorrect application behavior. Application validation is performed by using domain names or certificates.

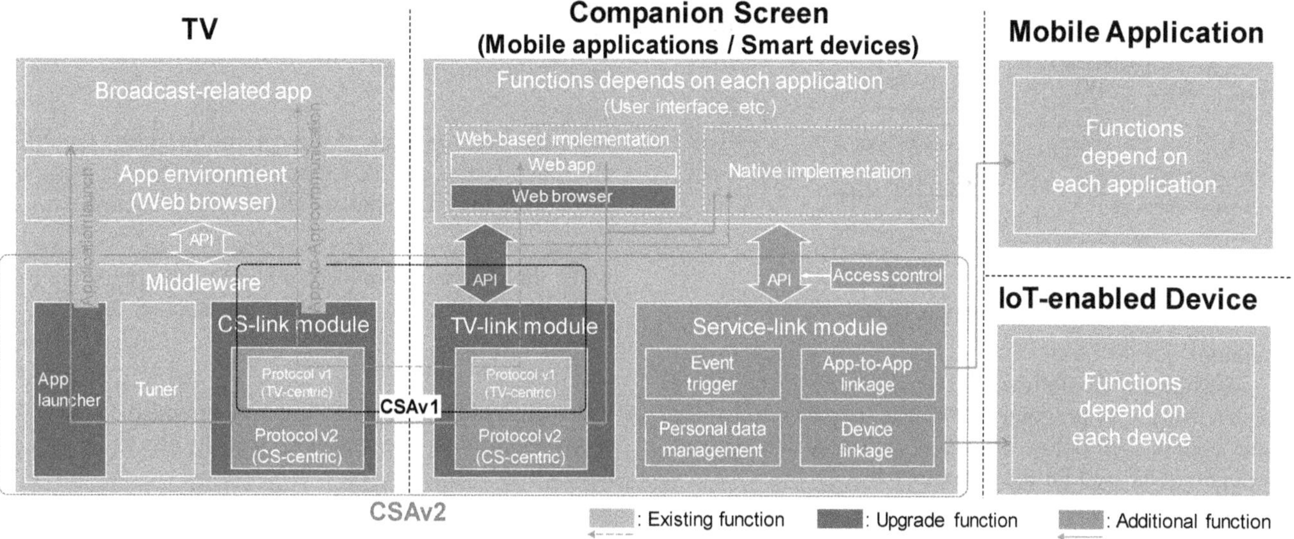

Figure 2. Function model of Companion Screen Architecture v2

EVALATION

We evaluated our proposed CSA by both prototyping and user testing.

Prototype

We prototyped software for a CS that supports CSAv2 and an upgraded Hybridcast TV. The software is implemented on HCApp as an extension in order to provide services on a smartphone. We also prepared limited software that can control the TV by smart speakers and smart watches. Next, we promoted a collaborative relationship with commercial broadcasters and service providers in Japan, and asked them to prototype service use cases with the HCApp.

In 2017, the partnership broadcasters and our study group demonstrated multiple use cases bridging TV viewing and life activities during our open house and at global and domestic exhibitions in the field of consumer electronics and broadcasting such as IBC, CEATEC and InterBEE. Through these prototyping and demonstration activities, we confirmed the feasibility of CSAv2. In this study, we show details of use cases conducted in front of a TV. Demonstration movies can be seen on our websites [14][15].

Prototype system

Figure 3 shows the architecture of the prototype system.

Hybridcast TV

We upgraded a commercially available Hybridcast TV to launch a Web browser and a broadcast-related application from a smartphone using the DIAL protocol.

Smartphone

HCApp, a NHK sports application, and SNS applications such as Twitter and LINE were installed on an Android smartphone. CSAv2 was implemented on HCApp. The NHK sports and SNS applications were used to provide notifications for the start of sports programs, video clips, etc.

IoT-enabled devices

Robot A is an intelligent ball that can rotate and flash. The brightness and color of the smart light emitting diodes (LEDs) can be controlled. Robot B can move its body and speak. Robot A uses the BLE communication protocol, while the other uses HTTP via Wi-Fi.

Modulator

A modulator transmits the broadcast signal of ISDB-T to the Hybridcast TV. The event message (EM) trigger data synchronized with the program are multiplexed on this signal.

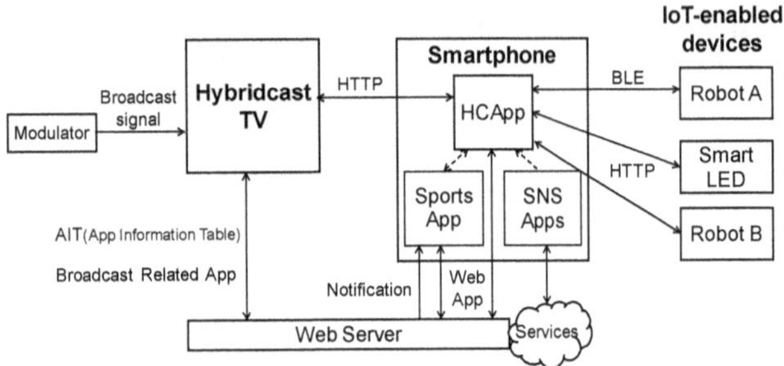

Figure 3. Prototype system

Scenario

We considered the following scenario, in which people watch a live soccer program on TV. The specific setup of the scene is described below. Figure 4 shows the sequence of user operations used for the scenario.

Scene 1

While watching NHK Educational TV (NHK E), a notification message that announces the start of a soccer program on NHK General TV (NHK G) is provided on the NHK sports and SNS applications.

Scene 2

The user taps the notification, causing the TV to tune into NHK G, and a broadcast-related application is launched on the TV.

Scene 3

After a few seconds, the soccer program begins. The broadcast-related application on the TV reports player information to HCApp as a TV-centric service. This is a typical multiscreen service on the current Hybridcast system.

Scene 4

A drop-down menu asking the user to select IoT-enabled devices that operate in conjunction with the TV program is displayed on HCApp in order to give the user a chance to choose those devices.

Scene 5

When events, such as a goal, occur, connected devices move or flash. This provides an enhanced feeling of actual participation to the user.

Scene 6

After the event is over, the program introduces the NHK sports application and the HCApp displays its link. When the user taps it, the NHK sports application is launched.

Scene 7

When the program introduces other TV programs, the user can make viewing reservations by tapping the link on HCApp.

Scene 8

Video clips of the game highlights are provided on the NHK sports application. The user can select any clip and play it on the TV.

Scene 9

Just before the beginning of a program that was reserved in Scene 7, a dialog box is provided on HCApp. When the user taps this dialog box, the TV turns on and the appropriate channel is selected.

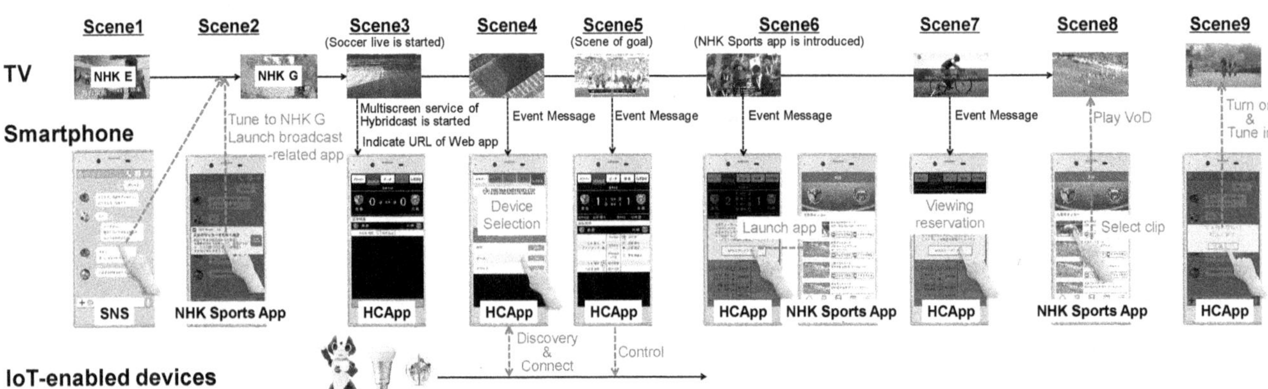

Figure 4. Sequence of user operations on prototype scenario in front of a TV

Implementation

These use cases are implemented by all CSAv2 functions, other than the personal data management function and access control mechanism.

`Scene 2`

We embedded the HCApp URL scheme with a control command for broadcast channel information and the URL of application information table (AIT) that indicates the location of the broadcast-related application as notification message parameters. When the message is tapped, HCApp is launched by the app-to-app communication function and HCApp issues a control command from the TV-link module to the CS-link module. Next, the middleware tunes the TV to the appropriate channel and launches the broadcast-related application on the TV.

`Scene 4`

The device-linkage function discovers and reports available devices on the Web application on HCApp.

`Scene 5`

The broadcast-related application on the TV can handle the EM multiplexed on the broadcast signal. Upon receiving the EM, the application transmits it to a Web application on HCApp. The control commands are described on the EM as text data and issued to the devices from the device-linkage function.

`Scene 6`

Upon receiving the EM, the Web application on HCApp issues a dialog box that includes the NHK sports application URL scheme. Tapping this link causes the HCApp to launch the NHK sports application using the app-to-app communication function.

`Scene 7`

As in Scene 6, the Web application on HCApp issues a dialog box that includes the program start time. When a user taps the dialog box, an event trigger function is called and the Web application sets the time and channel information as the event launch conditions.

`Scene 8`

In video clips, both the URL scheme of HCApp and the URL of AIT and VoD are embedded as button parameters. When a user taps the button, the HCApp is launched and the TV-link module communicates with the CS-link module, which then launches the broadcast-related application that works as the MPEG-DASH video player compliant with Media Source Extensions and Encrypted Media Extensions on the TV. This behavior is almost the same as Scene 2.

`Scene 9`

The event trigger function pushes a notification message to HCApp. When that message is tapped, the TV-link module communicates with the CS-link module, which then turns on the TV and tunes it to the appropriate channel.

Other use cases

We also prototyped a case aimed at targeting broadcast content usage outside the home. Specifically, when users are out driving, their car navigation systems notify them when they approach locations such as shops, restaurants, and scenic spots that were mentioned in TV programs that they had watched previously. In these use cases, a companion application obtains channel information from broadcast-related applications on TVs and stores it in the personal data management function as viewing history. Service providers supply a data set that includes the location names and latitude/longitude data of specific sites mentioned in each TV program. By matching the data sets and viewing history, personalized navigation data can be created. By transferring these data from a companion application to a car navigation system via the device-linkage function, users can enjoy expanded TV experiences in their cars.

We also implemented the CS TV-link module in an Android smart watch application and confirmed that various manufacturers' TVs could be controlled from the smart watch via voice and touch interactions. In addition, we verified connectivity between smart speakers (such as Amazon Echo and Google Home) and TVs by using a server-implemented TV-link module. The server is located in the same network segment as the TV and relays commands from the cloud service of these speakers to the local network. We also confirmed that users can control TVs by voice using smart speakers.

Partnership broadcasters also demonstrated various use cases. They found that bridging TV viewing and purchase behavior could be suitable for commercial broadcasters. For example, one broadcaster prototyped a method of bridging TV ad viewing and purchased goods at a sponsored chain store. In this model, a companion application implemented CSAv2 collects and manages TV ad viewing history by using a broadcast-related application. It also issues coupons when a user approaches the store by using the event trigger function.

Another broadcaster demonstrated a loyalty program for TV viewing and life activities in which users can receive loyalty points by viewing TV programs and ads, by recommending the programs to his/her friends on SNSs, and/or by visiting the sponsored locations, such as restaurants and tourist spots. The loyalty points can be used for purchasing transactional VoD contents, for example. In this model, a companion application implemented CSAv2 and its service mashups, including viewing and activity history.

Another broadcaster prototyped a connected toy that functions interactively with a cartoon program. This architecture is almost the same as the prototype described above. An important characteristic of this model is that the toy(s) and their actions relate directly to the cartoon, which not only creates a new program UX but also contributes to increasing the sales of the toy manufacturer.

Discussion

In our evaluations of the general versatility of CSAv2, we first ensured that it would be possible to combine multiple CSAv2 functions in order to successfully complete each use case. We then confirmed that each prototype system functioned with sufficient stability throughout the scenario and that the TV-link module could be implemented on the applications of smartphones, smart watches, and smart speakers. To accomplish this, it was necessary to ensure that the various connected devices were able to create the touch points required to access broadcast contents, as well as opportunities to process those contents for their users. The results of our prototyping and testing confirmed that CSAv2 has a sufficient level of general versatility and feasibility to create bridges between TV experiences and life activities.

Next, we considered UX improvements by observing each scene of our scenario. During Scenes 2, 7, 8, and 9, it was not necessary to use a remote control to turn on the TV, find the appropriate channel or video clip, or select the channel or play the VoD. In addition, during Scene 6, users were not required to find the NHK sports application on their smartphones. Based on the above points, we can conclude that CSAv2 reduces the number of user operations and has the potential to improve the UX.

We then considered enhanced business value for broadcasters and other enterprises. Focusing on a model for commercial broadcasters, we determined that a broadcaster and its sponsored enterprises such as stores, tourist spots, and toy manufacturers had new opportunities to generate synergy that would increase both their TV ratings and sales by using the CSAv2-implemented companion applications. Not only did the coupons, loyalty points, and toys work as user incentives, but they also provided a hub from which the broadcast service and Internet providers could provide information on real-life services and products.

By directly linking users' viewing histories and life activity history, each enterprise can better analyze the detailed effects of each service based on their behavior patterns. This is beneficial for users because they can be provided with personalized content and improved UX, and for broadcasters and sponsored enterprises because it allows them to strategize efforts for increasing TV ratings and/or related sales. Based on these considerations, it is clear that CSAv2 offers a variety of potential ways to create new business value.

User Tests

We evaluated the anticipation levels and satisfaction of user operations related to the access broadcast services from mobile application using CSAv2. The user tests consisted of an online questionnaire and a field test. Table 1 shows the conditions of examinees in both tests.

Age	20–59
Gender	Male/Female
Residence	Japan
Other	Users of both TVs and smartphones

Table 1. Conditions of examinees in user tests

Online questionnaire

Our online questionnaire was conducted on Nov. 27–28, 2017. The number of questionnaire respondents was 1000. In order to reduce age and gender bias, we began by defining each consumer segment and its sample size as shown in Table 2. Next, we sent out our questionnaire to examinees who met the conditions listed in Table 1, and handled their answers in the order of arrival based on Table 2.

In this questionnaire, we explored how the examinees used TV and smartphone in their daily lives, as well as their anticipation levels regarding the new function for CS-centric TV control, by showing them descriptions and illustrations (Figure 5) that explain situations related to their use.

	Male	Female
20s	125	125
30s	125	125
40s	125	125
50s	125	125

Table 2. Online questionnaire sample size

This is a new function that can turn on and tune into at TV from applications or Web pages on a smartphone. For example, you can watch a broadcast TV program just by tapping the "Watch on TV" button presented by a sports application, Web page, or embedded link on a comment of an SNS application, such as Twitter or LINE.

Figure 5. Description and illustration of the new function

We explored anticipation levels for this function on a scale of one to five. Figure 6 shows the results. The rates of positive ("Very positive" or "Positive"), neutral ("Neither positive nor negative"), and negative ("Negative" or "Very negative") were almost the same, at around 35% (Result 1).

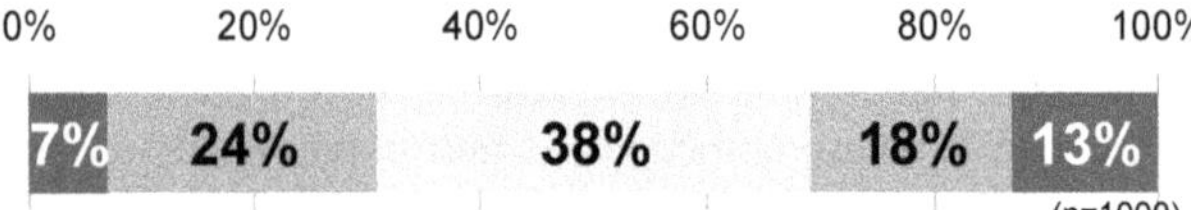

Figure 6. Anticipation levels for the new function

Also using a scale of one to five, we surveyed the presence or absence of regret experienced by users when missing a favorite or interesting broadcast program. From those results, we found that 83% of examinees had experienced such regret (Result 2). We then analyzed the relationship between anticipations related to the new function and the regret experience. Figure 7 shows the results. Here, it can be seen that there is a tendency for people who have experienced such regret to have higher anticipation levels than people who had not (Result 3).

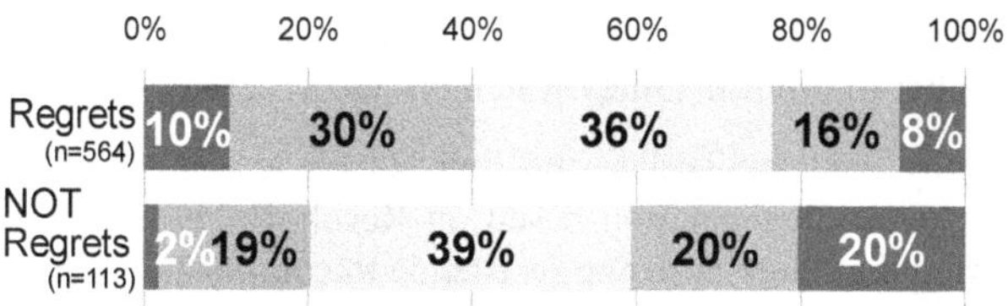

Figure 7. Relationship between anticipation regarding the new function and regret experience

Field test

We conducted field testing on Dec. 15–17, 2017. A total of 103 examinees participated. We defined each consumer segment and its sample size as shown in Table 3. Examinees were recruited from those who had met the conditions in Table 1 and lived in the Tokyo Metropolitan Area. We chose examinees on a first-come-first-served basis according Table 3. However, it should be noted that the online questionnaire examinees were different from the participants of this field test.

	Male	Female
20s–30s	26	26
40s–50s	26	25

Table 3. Field test sample size

Before participating in the field test, examinees were requested to complete the same questionnaire discussed above. During the test, they gained actual experience with the new function using a CSAv2-implemented prototype system in a situation similar to that shown in Figure 5. After the experience, we asked some questions about this function.

From the questionnaire answers, we checked user preferences regarding this field test. For anticipation levels before the test, 60% were positive, 19% were neutral, and 20% were negative (Result 4).

Questions and results after the experience are described below.

1. After the experience, we again asked them to express anticipation levels on a scale of one to five. The results shown in Figure 8 indicate that 94% of the all examinees, including 86% of the examinees who answered negative before this test, showed positive anticipation levels (Result 5).

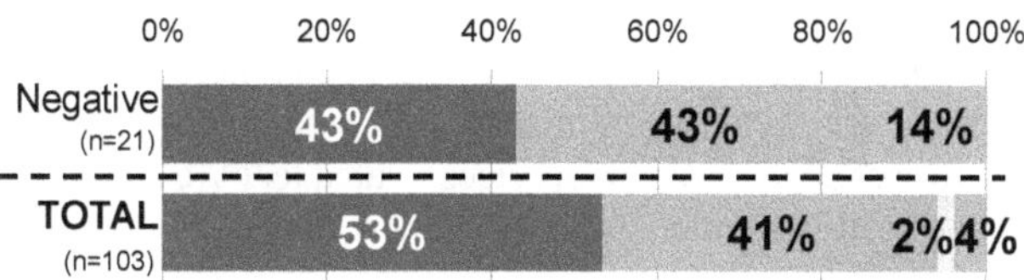

Figure 8. Anticipation levels for the new function after the field test experience

2. After the experience, we then asked examinees to give their before and after impression level changes regarding this function on a scale of one to five. The results, shown in Figure 9, indicate that 86% of all examinees, including 94% of the examinees who answered negative before this test, had improved impressions of the function (Result 6).

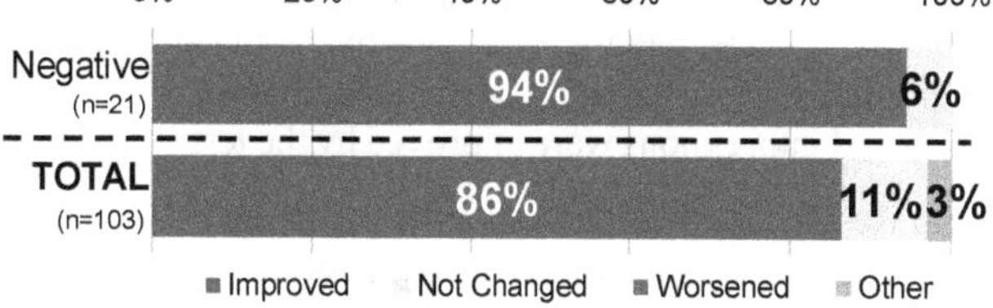

Figure 9. Change of impression about the new function before and after the experience

3. Then, once again using a scale of one to five, we asked the examinees whether it was possible that this new function would increase or decrease the number of times that they watched broadcast programs. The results shown in Figure 10 indicate that 78% of all examinees, including 67% of the examinees who answered negative before this test, said that they would probably increase the amount of time that they watched broadcast programs (Result 7).

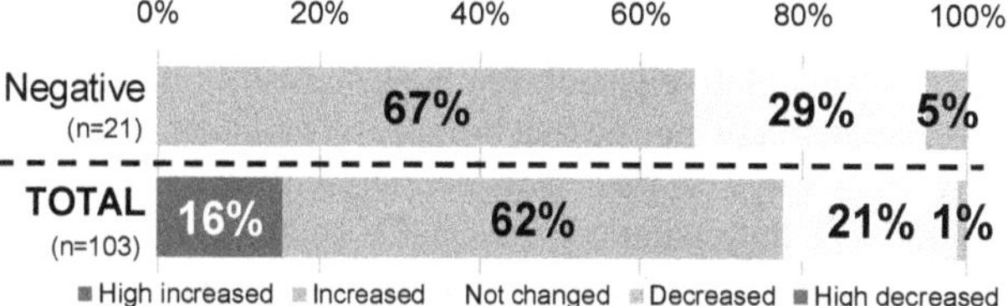

Figure 10. Possibility of increase or decrease in number of times to watch broadcast program by the new function

4. We then asked the examinees who had answered "Very positive" and "Positive" to describe the advantages of this function via an open-ended question. The most common answer, at 62%, was that they would be effective for reducing the number of inadvertently missed programs (Result 8). The second most popular answer, at 59%, was that this function facilitates easy operation and reduce the efforts needed to reach a broadcast program (Result 9).

5. We then asked all examines, via an open-ended question, to give their opinions and suggestions regarding this function. A number of typical opinions are shown below (Result 10).

   - The initial setup, such as pairing the device to a TV, should be made very simple.
   - Users should not have to install new applications in order to use this function.
   - It would be nice to have an additional function that allows users to continue watching a live event from

their smartphone if they must leave the vicinity of the TV.

Discussion

First, we performed a quantitative evaluation of anticipation levels and user satisfaction related to this function using Results 4, 5, and 6. From these results, it was clear that most people, even those who were negatively inclined before the actual experience, had increased positive anticipation levels. Additionally, it was found that the anticipation levels were raised and impressions were improved by the test experience.

From Result 1, we can see that anticipation levels before the experience were not always high. Therefore, it is clear that the promotional activities provided by the service are important for creating opportunities for people who were unaware of the potential usefulness of this function. This is because, after a single positive use, most people would be awakened to the convenience provided by the function and be more likely to use them continuously.

Second, we examined the influence of this function on user behavior by quantitatively evaluating Result 7. Here, we found that, in spite of the presence or absence of anticipation prior to the experience, more than 60% of the examines said this function would likely increase the number of times that they watched broadcast programs.

Third, we qualitatively analyzed the benefits of this function. Here, we begin by noting that broadcast is a linear media and there is always a risk that people will miss watching programs if they cannot get to a TV in time. From a UX design standpoint, the regret that ensues from missing favorite programs may decrease user satisfaction in the broadcast service. However, from Result 2, we can see that most people have experienced such regret.

On the other hand, Result 3 shows that more is expected from this function by people who have experienced missed program regret. Moreover, from Result 8, we can see that more than 60% of the positive examinees indicated that the primary advantage of this function is that it would help reduce the number of broadcast programs missed.

It was also said that the operability of the application or device significantly influences user satisfaction with the services. Accordingly, via prototype verification, we confirmed that this function could reduce the number of required user operations. Furthermore, through the actual experiences, as discussed in Result 9, we find that more than half of the positive examinees indicated that the ability of this function to smoothen the operations needed to reach the broadcast service was a powerful advantage.

From these results, we conclude that this function have the potential to increase user satisfaction by reducing opportunities to miss broadcast programs and by providing smoothened operations from mobile to broadcast services. We further concluded that these reasons for increasing user satisfaction might also affect user behavior by increasing the number of times that they watch broadcast services.

Finally, we will describe our observations aimed at improving this function based on Result 10. We begin by noting that there is strong resistance to complicated settings or the need to perform excessive operations on the mobile application, such as installation and initial setup. Difficulties here negate the simple operation advantages of this function and would likely cause user abandonment. Next, we can see that a combination of this and other functions, such as live streaming and program recommendations, could boost value of related applications and services.

The CSAv2 for a CS consists of a TV-link and a service-link module that is used as a software library. This architecture makes it easy to implement this function in existing applications. Therefore, we conclude that the CSAv2 has strong potential to smoothen paths from various services to broadcasts.

CONCLUSION

We proposed a system model and a companion screen architecture for connecting TV experiences and life activities by redesigning an existing IBB system. We also prototyped software that supports our proposed CSAv2. We then implemented this software on a companion application for smartphones, smart watches, and smart speakers, and then prototyped multiple use cases that involved connecting Internet or real-life services with various broadcasters using the proposed CSAv2. From the prototyping results, we confirmed that the proposed architecture has both the necessary feasibility and general versatility required for our envisioned system.

Moreover, via a questionnaire and field tests, we evaluated user needs and satisfaction levels regarding operations from a mobile device to a broadcast service using our proposed CSAv2. From these results, we confirmed that our CSAv2 is suitable for linear broadcast media and provides better satisfaction for users in front of the TV. We concluded that our proposed CSAv2 has an acceptable level of general versatility and improves broadcast accessibility from mobile and IoT services. Furthermore, it has the potential to increase the number of times that users watch broadcast programs and create new business value for broadcasters and their sponsored enterprises by bridging TV experiences and life activities.

The standardization of CSAv2 is nearly completed in Japan. In the future, we will continue to work with diverse business enterprises so that various services related to TV experiences can be easily provided anytime and anywhere.

ACKNOWLEDGMENTS

The authors would like to thank the relevant person of broadcasters who considered and prototyped service use cases using CSAv2.

REFERENCES

1. eMarketer. 2016. Average Time Spent per Day with Major Media by US Adults, 2012-2018. Retrieved April 10, 2018 from https://www.emarketer.com/Chart/Average-Time-Spent-per-Day-with-Major-Media-by-US-Adults-2012-2018-hrsmins/188929
2. eMarketer. 2016. US TV vs Digital Ad Spending, 2015-2020. Retrieved April 10, 2018 from https://www.emarketer.com/Article/US-Digital-Ad-Spending-Surpass-TV-this-Year/1014469
3. CNBC Catalyst. Why TV is still the most effective advertising medium. Retrieved April 10, 2018 from http://cnbccatalyst.com/why-moving-your-ad-spend-away-from-tv-can-cost-you-more-than-you-think/
4. A. Shokrpour and M. J. Darnell. 2017. How People Multitask While Watching TV. In *Proceedings of the ACM International Conference on Interactive experiences for TV and Online Video* (TVX '17). ACM. 12-19. DOI= https://doi.org/10.1145/3077548.3077558
5. IPTV FORUM JAPAN. 2014. IPTVFJ STD-0010 Integrated Broadcast-Broadband System Specification Version2.0. Retrieved April 10, 2018 from https://www.iptvforum.jp/en/download/input.html
6. ETSI. 2016. ETSI TS 102 796 v1.4.1 Hybrid Broadcast Broadband TV. Retrieved April 10, 2018 from http://www.etsi.org/deliver/etsi_ts/102700_102799/102796/01.04.01_60/ts_102796v010401p.pdf
7. H. Ohmata, M. Takechi, S. Mitsuya, K. Otsuki, A. Baba, K. Matsumura, K. Majima and S. Sunasaki. 2013. Hybridcast: A new media experience by integration of broadcasting and broadband. In *Proceedings of the ITU Kaleidoscope: Building Sustainable Communities (K-2013)*, S5.1, IEEE.
8. Christoph Ziegler. 2013. Second screen for HbbTV - Automatic application launch and app-to-app communication enabling novel TV programme related second-screen scenarios. In *Proceedings of the IEEE 3rd International Conference on Consumer Electronics Berlin (ICCE-Berlin 2013)*. IEEE. DOI=https://doi.org/10.1109/ICCE-Berlin.2013.6697990
9. Netflix. 2017. DIAL DIscovery And Launch protocol specification Version 2.1. Retrieved April 10, 2018 from http://www.dial-multiscreen.org/dial-protocol-specification
10. Louis Columbus. 2017 Roundup Of Internet Of Things Forecasts. Retrieved April 10, 2018 from https://www.forbes.com/sites/louiscolumbus/2017/12/10/2017-roundup-of-internet-of-things-forecasts
11. K. Ariyasu, H. Kawakita, T. Handa and H. Kaneko. 2014. Tactile sensibility presentation service for Smart TV. In *Proceedings of the IEEE 3rd Global Conference on Consumer Electronics (GCCE)*. IEEE. DOI=https://doi.org/10.1109/GCCE.2014.7031287
12. S. Nishimura, H. Kawanami, M. Kanbara and N. Hagita. 2017. A TV Chat Robot with Time-Shifting Function for Daily-Use Communication. In *International Conference on Social Robotics (ICSR)*. 516-525. Springer. Cham. DOI= https://doi.org/10.1007/978-3-319-70022-9_51
13. H. Ogawa, M. Ikeo, H. Ohmata, C. Yamamura and H. Fujisawa. 2018. System Architecture for IoT Services with Broadcast Content. In *Proceedings of the International Conference on Consumer Electronics 2018 (ICCE2018)*, 802-803.IEEE
14. NHK. 2017. Enriching Daily Activity by TV Content Connecting with IoT. Retrieved April 10, 2018 from https://www.nhk.or.jp/strl/open2017/tenji/2_e.html
15. NHK. 2017. Services and Technologies to Bridge Content and Daily Activity. Retrieved April 10, 2018 from https://www.nhk.or.jp/strl/open2017/tenji/14_e.html

Twickle: Growing Twitch Streamer's Communities Through Gamification of Word-of-Mouth Referrals

Jacob T. Browne
Twickle
San Diego, CA 92116, USA
jacobbrowne8@gmail.com

Bharat Batra
Twickle
San Diego, CA 92116, USA
bharat.batra@gmail.com

Abstract
Twitch.tv has grown to be one of the largest streaming platforms worldwide, hosting over 2 million active streamers. Many of these streamers are using their Twitch stream to earn a living, turning their streams into a business. However, growing a community that supports this endeavor remains a central challenge amongst streamers. In this paper, we present Twickle: a web-based leaderboard tool that leverages the gamification of word-of-mouth referrals to grow a streamer's community. An initial feasibility study with four streamers reveals that Twickle increases the amount of new viewers and is appreciated by the Twitch community. We address design opportunities for Twickle and outline future research.

Author Keywords
Twitch.tv; live streaming; leaderboard; viewer participation; online communities; referrals

ACM Classification Keywords
H.5.m. Information interfaces and presentation (e.g., HCI): Miscellaneous

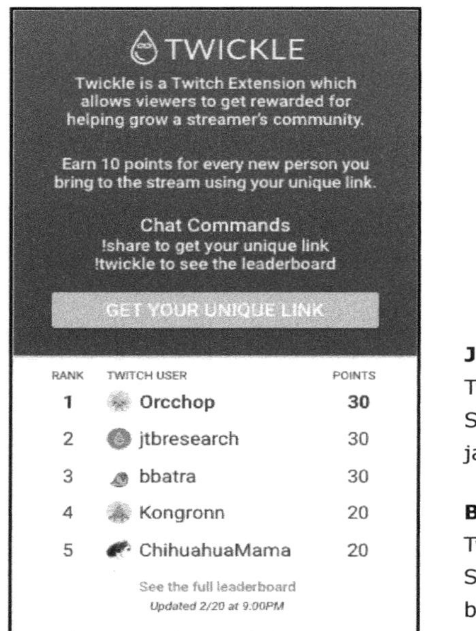

Figure 1: The streamer panel displays a brief explanation of Twickle, how to get points using Twickle, commands to use in chat, a button to get your unique link, and a minified top 5 version of the leaderboard. This panel would be located below the streamer's video feed on Twitch.

TVX '18, June 26–28, 2018, SEOUL, Republic of Korea

ACM ISBN 978-1-4503-5115-7/18/06.
https://doi.org/10.1145/3210825.3213554

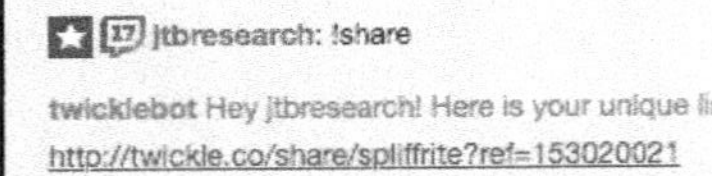
jtbresearch: !share
twicklebot Hey jtbresearch! Here is your unique link:
http://twickle.co/share/spliffrite?ref=153020021

Figure 2: A user has requested their unique link to share through the Twitch chat.

Introduction

Live-streaming platforms offer a way for content creators to broadcast live content to their viewers [11]. Twitch.tv, or Twitch, is the most eminent example, with over 2 million active streamers producing user-generated content [18]. Twitch streamers can display a live video feed of themselves and interact with viewers through a real-time chat interface [5]. Twitch recently incorporated interactive overlays and panels, known as "Extensions", which allow streamers to enhance their stream [17]. Twitch offers streamers a program to monetize their live content, starting as an "affiliate" after earning a certain amount of followers and consistent viewers, and later as a "partner" after the stream gains a consistent, growing viewership and strong sub-community [20, 21]. As an affiliate, a streamer can start accepting "subscriptions", which allow a viewer to pay a monthly fee to support the streamer [19]. Affiliates can also accept "bits", a virtual good that acts as a currency to transfer money to streamers [16]. As a partner, streamers begin making ad-revenue [20]. Becoming a partner is often the end-goal of many streamers, despite being competitive [9]. Successful streamers can earn amounts comparable to a full-time job, with top streamers making hundreds of thousands of dollars per year [6].

Streamers often face difficulty gaining new viewers [5, 7, 8]. Most channels plateau at a few viewers, with the top 10% of streams holding nearly 88% of the viewers on Twitch [7]. Pellicone and Ahn found the idea of "building community" as a major theme in their grounded theory analysis [9]. They mention that streamers suggest using other social media platforms to promote one's own stream as a method to foster a larger community [9].

Our research introduces an approach for building a streamer's community based off of previous research on word-of-mouth (WOM) referrals and gamification. To embody this approach in the context of growing a streamer's community, we created Twickle, a web-based leaderboard tool that leverages the gamification of WOM referrals. We seek to uncover if using this gamification technique can increase the number of new viewers in a streamer's community and offer the streamer insight into who is promoting their stream. We conducted a feasibility study in which four Twitch streamers used our tool during a streaming session. We found that Twickle generated new viewers and was appreciated by the viewers and streamers involved. In the following sections, we present related work, explain the design of the tool, discuss a small-scale feasibility study we conducted to get feedback from the Twitch community, and outline future research.

Related Work

Gamification and Leaderboards

Gamification is known to increase user engagement [14]. Deterding et al. define "gamification" as the "use of game design elements in non-game contexts" [3]. Leaderboards are a prominent example of gamification, increasing user motivation through the introduction of competition [4]. The most widely used leaderboard on Twitch is the "Streamlabs Leaderboard", a Twitch Extension which visualizes the top cheerers, subscribers, and viewers in a specific stream [15].

Word-Of-Mouth Referrals

A growing number of companies have utilized word-of-mouth (WOM) programs by giving customers incentive to share to their friends and families [2]. These WOM programs are "designed to motivate consumers to

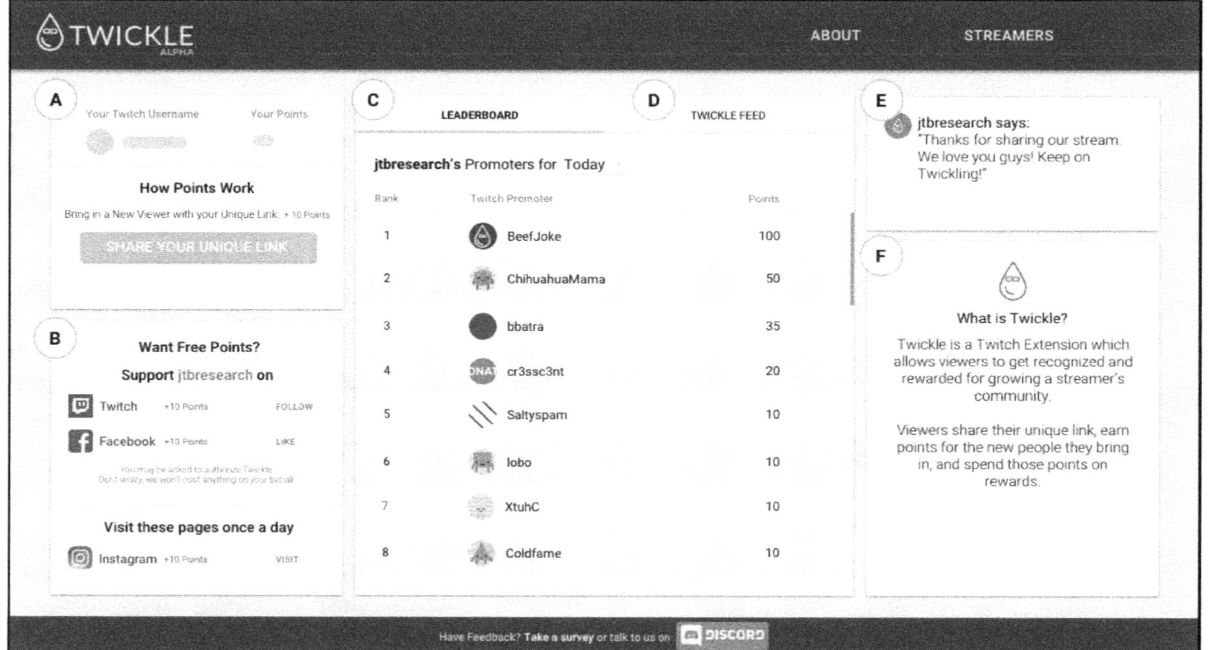

Figure 3: The Twickle Leaderboard Page. (A) User's point amount, how points work, and a button to get their unique link. (B) Links to get points for following, liking, and visiting a streamer's social media pages. (C) Twickle leaderboard. (D) Feed showing recent user activity. (E) Message from the streamer. (F) Explanation of Twickle.

spread positive WOM about products or services... to integrate customers into the sales force" [1]. WOM has become a major source of traffic for websites and users often discover content through the sharing of URLs between social groups [12]. Incentivized sharing in social networks has been shown to increase sharing behavior and referral likelihood [10, 13].

System Description

Twickle consists of 4 parts: a Streamer Panel, a Leaderboard Page, a Share Page, and a chatbot.

Streamer Panel

The panel has a brief explanation of Twickle, how to earn points, chat commands, a button to get your unique link, and the top 5 viewers (Figure 1). This provides users with a way to get to the leaderboard page and compare their point value to other viewers from a streamer's Twitch page. In displaying the top five users, we can incite a sense of competition to increase usage [4]. If users click the "get your unique link" button, they are taken to the leaderboard page.

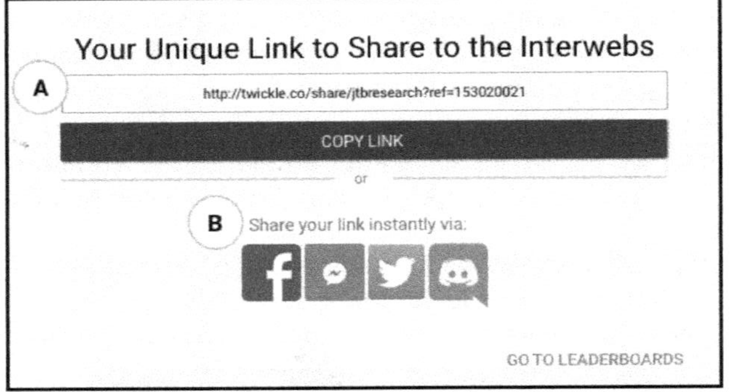

Figure 4: The Share Page. (A) Users can copy their unique link to share. (B) Users can share to social media.

Leaderboard Page
The leaderboard page offers the viewer's current point value, an explanation on how points work, and a button to get their unique link (Figure 3 (A)). The leaderboard page also offers an additional way to get points by liking, following, and visiting streamer's social media pages (Figure 3 (B)). We aim to help grow a streamer's community on other platforms by offering this functionality. The leaderboard exhibits a ranking of each viewer's point value (Figure 3 (C)). We placed this in the center of the page to draw attention and incite competition amongst viewers [4]. An additional view offers a dynamic feed of user actions (Figure 3 (D)). Streamers can also leave a message to their viewers (Figure 3 (E)). This allows streamers to personalize the leaderboard page in a way that reflects their community [5]. Lastly, a brief explanation of Twickle is shown (Figure 3 (F)).

Share Page
When users click the "share your unique link" button, they are taken to the share page (Figure 4). Viewers can copy their unique link (Figure 4 (A)). Below the link is a way to share it to different social media platforms (Figure 4 (B)). Promoting a stream on other platforms has been noted to increase its reach [9].

Chatbot
We hope to increase engagement by offering the functionality of Twickle in the Twitch chat, a medium viewers are already accustomed to [5]. From the streamer's Twitch page, viewers can type "!share" into the chat to get their unique link sent by the chatbot (Figure 4(A)). Additionally, viewers can get a link to the leaderboard page by typing "!twickle" into the chat.

Feasibility Study
We conducted a feasibility study with four Twitch Affiliate Streamers. Participants were chosen if they had on average 10 concurrent viewers each stream, a goal of obtaining partnership status, and an active subcommunity. Participants would use the leaderboard for one full streaming session, allowing their viewers the ability to share the channel using Twickle. Afterwards, we interviewed the participants to garner qualitative feedback regarding their experience during the session.

Through using Twickle, three streamers were able to garner new viewers through viewer-shared referrals during the streaming session. All participants expressed their interest and appreciation of our tool. Twickle helped them understand who in their community was promoting their stream successfully. In the interviews, two participants noted how nicely integrated Twickle was with Twitch, given the presence of the chatbot and streamer panel on their Twitch page.

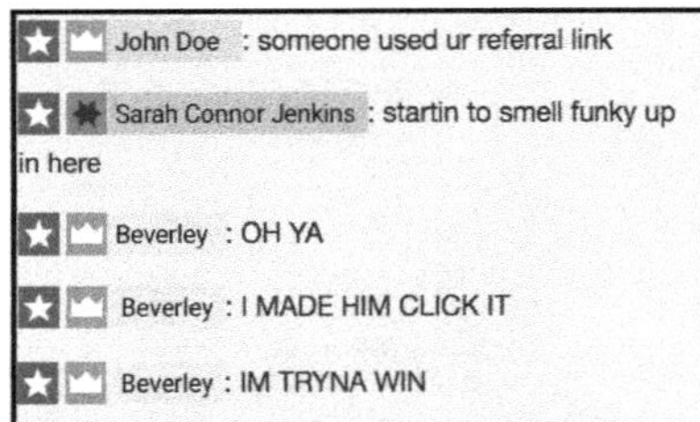

Figure 5: A Twitch chat log with viewers discussing why they chose to share using Twickle. Viewer John Doe notices a new viewer came in the stream through Viewer Beverley's referral, in which Viewer Beverley remarks, "IM TRYNA WIN".

During the streaming sessions, the overall viewer response to Twickle was accepting. One conversation between viewers in one of the streamer's chat indicates the competitiveness of our tool with one viewer noting, "IM TRYNA WIN" (Figure 5). Viewers tended to request a link to share when others in the chat requested a link. Additionally, a viewer tended to request their unique link more after their link had brought in their first new viewer.

The participants also noted some improvements for Twickle. One participant said he needed to be alerted when a new viewer arrived, to welcome the new viewer and thank the referrer. Another participant mentioned how he wanted to use Twickle as a point system for viewers to redeem stream related bonuses (as a music streamer, viewers would buy song requests to play during the stream using Twickle points). This would add incentive for viewers to share. Lastly, it was noted that the panel should be more interactive. Ideally, users would be able to copy their unique link right from the panel on the streamers Twitch page.

Conclusion and Future Work

This paper outlines the design of Twickle. Twickle aims to help Twitch streamers grow their communities through gamification of word-of-mouth referrals. Our initial user test showed that our tool helped streamers garner new viewers while increasing interactivity and competition amongst viewers to share the stream. Twickle also allowed streamers a better understanding of who is promoting their stream.

We will iterate on the design of Twickle and incorporate the user feedback. We plan to recruit more streamers of varying status to conduct a deeper evaluation of Twickle, focusing on its effectiveness and user behavior. We hope that these insights can inform the design of other online community building tools.

References

1. Eyal Biyalogorsky , Eitan Gerstner, Barak Libai, Customer Referral Management: Optimal Reward Programs, Marketing Science, v.20 n.1, p.82-95, December 2000
2. F. A. Buttle. Word of mouth: understanding and managing referral marketing. Journal of Strategic Marketing, 6(3):241–254, 1998.
3. Sebastian Deterding, Dan Dixon, Rilla Khaled, and Lennart Nacke. 2011. From game design elements to gamefulness: defining "gamification". In Proceedings of the 15th International Academic MindTrek Conference: Envisioning Future Media Environments (MindTrek '11). ACM, New York, NY, USA, 9-15. DOI: https://doi.org/10.1145/2181037.2181040
4. Juho Hamari, Jonna Koivisto, and Harri Sarsa. 2014. Does Gamification Work? -- A Literature Review of Empirical Studies on Gamification. In Proceedings of the 2014 47th Hawaii International Conference on System Sciences (HICSS '14). IEEE Computer Society, Washington, DC, USA, 3025-3034. DOI: http://dx.doi.org/10.1109/HICSS.2014.377
5. William A. Hamilton, Oliver Garretson, and Andruid Kerne. 2014. Streaming on twitch: fostering participatory communities of play within live mixed media. In Proceedings of the SIGCHI Conference on Human Factors in Computing Systems (CHI '14). ACM, New York, NY, USA, 1315-1324. DOI: https://doi.org/10.1145/2556288.2557048

6. E.Karakus. A Look Into Streaming, (2014) Retrieved February 26, 2018 from https://efekarakus.github.io/twitch-analytics/#/revenue

7. Mehdi Kaytoue, Arlei Silva, Loïc Cerf, Wagner Meira, Jr., and Chedy Raïssi. 2012. Watch me playing, i am a professional: a first study on video game live streaming. In Proceedings of the 21st International Conference on World Wide Web (WWW '12 Companion). ACM, New York, NY, USA, 1181-1188. DOI=http://dx.doi.org/10.1145/2187980.2188259

8. Pascal Lessel, Michael Mauderer, Christian Wolff, and Antonio Krüger. 2017. Let's Play My Way: Investigating Audience Influence in User-Generated Gaming Live-Streams. In Proceedings of the 2017 ACM International Conference on Interactive Experiences for TV and Online Video (TVX '17). ACM, New York, NY, USA, 51-63. DOI: https://doi.org/10.1145/3077548.3077556

9. Anthony J. Pellicone and June Ahn. 2017. The Game of Performing Play: Understanding Streaming as Cultural Production. In Proceedings of the 2017 CHI Conference on Human Factors in Computing Systems (CHI '17). ACM, New York, NY, USA, 4863-4874. DOI: https://doi.org/10.1145/3025453.3025854

10. J. J. Pfeiffer III and E. Zheleva, "Incentivized sharing in social networks," WOSS, 2012.

11. Karine Pires and Gwendal Simon. 2015. YouTube live and Twitch: a tour of user-generated live streaming systems. In Proceedings of the 6th ACM Multimedia Systems Conference (MMSys '15). ACM, New York, NY, USA, 225-230. DOI=http://dx.doi.org/10.1145/2713168.2713195

12. Tiago Rodrigues, Fabrício Benevenuto, Meeyoung Cha, Krishna Gummadi, and Virgílio Almeida. 2011. On word-of-mouth based discovery of the web. In Proceedings of the 2011 ACM SIGCOMM conference on Internet measurement conference (IMC '11). ACM, New York, NY, USA, 381-396.

13. Ryu, G. and L. Feick, A penny for your thoughts: Referral reward programs and referral likelihood. Journal of Marketing, 2007. 71(1): p. 84–94

14. Katie Seaborn and Deborah I. Fels. 2015. Gamification in theory and action. Int. J. Hum.-Comput. Stud. 74, C (February 2015), 14-31. DOI: http://dx.doi.org/10.1016/j.ijhcs.2014.09.006

15. Streamlabs. Leaderboard Panel Extension: show off your top supporters. (September 2017). Retrieved February 26, 2018 from https://blog.streamlabs.com/leaderboard-panel-extension-show-off-your-top-supporters-3d9933853ee8

16. Twitch. Cheer with Bits to celebrate and show support!. Retrieved February 26, 2018 from https://www.twitch.tv/bits

17. Twitch. Extensions: A Revolution in Live Streaming. (2017). Retrieved February 26, 2018 from https://www.twitch.tv/p/extensions/

18. Twitch. Frequently Asked Questions. (2017). Retrieved February 28, 2018 from https://www.twitch.tv/p/partners/faq/

19. Twitch. How to Subscribe. (November 2017). Retrieved February 26, 2018 from https://help.twitch.tv/customer/en/portal/articles/2812403-how-to-subscribe

20. Twitch. Joining the Affiliate Program. (February 13, 2017). Retrieved February 26, 2018 from: https://help.twitch.tv/customer/portal/articles/2785927-joining-the-affiliate-program

21. Twitch. Tips for Applying for the Partner Program. (March 2017). Retrieved February 26, 2018 from https://help.twitch.tv/customer/en/portal/articles/735127-tips-for-applying-to-the-partner-program

Touchable Video Streams: Towards Multi-sensory and Multi-contact Experiences

Seokyeol Kim
School of Computing
Korea Advanced Institute of Science and Technology
Daejeon, Republic of Korea
sy.kim@kaist.ac.kr

Jinah Park
School of Computing
Korea Advanced Institute of Science and Technology
Daejeon, Republic of Korea
jinahpark@kaist.ac.kr

TVX '18, June 26–28, 2018, SEOUL, Republic of Korea
ACM 978-1-4503-5115-7/18/06.
https://doi.org/10.1145/3210825.3213555

Abstract
Haptic feedback takes on an important role in providing spatial cues, which are difficult to convey solely by sight, as well as in increasing the immersion of contents. However, although a number of techniques and applications for haptic media have been proposed in this regard, live streaming of touchable video has yet to be actively deployed due to computational complexity and equipment limitations. In order to mitigate these issues, we introduce an approach to render haptic feedback directly from RGB-D video streams without surface reconstruction, and also describe how to superimpose virtual objects or haptic effects onto real-world scenes. Furthermore, we discuss possible improvements in software and appropriate device setups to extend the proposed system to support a practical solution for multi-sensory and multi-point interaction in streaming touchable media.

Author Keywords
RGB-D video streams; haptic feedback; multi-point interaction; telepresence

CCS Concepts
•Information systems → **Multimedia streaming; •Human-centered computing** → *Haptic devices;* Mixed / augmented reality;

Introduction

For human perception of the surrounding environment, the sense of touch is as important as visual sensation. With the importance of touch and the recent advances in media technology, visual contents, which are the mainstream of traditional media, gradually shift to multimodal interactive contents including haptic feedback. These changes range from entertainment to distance learning and telemedicine, which will ultimately improve people's satisfaction and reduce social costs.

However, there are still many challenges that need to be addressed in order for touchable media to become widespread. First, due to the nature of the human sensory system, haptic feedback requires a much higher refresh rate (over 1,000 Hz) than visual feedback. This rate can be achieved to some extent using well-suited preprocessing and space partitioning techniques, but it is difficult to apply these techniques in case of real-time interaction with unpredictable spatial data such as live video streams. Moreover, in terms of hardware, haptic interfaces have not yet been sufficiently standardized and the consumers' accessibility has been low as compared to visual displays which have been technically matured and mass-produced for a long time.

Proxy-based Haptic Rendering

When a virtual proxy, which is the avatar of the user, is in contact with an object, contact force feedback is determined by the displacement vector between a *haptic interface point* (HIP) and a *surface contact point* (SCP). In this, the HIP reflects the actual position of a haptic device, and the SCP represents the optimum position that minimize the potential energy from the HIP while preventing penetration into the surface. The god-object method [10] is one of the representative approaches of proxy-based haptic rendering, and we also adopt this method to our system.

To provide tangible experiences to video audiences, we propose a touchable video system for live streaming contents as illustrated in Fig. 1. In the proposed system, real-world scenes are captured by an RGB-D camera, and virtual objects or effects can be added to the scenes as needed. The video streams created in this manner are transmitted to the audience side via a network in a compressed form. Then the client terminal decodes the received data and renders visual and haptic feedback through the corresponding displays. In order to ensure real-time interaction, we perform proxy-based haptic rendering directly from unstructured point clouds, instead of reconstructing closed surfaces from the RGB-D video streams. The following sections briefly describe how we have designed and implemented the aforementioned features. In addition, we also suggest possible ways to extend the proposed system to support multisensory and multi-point interaction, and discuss appropriate hardware configurations for enjoying touchable video contents.

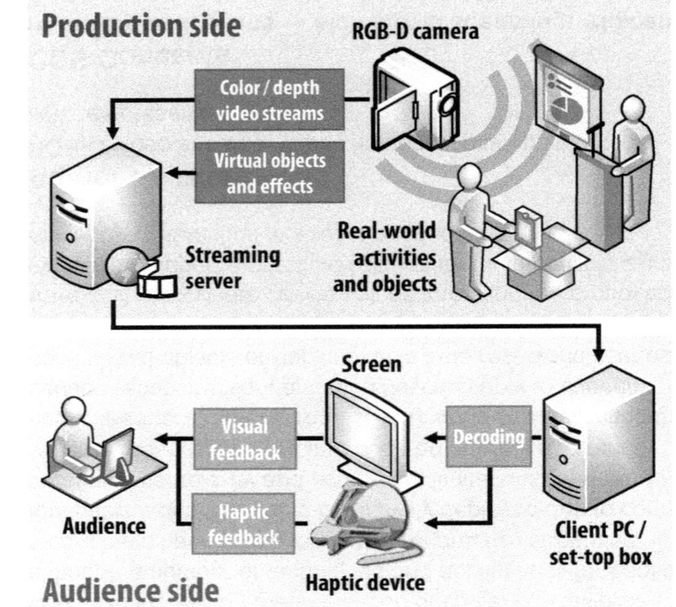

Figure 1: Overview of the production and consumption process of touchable video contents.

Haptic Interaction with RGB-D Video Streams

In a touchable video stream composed of RGB-D images, depth information is a main source of haptic feedback. A depth image itself is frequently used for representing dynamic objects in touchable video by virtue of fast and lightweight processing [3, 7]. However, most of the depth-based haptic rendering methods have difficulty in interacting with concave surfaces or backfaces. To overcome this issue and to enable more flexible interaction, the studies that utilize streaming point cloud data have begun to emerge [6, 8], and our system has also converted depth images into point clouds as a geometric representation for real-world dynamic objects.

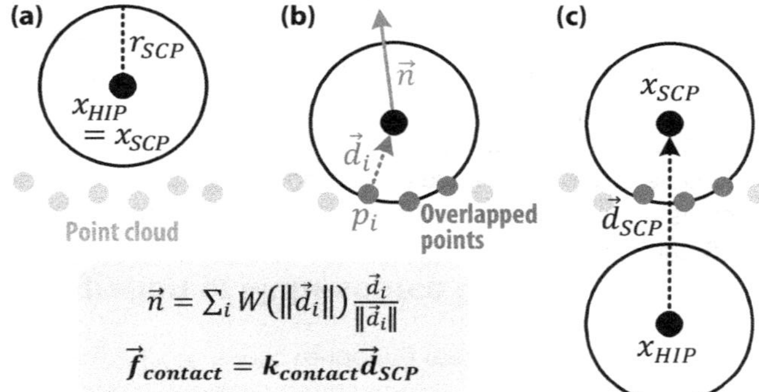

Figure 2: Collision handling with a point cloud. (a) Free motion (no collisions). (b) Surface normal estimation. (c) Contact force calculation.

In order to calculate force feedback from contact between a proxy and an object, information on the contact position and the penetration depth is necessary, but the problem is that point clouds have no definite surfaces nor any clues to the interior of the object. Under these conditions, we formulate a contact handing scheme based on the previous studies [8] to detect the collisions and estimate the surface of a target object. In an empty space, the HIP and the SCP are in the same position, and the system has no further tasks (Fig. 2-(a)). If there exists a point p_i inside a radius r_{SCP}, however, the HIP is regarded as in a contact state, and a surface normal $\vec{n}$ is estimated by using either the weighted sum of $\vec{d}_i$ or principal component analysis (Fig. 2-(b)). During contact, the SCP remains on the estimated surface, and the contact force is exerted along $\vec{d}_{SCP}$, where $k_{contact}$ is the stiffness coefficient of the object (Fig. 2-(c)). The interim results of this approach are shown in Fig. 3, and the more detailed description of contact handling is given in [5].

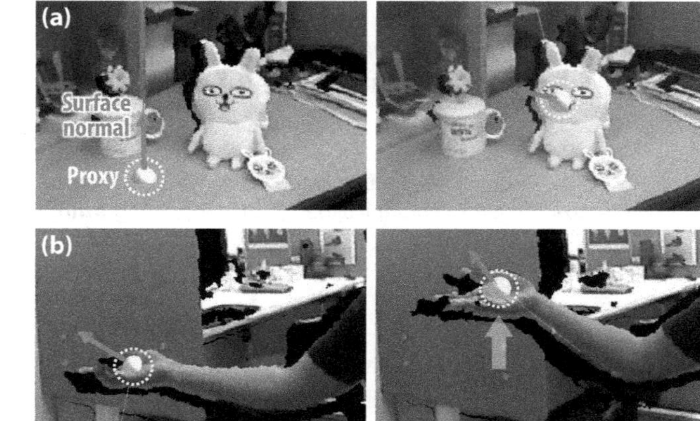

Figure 3: Practical examples of haptic interaction with RGB-D video. (a) Active exploration of the scene. (b) Passive motion by the remote object.

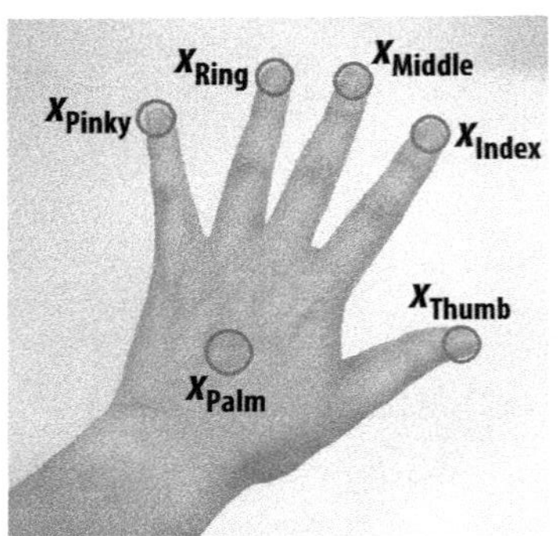

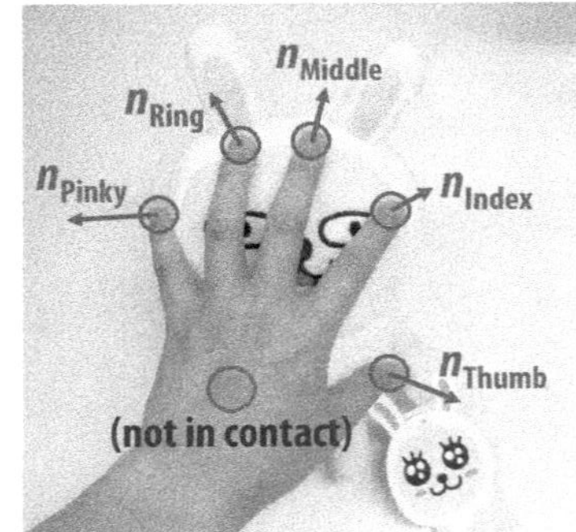

Figure 4: Possible interaction points (top) and contact information (bottom) for multi-fingered interaction.

Our prototype application still only supports 3-DOF single-point interaction, but we will extend it to provide multi-contact experiences by assigning individual proxies to each fingertip (Fig. 4). Although tool-mediated 6-DOF haptic rendering is also a remarkable way to broaden the bandwidth of information obtained from touch, this kind of multi-fingered interaction would be more natural in terms of directly touching objects with bare hands and more compatible with the existing 3-DOF haptic rendering methods.

Integration of Multi-source Data

Touchable video fundamentally contains the visual images and the shape information of target objects, but the stimuli felt in contact with an object are composed of more information besides the shape of the object. Thermal sensation is a representative example of such contact feedback. The surface temperature of a target object can be readily measured using a thermographic camera, and registration techniques for thermograms and point clouds have also been proposed [9]. We are working to combine these techniques with an appropriate thermal display to deliver more realistic feedback with touch.

Furthermore, the proposed system is capable of providing haptic feedback on virtual objects or effects as well as objects that exist in a real environment. For example, wind and water flow can be expressed as force fields, and it is also possible to guide the user's motion by using haptic constraints. In this kind of mixed-reality environment, a pivot point for determining the pose of virtual elements can be based on specific image features such as a fiducial marker (in a world coordinate system) or the origin of the view space (in a camera coordinate system). Since real-world and virtual objects are typically defined with different geometric representations, we use an integrated constraint solver [4] to handle the collisions with the heterogeneous surfaces together (Fig. 5). At the moment, it accepts relatively simple implicit surfaces and potential functions, but we plan to add support for more sophisticated surface representations in the near future.

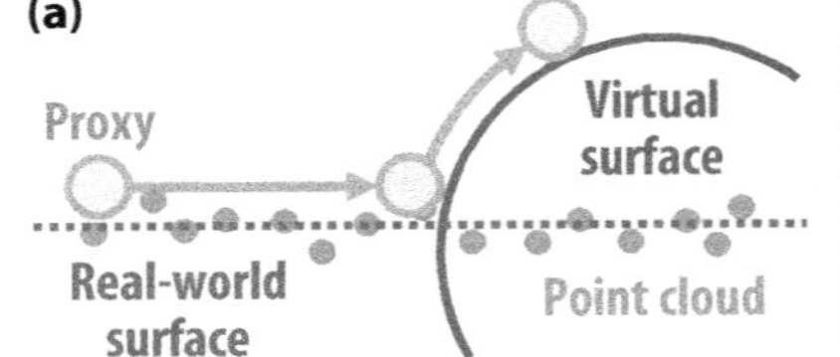

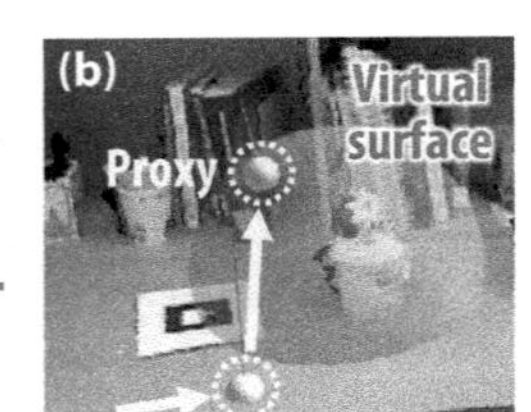

Figure 5: (a) Concept of haptic interaction with a mixed-reality environment. (b) Snapshot of actual interaction.

Appropriate Interfaces for Touchable Video

Two major barriers to the spread of touchable video are the functional constraints and the financial burden of haptic devices for customers. In recent years, however, affordable haptic devices have been released, and the types of interaction that these devices support are also diversifying. Among these haptic devices, we discuss suitable device configurations for touchable video systems.

Glove-type interfaces (Fig. 6-(a)) are commonly found in the conventional approaches related to telepresence and touchable video. They have a hardware structure specialized for multi-fingered interaction and have the advantage of providing multi-sensory feedback such as tactile, kinesthetic, and thermal stimuli depending on the mounted actuators. However, they are generally expensive, inconvenient to wear, and have sanitary concerns. Gloves equipped only with vibrotactile actuators can reduce the cost considerably, but they do not provide enough information to perceive the shape of target objects.

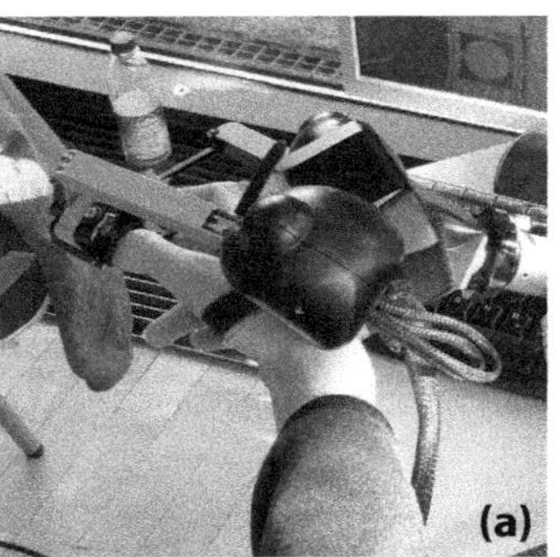

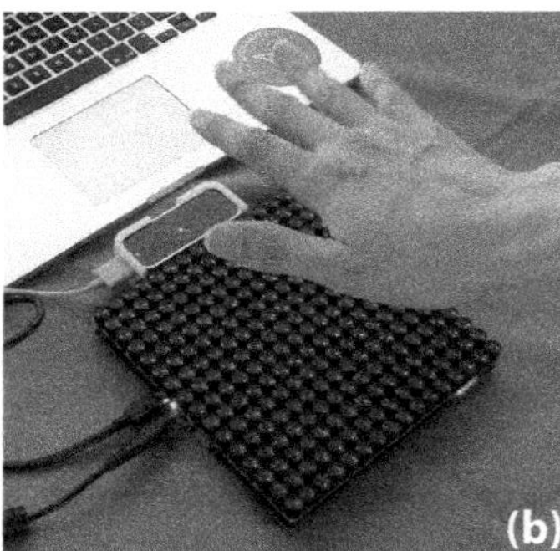

Figure 6: Haptic interfaces for multi-point interaction. (a) Haption HGlove^{TM}. (b) Ultrahaptics STRATOS Explore.

Meanwhile, ultrasound-based haptic devices such as UltraHaptics (Fig. 6-(b)) [2] offer a novel experience of multi-point mid-air haptic interaction, and various technical attempts have also been made to enhance the viewing experience of video contents using these mid-air haptic interfaces [1]. They do not need to be worn or even in contact and are relatively inexpensive, but they have some limitations on the spatial and temporal resolution of haptic feedback. Moreover, although they can provide a tactile hint like tickling sensation to the user, it is difficult to synthesize full kinesthetic feedback solely with acoustic radiation force.

These two representative interfaces for multi-point haptic interaction have their own unique characteristics, so the target contents and user base will also vary. Glove-type devices are considered to be suitable for individual users who want more realistic and immersive experiences. In the case of ultrasound-based devices, on the other hand, it is more likely to be appropriate for demonstration in a public place. We are currently focusing on mid-air interaction using ultrasound-based devices, but glove-type devices may also be a useful alternative depending on the situation.

Conclusion and Future Work

In this paper, we have presented a series of techniques for real-time haptic interaction with RGB-D video streams, and implemented the prototype of a touchable video system based on these techniques. At this point, the proposed system only allows a limited level of interaction, but we believe that more natural interaction metaphors lead to a better user experience in touchable video and thus make efforts to incorporate multi-sensory and multi-contact feedback into the system.

In addition to the future plans already mentioned in the text, various improvements will be made aiming at the practical use of the proposed system. The data acquisition process can be optimized through sophisticated vectorization and parallelization, and the computational burden that arises from multi-point interaction also can be reduced in a similar way. Another feature to consider adopting is sensor fusion. Besides contributing to multi-sensory feedback, it can also broaden the field of view and increase the robustness of spatial data. When all these improvements are made, a benchmark study will be conducted to assess the performance and user experience of the proposed system.

Acknowledgements

This work was supported by Institute for Information & Communications Technology Promotion (IITP) grant funded by the Korea government (MSIT) (No. 2017-0-00179, HD Haptic Technology for Hyper Reality Contents).

REFERENCES

1. Damien Ablart, Carlos Velasco, and Marianna Obrist. 2017. Integrating Mid-Air Haptics into Movie Experiences. In *Proceedings of the 2017 ACM International Conference on Interactive Experiences for TV and Online Video (TVX '17)*. 77–84.

2. Tom Carter, Sue Ann Seah, Benjamin Long, Bruce Drinkwater, and Sriram Subramanian. 2013. UltraHaptics: Multi-point Mid-air Haptic Feedback for Touch Surfaces. In *Proceedings of the 26th Annual ACM Symposium on User Interface Software and Technology (UIST '13)*. 505–514.

3. Jongeun Cha, Mohamad Eid, and Abdulmotaleb El Saddik. 2009. Touchable 3D Video System. *ACM Transactions on Multimedia Computing, Communications, and Applications* 5, 4, Article 29 (Nov. 2009), 25 pages.

4. Seokyeol Kim and Jinah Park. 2016. A Unified Virtual Fixture Model for Haptic Telepresence Systems based on Streaming Point Cloud Data and Implicit Surfaces. In *Proceedings of the 2016 16th International Conference on Control, Automation and Systems (ICCAS)*. 881–885.

5. Seokyeol Kim and Jinah Park. 2017. Robust Haptic Exploration of Remote Environments Represented by Streamed Point Cloud Data. In *Proceedings of the 2017 IEEE World Haptics Conference (WHC)*. 358–363.

6. Adam Leeper, Sonny Chan, and Kenneth Salisbury. 2012. Point clouds can be represented as implicit surfaces for constraint-based haptic rendering. In *Proceedings of the 2012 IEEE International Conference on Robotics and Automation (ICRA)*. 5000–5005.

7. Shahzad Rasool and Alexei Sourin. 2016. Real-time haptic interaction with RGBD video streams. *The Visual Computer* 32, 10 (Oct. 2016), 1311–1321.

8. Fredrik Rydén and Howard Jay Chizeck. 2013. A Proxy Method for Real-Time 3-DOF Haptic Rendering of Streaming Point Cloud Data. *IEEE Transactions on Haptics* 6, 3 (July 2013), 257–267.

9. Martin Weinmann. 2016. *Reconstruction and Analysis of 3D Scenes: From Irregularly Distributed 3D Points to Object Classes*. Springer International Publishing, Chapter Co-Registration of 2D Imagery and 3D Point Cloud Data, 111–140.

10. Craig B. Zilles and J. Kenneth Salisbury. 1995. A constraint-based god-object method for haptic display. In *Proceedings of the 1995 IEEE/RSJ International Conference on Intelligent Robots and Systems (IROS)*, Vol. 3. 146–151.

A Mediography Of Virtual Reality Non-Fiction: Insights And Future Directions

Chris Bevan
University of Bristol
Bristol, UK
chris.bevan@bristol.ac.uk

David Green
University of the West of England
Bristol, UK
david10.green@uwe.ac.uk

TVX '18, June 26–28, 2018, SEOUL, Republic of Korea

ACM ISBN 978-1-4503-5115-7/18/06.
https://doi.org/10.1145/3210825.3213557

Abstract

The emergence in recent years of consumer-accessible virtual reality (VR) technologies such as the Google Daydream, Oculus Rift and HTC Vive has led to a renewal of commercial, academic and public interest in immersive interactive media.

Virtual reality non-fiction (VRNF) (e.g. documentary) is an emergent and rapidly evolving new medium for filmmaking that draws from - and builds upon - traditional forms of non-fiction, as well as interactive media, gaming and immersive theatre.

In this paper, we present our ongoing work to capture and present the first comprehensive record of VRNF - *a Mediography of Virtual Reality Non-Fiction* - to tell the story of where this new medium has come from, how it is evolving, and where it is heading.

Author Keywords

VR; mediography; non-fiction; documentary.

ACM Classification Keywords

• **Human-centered computing~Virtual reality** • Applied computing~Media arts.

Introduction

Recent years have seen a surge of interest in virtual reality (VR) as a platform for non-fiction. From Nonny de la Peña's experiments in "immersive journalism" [9] to Google-funded projects at *New York Times* and *The Guardian*, journalists have been exploring the conceptual and technical potential of VR non-fiction for several years. Likewise, mainstream filmmakers such as Kathryn Bigelow, as well as broadcasters such as the BBC, have begun to embrace immersive technologies in their non-fiction media production practises. Since the release of the Oculus Rift DK1 in 2014, there has been a steady increase in VRNF projects. This is reflected in non-fiction categories appearing on VR distribution platforms, and a growing visibility of VRNF content at established international film festivals including *Sundance* and *Tribeca*.

The emergence of VRNF presents many challenges and opportunities for researchers, designers, developers, broadcasters, producers and curators of digital media alike. A key challenge across all of these sectors is the need for a deeper understanding of the principles and parameters of this nascent paradigm [18]. In this paper, we present our ongoing work to capture and present a comprehensive record of this new form of interactive experience; to tell the story of where it has come from, how it is evolving, and where it is heading.

Background & Related Work

VR is attracting widespread multi-disciplinary research interest. There is a corresponding groundswell of research into VRNF, with a particular focus on of the degree to which VR is able to create a heightened sense of "presence" [e.g. 11, 9, 4, 1, 13], "immersion" [e.g. 5, 10] and, perhaps, "empathy" [e.g. 16, 2, 17]. In online spaces, journalists, experts and the general public routinely dissect new developments and releases across a wide spectrum of VR genres [e.g. 19]. However, this online discourse is piecemeal, unstructured and subjective. There has been no systematic examination of the growing corpus of VRNF. Informed by [6], we argue a more systematic approach would be valuable across sectors and research disciplines. We have therefore created a database of VRNF and are developing an associated set of visualisations that illustrate the formal, thematic and technical trends in the growing corpus of VRNF.

A number of existing projects have informed our work. MIT Docubase [12] is a curated collection of ~300 documentary works (including a number of VR pieces), with associated metadata including, 'technologies' (e.g. *Depthkit*) and 'techniques' (e.g. *volumetric capture*). The Internet Movie Database (IMDb) [8] is a semi-moderated online database of video content, covering ~5m film and television productions, but (as yet) few VRNF pieces. The IMDb collects substantial technical metadata (e.g. camera details), but does not collect information on design techniques. Finally, the International Documentary Film Festival Amsterdam (IDFA) maintains a database of its own selected works [7]. This includes immersive / VR pieces, amongst a range of other interactive documentary forms.

While our work shares a number of characteristics with these projects, it differs in two key ways. *Firstly*, our focus is exclusively on VR non-fiction works, and a major contribution of our work is mapping how the unique affordances of VR are approached in the construction and design of this content. *Secondly*, our objective is to compile a systematic, historical record of

VRNF, from the earliest known example. Our scope is also wider in that we collect not only the high-level metadata of each title (title, director, release date etc.), but also detailed information about its structure (e.g. visual cues, interactivity, use of audio, CGI etc.) and form (e.g. distribution platform).

Methodology: "Mediography"

We have characterised this work as 'mediography'. The intended interpretation of this term is essentially analogous to 'bibliography' (i.e. *a history and systematic description of texts*), but recognizing more explicitly the nature of the content of study. In this section, we describe our inclusion criteria, search strategy and the scope of our cataloguing system.

Inclusion Criteria

Our inclusion criteria are twofold. The first considers how the content is presented (*is it VR?*). The second addresses whether or not a particular title is non-fictional (*is it VRNF?*).

To the first point, we acknowledge that the use of a head mounted display (HMD) is not essential to an immersive VR experience. However, as our research concerns the most recent wave of consumer VR technologies, we are restricting the scope of the content we are examining to panoramic visual imagery that is presented for viewing within a HMD. The most frequently encountered example of this is 360° or 'spherical' video content.

To the second point, the line between fiction and non-fiction is a fine one [14]. Our initial review of the VRNF landscape revealed many short (~10mins), linear 360° video pieces. These works are relatively easy to identify and catalogue as they closely resemble contemporary 2D documentary or journalistic works. However, there is also a proliferation of non-linear, CGI and interactive works that are less immediately recognisable as 'non-fiction'. For example, *Home - an Immersive Spacewalk Experience* (2016) is an interactive simulation of the International Space Station that - while based on a real environment and the people who work there - uses artistic license and game mechanics to provide a more interactive educational experience. Other works like *Notes on Blindness - Into Darkness* (2016) use artistic CGI to represent physical phenomena in different modalities. This formal diversity and the new affordances of the medium mean the line between fiction and non-fiction can be particularly fine.

Acknowledging that these definitions are both nebulous, we have initially adopted a broadly inclusive approach. We therefore currently include any piece that satisfies our technical criteria, self-presents as being non-fiction (e.g. 'journalism', 'documentary' etc.), or is referred to by an independent third party as VR non-fiction.

Search Strategy

Distribution channels for VRNF include media aggregation websites (e.g. *YouTube*), and platform-specific 'apps' (e.g. *Jaunt*). In addition to reviewing the VRNF content from each of these channels, our search strategy includes organic keyword search via search engines and social media (keywords: 'immersive', 'vr', 'documentary'). Finally, we are reviewing the programmes of international festivals (e.g. *Tribeca*), along with VR / technology-focussed publications such as *Engadget*, *VRFocus* and *Wired*.

App stores: The platform(s) from which a VRNF title is distributed (e.g. *Guardian VR*, *Oculus Store*, *Within*).

Film Festivals & awards: VRNF titles are increasingly visible in the programming of international film festivals, with titles often appearing at multiple venues. We capture where a given title is world-premiered, and every subsequent festival appearance.

Countries, directors & producers: VRNF titles can (and often do) have multiple directors, producers and countries of origin.

HMD platform(s): VRNF titles can be multi-platform, exclusive to one platform, or limited by technical requirements to a specific *set* of platforms.

Content: Refers to the internal composition of the title. See subsection "content tags".

Figure 1: Summary of additional title metadata captured in the Mediography

Metadata: What are we Capturing?
VRNF is attracting input from a diverse range of people with backgrounds in – amongst others - filmmaking, theatre and video games development. As a consequence, what constitutes 'best practice' in VRNF is the subject of rapid evolution and re-evaluation as practitioners collaborate and experiment (e.g. [3]).

To ensure our work is of value to the TVX/HCI communities, we felt it essential that the design of the Mediography reflect this emergent experimental quality. Thus, we catalogue not only high-level metadata (e.g. release date, director etc.), but also detail relating to how the content itself is designed, produced and presented. To this end, our database was designed from the outset to be flexible and extensible, allowing us to quickly expand the scope of our capture as our investigation develops.

Database Structure
The Mediography is a relational database, developed using the *Django* web development framework. At the core of the database is the 'film' table that stores the basic metadata for each title, including its {title}, {url}, {duration} and {release date}. Supplementing this, a number of tag-based fields are stored in separate tables via many-to-many relationships. This design decision offers a number of advantages. For example, it facilitates the rapid development of taxonomies through reusable tags. We can also expand these tables further with context-relevant additional fields as required. The additional tag-based tables are summarized in Figure 1.

"Content" Tags: Capturing the Construction of VRNF
As previously mentioned, a major contribution of the Mediography is that we seek to capture the techniques used to craft VRNF, both as they emerge and as they spread and evolve over time. Some of these techniques reflect technological affordances, while others reflect creative decisions. To ensure our tags are as comprehensive as possible, we are working with multiple stakeholders including an interdisciplinary research team and professional VRNF producers. While remaining a work in progress, we have currently identified 50 techniques, examples of which are presented in Figure 3.

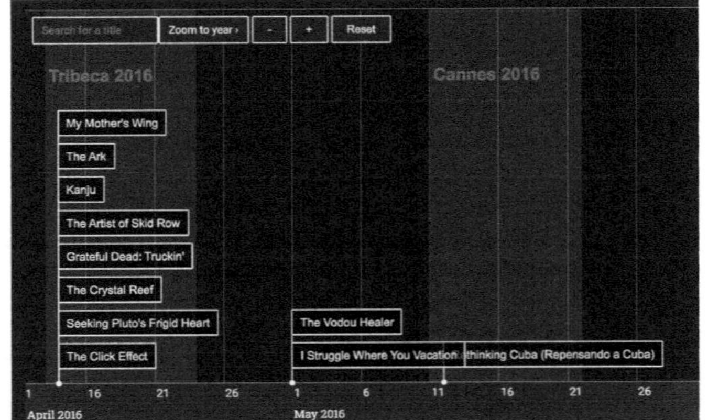

Figure 2: Prototype Mediography timeline UI.
http://vrdocumentaryencounters.co.uk/vrmediography/vrmediography

Design of the Mediography UI
Supporting the database is a web-based UI [19] that provides a public-facing means of exploring the data interactively. A key feature is an interactive timeline (Figure 2), which orders titles by date of

Viewer POV: E.g. first person, third person, omniscient.

Evidence of Physicality: E.g. visible arms or body, casting of shadows, visible breath etc.

Diegetic Annotation: E.g. text / maps / 2D screens / projections that are mapped to surfaces within a virtual scene (as opposed to a non-diegetic overlay).

Visual / audio prompting: Cues that explicitly guide viewer attention, such as arrows or spoken instruction.

Nonlinear narrative: e.g. branching narrative structure.

Figure 3: Examples of the content 'tags used in the Mediography (work in progress). These tags capture specific technical and / or design features of individual VRNF titles.

release, highlights award-winning pieces and indicates whether a piece was world premiered at a film festival.

A web-based platform provides a number of advantages. It provides accessible and up-to-date analytics based on live data, as well as showing how these factors have changed over time. It also enables stakeholders to highlight missing or inaccurate content.

Initial Findings and Tensions

While still a work-in-progress, our current dataset includes > 230 VRNF titles from 2012 to the present day. We have therefore been able to observe certain trends, tensions and issues from 2012-2017 (inclusive). Here, we highlight some of these initial observations.

Is there an appropriate duration for a VRNF piece?
Calculated across our whole dataset, the average duration for a VRNF piece is 8.7mins ± 0.3min (n=232). However, yearly averages have yet to settle, with values ranging from 7–12 minutes. While these durations align loosely to the film 'short' format, we also note that there currently exists little guidance on how long audiences are willing to spend viewing VRNF content. Though more research is required, the limited variation in durations we have observed might indicate a lack of confidence on the part of filmmakers to push the boundaries of the medium with longer pieces.

Towards a 'Shared Grammar' for VRNF
Through assembling the mediography, we have come to recognise that an exciting affordance of VRNF lies in its ability to mix traditional non-fiction media-making practises with other (traditionally fiction-focused) practises such as games and theatre in increasingly novel ways. Indeed, many of the most awarded VRNF projects to-date present unique configurations of elements. An example is *Spacewalk*, which combines game elements (ludology) and documentary conventions (narratology) in a non-linear narrative. As this convergence continues, we anticipate that there will be an increased need to identify the language that is emerging to describe VRNF content production, with particular attention on a number of terms currently used by previously independent disciplines that may be sources of potential misunderstanding or friction (e.g. 'diegesis', 'presence', 'empathy' etc.).

Next Steps

The focus of our current work is the completion of our content tag framework, and the collection of all VRNF titles released before 2018. We will then apply our framework across the corpus to conduct a deeper analysis of the VRNF content; an activity that will form the basis of a full paper that will detail the 'story so far'. In parallel, through this detailed examination of the VRNF landscape, we will seek to identify areas where research interventions may be most fruitful, and inform the design of a number of experimental VRNF commissions that will be developed in collaboration with our project partners over the next 18 months.

Acknowledgements

This research is funded by the UK EPSRC as part of the research project *Virtual Realities - Immersive Documentary Encounters* (ref: EP/P025595/1). For more information on the project and its partners, visit our website at http://vrdocumentaryencounters.co.uk.

References

1. Jakki O. Bailey, Jeremy N. Bailenson & Daniel Casasanto. 2016. When does virtual embodiment

change our minds? *Presence: Teleoperators and Virtual Environments,* 25(3), 222-233.

2. Paul Bloom. 2017. *Against empathy: The case for rational compassion*. Random House.
3. Andy Brown, Jayson Turner, Jake Patterson, Anastasia Schmitz, Mike Armstrong & Maxine Glancy. 2017. Subtitles in 360-degree Video. In Adjunct Publication of the 2017 ACM Intl. Conference on Interactive Experiences for TV and Online Video (TVX17). ACM, New York, NY, 3-8.
4. Julia Diemer et al. 2015. The impact of perception and presence on emotional reactions: a review of research in VR. *Frontiers in Psychology,* 6.
5. Valentina Feldman. 2016. Immersive paleoart: reconstructing dreadnoughtus schrani and remediating the science documentary for cinematic virtual reality. *In ACM SIGGRAPH 2016 Posters (SIGGRAPH '16)*. ACM, New York.
6. Arnau Gifreu-Castells. 2014. Mapping trends in interactive non-fiction through the lenses of interactive documentary. *In: Mitchell A., Fernández-Vara C., Thue D. (eds) Interactive Storytelling. ICIDS 2014. Lecture Notes in Computer Science*, vol 8832. Springer.
7. International Documentary Film Festival Amsterdam (IDFA). Retrieved from https://www.idfa.nl/en/collection/films
8. Internet Movie Database. Retrieved from http://www.imdb.com
9. Nonny De la Peña, et al. 2010. Immersive journalism: immersive virtual reality for the first-person experience of news. *Presence: Teleoperators and Virtual Environments,* 19(4), 291-301.
10. Mary F. Macedonio, Thomas D. Parsons, Raymond A. Digiuseppe, Brenda A. Weiderhold, and Albert A. Rizzo. 2007. Immersiveness and physiological arousal within panoramic video-based virtual reality. *Cyberpsychology & Behavior,* 10(4), 508-515.
11. Jamie McRoberts. 2017. Are we there yet? Media content and sense of presence in non-fiction virtual reality. *Studies in Documentary Film*, 1-18.
12. MIT Docubase. Retrieved from https://docubase.mit.edu/
13. Kate Nash. 2017. Virtual reality witness: exploring the ethics of mediated presence. *Studies in Documentary Film*, 1-13.
14. Bill Nichols. 2001. *Introduction to documentary*. Indiana University Press.
15. Non-Fiction Documentary VR: A Mediography. Retrieved from http://vrdocumentaryencounters.co.uk/vrmediography/vrmediography
16. Nicola S. Schutte & Emma J. Stilinović. 2017. Facilitating empathy through virtual reality. *Motivation and Emotion*, 41(6), 708-712.
17. Donghee Shin. 2018. Empathy and embodied experience in virtual environment: To what extent can virtual reality stimulate empathy and embodied experience?. *Computers in Human Behavior*, 78, 64-73.
18. Esa Sirkkunen, Heli Väätäjä, Turo Uskali, and Parisa Pour Rezaei. 2016. Journalism in virtual reality: opportunities and future research challenges. *In Proc. 20th International Academic Mindtrek Conference (AcademicMindtrek '16)*. ACM Press, New York, NY, 297-303.
19. Angela Watercutter. 2018. A VR movie set in space just landed a 7-figure deal at Sundance. Yes, you read that right. Retrieved March 1, 2018) from https://www.wired.com/story/vr-film-spheres-huge-sundance-deal

Content Unification in iTV to Enhance User Experience: The UltraTV Project

Pedro Almeida
Jorge Ferraz de Abreu
Sílvia Fernandes
Eliza Oliveira
Digimedia,
University of Aveiro
Aveiro, 3810-193, Portugal
almeida@ua.pt
jfa@ua.pt
silvia.fernandes@ua.pt
elizaoliveira@ua.pt

TVX '18, June 26–28, 2018, SEOUL, Republic of Korea

ACM ISBN 978-1-4503-5115-7/18/06.
https://doi.org/10.1145/3210825.3213558

Abstract
Recent changes in TV viewers' consumption habits are pushing to a point where industry content providers and producers must create new technological solutions to retain customers. To cope with these, the UltraTV project consortium developed an iTV concept, with a focus on the unification of content from different sources. This brings together traditional TV along with Over-the-Top content, aiming to provide an integrated solution that could foster the audiovisual consumption and ease the discovery of content. This paper presents the implemented solution and reports on the results of its evaluation using a Field Trial. Results provide valuable insights for a market-oriented version of the UltraTV concept, proving the feasibility and user demand for a profile-based content unification solution for future iTV solutions.

Author Keywords
Unification, interactive TV, personalization, user experience, usability.

ACM Classification Keywords
D.2.2 Design Tools and Techniques: User interfaces; D.4.7 Organization and Design: Interactive systems; H.5.1 Information interfaces and presentation (e.g., HCI): Multimedia Information Systems; H.5.m.

Information interfaces and presentation (e.g., HCI): Evaluation/methodology

Introduction

The current television experience is undergoing fundamental changes in the way viewers get constant access to TV content, increasingly supported by (Video) on Demand (VoD) services in addition to the traditional lineup of TV [1,2]. These transformations are leading to changes in the TV offering, increasing the challenges for commercial players to cope with the new users' expectations [3]. In this scope, the consortium of the UltraTV project (involving a major IPTV player, a University, and a R&D institution in the field of telecommunications) is developing an Interactive TV (iTV) concept. The focus is on the unification of content from different sources, bringing together traditional TV content (live and catch-up), with OTT content (from YouTube, Facebook, and Netflix), offering an integrated user experience (UX).

The main goal of this paper is to present the UltraTV concept and the results of a high-fidelity prototype assessment. It describes a Field Trial (FT) procedure, including the characterization of the participants' viewing habits, a report on the uses of the prototype, and the UX results gathered through different data collection instruments: the System Usability Scale (SUS), Self-Assessment Manikin (SAM), AttrakDiff, and a preliminary analysis of interviews, [4,5,6].

Motivational Factors

The growing relevance of non-linear video over linear TV is highlighted as the main change within audiovisual consumption in recent years [7], due to the increase in OTT offers and the convenience of mobile viewing as an alternative to the (big) TV screen. Advanced set-top boxes (STBs), Smart TVs or Media Players (e.g. Apple TV) offer OTT content in fragmented, proprietary applications with their UI and UX, forcing the user to jump from one app to another [8]. Furthermore, the convergence of online video and traditional content is taking over the iTV technological scenario, leading to the forgoing of pre-packaged UX and focusing on social and mobile proposals [9]. The pursuit of personalization and customization in iTV is still significantly confined to research, resorting to data from social networks and second screen applications [10].

Within this framework, personalization and a content-first approach, delivered on a content and source unified UI, may embody features that meet current users' media behaviors [11].

The UltraTV Project

Based on the identification of users' needs and the contexts of use, the prototype development was carried out in an iterative and continuous process. This approach allowed for the inclusion of users' suggestions and opinions, adopting a User-Centered Design methodology taking into consideration a Participatory Design approach. This process, extended for several months, took the product development through different design stages. This paper describes the final version and the users' feedback towards it.

Visually the home screen includes uppercase category titles, soft gradients, and visual and animated feedback. The home screen is structured into columns of content that are placed either according to genre/type of content, source or live TV

Luna is a framework developed by Craftwork https://craftwork.tv/products/luna/

Figure 2: A participant using the UltraTV STB in his house

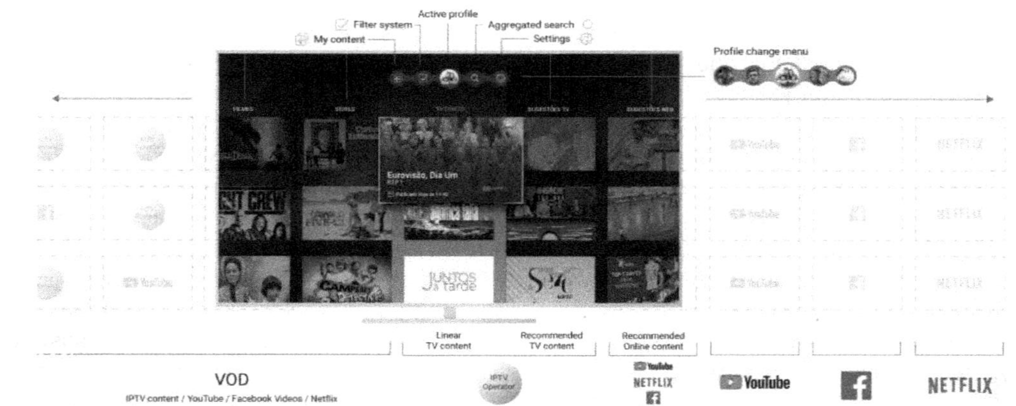

Figure 1: The home screen layout architecture –High fidelity prototype built for the field trial

Final prototype development

The Luna© framework, an application engine optimized for the development of context-oriented TV interfaces, was chosen as the implementation platform due to its performance, raw graphics speed, and time to product implementation. A functional STB-based prototype was built, benefiting from the feedback obtained from two former versions, evaluated by an experts' review and an in-lab assessment respectively. The goal of the team was to build an application that allowed for the unification of TV content, enhancing the entertainment experience offered to different viewer profiles. A closer look was given to younger generations, by providing content beyond the traditional broadcast and by trying to improve the viewing quality of OTT content on the TV screen for those who regularly used their mobile devices. The high-fidelity version of the prototype (see Figure 1) was supported by Web APIs capable of feeding the application with the IPTV's live content and VoD, along with OTT sources - YouTube, Facebook Videos and Netflix. With a MON-based framework [3], supported by the operator's channel offer, it can provide vast amounts of content, in contrast to limited OTT-based solutions like Apple TV. These features are the starting point to create a dynamic offering of contents, based on the user profile and consumption behaviors. For that the application promotes the use of individual or family profiles. As the main screen unifies the content on a single UI, it allows the user to have access to a diversified bundle of content with a reduced number of interactions. Content is displayed on a thumbnail and card-based grid, with reduced visual differentiation of content sources, mainly sorted by genre and other personalization. It also includes a unified search and cross-content recommendations.

Field Trial Evaluation

A Field Trial (FT) plays a crucial role in the validation of a product, allowing to test it in close to real conditions, possibly revealing problems that would not appear in controlled environments [12]. FTs are widely used for the assessment of the UX as an essential component of

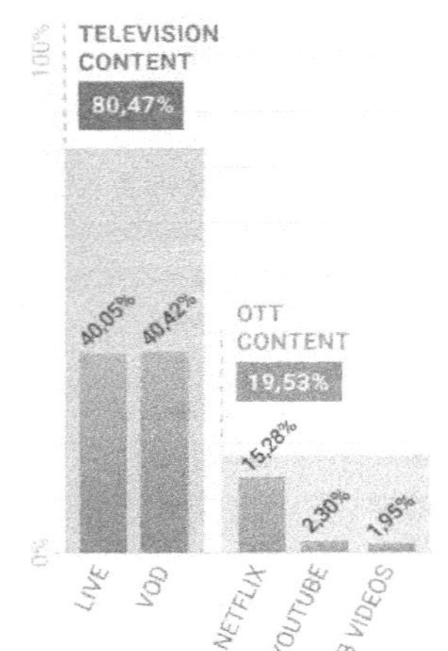

Figure 3: Time spent watching TV per content source

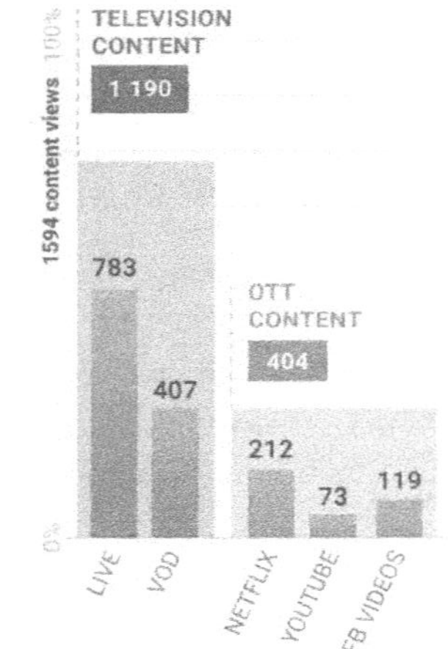

Figure 4: Number of videos watched per content source

an iterative process for the development and design of a product or service [13].

The UltraTV FT was carried out from January 12 to 31, 2018, using a total of 20 STBs. Participants included students and power users, ensuring viewers from different age ranges, especially in the UltraTV target audiences – "Millennials" and "Generation Z". Prior to the FT, a consumption habits characterization questionnaire was made. For the FT, Google Analytics was set up to log all interactions with the prototype. The UX evaluation, with an emphasis in the most significant dimensions in the iTV domain (Stimulation, Identification, Aesthetics and Emotional), was addressed by a combination of methods using SUS (System Usability Scale), AttrakDiff, SAM (Self-Assessment Manikin) and interviews [14].

Participants characterization
From the total of 20 STBs that started the FT, 12 STBs in 12 different houses were selected to be analyzed accounting for a total of 26 individual profiles and 9 family profiles. 8 STBs were not considered due to not complying with: i) having completed the characterization questionnaires, and, ii) using the system for at least 6 hours and registered more than 200 clicks, according to Google Analytics' data. The 26 valid participants include 15 male (57.69%) and 11 female (42.31%) evaluators, aged between 12 and 54 years old. Considering the completed level of education, high school education (38.46%) is most common, followed by a BA (26, 92%) and MA (19.23%). According to an age stratification with 5-year intervals, the sample was most illustrative of four groups: 26.92% between 20-24 years old and 19.23% between 15-19 years old. These are followed by ages between 30-34, and between 35-39 years (Generation X). Considering previous viewing habits at home, most participants watch TV with another adult (38.46%), with the family that includes children and adults (19.23%) or with roommates (19.23%). Only four participants reported watching TV alone (15.38%) and two mentioned watching TV with the children only (7.69%). For data analysis purposes participants were also grouped according to their family structure: a) families - 10 users (38.46%); b) couples - 8 users (30.77%); c) roommates - 5 users (19.23%); d) alone/single - 3 users (11.54%).

Results and discussion

This section presents the results gathered in the FT.

Audiovisual consumption
During the FT participants watched mostly regular TV content (Live and VOD), accounting for 80,47%, of which 40,05% corresponds to Live TV (see Figure 3). OTT content played a smaller role. However, considering that YouTube and Facebook Videos deliver shorter videos, when considering the number of videos (not the time spent watching them) Facebook and YouTube increase its influence (see Figure 4). The three users with the highest OTT time consumption are some of the youngest participants (12-20 years old), taking up to 70% of their consumption with online content. Older users (31-54 years old) watched significantly more Live and VoD content, with more than 75% of their consumption time being traditional TV content. STBs associated with family and couples' categories had the highest average consumption. Several users preferred to use a generic family profile instead of their profiles and confirmed that they felt UltraTV promoted common viewing practices.

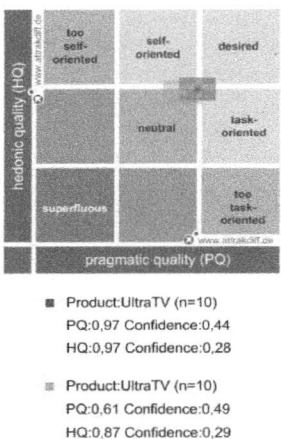

Emotional impact	
	SAM (1 to 5)
Satisfaction	3,23
Motivation	3,12
Feeling of control	3,77

Table 1: Global score for the SAM questionnaire

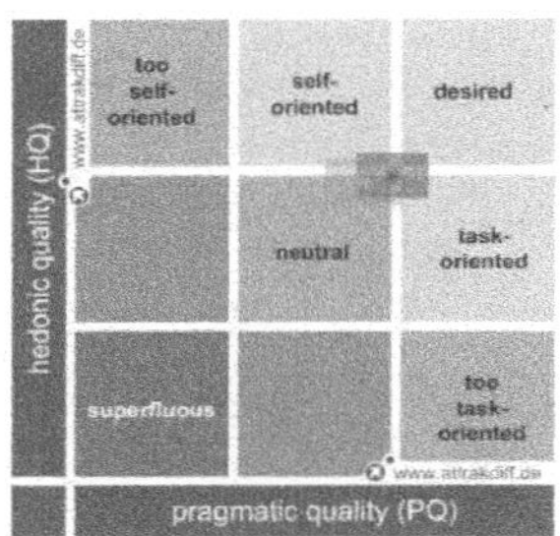

Figure 5: AttrakDiff Portfolio results – "Millennials" (orange) and "Generation Z" (blue)

Qualitative feedback revealed positive results. 76,92% of the participants stated that they would be willing to swap their current cable/IPTV service for a retail version of the UltraTV. Although most participants had limited previous contact with other OTT players and media centers, content aggregation solutions and the content discovery features were highly valued confirming the acceptance and valuation of such unified proposal. The need for better control of the system and the lack of some features (e.g. advanced catch-up TV features) and configuration options were considered negative to the UX.

SUS, SAM, and AttrakDiff evaluation
The prototype obtained 72.40 on the SUS scale (0 - 100). This score reflects the user's effectiveness and efficiency to perform tasks and their comfort in using the product. According to the SUS classification scale, the average value of the prototype usability is considered "Good" (72,40 out of 100). This reveals no major issues with usability in overall but indicates that there is room for improvement. The statement "I think I would like to use this product often" received the best answers, showing a relevant desire to use the prototype. The less positive scores on the statement "I found the system unnecessarily complex" reflected the participants' lack of control and difficulty in dealing with a significantly different TV interface.

Regarding the SAM questionnaire (see Table 1), participants showed an overall positive emotional relationship with the prototype. However, "motivation" and "satisfaction" show a more significant room for improvement. Younger participants (15-19 years old) got the highest SUS and SAM scores. Unification of sources could be a vital issue for the positive results.

Participants in the 30-34 age group gave the worst scores on the SUS and SAM scales. Being used to their operator's STB features, these participants may have missed their preferences and advanced catch-up features during the FT with the UltraTV STB. Regarding viewing dynamics, roommates were the family structure that best scored the prototype (SUS 78,50/ average SAM 4,07), while those who watched TV by themselves exhibited the lowest scores (SUS 60,33/ average SAM 2,67. The availability of profiles might have contributed to a personalized experience for families that share the same TV device. On the AttrakDiff questionnaire, "Millennials" and "Generation Z" provided positive results. Considering the hedonic and pragmatic qualities (see Figure 5), "Millennials" (orange) and "Generation Z" (blue), expressed similar confidence levels and approached the *desired* quadrant.

Conclusions

The emergent iTV ecosystem leans towards on-demand content without dismissing the viewing of the shared linear experience on the big screen, complemented by flexible access across mobile devices. The project acknowledges the identified challenges and tries to enhance the entertainment experience by focusing on unification and personalization features. The UltraTV prototype was tested in real conditions, with data provided by UX metrics. The quantitative results sustained the motivation of users to have access to an iTV solution that includes content beyond the traditional broadcast channels, upgrading the offer with OTT content. Positive feedback was higher in young generations. This provides essential insights towards the idea that unified iTV solutions may be decisive in retaining younger generations within the TV screen for collective shared viewing experiences.

Acknowledgements

This paper is a result of the UltraTV - UltraHD TV Application Ecosystem project (grant agreement no.17738), funded by COMPETE 2020, Portugal 2020 and the European Union through the European Regional Development Fund (FEDER). Authors are grateful to the project partners.

References

1. Abreu, J., Almeida, P., Teles, B. 2014. TV Discovery & enjoy: a new approach to help users finding the right TV program to watch. In *Proceedings of the 2014 ACM international conference on Interactive experiences for TV and online video* (ACM), 63-70.
2. Vanattenhoven, J., Geerts, D. 2015. Broadcast, Video-on-Demand, and Other Ways to Watch Television Content: a Household Perspective. In *Proceedings of the 2015 ACM international conference on Interactive experiences for TV and online video* (ACM), 1-10.
3. Abreu, J., Nogueira, J., Becker, V., Cardoso, B.: Survey of Catch-Up TV and other time-shift services: a comprehensive analysis and taxonomy of linear and nonlinear television. In: Telecommunication Systems, Vol. 64. pp. 57-74 (2017).
4. Brooke, J. SUS-A quick and dirty usability scale. In: Jordan, P.W., Weerdmeester, P.W., Thomas, P.W., McLelland, I.L. (eds.) Usability Evaluation in Industry, pp. 189–194. Taylor and Francis, London (1996).
5. Bradley, M.M., Lang, P.J.: Measuring emotion: the self-assessment manikin and the semantic differential. J. Behav. Ther. Exper. Psychiatry 25(1), 49–59 (1994).
6. Hassenzahl, M., Burmester, M., & Koller, F. (2003). AttrakDiff: A questionnaire to measure perceived hedonic and pragmatic quality. In J. Ziegler & G. Szwillus (Eds.), Mensch&Computer 2003. Interaktion in Bewegung (pp. 187–196). Stuttgart, Leipzig: B. G. Teubner.
7. Ericsson Consumer and Industry Insight Report: TV and Media 2017. A consumer-driven future of media. https://bit.ly/2yzN1Pp. (2017).
8. Abreu. J., Almeida, P., & Silva, T. (2015). A UX Evaluation Approach for Second-Screen Applications. In Applications and Usability of Interactive TV (pp. 105-120). Springer.
9. Montpetit, MJ., Klym, N. & Mirlacher, T. Multimed Tools Appl (2011) 53: 519. https://doi.org/10.1007/s11042-010-0504-4
10. Kim, J., Kim, I. & Jang, B. (2014). Research on User Customized Social Mobile Platform base on Personalized TV through IP Networks. International Journal of Multimedia and Ubiquitous Engineering. 9. 159-170. 10.14257/ijmue.2014.9.7.14.
11. Ericsson Consumer and Industry Insight Report: TV and Media 2016. The evolving role of TV and media in consumers' everyday lives. https://bit.ly/2pFxcQV (2016).
12. Field trials: what does this technic do?. Tools & Techniques. Retrieved January 29, 2018 from https://bit.ly/2I6Sb65
13. Monahan, K., Lahteenmaki, M., McDonald, S., Cockton, G. An investigation into the use of field methods in the design and evaluation of interactive systems. Proceedings of the 22nd British HCI Group Annual Conference on People and Computers: Culture, Creativity, Interaction (2008).
14. Bernhaupt, R; Pirker, M.: Evaluating User Experience for Interactive Television: Towards the Development of a Domain-Specific User Experience Questionnaire. HUMAN-COMPUTER INTERACTION - INTERACT 2013, PT II Book Series: LNCS, vol. 8118, pp. 642-659 (2013).

Viewers' Behaviors at Home on TV and Other Screens: An Online Survey

Jorge Ferraz de Abreu
Pedro Almeida
Ana Velhinho
Enrickson Varsori
Digimedia,
University of Aveiro
Aveiro, 3810-193, Portugal
jfa@ua.pt
almeida@ua.pt
ana.velhinho@ua.pt
varsori@ua.pt

Abstract
In a context where audiovisual consumption habits are continually transforming, mostly driven by Video On Demand services, this paper has the main goal of characterizing the motivational factors and behaviors related with the uses of multiple devices at home. The report is sustained in the results of an online survey carried out in Portugal, aiming to collect information about the online video and linear TV content consumption. Besides the regular TV contents, usually watched on a TV connected to a set-top box, the Computer was the most chosen device to watch all the other sources of content at home. Furthermore, 71,4% stated that they usually connect more than one device to the TV screen.

Author Keywords
Audiovisual consumption; Behaviors; iTV; Online data collection; Survey.

ACM Classification Keywords
A.1 Introductory and Survey; G.3 Probability and Statistics (e.g., Correlation and regression analysis); H.1.2 User/Machine Systems (e.g., Human factors); J.4 Social and Behavioral Sciences.

TVX '18, June 26–28, 2018, SEOUL, Republic of Korea

ACM ISBN 978-1-4503-5115-7/18/06.
https://doi.org/10.1145/3210825.3213559

Introduction

Driven by Video On Demand (VOD) services, audiovisual viewing habits have been changing, mostly the ones related to the increasing consumption of Over the Top (OTT) contents [1]. Concomitantly, the establishment of the new culture of *anywhere and anytime*, associated with the use of mobile devices, has led to a shift in the primary devices for audiovisual consumption [2]. At the same time, Pay-TV operators are making the traditional TV line-up more flexible, offering services such as "catch-up TV" and "time-shift" [1]. Pay-TV penetration in Portuguese households has reached a total of 89% in 2017, and it is expected to grow slowly but steadily up to 94% by 2021. For this, the IPTV services have had a relevant role since 2013 [3]. Taking into consideration that the information available in previous and current studies [4,5,6] was lacking a focus on the particular habits in the domestic consumption and screen preferences, namely regarding how the type of content to be watched influences the screen choices, an online questionnaire that could complement the studies with a more in-depth understanding of the uses of screens at home was prepared and disseminated. This paper has the main goal of presenting the results regarding the dynamics of audiovisual consumption on Portuguese households, based on preliminary results of the Portuguese version of the online survey, collected between January and February 2018.

Viewers Behaviors on the TV Ecosystem

Current studies, focused on consumption behaviors, revealed that the TV and media landscape suffered significant changes, leading to the establishment of different consumer profiles. Ericsson ConsumerLab points to six TV user groups that can be considered [4]. The classic "TV Couch Traditionalist" (heavy viewers of broadcasted TV using the large screen) is currently the less representative group with 13%, down from 40% in 2010. This decrease is in favor of other user groups such as the "Screen Shifters" (consumers of all kind of TV and video, anywhere and across devices) with 21% and the "Mobility Centric" (mobile screen users) already with 22% (a mere 5% in 2010). These TV groups are related to generational clusters categorized as the "Silent Generation" (ages 65+), "Baby Boomers" (ages 50-64)", "Generation X" (ages 35-49), "Millennials" (ages 21-34) and "Generation Z" (ages 15-20) [5]. As for device preference, the computer, tablet and mobile phone-based viewing are more popular among the youngest users. Although the TV screen is not dismissed, they adopt multiple screens viewing, along with multitasking practices [6]. Most of the Pay-TV operators are already offering non-linear TV content (from VOD and catch-up TV services). Despite this, users are increasingly subscribing on-demand services (SVOD) like Netflix or getting free online content (FVOD) made available online by leading video sharing platforms like YouTube or Facebook [4,5].

The online survey

Scope and delimitation

The central research question, which drove the design of this data collection instrument, was to know whether audiovisual content preferences are influencing the device's choice at home. The survey includes 20 closed questions structured in five sections: 1) sociodemographic characterization; 2) device usage; 3) online audiovisual (AV) content consumption; 4) TV consumption; 5) Television of the future: unification of contents. This approach aimed to determine the viewers' profiles, based on their projections or actual viewing behaviors about specific uses of the devices

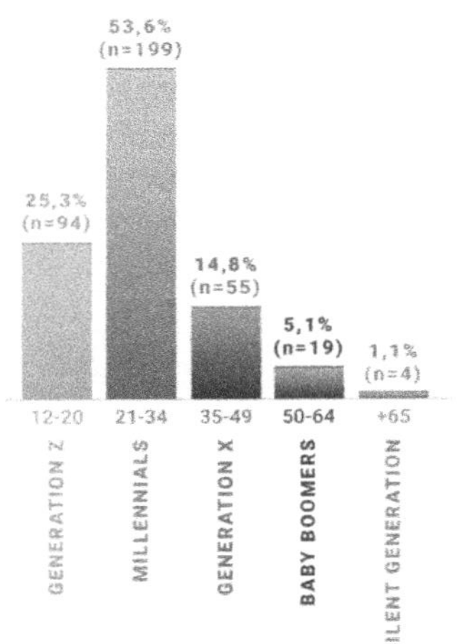

Figure 1 - Sample distribution by generations

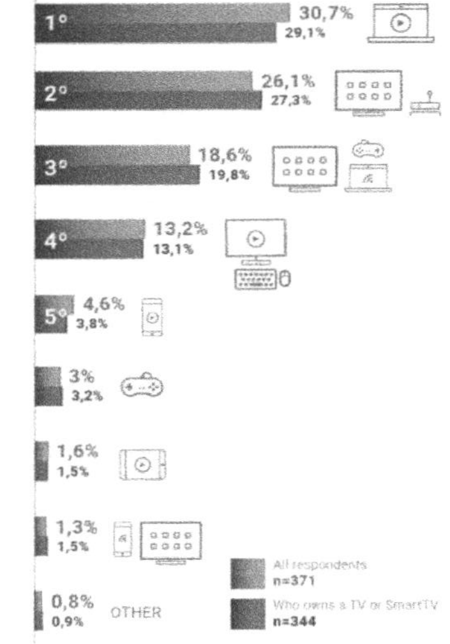

Figure 2 - Ranking of preferential device for watching audiovisual content at home (Question 1.3)

selected to watch audiovisual content. Although the scope of the survey is broader, including the dynamics of audiovisual consumption among different screens, for this paper the analysis is focused on the domestic environment, comprising a subset of questions.

The data collection was intentionally divided into three streams[1], a version for individuals living in Portugal (PT version), in Brazil (BR version) and other foreign countries (EN version). Only the data collected in the Portuguese version of the survey, between January and February 2018, is considered in this paper. The PT survey got 371 valid answers, with men representing 58,8% of the respondents. Regarding academic degrees, most of the individuals have a Bachelor´s degree (29,1%) or High school graduation (28,6%), 17,8% have a Master´s degree, 8,9% a Trade/technical/vocational training, 6,2% an Associate degree, 5,7% a Professional or doctorate degree and 3,8% up to 8th grade. Regarding the respondents' household occupation, it is mostly composed of adults with the following distribution: Family without children (49,9%); Family with adults and children (24%); Housemates (15,1%); Single (8,1%); Adult with children (1,1%), and; Other (1,9%). The age distribution ranged from 12 to 81 years old with an average age of 28 years old. For comparison with other studies [5], the sample was also analyzed regarding age clustering (Figure 1). Thus, the sample highlights three main clusters relevant to the study: Millennials (53,6%); Generation Z (25,3%) and Generation X (14,8%).

[1] PT: http://bit.ly/dinamicas_tv_ecras;
BR: http://bit.ly/br_dinamicas_tv_dispositivos;
EN: http://bit.ly/tv_screens_dynamics.

Results and discussion

The use of Devices for AV consumption at home

Regarding regular television viewing at home, 32% watch TV alone and 60,2% watch television with others, according to the following distribution: Family with other adults (38,8%); Alone (32%); Family with adults and children (13,7%); Housemates (6,5%), and; Single adult with children (1,1%). Some respondents said that they don't watch TV at home (7,8%). As for the preferential device to watch AV content at home (Figure 2), the three most common devices selected by the respondents were: the Laptop (30,7%), a set-top box connected to a SmartTV (26,1%) and to a Computer or Media Center, like Apple TV, Chromecast, Android TV, among others, connected to a SmartTV (18,6%). The ranking is the same for the group of 344 respondents (92,7%) that own a TV or SmartTV. Despite having a TV set they chose the Laptop as the preferential device at home (29,1%). The connection of devices to the TV screen was also examined. 71,4% stated that they usually do it and likely connect more than one device. The most used devices connected to the TV are the Laptop (42%), Smartphone (21%) and Media Center (20,8%). Among the reasons for choosing a specific preferred device for watching videos (at home), the "practical and convenient access" was the most valued reason (Figure 3) for all devices, with the exception of the Desktop Computer for which the main reason was the "access to other applications and functionalities" and the screencasting via smartphone and tablet, due to the "screen size".

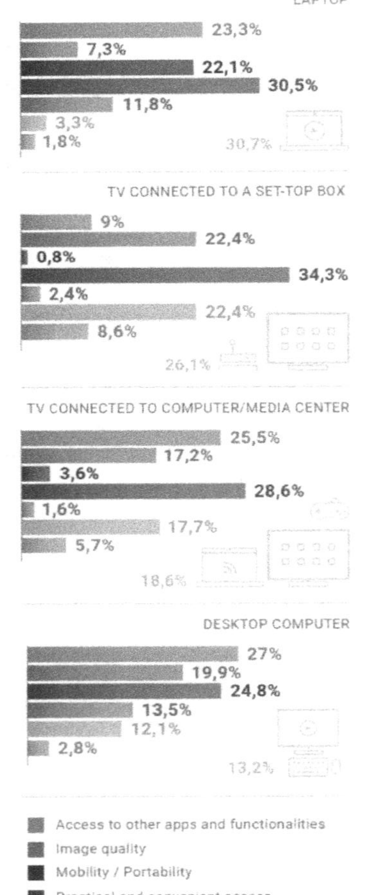

Figure 3 – Top 4 preferential devices and the main reasons for its use at home (Question 1.3 and 1.4)

Analysis of variance regarding generations

To support the reliability of the inferences, regarding generation clustering as a correlation factor towards the device's preferences, parametric tests were applied in specific questions of the survey: "1.3. *Select which device do you prefer to watch audiovisual content at home*" and "*1.8. Select the device you use to watch the following content according to its source*". One-way ANOVA was used to determine if there were significant differences in the means of the groups of the independent variable (generations) [7]. To sustain the results obtained by ANOVA, Levene´s test was used to verify the homogeneity of the variances, and in cases where the assumption of variance homogeneity is violated, Welch's robust test was applied considering *sig. values* that are different from 0 or 0,05. According to the parametric results[2], there is a statistical variance between generations and the choice of devices and content sources (question 1.3 and 1.8), supporting the different patterns of behavior that can be seen in Figure 4 and Figure 5. In case of question 1.3, both Levene and ANOVA have *sig*. 0, thus, there is homogeneity in the analyzed groups. In question 1.8, just the Facebook source (Levene with a *sig*. 0,06 and Robust Welch with 0,489) allow stating that there is no homogeneity among the variables, that is, there is a difference between the generations and the use of Facebook. As shown in Figure 4, there is a deviation between individuals with less than 34 years old (Generation Z and Millennials) that have chosen the Laptop as the preferred device (41,5% and 34,1%, respectively) and the Generation X with only 8,8% selecting this device as preferential. In this group, the Television or SmartTV connected to a set-top box or an antenna (49,3%) was the top preference. Considering the second preferred device, Generation Z pointed to the Desktop Computer, and the Millennials chose a Computer or Media Center connected to the TV set or SmartTV, suggesting an increasing appreciation of the large TV screen over smaller screens, possibly favoring size and image quality. The Computer, either Desktop or Laptop, for the youngest respondents may be related to multitasking practices and intensive use of such device due to their student activity. On the other hand, the set-top box or antenna connected to the TV set or SmartTV drops abruptly from 49,3% in Generation X to 13,8% in Generation Z preference. Moreover, despite the intensive use and ubiquitous presence of mobile devices in our daily lives, as shown in several reports [4,5,6], the Smartphone and Tablet were not a relevant option to watch AV content at home for these respondents.

Considering the source of the content, Figure 5 shows that the set-top box or an antenna connected to the TV is the most chosen device to watch television content among the three generations, mainly by Generation X (72,5%). Generation Z is the age group that spends the least time with television content, with 34% of the sample claiming they never or rarely watch content from TV channels. A considerable portion of the same age group never or rarely watches content from Netflix (35%) and Facebook Videos (29,6%). Regarding Netflix, Generation Z and Millennials focus the consumption on the Computer (46,9% and 35,5%, respectively), while Generation X presents a more distributed device choice. They prefer the screencast of devices on the TV (27,2%) or the TV connected to a

[2] http://socialitv.web.ua.pt/UltraTV/Parametric_test_surveyPT.pdf

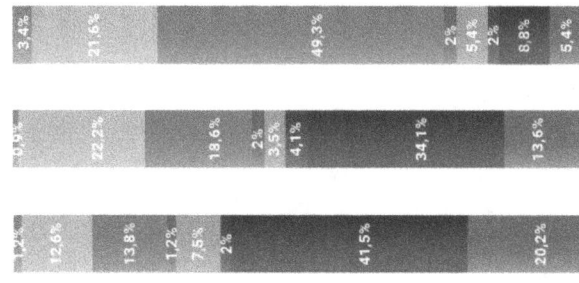

Figure 4 - Preferential device for watching AV content at home by generations (Question 1.3)

set-top box or antenna (16,3%) or even the Computer (10,9%). Content from Internet sources like YouTube and other websites (e.g., downloads and streaming platforms) are preferentially watched at home on the Computer by the three generations, except for Facebook content with a slightly higher preference for the Smartphone followed by the Computer.

Conclusion and Future Work

Having into account that the Pay-TV penetration in Portuguese households is estimated to grow up to 94% by 2021 [3], IPTV services qualify as a relevant context for research and development of more adapted services, regarding the recent consumers' behaviors. Concerning the use of devices, essential targets are expanding groups such as the "Screen Shifters" and "Mobility Centric", that together represent almost half of the AV consumers according to a 2017 study [4]. The preliminary results from the Portuguese version of the presented online survey highlight some insights regarding devices preference at home, depending on the content source and age, with focus on the three most relevant age groups for this study – Generation Z, Millennials and, Generation X.

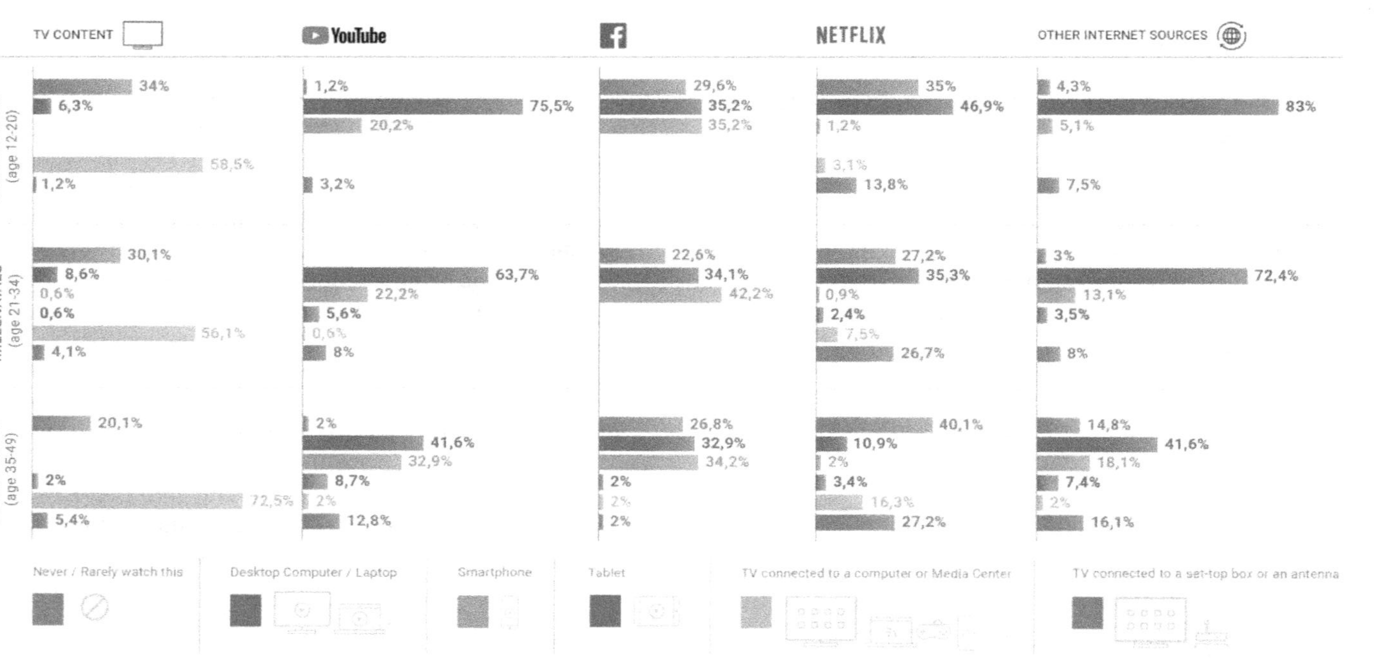

Figure 5 - Generation distribution of preferential device for watching audiovisual content at home by source (Question 1.8)

Based on a sample of 371 participants, 74% of the respondents claimed to watch television together, and 71,4% stated that they usually connect more than one device to the TV screen. The most used devices connected to the TV are the Laptop (42%), Smartphone (21%) and Media Center (20,8%). Globally, the Computer continues to be a preferred device to get Internet-based content sources at home, although the use of connected devices to the TV screen points to the resurgence of the television due to the larger dimension and high-quality image. These results allowed to get an overview of the Portuguese context focused on motivational factors at home, disregarded by other European studies. Briefly, the results from the English and Brazilian version of the online survey may provide further insights based on comparison and verification of possible correlations with geographic and cultural patterns, dependent on each country's consumption dynamics and media landscape. The validation of the hypothesis and correlations drawn from the online survey, allow not only to understand the dynamics of audiovisual consumption regarding the 'future of television', but also to sustain product-oriented practices based on the synergies between behavioral factors, technological innovations and industry trends regarding audiences' needs and user experience.

Acknowledgments

This paper is a result of the UltraTV - UltraHD TV Application Ecosystem project (grant agreement no.17738), funded by COMPETE 2020, Portugal 2020 and the European Union through the European Regional Development Fund (FEDER). Authors are grateful to the project partners.

References

1. Abreu, J., Nogueira, J., Becker, V., Cardoso, B. 2016. Survey of Catch-up TV and other time-shift services: a comprehensive analysis and taxonomy of linear and nonlinear television. *J. Telecommunication Systems. Res.* 61, 4 (Mar. 2016), 627-908. http://dx.doi.org/10.1007/s11235-016-0157-3
2. Vanattenhoven, J., Geerts, D. 2015. Designing TV Recommender Interfaces for Specific Viewing Experiences. In *Proceedings of the 2015 ACM international conference on Interactive experiences for TV and online video*, ACM, 185-190. http://dx.doi.org/10.1145/2745197.2755522
3. Ovun. 2017. Portugal Update April 2017. Retrieved January 29, 2018 from http://bit.ly/PTUpdate2017
4. Ericsson Consumer and Industry Insight Report: TV and Media 2017. 2017. A consumer-driven future of media. Retrieved January 29, 2018 from https://www.ericsson.com/en/networked-society/trends-and-insights/consumerlab/consumer-insights/reports/tv-andmedia-2017.
5. Nielsen Company. The Battle for Eye Space in a TV-Everywhere World. 2015. Retrieved March 20, 2018 from www.nielsen.com/content/dam/corporate/Italy/reports/2015/Nielsen%20Global%20Digital%20Landscape%20Report%20March%202015.pdf
6. ERC. 2016. As novas dinâmicas do consumo audiovisual em Portugal. Retrieved March 20, 2018 from http://www.erc.pt/documentos/Estudos/ConsumoAVemPT/ERC2016_AsNovasDinamicasConsumoAudioVisuais_web/assets/downloads/ERC2016_AsNovasDinamicasConsumoAudioVisuais.pdf
7. Field, A. 2018. Discovering Statistics Using IBM SPSS Statistics (5th Edition). London: Sage Publications.

Personalising the TV Experience with Augmented Reality Technology: Synchronised Sign Language Interpretation.

Vinoba Vinayagamoorthy
Maxine Glancy
Paul Debenham
Alastair Bruce
BBC R&D
London, United Kingdom
vinoba.vinayagamoorthy@bbc.co.uk
maxine.glancy@bbc.co.uk

Christoph Ziegler
Richard Schäffer
IRT
Munich, Germany
ziegler@irt.de

TVX '18, June 26–28, 2018, SEOUL, Republic of Korea

ACM ISBN 978-1-4503-5115-7/18/06.
https://doi.org/10.1145/3210825.3213562

Abstract
This paper explores the potential of augmented reality technology as a novel way to allow users to view a sign language interpreter through an optical head-mounted display while watching a TV programme. We address the potential of augmented reality for personalisation of TV access services as part of closed laboratory investigations. Based on guidelines of regulatory authorities and research on traditional sign language services on TV, as well as feedback from experts, we justify our two design proposals. We describe how we produced the content for the AR prototype applications and what we have learned during the process. Finally, we develop questions for our upcoming user studies.

Author Keywords
Accessibility, AR, Companion Screen, Connected Experiences, HoloLens, Interaction Techniques, Second Screen, Sign Language, Synchronisation, Television

Categories and Subject Descriptors
• Human-centered computing~Mixed / augmented reality • Human-centered computing~Empirical studies in accessibility

Introduction

BBC R&D and IRT have been exploring how to customise and personalise the experience of viewing programme content on connected TVs by, in tandem, delivering additional (companion) content, to personal devices via IP [1, 2]. So far, our investigations have focused on devices like a mobile phone or tablet. However, with the rise in popularity of optical head mounted displays, augmented reality (AR) applications enable a way to make experiences that might spill out beyond the frame of a TV thereby extending the real estate of the TV screen. As a probative part of a closed laboratory study, we chose to look at placing a video stream of a sign language interpreter just outside the TV frame synchronised to the programme content within the TV frame.

Traditional access services undoubtedly enhance the experience for many users but they remain an intrusive option which can't be customised and controlled beyond turning them on/off in the case of subtitles and audio description. Considering that the TV might be a shared device watched by others, potentially with different personal preferences, how can access services be delivered without imposing one users' preference on the whole group [4]? Even if the social issues are mitigated through compromise, there are users who experience different types of impairments at different times during their lives or under different conditions. Some users experience multiple impairments often with increasing age. Add in personal preferences, such as not being able to proficiently read subtitles because English is not the users' first language or wanting to watch a particular programme on the all of the screen real estate available to the user [4], it becomes obvious that there may be merit in being able to present personalised augments, including potentially some access services, to the TV experience outside the TV frame.

In this paper, we focus on describing the process we undertook while designing a companion application on the HoloLens [7] which displayed a sign language interpreter to accompany a programme. We discuss justifications behind our selections and the challenges we faced in creating a suitable representation of the sign language interpreter in AR.

Augmenting the TV

Studies have shown that there are particular UI design principles which have been key to building an optimal user experience. As part of 2Immerse [1], we explored the role of synchronisation, placement of content and flow of attention in multi-device experiences.
Previously, BBC R&D also investigated the potential of using large scale displays and augmented spaces around the TV to provide users with more content in a suitable configuration [3]. The HoloLens [7] potentially allow us to personalise spaces outside the TV frame and enable users to access synchronised content (inc. sign language interpretation) on the same visual plane as the TV, potentially at the same focal length.

Accessibility and the TV

There is a significant percentage of the population for whom access services remain invaluable as a means to better consume our audio-visual content. Broadcasting in European countries like, the UK and Germany, is subject to regulation on various fronts including guidelines on access requirements [8]. These regulations provide us with a starting point to design novel ways of making our content more accessible.

Figure 1: Capturing the interpreter using blue LED lights and Chromatte (reflective cloth) at BBC R&D.

Figure 2: Capturing the interpreter using a green studio set-up at IRT.

Figure 3: In-Vision interpreter as seen on a typical interpreted content piece.

The Use Case: Sign Language delivered in AR

We carried out a review of literature relevant to the use of current signing for TV practice. This included industry guidelines, recommendations and reports from organizations and academic studies. As far as we can tell, there are no official guidelines for the presentation of sign language interpreters on TV from the German regulation authorities, so we looked to UK-based legislation [8] and a review of prior work [5, 6, 9, 10].

Some recurring themes emerged to include the quality of the signing, the prominence and presentation of the interpreter, the scale and position of interpreter within the TV frame, the interpreters' relationship with the TV content, problems associated with *'cutting off the singing'* and *'overlap with the TV content'*, and the continuity and synchronisation of the signing with the TV content. These were all challenges that were continuously considered through while designing the HoloLens companion application to the TV.

The programmes used on the TV by BBC R&D[1] and IRT[2] were both set in the Sahara and chosen because we were able to extract a segment with a self-contained sub-story which worked well for a relatively short experience piece. We worked with BSL & DGS[3] sign language interpreters to capture their interpretations of the aforementioned programmes in the form of videos (Figure 1 and Figure 2). The captured videos were processed to extract 2D video cut-outs of the interpreter (referred to as *AR Interpreter* in this paper) using Chroma-Keying. We consider different design formats in order to design optimal ways to present the AR interpreter to a user wearing a HoloLens while also watching a programme on a TV.

Capturing Content

Our review revealed the importance of the interpreters' relationship with the content. In addition to 'ease of shifting attention', a relationship can be demonstrated via the direction of the interpreters' gaze and their synchronized interaction with the TV content. This was tackled during the capture process.

Direction of Gaze –Designing with the Interpreter

While resting (not actively signing), in-vision interpreters usually direct their gaze towards the TV content, as if watching it with the viewer. In the studio, during the capture process, we discussed the possibility of recording a variety of 'directions of gaze' with the interpreter. The interpreter was filmed gazing in 3 directions:

- Facing into the camera –as if looking at the viewer;
- Looking horizontally to her right - so the interpreters' eyes were level with the presenter's eyes on the TV;
- Looking down diagonally to the bottom right –as if standing by the side of a TV placed on a stand.

Ensuring Synchronisation Interaction

If the user feels a delay between the TV content and the signing, this can break the continuity of the experience. [8, 9]. In the UK, steps were taken during

[1] *Morocco To Timbuktu: An Arabian Adventure*, BBC Two

[2] *Herausforderung Wüste: Sinnsuche in der Sahara,* Bayrischer Rundfunk (BR)

[3] British Sign Language (BSL) and Deutsche Gebärdensprache (DGS) are the sign languages of the deaf community in the U.K. and Germany respectively. They are distinct languages and recognised as such by the government.

Appearance: *"The signer should use a style of interpretation and wear clothing that is appropriate to the style of the programme ... It is important that signers' clothing allows them to be seen distinctly against the picture" [8]*

Quality: *"Sign language presenters, reporters and interpreters should be appropriately qualified, both to use sign language of native competency, and to communicate effectively through television" [8]*

Technique: *"The signer should use appropriate techniques to indicate whose speech he or she is interpreting, and to draw attention to significant sound effects" [8]*

Size: *"The image of the signer superimposed upon the original programme should generally appear on the right hand of the screen and occupy a space no smaller than one sixth of the picture." [8]*

the capture shoot to ensure synchronization. We playing the documentary content in front of the BSL interpreter for use as cues. We recorded the programme sound via a live microphone, allowing us a way to initialise alignment during processing.

In Germany, the capture process was slightly different. A deaf DSG interpreter read multi-line subtitles from a TV-screen with the original video in the background. An additional hearing interpreter checked if the deaf interpreter was in sync with the TV's audio. This was to comply with an agreement between hearing and deaf interpreters in Germany, that recorded content shall only be interpreted by deaf interpreters.

Signing Space
In-vision interpreters restrict their signing space to a 'safe-zone' to guarantee that the signing is not 'cut-out' of the content within the TV frame [9]. The HoloLens has quite a small field-of-view, similar in shape to a letter box, so it would be difficult for the user to see the TV and the AR interpreter within it. So, the interpreter was asked to maintain the use of a 'safe-zone' while signing during the capture process.

Placement of Content in AR

After Chroma-keying the captured interpretations of the content, we considered the best way to present the AR interpreter in a synchronised sign language interpreted TV+HoloLens experience.

Prominence and Presentation of the Interpreter
To ensure the prominence of the interpreter, and get a crisp Chroma-keying outline of the interpreter in the HoloLens, we took some precautionary measures. The interpreter could not wear the same colour as the backdrop against which they would be Chroma-keyed - blue in the U.K (*Figure 1*) & green in Germany (*Figure 2*). The interpreters were asked to avoid black since it appears transparent in the HoloLens. We wanted the AR interpreters to have enough contrast against real world spaces so we chose to avoid dressing the interpreter in white and light neutral colours. No jewellery was allowed, to avoid the impact of reflective surfaces on the capture quality. The interpreters' hair was neatly combed or tied back, to avoid a 'fuzzy' outline in the Chroma-keying process.

Signing Quality & Techniques
The quality of the signing is more important than the presentation of the interpreter [5, 8, 9]. This concerns the interpreters' ability to give full translations of the content, without the user feeling as if there are details missing. We sent the qualified interpreters a copy of the script and links to the documentary footage several days before the capture shoot. This was crucial to let them get familiar with the content.

Size, Position and Scale
The interpreter should not dominate the screen, and should not obscure the TV content [6, 8, 9, 10]. Traditionally on TV, in-vision interpreters appear in half body (head to hip - Figure 3) or 2/3 body (head to mid-thigh) formats on the right hand side of the TV screen. Full-body (head to toe) formats are not used because the clarity of the interpretations is reduced.

In an Augmented TV space, we didn't have to compromise between the size of the interpreter and the space available for the content. We explored the half body and 2/3 body formats, in the HoloLens, by scaling the Chroma-keyed video cut out of the interpreter to

Language: "*So far as possible, interpretation and voice-overs of signed programmed should be synchronised with the original speech / sign language"* [8]

Figure 4: Half Body AR interpreter at BBC R&D – View through the HoloLens. The user sees the half body AR interpreter 'sitting' on the TV stand on the right hand side of the TV.

Figure 5: Similar Half Body AR interpreter at IRT – View through the HoloLens.

match the height of the TV-screen. This meant that the top of the AR interpreters' head was level with the top of the TV frame, while the bottom half of the AR interpreter was placed on the surface on which the TV stood (Figure 4 and Figure 5). Eventually, we considered the 2/3 body format too similar to the half body format.

We explored three scales of the full-body AR interpreters. A life size version of the AR interpreter in which the AR interpreters' head was well above the TV frame while the AR interpreters' feet was on the floor. However, the narrow field of view of the HoloLens made it difficult to easily shift attention between the AR interpreter and the content on the TV. We considered a full-body interpreter scaled to the height of the TV, however, the clarity of the signing diminished with the reduced scale. The third version of the full-body AR interpreter was slightly less than life size version. In this case, the top of the AR interpreters' head was level with the TV frame while the AR interpreters' feet stood on the floor of the room. This compromise allowed the top half of the full body AR interpreter to be placed in parallel with the height of the TV frame and allow the AR interpreters' legs to be included in the HoloLens environment (Figure 6 and Figure 7).

Distance & Overlap
Similar to in-vision concerns [8], we did not want too much overlap between the AR interpreter and important parts of the TV content. However, we were also aware that the distance between the interpreter and the TV content needs to allow users to shift attention between the two entities. If the distance is increased, shifting attention becomes tiresome and the connection is broken. The 'ease of shifting attention vs overlapping' was of key importance [9].

In both our designs, the interpreter was positioned to the right of the TV frame, slightly overlapping the frame (to no more than $1/6^{th}$) reducing the distance between the AR interpreter and the TV content.

Choosing the Interpreters' Direction of Gaze
We invited a colleague with BSL skills to review the AR interpreters' position and scale, to review the clarity of the signing, and which of the 3 'directions of gaze' were most suitable. The condition in which the AR interpreter was gazing along a horizontal line to the TV screen, in the half-body and full-body designs, was favoured.

Discussion
The slightly less than life size full-body format and the half-body format seemed the best two designs to study in further user experiments. These two designs also seemed diverse enough to not be seen as slight variations of the same thing. All designs were placed on the right hand side of the TV frame in keeping with Ofcom recommendations [8] and prior studies [5, 6]. The aim is to maintain a 'connection' between the interpreter and the content, and in-turn the 'continuity' between the user, the interpreter and the content.

Limitations
The HoloLens will be a new technology for participants in the study – introducing the novel factor. It is anticipated that participants will respond to the physical effects of wearing the HoloLens, which can be heavy and uncomfortable, especially if wearing spectacles. The HoloLens has a limited field of view, and this could compromise the presentation of the AR Interpreter.

Figure 6: Full Body AR interpreter at BBC R&D – View through the HoloLens. The user sees the AR interpreter 'standing' on the floor on the right hand side of the TV.

Figure 7: Similar Full Body AR interpreter at IRT – View through the HoloLens.

Users will have to be briefed beforehand in order to properly tease out what factors are used to evaluate our designs.

Conclusion and Future Work

We have presented two potential designs for AR interpreters for use in viewing sign language interpreted content on TV+HoloLens experiences. In addition to the design work, BBC R&D and IRT are working together on explorative ongoing laboratory-based user studies with three goals.

- Gain an early understanding of how members in the BSL and DSG communities respond to accessing sign language interpretations through the HoloLens in AR,
- If there are any differences due to the way sign language interpretations are consumed across two cultures and
- Confirm the reproducibility of our design approach and methodology of our ongoing studies.

Acknowledgements

The research leading to these results received funding from the European Union's H2020-ICT-2015 programme under grant agreement number 687655 (2-IMMERSE). We thank our colleagues who generously gave invaluable support and advice. We would also like to thank Dominique Ferdinand from Roger Beeson's London BSL Interpreters, Kilian Knörzer of Spectrum11 and Michaela Nachtrab from Swiss Txt for their help.

References

1. 2-Immerse Home Page. 2-Immerse. Retrieved March 27, 2018 from https://2immerse.eu/.
2. BBC R&D - Companion Screens: Creating a viewing experience across more than one screen. BBC R&D Blog Post. Retrieved March 27, 2018 from http://www.bbc.co.uk/rd/projects/companion-screens.
3. BBC R&D – Unconventional Screens: Exploring the potential of future display technologies. BBC R&D Blog Post. Retrieved March 27, 2018 from https://www.bbc.co.uk/rd/projects/unconventional-screens.
4. Mike Armstrong. Object-Based Media and Accessibility. 2018. BBC R&D Blog Post. Retrieved March 27, 2018 from https://www.bbc.co.uk/rd/blog/2018-01-accessibility-object-based-media
5. Matthew Dye. The Digital Age: Digital and Signed TV. Deaf Studies Trust. 2000
6. Hbb4All. D6.4 – Pilot-D Evaluation and Recommendations. 2017. Retrieved March 29, 2018 from http://pagines.uab.cat/hbb4all/content/deliverables
7. Microsoft. Microsoft HoloLens. Retrieved March 28, 2018 from https://www.microsoft.com/en-gb/hololens
8. Ofcom. The Ofcom Code on Television Access Services. 2017. Retrieved March 27, 2018 from https://www.ofcom.org.uk/tv-radio-and-on-demand/broadcast-codes/tv-access-services
9. Benice Woll. Sign Language on Television. Centre for Deaf Studies, University of Bristol. 1991.
10. Yan Wu, Elain Price and Leighton Evans. Digital Television and Deaf/Hard of Hearing Audiences in Wales. Research Institute for Arts and Humanities, Swansea University. 2014. Retrieved from March 29, 2018 from http://www.swansea.ac.uk/riah/research-projects/dtv-wales-survey/

Educational Online Video: Opportunities and Barriers to Integrate it in the Entertainment Consumption Routines

Carolina Almeida
CIC.Digital- DIGIMEDIA
University of Aveiro
Campus Universitário de Santiago
3810-193 Aveiro, Portugal
carol@ua.pt

Pedro Almeida
CIC.Digital- DIGIMEDIA
University of Aveiro
Campus Universitário de Santiago
3810-193 Aveiro, Portugal
almeida@ua.pt

TVX '18, June 26–28, 2018, SEOUL, Republic of Korea

ACM ISBN 978-1-4503-5115-7/18/06.
https://doi.org/10.1145/3210825.3213563

Abstract
General population and particularly teenagers are increasingly using mobile devices for video consumption instead of the regular TV set. Considering that the top motivation for video consumption is to seek for entertainment, there is an opportunity to try to capture some of those moments for educational content enriched with some entertainment characteristics. This study aims to identify narrative and technical characteristics to incorporate in educational informal videos, designed for new media platforms by analysing the preferences of teenagers aged from 12 to 16 years old that attend the Portuguese public school system. Furthermore, the research team expects to understand if educational videos enriched with the referred characteristics are able to be included in entertainment consumption routines of these viewers. Some of the most valued characteristics are the comic approach, the integration of animations, the relaxed yet clear presenter style and the low level of scientific detail in video explanations.

Author Keywords
Online video; informal learning; educational video; teenagers

ACM Classification Keywords
• Information systems~Multimedia content creation

Introduction
Nowadays teenagers spend several hours a week or even a day watching online videos. Studies are focused mainly in users with 16 years old or more, but the results point to an increasing trend that may be even stronger in younger audiences. Some reports point that, since 2015, video consumption has been growing, in all age ranges, in online/streaming platforms while linear TV consumption has been decreasing [5,8]. This trend seems to be even stronger when considering younger users. Regarding the content genres, these consumption moments have been privileging entertainment content. Educational videos are watched on YouTube by 32% of US users, music videos are watched by 72% and entertainment videos are watched by 64% of American users [13]. Taking the referred changes in consideration, namely the long hours spent on mobile devices watching videos, an opportunity to use a part of those moments for informal learning activities may be foreseen. But, in order to achieve such goals, there is a need to understand what features and characteristics of videos may be integrated in educational videos for it to be appealing for the younger generations (aged from 12 to 16). Therefore, a study was conducted in order to identify narrative and technical guidelines for the production of educational content for informal consumption. First a study about the teenagers' preferences about existing videos was carried. In this phase, a focus group was arranged with the purpose of showing teenagers different narrative and technical characteristics, embedded in segments of existing entertainment videos to get their opinions on the characteristics most valued by them [2]. Later some educational videos with entertainment characteristics about topics of the Portuguese curricular program of natural sciences [10] were produced in order to validate the set of characteristics previously identified. These videos were designed for informal consumption but other uses like as study complements or as a resource in classrooms were not excluded. It is important to underline that the dissemination and evaluation of the videos took place in February 2018.

Literature Review
Viewing habits

When considering viewing habits, most of the studies consider the population above 18 years old, but still some also focus on the younger population. According to recent data, 91% of the Americans aged between 18 and 29 years old use YouTube® [11]. According to the "TV and media 2017" report [6], conducted in countries like Spain, USA and UK that analysed, among others, people aged between 16 and 19 years old, concluded that they spend 33 hours a week on video consumption, 54% of it is spent watching on-demand content and 21% is spent on UGC or e-sport content. According to a 2015 study that analysed the adult population in the USA, the main motivation for watching online video is entertainment, followed by the need to escape from the daily tasks and on third place the willingness to learn something new [14]. Similar conclusions were found in a study conducted by Khan [9] which aim was to identify the motivation factors that drive viewers to online video, with the analysis of

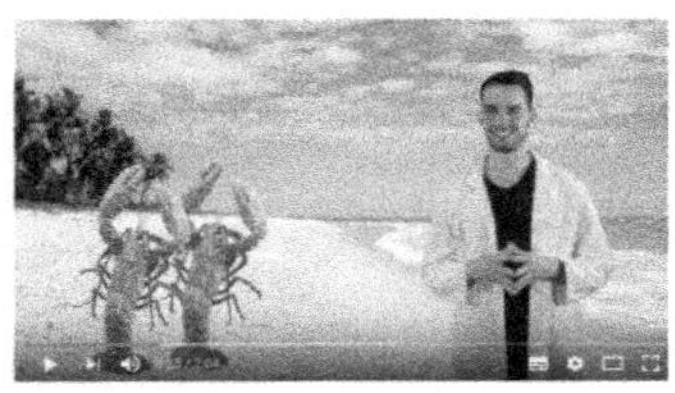

Figure 1 - One of the published videos "PARA ONDE FORAM AS MONTANHAS?" - Where did the mountais go?. http://bit.ly/2oxfHlo

users sense of gratification associated to those practices. Besides seeking relaxation and entertainment (3,49 in a scale from 1 to 5, being 5 the highest score), the motivation to learn new things was also an important driver with 3,03. "Consumer Barometer by Google" [7] points that 23% of the online video consumers watch videos with the intention to learn something new. But, despite these opinions, when analyzing the top content genres of online video consumption, it is perceived that educational videos are not on the top preferences. Music, comedy, gaming, fashion or films and animations are the preferred genres. Educational videos seem to be having difficulties in capturing the younger viewers time, especially at their relaxed, informal consumption moments [15,16].

Characteristics of educational informal videos

The attractiveness of educational videos has been pursued either in academic studies or by the industry. According to Schneider et al [12] literature review most of the educational entertainment videos are 2 to 3 minutes long, are narrative and humorous, have animations, background music and sound effects. Douglas et al [4] studied the inspirations that were taken into consideration in the development of new videos (like whiteboard videos) to the Massive Online Open Courses (MOOCs) and Physics courses of Georgia Institute of Technology. The authors concluded that the videos were mostly influenced by other (non-educational) informal and entertainment videos [4] and by this were a more engaging and expressive way of presenting content to students. Regarding multi genre videos, West [17] synthetizes some elements of viral videos: short duration (< than 3 minutes), comic elements, surprise effect, irony and musical elements are common to those videos. Despite some of the presented studied being about formal videos [4] or entertainment ones [17] the conclusions are useful assets for the development of this study and the creation of new educational videos about natural sciences with entertainment characteristics.

Methodology

The research is grounded on a Design Based Research [1] approach developed in collaborative cycles of definition and redefinition of an intervention. The study comprises two main phases. The results of the first phase allowed for the research team to create and produce a total of three videos, integrating the identified characteristics, to be published and available to the general public, and to be evaluated by a group of teenagers. The videos addressed natural sciences topics, specifically about tectonics plates and plate boundaries. The developed videos were targeted at teenagers aged between 12 and 16 years old, attendees of the 3rd cycle of studies grades). The videos pretended to validate the previously identified preferences: use of a comic style, use of animations and infographics, use of a relaxed presenter, integration of sound effects, a clear and relaxed or comic speech with plain language, the use of virtual scenarios, all in a short (<3 min) duration video [2]. Therefore, phase 2 included: i) the pre-production and production of the videos; ii) the development of a dissemination strategy for its promotion, and; iii) the evaluation of the videos and the dissemination strategy. For the evaluation of the produced videos, a non-probabilistic or intentional sample was selected, a group of 8 students ranging from 13 to 14 years old. In order to operationalize this stage, a pre-test was settled. It comprised the publication of the videos in

Informal video characteristics valued by teenagers
• Comic style • Animations • Relaxed presenter • Clear speech • Low level of detail in explanations • Examples • Use of sound effects • Short duration

Table 1 - Most valued video characteristics identified in the previous phase and validated on the current phase

YouTube®, at intervals of one to two days, and the dissemination of those contents via a Facebook® page and an Instagram® profile, with more emphasis on the Facebook® page. Four teenagers participated in an evaluation session that comprised: i) watching the video; ii) completion of a questionnaire; iii) participation in a focus group. Data collection comprised statistical data from the online platforms as well as qualitative data coming from the evaluation session. This pre-test allowed validating the data collection instruments along with the methodological set-up. Is also allowed to get feedback on the dissemination activities and the need for a deeper work on the dissemination phase. Based on the results a new dissemination strategy was defined with the purpose of understanding if a well-defined strategy, following practices of the main entertainment channels, would make a difference for the integration of this kind of content in the entertainment video consumption routines. Additional image and video contents were produced to enrich the posts on Instagram® (http://bit.ly/2oA02kA), Twitter® (https://twitter.com/CoisaCiencia) and Facebook® (https://www.facebook.com/coisaciencia/) and attract viewers to the main videos. Posts were scheduled in order to promote the number of views of the videos published on YouTube® (http://bit.ly/2xAX41y) on intervals of two days between each video during two weeks. In the final evaluation session, following the pre-test structure, eight participants evaluated the videos and the dissemination strategy. Considering that not all the participants had previously watched all the videos (despite being exposed to the dissemination strategy), the session started with the video viewing, followed by the administration of a questionnaire with questions about the dissemination strategy and the video characteristics and attractiveness. Finally, a focus group was promoted. Quantitative data from the platforms and qualitative data from the session were collected. The transcripts of the focus group were analysed, the answers to the questionnaire and data from the platforms were submitted to descriptive statistic.

Results

Five female and three males, four of them with 13 and four with 14 years old participated in the evaluation session. Five attended the 8th grade, two the 9th and one the 7th grade. According to the questionnaire all participants had a smartphone and online entertainment video viewing habits on a daily basis (five of them stated watching 1 to 2 hours a day; two watched less than an hour, and; one 3 to 4 hours). According to the answers to the questionnaire and the transcripts, the video consumption during the dissemination phase wasn't constant. The most watched video was the first and the viewing time showed a decreasing tendency in the second and third videos. All the participants said that they use YouTube® and Fabebook® daily, five said that they use Instagram® and Twitter®. Six of them interacted with the project YouTube® channel "Coisa Ciencia", three of them with the Instagram® profile and two with the Facebook® page. Only two followed the Twitter® channel. Considering the characteristics of videos, participants highlighted, during the focus group, as pleasing characteristics the ones referred in Table 1. Besides that, some participants stated that the second and third videos could be longer in order to detail the concepts explanation (video #2) and to extend the entertainment due to the comic style (video #3). One participant stated that the explanation in video #1 could be improved and another stated that the thematic, a school topic, wasn't interesting as subject of an entertainment video. Three of the eight participants showed motivation to subscribe the channel and watch videos a few times a week, three to watch once or twice a week, one to watch videos like the presented ones on a monthly basis and another only occasionally. On the questionnaire all the participants considered to be partially or totally available to watch videos like the presented ones in classroom or during their study time. When asked about including this type of video on their entertainment routines, half of them agreed and the other half disagreed with this scenario. Besides the answers to the questionnaire, during the focus group, several participants stated they would only watch this type of content sporadically without replacing the usual entertainment content in favour of educational informal videos like the presented ones. When asked about the possibility of including videos like these ones in their study routines or in the classroom, as educational resources, all of them agreed with that scenario. Furthermore, some stated that the project videos were of higher quality compared with some video resources already in use in Portuguese classrooms and provided by the main educational publishers.

Preliminary Conclusions

This study adopts a descriptive approach with a restricted sample of the teenagers' population. Despite conclusions not being able for full generalization, it introduces insights that may be useful for educators and online video creators. Furthermore, similar studies with different samples can be conducted, in a near future, to try to validate it in different contexts. These results allow to complement the conclusions of the previous phase of this study, namely about the identification of the characteristics of an educational video designed to be consumed in informal contexts [2,3]. Confirming the first phase results, the most valued characteristics were the comic style, the use of animations, the relaxed presenter with clear speech and low level of detail in explanations and also the use of sound effects and short duration of videos. It was also possible to understand that there is some resistance concerning the integration of such educational or informative videos on teenagers' informal video consumption routines. But, it was possible to understand that an educational content will have a grater chance of being watched if these characteristics are integrated and if it is recommended by a professor or tutor as study resource both in formal classroom environment or in non-formal contexts of study. This insight will be further analysed by means of a study that will be carried with teachers. These preliminary results can be useful to educators or other producers interested in developing videos about scientific topics to disseminate in non-formal contexts.

Acknowledgements

This paper reports on a research developed within the PhD Program Technology Enhanced Learning and Societal Challenges, funded by Fundação para a Ciência e Tecnologia, FCT I. P. – Portugal, under contract # PD/00173/2014 and # PD/BI.

FCT PhD PROGRAMMES

References

1. J Van den Akker. 1999. Principles and methods of development research. In *Design approaches and tools in education and training*, J. Van den Akker, R.M. Branch, K. Gustafson, N. Nieveen and T. Plomp (eds.). Springer Science + Business Media, B. V., Dordrecht, 1–14. https://doi.org/0.1007/978-94-011-4255-7
2. Carolina Almeida and Pedro Almeida. 2017. Online educational videos: The teenagers' preferences. In *Applications and Usability of Interactive TV*, 65–76. https://doi.org/10.1007/978-3-319-63321-3_5
3. Carolina Almeida and Pedro Almeida. 2017. Preferences of Teenagers About Online Video: How To Incorporate Educational Informal Videos in Their Daily Consumption Routines. *Inted2017: 11th International Technology, Education and Development Conference*: 1526–1532. https://doi.org/10.21125/inted.2017.0493
4. Scott Samuel Douglas, John Mark Aiken, Edwin Greco, Michael Schatz, and Shih-Yin Lin. 2017. Do-It-Yourself Whiteboard-Style Physics Video Lectures. *The Physics Teacher* 55, 1: 22–24. https://doi.org/10.1119/1.4972492
5. Ericsson ConsumerLab. 2016. *Tv and Media 2016*. Retrieved from http://bit.ly/2f4kFzy
6. Ericsson ConsumerLab. 2017. *Tv and Media 2017*. Retrieved from http://bit.ly/2zON4rI
7. Google. How-To Video Users. *Consumer Barometer with Google*. Retrieved February 27, 2018 from http://bit.ly/29MQ7Rp
8. Interactive Advertising Bureau (IAB). 2015. *Mobile Video 2015: A global perspective*. Retrieved from http://bit.ly/2EXuaxi
9. M. Laeeq Khan. 2017. Social media engagement: What motivates user participation and consumption on YouTube? *Computers in Human Behavior* 66: 236–247. https://doi.org/10.1016/j.chb.2016.09.024
10. Jorge Bonito Morgado (Cord), Margarida Silva, Marta Figueira, Dulce Rebelo, Marta Serrano, José Mesquita, and Hugo Rebelo. 2013. *Metas Curriculares de Ciências Naturais para 5.o, 6.o, 7.o e 8.o anos*. Retrieved from http://bit.ly/2CPU7wB
11. Pew Research Center. 2018. *Who uses Pinterest, Snapchat, YouTube and WhatsApp*. Retrieved from http://pewrsr.ch/2oAKhKh
12. Frank M. Schneider, Carina Weinmann, Franziska S. Roth, Katharina Knop, and Peter Vorderer. 2016. Learning from entertaining online video clips? Enjoyment and appreciation and their differential relationships with knowledge and behavioral intentions. *Computers in Human Behavior* 54: 475–482. https://doi.org/10.1016/j.chb.2015.08.028
13. Statista. Types of video content watched on Facebook and YouTube among internet users in the United States as of March 2016. Retrieved March 29, 2018 from https://bit.ly/2pOzWvF
14. Statista. 2015. *Most common motivations for watching online videos in the United States in 2015*. Retrieved from http://bit.ly/2GQjJw1
15. Statista. 2015. Most popular YouTube video categories based on female Millennial user engagement as of December 2013. Retrieved April 27, 2016 from http://bit.ly/1STPvMW
16. Statista. 2015. Most popular YouTube video categories based on male Millennial user engagement as of December 2013. Retrieved April 27, 2016 from http://bit.ly/1VVBFKQ
17. Tyler West. 2011. Going Viral : Factors That Lead Videos to Become Internet Phenomena. *The Elon Journal of Undergraduate Research in Communications* 2, 1: 76–84.

Understanding Blind or Visually Impaired People on YouTube through Qualitative Analysis of Videos

Woosuk Seo
University of Michigan
Ann Arbor, MI 48109, USA
seow@umich.edu

Hyunggu Jung
Kyung Hee University
Yongin-si, Gyeonggi-do 17104, Republic of Korea
hgjung@khu.ac.kr

TVX '18, June 26–28, 2018, SEOUL, Republic of Korea

ACM ISBN 978-1-4503-5115-7/18/06.
https://doi.org/10.1145/3210825.3213565

Abstract

In this paper, we analyzed videos to explore blind or visually impaired (BVI) people on YouTube. While researchers found how BVI people interact with contents and other people on social media platforms (e.g., Facebook), little is known about the experience of BVI people on video-based social media platforms (e.g., YouTube). To use videos as a mean of identifying the needs of BVI people on YouTube, we collected and analyzed a specific type of video called Visually Impaired People (VIP) Tag video. This Tag video has a set of structured questions about eye condition and experience as a BVI person. Based on the qualitative analysis of 24 VIP Tag videos created by BVI people, we found how they create videos and why they joined YouTube. In conclusion, we present how video-content analysis can be used to create an inclusive video-based social media platform.

Author Keywords

YouTube; blind; visually impaired; video; accessibility.

Categories and Subject Descriptors

• Human-centered computing~Collaborative and social computing systems and tools • Human-centered computing~Interaction design.

VIP Tag Video Questions

1. What medical condition caused you to be blind or visually impaired?

2. In three words, describe your vision.

3. What is the hardest thing to do being blind or visually impaired?

4. What is the best part about being blind or visually impaired?

5. What question do you get asked most about or because of your vision?

6. Do you have a cane, a guide dog, or neither?

7. What one piece of advice would you give to someone who is losing, going to lose, or has lost their vision?

8.What is on piece of advice you would you give to a sighted person about interacting with a person who is blind or visually impaired?

Introduction

Along with the growth of camera technology, video has become a trending medium on social media platforms. Facebook added a new section specifically for video content while YouTube has become the largest video platform with 1.32 billion users [10]. Each day those YouTube users watch a billion hours of video and generate billions of views [10]. Instead of text-only description, people began to share their stories and experiences through videos.

With its increasing popularity, videos are often used as a source of research data. Researchers have leveraged videos to understand target populations when interacting with media. They collected and analyzed videos created by people with various backgrounds, such as people with chronic diseases, disabilities, or anorexia [1, 2, 3, 7]. In addition to interviews and focus groups, videos offer supplementary information about the target group. On the other hand, some researchers aimed to understand and improve the experiences of BVI people on social media platforms, such as Facebook and Twitter [4, 8, 9]. While these studies focused on text-based or picture-based contents, a recent study revealed that BVI people upload their videos and connected with other people through videos on YouTube [6].

Nevertheless, little is known about the video experiences of BVI people and their motivation for using video-based social media platforms (e.g., YouTube). To address the gap, we collected and analyzed a specific type of video that they created, VIP Tag videos. The goal of our research is to create inclusive video-based social media platforms by

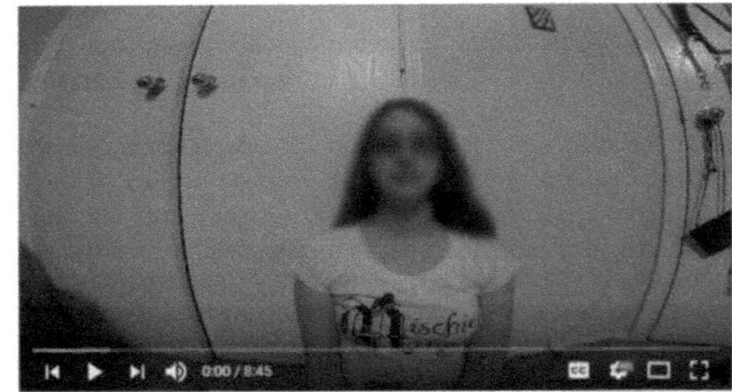

Figure 1: The creator of Visually Impaired People Tag is explaining about the Tag video and the ten questions.

analyzing video contents posted by BVI people on YouTube. This study aims to understand BVI people on YouTube by answering the following questions:

RQ1: What contents do BVI people create on YouTube?
RQ2: How do BVI people create videos?
RQ3: Why do BVI people upload videos?

In particular, we present an additional method to identify the needs of BVI people and to improve their video experiences. In the next sections, we describe the characteristics of video data and present methods to collect and analyze the data. We then demonstrate the findings on different aspects of BVI people and their videos on YouTube. The conclusion section is followed by presenting the contribution of this study and future studies to support BVI people on video-based social media platforms.

VIP Tag Video Questions

9. Why did you join YouTube?

10. Name three people to do this next.

Keyword Search

Related Videos

Tagged Vloggers

24 videos

Figure 2: We collected 24 Visually Impaired People (VIP) Tag videos from YouTube.

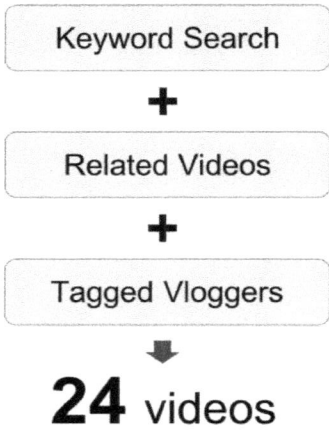

Video Sample

A VIP Tag video contains the responses of a video blogger (i.e., vlogger) to the structured ten questions about their eye condition and experience as a BVI person (see Sidebar). It was initially created by a visually impaired vlogger in 2015 (see Figure 1). In the video, the vlogger answers them while sharing his or her experience with the audience. At the end of the video, the vlogger should mention or tag three other vloggers to do the same Tag video. Among various types of Tag videos, VIP Tag videos encourage BVI vloggers to introduce themselves to the audience on video-based platform since the questions help them share their stories one at a time. We decided to analyze VIP Tag videos since we could confirm that the vloggers who created the videos are all blind or visually impaired. In addition, one of the question about joining YouTube overlaps with our research question.

Method

To identify VIP Tag videos on YouTube, we used the keywords ("visually impaired" OR "vip") AND ("tag"). We then collected the VIP Tag Videos that contain "visually impaired" or "VIP" in title. When we found first several VIP Tag videos, we tracked the tagged vloggers to find more VIP Tag videos. We also found additional videos from the list of the related videos which was shown next to each VIP Tag video. Overall, we collected 24 videos created individual BVI person (see Figure 2). From each video, we collected the meta-data, including the number of views, length of the video, and video effects. In this paper, we define video effects as any extra features applied to raw videos (i.e. background music). To analyze qualitative data, we transcribed videos and collected statements describing experiences of participants on YouTube. We used an open coding technique [5] by reviewing transcripts and highlighting excerpts. After each researcher coded the half of the statements, both researchers conducted an affinity diagramming session to identify key insights, themes, and patterns that occurred in the data repeatedly.

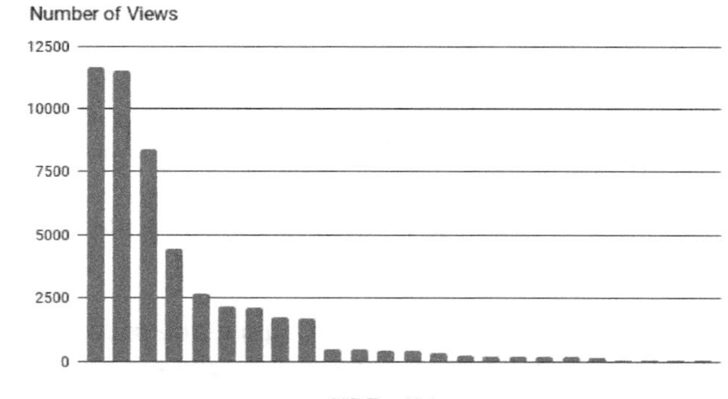

Figure 3: Only some of the videos are popular with high number of views. The highest number of views is 11,659 while the lowest one is 46.

Findings

The collected 24 videos were uploaded by individual BVI people on YouTube between June 2015 and March 2017. The average length of the videos was 13 min 27 sec (SD: 6 min 44 sec). The average number of views was 2,076 (SD: 3,476). This high standard deviation of the number of views indicates that only a few videos are popular while some are not, though all of the videos have a similar content structure (see Figure 3). Based on the analysis of the videos, we identified three themes which correspond to the research questions.

What contents do BVI people create on YouTube?
We found that a type of content that BVI people create is the description of themselves and their experiences. BVI vloggers shared their current eye conditions in their videos. They explained how they became blind or visually impaired and what they can do in daily life. In addition, they also shared their best experience as a BVI person. For example, they do not judge others by the appearance. Instead, they focus more on the personality: *"I'm not constantly thinking about someone's looks or their appearance or how they dress. I'm thinking about their personality." (P11)*

Some of them described that they can be themselves and do anything they want since they do not worry about reactions from other people. Being humble and meeting other BVI people are also good experiences that they had as BVI people*: "I would say getting to see how I overcome challenges and also getting to meet others that are visually impaired and getting to learn from them and just getting to experience life a little different." (P8)*

On the other hand, they also shared their experience with activities that are hard to be done as a BVI person. For example, while they manage to complete in the end, daily chores such as brushing teeth, putting up makeup, and vacuuming take them longer time than people with vision: *"I can do them [daily chores], it just takes me a lot longer to do." (P12)*

Moreover, many of them pointed out that there are difficulty in communication. It is hard to explain their vision whenever they talk to new people. Even in a conversation, they cannot read non-verbal communication, such as body language, facial expression or eye contact, so that they lose so much information: *"I can't always judge their expressions or the looks in their eyes to always accurately gauge how they're feeling." (P25)*

Furthermore, many BVI vloggers are struggling against many social issues. They are trying hard to overcome the stereotypes of BVI people, to find alternative accessible way in daily life, and to live in the society where it does not understand the spectrum of blindness*: "The worst part about being blind or visually impaired is just the lack of open-mindedness in society, and the lack of understanding or awareness about the spectrum of blindness." (P15)*

As shown above, BVI vloggers utilized videos to present themselves. Motivated by the questions of Tag videos, BVI vloggers tend to describe themselves with personal story and experience. Although a Tag video seems to be structured with the set of the same questions, the answers are different as each BVI vlogger has a unique experience and a different perspective.

How do BVI people create videos?
We found that 23 out of 24 videos are recorded with proper orientation. Most BVI vloggers in the videos faced directly into the camera. It is hard to determine how they record the videos unless they mentioned it in their videos like P24 did: *"My husband is taking the video for me and is going to read the questions." (P24)*

On the other hand, only one person, P2, had difficulty in adjusting the camera. Her video was dark and dim so that it was difficult to identify what she was doing. Since she knew this issue, she acknowledged the audience that the video would not be oriented properly:

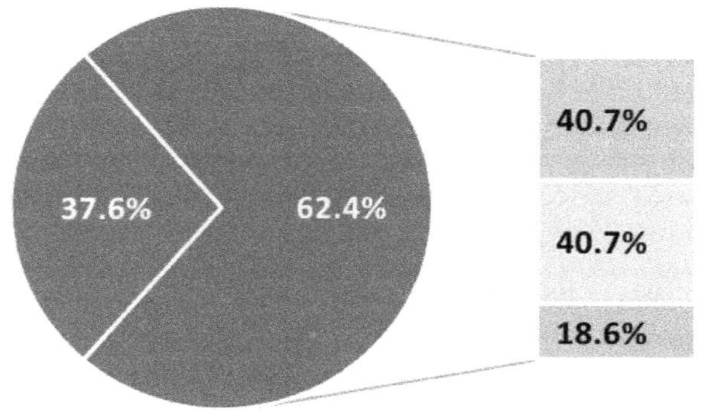

Figure 4: This pie chart shows the percentage of 24 videos with video effects, such as Intro, BGM, and Text decoration.

"First of all, as I say in every video, I am blind and cannot see or adjust it [camera]." (P2)

For video effects, we identified three basic effects that BVI people used: Intro, Background music, and Text decoration. These features are not provided by YouTube, but frequently used in videos. Of 24 videos, 62.4% of the videos had at least one effect (see Figure 4). 40.7% of them had intro and another 40.7% had background music (BGM) while 18.6% of them had text decorations. The use of these additional features demonstrates that BVI people are interested in editing and making their videos more visually appealing.

Why do BVI people join YouTube?
Many BVI people use YouTube to watch videos for entertainment and information. In addition, we found that BVI people joined YouTube due to two important reasons: 1) to support other BVI people and 2) to educate sighted people. First, they wanted to provide social support to those who have similar eye condition. By sharing their daily life and experiences, they tried to make other BVI people feel less alone: *"One person will stumble upon this video and they'll feel less alone. (P17)". "I joined YouTube to share my story. So, others [BVI people] know that they're not alone." (P8)*

In addition, they knew how to support the other BVI people as they already had similar experiences. They were able to understand what other BVI people suffered from and how to help those people: *"The only person who truly understand how their disability affects them is the disabled person themselves." (P25)*

Second, BVI people joined YouTube to overcome stereotypes and educate the community of sighted people. In their VIP Tag videos, BVI people delivered messages that they wanted to create awareness and educate people about blindness and visual impairments: *"I wanted to educate the public on blindness and how just because I can't see or someone else can't see doesn't mean that we can't do things. (P11)". "The big thing is to educate people about blindness awareness [and] what we really can do because right now people think that anybody with a disability is not able to do anything." (P13)*

Although BVI people have difficulties in interacting with video-based social media platforms, they were eager to leverage videos as a medium to support other BVI people and to educate sighted people to correct inappropriate stereotypes of BVI people.

Conclusion

Overall, our research aims to make video-based social media platforms accessible to support BVI people. The primary contribution of this study is to present an approach to understand BVI people on video-based social media platforms. We conducted a qualitative analysis on a specific type of online videos created by BVI people and identified the contents of the videos. This study shows that the method of analyzing the videos created by BVI people could be a supplementary strategy to identify their needs while using video-based social media (e.g., YouTube).

Future work still remains to conduct multiple studies to understand experiences of BVI people when interacting with other people through online videos. While we only focused on analyzing the contents of videos, comments on the videos may provide additional information to understand the interaction between vloggers and viewers. Also, we plan to recruit active BVI vloggers on YouTube and conduct interviews with them to collect additional qualitative data to identify challenges they face when interacting with other people through online videos.

References

1. Anthony, L., Kim, Y. and Findlater, L. Analyzing User-Generated YouTube Videos to Understand Touchscreen Use by People with Motor Impairments. *Proceedings of the SIGCHI Conference on Human Factors in Computing Systems - CHI '13, (2013).*
2. Hibbard, E. and Fels, D. The Vlogging Phenomena: A Deaf Perspective. *The proceedings of the 13th international ACM SIGACCESS conference on Computers and accessibility - ASSETS '11, (2011).*
3. Huh, J., Liu, L., Neogi, T., Inkpen, K. and Pratt, W. Health Vlogs as Social Support for Chronic Illness Management. *ACM Transactions on Computer-Human Interaction 21, 4 (2014), 1-31.*
4. Morris, M., Zolyomi, A., Yao, C., Bahram, S., Bigham, J. and Kane, S. "With most of it being pictures now, I rarely use it": Understanding Twitter's Evolving Accessibility to Blind Users. *Proceedings of the 2016 CHI Conference on Human Factors in Computing Systems - CHI '16, (2016).*
5. Patton, M. Qualitative Research & Evaluation Methods. Sage, Thousand Oaks, Calif., 2009.
6. Seo, W. and Jung, H. Exploring the Community of Blind or Visually Impaired People on YouTube. *Proceedings of the 19th International ACM SIGACCESS Conference on Computers and Accessibility - ASSETS '17, (2017).*
7. Veer, E. Hiding in plain sight: 'Secret'Anorexia Nervosa Communities on YouTubeTM. *ACR North American Advances 38, (2011), 256-261.*
8. Voykinska, V., Azenkot, S., Wu, S. and Leshed, G. How Blind People Interact with Visual Content on Social Networking Services. *Proceedings of the 19th ACM Conference on Computer-Supported Cooperative Work & Social Computing - CSCW '16, (2016).*
9. Wu, S. and Adamic, L. Visually Impaired Users on An Online Social Network. *Proceedings of the 32nd annual ACM conference on Human factors in computing systems - CHI '14, (2014).*
10. YouTube for Press, 2017. Retrieved September 14, 2017 from https://www.youtube.com/yt/about/press/.

Collecting Observational Data about Online Video Use in the Home Using Open-Source Broadcasting Software

Steven Schirra
Twitch
San Francisco, CA 94104
sschirra@twitch.tv

Danae Holmes
Twitch
San Francisco, CA 94104
hdanae@twitch.tv

Alice Rhee
Twitch
San Francisco, CA 94204
alrhee@twitch.tv

TVX '18, June 26–28, 2018, SEOUL, Republic of Korea © 2018 Copyright is held by the owner/author(s). ACM ISBN 978-1-4503-5115-7/18/06.
https://doi.org/10.1145/3210825.3213568

Abstract
Capturing contextual data about online media consumption in the home can be difficult, often requiring site visits and hardware installation in the field. In this paper, we present an exploratory study in which we use free, open-source broadcasting software and participants' existing computer hardware to capture remote, contextual video data inside the home. This method allows participants to simultaneously capture live recordings across multiple computer screens—as well as themselves and their home viewing environment—while watching long-form online video. We discuss the affordances and challenges of this method for researchers seeking to capture contextual data remotely.

Author Keywords
Remote contextual inquiry; multitasking; multi-screening; multiple monitors; research methods; Open Broadcaster Software (OBS); online video; livestreams; Twitch; multiple monitors; in-home observation.

ACM Classification Keywords
Human-centered computing~User studies

Introduction

Understanding the evolving context for television in the home has significant implications for the ways we design the next generation of interactive video experiences. Topics such as multi-tasking and multi-screening have been of continued interest to the TVX community [e.g. 2, 5, 6] as researchers seek to better understand the ways viewers divide their attention between media content, multiple screens and applications, and everyday household activities.

In our research on Twitch—a videogame-focused livestreaming platform that allows users to broadcast and watch live digital content and interact with each other via chat—we see many analogues between viewing practices for television and long-form online video. Many live broadcasts on Twitch span multiple hours, and we often hear reports from Twitch users about multi-screening and multitasking activities they engage in during a typical viewing session. These reports include activities such as simultaneously playing a videogame while watching a broadcaster play the same videogame on Twitch; participating in multiple live discussions about a broadcast across multiple communication channels (e.g. Twitch and Discord); and watching Twitch on auxiliary computer monitors while working or studying.

To better understand these content practices, we conducted an exploratory study with eight Twitch users in which observational video data from the user's viewing environment and their computer screen(s) was collected remotely using open-source broadcasting software. In this paper, we describe our process, report early results, and describe the limitations of this method.

Related Work

Several recent studies describe methods for observing and quantifying content viewing behaviors in the home beyond self-reported data. Rigby et al. [5] installed surveillance cameras in four households to understand viewers' multitasking behaviors while watching TV. Two cameras collected video data from the participants' television screen and viewing area, allowing for qualitative coding of both the television content and the participants' multitasking behaviors during broadcasts. They found that households had large variations in their multitasking behaviors, from frequent but short device uses, to infrequent but long device uses—to no device use at all.

Shokrpour and Darnell [6] installed cameras in ten households with the same configuration described above to collect observational multitasking data. They coded their video for a variety of observations, including multitasking frequency, type of multitasking behavior, and timing of multitasking in relation to the TV show. They found that multitasking occurred in 40% of television viewing time, with 36% of multitasking activities happening on a second device.

These studies describe several limitations of camera-based video observation for understanding viewing behaviors. In both studies, a researcher needed to travel onsite to the participant's home to physically set up the hardware, and later to collect the recordings. Rigby et al. [5] note that the recording equipment sometimes malfunctioned, and that image quality was lower than desired, making nuanced movements from participants difficult to discern.

Holtz et al. [2] describe a novel method for quantifying multi-screening while watching television. Their study used a combination of app logging on participants' smartphones, location tracking within the home, and "sound print" detection to identify how frequently users were multi-screening, what apps they were using, where they were in the home, and what content they were viewing. This allowed the researchers to build minute-by-minute profiles of device use per household member; however, this method also required onsite installation of dedicated hardware for data capture.

For a globally distributed participant base, remote observation methods offer contextual data without the need for onsite travel and hardware installation. Building off of Holtzblatt and Beyer's [3] foundational work on contextual inquiry, English and Rampoldi-Hnilo [1] describe Remote Contextual Inquiry (RCI) as a method for collecting contextual information using web-conferencing and screen-recording software. Through the web-conferencing software, users can share a live view of their personal computer setup and activities for observation by a remote researcher.

In the current study, we aimed to collect the types of deep, contextual qualitative data afforded by in-home video capture, while still providing the ability to observe the viewing practices of our global audience remotely.

Recording Software Considerations

To ensure naturalistic video data collection, we considered several factors in selecting a recording process for this research. We wanted to capture video of both the participant and their environment, as well as the participant's monitor setup. (Including support multiple-monitor setups, which are common among Twitch viewers.) We also needed a tool that allowed participants to capture video asynchronously and save the files locally so they could be transferred later to the researcher. Finally, we needed a recording tool that participants could install on their computers at no cost, was compatible with common consumer recording peripherals (webcam, microphone), and was easy to learn in an onboarding session.

We ultimately chose Open Broadcaster Software (OBS) [4] for our research. Not only was this software free and open-source across Windows, MacOS and Linux, but it also included the ability to build, record and save dynamic video scenes including multiple local monitors, plus the participant's webcam and microphone.

Methods

Participants

We recruited eight Twitch viewers from an internal participant database with varying degrees of monthly platform use (low, moderate, and heavy). As part of the screening process, potential participants described their common Twitch multitasking behaviors and the desktop computer equipment they owned. Because the goal of this research was to test our data collection method, we constructed a purposive sample of users with a variety of self-reported viewing behaviors and desktop setups. We also selected users with high-end computer systems, due to the high level of resources needed to capture video.

Procedure

The study was conducted over the course of seven days, including a one-hour onboarding session at the beginning of the study, and a one-hour retrospective

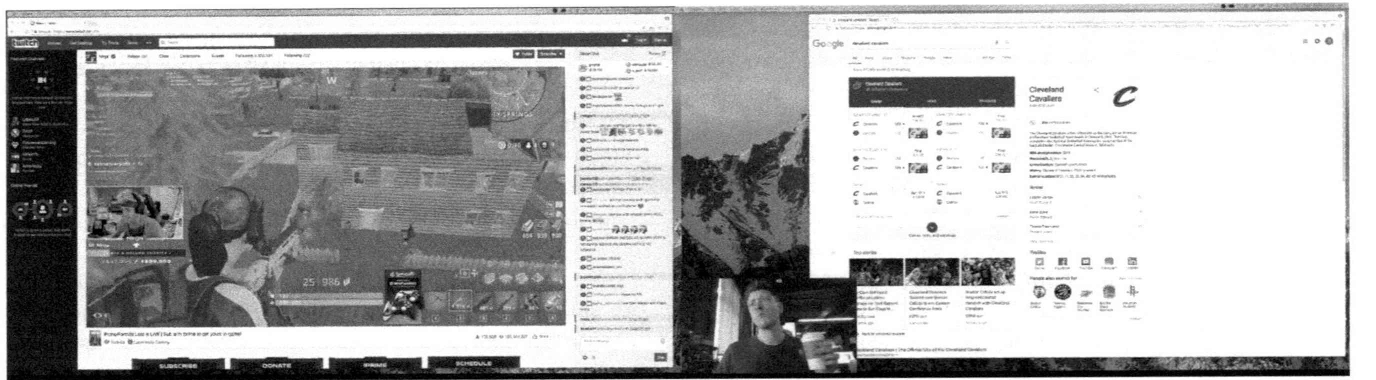

Figure 1. A screenshot of an example multi-monitor recording layout in OBS that participants used during the study. The recording showed computer activity on each monitor with a small overlay of the participant in the corner of one of the monitors.

interview. All participants received a gratuity for their time.

Onboarding

To onboard users to the study, we conducted a one-hour introductory session with participants over Skype to explain the study and help them install and set-up OBS on their computer. After installing the software, the researcher walked the participant through the process of building a scene in OBS to include their monitors, webcam, and microphone. Setting up OBS generally took about 20 minutes, including time for troubleshooting. After installation and set-up, participants recorded a test video with the software and uploaded it to a secure file-sharing site. The researcher could then download the video, check the video and audio quality, and troubleshoot any additional quality issues with the participant. Participants then received verbal and written instructions of the study.

Recording Viewing Sessions

After onboarding, we asked participants to record all Twitch sessions using OBS over a seven-day period. Participants then uploaded each completed video to a secure file-sharing site over the seven days. To protect participant privacy, we instructed participants to only send us video recordings they were comfortable with sharing and allowed them to omit any sessions that contained sensitive information or that made them feel uncomfortable.

Retrospective Interviews

We conducted one-hour retrospective interviews at the end of the seven-day collection period to clarify key moments seen in the video data, and to gain a deeper understanding of their motivations for viewing.

Results

We received 87 contextual video files from participants over seven days, with 168 hours of observational video data total. For each video, we coded and time-stamped all observable multitasking activities. We then identified and characterized high-level themes across our corpus of video data.

Key Observational Themes

Web Browsing: Viewing and interacting with websites outside of Twitch (not including online shopping)

Discord: Participants viewed or engaged in chat on the Discord chat application.

Checking Email (Desktop Only)

Eating and Drinking

Playing Videogame: Participants were playing a video game during a Twitch viewing session

Shopping Online: Participants browsed online retail websites, such as Amazon and eBay

Smartphone Use: Participants were engaged on their smartphone by touching/typing or talking on the phone

All participants were observed engaging in multitasking activities during Twitch viewing sessions. Six of our participants had multi-monitor setups for their computers, which supported this multitasking behavior. For most participants, Twitch occupied its own monitor, while other tasks, such as web-browsing and videogames were completed on a second monitor.

Even in circumstances where another task was occupying their attention visually, participants followed-along with the audio of the Twitch broadcast in the background. Various audio cues (e.g. a strong vocal reaction from a Twitch broadcaster) brought their attention back to Twitch. As P1 stated, "It's definitely easier with audio—you can hear what's going on. During the down time of a certain task, I can switch over and read any updates, or if there's something I want to look at I can switch over and watch."

The three most common multitasking activities observed in this study were web browsing/shopping online, monitoring or participating in chat on the Discord app, and playing videogames.

Observing these behaviors on video provided deeper context about how multitasking supports and enhances Twitch viewing. For example, because most Twitch livestreams consist of long-form user-generated content, there are often lulls or downtime as the Twitch broadcaster takes a break or switches games. Participants played their own videogames as a way of occupying their time during these slow periods. Similarly, many turn-based videogames have downtime where the player is waiting on an opponent to take an action, and during this downtime in the game, the participant was focused on Twitch. We observed this behavior for participants playing the popular turn-based card game *Hearthstone* during Twitch viewing sessions. As P4 stated, "I almost can't play games without having something going-on on the other [monitor] right now."

We also observed gameplay and Twitch interaction happen simultaneously as participants played games directly with Twitch broadcasters, such as the online trivia and party games in *Jackbox Party Pack*, or more traditional games such as chess.

The sociality of the Twitch platform was often discussed by participants as a key reason to have a dedicated monitor for Twitch viewing. P2 said, "I find that the benefit with watching Twitch instead of binge-watching Netflix on one screen and playing a game on the other, is that I get to have that social interaction." Similarly, P6 said "I would prefer to be entertained in a way where I can actually have some social interaction."

Participants also engaged both in Twitch's native chatroom and related auxiliary chat servers within the Discord app. This included participating in external chatrooms directly related to the specific Twitch channel they were watching, checking in with other Twitch communities that they were not currently watching, or chatting in servers about related topics. For example, one participant was observed chatting in a Discord channel about Japanese culture while watching Japanese-language Twitch streams.

Discussion

Overall, this remote asynchronous data collection method provided detailed contextual information around Twitch viewing sessions. The study provided insight into the types of multitasking behaviors that occur while viewing a broadcast—and what those behaviors look like in practice. Using OBS to create video recordings allowed us to adequately capture the activity across multiple monitors while still observing the participant, their viewing environment, and where their attention was focused during a broadcast.

The videos collected were of high-enough quality for researcher to observe nuanced attentional cues, as well as see the full content of multiple monitors in a single video file. This addresses some of the challenges with observational video fidelity discussed in past work [5]. The participant onboarding process for the OBS software was also simple enough that it could be completed remotely with the assistance of the researcher.

It is important to note that this method has multiple limitations that researchers should consider. One key limitation is creating high-fidelity recordings with OBS can require a significant amount of computing resources, and lower-end PCs may not be able to handle video capture while doing other tasks. Because many Twitch users own high-end gaming PCs with adequate resources, this was not an issue in the current study. Alternate methods should be used for users with less powerful PCs.

Hours-long recording sessions with OBS can require multiple gigabytes of local hard drive space, so it is important to ensure that participants have adequate storage as part of the screening process. This can also result in lengthy video upload times for participants sending their files to researchers.

Conclusion

In this paper, we have presented a novel method for capturing observational video data remotely using open-source software and participants' existing PC equipment. We were able to successfully collect video data across multiple computer monitors and within the participant's viewing environment to understand multitasking behaviors. While this method is currently limited by the computing power of the participant's PC, it shows promise for user groups where the use of high-end computing equipment is common.

References

1. Jeff English and Lynn Rampoldi-Hnilo. 2004. Remote contextual inquiry: A technique to improve enterprise software. In *Proc. Human Factors and Ergonomics Society 48th Annual Meeting*. HFES, Santa Monica, CA, USA, 1483-1487.
2. Christian Holz, Frank Bentley, Karen Church, and Mitesh Patel. 2015. "I'm just on my phone and they're watching TV": Quantifying mobile device use while watching television. In *Proc. TVX '15*. ACM, New York, NY, USA, 93-102.
3. Karen Holtzblatt and Hugh Beyer. 1993. Making customer-centered design work for teams. *Commun. ACM* 36, 10 (October 1993), 92-103.
4. Open Broadcaster Software. https://obsproject.com.
5. Jacob M. Rigby, Duncan P. Brumby, Sandy J.J. Gould, and Anna L. Cox. 2017. Media Multitasking at Home: A Video Observation Study of Concurrent TV and Mobile Device Usage. In *Proc.* TVX '17. ACM, New York, NY, USA, 3-10.
6. Auriana Shokrpour and Michael J. Darnell. 2017. How People Multitask While Watching TV. In *Proc. TVX '17*. ACM, New York, NY, USA, 11-19.

A Study on User Experience Evaluation of Glasses-type Wearable Device with Built-in Bone Conduction Speaker: Focus on the Zungle Panther

Ayoung Seok
Sogang Univ, 35 Baekbeom-ro
Mapo-gu,Seoul, Republic. of Korea
say0420@sogang.ac.kr

Yongsoon Choi
Sogang Univ, 35 Baekbeom-ro
Mapo-gu,Seoul, Republic. of Korea
yongsoon@sogang.ac.kr

TVX '18, June 26–28, 2018, SEOUL, Republic of Korea

ACM ISBN 978-1-4503-5115-7/18/06.
https://doi.org/10.1145/3210825.3213569

Abstract

The current HDM-oriented glasses wearable devices are inconvenient to use in real daily life that it needs both miniaturization and weight lightening. Glasses-type wearable devices are expected to develop into glasses-type devices. There is a lack of research on evaluation of user experience of VR(Virtual reality), AR(Augmented reality), television and game using glasses-type devices and design guideline. This research used Zungle Panther, a glasses-type wearable device with built-in bone conduction speaker to research user experience evaluation model needed for AR·VR content of the near future to be used in daily user life, and to research design guideline needed for glasses-type device guideline for near-future content including TV and online videos.

Author Keywords

VR; AR; Wearable; Bone conduction; Smart glass; Glasses-type device; TV; Online video; User Experience

ACM Classification Keywords

H.5.2. User Interfaces: Evaluation/methodology; H.5.2. User Interfaces: Style guides

INTRODUCTION

AR·VR technologies are C-P-N-D ecosystem industry with content, platform, network and device combined together. They are expected to create new added value by being applied to various industries. Especially, for the vitalization of the industry, killer-content and equipment to enhance public preference are absolutely needed. It is anticipated that killer content AR·VR games and movies maximizing immersion and realism beyond the limits of time and space will appear to lead the development of media entertainment industries. Recently, media corporations as well as video and game corporations have been active as well that there are more investments into AR·VR startups by giant media companies including Walt Disney, Comcast, Time Warner and 20th Century Fox.[1]

However, only 4 to 6 percent of consumers from developed nations plan to purchase AR·VR products or services within the next 6 months. Due to the price of the equipment or technological instability, the public preference and accessibility are still low. The currently launched display equipment including Oculus and HTC Vive are HMD type that people wearing glasses have difficulty wearing these products. Due to the heavy weight, users also feel discomforted with prolonged usage that enhancements are needed.[1]

Due to the development of technology, HMD enabling its users to experience the immersion and realism of AR ·VR video content will develop as glasses-type devices.[2][3]

This research uses Zungle Panther acknowledged in the market as glasses-type wearable device with built-in bone conduction speaker to extract user experience factors of glasses-type device design needed by AR·VR video content consumers to consume content in real daily life and studies design guideline based on the factors.

GLASSES-TYPE DEVICES DESIGN

Understanding of HMD Devices

HMD, a type of glasses-type wearable device is one of the most necessary equipment to enhance the immersion and realism of AR·VR video content. HMD is one of the core parts of smart devices including wearable devices that its influence on real daily life would become greater. With the development of the TV industry, glasses-type wearable devices providing attractive user experience with experiential content will be playing the role of complementary companion devices. There are various products launched in the market.[4]

However, there are more developments needed in the aspects of quality, size, weight, battery span, wearability or user experience. There are various forms of fusion including fusion of wired and wireless networks, fusion of platforms including Facebook, fusion of multimedia content and fusion of broadcasting communication services. In this process, for the consumption of new AR·VR content, new forms of UI, UX and real-experience devices supporting the five senses of human beings are needed. Due to the characteristics of AR·VR content needing dynamic and natural movements, the current wired devices are limited that lighter wireless devices need to be introduced and launched with the development of 5G, Giga Internet and UHD broadcast. Glasses-type

Figure 1: Galsses-type wearable devices utilizing microphone and bone conduction auido Zungle Panther.

wearable devices are appropriate alternatives. They will help expand the scope of content development and cope effectively against the demands of users.[3][5]

Sample of Glasses-type device Usable in Future Daily Life

With the development of AR·VR TV and video content, there will be devices with various technologies applied. Especially, glasses-type wearable devices utilizing microphone and bone conduction audio to allow its users to interact with AR·VR media content and both listen at the same time will dominate the market.[2]

This research selected glasses-type wearable devices providing glasses functions, voice functions and listening functions similar to the functions of glasses-type devices in conducting the research.

Zungle Panther, currently commercialized smart glasses recording second in sales in the market for general consumers having bone conduction speakers was selected as a sample. The reason was that it recorded sales of over 70,000 dollars in glasses-type wearable market, which was not getting enough attention after Google Glasses, and was being acknowledged in both public preference and accessibility with design considering user experience compared to other glasses-type wearable devices.

Panther could be paired with all other smart devices with Bluetooth that the user is able to enjoy any content with it, including TV, video and music. Also, due to built-in bone conduction speaker, the product is appropriate for enjoying AR·VR video content. The reason is because while other HMD products block external sounds that it may cause safety accidents or cause trouble controlling the device, Panther is an open-year solution enabling its users to listen to external sounds that there is no difficulty controlling the product alone, and the users are able to listen in safe environments. Also, in interaction with TV or online videos, its built-in noise-cancelling microphone allows input through voice that the device is appropriate for AR or MR video content interacting with virtual content.[6]

GLASSES-TYPE WEARABLE DEVICE WITH BUILT-IN BONE CONDUCTION SPEAKER – USER EXPERIENCE EVALUATION DESIGN

User Experience Evaluation Model

According to the definition of NNGroup, "user experience" refers to the addition of all experiences in interaction of users with products, services and companies providing them. Also, "user experience evaluation" refers to survey exploring problems to develop or enhance user interfaces for the users to easily and usefully use product or service functions.[7]

As for models related to user experience model, Heuristic of Jakob Nielson developed as usability evaluation model for web and Honeycomb of Peter Morvile are the most frequently used. To develop user experience evaluation model appropriate for glasses-type wearable devices, past researches have been viewed.

Researches on HMD and glasses-type wearable are mostly related to technological enhancements and VR content. In the research of Kim Whiwoon (2009), free-

Item	Detailed Item
Useful	Utility, Offer informative feedback, Design for multiple & dynamic contexts, Device From factor, Companion Device, Device Screen, Application
Usable	Usability, Enable frequent users to use shortcuts,Support internal locus of control, Reduce short-term memory load, Design for speed & recovery, Device Control (Gesture, Voice)
Desirable	Aesthetic, Design for enjoyment, Device Accessory
Findable	Design dialogs to yield closure, Reversal of actions, Design for 'top-down' interaction, Device sensor
Accessible	Availability, Consistency, Design for limited & split attention, Design for small devices,
Credible	Offline issues, Error prevention and simple error handling
Valuable	Allow for personalization
Audible	Contrast of sound, Loudness, Resolution, Softness & Sharpness, External Sound

Table 1: User Experience Evaluation Model

form surface prism lens was used to suggest 8 basic types, and 1 design was suggested after a survey.[8] Chae daeil (2011) measured form, functional and emotional satisfaction of exhibition viewing device with AR technologies applied to suggest design type suitable for the design concepts of emotional satisfaction, affordance and interface.[9] Jun Gong(2004) suggested a total of 15 interface design guidelines of mobile devices. This is based on the 8 interface design guidelines of Shneiderman and was composed of 8 interface design guidelines, 4 revisions and 7 additions.[10]

User Experience Evaluation Items for Glasses-type Wearable Devices with Built-in Bone Conduction Speaker

For the user experience evaluation model of glasses-type wearable product with built-in bone conduction speaker, Honeycomb's evaluation criteria was used. However, considering that it's an evaluation criteria for web usage, total of 27 items from smart watches' usability evaluation criteria used in Kim Gayeon (2015)'s research,[11] Guidelines for Handheld Mobile Device Interface Design developing existing heuristics to be suitable for mobile devices,[10] and evaluation items from wearable glasses UX guide considering field of view were categorized based on Honeycomb.[12] Considering that there is a built-in bone conduction speaker, "Audible" category was added to deduct a total of 8 UX evaluation criteria for glasses-type wearable device with built-in bone conduction speaker.

USER EXPERIENCE EVALUATION OF GLASSES-TYPE WEARABLE DEVICE WITH BUILT-IN BONE CONDUCTION SPEAKER

Experiments Plan

In experiments subject selection, this research recruited 5 users without usage experience of glasses-type wearable devices to evaluate user experience of glasses-type wearable devices usable in real daily life.

In participation of each participant in experiments, Panther, a glasses-type wearable device with built-in bone conduction speaker was worn (with lens removed) and TV and online video content were experience as in real daily life. Game and TV content were enjoyed for 30 minutes each through smartphones. Immediately afterwards, the prepared survey was conducted based on the user experience evaluation model for glasses-type wearable device with built-in bone conduction speaker. The scenes of users enjoying game and TV content were recorded by a camera, and after survey evaluation, participants and researchers conducted in-depth interview after the survey while viewing the recorded video and the finished survey. The content of the survey is as follows.

To provide an environment closest to the daily lives of participants, the researchers visited the personal spaces of study participants. Each experiment allotted 10 minutes for setting the environment, 30 minutes in enjoying games and TV content utilizing smartphones after wearing Panther, and 20 minutes for completing the survey. After the experiment, 10 minutes break was given. Afterwards, in-depth interview was conducted for 30 minutes.

Result of Experiments

Item	Detailed Item
Useful	Is the product useful for watching TV? Is the product functioning suitable for the glasses form?
Usable	Is there any difficulty for everyone to use? Is it convenient for normal movements? Can the desired functions used at appropriate times?
Desirable	Is the design of the product itself likable? Is the product attractive compared to different glasses type products? Is the product visually conveniently designed?
Findable	Can the circumstances for using the product easily discerned? Is it convenient to return to previous work? Is it easy to find desired content?
Accessible	Is there coherence in the product's motion? Is there no difficulty in motion while watching TV? Is necessary information shown appropriately considering the small size of the glasses-type product?
Credible	Are there alarms shown and measures taken in case of product error? Are services related to the purchase of the product reliable?
Valuable	Can the product be modified according to personal tastes and circumstances of usage? Does the usage of the product add joy to TV watching and gaming? Does the product provide better experiences compared to TV and games? Do you favor the usage of bone conduction products?
Audible	Is the definition of TV and games appropriate? Are the sounds of TV and games heard vividly? Is the volume of the TV and game sound appropriate? Is the sound range of the TV and game sound sufficiently wide? Are there no inconveniences in listening to the external sounds during motion?

Figure 2: Survey questions of Experiments

Satisfaction of the product design was the most frequent issue on the in-depth interview. Existing glasses-type wearable devices had low aesthetic sense that there seemed to be difficulties in using the product in real daily life, but for Panther, it was not a problem.

"It looks like a normal pair of sunglasses rather than a wearable device. Google Glasses seem to be for early adopters. But for Panther, I think I can wear it for fashion purposes. I also like that you can choose the color of the glasses frame and lens as well."

Also, though enjoying TV programs or games for prolonged periods with earphone or headphones caused inconveniences of the headphones being heavy and large sounds being transmitted directly to the ears, glasses caused no inconveniences with long-term enjoyment of content or enjoying other activities. With the bone conduction speaker, fear against trouble of hearing was resolved as well.

"No matter how good a pair of headphones is, it will cause my necks to ache because it's heavy. Also, I disliked large sounds being transmitted to my ears directly that I was concerned that I might have trouble hearing sounds later. But with bone conduction speaker, that fear against trouble hearing could be resolved, too."

As for sound, functions like high-quality headphones could not be anticipated, but the sound was sufficient to enjoy TV and games. Another characteristic was that because sound was being transmitted through bone conduction, sounds from within the content and sounds from the real world could be heard at the same time that it would be appropriate for circumstances where the users had to interact with the virtual reality and the real world.

"It was awkward at first because I could hear sounds from both the TV or games and the sounds from the real world. But I got used to it soon. It's natural to hear sounds from around me, but the sounds being blocked caused inconveniences. When I plan strategies with friends or when I have to hear external sounds while enjoying VR or AR content, it's much stable and comfortable."

Also, there were opinions that users would want to choose device sizes as people have different head sizes, and that they would like different functions added to it. Also, there were opinions that the device could get rid of negative image(geek, nerd) about people using smart devices (wearable device).

CONCLUSION

This design utilized microphone and bone conduction speaker as glasses-type product for the design of glasses-type device allowing users to enjoy AR·VR media content in real daily life. For this purpose, Zungle Panther optimized for interaction was used to research the user experience evaluation of glasses type wearable devices with built-in bone conduction speaker.

As for the result of the experiment, the device was useful in terms of user experience compared to other wearable devices. Especially, the fashionable design and the light weight of Panther unlike other products influenced the evaluation. Also, with the usage of bone conduction speaker, it was first awkward to hear the sounds from the content (virtual reality) and the environment (real daily life), but in interactions, it was more useful.

Also, though the sense of vision and the sense of hearing are in interactive roles in enjoying AR·VR content with glasses-type wearable devices, there is no specific design guideline about the sense of hearing. Therefore, category of "Audible" was added to the user experience evaluation model to suggest direction to make the experience for users more attractive.

It is anticipated that the user experience model for glasses-type wearable device with built-in bone conduction speaker would provide a good guide in designing glasses-type wearable device playing an important role in experiencing media content utilizing AR·VR in the future.

FUTURE WORK

This study had five study participants and had the characteristic of a pilot study before the actual study. Thus, there were limitations of the study being conducted around qualitative evaluation rather than quantitative evaluation. In future studies, quantitative studies with the evaluation subjects expanded will be carried out to evaluate the validity the user experience evaluation model and to complement the model. Also, continuous research will be conducted with the launch of new glasses-type wearable devices when Google and Apple launch their own glasses-type wearable devices to suggest design directions for the ideal glasses-type wearable devices.

REFERENCES

1. AR·VR Industry Status and Implications of Domestic and Foreign. VIP Report. Hyundai Research Institute. 17-14. (April 2017).

   http://hri.co.kr/upload/publication/201743182547[1].pdf
2. Cho, Sung sun. 2017. Next-generation display-Development trend of Micro LED. ICT Spot Issue. IITP(Institute for Information & communications Technology Promotion). (July 2017). https://www.nipa.kr/know/periodicalView.it
3. Mike Elgan. 2017. *Why Apple will make smart glasses.* IT WORLD from IDG. https://www.itworld.com/article/3160049/wearables/why-apple-will-make-smart-glasses.html
4. Kim, Jang seok. 2017. A Study on the Design of HMD(Head Mounted Display). *Journal of Cultural Product & Design.* Vol. 51. 2017 pp. 57-67
5. Kim, DoHoon. 2012. Ecosystem of Smart Media. Information & Communications Magazine. 29(10), 3-8. (September 2012)
6. Zungle. Retrieved March 1, 2018 from https://www.zungleinc.com/
7. Don Norman & Jakob Nielsen. The Definition of User Experience(UX). Retrieved March 1, 2018 from https://www.nngroup.com/articles/definition-user-experience/
8. Kim, Hwi Woon. 2009. Study of HMD using free-form surface prism lens. Master's Thesis. Korea Polytechnic University, MA, Republic of Korea.
9. Chae, Daeil. 2010. A Study about Art Exhibition Viewing Device Design Using Augmented Reality Technology. Master's Thesis. Honing University, MDes(Industrial design), Republic of Korea.
10. Jun Gong. 2004. Guidelines for handheld mobile device interface design. In *Proceedings of the DSI Annual Meeting,* , pp. 3751-375 6, 2004.
11. Kim, Ga Yeon. 2015. A Study on User Experience and Usability of Apple-Watch as Wearable Devices. Korea Science & Art Forum, 21, 19-29.
12. Son, Minji. 2015. Wearable Glass UX Design Guide Based on Human FOV(Field of View) Principle. Journal of Korea Design Knowledge 33, 2015.3, 235-244

Dynamic Subtitles in Cinematic Virtual Reality

Sylvia Rothe
LMU Munich
Munich, Germany
sylvia.rothe@ifi.lmu.de

Kim Tran
LMU Munich
Munich, Germany.
ki.tran@campus.lmu.de

Heinrich Hußmann
LMU Munich
Munich, Germany
hussmann@ifi.lmu.de

TVX '18, June 26–28, 2018, SEOUL, Republic of Korea
ACM 978-1-4503-5115-7/18/06.
https://doi.org/10.1145/3210825.3213556

Abstract

Cinematic Virtual Reality has been increasing in popularity in recent years. Watching $360°$ movies with a Head Mounted Display, the viewer can freely choose the direction of view, and thus the visible section of the movie. Therefore, a new approach for the placements of subtitles is needed. There are three main issues which have to be considered: the position of the subtitles, the speaker identification and the influence for the VR experience. In our study we compared a static method, where the subtitles are placed at the bottom of the field of view, with dynamic subtitles, where the position of the subtitles depends on the scene and is close to the speaking person. This work-in-progress describes first results of the study which point out that dynamic subtitles can lead to a higher score of presence, less sickness and lower workload.[1]

Author Keywords

Cinematic Virtual Reality, 360-degree video, subtitles, dynamic subtitles, static subtitles, speaker identification, presence, sickness, task workload, screen-referenced subtitles

CCS Concepts

•Human-centered computing → User interface programming; *Virtual reality;*

[1] The term dynamic subtitles is based on [2]. In the future we will use the term world-referenced subtitles (static subtitles: screen-referenced).

Introduction

$360°$ movies are attracting widespread interest and have many possible applications, e.g. telling stories about exciting locations in the world or ancient places of interest in history. In Cinematic Virtual Reality (**Cinematic VR**), the viewer watches a $360°$ movie using a Head Mounted Display (**HMD**). Therefore, the viewer is inside the movie and has the possibility to look around. For watching movies in foreign languages, but also for supporting hearing-impaired viewers, subtitles are needed. Not all rules of subtitling can be transformed from traditional movies to Cinematic VR. The freedom of the viewer to choose the viewing direction requires new approaches for subtitling.

In traditional movies, usually **static subtitles** are used. These subtitles are mostly at the bottom of the movie and do not change their position. This method is also called center-bottom subtitles [7]. For reducing head and eye movements during watching movies with subtitles, there are attempts to use **dynamic subtitles** placed near the speaker. The position of these subtitles is dynamically changing and depends on the scene. Other names for these subtitles are speaker following subtitles [7] or positioned subtitles [1].

Regarding subtitles in Cinematic VR there are three main issues. The first issue is the **position** of the subtitle. The viewer can move the head, thereby the field of view (**FoV**) is changing. There is no bottom in a $360°$ image, so the standard location for static subtitles is missing. Using the bottom of the display is one approach for static subtitles in Cinematic VR. Dynamic subtitles can benefit from more space between the speakers in Cinematic VR. In traditional movies usually there is only little room between dialog partners, if they are in the same shot. In other cases, only one person can be seen in one shot - the dialog partner in the next one. In Cinematic VR all talking persons are on the image at the same time with some distance to each other - so the eye movements between speaking persons and bottom-based subtitles are mostly greater than for subtitles placed between the persons.

The second issue is **speaker identification**. The problem of speaker identification is more relevant in Cinematic VR than in traditional videos, as all persons in the room are visible in the $360°$ image at the same time, even if the viewer sees just a part of it. Placing the subtitles near the speaker, helps to identify the speaker, however the viewer is restricted in the choice of the viewing direction when reading the subtitles. In our experiments we used speaker names for the static method and placements close to the speaker for the dynamic method to indicate the speaker.

This leads to the third issue - the **VR experience** - which includes topics such as presence, sickness and workload. Watching the movie using a HMD, the viewer is inside the scene - part of the surrounding scenery. Since subtitles do not belong to this scenery, the presence could be reduced and additional workload or sickness could be caused.

Searching for a subtitling method in Cinematic VR, the following issues have to be taken into account:

- The subtitles have to be easily readable, and should support the viewer's understanding of the story.
- The subtitles have to be understandable with an easy way for speaker identification.
- The subtitles should not destroy the VR experience - with as little eye strain as possible, less sickness and high presence.

Since speaker identification is an important issue for subtitling, especially in Cinematic VR, we chose scenes with more than one speaker: one dialog scene with two people and a meeting room scene with several people. We compared different subtitle methods for these scenes.

As a first approach to this topic, we started studies for viewers with normal hearing abilities watching movies in foreign languages. We are aware of the fact that not all of our findings can be adapted to subtitles for **hearing-impaired** viewers. For parts of our user study we had one deaf participant, who gave us valuable hints for our further research. We did not include this data in our analysis, as we decided to work out subtitles methods for this specific user group in the near future.

Related Work

Placement of Subtitles in Traditional Videos

Kurzhals et al. [7] compared center-bottom subtitles with dynamic (speaker-following) subtitles in traditional videos. Dynamic subtitles led to higher fixation counts on points of interest and reduced saccade lengths. The participants had the subjective impression of understanding the content better with dynamic subtitles. In their experiments the audio was muted. Since in Cinematic VR, audio is an important cue for hearing people to recognize something new in the scene, even outside the FoV, we did not adapt this approach. Instead, we manipulated the audio.

Several studies investigated the placement of dynamic subtitles in traditional videos for reducing the switching rate and distance between regions of interests and subtitle [1, 2, 5]. In our work we investigate if dynamic subtitles are applicable in Cinematic VR environments.

Brown et al. [2] analyzed the eye tracking data for subtitles in regular videos. They found out that gaze patterns of people watching dynamic subtitles were more similar to the baseline, than watching with traditional subtitles. Most of the participants were more immersed and missed less of the content. However, a few people preferred traditional subtitles, because they found dynamic subtitles more distracting. Another mentioned disadvantage was that for viewers who do not need subtitles, dynamic subtitles are more disruptive. This weakness is not relevant for Cinematic VR, as every viewer can choose if subtitles are desired, in contrast to traditional videos, where several people can look at the same display.

Speaker Identification in Traditional Videos

Another problem besides placement of subtitles is the identification of speakers in cases where there are more than one speaker. To place the subtitles near the speaker is one of the methods which can help to solve the problem. Vy and Fels [8] compared subtitles including speaker names with subtitles next to the speaker. In their experiments the participants felt distracted by subtitles following the speakers who change the place. Speaker names were helpful for most participants, but not for deaf viewers, who are not aware of the voices and do not usually identify people by names, but rather by visual characteristics. A conclusion of the paper is that hearing-impaired persons need different methods of subtitling than hearing persons. Since our participants were hearing people we used names for speaker identification in the static method.

Static Subtitles in 360° Videos

In their work-in-progress Brown et al. [3] suggested four static methods of subtitling. We implemented these methods and compared them in a prestudy. All participants chose the Static-Follow method - where the subtitles are moving with the head of the viewer - as the most comfortable and best working. Hence, in our main study we compared this method with dynamic subtitling. For this presence, simulator sickness and task workload was measured and a semi-structured interview was carried out.

User Study

In our study we compared static and dynamic subtitling. For the **static subtitles**, the texts are fixed in front of the viewer and statically connected to the head movements. In our experiments they are $12.5°$ below eye level. For speaker identification, the name of the speaker was added at the beginning of the text.

The position of the **dynamic subtitles** is near the speaker. It depends on the scenario where the subtitles are placed. Thus, the viewer has to look in the direction of the speaker to read the text.

Figure 1: The scene of talk video

Figure 2: The scene of the meeting video

Participants and Material
34 paid participants (26 men, 8 women, average age 22.9, 11 VR beginners) watched the videos using an Oculus Rift. They saw two short scenes recorded in a TV studio (3min length overall). In the first scene (Figure 1) two people talk to each other - we call this the "talk" video. In the second scene (Figure 2), there are several people in a meeting room, others are coming and leaving. This video is called the "meeting" video. We wanted to make sure, the participants did not understand the spoken text, therefore the audio was manipulated.

Study Procedure
After a general questionnaire part, every participant saw the same two short videos, each of them with one of the two methods. The order of videos and methods was counterbalanced.

All the head movements were tracked. After each video the task workload, sickness and presence parts of the questionnaire were answered.

Task workload: The workload was studied using the NASA-TLX questionnaire [4], where all six sub-scales were used: (1) Mental Demand, (2) Physical Demand, (3) Temporal Demand, (4) Performance, (5) Effort, (6) Frustration. In addition to the overall load, the subscale rates of each single item were compared for finding possible reasons for increased workload.

Simulator sickness: For measuring simulator sickness a reduced questionnaire of the Simulator Sickness Questionnaire (SSQ) of Kennedy et al.[6] was used. Since not all questions are relevant for Cinematic VR, six items were selected: (1) general discomfort, (2) fatigue, (3) headache, (4) eye strain, (5) difficulty focusing, (6) nausea, (7) difficulty concentrating.

Presence: To investigate the presence, we used parts of the presence questionnaire (PQ) of Witmer and Singer [9]. Since the PQ was developed for general Virtual Environments with interactivity and movement, we chose some of the questions which are relevant for Cinematic VR.

The questionnaire ended with some questions comparing the two methods. After each video a semi-structured interview was held and recorded.

First Results

Asking the participants directly about the preferences for the two subtitling methods, the results were well-balanced. However analyzing the scores of the NASA-TLX, SSQ and PQ questionnaires we could find some differences, which need a closer inspection. For some items dynamic subtitles led to a higher score of presence, less sickness and lower workload. Additionally, we got important hints for problems which we will investigate in the future.

Figure 3: Heatmap of the head tracking data for the talk video with dynamic subtitles. There is a cluster in the area of the subtitles.

Figure 4: Heatmap of the head tracking data for the talk video with static subtitles. The viewers are looking more around than in the dynamic case

In the comment part of the questionnaire and the semi-structured interview the following statements were mentioned :

Static Method, positive:

- "I can decide where to look."
- "This method is similar to the method in TV."
- "The subtitles are always visible."

Static Method, negative:

- "It is difficult to assign the speaker."

Dynamic Method, positive:

- "Subtitles can be assigned more easily to the speaker."
- "Speakers and subtitles can be seen simultaneously."
- "It is a more natural experience".
- "It is easier to absorb the content."

Dynamic Method, negative:

- "I am forced to look at the speaker."
- "It is sometimes difficult to discover the speaker."
- "I did not know where the next subtitle will appear."

Inspecting the heatmaps of the head tracking data, we found differences for the talk scene (Figure 3 and Figure 4). In time intervals where people were speaking, the data of the dynamic methods are more concentrated around the speakers, which means less head movements.

Discussion

Static subtitles make it easier to look around but more difficult to absorb the content. For speaker identification the dynamic method is preferred. The viewer can see the speaking person and read the subtitles simultaneously without extensive eye movements. From there, it is easier to capture the content. However, if the speaking person is changing and the following person is not in the FoV, it needs some effort to find the new speaker and subtitle. If there is more than one speaking person in the movie, it is difficult to match the subtitles to the speakers using the static method. So it is more difficult to understand the story.

Even if the participants did not prefer one of the methods in the comparison part of the questionnaire, the questions about the VR experience result in better scores for the dynamic method. One reason could be that dynamic subtitles are integrated in the movie and static subtitles are part of the display. Participants noted, that dynamic subtitles are "more natural , it coincides more with the real life". Comparing the data regarding task workload, sickness and presence the dynamic subtitling method was more comfortable in several cases. There is less eye strain because the subtitles are placed near the speaking persons and the viewer is not forced to switch to the bottom of the FoV.

Conclusion and Future Work

We explored two types of scenes: a dialog of two persons and a group of speaking people. The protagonists did not change their positions during the conversation. For moving protagonist, who are speaking, dynamic subtitles need to move accordingly. Such scenarios require further testing.

The participants of this study were hearing people. So, the results can be helpful for finding subtitle methods for foreign languages. Because we want to continue our work with subtitles for hearing-impaired people, we had one deaf person at the end of our user study, who tried out the investigated methods. As we expected, the problem of speaker identification needs much more effort than for hearing people. For hearing people the voices of the protagonists are an aid which is not available for deaf people. Different colors, fonts or signs are already used in subtitling of traditional movies and could be adapted. However, the problem of speaker identification in Cinematic VR is harder than in traditional movies and needs more research.

For logging the viewing direction we used head tracking. The additional usage of an eye tracker could lead to more detailed results in the analysis of the viewing direction.

Both methods - static and dynamic subtitling - are helpful for understanding movies in foreign languages. Even if our work is just a first approach and we investigated just two special scenes, the result of this study encourages further studies in this field. We think there is much potential in dynamic subtitles which are not used in Cinematic VR at the moment. However, none of the investigated methods meet all requirements for each scenario in Cinematic Virtual Reality. A combination of the methods depending on the requirements could be a new approach. Additionally, the subtitling methods could be expanded with techniques of attention guiding to facilitate speaker identification.

Even if we are just at the beginning of finding useful subtitle methods for Cinematic VR, these techniques are also important in other areas such as Augmented Reality and other fields of Virtual Reality.

REFERENCES

1. M Brooks and M Armstrong. 2014. Enhancing Subtitles. *TVX2014 Conference, Brussels* (2014), 25–27.
2. Andy Brown, Rhia Jones, Mike Crabb, James Sandford, Matthew Brooks, Mike Armstrong, and Caroline Jay. 2015. Dynamic subtitles: the user experience. In *Proceedings of the ACM International Conference on Interactive Experiences for TV and Online Video*. ACM, 103–112.
3. Andy Brown, Jayson Turner, Jake Patterson, Anastasia Schmitz, Mike Armstrong, and Maxine Glancy. 2017. Subtitles in 360-degree Video. In *Adjunct Publication of the 2017 ACM International Conference on Interactive Experiences for TV and Online Video*. ACM, 3–8.
4. Sandra G Hart and Lowell E Staveland. 1988. Development of NASA-TLX (Task Load Index): Results of empirical and theoretical research. *Advances in psychology* 52 (1988), 139–183.
5. Yongtao Hu, Jan Kautz, Yizhou Yu, and Wenping Wang. 2015. Speaker-following video subtitles. *ACM Transactions on Multimedia Computing, Communications, and Applications (TOMM)* 11, 2 (2015), 32.
6. Robert S Kennedy, Norman E Lane, Kevin S Berbaum, and Michael G Lilienthal. 1993. Simulator sickness questionnaire: An enhanced method for quantifying simulator sickness. *The international journal of aviation psychology* 3, 3 (1993), 203–220.
7. Kuno Kurzhals, Emine Cetinkaya, Yongtao Hu, Wenping Wang, and Daniel Weiskopf. 2017. Close to the Action: Eye-Tracking Evaluation of Speaker-Following Subtitles. In *Proceedings of the 2017 CHI Conference on Human Factors in Computing Systems*. ACM, 6559–6568.
8. Quoc V Vy and Deborah I Fels. 2010. Using placement and name for speaker identification in captioning. In *International Conference on Computers for Handicapped Persons*. Springer, 247–254.
9. Bob G Witmer and Michael J Singer. 1998. Measuring presence in virtual environments: A presence questionnaire. *Presence: Teleoperators and virtual environments* 7, 3 (1998), 225–240.

Augmenting the Radio Experience by Enhancing Interactions between Radio Editors and Listeners

Sandy Claes
VRT innovation
Brussels, Belgium
Sandy.claes@vrt.be

Rik Bauwens
VRT innovation
Brussels, Belgium
Rik.bauwens@vrt.be

Mike Matton
VRT innovation
Brussels, Belgium
Mike.matton@vrt.be

 ACM ISBN 978-1-4503-5115-7/18/06.
https://doi.org/10.1145/3210825.3213560

Abstract
Radio has a long history of being a one-way communication channel from radio station to listener. Recent technological advancements, such as online radio, enable the listener to interact more easily with radio stations, potentially augmenting the overall radio experience of the listener. In turn, the editorial teams of radio stations are challenged with the streams of incoming messages. In this paper, we report on the results of an initial, exploratory co-design process that aimed at mapping needs and values of both end-users, i.e. listeners and radio editors towards interaction. Specifically, we organized 6 co-design workshops at radio stations of 3 different countries. Results demonstrate how needs of both type of end-users overlap. The paper is concluded with 5 general points of attention, i.e. relevant feedback, co-creation of content, personal services, content on demand and being part of a community, which form the basis for the continuation of our work.

Author Keywords
Co-design; contextual inquiry; interactive radio.

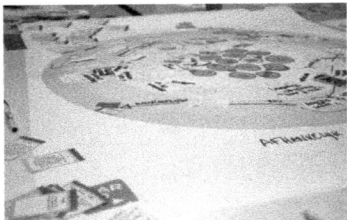

Figure 1. Process of co-design workshop with radio makers at VRT: Map (above), inspiration cards (second), group 1 (third) and a resulting concept (below).

ACM Classification Keywords

H.5.m. Information interfaces and presentation (e.g., HCI): Miscellaneous.

Introduction

Radio is a resilient medium; early predictions of its demise have so far been proven wrong. Yet radio is still largely a one-way communication system that allows individual listeners to passively consume radio content provided by radio broadcasters without any interaction or participation [1]. As a result, opinions and feedback of listeners are often ignored. This power imbalance between radio broadcasters and listeners is even more noticeable in an age of audience participation [5].

In this work-in-progress, our goal is to understand how i) radio makers (including hosts, editors, online managers and so on) and ii) listeners currently interact with each other, thereby defining problems and opportunities that can serve future potential of interactive radio. First, we organized observations at 3 European radio stations, followed by 6 co-design workshops with radio makers and listeners. The results of these workshops were analysed, and informed the next steps of an on-going research project on the potential of interactive radio.

Study set up

The study took place at 2 public broadcasters, which both house 5 or more radio stations (i.e. VRT in Belgium, NPO in The Netherlands) and 1 independent city radio station (i.e. StadtFilter in Switzerland), which also gave us the opportunity to reflect on similarities and differences. At these 3 locations, we first observed radio hosts and editors during at least one radio show after which informal interviews with the editorial team were taken. These contextual inquiries [3] took place in November and December 2017.

On air, interaction is triggered by radio hosts through questions, provocations, competitions and so on. An editorial team then receives messages of listeners through different communication channels in a chronological way (e.g. SMS text messages, tweets, e-mail, guestbook, phonecalls, VRT's own chatbot channel). We learned editors have difficulties to keep an overview of the incoming topics (such as traffic situations, opinions on a radio item or song, random thoughts, etc.). Also, it was too time-intensive for the editorial team to reply to all incoming messages, causing editors rarely to reply to listeners (e.g. only reply when incoming message will be treated in the show). We also noticed how incoming messages with visuals (e.g. a picture) were noticed quicker and interpreted more easily. Through this inquiry we also identified key values of interacting with listeners (i.e. recruiting, connect, inform, engage, respond), which informed the following co-design approach.

Co-design approach

At each of the 3 locations, 2 co-design workshops were set up: 1) with radio makers, and 2) with listeners. These co-design workshops were facilitated by the Map-it method [4], and guided by the research question: "How can we augment radio experiences through interaction?" Participants of the workshop were divided in two groups and each group was assigned to one moderator. A large (A0-sized) map covered each table (see Figure 1). Each participant also received sticker sheets, based on a pre-defined template. All moderators followed the same script and only intervened for timing reasons. They made sure the participants felt comfortable to speak freely (e.g. by creating a cosy living room atmosphere). For the workshop with listeners, informed consents were requested to be signed before the start of the workshop.

In the workshops with radio makers, the script departed with asking participants to identify values,

Nr.	Profession
V1	Editor
V2	Innovation manager
V3	Radio host
V4	Researcher
V5	Radio host
V6	User researcher
V7	Editor
V8	Project leader
V9	Editor
V10	Radio host
V11	CTO
V12	Radio host
V13	User researcher
N1	Online Editor
N2	Online web editor
N3	Education Coordinator
N4	Service manager online
N5	Editor in Chief
N6	Online editor
N7	Online editor
N8	Online producer
S1	Editor (Online)
S2	Editor/Instructor
S3	Editor(News)

Table 1. Overview of participating radio makers of VRT (V), NPO (N) and StadtFilter (S).

needs and frustrations related to the research question. In the workshops with listeners, the script departed with the presentation of some initial concepts on interactive radio that were defined earlier by radio professionals. (i.e. receiving notifications on preferred music, a radio broadcast that adapts to the listeners' daily journey and a button to skip music that is not preferred by the listener). Participating listeners could give their opinion (including needs, values and frustrations) on these concepts.

This first round formed the starting point for an ideation round that was guided by inspiration cards [2], that were focused on technology (e.g. chatbots, Artificial intelligence and voice control) and on out-of-the box concepts (e.g. a radio that sings on your birthday, a radio that can go back in time). Then, resulting concepts were exchanged between groups, and discussed by means of distributing likes and dislikes.

Results of the workshops were further contrasted to each other, and then analysed, coded and categorized, informed by a grounded theory approach [6]. To avoid bias in the interpretation of the data, all sessions were transcribed, and the analysis was organised collectively in a group of 5 researchers.

Workshops with radio makers

As shown in Table 1, 24 radio makers (of which 12 female) participated in one of the 3 co-design workshops. These radio makers have various responsibilities (e.g. an editor of online content, the host of a show) and are connected to different types of radio stations (e.g. station that aims at youth, fans of classical music or rock music etc.).

One of the frustrations of an editor of a radio station that aims at youth (i.e. 16 – 28 years old) is that listeners do not like to call or be called, which potentially affects their number of interactions. They currently overcome this by letting their listeners respond via audio or video messages.

Another frustration is that radio studios are grey and dull. Radio makers believe that hosting a show at events such as music festivals result in better radio shows, as radio hosts are able to immediately see how listeners respond to their efforts towards finding interaction.

At the moment, editors rely on the discussions that emerge on their radio stations' Facebook page to find out what is relevant for their listeners. However, often these discussions became less relevant when the radio show is actually broadcasted. One of the editors felt the need to be on top of these discussions, in order to be able to host a relevant debate.

Another need of radio makers is that many questions and remarks from listeners are received during a show but also when a show has just ended. Because then another program already started, editors are already focusing on the next show and do not have time to answer these questions.

A need that is particularly noticeable at StadtFilter, as a small radio station, is to enlighten the work towards social media. They envisioned a central social media exchange button to easily distribute content to all channels.

Workshops with listeners

As shown in Table 2, 22 listeners (of which 9 female) participated in one of the 3 co-design workshops. Listeners varied in age (AVG. 35 y.o., SD. 15), experience levels towards interaction with radio station (e.g. calling, sending text or chatbot messages) and type of station.

Lt.	Profession
VA	Administrative assistant
VB	Scientific assistant
VC	Student
VD	Unemployed
VE	Student
VF	Unemployed
VG	Office clerk
VH	Office clerk
VI	Radio host
VJ	Developer
NA	Director
NB	Student
NC	Test engineer
ND	Student
NE	Project leader
NF	Administrative
NG	Actor
SA	Software programmer
SB	Facility manager
SC	Student
SD	Allrounder
SE	Designer

Table 2. Overview of participating listeners of VRT (V), NPO (N) and StadtFilter (S).

Listeners do not often feel the need to spontaneously contact the radio station. They feel their message would be lost in the many other messages a broadcaster might receive. Listeners questioned out loud if they could see the number of responses on a particular topic, similar as you could recognize the amount of likes on Facebook, which they envisioned to be a trigger to react more often.

In general, all listeners experienced radio as a "mystery"; they like that when they listen to the radio they do not have to select playlists or think of what topic they would like to learn more on. Listeners also appreciated that radio is broadcasted to everybody at the same time, thereby enabling them to feel connected to strangers in traffic jams (as they recognized them listening to the same radio station). To protect this collective experience, yet still meet their need more personal music, they envisioned 'smaller, sub communities' that could be receive songs that fit their music taste.

Discussion

Similarities between radio makers and listeners

Also, listeners raised the point that radio items are not always relevant, or might take too long. To give feedback to the radio makers, they envisioned an application to give feedback. This concept overlaps with the needs defined by several radio makers (of VRT and StadtFilter).

As listeners found it frustrating to miss interesting content, they were also wondering if the rich content could be explored on a later basis. They envisioned concepts (such an application that would push older items that are linked to a particular location) to discover content of the radio archive. Similarly, radio makers also referred to the radio archive as a potential source of information for more personalized services.

Similarities between broadcasters

It was not the scope of this study to compare results of three radio broadcasters in detail, yet results revealed 3 interesting insights.

In all workshops with radio makers, the work effort concerning maintaining social media contacts was named as a frustration. In the large-scaled stations, dedicated online editors take care of content for each social media channel. In the small-scaled station, this work is done by radio hosts. They all recognize opportunities to automate these interactions.

On the other hand, in all workshops with radio makers, a certain fear towards chatbot technology was expressed. Radio makers fear they would misinterpret messages of listeners, and respond not according to the values of the radio station.

In the workshops with listeners, all participants expressed a general requirement to respect the community (as examplified in the concept on smaller communities) and background functions of radio (illustrated by concepts that deal with radio as a mistery).

Points of attention

Our analysis led to 5 specific points of attention that will shape the design process in the next stage, i.e. prototyping:

A **Facilitating relevant feedback**: Several concepts (e.g. instant feedback for users and real-time feedback for radio makers, content proposal from users) concerned the need to understand the listener, and to find out what is relevant at a certain moment.

B **Co-creating content**: Three concepts further built upon this need to understand the listener by allowing him to co-create radio items or compose their 'own' radio show.

C **Allowing personal services for listeners**: Other concepts (e.g. a pause function, personal radio based on GPS location) focus on creating personalised radio experiences.

D **Providing content on demand for listeners and radio makers:** Several concepts (e.g. a podcast service) focused on the ability to filter content and explore the radio archive.

E **Feeling part of a community**: Some concepts (e.g. smaller sub communities) were concerned to protect radio as a collective experience, and proposed solutions to strengthen this community aspect.

Next steps

This exploratory study is framed within a larger design research project on the interactive potential of radio. Our next steps will include the definition of i) user scenarios and ii) prototypes. For i), we will cluster the concepts from the workshops and write a scenario for each of the above mentioned attention points. For ii), we foresee a workshop with the 3 broadcasters and other industrial stakeholders (e.g. radio software developers) to collaboratively identify the needed interfaces and rank according to their preferences. Then, we plan to pilot these prototypes within the stations of the broadcasters, and iteratively refine the concepts.

Conclusion

In this paper, we presented the results of contextual inquiries at radio stations of 3 European broadcasters, and 6 co-design workshops with radio makers and listeners, guided by an exploratory research question concerning the potential of interactive radio. These workshops resulted in several concepts, which were thoroughly discussed, filtered and categorized in a group-analysis. The resulting attention points, i.e. 1) facilitating relevant feedback, 2) co-creating content, 3) allowing personal services, 4) providing content on demand for listeners and radio makers and 5) feeling part of a community, inform the next, prototyping activities of our study.

Acknowledgements

The research leading to these results was carried out in the MARCONI project (H2020 research and innovation programme under grant agreement 761802).

References

1. Angeliki Gazi, Guy Starkey, and Stanislaw Jedrzejewski. 2011. *Radio content in the digital age: The evolution of a sound medium*. Intellect Books.
2. Kim Halskov and Peter Dalsgaard. 2007. The emergence of ideas: the interplay between sources of inspiration and emerging design concepts. *CoDesign* 3, 4: 185–211.
3. Karen Holtzblatt and Sandra Jones. 1993. Contextual inquiry: A participatory technique for system design. *Participatory design: Principles and practices*: 177–210.
4. Liesbeth Huybrechts, Katrien Dreessen, and Selina Schepers. 2012. Mapping design practices: on risk, hybridity and participation. In *Proceedings of the 12th Participatory Design Conference: Exploratory*

Papers, Workshop Descriptions, Industry Cases-Volume 2, 29–32.
5. Guy Starkey. 2013. *Radio in context*. Palgrave Macmillan.
6. Anselm Strauss and Juliet M. Corbin. 1997. *Grounded theory in practice*. Sage.

Taxonomies in DUI Design Patterns

Mubashar Iqbal
Tallinn University
Narva mnt 25, Tallinn
Estonia
mubashar@tlu.ee

Ilja Šmorgun
Tallinn University
Narva mnt 25, Tallinn
Estonia
ilja.smorgun@tlu.ee

David Jose Ribeiro Lamas
Tallinn University
Narva mnt 25, Tallinn
Estonia
drl@tlu.ee

TVX '18, June 26–28, 2018, SEOUL, Republic of Korea
ACM 978-1-4503-5115-7/18/06.
https://doi.org/10.1145/3210825.3213561

Abstract

Recently a library of design patterns[1] was created to aid researchers and designers in specifying Distributed User Interfaces (DUIs). The patterns provide an overview of the solutions to common DUI design problems without requiring a significant amount of time to be spent on reading domain-specific literature and exploring existing DUI implementations. Among the main limitations of the library's current implementation is the significant overlap among design pattern descriptions and their relationships not being sufficiently clear. To address this, a systematic approach was undertaken to remove the overlaps among the design patterns, as well as to clarify their relationships by creating a taxonomic structure. The results of this study open several research directions to advance the current work on DUI design patterns.

CCS Concepts

•Human-centered computing → HCI theory, concepts and models; User interface toolkits;

Author Keywords

Distributed user interfaces, design patterns, taxonomy design, cross device interaction, natural language processing, thematic analysis

[1] http://idlab.tlu.ee/patterns

Table 1

Hyperdrag

Cross-Device Drag and Drop

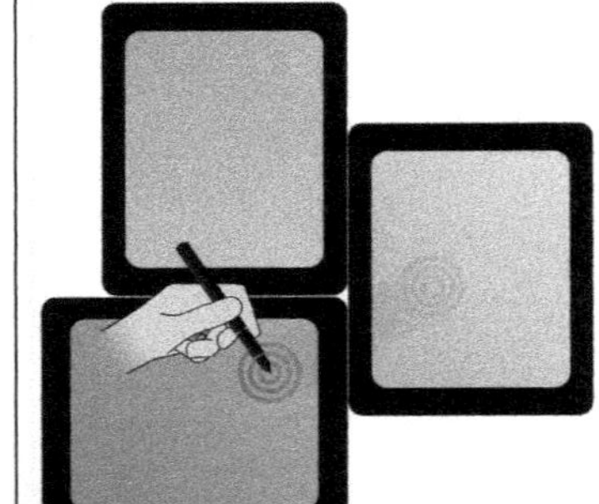

Hyperdrag & Cross-device drag and drop are duplicate patterns as both are using the same drag and drop technique, but are listed in the pattern library as separate entities, because they originate from different research papers.

Introduction

The rapid evolution of technology, popularity and diversity of devices has completely changed our ways of interaction. Multi-device environments enable interactions across devices, while also supporting the control of embedded systems from mobile devices. DUIs facilitate this ubiquitous control and can completely share the components of an application's user interface between different devices and not just the information between two different user interfaces [4].

This research focuses on proposing a taxonomy for a recently developed DUI design patterns library that aim to support the process of designing DUIs by introducing HCI experts to working solutions to recurring DUI design problems. The patterns belonging to the library are derived from a systematic literature review that covered a wide range of examples of applying DUIs in a diverse set of contexts, including but not limited to collaborative work, multi-device based reading, interactive walls & screens, gaming and entertainment. Whatever the diverse settings, activities, and device configurations users encounter, DUIs are meant to gracefully scale and adapt to those circumstances to enable user to stay engaged and efficient.

The term design pattern was introduced by Christopher Alexander back in the 1970's and the purpose is to provide a reusable solution to commonly occurring design problems, speed up the design and development process. Same applies in the context of HCI, where design patterns provide an effective reusable approach to design interactive systems.

Shmorgun [9] collected a set of patterns to aid the design of DUIs. In the current version of the DUI design pattern library, a total of 47 design patterns are listed. A major shortcoming of the pattern library is that a significant number of the patterns are overlapping and their relationships are not clear enough to facilitate the effective finding of the most relevant pattern for solving a particular design problem. The reason for this is that no clear classification or taxonomy was previously created to structure the design patterns. According to Niu [7], a taxonomy is a knowledge organisation system serving as the backbone for organising the concepts and applying the findings of a knowledge field. Fincher [2] also highlighted the importance of a taxonomy in their four principles of pattern languages, where they mentioned that design patterns should have a taxonomy to enable the reader to easily find the pattern(s) they need.

According to Usman [10], knowledge classification has supported the maturation of different fields by:

- Easing the sharing of knowledge [6] & [11];
- Providing a better way to understand the interrelationships between the objects of a knowledge field [6];
- Helping to identify knowledge field gaps [6] & [11];
- Supporting the decision-making process(es) [6].

The purpose of this research is to mature the structure of the DUI design patterns library by removing the duplicate design patterns and to create a taxonomy where each design pattern should be organised in a way that will minimise redundancy, possibly leading to a grouping or eventually merging of similar patterns.

To achieve this goal, the first step was to investigate the possible overlaps among the existing set of DUI design patterns. For this purpose, a Natural Language Processing (NLP) tool was developed for extracting and analysing each design pattern research paper to find the potential codes (also referred to as core concepts) that can be used for creating a design pattern description. Based on the generated

Table 2

Design Patterns High Level Categories

1. Gesture Control
2. Connectable
3. Proxy
4. Ubiquitous Interaction

Design Patterns

1. Drag and drop
2. Drag and pick
3. Lift and drop
4. Bumping
5. Throwing
6. Shuffling
7. Pinch
8. Portals
9. Connector
10. Perspective aware
11. Assistive
12. Proximity

Set of newly created design patterns & higher level categories

codes thematic analysis sessions were conducted with domain experts to get a set of higher level themes and categories that could be used for organising all relevant design patterns in a clear hierarchy.

The outcome of this study is the creation of a taxonomic structure that clarifies the relationships between the design patterns by removing duplicate and merging similar ones.

Related Work

Content analysis is often used for deriving a taxonomy from a large amount of textual materials [7]. Krippendorf [3] defines content analysis as a research technique for building valid and replicable inferences from texts to the context of their use. Content analysis gained popularity in the 1960s [7], originating from social sciences, where it has been used for studying the content of the communication.

Yao [12] built an algorithm for extracting the tags Del.icio.us to demonstrate the performance of the taxonomy construction and evolution. The resulting taxonomy reflected the evolution of user interests in regards to online resources. In another study, Chilton [1] presented a cascade algorithm technique, a novel crowd algorithm that produces a global understanding of large datasets. The cascade algorithm technique creates human-readable category labels and associates items with each category.

Niu [7] focused on the involvement of domain experts in intensive interviews, iterative development and competency questions to formulate a taxonomy. These approaches facilitate the development of the taxonomy in a more theoretical sense, which makes the results more solid as compared to solely using content analysis. Niu [7] used the ontology annotation tool (OAT) in their study as it is widely used for NLP tasks. After performing the data processing, the concepts were identified from the text and each concept was put into the appropriate root concept class.

Contribution

The main contribution of our study is a revised taxonomy structure of the DUI design pattern library that removes the overlaps among design patterns and facilitates clearer navigation and easier discovery of patterns. As part of this research, we also developed a text processing tool that derives the themes from the research papers describing DUI interaction techniques. These themes can later be used for composing new design pattern descriptions.

Revised Taxonomic Structure

Four new hierarchical taxonomy structures were created[2] to better organise the set of design patterns available in our library.These taxonomy structures are divided into four different levels (categories, families, design patterns, and interaction variations).

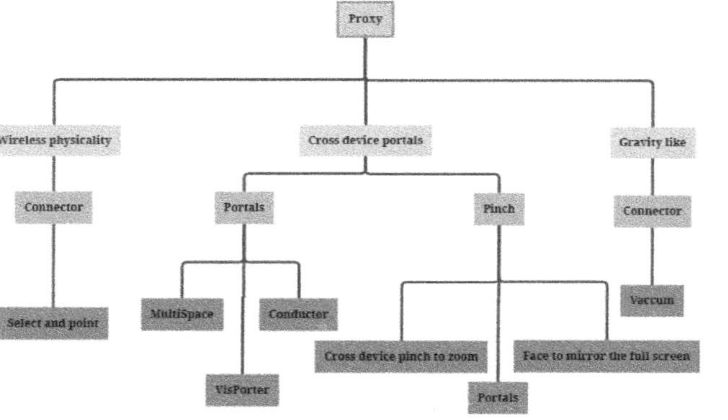

Figure 1: The taxonomy structure of the Proxy design pattern

[2]Follow this link to view all four taxonomic structures http://idlab.tlu.ee/patterns/index.php/Thesis_Resources

Table 3

Text Processing Services

Google Natural Language APIs, derive insights from unstructured text by using Google's machine learning algorithms.

Microsoft Cognitive Services, easily evaluate sentiment and topics from the text to understand what users want.

IBM Alchemy Language, a collection of APIs that offer text analysis through natural language processing.

Python NLTK, a leading platform for building Python programs that work with human language data.

NlpTools, same as NLTK, NlpTools is a library for natural language processing written in PHP.

The levels of the taxonomy structure are as follows:

- **Level 1** shaded in blue and represents the main category.
- **Level 2** shaded in grey and represents design pattern families that were generated by Mercer et al. [5]. A total of 9 families are listed in the Semantic MediaWiki. Our design patterns were initially grouped into these families.
- **Level 3** shaded in pink and represents the newly created design patterns.
- **Level 4** shaded in red and represents the different interaction variations that were collected from the design pattern research papers.

Research Methodology

The overall research methodology consisted of four phases.

Text Analysis

A web-based text processing tool was developed to analyse the research papers describing DUI design patterns. Mostly an open source technology stack was used for showing data in an organised tabular form, while the PDFParser module was used for parsing and extracting the text from the research papers. The TextRazor API was used for natural language processing.

A brief technology review was conducted to the select the most suitable NLP service. Six different services were reviewed and the TextRazor NLP API was selected based on its concept extraction capability, stable and solid performance, precision and recall of concepts [8].

Data Collection

Based on the NLP text processing of each design pattern research paper a total of 13,834 core concepts (initial codes) were generated and stored in the database, these were later shrunk to 3,406 by removing all abstract and interchangeable terms. All duplicate design pattern codes were also removed after being identified through cross comparison.

Data Analysis

The initial codes of each design pattern were cross compared[3] with other design patterns to find possible duplicates, overlaps or similar terms.

Afterwards, thematic analysis sessions were conducted with domain experts in order to identify the potential themes those were later used for formulating the root concepts, remove unnecessary overlaps, and merge design patterns based on similarities.

Further, social network analysis (see Figure 2) was performed to determine how the themes are grouped together and to visualise the relation of the different themes to the design patterns.

Categorisation and Findings

As a result of cross-comparisons, 12 duplicate design patterns were identified and removed based on the 100% similarity in the initial codes. This is due to the fact that these patterns were compiled based on the same research paper, but listed as separate entities in the DUI pattern library.

After removing the duplicates 35 unique design patterns remained and a set of 3,406 codes was identified and later

[3] A software tool was built to dynamically compare sets of design pattern codes. 1,081 cross comparisons were performed for the 47 design patterns.

used for thematic analysis.

By conducting the thematic analysis of the 35 design patterns with 18 domain experts 31 unique themes were created. These themes were later used to identify a set of 12 design patterns (see Table 2) and 59 different interaction techniques (as described in the related research papers). The emerging taxonomy also included the 9 pattern families those were previously identified in a study by [5].

The social network analysis led to the identification of the four higher level categories (see Table 2 & Figure 2).

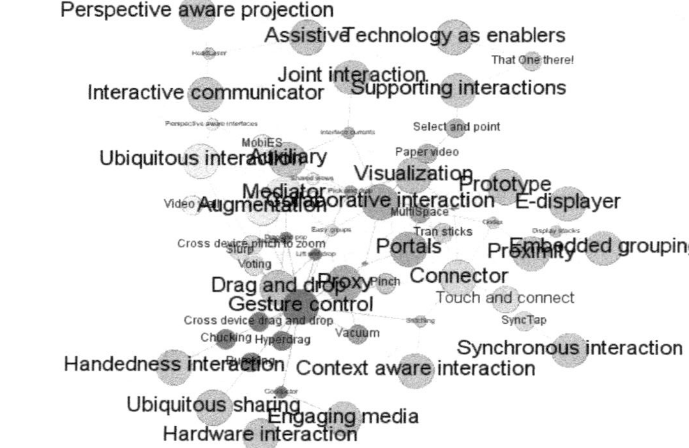

Figure 2: Themes social network analysis

By visualising the central themes and the connected design patterns in Gephi, the central themes were later used as the top part of the emerging DUI pattern taxonomy (see Figure 1).

Discussion and Future Work

The aim of this study was to remove the overlaps among the DUI design patterns and clarify their relationships, leading to the creation of a clear taxonomy. This goal was achieved by developing a text processing tool for extracting the initial codes from the associated design pattern research papers. Later thematic analysis sessions and social network analysis were used to get a set of higher level themes and categories.

As a result of this study, a number of overlaps in the design pattern descriptions were removed and the pattern library gained a clearer taxonomic structure.

Our current study has a number of limitations that should be pointed out. 1) No working prototype of the DUI design patterns was available at the time of the study and because of this it was difficult to introduce the participants to the notion of DUIs. 2) The newly created taxonomy has not been formally validated yet. Without validation, it is difficult to claim that the proposed taxonomy will contribute to better understanding, ease of identification and selection of design patterns. 3) Our taxonomic structure was developed without expert feedback, which is critical for uncovering the potential shortcomings in our process. Overcoming these limitations will contribute to stronger and more interesting results.

As part of the future work, our aim is to validate the newly created taxonomy. According to Usman [10], validation strengthens the reliability and usefulness of taxonomies. Another research direction is to investigate how users navigate the design pattern library after the new taxonomy has been implemented and to assess the level of cognitive load that they experience when searching for the desired patterns while solving specific design problems.

REFERENCES

1. Lydia B. Chilton, Greg Little, Darren Edge, Daniel S. Weld, and James A. Landay. 2013. Cascade: Crowdsourcing taxonomy creation. *Proceedings of the SIGCHI Conference on Human Factors in Computing Systems* (2013), 1999–2008. DOI: http://dx.doi.org/10.1145/2470654.2466265
2. Sally Fincher and P. Windsor. 2000. Why patterns are not enough: some suggestions concerning an organising principle for patterns of UI design. *CHI'2000 Workshop on Pattern Languages for Interaction Design: Building Momentum* (2000), 1–6. http://scholar.google.com/scholar?hl=en
3. Klaus Krippendorff. 2004. *Content Analysis: An Introduction to its Methodology.* DOI: http://dx.doi.org/10.2307/2288384
4. Jérémie Melchior. 2011. Distributed user interfaces in space and time. *Proceedings of the 3rd ACM SIGCHI symposium on Engineering interactive computing systems - EICS '11* (2011), 311. DOI: http://dx.doi.org/10.1145/1996461.1996544
5. Eduardo Mercer. 2015. Towards a Pattern Language for Describing Distributed Interactions Hajutatud interaktsioone kirjeldav mustrikeel. (2015), 48. http://idlab.tlu.ee/patterns/
6. Juristo; Sira Vegas; Natalia and Victor R. Basil. 2009. Maturing Software Engineering Knowledge through Classifications: A Case Study on Unit Testing Techniques. 35, 4 (2009), 551–565. http://ieeexplore.ieee.org/document/4775907/
7. Jia Niu and Raja R.A. Issa. 2015. Developing taxonomy for the domain ontology of construction contractual semantics: A case study on the AIA A201 document. *Advanced Engineering Informatics* 29, 3 (2015), 472–482. DOI: http://dx.doi.org/10.1016/j.aei.2015.03.009
8. Giuseppe Rizzo, Marieke Van Erp, and R Troncy. 2014. Benchmarking the Extraction and Disambiguation of Named Entities on the Semantic Web. *Lrec-Conf.Org* (2014), 4593–4600. http://www.lrec-conf.org/proceedings/lrec2014/pdf/176
9. Ilya Shmorgun, David Lamas, and Eduardo Mercer. 2016. Towards a Pattern Language for Distributed User Interfaces. *Proceedings of the 2016 CHI Conference Extended Abstracts on Human Factors in Computing Systems - CHI EA '16* (2016), 2712–2718. DOI: http://dx.doi.org/10.1145/2851581.2892304
10. Muhammad Usman, Ricardo Britto, Jürgen Börstler, and Emilia Mendes. 2017. Taxonomies in software engineering: A Systematic mapping study and a revised taxonomy development method. *Information and Software Technology* 85 (2017), 43–59. DOI: http://dx.doi.org/10.1016/j.infsof.2017.01.006
11. Claes Wohlin. 2014. Writing for synthesis of evidence in empirical software engineering. *Proceedings of the 8th ACM/IEEE International Symposium on Empirical Software Engineering and Measurement - ESEM '14* (2014), 1–4. DOI: http://dx.doi.org/10.1145/2652524.2652559
12. Junjie Yao, Yuxin Huang, and Bin Cui. 2009. Constructing evolutionary taxonomy of collaborative tagging systems. *Proceeding of the 18th ACM conference on Information and knowledge management - CIKM '09* (2009), 2085. DOI: http://dx.doi.org/10.1145/1645953.1646314

Smartphone-like or TV-like Smart TV? The Effect of False Memory Creation

Hyejeong Lee
ImagineX Lab, A&TECH
Hanyang University
Seoul, Korea
lhj4625@hanyang.ac.kr

Hokyoung Ryu
ImagineX Lab, A&TECH
Hanyang University
Seoul, Korea
hryu@hanyang.ac.kr

Jieun Kim*
ImagineX Lab
Hanyang University
Seoul, Korea

TVX '18, June 26–28, 2018, SEOUL, Republic of Korea

ACM ISBN 978-1-4503-5115-7/18/06.
https://doi.org/10.1145/3210825.3213564

Abstract
False belief pertains to what users believe falsely in their mental model about remembering novel features with no prior experience. The current study investigated how the False Belief technique can be employed to extract a first-time smart TV user's mental model. Smart features formed by a group of users' false memories (n=41) were monitored to see how the users' mental model changed with retention intervals (immediate, short, and long delays). The findings showed that a gist trace formed in the first-time use cannot last long (1 month) because of the greater false belief effect. Practical implications of these findings should be furthered to improve the apparent adoption obstacles in smart-TV use.

Author Keywords
Smart TV; mental model; schema; false memory; feature selection

ACM Classification Keywords
Human-centered computing---Human computer interaction (HCI)---HCI design and evaluation methods---User models

Background
"They all favored novel smart TV functions, but they have never used them [5]."

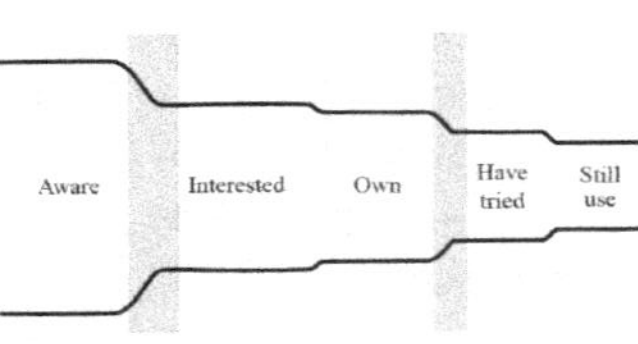

Figure 1: Two bottlenecks in the smart-TV adoption funnel (revised from [7])

This is a rather paradoxical user attitude in the smart-TV market. Despite the active increase in the supply of smart TVs, surveys have reported that actual usage remains marginal. Figure 1 illustrates the major bottlenecks in the smart-TV adoption funnel [5]. The first concern is awareness regarding what a smart TV actually is. The second, which is now a serious concern, is that over 50% of smart-TV owners have never tried to use the smart features of their TV, except at the first installation, thanks to many alternatives available (e.g., set-up box, smart phone).

Many critics of current smart TVs [3] suggest that success would only be guaranteed when a distinct smart TV feature is introduced and adopted by the user, and when this can form a unique mental model for the smart TV. Otherwise, the mental model of the smartphone would present a rather negative transfer effect, owing to which, many users would not employ the features on the smart TV because they already have the same features on their smartphone. This is a very plausible account, but it has not yet been examined whether smart-TV users actually apply the smartphone mental model to the use of smart TVs.

Method

To reflect this, we proposed a new technique, tentatively called, the false belief technique. Built upon the Deese–Roediger–McDermott (DRM) paradigm [8], this technique is designed to examine a first-time users' mental model of smart TV features. First-time users' mental model would be based on their beliefs about what they think they know. Here, it is important to note that people often have distorted memories [4], where they fail to distinguish what they have actually experienced from what they remember falsely. Thus, a false belief pertains to what users believe falsely in their mental model about remembering features that they have never encountered, even though they were not familiar with the product [3].

The experiments were designed using the DRM procedure developed by Tulving [11] and Roediger et al. [9]. The DRM procedure involves the visual presentation of a list of smart TV features (e.g., Skype, App, On TV, VOD), and it allows first-time users to explore the smart TV. In this training session, they were able to experience all the presented features. As suggested in the DRM paradigm, immediately after or days later, they were given a pen-and-paper recognition memory test: a list of features comprising smart TV features learnt plus non-studied feature items (including critical lure items that a design team tries to add in the new product, such as Home Shopping, Fitness, and 3D Experience). In the memory test, a remember/know judgment task was used to determine whether the participants recognized a feature item based on their memory or based on familiarity. Thus, they were first asked if they had seen a feature before (old) or if they had not seen it (new). Subsequently, for items that they classified as "old," the participants were asked to judge if they can mentally relive the experience of the item being presented (remember), or if they were confident that it occurred without having a detailed memory of the event (know). For each question, they were asked to rate their confidence to identify the criteria that the participants would adopt.

This DRM procedure would reveal the gist of memories from the first-time exploration that are incorporated into a mental model of a smart TV. Indeed, the robustness of the DRM paradigm has been confirmed in

Studied Items	Nonstudied items: Critical lure	Nonstudied items: Weakly related lure
Motion recognition	Most popular channel in real time	TV built-in camera
Voice recognition	Personal favorite channels	Screen capture
Interactive voice response	Internet broadcasting	Home shopping
Apps	Schedule recording	Home appliance control
Game	Art mode	Screen off memo
Skype	Split View	Voting
Screen Mirroring	3D experience	Fitness
Video On-demand	Showing captions	Karaoke
Social	Speaker mode	Remote self-diagnosis
Web browsing	Time shift	TV remote finder

Table 1: The apparatus used for the remember/know judgment task

many areas of research [4] [10]. Furthermore, it revealed that people not only confidently recognized the non-presented item but that they consciously remember this lure appearing on the list, rather than relying on some feeling of familiarity.

Experiment

Participant/Apparatus/Procedure

We recruited 41 participants (28F/13M) aged between 19 and 29 years with no experience with using a smart TV. Participation was voluntarily, and those who completed the experiment were compensated with $25. Table 1 presents the 30-item recognition test that included 10 studied and 20 nonstudied items. The nonstudied items comprised the latest smart TV and new imaginative features of the design team's interest. The nonstudied items included the following two types: i) ten critical lures related to the basic TV function and viewing experience and ii) ten weakly related lures that are similar to App or smartphone widget-like functions, not necessarily related to TV viewing.

The experiment consists of the sessions: training session, immediate recognition test (remember/know judgments), and delayed recognition test. In the training session, the participants watched narrative video clips that explained the smart TV features listed in Table 1. The video was repeated twice with no interruptions (https://youtu.be/JMtFa71FumQ). All the participants were instructed to try to remember as many features as possible for the subsequent recognition test that would follow either immediately or after a delay of a few days, weeks, or a month. At the end of the video-conditioned smart TV training session, the participants were asked to complete the product comprehension test obtained from van den Hende et al. [12]. The remember/know recognition memory test was conducted at six different retention intervals, including immediate (no delay), and a 2-day, 5-day, 1-week, and 1-month delay. The remember/know instructions were based on those used by Gardiner and Richardson-Klavehn [1].

Results and Discussion

Remember/know judgments

Table 2 presents the principal findings, including the mean recognition proportion for studied items, critical lures, and weakly related lures, and the effect of retention interval over time. The results revealed an accurate memory for studied items (hits) and false memory for crucial lures and weakly related ones (false alarms). We examined group differences at each retention interval using the Chi-square test.

The overall hit and miss rates for the studied items in the immediate condition were 0.92 and 0.08 respectively. The hit rates for the studied items declined slightly over the retention intervals; whereas, the false alarm rates for both critical and weakly related lures increased with greater delays. This is consistent with the finding that the wrongly formed belief is more persistent over time than the correct memory is, unless the latter is fixed by repeated experiences or information [7] [10]. The mean proportions of "remember" judgments for studied items exceeded the "know" judgments at all retention intervals. In comparison, the "know" judgments were more frequent for the nonstudied lures (critical and weakly related lures) at all retention intervals. We found that the frequency of remember judgments tended to decrease while that of know judgments tended to increase with the longer retention intervals for the studied and nonstudied items.

Interestingly, a statistical significance was only found only for the immediate and 1-month delay retention intervals in the false alarms for both critical and weakly critical lures ($p = .0349$, $p < .05$ for critical lures; $p = .0098$, $p < .01$ for weakly critical lures). These results revealed that the participants had more difficulties in retaining new correct information after a 1-month delay. However, imaginary or false memories would appear and be systematically reinforced over time. In a similar vein, Nielsen Norman Group's [6] addressed this inertia in users' mental model.

False belief with retention intervals

Figure 2 and Figure 3 illustrate the distribution of the confidence ratings for the Remember/Know and New judgments, separately for the critical and weakly related lures. We were particularly interested in the changes of users' responses between the immediate and 1-month delay recognition tests, where the retention interval uniquely showed significant differences (see Table 2).

Retention interval	Response Old			Response New
	Overall	Remember	Know	
Immediately after				
Studied	0.92	0.84	0.08	0.08
Items	*hit*	*strong hit*	*weak hit*	*miss*
Critical	0.19	0.08	0.11	0.81
Lures	*false alarm*	*strong false alarm*	*weak false alarm*	*correct rejection*
Weakly Related	0.02	0.01	0.01	0.98
Lures	*False alarm*	*strong false alarm*	*weak false alarm*	*correct rejection*
2 days later				
Studied	0.90	0.84	0.05	0.10
Critical_L	0.22	0.08	0.14	0.78
Weak_L	0.03	0.01	0.02	0.97
5 days later				
Studied	0.88	0.83	0.05	0.12
Critical_L	0.25	0.12	0.13	0.75
Weak_L	0.05	0.02	0.02	0.95
1 week later				
Studied	0.90	0.80	0.10	0.10
Critical_L	0.24	0.12	0.12	0.76
Weak_L	0.03	0.01	0.02	0.97
2 weeks later				
Studied	0.90	0.79	0.12	0.10
Critical_L	0.25	0.11	0.14	0.75
Weak_L	0.06	0.03	0.03	0.94
1 month later				
Studied	0.90	0.77	0.14	0.10
Critical_L	0.32	0.14	0.18	0.68
Weak_L	0.11	0.03	0.08	0.89

Table 2: Proportion of studied items, critical lures, and weakly related lures with reference to different retention intervals, broken down into proportions of Remember/Know and New Judgments

Remember/know false alarms represent incorrect answers for the nonstudied items. The larger the number of participants who answered Old and that of participants having full confidence in their answers, the more likely was it for the feature to match with the participant's expected mental model. In turn, new/correct rejection responses represent the opposite of the remember/know false alarms. Specifically, larger the number of participants who answered New with higher confidence, less likely was it for the feature to match with their mental model of a smart TV. For instance, if the Apps feature was strongly imprinted in their mental model, they would say Old (the feature was presented in the experiment) with high confidence.

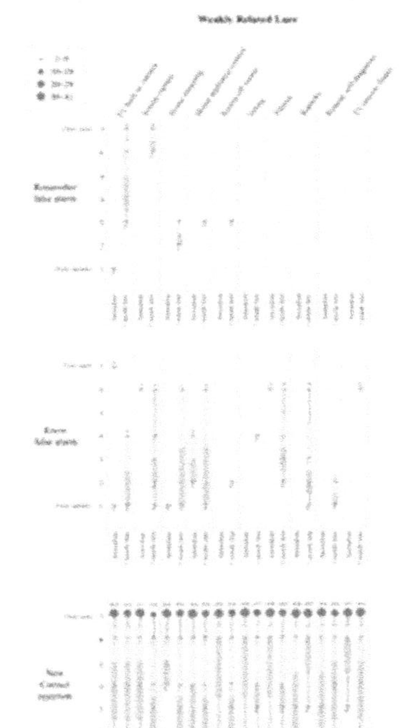

Figure 3: Distribution of confidence ratings for weakly related lures immediate after and 1 month later

Otherwise, they would say New (miss) or Old (hit) with lower confidence. The latter can thus be thought to have a weaker imprint on their mental model. Thus, the present findings reveal each feature's imprinting level in the users' mental model, and identify the features that might have a stronger impression on users' minds.

Regarding the high confidence for false alarms for critical lures (i.e., items that received a rating of 6 or 7) in the immediate recognition test, half of the participants (20) made at least one high-confidence remember judgment on the following critical lures: most popular channel in real time, personal favorite channels, internet broadcasting, schedule recording, art mode, spilt view, and speaker mode. Only four participants made at least one low confidence (a confidence rating of 1 or 2) of weakly related lures (TV built-in camera) in the immediate test. In comparison, the results of the know judgment showed that the high and low confidence rates for critical lures in the immediate test differed marginally (12 and 16 participants, respectively). Note that know judgments in the recognition test do not simply reflect guessing at least when majority of the participants made the know judgment with a high confidence rate of 6 or 7. Retention interval strongly influenced the know judgment for both critical and weakly related lures. At least one knows judgment was made for each critical

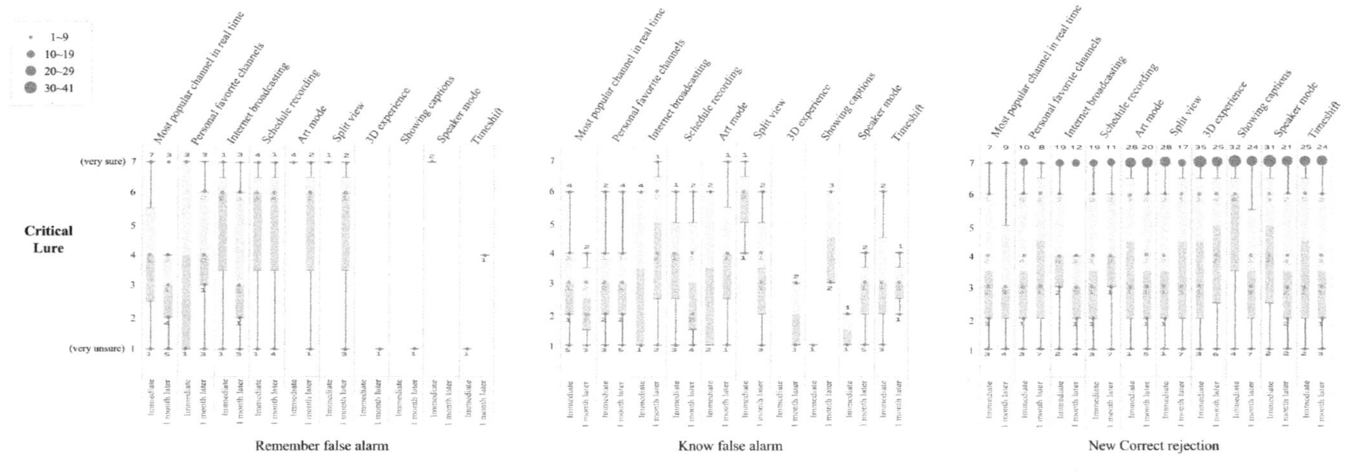

Figure 2:Distribution of confidence ratings for critical lures immediate after and 1 month later

and weakly related lure after a 1-month delay, with a wide range of confidence rates.

In comparison, the four critical lures of 3D experience, Showing captions, Speaker mode, and Time shift were newly marked as remembered after the 1-month delay; however, except for Showing Captions, the rest of three critical lures were answered with low confidence. It should be noted that all five participants who made the remember judgment with high confidence (6 or 7) for Screen capture (weekly related lure) initially answered new-correct rejection in the immediate test, with a strong confidence rate (very sure, 7 point). This finding confirms the effect of false beliefs in users' mental model over time, when the new training or experience has not been inserted.

Conclusions

The false belief technique developed in the present study exhibited two contrasting benefits against the conventional feature selection methods used in previous studies. First, unlike the previous methods used to examine users' mental models, their schema for the smart TV can be collected in a rather unconscious way by using the false belief technique.

Acknowledgements

This research was supported by Basic Science Research Program through the National Research Foundation of Korea (NRF) funded by the Ministry of Science, ICT & Future Planning (No. NRF-2016R1D1A1B03931389

References

1. Gardiner, J. M., & Richardson-Klavehn, A. 2000. Remembering and knowing. *The Oxford handbook of memory*, New York: Oxford University Press. 229-244.
2. Gina Ghensi. Most smart-TV owners do not connect their TVs to the internet: Manufacturers must respond. Retrieved May 28, 2013 from http://www.analysysmason.com/About-Us/News/Insight/smart-TV-May2013/#.UjbQctK-1cb
3. Lee, J., & Ryu, H. 2014. I remember/know/guess what i saw: a false belief technique to features selection. In CHI'14 Extended Abstracts on Human Factors in Computing Systems, ACM, 2593-2598.
4. Loftus, E. F. 1996. Memory distortion and false memory creation. *Journal of the American Academy of Psychiatry and the Law Online*, 24, 3, 281-295.
5. McKinsey. Connected TV Quantitative Survey. Retrieved 2012
6. Nielsen Norman Group. 2010. Mental Models. Retrieved October 18, 2010 from https://www.nngroup.com/articles/mental-models/
7. Payne, D. G., Elie, C. J., Blackwell, J. M., & Neuschatz, J. S. 1996. Memory illusions: Recalling, recognizing, and recollecting events that never occurred. *Journal of Memory and Language*, 35(2), 261-285.
8. Reyna, V. F., Holliday, R., & Marche, T. 2002. Explaining the development of false memories. *Developmental Review*, 22(3), 436-489.
9. Roediger, H. L., & McDermott, K. B. 1995. Creating false memories: Remembering words not presented in lists. *Journal of Experimental Psychology: Learning, Memory, and Cognition*, 21, 4, 803.
10. Seamon, J. G., Luo, C. R., Kopecky, J. J., Price, C. A., Rothschild, L., Fung, N. S., & Schwartz, M. A. 2002. Are false memories more difficult to forget than accurate memories? The effect of retention interval on recall and recognition. *Memory & Cognition*, 30(7), 1054-1064.
11. Tulving, E. 1985. Memory and consciousness. Canadian Psychologist. 26, 1-12.
12. Van den Hende, E. A., Schoormans, J. P., Morel, K. P., Lashina, T., van Loenen, E., & de Boevere, E. I. 2007. Using early concept narratives to collect valid customer input about breakthrough technologies: The effect of application visualization on transportation. *Technological Forecasting and Social Change*, *74*(9), 1773-1787.

Experiencing Virtual Reality Together: Social VR Use Case Study

Simon Gunkel
Hans Stokking
Martin Prins
Omar Niamut
TNO, Den Haag, Netherlands
simongunkel@googlemail.com
hans.stokking@tno.nl
martin.prins@tno.nl
omar.niamut@tno.nl

Ernestasia Siahaan
Pablo Cesar
CWI, Amsterdam, Netherlands
E.Siahaan@tudelft.nl
P.S.Cesar@cwi.nl

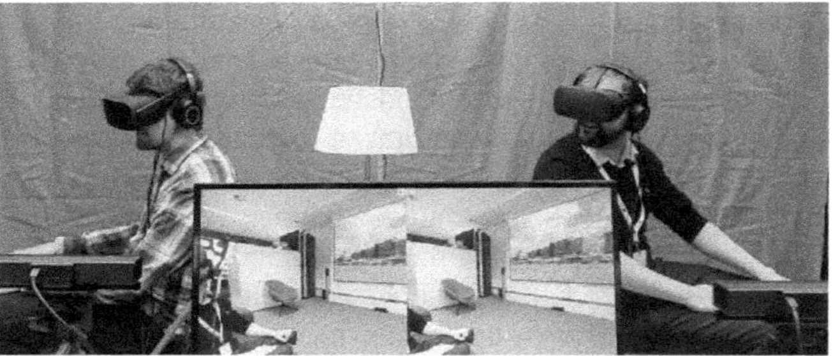

Figure 1: Two participants trying a Social VR Experience. In a virtual environment, they appear to sit next to each other on an office couch, and can interact with each other.

TVX '18, June 26–28, 2018, SEOUL, Republic of Korea
ACM 978-1-4503-5115-7/18/06.
https://doi.org/10.1145/3210825.3213566

Abstract

As Virtual Reality (VR) applications gain more momentum recently, the social and communication aspects of VR experiences become more relevant. In this paper, we present some initial results of understanding the type of applications and factors that users would find relevant for Social VR. We conducted a study involving 91 participants, and identified 4 key use cases for Social VR: **video conferencing**, **education**, gaming and watching movies. Further, we identified 2 important factors for such experiences: **interacting within the experience**, and **enjoying the experience**. Our results serve as an initial step before performing more detailed studies on the functional requirements for specific Social VR applications. We also discuss the necessary research to fill in current technological gaps in order to move Social VR experiences forward.

CCS Concepts

•Information systems → Web conferencing; *Multimedia information systems;* **•Human-centered computing → Virtual reality;**

Author Keywords

Virtual Reality; VR; Social VR; Use Case; Requirements; WebRTC; WebVR; Immersive Virtual Environments

Introduction

With the increased interest for Virtual Reality in the market (both in terms of hardware and software), interest in Social VR has also emerged. This is showcased through VRChat, which attracted "10000 concurrent users" in January 2018[1]. The demand for more Social VR is not surprising as humans are highly social beings. However, current VR systems that allow communication in VR (Facebook Spaces, VRChat and AltspaceVR, to name a few) have severe limitations when it comes to communication interactions [9]. One limitation is that users are represented as artificial (sometimes comic-like) avatars. Even though this might be beneficial for some use cases, this might not be beneficial for many communication settings such as business meetings, or sharing experiences with family or friends. Based on current scientific literature and industrial approach, it is still unclear which use cases are relevant to the different methods users can be represented. Thus, more research is necessary to better understand Social VR requirements.

Figure 2: Example view inside VR, showing the other user and a movie projection space

As a first step to close above gap, we conducted a Social VR study where participants tried a photo-realistic Social VR experience [4, 5] in sessions of 3-10 min followed by a questionnaire and informal discussion. In the VR environment, users sit beside each other on a couch in a 360-degree 2D VR environment and consume a 2D video (see Figure 2), while being able to hear and see each other as photo-realistic video streams. The experience was created to give people a better idea of Social VR. The main contribution of this paper is the study of use cases in Social VR. In this study, we identified 4 key use cases for Social VR: **Conferencing**, **Education**, Gaming and Watching Movies. Further, we identified important factors for such experiences: **interacting within the experience**, **enjoying the experience**, sharing the experience, and being able to move. Our results can guide future studies on more detailed functional requirements, which is essential to design Social VR interfaces and experiences.

[1] https://twitter.com/vrchatnet/status/949453320200052737

Related Work

In the past years, virtual reality saw renewed interest within research communities and industry with the rise of high-quality but affordable HMDs. This has led to new initiatives in shared and social VR experiences as well [10]. Communication has been studied in different virtual environments in the past, for example via large screens, and calibrated camera rigs [6]. This is, by systems that represent users as graphical avatars to create large shared virtual environments, of which [1, 7, 11] give some overview. The realism of avatars in such virtual spaces has also been studied [3].

However, it is not widely understood how such virtual experiences map to the current VR hardware and to collaborative use cases like remote media sharing [2]. One recent work that compares face-2-face communication with embodied virtual reality [12], shows that both "embodied VR provides a high level of social presence" similar to face-to-face interaction, and VR experiences appear to be lonely if other users are not shown. In our preliminary work [4, 5], our main focus has been on using 2D video streaming and web technologies as a basis to bring people together in virtual environments. We have shown that photo-realistic shared and Social VR experiences can be created by using current off-the-shelf equipment and by using a WebVR-based framework. What is currently not studied in literature is which use cases will most likely benefit from Social VR experiences, which we like to address with this paper. Further studies are needed to compare different user representations (like animated avatars versus more photo-realistic 2D and 3D approaches), which is out of scope of this paper.

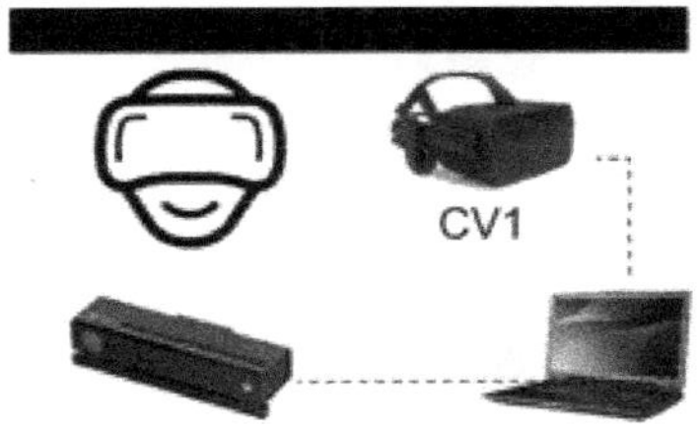

Figure 3: Scheme of our technology setup for each user of the Social VR experience.

Table 2: Details of participants

Total participants: 91
Experienced VR before: 80
Gender distribution: 20 F, 69 M, 2 N/A
Age range: 20 between 18 and 30, 49 between 30 and 45, 21 between 45 and 60

Table 1: Questionnaire Items for Requirements Gathering and their Response Format

Question	Response format
Are you interested in Social VR experiences?	For each option, 7-point scale with labels: not interested at all - low interest - slightly interested - neutral - moderately interested - very interested - extremely interested
Would you like to experience the following topics in Social VR? Sports - Movies - Theatre - Video games - Education - Music experiences - Live TV Shows - Video conferencing - Dating - Adult Entertainment	
Is there anything else you would like to experience within a VR environment?	Free response format
In a VR experience, how important would it be for you to...	For each option, 7-point scale with labels: not important at all - low important - slightly important - neutral - moderately important - very important - extremely important
...share the experience with someone?	
...interact within the experience?	
...enjoy the overall the experience?	
...being able to move within the experience?	

Requirements Gathering

To understand user expectations for Social VR, we performed a requirements gathering and analysis. We conducted our requirements gathering at the European VR exhibition, VR Days 2017 in Amsterdam. In this way, we ensured that our participants at this stage are people who at least have an interest in VR, and/or have experience using VR applications. Table 2 shows details of our participants.

Method

We conducted our requirements gathering using a survey/questionnaire method.Table 1, gives an overview of the questions we asked, along with their response format or scaling method.

Before filling out our questionnaire, participants were asked to try out our Social VR demo, so that they have an understanding of our Social VR application concept. The demo was done in pairs. Each time, two participants were asked to sit with their backs against each other (to simulate being away from each other/remote). The experimenters would help each participant put on head mounted displays (HMDs), headsets and microphones, and make sure that each of these worked properly for the participant. Once this was done, participants could then start their experience in the virtual environment. When a participant did not have a partner to do the demo with, one of the experimenters would perform the demo together with him/her. In the virtual environment, the two participants would appear to be sitting side by side on an office couch. They could see each other and communicate verbally with each other. Moreover, they could see a screen in front of the couch, and could either watch a video clip together or play a game together on the screen. Figures 1, 2 and 3 show the setup of our demo. The screen in Figure 1 shows the view of the participant within the HMD. After trying out the demo and taking off all the equipment, participants were then asked to fill in our questionnaires through a tablet device.

Technology Setup

The demo experience is completely based on web technologies. Our main motivation to utilize web technology is to allow an easy, widespread deployment and low entry burden for end users and developers. For this reason, we currently use off-the-shelf hardware and state-of-the-art

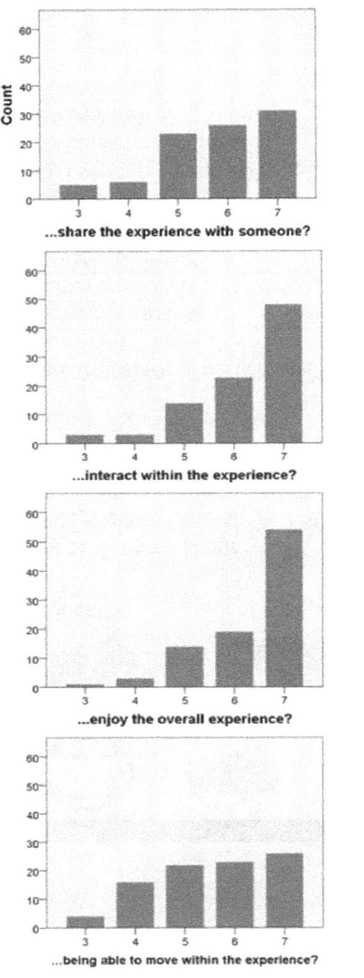

Figure 4: Example view inside VR, showing the other user and a movie projection space

web technologies. In our setup (Figure 3, each user has a specific and similar setup. Each user has a laptop (MSI GT62VR), Oculus Rift HMD (CV1), Kinect camera, headset (Sennheiser HD 201), unidirectional microphone (Power Dynamics PDT3), and gamepad (Xbox 360). It is important to note that the physical environment of the user is aligned with the virtual environment, i.e. if the user looks into the camera, he will look at the other person in the virtual environment. In the virtual environment, the users sit on either the left or right side of a sofa. Thus, the view in the virtual room is different for each of the users. Furthermore, the other user is placed to the right or left of the user according to their view. The placement of users is done by alpha-blending people into the environment based on WebGL shaders. We use this system to record users with a Kinect 2 RGB-plus-depth camera, replace the background with an alpha channel before transmission, and apply alpha-blending after reception to remove the background in the receiving browser (leaving us with a transparent image showing just the user without his/her physical background). Currently, for capture and transmission we use a resolution of 960x540 pixels.

Results

Interest in Social VR Experiences. In our survey 47.25% of the participants expressed that they are extremely interested in Social VR experiences. Only 6 people were neutral or slightly interested, while no people had low to no interest.

Important factors in (social) VR experiences. Figure 4 shows the histogram of responses for the questionnaire items asking users what they would consider to be the most important factors in (social) VR experiences. Based on the charts, "interaction within the experience" and "enjoyment of overall experience" seem to be considered extremely important by more than half of our participants.

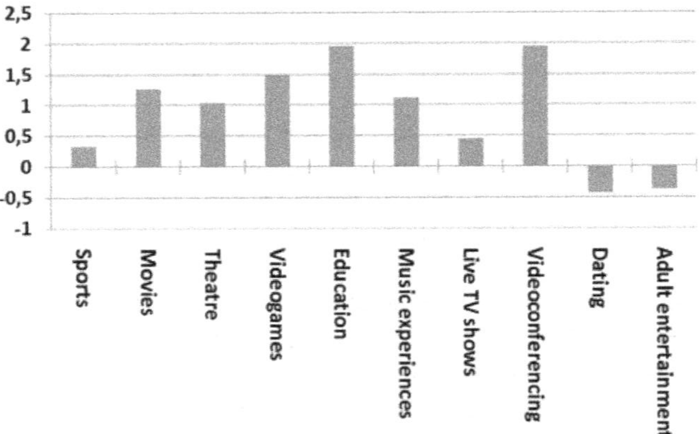

Figure 5: Users interest in Social VR for different application contexts.

Potential application contexts for Social VR experiences. To compare the responses for Q3 (see Table 1), we coded the responses into the score range [-3,3], with neutral (the middle of the scale) as 0 value. We then took the average score across participants and plotted a chart comparing the average scores (Figure 5). Figure 5, shows an overview of the results for the different application contexts proposed in our questionnaire. From the charts, we see that the highest interest is shown for video conferencing and education applications, followed by video games, music experiences and movies.

Discussion & Future Work

Our demo and requirements analysis aims at understanding users' interest in Social VR experiences, specifically on the types of applications that users (who are already familiar with VR experiences) would find most benefiting from our setup, and important factors to consider in a Social VR

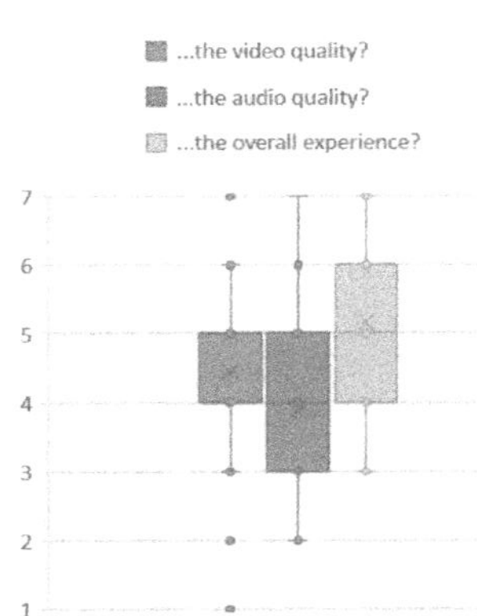

Figure 6: Users response when asked about audio, video, and overall quality of the experience.

Experience. From our results, perhaps not surprisingly, the two most interesting applications to users (i.e. education and video-conference) are those that involve a lot of face-to-face conversations or interactions in non-remote/real world settings. However, the same level of interest was not shown for two other cases with high face-to-face interactions in real world settings: dating and adult entertainment. Our guess is that there are more factors besides realistic representations that need to be considered for dating and adult entertainment in VR.

Users found enjoyment and interaction within the experience as the most important factors among the four factors that we asked them (see Figure 4). However, it is possible that people did not consider the importance of moving in Social VR, based on our example demo. This is, our demo presented an application where users are sitting together on a couch, to watch a video or play a game. The importance of the different factors are suggested through users' responses when asked to rate the system's quality of the experience (QoE, see Figure 6). Users tend to rate the overall experience higher than the audio and visual quality. This hints at users considering more factors other than what they see or hear in the VR setup. At this stage, we cannot yet pinpoint whether these additional factors are due to the enjoyment or interaction in experiencing Social VR. However, our results show that people are interested in Social VR and the need to further investigate the different factors that influence the QoE in Social VR experiences.

One possible down-point of our setup is that the results could suffer from a first-timer effect: people only spent a short time in our setup, and it was the first time they experience Social VR. Additionally, the use case presented in the demo did not yet represent a real application, rather then a Social VR concept. In the future, we plan to do user evaluations in a more controlled setting, and incorporate use cases from the real world where users follow a specific task for a longer period of time, for example half an hour to an hour. We also plan to have a group of users use it on a number of occasions, to see if repeated experiences would change their perception of our Social VR environment.

Our approach of capturing users with a depth-camera and blending them in the VR space appears to be promising to use. The current limitations (low resolution for participants representation of 960x540 pixels in 2D, users do not see eye gaze but others wearing a headset, and no self-view) seem to not hinder our participants from both communicating as well as consuming the immersive experience. One of our future work is to solve the technological limitation such that users will be able to see each other's full face (i.e. removal of HMD image), and that users will be able to see their own body parts (self-representation).

In our setup, we used a photo-realistic representation of the environment and users. Nevertheless, there are other types of representations that can be used in VR, such as mesh-based or point cloud-based avatars [8]. Together with industrial partners, we are planning to perform studies that compare different technologies for Social VR representations. Further, we like to investigate how this technologies map to real application use-cases, particularly related to education, collaboration and live events (e.g. sports).

Conclusion

With the results of this paper, it is clear that we are still at the initial stages of creating Social VR experiences for the general user. The study presented in this paper provides important insight into the types of applications relevant to users within Social VR experiences, such as video conferencing and educational applications. Moreover, the paper outlines a general idea of the factors that need to be considered when designing Social VR experiences, such as enjoyment and interactivity. More studies will need to be performed to obtain more detailed requirements for specific application contexts. We plan to follow up on this study by performing experiments both related to use-cases and technical choices in Social VR, such as different user representation types in VR, and image processing to remove the HMD within the user representation.

Acknowledgements

This paper was partly funded by the European Commission as part of the H2020 program, under the grant agreement 762111, "VRTogether" (http://vrtogether.eu/).

REFERENCES

1. Steve Benford, Chris Greenhalgh, Tom Rodden, and James Pycock. 2001. Collaborative virtual environments. *Commun. ACM* 44, 7 (2001), 79–85.
2. Azadeh Forghani, Gina Venolia, and Kori Inkpen. 2014. Media2gether: Sharing media during a call. In *Proceedings of the 18th International Conference on Supporting Group Work*. ACM, 142–151.
3. Maia Garau, Mel Slater, Vinoba Vinayagamoorthy, Andrea Brogni, Anthony Steed, and M Angela Sasse. 2003. The impact of avatar realism and eye gaze control on perceived quality of communication in a shared immersive virtual environment. In *Proceedings of the SIGCHI conference on Human factors in computing systems*. ACM, 529–536.
4. Simon Gunkel, Martin Prins, Hans Stokking, and Omar Niamut. 2017a. WebVR meets WebRTC: Towards 360-degree social VR experiences. In *Virtual Reality (VR), 2017 IEEE*. IEEE, 457–458.
5. Simon NB Gunkel, Martin Prins, Hans Stokking, and Omar Niamut. 2017b. Social VR Platform: Building 360-degree Shared VR Spaces. In *Adjunct Publication of the 2017 ACM International Conference on Interactive Experiences for TV and Online Video*. ACM, 83–84.
6. Peter Kauff and Oliver Schreer. 2002. An immersive 3D video-conferencing system using shared virtual team user environments. In *Proceedings of the 4th international conference on Collaborative virtual environments*. ACM, 105–112.
7. Jason Leigh, Andrew E Johnson, Thomas A DeFanti, Maxine Brown, M Dastagir Ali, Stuart Bailey, Andy Banerjee, P Benerjee, Jim Chen, Kevin Curry, and others. 1999. A review of tele-immersive applications in the CAVE research network. In *Virtual Reality, 1999. Proceedings., IEEE*. IEEE, 180–187.
8. Rufael Mekuria, Kees Blom, and Pablo Cesar. 2017. Design, Implementation, and Evaluation of a Point Cloud Codec for Tele-Immersive Video. *IEEE Transactions on Circuits and Systems for Video Technology* 27, 4 (2017), 828–842.
9. J. Outlaw and B. Duckles. 2017. Why Woman Don't Like Social Virtual Reality. (2017). `https://extendedmind.io/social-vr`
10. Tekla S Perry. 2016. Virtual reality goes social. *IEEE Spectrum* 53, 1 (2016), 56–57.
11. Ralph Schroeder. 2012. *The social life of avatars: Presence and interaction in shared virtual environments*. Springer Science & Business Media.
12. Harrison Jesse Smith and Michael Neff. 2018. Communication Behavior in Embodied Virtual Reality. (2018).

As Music Goes By in versions and movies along time

Acácio Moreira
LASIGE, Faculdade de Ciências
Universidade de Lisboa
1749-016 Lisboa, Portugal
acacio.moreira@gmail.com

Teresa Chambel
LASIGE, Faculdade de Ciências
Universidade de Lisboa
1749-016 Lisboa, Portugal
tc@di.fc.ul.pt

Abstract

Music and movies have a significant impact in our lives and they have been playing together since the early days of the moving image. Music history on its own goes back till much earlier, and has been present in every known culture. It has also been common for artists to perform and record music originally written and performed by other musicians, since ancient times. In this paper we address the relevance and the support to access music in versions and movies along time, and introduce As Music Goes By, an interactive web application being designed and developed to contribute to this purpose, aiming at increased richness and flexibility, the chance to find unexpected meaningful information, and the support to create and experience music and movies that keep touching us.

Author Keywords

Music; Movies; Versions, Covers and Standards; Time; Genres; Emotions and Mood; Popularity; Hyperlinking; Video; Visualization; Interactive Media Access; Synchronicity and Serendipity.

ACM Classification Keywords

H.1.2. User/Machine Systems: Human factors; H.5.1. Information Interfaces and Presentation (e.g. HCI): Multimedia Information Systems – video, audio; H.5.2. (e.g. HCI): User Interfaces – graphical user interfaces, input devices and strategies, user-centered design.

TVX '18, June 26–28, 2018, SEOUL, Republic of Korea

ACM ISBN 978-1-4503-5115-7/18/06.
https://doi.org/10.1145/3210825.3213567

Concepts

Cover versions, cover songs, or simply covers, have been a quite relevant part of music history [12]. Although technically sonatas and piano concerts, originally from other artists, would also be covers, they do not usually go by that name. The same happening with *Jazz standards*: widely known by listeners and musicians, as an important part of their musical repertoire. It is in pop music and even in traditional folk music that the term *cover* is used more often. For the sake of consistency, we will adopt the terms **cover** and **original versions**, independent of musical genre. Note that the term *version* may refers to both original and cover, but if a song is a version of another one, it is not the original.

Colors	Music Genre
	Classical
	R&B and Soul
	Electronic
	Blues
	Adult Standards
	Jazz
	Easy Listening
	World Music
	Folk
	Country
	Religious
	Comedy
	Movie Scores & Musicals
	Latin
	Rock
	Hip Hop
	Pop

Table 1: As Music Goes By: Color map for genres, in highlight and no-highlight shades.

Introduction

Music has been present in every known culture, and it is a ubiquitous companion to people's everyday lives. Listening to music is one of the most popular yet enigmatic leisure activities. According to [20], people listen to music to regulate arousal and mood, to achieve self-awareness, and as an expression of social relatedness. It affects our cognitive development, influences our perception of taste, can make us feel good, fosters feelings of flow, increases hope, and aids productivity [17]. It is no wonder that we treasure music so much and that it has been created, performed, and recorded since technology has allowed.

It has also been common for artists to perform and record music originally written and performed by other musicians, since ancient times [12]. New artists and bands often start versioning, or covering, their favorite songs, making them their own, on the journey to find their own musical identity. It is also common for artists to inprint their individual style to favorite songs, to revive songs' popularity long after the original version, or even as tributes. There are covers that are career-making or career-breaking, one-hit wonders, and those that become more popular than the original.

Music has always played a significant role in movies, or films, also seen as important sources of entertainment, learning and inspiration, with significant emotional impact [4,15,1]. Music was originally used to enhance mood and aid narrative and meaning, becoming an essential part of the movie itself [7]. Music was written especially for the movies, or consisted of well-known favourites from classical and popular repertoires, gradually leading to a creative industry and theories on how music works with film. Prominent directors like Tarantino and the Coen brothers contributing to a widespread trend of using existing music in movie productions.

In this paper we address the relevance and the support to access music in versions and movies along time, by related work and our own. We also introduce As Music Goes By, an interactive web application we are designing and developing in this context, aiming at increased richness and flexibility, and end with reflections and perspectives for future work.

Related Work

Music Information Retrieval & Visualization became a very relevant area when music digital collections were becoming large. Langer's survey [11] identified motivations, common ideas and techniques to solve main problems, and presented examples. In spite of the lack of "the" best-working method, visualization usually relied on music similarity, hierachical structures, and tracks often based on time-bars along the music; with search methods aiming at Query-By-Example, Query-By-Humming, Query-By-Rhythm, and Query User Interfaces based on parameters or symbolic representations. Musicmap(.info) aims to provide the ultimate genealogy of popular music genres, based on an interactive visualization along time, genre relations, and textual descriptions, aiming at a balance between comprehensibility, accuracy and accessibility. The focus are the genres, in depth, not particular songs or movies. Music Timeline [14] is an interactive visualization tool of artists and genres over the decades, centered around an area chart. It uses aggregated data from Google Play Music to show how artists and genres have gained and dropped popularity. Users can highlight key artists in each genre, read their stories, and listen to the music on Google Play.

SecondHandSongs(.com) claims to be the largest and most accurate database (DB) of cover songs, about who performed the originals and cover or sample versions, songwriters, releases, popularity, videos and

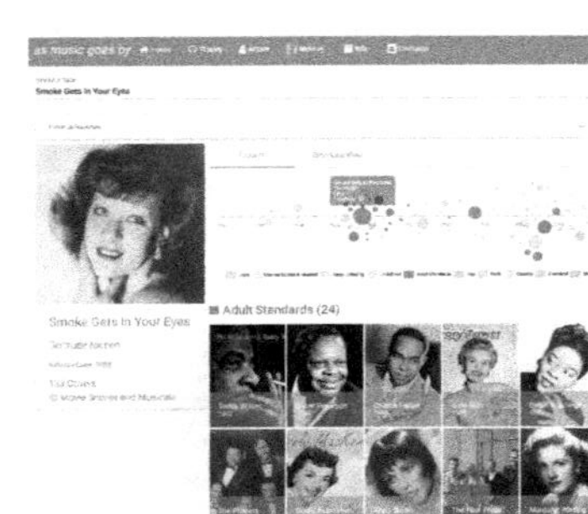

Figure 1- Music View in Timeline Tab: with original version (top, left) for Smoke Gets in Your Eyes; the different versions along time, with circle size for popularity, and color for genre, Adult Standards selected, in blue (top, right); and the list of versions in the selected genre listed by date, in the example (bottom, right).

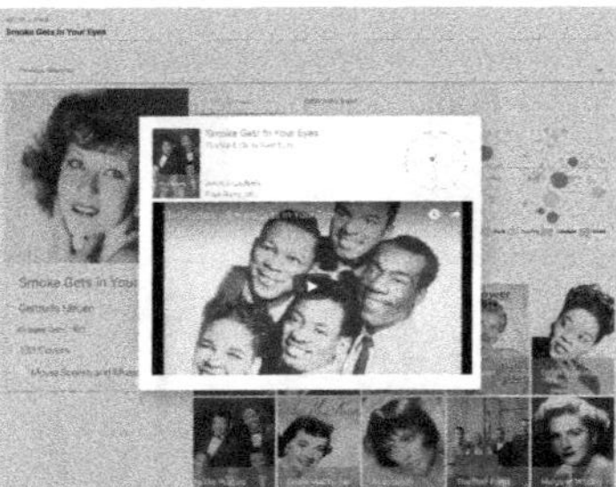

Figure 2 - Music Video Player View: when selected, a version is presented with detailed information (title, artist, date, genre, popularity & mood), and a video from youtybe can be played. In e.g., the most popular (60/100) version. from The Platters. 1958.

web covers. Data is crossreferenced with other DBs, like Discogs, RateYourMusic, Echonest, Spotify, and iTunes. The web interface allows to search by song and by artist. Results are presented in lists that can be explored to watch and listen to the musics. Users can also participate in discussions, contribute to the DB, play quizzes, and compare in a random selection a pair of original and cover song, introducing a touch of surprise to the experience. It involves users in the DB updating, in spite of the work in the area of audio processing for version identification, like [19] that compares the use of different musical representations to demonstrate that: harmony remains the most reliable for version identification, but in some cases melody and bass line descriptions can improve performance. In another perspective, Smule (.com) is about creating social music experiences. It supports creating, sharing, discovering, participating, and connecting with people, around the world, making music and often singing covers in duets. It then allows to search and access all the covers of the same music.

Inskip et al. [8] examined and discussed the classification of commercial popular music for use in films. They analized the metadata used by systems, choices for user queries, and music facets derived from musicological literature on semiotic analysis of popular music, finding that genre, subject and mood are used widely, along some musical facets, in some systems. Previously [7] they had discussed the use and matching of music in films, advertising and TV programs, focusing on communication and meaning of the music, with the aim to inform and improve decision making. Although final decision is partly intuitive and determined by creative professionals, search by content and context was found important. Whatsong (what-song.com), since 2008, provides the official soundtrack and list of songs, from movies and TV shows, with scene descriptions. Can be searched by artists, movies and shows, not songs. Content is generated from admins and users, videos are from youtube, and audio samples from Spotify and iTunes. More recently, Tunefind(.com) (TF) and Sweet Soundtrack(.com) (SS) also find music in TV shows and movies, by author or by shows and movies, not by song. Results are presented in lists, and for each movie or show, song can be accessed from iTunes or Amazon. In addition, SS lists all the songs in each movie, all the movies for each song, and all the songs for each artist, alowing to browse across movies that share the same songs or artists. In TF, the information comes from professionals (Music Supervisors), or may be submitted by users, Tunefind community voting on accuracy. All of them allow to search, sometimes play, but they barely present visualizations for overviews and comparison, and don't support music versions or scene indexing in the movies. With video timelines like those found in video players. On the other side of the spectrum, richer approaches like Story Curves [10] visualize nonlinear narratives of movies by showing the order in which events are told comparing them to their actual chronological order.

Music and movies are among the most used media to improve emotional states. In [3] we present work related with accessing music based on mood, as consumers, like www.rockola.fm. Rothera et al. [22] explored the creator's perspective, in Flutter, an app using music to help those dealing with loss of loved ones, by expressing themselves in a safe, positive environment. In [15,1] we made a literature review of models of emotions, emotional classification of movie content and their impact on viewers, video access and visualization, and eliciting and visualizing emotions. In summary, some related work exists, but not so much allowing to access movies based on emotions. In our own work in iFelt, we addressed movie classification and access based on the emotions felt by

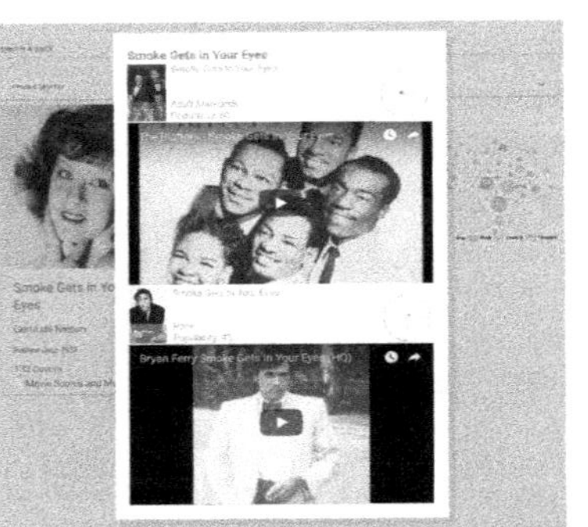

Figure 3 – Music Compare View. A second version was chosen to allow comparison. In the e.g. Bryan's Ferry, 1974, also very popular (45), in rock genre, and more positive emotion (higher valence). Both can be played.

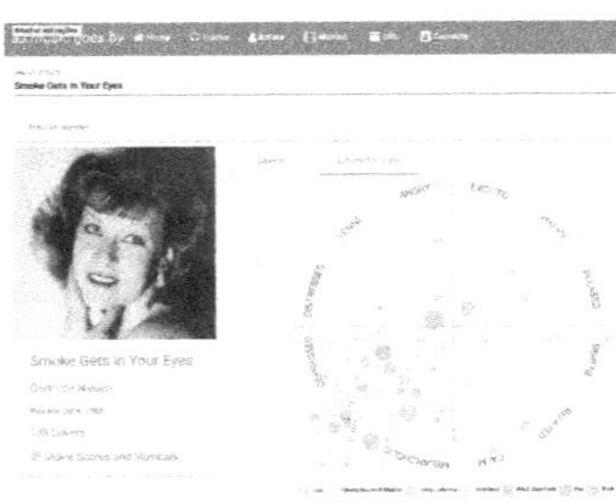

Figure 4 - Music View in Emotions Tab, representing each version in the emotional circumplex, based on valence and energy. Again, circle size used for popularity and color for genre.

the user. Movie Clouds [3] allows to access, explore and watch movies based on their content, mainly in audio, and subtitles, and with a focus on emotions expressed in the subtitles, in the mood of the music, and felt by the users. As a follow-up [9] we enriched the design of interactive spatiotemporal visualizations to enhance movie browsing, and in Media4Wellbeing [1] we are taking a step further to include other media (also music) and the sense of wellbeing.

As Music Goes By

This interactive web application is being designed and developed to allow users to search, visualize and explore music and movies from complementary perspectives that highlight the music in its different versions, the artists, and the movie soundtracks they belong to. Relevant properties are highlighted, including popularity, genre and emotional impact. It is possible to compare versions of the same song, see which songs or artists have more versions, find the original versions, performers and authors, see the mood of the songs, and the movies and scenes they appear in. At all times, the user can listen to and watch the music clips of the songs, and access and watch the movie scenes where they play.

Music Genres and Colors

We defined 17 genres to aggregate from the Spotify API subgenres (table 1). We used the list in [13], and aggregated the less known regional music in World Music. Three new genres were added: Adult Standards, since they may be linked with different genres, and the Religious and Movie Scores & Musicals. In a UC Berkeley study [16], participants consistently picked bright, vivid, warm colors to go with upbeat music, and dark, dull, cool colors to match the more somber pieces. According to [6] color-genre mapping is not consistent, probably due to cultural bias. We do not aim at providing a definite mapping, but to adopt a consistent one that is aligned with previous work and what is commonly accepted or familiar. The genres were colored according to [16] and partially [6], and text labels used to help identification.

Emotion Representation and Visualization

We adopt Russell's circumplex [18,1], based on the valence and arousal dimensional model for emotions. The position of each song is determined by the audio features of Valence (for valence) and Energy (for arousal) provided by the Spotify API [21], and described as: Valence (0-1), the musical positiveness conveyed. High valence sounds more positive (happy, cheerful or euphoric) and low valence sounds more negative (sad, depressed or angry); and Energy (0-1), a perceptual measure of intensity and activity. Typically, energetic songs feel fast, loud, and noisy. Perceptual features contributing to this attribute include dynamic range, perceived loudness, timbre, onset rate, and general entropy.

Views and Interaction

The home page provides users with overview visualizations for a high level perception of the relations between artists, versions and music genres, the proportion and evolution of genres, popularity, and covers vs originals along time. The users can also search and browse the results and the interactive visualizations to access more detailed views.

These views are presented and described in the figures. Here we provide a brief overview. Figs.1-4 present the Music View, accessed when users selects one music/song, Smoke Gets in Your Eyes in this case. The user is presented with tabs for different perspectives. Once the user clicks a genre, the versions in that genre are displayed in a list below, with title and background in the genre color (e.g. Adult Standards, with 24 versions, in blue). Timeline and list are synchronized, on over a

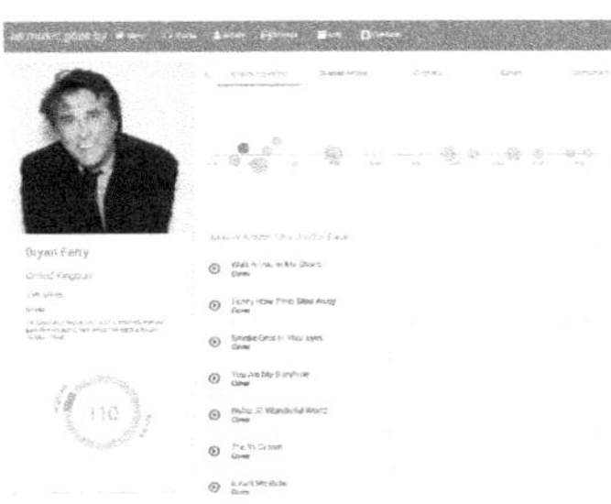

Figure 5 – Artist View in Album Timeline Tab. On the left, personal data (photo, name, country, birth), all the genres, percentage and number of covers and originals, with more details on over; on the rigth, the tab for the album timeline, showing albums released by this artist along time, with popularity represented by size of the circles (top);
and the list of tracks for the selected/clicked album, highlighting if it is a cover or an original version (bottom). From this view, users can access all the songs that Bryan authored or covered (in different tabs), and all the movies that have any of his versions. All views allowing to play and compare musics, and access related views of Music, Artists and Movies.

song in the list highlights that song in the timeline and the other way around. When the user clicks on one song (e.g. cover by The Platters), it opens a Player View with more details about the song and a vídeo that can be played (Fig.2). The user can also compare two versions (Fig.3), by selecting them in the list or the timeline. Fig.4 presents Music View in Emotions tab.

In the Artists View, overviews and search are available. Selecting an artist leads to the Artist View (Fig.5). In the Movies Views, users have overviews and search for movie soundtracks, giving access to Movie Views (Figs.6-7). To allow easy exploration of the songs, users can click on songs titles, artist names or movie titles anywhere on the application to access the detailed views.

Architecture and Technologies

A three tier architecture is used, with Data Layer (Mongo DB, external APIs), Business Logic Layer (NodeJS, Express) and Presentation Layer (AngularJS, D3). It relies on external REST APIs to collect data, at this point from Spotify (tracks, artists, albums, images, popularity and audio features) and SecondHandSongs (original and cover versions, and YouTube links for the songs).

Reflections and Perspectives

This paper presented As Music Goes By, a web application being designed and developed with the aim to propose a richer way to access and relate music and movies along time. The way we see it differing from and contributing to the scenario of existing applications is trough flexibility and richness. We propose to add the ability to interact with visualizations that provide overviews and alow to navigate music in its different versions and genres, the artists and the movies they play in, along time. The time when each music was created, versioned, and featured in the movies; and the time inside each movie, when they are actually played and can be watched in context. There is also a focus on genres, emotions and popularity, reflecting the impact that these media have on us, and following on our previous work on movies, media and wellbeing [1].

For the future, we plan to refine, evaluate and extend the interactive features being designed. To develop visualizations further, with more integrated overviews, enrich relations among music (versions, genres, and albums),artists and movies, making it easy to go through, relate and find them based on common features (e.g. artists that covered the same music or musician, or songs that appear in similar movies, or songs created or popular at the times along the narratives of the movies, following up on [10]), increasing the chances and opportunities to find unexpected meaningful information, by chance, synchronicity or serendipity [2]. This could be enhanced by richer content processing (e.g. subtitles, lyrics, quotes, and audio) [3], and emotional impact [1]; and the flexibility of access from diverse media, modalities and contexts, e.g. while listening to a music (identifying the version, like in Shazan, through query by example, or by humming); or when feeling blue; or while watching a movie or music clip, to reach at related or recommended information.

A challenge is the way to collect and maintain this huge information space, and we see it as an evolution of current databases and services, relying on information processing, professionals and users for contributions, e.g. Secondhand Songs and [5]. We envision a service that can be valuable for everyone, the general public, interested in music and movies, for entertainment, curiosity and inspiration, as well as to professionals and content creators, e.g. to raise awareness about the way music has evolved and has been used in movies, and as a support to help them choose or create music and movies that keep touching us.

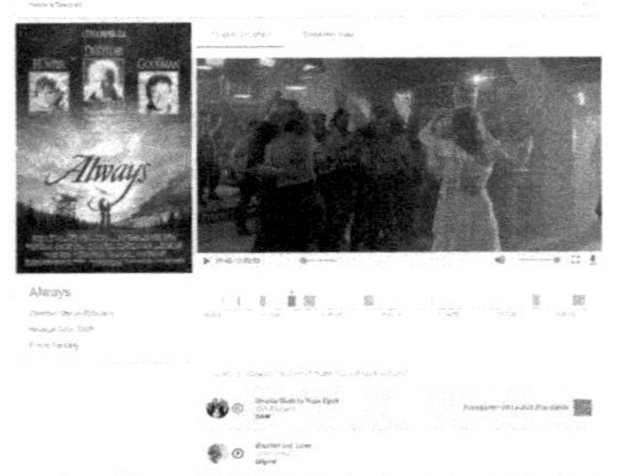

Figure 6 - Movie View in Timeline Tab, for Always. highlighting Smoke Gets in Your Eyes in the soundtrack, in The Platters' version. Soundtrack lists titles, artists, cover/original, popularity and genre (bottom), synchronized with the timeline, representing when each song plays, highlighting current one, and allowing to index and play them (top).

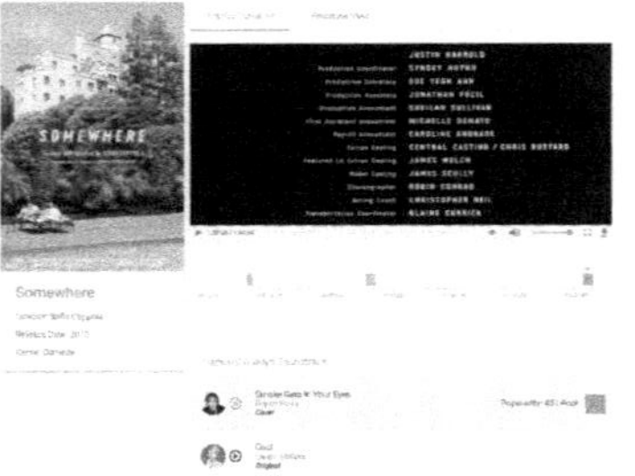

Figure 7 - Movie View for Somewhere. highlighting Smoke Gets in Your Eyes in Bryan Ferry's version.

Acknowledgements

This work is partially supported by FCT through LASIGE funding ref.UID/CEC/00408/2013, and by FCT and MCE Portugal (PIDDAC) under grant UID/BIO/00645/2013.

References

1. Bernardino, C., Ferreira, H.A., and Chambel, T. 2016. Towards Media for Wellbeing. In *Proc. of ACM TVX' 2016*, ACM. 171-177.
2. Chambel, T. 2011. Towards Serendipity and Insights in Movies and Multimedia. In *Proc. of Intern. Workshop on Encouraging Serendipity in Interactive Systems*. Interact'2011. 12-16.
3. Chambel, T., Langlois, T., Martins, P., Gil, N., Silva, N., and Duarte, E. 2013. Content-Based Search Overviews and Exploratory Browsing of Movies with MovieClouds. *IJAMC*, InderScience, 5(1): 58-79.
4. Chambel, T., Oliveira, E., and Martins, P. 2011. Being Happy, Healthy and Whole Watching Movies that Affect our Emotions. *Proc. of ACII 2011*, 35-45.
5. Gomes, J.M.A., Chambel, T., and Langlois, T. 2013. SoundsLike: Movies Soundtrack Browsing and Labeling Based on Relevance Feedback and Gamification", In *Proc. of EuroiTV'2013*, ACM, 59-62.
6. Holm, J., and Siirtola, H. 2012. A Comparison of Methods for Visualizing Musical Genres. Proc. of 16th International Conference on Information Visualisation, 636-645.
7. Inskip, C., MacFarlane, A., and Rafferty, P. 2008. Music, movies and meaning: communication in film-markers' search for pre-existing music, and the implications for music information retrieval. *Proceedings of ISMIR' 2008*, 477-482.
8. Inskip, C., MacFarlane, A., and Rafferty, P. 2010. Organising music for movies. *Aslib Proceedings*, 62(4/5), 489-501.
9. Jorge, A., Correia, N., and Chambel, T. 2017. Designing Interactive Spatiotemporal Visualizations to Enhance Movie Browsing. *Proc. of Interact*. 352-5.
10. Kim, N.,W., Bach, B., Im, H., Schriber, S., Gross, M., and Pfiste, H. 2018. Visualizing Nonlinear Narratives with Story Curves. *IEEE Trans. on Visualization and Computer Graphics*,24(1):595–604.
11. Langer, T. 2010. Music information retrieval & visualization. *Trends in Information Visualization*.
12. Maehner, J. 2015. Under The Covers: Second Hand Songs That Matter, *Cuepoint*. Retrieved April 2nd, 2018 from: https://medium.com/cuepoint/under-the-covers-5ffe85ac96d0
13. Music Genres List. Retrvd Feb 2, 2018: https://en.wikipedia.org/wiki/List_of_popular_music_genres
14. Music Timeline https://music-timeline.appspot.com
15. Oliveira, E., Martins, P., and Chambel, T. 2013. Accessing Movies Based on Emotional Impact. *ACM/Springer Multimedia Systems Journal,* ISSN: 0942-4962, 19(6), Nov. 559-576.
16. Palmer, S. E., Schloss, K.B., Xu, Z., and Prado-León, L. R. 2013. Music–color associations are mediated by emotion. Proceedings of the National Academy of Sciences.
17. Reflectd. 2014. The Psychology of Music: Why We Listen to Music and How It Affects The Mind. http://reflectd.co/2014/06/17/the-psychology-of-music
18. Russell J., (1980) A circumplex model of affect. *Journal of Personality and Social Psychology*, 39:1161–1178.
19. Salamon, J., Serrà, J., and Gómez, E. , Melody, 2012. Bass Line, and Harmony Representations for Music Version Identification. In AdMIRe'12 Workshop: "The Web of Music". *Proc. of WWW 2012 Companion*, ACM, 887-894.
20. Schäfer, T., Sedlmeier, P., Städtler, C. and Huron, D. 2013. The psychological functions of music listening. Front. Psychol. 4:511.
21. Spotify Audio Features. https://developer.spotify.com/web-api/get-audio-features/
22. Stinson, E. 2015. A Music-Making APP Designed to Help Teens Deal with Death, *WIRED*, Design 1(15).

ImAc: Enabling Immersive, Accessible and Personalized Media Experiences

Mario Montagud
I2CAT Foundation
Barcelona, Spain
mario.montagud@i2cat.net

Juan A. Nuñez
I2CAT Foundation
Barcelona, Spain
juan.antonio.nunez@i2cat.net

Isaac Fraile
I2CAT Foundation
Barcelona, Spain
isaac.fraile@i2cat.net

Sergi Fernández
I2CAT Foundation
Barcelona, Spain
sergi.fernandez@i2cat.net

TVX '18, June 26–28, 2018, SEOUL, Republic of Korea

ACM ISBN 978-1-4503-5115-7/18/06.
https://doi.org/10.1145/3210825.3213570

Abstract
The integration of immersive contents and consumption devices within the TV landscape brings new fascinating opportunities. However, the exploitation of these immersive TV services is still in its infancy and ground-breaking solutions need to be devised. A key challenge is to enable truly inclusive experiences, regardless of the sensorial and cognitive capacities of the users, their age and language. In this context, ImAc project explores how accessibility services (subtitling, audio description and sign language) can be efficiently integrated with immersive media, such as omnidirectional and Virtual Reality (VR) contents, while keeping compatibility with current standards and technologies. This paper provides an overview of the project, by focusing on its motivation, the followed user-centered methodology and its key research objectives. The end-to-end system (from production to consumption) being specified, the envisioned scenarios and planned evaluations are also briefly described.

Author Keywords
Accessibility Services, Immersive Media, Multi-Screen Scenarios, Spatial Audio, Subtitles, Virtual Reality.

ACM Classification Keywords
Information systems applications: Information systems applications

ImAc: Immersive Accessibility

Goal: Seamless integration between accessibility services and immersive media, by enabling personalization and keeping compatibility with current technologies and standards.

Immersive Contents: High-Resolution Media, 360º Video, and Spatial Audio.

Accessibility Contents: subtitling, audio description, and sign language interpreting. Assistive technologies (e.g. voice recognition, guiding mechanisms). Adapted User Interfaces (UI). Personalization.

Use Cases: Single- and Multi-Screen Scenarios, combining traditional and VR consumption devices.

Figure 1: ImAc logo.

Introduction

Research on TV-related content consumption is being intense in the last years. One of the most active research topics consists of enabling successful and coherent multi-screen experiences (e.g. [1, 8, 9]). A step beyond, the integration of omnidirectional contents and devices within the TV landscape can open the door to new fascinating scenarios (e.g. [3]).

These customizable, interactive and immersive multi-screen TV experiences can increase the users' engagement, but also bring new challenges. A key requirement of every emerging media technology and scenario is to consider accessibility, in order to ensure a proper narrative, interpretation of contents and usability, regardless of the sensorial and cognitive capacities of the users, their age, language, and/or other specific impairments and difficulties. This will contribute to a global e-inclusion, offering equal opportunities of access to the whole consumers' spectrum, while ensuring compliance with regulatory guidelines (e.g. Human Rights Obligations). In this context, subtitles play a key role in TV-related scenarios to better interpret the audiovisual contents. Previous works have targeted at proposing solutions for an adaptive and customizable presentation of subtitles, even in multi-screen scenarios (e.g. [6, 7]) and for 360º videos (e.g. [2]). However, many challenges still need to be overcome in order to efficiently integrate accessibility services (not only subtitling, but also audio subtitling, sign language interpreting and audio description) in immersive environments.

ImAc is a H2020 European project (www.imac-project.eu), October 2017-March 2020, that explores how accessibility services can be efficiently integrated with immersive media, such as omnidirectional and Virtual Reality (VR) contents, while keeping compatibility with current standards and technologies. The idea of ImAc is not to consider accessibility as an afterthought, but as a key aspect in the specification and deployment of end-to-end immersive systems and services. It involves overcoming existing limitations in current technologies and systems in order to enable truly inclusive, immersive and personalized multi-screen experiences, adapted to the particular needs and/or preferences of the consumers.

Among others, ImAc aims at providing efficient solutions and/or meaningful insights to the following research questions:

- What are the requirements in order to enable truly accessible and inclusive immersive services?
- How current (immersive) technologies and systems can be augmented in order to seamlessly integrate and support accessibility services?
- What personalization features should be provided in order to meet particular users' needs and/or preferences?
- To what extent accessibility services in immersive environments contribute to a higher e-inclusion and to equal opportunities?
- What scenarios and use cases would be (more) benefited by a seamless integration between immersive and accessibility services?
- What kind of assistive technologies should be adopted?
- Which presentation modes for accessibility contents are better suited in the envisioned scenarios?

Presentation of Accessibility Contents in Immersive Environments:

A proper presentation of accessibility contents when consuming immersive media can contribute to a higher e-inclusion, but is more complex than for traditional media. On the one hand, there is more information to process and users can get overwhelmed. On the other hand, the presentation is no longer purely time-based, but involves a spatial dimension, determined either by the user's viewing point or by the direction where the main action is taking place. Therefore, proper presentation modes will be considered to assist to a higher comprehension and to guide users. The most proper presentation modes may depend on the specific users' profiles, their sensorial capacities and preferences. Therefore, adaptability and personalization become essential in this context.

- What are the comfortable viewing fields for accessibility contents, especially when using Head Mounted Displays (HMDs)?
- What benefits are provided (e.g., in terms of usability, content comprehension, level of immersion and engagement...)? How to properly evaluate and determine them?

The remaining of the paper provides a brief overview of the ImAc project. Its relationship with other related projects is indicated in Section 2. The employed methodology is described in Section 3. The end-to-end system to be specified and implemented, focusing on the consumer side, is introduced in Section 4. The envisioned scenarios, use cases and pilot evaluations are then presented in Section 5. Finally, conclusions and the planned roadmap are provided in Section 6.

Relationship with other Projects

ImAc departs from the expertise, insights and contributions from other recent related projects. On the one hand, HbbTV4all project has addressed accessibility in the emerging connected hybrid broadcast broadband media ecosystem, within the umbrella of Hybrid Broadcast Broadband TV (HbbTV) standard [4]. ImAc seeks the same success story within immersive environments. On the other hand, ImmersiaTV targets at overcoming existing challenges to enable customizable and immersive multi-screen TV experiences. By considering the current heterogeneity in terms of contents and consumption devices, with a special focus on omnidirectional media, ImmersiaTV proposes backward-compatible and standard-compliant re-definitions to the end-to-end chain to make these new experiences a reality.

Methodology

ImAc is built around three 3 pillars: 1) requirements gathering, 2) development and integration; and 3) validation and dissemination. A simplified diagram of the chosen methodology is illustrated in Figure 1. It must be remarked that the project follows a user-centric approach, in which end-users, professional users and stakeholders are involved since the beginning of the project through the organization of workshops, focus groups, evaluations, and the attendance to events. This allows determining with higher precision the accessibility requirements, desired features and scenarios, as well as the required new technologies or extensions to existing ones in order to maximize usability and deployment. The ImAc platform specification, services to be developed, in addition to the deployed pilots, will be based on the gathered insights from the user-centric activities.

The pilots and evaluations will allow validating the contributions and results, but also refining the gathered requirements, functionalities and architecture of the ImAc platform.

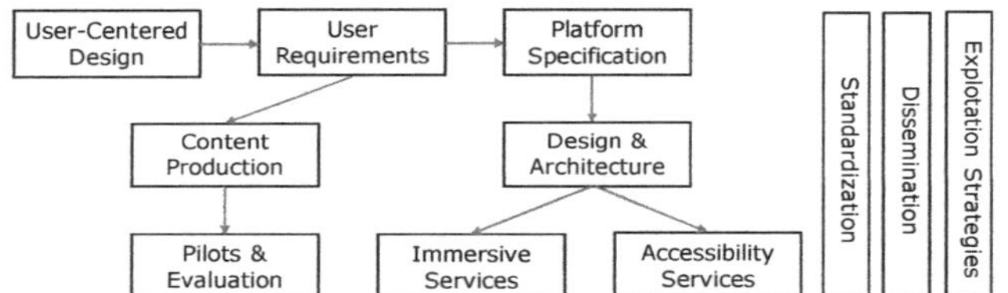

Figure 1: Methodology followed in ImAc.

End-to-End ImAc System

This section provides an overview of the end-to-end ImAc system specification and functionalities, derived from the functional requirements gathered in the conducted user-centric activities and their transformation into technical requirements. Exhaustive details about the architecture, components and modules of the system are not provided, as they are still being currently specified. Basically, the system is divided into four parts (Figure 2): production/edition, management, preparation/distribution and consumption. The key modules / functional blocks in these parts are indicated in Figure 2, where green color indicates these components are under the umbrella of ImAc, orange indicates they have been developed in other projects (e.g. ImmersiaTV), and white that are out-of-scope of the project, but form part of the end-to-end workflow in typical systems.

Content Production: tools for the production, authoring and edition of accessibility contents, and for their integration with classical and immersive media services. It includes the definition of metadata and signalization to be provided to the Service Prover part.

Service Provider: where the management of programs is handled, including Media Asset Management (MAM), linking of additional contents to main TV programs and scheduling playout.

Content Preparation & Distribution: handles distribution via various technologies. This part covers content encoding and packaging, signalization, and distribution via DVB and IP-based CDNs (e.g. using DASH [5]).

Content Consumption: includes all required components for the presentation of the available ImAc contents, including traditional, immersive and accessibility contents, to end-users. In ImAc, traditional TV contents will be played out on connected TVs. The immersive (360º videos and spatial audio) and accessibility contents will be played out on companion screens (e.g., tablets, HMDs...) via a web-based player being developed. The player will support different presentation modes and include customization options. Different interaction functionalities and modalities will be also provided. In addition, inter-media and inter-device sync functionalities will be provided to enable a time-aligned presentation of all contents across the involved devices. A high-level overview of the components of the ImAc player is provided in Figure 3.

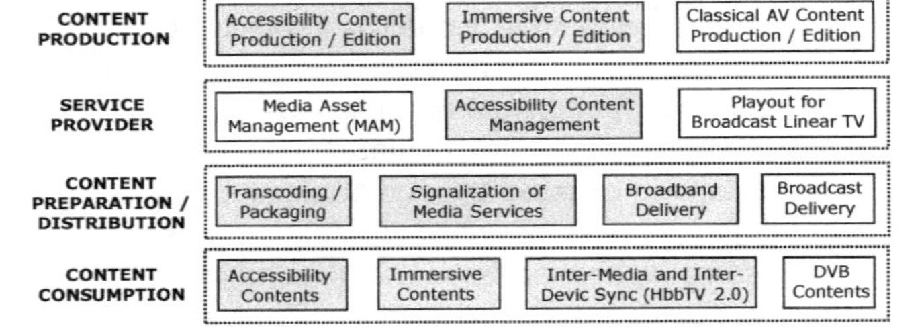

Figure 2: Main components of the ImAc system.

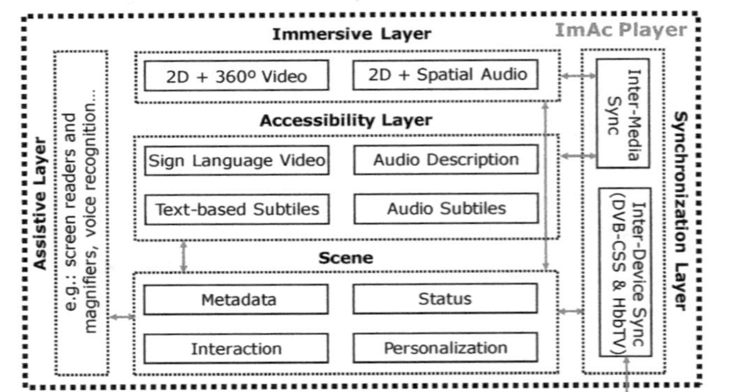

Figure 3: Main Components of the ImAc player.

Scenarios and Pilots

ImAc considers both single- and multi-screen scenarios, composed of a main TV and companion screens (e.g., tablets, smartphones, HMDs). In the latter scenarios, proper discovery, association, app launching and media sync solutions will be provided (Figure 4).

The user-centered activities will determine the contents to be created, specific scenarios to be developed and demonstration pilots to be set up (Figure 1). As part of its objectives, ImAc will perform two (large scale and open) national pilots plus a cross-national one.

In addition, in a joint initiative with ImmersiaTV, ImAc has participated in an extra pilot: an immersive recording of "Roméo et Juliette" at the Gran Teatre del Liceu Opera House, in Barcelona. The goal is to create a ground-breaking product that allows consumers enjoying an opera performance in a highly interactive, immersive, personalized and accessible manner. In particular, multiple video cameras (4 360º, 2 320º, 4 170º, and 5 directive cameras) and more than 80 audio sources (including 3D –Ambisonics– and binaural formats), distributed both on and off the stage, were used in the recording. This allows experiencing the opera performance from the preferred viewpoint, using the preferred media formats and devices, and being able to dynamically switch between viewpoints and devices. In relation to this, the presented audio matches the selected camera position and current viewpoint, providing detailed sound landscapes and thus highly immersive and realistic experiences. Finally, a customizable, adaptive and assistive presentation of accessibility contents related to the 360º videos is also supported. Regarding subtitles, different colors for each speaker can be added, and different font sizes and languages can be dynamically selected. Subtitles are, by default, presented at the bottom region, as in typical video players. However, it is also possible to present them at the top region of the player (Figure 5). This presentation option is known as super-titles or surtitles, and is typically used and preferred in musical and theatre performances. In order to properly identify the active speaker(s) and main actions while freely exploring the 360º area, different guiding mechanisms are provided, such as adding arrows, a compass, or sided text. Similar guiding mechanisms are also provided for sign language (Figure 6) and audio description. The playback of all the selected contents will be accurately synchronized, regardless on the number and types of consumption devices being used in multi-screen scenarios (Figure 7). A demo video can be watched at: https://goo.gl/xpqVPF

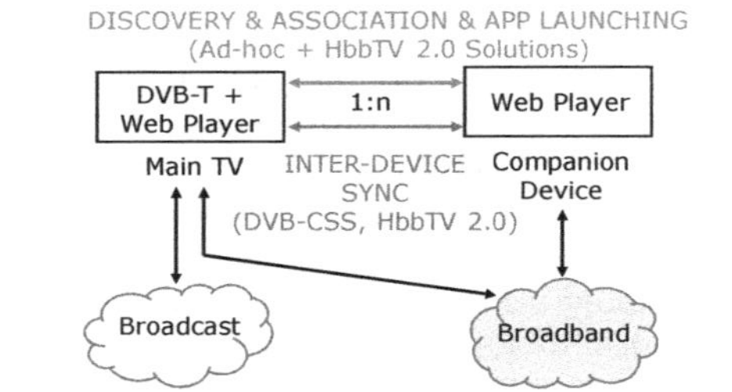

Figure 4: Functionalities in the multi-screen scenarios.

Figure 5: Presentation of Subtitles in 360º Environments.

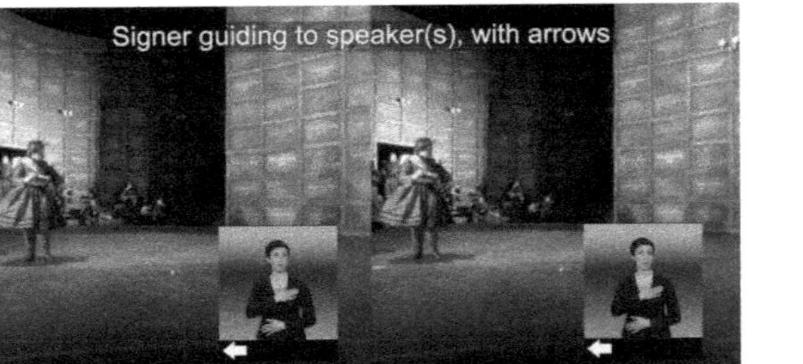

Figure 6: Presentation of Sign Language Videos in 360º Environments.

Figure 7: Immersive, Accessible and Personalized Multi-Screen Scenarios considered in ImAc.

Conclusions and Future Work

This paper has provided an overview of the ImAc project, by focusing on its motivation, the followed user-centered methodology and its key research objectives. The end-to-end system being specified, the envisioned scenarios and planned evaluations have been also briefly described. As the project advances in time, it is expected to refine the research objectives and plan, to achieve relevant contributions and to reach a big impact.

Acknowledgements

This work has been funded by European Union's Horizon 2020 program, under agreement nº 761974 (ImAc project).

References

1. F. Boronat, D. Marfil, M. Montagud, J. Pastor, "HbbTV-Compliant Platform for Hybrid Media Delivery and Synchronization on Single- and Multi-Device Scenarios", IEEE Transactions on Broadcasting, vol. PP, no. 99, pp. 1-26, 2017.
2. A. Brown, J. Turner, J. Patterson, A. Schmitz, M. Armstrong, M. Glancy, "Subtitles in 360-degree Video", ACM TVX '17, June 2017.
3. D. Gómez, J.A. Núñez, M. Montagud, S. Fernández, "ImmersiaTV: Enabling Customizable and Immersive Multi-Screen TV Experiences", ACM MMSYS'18, June 2018.
4. Hybrid Broadcast Broadband TV (HbbTV) 2.0.1 Specification, HbbTV Association Resource Library, https://www.hbbtv.org/resource-library, July 2016.
5. ISO/IEC 23009-1: 2012. Information Technology. Dynamic Adaptive Streaming over HTTP (DASH). Part 1: Media Presentation Description and Segment Formats. April 2012.
6. M. Montagud, F. Boronat, J. González, J. Pastor, "Web-based Platform for Subtitles Customization and Synchronization in Multi-Screen Scenarios", ACM TVX '17, June 2017.
7. A. Rodriguez, G. Talavera, P. Orero, J. Carrabina "Subtitle Synchronization across Multiple Screens and Devices", Sensors, 12(7), June 2012
8. V. Vinayagamoorthy, R. Ramdhany, M. Hammond, "Enabling Frame-Accurate Synchronised Companion Screen Experiences", ACM TVX '16, June 2016.
9. C. Ziegler, et al., "On Time or Not on Time: A User Study on Delays in a Synchronised Companion-Screen Experience", ACM TVX '17, June 2017.

Care TVX: Challenges and Design to Improve TV in In-Hospital Environment and for Visually Impaired People

Toinon Vigier
LS2N UMR CNRS 6003
Université de Nantes
Nantes, France
toinon.vigier@univ-nantes.fr

Patrick Le Callet
LS2N UMR CNRS 6003
Université de Nantes
Nantes, France
patrick.lecallet@univ-nantes.fr

Jieun Kim
Imagine X lab
Hanyang University
Seoul, South Korea
jkim2@hanyang.ac.kr

Hokyoung Ryu
Imagine X lab, Hanyang University
Seoul, South Korea
hryu@hanyang.ac.kr

Seongil Lee
Sungkyunkwan University
Suwon, South Korea
silee@skku.edu

ABSTRACT

The overarching goal of this workshop is to bring together practices and research in medical fields with media contents developers, designers, and UI/UX/QoE researchers, as well as hospital practitioners as ophthalmologists and psychiatrists. Discussions will relate to:

- how new visual experience and media contents can improve the in-hospital experience of in-patients, caregivers, and medical staffs;
- how better understanding of visual impairments (e.g. for elderly) can help to design more inclusive TV experience.

The starting point will be the cases and experiences of Care TVX, followed by a multidisciplinary discussion on "challenges and design considerations to adjusted or new hospital and care practices", led by workshop participants. The outcome of the workshop will be a collection of best practices in the form of position papers and online content.

Author Keywords

Care; Hospital Environment; In-patient experience; Visual impairments; Immersive Media & Visual Contents; Co-Design

ACM Classification Keywords

Human-centered computing---Human computer interaction (HCI)---Accessibility---Accessibility technologies; 500.

TVX '18, June 26–28, 2018, SEOUL, Republic of Korea

ACM ISBN 978-1-4503-5115-7/18/06.
https://doi.org/10.1145/3210825.3213551

INTRODUCTION

An increasingly rich range of features and functionality is now available through smart televisions, interactive and immersive multimedia. These new technologies disrupt most of our social and individual attitudes, practices and experiences in everyday life, at home, at work or at school, in transport, etc. What about in hospital and for aged patient population?

1. Television has long been the primary form of in-room entertainment in hospital. However, surprisingly, there has been limited research and practices examining how TV can help improve care environment tailored to patients. Using new interactive TV screen and media contents, patients and care-givers can watch both clinical and non-clinical channels, make requests across the spectrum of hospital services, view appointment, use the internet- among other features. Along with significant benefit, the new technology brings new challenges and considerations for adjusted or new practices in hospital. Part of the workshop aims to address how new TV and media contents can improve the in-hospital experience of in-patients, caregivers, and medical staffs.
2. With ageing population, epidemiology studies report increases of both DLMA and Glaucoma cases, with consequences of loss of either peripheral or foveal vision. At the age of immersive media stressing more and more visual field, such visual impairments must be better understood to avoid digital exclusion and adopt ad hoc mitigation solutions.

Our half-day workshop on "Care TVX now playing" will bring together media contents developers, designers, and UI/UX researchers, and medical staffs.

WORKSHOP TOPICS

This workshop will present a selection of high quality position papers and demos addressing, but not limited to, the following topics:

- Co-design methodologies (with health care professionals and patients) for interaction design in hospital
- New multimedia and visual experiences (interactive visit, serious-games, immersive and interactive environments...) to improve in-patient experience (social engagement between in-patients and medical staffs, in-patient well-being and empowerment, better acceptation of medical acts and treatments...)
- Multimedia and interactive services to assess in-patient physical and mental state
- Studies of foveal and peripheral vision impairments, impact on immersive media experience
- New VR opportunities for visually impaired and elderly populations
- UX and QoE studies for Care TVX.

FORMAT AND DURATION

- Welcome and Introduction of participants

Welcome of workshop organizers with a brief introduction to the workshop topics. Short introduction of the workshop participants.

- Session 1: New TVX in hospital context
  - Paper 1: Value Sensitive Design for Clinical Dashboard in the Medical Context
  - Paper 2: New VR and AR experiences for the personalization of care in psychiatry: the example of ReViSTIM-X project
- Session 2: New TVX and accessibility for visually impaired people
  - Keynote 1: Accessibility Standards of TV and multimedia contents
  - Keynote 2: Visual attention in TVX: impact of retinal deficiencies
  - Keynote 3 & Industry Demo: Samsung Relúmĩno Project Demo: smarter vision for partially sighted people with Gear VR headset
- Panel Discussion & Wrap-up

The workshop provides an open forum for the discussion on and advancement of the state of the art. It highlights areas the industry needs to address in terms of practice, standards and recommendations.

WORKSHOP ORGANIZERS

Toinon Vigier obtained a PhD in July 2015 from the Ecole Centrale de Nantes in the Ambiances Architectures and Urbanity lab, where she focused on virtual reality for urban studies. She was then a postdoctoral fellow in the Image Video and Communication team at Université de Nantes. She worked mainly on video quality in the European project UltraHD-4U. Since September 2016, she is an Associate Professor at Université de Nantes in the Image Perception Interaction research team of the Laboratory of Digital Sciences in Nantes (LS2N). Her research mainly focuses on the study, the analysis and the prediction of the quality of experience for immersive and interactive multimedia. Her research mainly focuses on the study, the analysis and the prediction of the quality of experience for immersive and interactive multimedia. She is also involved in a lot of interdisciplinary research projects gathering computer scientists with designers, artists, psychiatrists or psychologists.

Patrick Le Callet is a Professor at Université de Nantes (Polytech Nantes, Engineering School) in the Image Perception Interaction research team of the Laboratory of Digital Sciences in Nantes (LS2N). Since January 2017, he is one of the seven members of the steering Board the CNRS LS2N lab (450 researchers), as representative of Polytech Nantes. He is also since 2015 the scientific director of the cluster "West Creative Industries", a five-year program gathering more than 10 institutions (including 3 universities). "West Creative Industries" aims to strengthen Research, Education & Innovation of the Region Pays de Loire in the field of Creative Industries. His current centers of interest are Quality of Experience assessment, Visual Attention modeling and applications, Perceptual Video Coding and Immersive Media Processing. He is co-author of more than 250 publications and communications and co-inventor of 16 international patents on these topics.

Jieun Kim is an Assistant Professor at the Graduate School of Technology and Innovation Management, and jointly affiliated with the Department of Arts & Technology, at Hanyang University in Korea. She received the M.S and Ph.D. degrees in Industrial Engineering from Arts et Métiers ParisTech in 2008 and 2011, respectively. Her current research focuses on Human-Computer Interaction in medical fields. The interests include rehabilitation design for the elderly, patient empowerment, and caring systems in hospital environment.

Hokyoung Ryu is a Professor in Department of Arts \& Technology at Hanyang University. His research interest includes Practitioner's HCI and designing issues, cognitive information design, and learning technology and game-based learning (e.g., serious games) finding creative and innovative outputs thus far.

Seongil Lee is a Professor at the department of systems management engineering of sungkyunkwan university in suwon, korea. He holds a ph.d. degree in industrial engineering from the university of Wisconsin-Madison in 1995. His areas of interest are human factors engineering, human-computer interaction, and universal design in ICT.

360° Video Storytelling and Virtual Reality Workshop

Lily Díaz-Kommonen
Media Lab Helsinki
Aalto University, Finland
lily.diaz@aalto.fi

Mirjam Vosmeer
Amsterdam University of Applied Sciences
The Netherlands
m.s.vosmeer@hva.nl

Ji-Hye Lee
Media Lab. Seoul
Republic of Korea
jihyelee1129@hotmail.com

Stefan Pham
Fraunhofer FOKUS, Germany
stefan.pham@fokus.fraunhofer.de

Louay Bassbouss
Fraunhofer FOKUS, Germany
louay.bassbouss@fokus.fraunhofer.de

Andrea Mancianti
Media Lab Helsinki
Aalto University, Finland
andrea.mancianti@aalto.fi

ABSTRACT

The purpose of this joint workshop is to bring together a diverse group of researchers and practitioners for focused discussion and knowledge sharing in 360° video storytelling and virtual reality.

Author Keywords
Virtual Reality; Television, 360 video streaming; Storytelling

ACM Classification Keywords
Human-centred computing---Human computer interaction (HCI)---Interaction paradigms---Virtual reality;500.

INTRODUCTION

The purpose of this joint workshop is to gather together a diverse group of researchers and practitioners working in 360° video storytelling and virtual reality. During the morning session, researchers from three different institutions present an overview of their work on VR and the practical and theoretical issues that they have been confronted with. Five participants will then be invited to present the paper that they have sent in for this workshop. In the afternoon sessions, participants can choose to focus on one of the three workshop themes that are introduced below. In the final part of this full day workshop, all researchers will join forces again to discuss the outcomes of their explorations.

Virtual Reality Workshop

In virtual reality, embodiment seems to be an active topic of discussion among the engineers, scientists and the artists and designers. From a new media perspective, the questions emerge such as how much attention should we pay to the user? How to 'construct' a working vision of who the user is? How does this affect the way we work (e.g. the way that we gather data and the way this might influence the resulting applications?). These are interesting questions to ponder when developing user studies in virtual reality. In this session we will use participatory design method to generate a research and development agenda; the research questions that we must answer and the techniques and designs that we would like to invent in order to maximize the value of integrating user's active engagement and virtual reality environment. Therefore, we will investigate themes about embodiment in VR including aspects of cognitive enhancement, physical sense and interaction between multiple bodies and agents.

Virtual Reality Meets Television

In this session we aim to collaboratively develop an (imaginary) concept for a VR experience that could accompany an existing television show. This workshop is intended for both students and professionals working in creative industries. During the session, the focus will be on developing and analyzing concepts and narratives, rather than on dealing with technical issues. By discussing the 'do's' and 'don'ts' for producing VR content we will gather insights into how different audiences may engage with VR and how virtual reality can be used to create mixed media experiences that allow audiences to enjoy their favorite television shows from a new perspective.

360° Video Streaming & Storytelling Workshop

360° streaming covers the content preparation, delivery and consumption of 360° video material. 360° video can be consumed on any device, whether it's a head-mounted display (HMD), TV set or a second-screen device. This part of the workshop addresses the challenges heterogeneity of devices, network characteristics and interaction methods. For example, streaming latency and user input are different for a HMD than for a TV set. 360° storytelling is also a topic addressed in this workshop. It starts with the recording of the video using an array of cameras and useful viewing directions and ends with the way that the 360° video is

TVX '18, June 26–28, 2018, SEOUL, Republic of Korea

ACM ISBN 978-1-4503-5115-7/18/06.
https://doi.org/10.1145/3210825.3213552

presented to the user. 360° storytelling can for example be enhanced with interactive overlays or voiceovers. The workshop will discuss this challenge together with innovative storytelling concepts, tools and players to guide and direct the viewer in a 360° video on the different kind of playback devices and by considering the different input capabilities of these devices (motion, remote control, keyboard, mouse, device orientation, etc.)

SUBMISSIONS AND CONTRIBUTIONS

The workshop features a list of different activities – including regular presentations on the topics in 360° video streaming, storytelling, VR, immersive experience, and its creative applications, and interactive group-work. The workshop concludes with a panel discussion in which we discuss future opportunities of immersive media. Authors were asked to submit a short paper (2,000 – 4,000 words) in the extended ACM abstract format. Submitted papers have undergone a peer-review process.

DISSEMINATING THE CALL FOR CONTRIBUTIONS AND ATTRACTING PARTICIPANTS

We distributed the call among a diversity of networks worldwide involving art, design and digital media technologies including the following: Aalto University and other Nordic institutions; ACM Siggraph Digital Arts Community; Ars Electronica; Cumulus art and design network; Leonardo and Laser networks; PhD Design List; W3C; EU projects.

WORKSHOP ORGANIZERS

Lily Díaz-Kommonen (a.k.a Lily Díaz) is Professor in New Media at Aalto University, School of Design, Art and Architecture. Since 1998, she leads the Systems of Representation research group that works in areas such as visualization and design of interfaces for virtual reality. She is currently on the editorial board of Journal of Visual Arts Practices (Taylor Francis) and associate editor for She-Ji. The Journal of Design, Economics and Innovation (Elsevier). In her work she seeks to combine anthropology and new media to promote human-centered design and works primarily with qualitative methods, including design research. See also https://people.aalto.fi/lily.diaz.

Mirjam Vosmeer has an academic background in media psychology, communication science and film studies. In 2013 she started her VR-research project Interactive Cinema at the Amsterdam University of Applied Sciences. As coordinator of the Interaction & Games Lab in Amsterdam, she strives to connect academic research, education and local industry partners within the field of VR. In 2016, she received a grant from the Dutch government to set up her research project Storytelling for 360 Media, in collaboration with the Dutch Film Academy. Since 2018, she is also affiliated with the Norwegian Film School in Lillehammer as PhD-coach for VR projects.

Ji-Hye Lee is an interactive media experience designer and researcher. Currently she works as a creative director at Media Lab. Seoul. She holds PhD in Film and Digital Media Design from Hong Ik University in Seoul, South Korea (2015), working as a visiting professor in Seoul National University of Science and Technology and a visiting researcher in Aalto University (fall, 2017). She has published several journals in a field of convergence between AR/VR, design and UX research including Investigating Socio-cultural Specificity of Mobile Augmented Reality (2017), Context-based Design Methodology For Augmented Reality Contents (2017), and Augmented Reality and Art (2018 Spring). Currently she is leading several governmental projects regarding use of digital technologies in the cultural sector.

Stefan Pham studied Computer Science at the Technical University of Berlin (TUB). He received his diploma degree (Dipl-Inf.) at Fraunhofer Institute for Open Communication Systems (FOKUS) in 2011. Currently, he is employed as Senior Project Manager at the Business Unit Future Applications and Media (FAME) and specializes in the R&D of topics dealing with Internet-delivered media, TV and cross-platform Web apps. He has been involved and managed various industry as well as publicly funded projects.

Louay Bassbouss is a scientist and senior project manager R&D in the business unit Future Applications and Media (FAME) of the Fraunhofer Institute for Open Communications Systems (FOKUS) in Berlin. his diploma degree in computer engineering from the Technical University of Berlin in 2008. His main research focuses on developing future web technologies in the fields of cross-device & cross-platform applications, 360° video streaming and rendering technologies and Web of Things. Louay has actively participated in many standardization activities by W3C and HbbTV (Hybrid broadcast broadband TV) especially in the W3C Second Screen Working Group and HbbTV 2.0 Companion Screens Task Force. He is also a test facilitator of the W3C Presentation API.

Andrea Mancianti is a composer, performer and media artist mostly devoted to work with real-world phenomena (sound, movement and space) and digital tools. Holds an MA in composition and music technology (2012, Conservatory of Florence) and a BA in Philosophy (2006, La Sapienza, Rome). He also participated to the IRCAM's Cursus 1 in Paris (2013-2014). Currently he is a PhD candidate in the Department of Media, of Aalto University, Helsinki, researching embodied performative applications of VR. With media artist Roberto Pugliese is a founding member of quietSpeaker studio, a duo creating audiovisual performances and interactive installations. His works have been performed in Europe and USA, for institutions such as Ircam (Paris), Biennale Musica (Venice), Impuls and KUG (Graz), Muziekcentrum De Bijloke (Ghent), Centre Henri Pousseur (Liege), STUK (Leuven), Boston University, Nuova Consonanza (Roma), Sibelius Academy (Helsinki) and others.

Author Index

NOTES

www.ingramcontent.com/pod-product-compliance
Lightning Source LLC
Chambersburg PA
CBHW061356210326
41598CB00035B/6004

9781450361651